The Sentencing Process

The International Library of Criminology, Criminal Justice and Penology
Series Editors: Gerald Mars and David Nelken

Titles in the Series:

The Origins and Growth of Criminology
Piers Beirne

Comparative Criminology
Piers Beirne and David Nelken

The Psychology and Psychiatry of Crime
David Canter

Offender Rehabilitation
Francis T. Cullen and Brandon K. Applegate

International Criminal Law and Procedure
John Dugard and Christine van den Wyngaert

Crime and the Media
Richard V. Ericson

Psychological Explanations of Crime
David P. Farrington

Terrorism
Conor Gearty

Criminal Careers, Vols I & II
David F. Greenberg

Social Control: Aspects of Non-State Justice
Stuart Henry

Professional Criminals
Dick Hobbs

Crime, Deviance and the Computer
Richard C. Hollinger

Race, Crime and Justice
Barbara A. Hudson

Fraud: Organization, Motivation and Control
Michael Levi

Violence
Michael Levi

Radical Criminology
Michael Lynch

Street Crime
Mike Maguire

Occupational Crime
Gerald Mars

Theoretical Traditions in Criminology
Ross Matsueda

Alternatives to Prison
Roger Matthews

The Sociology of Punishment
Dario Melossi

Gender, Crime and Feminism
Ngaire Naffine

White-Collar Crime
David Nelken

Comparative Criminal Justice
David Nelken and Richard K. Vogler

Organized Crime
Nikos Passas

Uses and Abuses of Criminal Statistics
Kenneth Pease

Policing, Vols I & II
Robert Reiner

Victimology
Paul Rock

Criminal Policy Making
Andrew Rutherford

Prosecution in Common Law Jurisdictions
Andrew Sanders

Drugs, Crime and Criminal Justice, Vols I & II
Nigel South

Youth Crime, Deviance and Delinquency, Vols I & II
Nigel South

Rape and the Criminal Justice System
Jenny Temkin

The Sentencing Process
Martin Wasik

Sex Crimes
Donald West

The Sentencing Process

Edited by

Martin Wasik

Professor of Law
University of Manchester

Dartmouth
Aldershot · Brookfield USA · Singapore · Sydney

Published by
Dartmouth Publishing Company Limited
Gower House
Croft Road
Aldershot
Hants GU11 3HR
England

Dartmouth Publishing Company
Old Post Road
Brookfield
Vermont 05036
USA

British Library Cataloguing in Publication Data
The sentencing process. – (The international library of
criminology, criminal justice and penology)
1. Sentences (Criminal procedure)
I. Wasik, Martin
345'.0772'026

Library of Congress Cataloging-in-Publication Data
The sentencing process / edited by Martin Wasik.
p. cm. — (The international library of criminology, criminal justice and penology)
A collection of essays originally published in law journals from 1963 to 1994.
Includes bibliographical references.
ISBN 1-85521-784-8 (hb)
1. Sentences (Criminal procedure) I. Wasik, Martin. II. Series: International library of criminology, criminal justice & penology.
K5121.Z9S465 1996
345'.0772—dc20
[342.5772]

96-43131
CIP

ISBN 1 85521 784 8

Printed in Great Britain by Galliard (Printers) Ltd, Great Yarmouth

Contents

Acknowledgements

The editor and publishers wish to thank the following for permission to use copyright material.

Blackwell Publishers for the essay: John Baldwin and Michael McConville (1978), 'Sentencing Problems Raised by Guilty Pleas: An Analysis of Negotiated Pleas in the Birmingham Crown Court', *Modern Law Review*, **41**, pp. 544–58.

Cornell Law Review and Fred B. Rothman and Company for the essay: Deborah Young (1994), 'Fact-Finding at Federal Sentencing: Why the Guidelines Should Meet the Rules', *Cornell Law Review*, **79**, pp. 299–373. Copyright © 1994 by Cornell University. All Rights Reserved.

Georgetown University Law Center for the essay: Donald J. Hall (1991), 'Victims' Voices in Criminal Court: The Need for Restraint', *American Criminal Law Review*, **28**, pp. 233–66. Reprinted with the permission of the publisher. Copyright © 1991 by Georgetown University.

Harvard Law Review Association for the essay: Stephen J. Schulhofer (1984), 'Is Plea Bargaining Inevitable?', *Harvard Law Review*, **97**, pp. 1037–107. Copyright © 1984 by The Harvard Law Review Association.

The Law Book Company Limited for the essays: Janet Martin (1991), '"A Balanced Performance" on Sentence – Some Comments on the Modern Role of Defence Counsel in the Sentencing Process', *Criminal Law Journal*, **15**, pp. 261–81; I.G. Campbell (1985), 'The Role of the Crown Prosecutor on Sentence', *Criminal Law Journal*, **9**, pp. 202–31. Richard Fox and Arie Freiberg (1989), 'Sentences Without Conviction: From Status to Contract in Sentencing', *Criminal Law Journal*, **13**, pp. 297–323.

Oxford University Press for the essays: Martin Davies (1974), 'Social Inquiry for the Courts', *British Journal of Criminology*, **14**, pp. 18–33; Martin Wasik (1985), 'Rules of Evidence in the Sentencing Process', *Current Legal Problems*, **38**, pp. 187–209.

Sweet & Maxwell Limited for the essays: D.A. Thomas (1970), 'Establishing a Factual Basis for Sentencing', *Criminal Law Review*, pp. 80–90; D.A. Thomas (1963), 'Sentencing – The Case For Reasoned Decisions', *Criminal Law Review*, pp. 243–53; Brian W. Ewart and D.C. Pennington (1988), 'Reasons For Sentence: An Empirical Investigation', *Criminal Law Review*, pp. 584–99; Nigel Stone (1992), 'Pre-Sentence Reports, Culpability and the 1991 Act', *Criminal Law Review*, pp. 558–67.

University of Cincinnati for the essay: Marvin E. Frankel (1972), 'Lawlessness in Sentencing', *University of Cincinnati Law Review*, **41**, pp. 1–54. Copyright © 1972 by Marvin E. Frankel.

Vanderbilt University School of Law for the essay: Michael H. Tonry (1982), 'Criminal Law: The Missing Element in Sentencing Reform', *Vanderbilt Law Review*, **35**, pp. 607–41.

The Yale Law Journal Company for the essay: Peter B. Pope (1986), 'How Unreliable Factfinding Can Undermine Sentencing Guidelines', *Yale Law Journal*, **95**, pp. 1258–82. Reprinted by permission of the Yale Law Journal Company and Fred B. Rothman & Company.

Every effort has been made to trace all the copyright holders but if any have been inadvertently overlooked the publishers will be pleased to make the necessary arrangement at the first opportunity.

Series Preface

The International Library of Criminology, Criminal Justice and Penology, represents an important publishing initiative designed to bring together the most significant journal essays in contemporary criminology, criminal justice and penology. The series makes available to researchers, teachers and students an extensive range of essays which are indispensable for obtaining an overview of the latest theories and findings in this fast changing subject.

This series consists of volumes dealing with criminological schools and theories as well as with approaches to particular areas of crime, criminal justice and penology. Each volume is edited by a recognised authority who has selected twenty or so of the best journal articles in the field of their special competence and provided an informative introduction giving a summary of the field and the relevance of the articles chosen. The original pagination is retained for ease of reference.

The difficulties of keeping on top of the steadily growing literature in criminology are complicated by the many disciplines from which its theories and findings are drawn (sociology, law, sociology of law, psychology, psychiatry, philosophy and economics are the most obvious). The development of new specialisms with their own journals (policing, victimology, mediation) as well as the debates between rival schools of thought (feminist criminology, left realism, critical criminology, abolitionism etc.) make necessary overviews that offer syntheses of the state of the art. These problems are addressed by the INTERNATIONAL LIBRARY in making available for research and teaching the key essays from specialist journals.

GERALD MARS
Professor in Applied Anthropology, University of Bradford School of Management

DAVID NELKEN
Distinguished Research Professor, Cardiff Law School, University of Wales, Cardiff

Introduction

Overview

Recognition of the sentencing process as forming an important field of study in its own right is relatively recent. The earliest essay in this volume dates from 1963, but the topic was beginning to receive more systematic attention, across different jurisdictions, by the early 1970s. At about that time practitioners and academics, both in the UK and in the US, were realizing that, while much reforming effort had been directed towards the substantive criminal law and its procedure, little had thus far been done about the law and procedure of sentencing.[1] A rather sharp distinction between the 'trial stage' and the 'sentencing stage' had hitherto been assumed,[2] at least within the Anglo-American tradition.[3] Characteristic of the trial stage were adversarial proceedings and the operation of strict rules of admissibility and proof. When it came to sentencing, however, these same rules of admissibility and proof were substantially relaxed. The predominant sentencing aims at that time were utilitarian, particularly the rehabilitation of the offender. Indeterminate sentences predominated, allowing judges and parole boards considerable discretion over the form and length of sentence. This also meant that, at the sentencing stage, the adversarial contest largely gave way to a diagnostic or 'problem-solving' model. Information about the background, personal circumstances and motivation of the defendant, much of which material was 'soft' and untested, was presented to the sentencer and used as the basis for the sentence to be imposed. At the time of writing his classic article in 1972 (reprinted here as Chapter 1), Judge Marvin Frankel felt moved to describe sentencing as 'a wasteland in the law' (p. 56).[4] He saw a sentencing procedure and practice which was highly discretionary and, since it was so subjective to the preferred approach of the individual judge, one which generated massive disparity in outcome. The purpose of this volume is to describe and assess developments and reform in the sentencing process which have taken place since that essay was written.

Part I: Establishing Facts and Providing Reasons

In his famous law review article, 'Lawlessness in Sentencing' (1972), Judge Marvin Frankel's criticisms are widely targeted and vividly expressed. He speaks of 'extravagant powers' conferred upon 'variable and essentially unregulated judges' (p. 3). He notes the absence of consensus on sentencing aims, the uncertain relevance of various aggravating and mitigating factors in sentencing, the lack of qualification, experience and training of sentencers, the excessive reliance upon indeterminate sentencing, and the existence of widespread sentencing disparity. He argues that '... by substantive controls and through procedural revisions the unchecked powers of the untutored judge should be subject to a measure of regulation' (p. 43). While Frankel's essay makes a remarkable clarion call for reform, it is fair to say that it is somewhat stronger on criticism than on substantive reform proposals. There are two principal suggestions for change. The first is the need to develop a regular practice of appellate sentence review, which was largely non-existent in America at that time.[5] The second is the setting up of a National Sentencing Commission charged with the study of sentencing, corrections and parole and with the formulation of associated laws and rules (p. 53). Although he does say that '... the whole sentencing *procedure*, from first to last, could stand a fresh look, with a view to revision' (p. 54; emphasis added), Frankel offers a few specific proposals for procedural reform, such as the assignment of numerical weights to mitigating and aggravating factors, more efficient organization of pre-sentence reports, and sentencing to be carried out by three-member panels, only one of whom should be a judge.

Chapter 2 in this collection, 'Establishing a Factual Basis for Sentencing' by David Thomas, published in 1970, must certainly also be regarded as a landmark essay. In contrast to much of the earlier published material, which had stressed the demarcation between trial and sentencing stages, Thomas began to redress the balance by demonstrating the close relationship between the substantive law and sentence decision-making. He shows that the trend in 20th-century criminal law reform – towards drafting broader offences with fewer sub-divisions – means that important gradations of harm and culpability must be established during the sentencing process.[6] It is a fundamental requirement of fairness in the sentencing process, he argues, that the judge should base sentence selection upon a reliable finding of facts. Yet establishing guilt in respect of a broadly-defined offence may still leave much unresolved. The jury's verdict, while providing the essential starting point for sentence, may sometimes be ambiguous or unhelpful. Suppose the defendant is charged with murder. Alternative versions of the facts have been advanced during the trial. It may be that the defendant has killed the victim after being provoked, and there is evidence that he was suffering from diminished mental capacity. The defence has also suggested a lack of intent to kill or cause serious harm. The jury, having heard the evidence, returns a verdict of manslaughter – but what is the factual basis for that result? Manslaughter is a very broad offence.[7] The sentence appropriate for a killing under diminished responsibility is likely to be different from one based on lack of intent, or on provocation. Facts which have not been strictly relevant to guilt will nonetheless be important in determining the sentence.[8]

Matters are often more uncertain where there has been a guilty plea. Suppose that the defence claims that the defendant assaulted the victim only after being provoked. This version is denied by the victim. The defendant's guilty plea will not resolve the underlying factual dispute since, in most jurisdictions, provocation is relevant in assault as a matter of mitigation rather than excuse. What seems to be needed here is a reliable post-conviction procedure for adjudication of the provocation issue. In his analysis David Thomas shows that '... procedures directed to establishing an account of the facts of the offence for the purposes of sentencing are one of the weakest links in our system of criminal procedure' (p. 57).[9] He shows how, contrary to his basic tenet that sentence should be based on the offence to which the defendant has pleaded guilty, or has been convicted according to the criminal standard of proof, possession of drugs (for example) can be made subject to the much higher sentences available for supplying those drugs where the sentencer has heard fresh, and disputed, material during the sentencing stage.[10] As Thomas says: '... this amounts in effect to sentencing him without indictment, evidence, cross examination or jury decision' (p. 66). Thomas offers a range of possible solutions for the procedural shortcomings identified, as follows:

1. the 'reconstruction' of substantive law to eschew over-broad offences, to achieve 'a reasonable degree of gradation of offences within the same category';
2. the development of a more sophisticated means of determining disputed issues of fact in the sentencing hearing, especially a recognition of the need for 'a separate hearing after conviction ... of any issue relevant to sentence which remains in dispute and has not been determined by the conviction'; and
3. a requirement that sentencers state explicitly the factual basis for sentences which they pass (p. 67).

In fact, as we shall see, although in the years since Thomas's essay was written there has been no take-up of his first suggestion, much progress has been made in respect of the second and third. In England, through an important series of decisions, the Court of Appeal has adopted Thomas's second proposal – to establish better post-conviction machinery for determining disputed issues of fact. There has also been an increase in the range of circumstances in which sentencers are required, by statute, to give reasons for what they do. These developments are considered further below.

The relationship between the substantive criminal law and the sentencing process was the first of Thomas's main concerns, an issue further addressed in an important 1982 paper by Michael Tonry: 'Criminal Law: The Missing Element in Sentencing Reform' (Chapter 3). The essay is a carefully considered analysis of these issues from the American perspective. Although writing only ten years after Frankel, Tonry surveys a sentencing scene in America which has been transformed. In reaction against disparity and the lack of direction in sentencing, the decade witnessed decisive moves against indeterminate sentencing, and also against the pursuit of rehabilitation as the predominant sentencing aim.[11] Tonry describes the move away from 'unstructured discretion and absence of official accountability' (p. 71), explaining that while '... indeterminate sentencing retained general acceptability for three quarters of a century [it] lost most of its credibility within a few years'. He identifies the principal causes of this change to be '... developments such as the prisoners' rights and civil rights movements, loss of faith in the rehabilitative ideal, and demands throughout the legal system for greater accountability in official decision-making processes' (p. 73). One should also add to this list the emergence in the mid-1970s of the penal theory of 'desert', according to which sentences should be proportionate to the gravity of the crimes committed.[12]

At the time of writing his essay, the 'sentencing reform movement' was well under way in the US. Tonry summarizes these changes: the development, in different State jurisdictions, of descriptive sentencing guidelines, presumptive sentencing, mandatory minimum sentences, here and there the introduction of appellate review, and parole guidelines (in some States, the abolition of parole altogether). Analysis of the plethora of sentencing system designs in the US is a subject that has subsequently occupied many writers,[13] but much in the detail of the different schemes need not concern us here. Part IV of his essay is of particular relevance to this volume. Here he shows that, despite the many changes under way in the stampede for sentencing reform, it is the procedural safeguards in the sentencing process which have been largely overlooked. Sharp distinctions between trial and sentencing procedures remain. During the trial '... constitutional rights, the law of evidence, and the criminal burden of proof, provide the defendant with important procedural safeguards ... [but] defendants have virtually no rights at sentencing ...' (p. 71). Although 'determinate sentencing has drawn tighter the relationship between crime and punishment' (p. 100), the sentencing judge remains entitled to consider *any* information[14] about the offence or the offender which he considers relevant '... including allegations of prior criminality that did not result in arrest, that resulted in arrest but not conviction, or even that resulted in a dismissal or an acquittal at trial' (p. 86). There are clear parallels with Thomas's argument in relation to criminal law offence structures. Tonry agrees that the substantive law often fails to address gross distinctions within a broad statutory offence. This failure creates 'a shadow criminal law within the sentencing process that distinguishes among cases in ways that the criminal law does not' (p. 89).[15]

There are institutional difficulties in American sentencing arrangements which generate even greater problems than those identified in the English writings. Tonry explains that, while the defendant may have pleaded guilty to, say, theft, the sentencing judge is entitled to sentence on the basis of what 'really happened' in the case, to look behind the guilty plea and perhaps hear evidence of the defendant's 'relevant conduct' – a practice which has come to be known as 'real-offense sentencing'.[16] Since, as we shall see, the vast majority of convictions in the US result from negotiated guilty pleas, the offence of conviction can be regarded by judges as of little real consequence and may to a large extent be ignored when sentence is passed. The defendant who pleads guilty to theft may end up being sentenced for robbery. The real problem here lies further back in the criminal justice system than the sentencing stage (see Chapter 12 in this volume). Heavy reliance upon plea negotiation within the system can place considerable power in the hands of the prosecutors who find themselves able to manipulate mandatory or presumptive sentencing guidelines. By dismissing some charges in return for guilty pleas on others, they can, in effect, guarantee a particular sentence outcome for the defendant.[17] The 'relevant conduct' notion is, in part, designed to circumvent that problem. It permits a defendant to be sentenced on the basis that, despite the plea agreement, he *was* really involved in a robbery rather than a theft, or *was* really involved in the supply of drugs rather than simple possession. A more severe penalty appropriate to the relevant conduct is then passed. In an empirical study which shows that American judges have long informally taken account of 'relevant conduct', Wheeler et al. quote one federal judge as saying that what mattered to him in sentencing was 'the total picture of what was going on, not ... the slice selected by the prosecution for inclusion in the indictment'.[18]

Sentencing for 'relevant conduct' remains a substantial issue of justice in the United States today. In his essay Tonry outlines the landmark sentencing guidelines adopted by the State of Minnesota (for further details, see Chapter 14 in this volume). At the drafting stage, the Minnesota Sentencing Guidelines Commission made a policy decision that, notwithstanding problems created by the process of plea bargaining, the presumptive sentence to be passed should be determined by the *offence of conviction* rather than on the basis of wider, or substantively different, 'relevant conduct' alleged against the defendant during the sentencing hearing.[19] The Model Sentencing and Corrections Act, however, took a different approach, permitting the sentencing judge to hear and to take into account behaviour alleged against the defendant unrelated to the offence – so-called 'real offense sentencing'. Professor Tonry is not alone in regarding real offence sentencing as 'fundamentally flawed' since it involves sentencing a defendant on the basis of facts which, at best, have only been established by a preponderance of evidence[20] at a sentencing hearing; at worst, it can be based on little more than unsubstantiated hearsay. Five years after his essay was published, the American Federal Sentencing Guidelines nonetheless elected to adopt a system of real offence sentencing,[21] a decision which has since drawn considerable fire from critics, both judicial and academic.[22] The Federal Guidelines themselves withstood constitutional challenge in 1989,[23] but remain deeply unpopular.

Rooted in the principles of natural justice in administrative law is the argument that no decisions affecting rights should be made without the provision of *reasons*. Reasons provide the basis upon which the correctness of the decision can be assessed and an appeal can be brought, if necessary. The requirement also serves to focus the mind of the decision-maker, requiring him/her to articulate the process of thought which led to the decision.[24] Trials are held in public, and the public has an interest in knowing the reasons for sentences passed. Yet it is a striking fact that the giving of reasons for sentencing decisions has only recently come to be seen as a matter of basic justice, despite the fact that people's liberty can be so fundamentally affected. In his essay published in 1963, 'Sentencing – The Case For Reasoned Decisions' (reprinted as Chapter 4), David Thomas sets out a convincing framework for the importance of giving reasons in the sentencing process. Nearly 30 years later, the Council of Europe similarly recommended that

> Courts should, in general, state concrete reasons for imposing sentences. In particular, specific reasons should be given when a custodial sentence is imposed. When sentencing orientations or starting points exist, it is recommended that courts give reasons when the sentence is outside the indicated range of sentence.[25]

Presumptive sentencing guidelines in the US generally require reasons to be given for the passing of any sentence falling outside the specified range, and such decisions may be subject to appellate review. While a statutory requirement to give reasons for sentence is a considerable step forward, it may not, in itself, be enough. Reasons may be peremptorily given, or expressed merely in a formulaic manner sufficient to comply with the legal requirement but offering no real explanation of the decision. As Fitzmaurice and Pease have explained, in the judicial context '... reasons tend to become bland, brief and standard'.[26] The Council of Europe Recommendations acknowledge that point in stating that 'What counts as a reason is a motivation which relates the particular sentence to the normal range of sentences for the type of crime and to the declared rationales for sentencing'. Thus, a moralistic sentencing homily by the judge will not count as a reason,[27] nor will a brief formulaic recitation.

In England, section 1(4) of the Criminal Justice Act 1982 introduced a provision whereby sentencers were required to articulate their reasons for imposing a custodial sentence upon a young person. The statute provided three such reasons, and sentencers were required to state in open court (and, in the case of magistrates' courts, record in the court register) which of those specified criteria they had relied upon in reaching their custody decision.[28] The requirement to give reasons was, in general, welcomed by court personnel, reflecting a general view that the criteria simply reflected 'what we had been doing all along'. Nonetheless, evidence from 12 magistrates' courts, compiled by Elizabeth Burney in 1985, found that, in 60 per cent of the sample of cases examined, the reasons provided were incomplete, invalid or not given at all.[29] The custody justifications in the 1982 Act have been superseded by those of the Criminal Justice Act 1991 (see below). The final paragraph of David Thomas's 1963 essay contains a plea for statutory change, indicating that a statutory requirement to give reasons '... could be imposed in the context of sentencing by a single section' (p. 115). In fact, there has been no such broad provision in England, with Parliament instead proceeding by way of a number of separate requirements. Thus, a sentencer passing a custodial sentence today will typically be required to explain:

1. the criterion on the basis of which custody is justified,
2. the reason why that criterion is satisfied,
3. an explanation of this to the offender in ordinary language in open court,[30]
4. the reason why a compensation order has not been passed,[31] and
5. the extent to which the defendant's guilty plea has been reflected in the sentence passed.[32]

Thirty years on, Thomas is now critical of the piecemeal statutory approach to the provision of reasons.[33] Despite all the changes, there are still examples of Crown Court judges passing sentence without divulging any reasons at all.[34]

The final essay in Part I is an empirical investigation into the giving of reasons by the court for sentences passed. Although there have been several such studies over the years,[35] 'Reasons for Sentence: An Empirical Investigation' by Brian W. Ewart and D.C. Pennington is one of the best examples, drawing as it does upon a broad selection of cases from both magistrates' courts and the Crown Court in England. The authors found that in magistrates' courts at least, one single reason for sentence was given in 66 per cent of cases, while for Crown Court sentencing the figure was 92 per cent. As perhaps might have been expected, reasons tended to relate to characteristics of the current offence (especially its 'seriousness'), offender culpability (such as degree of involvement in the crime) and the previous record of the offender. The researchers found a reasonably high degree of 'internal consistency' in the sentencing explanations which were given. Herein may lie a difficulty with this kind of assessment. As Fitzmaurice and Pease pointed out,[36] there is a need to be sceptical about the reasons provided by decision-makers, since reasons which people present afterwards may be different from those which actually motivated them at the time. Reliable evidence from the field of psychology shows that verbal explanations of past behaviour, whether in sentencing or in any other complex situation, cannot confidently be accepted as accurate.[37] There is also the point, of course, that the crucial decision about sentence (say, custody or not) may be made very early in the process, perhaps impressionistically, with rationalizations only being filled in later. Thus reasons become '*post hoc* justifications of what was actually done, rather than accurate representations of why it was done'.[38]

Part II: Having a Say on Sentence

Sentencing procedure arrangements vary considerably from one jurisdiction to another but, before passing sentence, the sentencer will almost always require more detailed information about the circumstances of the offence and the personal characteristics of the offender. At the very least, information will be provided about the offender's previous convictions, if any. In England, an antecedents statement is prepared by the police, with the assistance of the

Crown Prosecution Service, for the sentencing court. This now largely standard-form document contains details of the defendant's age, education, employment and domestic circumstances.[39] Attached to the antecedents form is a list of previous convictions, which should also reveal whether the defendant is currently serving either a community or a suspended sentence, a matter which may crucially affect the sentence to be passed. Old ('spent') convictions are generally not referred to.[40] Formal cautions (which are, strictly, *not* convictions) received by the offender during the previous three years are listed separately for the court.[41] In most cases the antecedents information is non-contentious, having been obtained from police records and an interview with the defendant. Occasionally, however, an inaccuracy of some sort may occur.[42] Since the defendant is to be sentenced on the basis of that information, he/she should have an opportunity to challenge it.[43] In one American case a defendant was sentenced on the basis that he had a very serious criminal record. The record had, in fact, been wrongly attributed to him, but this error was not discovered until much later since the defence had not seen the report in advance and had been given no opportunity to challenge the information provided.[44] Again, procedural constraints should prevent irrelevant or unsubstantiated material from being put into court under cover of a factual statement about the circumstances of the offence or the offender. In England there is a strict rule that previous arrests, charges or prosecutions of the defendant which have not led to conviction should not be referred to in the antecedents, still less any previous acquittals.[45] In the United States, by contrast, previous arrests (rather than convictions) have traditionally been used as the standard point of reference.

Most sentencing systems also provide for oral or written reports to be given, where appropriate, about the background and circumstances of the offender. Medical or psychiatric reports will be called for in some cases.[46] Where a juvenile is being sentenced, a report from his/her educational establishment may be given. Where the defendant has been held in custody awaiting trial or awaiting hearing of an appeal against sentence, there may be a report from that institution. In the Anglo-American tradition, predominant amongst the documents presented at sentence are the pre-sentence reports. In England, a range of situations exists in which the sentencer is under a duty (exceptional cases apart) to call for and to consider a pre-sentence report before passing sentence.[47] These reports are prepared by probation officers or social workers, and they provide fuller details of the defendant, her employment, financial and domestic circumstances, and her attitude towards the offence.[48] In some jurisdictions the report writer may indicate, or advise, an appropriate sentencing option for the judge to consider.

The first two essays in Part II of this volume discuss this kind of expert report. Although both are drawn from the same jurisdiction – England – they illustrate the changing role of these reports over the last 25 years. The first, 'Social Inquiry for the Courts', written by Martin Davies in 1974, describes the traditional role of the 'social inquiry report' as it was then called. These reports were widely used by the courts during the 1960s and 1970s when, as we have seen, an individualized (diagnostic) model of the sentencing process was dominant. Social inquiry reports, prepared by probation officers who were largely drawn from a social work ethos, became increasingly influential contributions to the sentencing process during that period. Although regulated by various Home Office Circulars and by local and national probation service guidelines, their style, content and approach essentially dated from the recommendations of the Streatfeild Report of 1961, which clearly espoused a diagnostic and treatment rationale for sentencing.[49] As well as describing the background of the offender, social inquiry reports provided information for sentencers (such as on the availability of local projects to which offenders might be assigned), and also tendered advice. Most reports concluded with a 'recommendation' on sentence. Research has demonstrated a high correlation (in the order of 80 per cent or more) between report recommendations and sentences passed.[50] The social inquiry report was hardly a 'neutral' document,[51] being used on occasion 'as an additional plea of mitigation' (p. 140) and having particular relevance and influence in marginal custody cases. Davies indicates the importance of the working relationship between probation officers (report writers) and 'their' courts. Where that relationship was close, officers would be trusted, treated as appropriate 'experts' to guide the court, and their recommendations would habitually be relied upon. Where attitudes were more suspicious, probation officers would be seen as 'soft', on the side of the offender, and as tending to usurp the function of the court. In such cases, recommendations for the avoidance of custody might well be rejected by the court as 'unrealistic'.[52] Davies concludes on an upbeat note by suggesting that 'if, during the next decade, treatment research begins to pay dividends ... the role of the probation officer as a sentencing adviser will become even more significant than it is now ...' (p. 149).

By 1992, however, the date of 'Pre-Sentence Reports, Culpability and the 1991 Act' by Nigel Stone (Chapter 7), the penal climate in England had changed considerably. Disillusionment with the rehabilitative model had grown. The rejection of indeterminate sentencing in the United States had been mirrored in England by the adoption of 'just deserts' as the guiding principle in sentencing policy. The central recommendations of an important White Paper published in 1990,[53] which endorsed that principle, were implemented in the Criminal Justice Act of 1991. That Act, though somewhat watered down by later amendment,[54] requires that, in the great majority of cases, priority be given to the seriousness of the offence rather than to utilitarian goals such as rehabilitation or deterrence. The Act, in effect, describes a 'sentencing pyramid', with custodial sentences at the top, below which come community sentences, then fines, and finally lenient disposals such as discharges. Before passing sentence in any case, the Act requires the sentencer to address offence seriousness. Thus, the level of a fine should comport with the *seriousness* of the offence;[55] a community sentence should not be imposed unless the offence is '*serious* enough' to warrant it,[56] and a custodial sentence normally cannot be passed unless the offence is 'so *serious* that only such a sentence can be justified' for it.[57] This shift in sentencing philosophy, taken together with a number of more direct attacks upon the social work roots of the probation service,[58] have required a recasting of social inquiry reports (renamed pre-sentence reports by the 1991 Act). Instead of investigating and detailing the background of the offender, the report must now be addressed to the sentencer's concerns which, as stated, are primarily seriousness of offence. Stone points out the problems which report writers may face in distinguishing between factors affecting offence seriousness and those which may mitigate but are not directly related to seriousness.[59] He also hints at potential issues of proof, where material in the report might be subject to evidential challenge in the sentencing process. While there has been some discussion of this important point elsewhere,[60] the question has so far not been squarely before the appellate courts in England. This point is taken up again in Part III.

The subject matter of the third and fourth essays in Part II are the respective roles to be played at sentencing stage by counsel for the defence and counsel for the prosecution. As with the last pair of essays, these two accounts are taken from the same jurisdiction, this time Australia. The role of defence counsel at sentencing stage is the subject of Janet Martin's '"A Balanced Performance" on Sentence – Some Comments on the Modern Role of Defence Counsel in the Sentencing Process' (1991). She comments that, in Australia, 'the sentencing process tends to be a relatively crude affair; ... there is still no uniform procedure which governs the sentencing hearing and there is not always agreement as to the functions and aims of defence counsel' (p. 161). Martin observes that, although in 1988 the Australian Law Reform Commission recommended more formal regulation of sentencing procedure,[61] 'there has been no consistent development along these lines' (p. 168). Her investigation confirms the existence of significant variations in the quality of information put before judges on sentence, and in particular raises the issue of sentencing legally unrepresented defendants. Recognizing the gradually increasing role of the prosecution on sentence, the author argues that defence representation on sentence should be mandatory and the defence role better defined.

A key responsibility for the defence lawyer in sentencing is the presentation of a plea in mitigation on behalf of the defendant. The defendant may make a personal statement to the court but, when represented, this task usually falls to the advocate.[62] While it has been argued that the purpose of the plea in mitigation is to assist the court 'to arrive at what seems the least punishment consistent with justice',[63] Martin argues that most defence lawyers see their purpose as achieving the sentence which is most favourable to their client.[64] In England, Comyn J. commented in one appeal case that defence mitigation is '... purported to be the province of the most junior of counsel' but 'is in fact amongst the most difficult tasks any barrister can ever face'.[65] The plea in mitigation is generally a single address to the court, but the advocate may, exceptionally, decide to call evidence, including evidence from the defendant, to establish the facts being urged in mitigation.[66] In England, Shapland found that factors most often mentioned by advocates in pleas of mitigation were (i) reasons for commission of the offence (e.g. provocation, domestic circumstances); (ii) the relative seriousness of the offence; (iii) the offender's attitude to the offence (especially contrition); (iv) the defendant's personal circumstances both at the time of the offence (employment, etc.) and in the future (e.g. employment prospects, family support); and (v) previous record (stressing, where possible, lack of criminal record, existence of a 'gap' in offending or the 'out of character' nature of the offence). Courts generally have considerable discretion in taking account of personal mitigation factors, which in some instances may reflect credit upon the defendant but be unrelated to the offence.[67] Martin discusses the code of conduct and professional standard appropriate to the defence lawyer when placing material before the court in mitigation, commenting that 'defence lawyers may have difficulty in knowing whether, in particular situations, their duty to the court or their duty to the client prevails' (p. 176). Advocates should never knowingly deceive the court (see, further, the author's discussion of the case of *Rumpf*[68]), put it to unnecessary expense, nor waste its time. There is a clear obligation on counsel to inform the court of any relevant statute or case law which might otherwise be overlooked, whether or not it helps their particular argument.[69] On the other hand, there seems to be no duty to disclose facts (rather than law) which work to the client's detriment if these have not been identified by the prosecution.

'The Role of the Crown Prosecutor on Sentence' is the subject of Chapter 9 by I.G. Campbell

(1985). The prosecutor's role is one which varies considerably from one jurisdiction to another; in England, for instance, the prosecutor's rôle has traditionally been restricted at sentencing stage. For example, the prosecutor is not permitted to address the judge to point out either the public's interest or the victim's interest in dealing severely with the defendant,[70] still less to argue for a particular sentence. In the US, however, it is customary for prosecutors to address the bench on sentence. Writing from an Australian perspective, Campbell offers a balanced view of the proper role to be adopted by the prosecutor. He notes the 'traditional reticence' on the part of prosecutors in sentencing, but reports that this is changing.[71] The development of a Crown appeal against sentence seems to be regarded as a *sine qua non* of the prosecutor assuming a more active role in sentencing. Now that there are such rights of appeal (to different extents) in Australia, Canada and much more recently in England, the current certainly seems to be moving in this direction.[72] Apart from bringing appeals against lenient sentences, the Crown is crucially involved in other sentence-related matters.[73] Another important factor is the increasingly adversarial nature of sentencing hearings. As one judge of the South Australian Supreme Court has stated:

> ... Crown Counsel should participate in the sentencing process. At the present time, we hear only the prisoner's argument on sentencng. I, for one, would welcome the assistance of the prosecutor. At least then I would not have the task of fossicking out the facts and thinking up the argument against the prisoner.[74]

Campbell argues, however, that the role of the prosecutor at sentencing stage should continue to be limited, consistent with being a minister of justice, striving neither for a conviction nor for a severe sentence, but rather assisting the court impartially to ensure that justice is done between the interests of the state and those of the defendant.[75] He suggests that the prosecutor's duty is to assist the court (i) by accurately presenting relevant facts, including furnishing the sentencer with the defendant's antecedents and prior record and (ii) in avoiding error, where appropriate by advising as to current sentencing principles and policy.[76] Whether the prosecutor should have a role in recommending a specific sentence varies from one jurisdiction to another. There is a willingness for this to happen in Canada, but not yet in Australia or in England.[77] In Australia, as Campbell points out, there have been numerous appellate criticisms of prosecutors' failures to advise sentencers of the unsuitability of community sentences in particular cases. This comes very close to saying that prosecutors should argue for custodial sentences. Another issue is whether, or to what extent, the prosecutor should be responsible for bringing issues relating to the victim to the sentencing court's attention. To what extent should the prosecutor act as the victim's advocate? Perhaps a reasonably clear distinction can be drawn between presenting a factual argument for making orders (such as compensation orders[78]) in the victim's favour, and acting more generally to press the victim's views, such as on the punishment to be imposed.

This last point leads into the final essay in Part II, selected from a rapidly growing literature on the question of the victim's role in the sentencing process. In 'Victims' Voices in Criminal Court: The Need for Restraint' (1991), Donald Hall examines a number of recent developments which, although different in design and scope, have all been geared to giving victims a greater say in the sentencing process. These initiatives stem from a long-standing concern that victims of crime are generally overlooked in the criminal justice system. Greater efforts have been made in recent years, across different jurisdictions, to try to ensure that victims are informed about the progress of 'their' case and that they receive such practical advice, assistance and counselling as is required.[79] Each jurisdiction has to establish procedures to determine the appropriate agency to assume responsibility for this matter: is it the task of the police, or the prosecutor, or some other state or voluntary agency? All too often, it seems, victims still do not receive the basic information nor even the degree of consideration which is surely their due.[80]

The extent to which victims' legitimate concerns ought to be recognized by according them a specific role within the sentencing process is much more problematic, though under discussion at present in a range of jurisdictions. Should victims be given a voice, perhaps in the form of a legal right, to influence the way that the defendant is treated by the prosecutor,[81] the judge, the jury and parole officials? Hall identifies some jurisdictions where the victim's views on sentence severity may be presented and formally taken into account by the judge when passing sentence. In a number of others, so-called 'victim impact statements' are prepared and made available to the court, so that the sentencer is made fully aware of any especial degree of suffering occasioned by the offence.[82] In a handful of recent appellate decisions in England, the Court of Appeal has commented upon information tendered to the sentencer describing the particular impact of the crime on the victim, but no clear view on the appropriateness of this practice has yet emerged.[83] There does now appear to be some political will to permit the use of victim impact statements in England.[84]

This trend has perhaps proceeded furthest in the United States. In a thorough review, written from the American perspective but making extensive reference to developments elsewhere, Hall argues that we should be very careful in venturing too far down this road. He identifies a number of problems. First, it is not clear that most victims really want these specific rights; they simply want to be taken more account of. It seems that while about half cooperate in the preparation of a victim impact statement, far fewer take advantage of a right to be directly involved in the sentencing process. Of those that do address the court on sentence, some, perhaps predictably, argue for the harshest penalty available. Others turn out not to be particularly punitive.[85] In the studies surveyed in Chapter 10, judges differed over their perception of the value of victim impact statements and victim allocution. A few said that they lent substantial weight to the victim's views, and most thought that they had some impact on their decision-making. The US Supreme Court has grappled, rather inconclusively, with the relevance or otherwise of victim impact statements entered by the relatives of deceased victims in capital homicide cases. In *Booth* v *Maryland*,[86] by a five to four vote, the majority of the Supreme Court held that information from the victim's family about the personal characteristics of the victim and the emotional impact of the crime on the whole family were in principle irrelevant to the sentencing decision. The minority felt, however, that this was legitimate information about the degree of harm which had been caused by the defendant and should be taken into account in fixing the punishment.

A second problem with allowing the victim a say on sentence is that the practice lends undue weight to 'harm' issues in sentencing, relegating the 'culpability' element in seriousness assessment to a subsidiary role, thus leading to 'disparate treatment of similarly-situated defendants' (p. 228). Both elements are clearly relevant to gauging crime seriousness, but sometimes the consequences of a defendant's actions produce far more (or far less) harm than could have been expected. When this happens, should the sentence level be driven primarily by what was foreseen (or should have been foreseen) by the defendant, or by the actual results?[87] The third argument made by Professor Hall for restricting the rights of victims to have a say on sentence is that sentencing is primarily a matter of 'collective judgment'. Since the individual victim is only a part of the broader society (albeit that part most directly affected by the offender), they should be entitled to no special input on sentence.

There is, of course, no guarantee that the victim's preferences will carry the day in court: it might make matters worse for a victim to be consulted, but then have his/her opinion rejected. Moreover, if the victim's positive qualities are cited, should not the defence be allowed to identify negative qualities? In many cases this would be sure to cause anger and distress to the victim or to his/her family, and might start an acrimonious exchange which, in terms of determining the proper sentence, would be little more than a side-issue.

III: Issues of Evidence and Process

Part III, the longest section of this book, takes up a number of issues touched upon in Parts I and II. However, its main concern is with the current state of the evidential and procedural standards which govern the sentencing stage of criminal trials. The first two chapters, which address the significance of guilty pleas, are taken from the voluminous literature on this subject. The percentage of offenders who enter a plea of guilty, either to the original charge brought against them or to a lesser charge, is, in many jurisdictions, very high. Data from the UK, from Australia and from a number of States in the US show that the number of cases in which a guilty plea is 'negotiated' and customarily accepted runs at about 90 per cent of those prosecuted.[88] From this arises what, in practical terms, is perhaps the most important element of sentencing procedure – the routine granting of a significant 'discount' on sentence to (most of) those offenders who plead guilty. In England, the Court of Appeal has approved a reduction of between one-quarter and one-third in light of a guilty plea, apart from certain exceptional cases such as where the defendant has been caught 'red-handed' and has no realistic alternative but to plead guilty.[89] The principal advantage claimed for the sentencing discount, of course, is that it oils the machinery of the criminal justice system – providing an incentive for defendants to admit their guilt rather than contest the case, thus saving the time, expense and possible distress (for witnesses) of a contested trial.

In those jurisdictions where 'plea-bargaining' is endemic, it is usually assumed that, were the discount system to be reduced significantly or removed altogether, there would be less (or no) incentive for defendants to plead guilty and most would prefer to have their 'day in court'.[90] On the other hand, negotiations over plea occur behind the scenes with little formal control, making the practice difficult to regulate. Indeed, where the system is perceived to have advantages for all, there may be little incentive to regulate it. With the prevalence of the discount principle, many defendants undoubtedly feel under pressure to plead guilty even though they may originally have intended to contest their case. Some who are innocent also plead guilty.

In the 1970s, John Baldwin and Michael McConville carried out path-breaking empirical research into the extent to which plea bargaining (the existence of which was vehemently denied by the legal establishment) was occurring in England at that time. The protestations of the legal community over the findings of this research now seem rather quaint. Those seeking a full account of the findings should, of course, read the authors' original report.[91] The short essay by Baldwin and McConville included as Chapter 11 in this volume, 'Sentencing Problems Raised by Guilty Pleas' (1978), provides an analysis, informed by their empirical research, of the problems which beset the whole of the sentencing process as a result of plea-bargaining. Their main point is that, at the end of the process of plea negotiation, the version of the facts presented to the court for sentence can be 'quite inconsistent' with what really happened. The authors comment that 'One of the most common complaints voiced by ... defendants was that the account of the offence in court frequently bore little relation to the facts' (p. 250). Thus,

> Defendents knew what in broad terms the prosecution was alleging, but they usually believed that their plea was based, and would be accepted by the court as being based, on the facts as *they* understood them. It therefore came as a shock to many of them to find in court that the prosecution version of the facts of the offence was quite inconsistent with their own (p. 251).

Some of the examples given by the authors suggest that defendants were being dealt with on the basis of facts so elaborated by the police that they were barely recognizable. But factual discrepancies can cut both ways. The compliance of prosecution and defence lawyers (and, most problematically, judges[92]) in the avoidance of contested trials sometimes leads to defendants pleading guilty to a version of the facts which scarcely does justice to the seriousness of the crime or the extent of injury inflicted on the unfortunate victim.[93] Even though plea-bargaining is usually presented as an inevitable element in any sizeable criminal justice system, Baldwin and McConville conclude by arguing for reform of the informal arrangements by which '... the account of the offence in court appears to bear an uncertain relation to the crime committed' (p. 263).

Elsewhere, however, the same authors have pressed more openly for the abolition of the sentencing discount altogether.[94] Proposals of this sort are usually dismissed with the response that change is impractical: the courts are under such pressure from the volume of cases waiting to be dealt with (and not forgetting that defendants may be held on remand for long periods awaiting a trial date) that the system is reliant upon the great majority of defendants entering prompt guilty pleas. Concerns over these waiting times, and also over the number of contested cases which 'crack' on the day of trial and turn into guilty pleas,[95] has led to recent proposals in England that the sentencing discount be further graded and formalized to provide a stronger incentive to defendants to plead guilty early.[96] At the time of writing, this proposal has not been acted upon.

Chapter 12, 'Is Plea Bargaining Inevitable?' by the American academic Stephen Schulhofer (1984), provides a challenge to the prevailing orthodoxy on plea bargaining. Overtly, this paper does not address sentencing at all. It does, however, challenge all of the common assumptions about the inevitability of plea bargaining by describing the practical operation of one American jurisdiction in which the State has implemented policy guidelines to forbid negotiation on plea.[97] These guidelines are almost always complied with: judges rarely, if ever, grant more lenient sentences in return for guilty pleas whose rate is consequently relatively low, running at around 35 per cent. Most defendants who choose to contest their case opt for a 'bench trial' (presided over by a judge, sitting without a jury). These trials are short, lasting on average about 45 minutes, roughly twice the length of time normally devoted there to a guilty plea. Inevitably, a few of the bench trials are 'quite hopeless' (p. 310). Procedure in the remainder varies; some are regarded as 'slow guilty pleas' in which the main purpose seems to be to elicit facts relevant to sentence, but in an adversarial setting. Others, however, are keenly contested. Schulhofer concludes that

> ... the conditions necessary for the successful abolition of plea bargaining are achievable. Bargaining by trial prosecutors and defenders can be stopped, tacit judicial concessions need not emerge to take its place, and contested trials can be provided within available resource constraints (p. 322).

More generally, Schulhofer raises the relationship between plea negotiation and the generation of sentencing guidelines.

It will be recalled that, in Chapter 2, David Thomas called for the development of a more sophisticated means of determining disputed issues of fact in the sentencing hearing. The essays in this volume now return to that theme. Martin Wasik's 'Rules of Evidence in the Sentencing Process', originally published in 1985, traces developments in this area, mainly with respect to the case-law in England, but also to changes elsewhere. Fifteen years after Thomas's article, it was fairly clear from cases in England that, whenever disputed issues of fact arose in the sentencing hearing, such that choosing between prosecution and defence versions would make a significant difference to the sentence to be imposed, the burden of proof lay on the prosecution to establish its version of the facts beyond reasonable doubt. The watershed case was *Newton*.[98] There the defendant pleaded guilty to an offence of buggery, committed on his wife. He claimed that his wife had consented to the act, but pleaded guilty since, as the law then stood, consent was no defence to this offence.[99] The defence denied that his wife had consented. The sentencing judge heard no evidence on this issue but, accepting the prosecution version of the facts, imposed a custodial sentence of eight years. The Court of Appeal reduced sentence to one year, stating that the judge should either have invited submissions from counsel on the issue of consent, or heard evidence himself on both sides before deciding which version was correct. Subsequent cases have confirmed that, when such a so-called '*Newton* hearing' is conducted, the burden is on the prosecution to establish its version beyond reasonable doubt.[100]

The defence should notify the prosecution, and the court, in advance that a plea of guilty is to be tendered, but that the prosecution version of the facts will be challenged. This allows the prosecution time to assemble witnesses.[101] Where the defence takes this option, however, the sentencing discount normally afforded by the guilty plea is placed at risk. Much of it will be lost if the defence version is eventually rejected by the sentencer, particularly where the victim of a sexual offence has been required to give evidence at a *Newton* hearing.[102] The decision to hold a *Newton* hearing is one for the court; the sentencer may order one notwithstanding the reluctance of defence counsel[103] and even if both sides have reached an agreement on the facts.[104] The recent decision in *Beswick*[105] is of particular importance here. In that case an agreement had been reached between prosecution and defence on the facts, but the judge declined to give it effect. The Court of Appeal stated clearly that:

1. The court should always sentence the defendant on a factual basis which was the true one. The Prosecution should not lend itself to any agreement with the defence which was founded on an untrue set of facts.
2. If that appeared to have happened, the judge was entitled to direct a *Newton* hearing to determine the true facts. The judge was entitled to expect the full assistance of both counsel in the presentation and testing of evidence at that hearing.

As far as the hearing itself is concerned, the cases – several of which have been decided since 1985 – establish that, in most of its features, the hearing resembles a 'mini-trial' in terms of the factual issues. Thus, witnesses may be called. The defendant may choose to give evidence. The defence may 'sit back' to see if the prosecution can discharge its burden. The hearing should follow normal adversarial lines, with the judge presiding over it as if directing a jury.[106] The judge should not assume an inquisitorial role. At least some of the rules of evidence normally applicable at trial also apply in the *Newton* hearing. In *Gandy*,[107] where the defendant pleaded guilty to violent disorder, the issue relevant to sentence was whether it had been the defendant, or another person involved in the disorder, who had thrown a glass at the victim causing the loss of an eye. The Court of Appeal thought that the *Turnbull* guidelines[108] (applicable for the guidance of juries in trials where identification is at issue) were also of value at the sentencing stage.

It should be noted that not every case of factual dispute requires a full *Newton* hearing. As is clear from the Court of Appeal's observations in *Newton* itself, if the factual divergence is insignificant, no hearing is necessary.[109] A second situation is where the defence version is so implausible that the judge can safely reject it out of hand.[110] A third is where the defence advances an important matter in mitigation which the prosecution is not in a position to dispute. In one case,[111] the defendant pleaded guilty to possession of drugs with intent to supply, but said that he had been acting under a threat of violence. The defence called no evidence. The prosecution did not accept the mitigation but could call no evidence either. The Court of Appeal held that this was a 'reverse-*Newton*' situation where the burden of proof was on the defence, on the balance of probabilities. Having looked at the facts of the case, the judge was entitled to reject the defendant's story.

The last three essays in this volume all pursue the discussion of whether, or to what extent, formal procedural and evidential rules existing in the trial process should be carried forward into the sentencing stage. As we have seen, certain exclusionary rules, such as that on hearsay, have traditionally been relaxed or ignored at sentencing. If the real danger of hearsay is that lay members of a jury may place too much weight on it, that danger disappears at sentencing stage. There are other arguments against hearsay evidence, however – such as the lack of opportunity to cross-examine whoever has made the statement – which still have validity at sentencing.[112] Again, what should the approach of the courts be to hearsay evidence contained in pre-sentence reports? Should other traditional rules (such as those relating to burden and standard of proof, corroboration, unlawfully obtained evidence, restrictions on the presentation of expert evidence, etc.) apply in the same way, and to the same extent, at sentencing stage? In recent years, there has been a trend to relax certain of the evidential rules at trial stage. In England, for example, most of the formal rules on corroboration have been abolished and replaced by a general discretion in the judge to explain to a jury why it might treat the evidence of a particular witness with caution.[113] This suggests a general move away from resolving evidential questions by way of admissibility to dealing with them in terms of weight.[114] There has been no discussion of the implications of these changes for evidential issues on sentence.

The *Newton*-related cases considered above do touch on evidential questions, but the matter has been little discussed in England. There is a richer literature in the United States. In Chapter 14, 'How Unreliable Factfinding Can Undermine Sentencing Guidelines' (1986), Peter Pope argues that the guiding principle of sentencing grids (such as the Minnesota grid, upon which he focuses) is that 'they yield a specific sentence when applied to a specific factual situation'. However, the guidelines movement has paid insufficient attention 'to the procedures that develop the facts to which guidelines are applied' (pp. 365, 363); these, he claims, 'are often unreliable and erratic' (p. 367). The familiar distorting effects of guilty plea negotiations are referred to, whereby a truncated version of the facts may work either to the defendant's benefit or disadvantage. Pope reports on the slack manner in which facts of cases are recorded by the police and by lawyers, and the cursory way in which advocates peruse the facts before starting to negotiate the 'cop out' (guilty plea). He mentions the limited success of pre-trial discovery laws in America where, in some jurisdictions, defence counsel is granted 'only a quick look at the prosecutor's file' (p. 372). 'Sentence-bargain' and 'charge-bargain' agreements are, he says, often reached on distorted or wholly inaccurate versions of the facts of the case, with the defendant being given no opportunity to challenge the official 're-construction' of what actually happened. There is then a short, though valuable, discussion of pre-sentence reports which, Pope claims, are 'likely to be the most complete written version of the offense that a judge will see' (p. 377). It seems that such reports can often be partial, omitting information or containing erroneous data. (This compares with the earlier discussion by Davies in Chapter 6 of partiality in social inquiry reports in England.) The style and background of probation officers in the US mean that any bias is likely to be against the defendant rather than in his favour;[115] alternatively, there may be over-reliance by the probation officer upon information in the prosecutor's file.

Pope argues that the development of principled sentencing guideline systems should clarify those facts which crucially affect sentence, thereby providing the opportunity for lawyers to assemble them properly in every case: 'Focusing the lawyers' attention on the salient facts should raise the quality of sentencing litigation and bring more information to the judge' (p. 384). Pope's essay was written before the promulgation of the Federal Sentencing Guidelines.

The next chapter, 'Fact-Finding at Federal Sentencing: Why the Guidelines Should Meet the Rules' by Deborah Young, was published in 1994 and places those important and controversial guidelines centre-stage. Her (by now familiar) claim is that 'despite the goal of fair sentencing, Congress, the Sentencing Commission and the courts have failed to impose the necessary standards to ensure fair and reliable fact-finding' (p. 389). Young argues that, since the history of appeals to various constitutional protections has failed to generate a fair and coherent sentencing procedure, the time is now right to tackle the problem in a different way – by incorporating the much stricter evidential standards applicable at trial into sentencing. The method suggested is the extension of the Federal Rules of Evidence into the sentencing stage of criminal trials.

Young provides a valuable and thorough review of the history of fact-finding in sentencing within the American context. She suggests that, since the Federal Sentencing Guidelines were implemented, defendants have increasingly sought to challenge the low standards applicable to fact-finding at sentencing; they have objected to the use of hearsay evidence in pre-sentence reports and antecedents material, and especially to material directed to show 'relevant conduct' (for discussion, see Chapter 3 by Tonry). The pre-Guidelines law indicated that the standard of proof at sentencing was the balance of probabilities. As Young points out, this allows the state 'to obtain a much higher sentence for a much lower level of proof and expenditure of resources' (p. 428). Subsequent appeals against sentence in this area have failed to force a departure from the earlier law, although some cases indicate that, if the factual material points not just to aggravation of the offence but really implicates the defendant in a *greater crime*, then the higher, criminal, standard should be used. Sentencing courts should apparently be able to recognize such cases themselves and apply the higher standard when appropriate (p. 408). This method of handling the standard of proof seems, with respect, dubious. Although advocating that Federal Rules of Evidence (such as that restricting the admissibility of hearsay) should be applicable at the sentencing stage, Young concludes, perhaps surprisingly, that the standard of proof in the sentencing hearing should remain the balance of probability.

The arguments advanced by Young (p. 440 *et seq.*) deserve close attention. They are based on giving priority to 'reliable' fact-finding at sentencing, the argument being that to raise the standard of proof will produce a higher overall number of factual errors, most of which will work in the defendant's favour. The problem, of course, is that there can be no logical basis for different standards at trial and at sentence since, according to how the offence is defined, the legislature may choose to allocate a particular issue to either stage. For example, the law may prescribe a single offence of robbery where possession of a firearm would constitute an aggravating factor on sentence, or it may provide for two offences of robbery, the greater being made out only where the defendant was carrying a gun. If the question of whether the defendant was armed is disputed between prosecution and defence, surely the fact should be established to the same standard, whether dealt with during trial or considered at the sentencing stage.[116] This brings us back to two important questions: whether a particular factor is to be regarded as part of the offence or as an 'aggravation', and the appropriate gradations within criminal offences (as raised in Chapters 2 and 3 by David Thomas and Michael Tonry).

The final chapter by Richard Fox and Arie Freiberg, 'Sentences Without Conviction: From Status to Contract in Sentencing' (1989), is, in a sense, both the narrowest and broadest of the essays collected here. It is narrow in that it addresses a rather special form of sentencing provision (marginal in most jurisdictions, but apparently of increasing significance in Australia) whereby the sentencer may pass sentence with or without proceeding to convict the defendant, or without recording such conviction.[117] One purpose of such provisions is to reduce the various stigmas attendant on conviction, such as damage to the defendant's employment prospects. Another purpose is to identify a case of 'technical' guilt where an absolute or conditional discharge may demonstrate the court's view that the prosecution, on balance, should never have been brought.[118] The authors draw attention to the change in a defendant's status occasioned by 'conviction', irrespective of the 'sentence' imposed; they also present an interesting analysis of the problems which arise when these sentencing powers are used to 'vacate' a conviction. The essay becomes broader in scope by raising as it does the rather ambiguous meanings of the terms 'conviction' and 'sentence', and the uncertain relationship between them. As Fox and Freiberg point out,

> A conviction is not merely a judicial alteration of legal status carrying with it collateral legal consequences such as civil disabilities, the risk of enhanced punishment for later crime, and the possible diminution of standing as a witness. It also represents an ethical statement or judgment of moral culpability which, in communal eyes, provides a declaration that the defendant is a person worthy of punishment, or in need of some other form of state intervention in the interest of suppressing crime' (p. 469).

It is precisely because of this that all substantial matters relating to culpability should be determined prior to conviction, either as elements requiring proof in the definition of the offence, or as elements within the available defences. A key objection to offences of strict liability is that they tend to undermine the 'judgment of moral culpability' inherent in conviction by moving consideration of *mens rea* from the trial stage, where it should surely be, to the sentencing stage.[119] On the other hand, we should not overburden juries with multiple detailed determinations of fact. Thus secondary issues of culpability and harm – which are insufficient to affect liability but sufficient to be taken account of in the 'fine tuning' of sentencing – will require proper scrutiny at the sentencing hearing. As we can see from the essays in this volume, the importance of adopting fair and appropriate judicial procedures for resolving disputed matters at the sentencing stage cannot be overstated. Yet the essays also demonstrate that, in the implementation of sentencing reforms, this is the element most frequently compromised or overlooked.

Notes

1. For example, the American Law Institute (1962), *Model Penal Code*. The Code provides only the broadest parameters for sentencing: sections 6 and 7. See further M. Tonry (1988), 'Sentencing Guidelines and the Model Penal Code', *Rutgers Law Journal*, **19**, 823.
2. See, for example, S. Glueck (1928), 'Principles of a Rational Penal Code', *Harvard Law Review*, **41**, 453 at p.475: 'The treatment (sentence-imposing) feature of the proceedings must be sharply differentiated from the guilt-finding phase'. Judge Marvin Frankel comments that: 'We tend with heady logic to think of guilt or innocence as sharply separate from questions of punishment': M. Frankel (1972), 'Lawlessness in Sentencing', p.27 in this volume.
3. See T. Weigend (1983), 'Sentencing in West Germany', *Maryland Law Review*, **42**, 37, especially Part III, describing an inquisitorial system where 'the guilt-finding and sentencing functions are not separated' (at p.61), but where 'the great majority of German legal writers in the last decade have called for the introduction of a two-phase proceeding patterned after the Anglo-American model' (at p.61).
4. See also M. Frankel (1972), *Criminal Sentences: Law Without Order*, and Judge T. Levin (1966), 'Towards a More Enlightened Sentencing Procedure', *Nebraska Law Review*, **45**, 499.
5. The UK is suggested as a model for such a system. For analysis of appellate guidance in sentencing cases in England, see D. Thomas (1970), *Principles of Sentencing* (2nd ed., 1979).
6. These points are more fully developed in his later essay, 'Form and Function in Criminal Law' in P.R. Glazebrook (ed.) (1978), *Reshaping the Criminal Law*, p.21.
7. See further M. Wasik [1994], 'Form and Function in the Law of Involuntary Manslaughter', *Criminal Law Review*, 883.
8. The sentencer might ask the jury to explain its reasons, but this practice has been generally disapproved in England: *Larkin* [1943] K. B. 174; though see *Frankum* (1984) 5 Cr. App. R. (S.) 259.
9. See also R.G. Fox and B.M. O'Brien (1975), 'Fact-Finding for Sentencers', *Melbourne University Law Review*, **10**, 163.

10 *Wilkins* (1977) 66 Cr. App. R. 49.

11 Discussed in detail in F. Allen (1981), *The Decline of the Rehabilitative Ideal: Penal Policy and Social Purpose*.

12 See A. von Hirsch (1975), *Doing Justice* and (1986), *Past or Future Crimes*. These matters are analysed in detail in the essays and commentary in A. von Hirsch and A. Ashworth (1992), *Principled Sentencing*. Also P.A. Ozanne [1982], 'Bringing the Rule of Law to Criminal Sentencing: Judicial Review, Sentencing Guidelines and a Policy of Just Deserts', *Loyola University Law Journal*, **13**, 721.

13 The literature on the American sentencing guidelines movement is very large. For comprehensive reviews see M. Tonry (1987), *Sentencing Reform Impacts*; M. Tonry, 'Sentencing Guidelines and Sentencing Commission: The Second Generation' in M. Wasik and K. Pease (eds) (1987), *Sentencing Reform*, p.22; R.S. Frase, 'Sentencing Guidelines in Minnesota and Other American States: A Progress Report' in C. Clarkson and R. Morgan (eds) (1995), *The Politics of Sentencing Reform*, p.169.

14 See *Williams* v *New York* 337 U.S. 241 (1949).

15 See also J.C. Coffee (1975), 'The Future of Sentencing Reform: Emerging Issues in the Individualisation of Justice', *Michigan Law Review*, **73**, 1361.

16 M. Tonry (1981), 'Real Offense Sentencing', *Journal of Criminal Law and Criminology*, **72**, 1550.

17 A.W. Alschuler (1978), 'Sentencing Reform and Prosecutorial Power', *University of Pennsylvania Law Review*, **126**, 550; M. Tonry and J.C. Coffee, 'Enforcing Sentencing Guidelines: Plea Bargaining and Review Mechanisms' in A. von Hirsch, K. Knapp and M. Tonry (eds) (1987), *The Sentencing Commission and its Guidelines*, p.142.

18 S. Wheeler, K. Mann and A. Sarat (1988), *Sitting in Judgment*, at p.17.

19 See K. Knapp (1984), 'What Sentencing Reform in Minnesota Has and Has Not Achieved', *Judicature*, **68**, 181; D. Parent (1988), *Structuring Criminal Sentences: The Evolution of Minnesota's Sentencing Guidelines*; R.S. Frase (1991), 'Sentencing Reform in Minnesota, Ten Years On', *Minnesota Law Review*, **75**, 727.

20 *McMillan* v *Pennsylvania* 477 U.S. 79 (1986).

21 See United States Sentencing Commission (1992), *Federal Sentencing Guidelines Manual*; S. Breyer (1988), 'The Federal Sentencing Guidelines and the Key Compromises Upon Which They Rest', *Hofstra Law Review*, **17**, 1.

22 Judge G.W. Heaney (1991), 'The Reality of Sentencing Guidelines: No End to Disparity', *American Criminal Law Review*, **28**, 161. M. Tonry, 'Judges and Sentencing Policy: The American Experience' in C. Munro and M. Wasik (eds) (1992), *Sentencing, Judicial Discretion and Training*, 137, noting at p.145 that 'Every other major American sentencing commission considered and rejected the "relevant conduct" approach on the basis that prosecutorial manipulation of guidelines, however desirable, is less undesirable than a sentencing policy that trivialises the significance of convictions based on proof beyond reasonable doubt or a voluntary, informed, confession'. Also M. Tonry and J.C. Coffee, 'Hard Choices: Critical Tradeoffs in the Implementation of Sentencing Reform Through Guidelines' in M. Tonry and F.E. Zimring (eds) (1983), *Reform and Punishment: Essays on Criminal Sentencing*. A defence of the 'relevant conduct' approach is provided by W.W. Wilkins and J.R. Steer (1990), 'Relevant Conduct: The Cornerstone of the Federal Sentencing Guidelines', *South Carolina Law Review*, **41**, 495.

23 *Mistretta* v *United States* (1989) 109 S. Ct. 647. The decision is discussed in detail in I.H. Nagel (1990), 'Structuring Sentencing Discretion: The New Federal Sentencing Guidelines', *Journal of Criminal Law and Criminology*, **80**, 883.

24 A point made by Frankel in Chapter 1, p.11 *et seq.*

25 Recommendation No. R(92) 17, 1992, para. E.

26 C. Fitzmaurice and K. Pease (1986), *The Psychology of Judicial Sentencing*, p.36.

27 See S. White [1971], 'Homilies in Sentencing', *Criminal Law Review*, 690.

28 By section 1(4A) these were that: '(a) he has a history of failure to respond to non-custodial penalties and is unable or unwilling to respond to them; or (b) only a custodial sentence would be adequate to protect the public from serious harm from him; or (c) the offence ... was so

serious that a non-custodial sentence for it cannot be justified'.

29 E. Burney [1985], 'All Things to All Men: Justifying Custody Under the 1982 Act', *Criminal Law Review*, 284. There is a story that some magistrates' courts had rubber stamps bearing the legend 'nature and gravity of the offence': Fitzmaurice and Pease, 1986, p.36.

30 Criminal Justice Act 1991, s.1(4). See further *Baverstock* [1993] 1 W.L.R. 202.

31 Powers of Criminal Courts Act 1973, s.35(1).

32 Criminal Justice and Public Order Act 1994, s.48.

33 See, for example, 'Viewpoint' (1994), *Sentencing News*, 26 April 1994, p.12 and (in respect of further legislative requirements to give reasons when sentencing young offenders), 'Viewpoint' (1994), *Sentencing News*, 26 July 1994: 'It remains to be seen whether any court will be able to cope with this combination of requirements, and what the ... defendant will make of the explanations if they are given'.

34 Examples are *Newman* (1979) 1 Cr. App. R. (S.) 252 and *A.G.'s Reference (No. 23 of 1992)* (1993) 14 Cr. App. R. (S.) 759. In the latter case, 'The learned recorder did not specify any reasons or explain the process by which she arrived at that sentence. It may be that if those who have to pass sentence do give some reasons for the sentence they pass, that brings them to consider the effect which the sentence they are minded to impose might have and the public perception of it.'

35 See, for example, S. White [1971], 'Homilies in Sentencing', *Criminal Law Review*, 690; J.P. Spreutels [1980], 'Giving Reasons for Sentence in the Crown Court', *Criminal Law Review*, 486.

36 Fitzmaurice and Pease (1986), p.37 *et seq.*

37 R.E. Nisbett and T.D. Wilson (1977), 'Telling More Than We Can Know: Verbal Reports on Mental Processes', *Psychological Review*, **84**, 227. See also C. Corbett, 'Magistrates' and Court Clerks' Sentencing Behaviour: An Experimental Study' in D.C. Pennington and S. Lloyd-Bostock (eds) (1987), *The Psychology of Sentencing*, p.204, commenting at p.212 that '... there is not necessarily a relationship between stated and unstated reasons or between stated reasons and behaviour ...'.

38 Fitzmaurice and Pease (1986), p.40. A possible example is *Keogh* (1994) 15 Cr. App. R. (S.) 279, where the defendant pleaded guilty to obtaining goods to the value of £35 from a shop by deception. The sentencer imposed one month's immediate imprisonment, explaining that the offence 'was so serious that only [a custodial sentence] can be justified': Criminal Justice Act 1991, s.1(2)(a). This seems dubious; the sentence may be better explained by the fact that Keogh was at the time subject to a suspended sentence, for stabbing.

39 *Practice Direction (Crime: Antecedents)* [1993] 1 W.L.R. 1459.

40 Rehabilitation of Offenders Act 1974; *Practice Direction (Crime: Spent Convictions)* [1975] 1 W.L.R. 1065.

41 Home Office Circular 59/1990.

42 A study of magistrates' courts published in 1981 found that practice varied as to the amount of antecedent information, or the number of previous convictions, which were actually read out in court. There were many cases in which information about the defendant's previous convictions was inaccurate or, more likely, out of date: J. Shapland (1981), *Between Conviction and Sentence*, pp.123–30.

43 *Van Pelz* [1954] K.B. 157; *Sargeant* (1974) 60 Cr. App. R. 74.

44 *State* v *Pohlabel* 61 N.J. Super 242, 160 A. 2d. 647 (1960).

45 *Burton* (1941) 28 Cr. App. R. 89.

46 This is a requirement in England before a medical disposal, such as a hospital order, can be imposed: Mental Health Act 1983, s.37. The defendant has no right to see the report but he, or his legal adviser, should be told of its contents: Mental Health Act 1983, s.54(3). A report should be ordered before any person who appears to have symptoms of mental disorder is given a custodial sentence: Criminal Justice Act 1991, s.4(1). See also R.D. Mackay [1986], 'Psychiatric Reports in the Crown Court', *Criminal Law Review*, 217.

47 Criminal Justice Act 1991, s.3(1) (custodial sentences) and s.7(3) (certain community sentences), as amended by the Criminal Justice and Public Order Act 1994 (requirement may be dispensed

with where the defendant is 18 or over and the report is 'unnecessary').

48 Criminal Justice Act 1991, s.3(5). A revised set of National Standards for Pre-Sentence Reports was issued in 1995.

49 *Report of the Interdepartmenal Committee on the Business of the Criminal Courts*, 1961, Cmnd. 1269: 'Our cardinal principle throughout is that sentences should be based on reliable, comprehensive information relevant to what the court is seeking to do' (para. 336). See also the extract from para. 278, quoted in Davies's article, p.142.

50 See J. Thorpe and K. Pease (1974), 'The Relationship Between Recommendations Made to the Court and the Sentences Passed', *British Journal of Criminology*, **14**, 18; J. Thorpe (1979), *Social Inquiry Reports: A Survey*, Home Office Research Study No. 48; J. Roberts and C. Roberts (1982), 'Social Inquiry Reports and Sentencing', *Howard Journal*, **21**, 84.

51 J. Thorpe (1979), *Social Inquiry Reports*, Home Office Research Study No. 48, found a tendency of probation officers to omit details from their reports which might tell against their recommendation.

52 See B. Harris [1979], 'Recommendations in Social Inquiry Reports', *Criminal Law Review* 78; for examples see *Blowers* [1977] Crim L.R. 531; *James* [1982] Crim L.R. 59.

53 Home Office (1990), *Crime, Justice and Protecting the Public*, Cm. 965. See M. Wasik and A. von Hirsch (1990), 'Statutory Sentencing Principles: The 1990 White Paper', *Modern Law Review*, **53**, 508.

54 In the Criminal Justice Act 1993. See M. Wasik (1993), 'England Repeals Key Provisions of the 1991 Sentencing Reform Legislation', *Overcrowded Times*, **4**, 1, 16–17; A. Ashworth and B. Gibson [1994], 'The Criminal Justice Act 1993: Altering the Sentencing Framework', *Criminal Law Review*, 101; D. Moxon (1993), 'England Abandons Unit Fines', *Overcrowded Times*, **4**, 5, 10–11.

55 Criminal Justice Act 1991, s.18(2).

56 Criminal Justice Act 1991, s.6(1).

57 Criminal Justice Act 1991, s.1(2)(a). The alternative ground for the imposition of custody (in s.1(2)(b)) is 'where the offence is a violent or sexual offence, that only such a sentence would be adequate to protect the public from serious harm from him'. For analysis of various aspects of the Act, see A. Ashworth, 'The Criminal Justice Act 1991' in C. Munro and M. Wasik (eds) (1992), *Sentencing, Judicial Discretion and Training*, p.77; D.A. Thomas [1992], 'Custodial Sentences', *Criminal Law Review*, p.232; A. Ashworth [1992], 'Non-Custodial Sentences', *Criminal Law Review*, p.242; M. Wasik and R.D. Taylor (1993), *Blackstone's Guide to the Criminal Justice Act 1991*, 2nd ed., Chaps 1 and 2.

58 Home Office (1990), *Supervision and Punishment in the Community*, Cm. 966, especially Chap. 3: 'A New Basis for Probation Work'. The government has also removed the requirement of social work training for those intending to become probation officers.

59 See further M. Wasik, 'Rethinking Information and Advice for Sentencers' in C. Munro and M. Wasik (eds) (1992), *Sentencing, Judicial Discretion and Training*, p.173.

60 R.L. Goldman and J.W. Mullenix (1978), 'A Hidden Issue of Sentencing: Burdens of Proof for Disputed Allegations in Presentence Reports', *Georgetown Law Journal*, **66**, 1515.

61 A.L.R.C., Report No.44, *Sentencing*, 1988, Chap. 6.

62 Denial of the offender's right to speak in mitigation is a denial of natural justice: *Parole Board, ex parte Birnie* [1988] W.A.R. 249.

63 Sir David Napley (1975), *The Technique of Persuasion*, 2nd ed., p.140.

64 See also E.L. Greenspan, 'The Role of the Defence Lawyer in Sentencing' in B.A. Grossman (ed.) (1980), *New Directions in Sentencing*, p.265.

65 *Gross* v *O'Toole* (1982) 4 Cr. App. R. (S.) 283.

66 In England, a few situations occur in which the sentencer should give notice to the defence of a particular sentence which may be imposed, so that the mitigation may address that particular point: e.g. where a life sentence (*Morgan* (1987) 9 Cr. App. R. (S.) 201) or a longer-than-normal sentence for a violent or sexual offence (*Baverstock* [1993] 1 W.L.R. 202) is being considered.

67 See A. Ashworth (1994), 'Justifying the Grounds of Mitigation', *Criminal Justice Ethics*, **13**,

5, who discusses, *inter alia*, 'acts of heroism' carried out by the defendant. An example is *Reid* (1982) 4 Cr. App. R. (S.) 280.

68 [1988] V.R. 466.

69 In *Ahmed* (1993) 15 Cr. App. R. (S.) 286, the Court of Appeal said that the judge could have been prevented from making an error on sentence if defence counsel had referred to relevant Court of Appeal decisions during the plea in mitigation.

70 Thus there is no 'plea in aggravation'.

71 A practical guide for prosecutors is provided by I.D. Temby Q.C. (1986), 'The Role of the Prosecutor in the Sentencing Process', *Criminal Law Journal*, **10**, 199. For other discussions of this issue, see A. Ashworth [1979], 'Prosecution and Procedure in Criminal Justice', *Criminal Law Review*, 480; G. Zellick [1979], 'The Role of Prosecuting Counsel at Sentencing', *Criminal Law Review*, 493.

72 See D. Thomas [1972], 'Increasing Sentences on Appeal – the Case for Re-Examination', *Criminal Law Review*, 288.

73 Such as the choice of charge and mode of trial. See Campbell, p.210, where the author points to 'an inescapable relationship between charge bargaining and the prosecution role in sentencing', echoing a discussion to be found in several of the contributions to this volume.

74 *Cartwright* (1979) 21 S. A. S. R. 564, *per* Sangster J. at p.566.

75 See also A. Ashworth (1995), *Sentencing and Criminal Justice*, 2nd ed., at p.304: '[P]rosecutors should act in the spirit of a minister of justice, not striving for severity but adopting a balanced view in the public interest'.

76 In England the Court of Appeal has said that there is a duty upon prosecuting counsel, as well as defence, to assist the sentencer to ensure that no order is made which the court is not authorized to make: *Komsta and Murphy* (1990) 12 Cr. App. R. (S.) 63. The prosecutor should also ensure that the sentencer is made aware of any relevant sentencing guideline case (*Panayioutou* (1989) 11 Cr. App. R. (S.) 535) or sentencing legislation, to ensure that the judge is 'kept on the rails' (*Johnstone*, *The Times*, 18 June 1996).

77 See pp.203–4. Making prosecution recommendations against a defendant unrepresented on sentence may present a particular difficulty.

78. In England, prosecution counsel must be ready to provide all relevant information about the victim's injury, damage or loss: *Horsham JJ, ex parte Richards* (1985) 7 Cr. App. R. (S.) 158. It is *not* the responsibility of the prosecutor to investigate the defendant's ability to pay compensation: *Phillips* (1988) 10 Cr. App. R. (S.) 419. Research into the award of compensation by magistrates' courts shows that the initiating role of the prosecutor is of great importance: J. Shapland, J. Willmore and P. Duff (1985), *Victims in the Criminal Justice System*.

79 J. Shapland, J. Willmore and P. Duff (1985), *Victims in the Criminal Justice System*.

80 J. Shapland and D. Cohen [1987], 'Facilities for Victims: The Role of the Police and the Courts', *Criminal Law Review*, 28; M. Maguire and J. Pointing (eds) (1988), *Victims of Crime: A New Deal?*; T. Newburn and S. Merry (1990), *Keeping in Touch: Police-Victim Communication in Two Areas*, Home Office Research Study No. 116.

81 By being accorded a right to express a view on plea agreements, as in Florida. In England, the Director of Public Prosecutions has said that victims of violent crime will henceforth be asked their opinion on whether their alleged attackers should be prosecuted: 'Victims to Have a Say Over Prosecution', *The Times*, 22 February 1995.

82 Preparation of victim impact statements is authorized or mandated in 42 US States, over half of which also provide the victim with an opportunity to make an oral statement at the sentencing hearing: Hall, n.8, pp. 214–15.

83 Compare *A.G.'s Reference (No. 19 of 1992)* (1993) 14 Cr. App. R. (S.) 330 with *Hobstaff* (1993) 14 Cr. App. R. (S.) 605 and *O's* (1993) 14 Cr. App. R. (S.) 632. See D. Thomas (1993), 'Sexual Offences – Proving Damage to the Victim', *Sentencing News*, 27 July.

84 The current Home Secretary, Michael Howard, has expressed support for the idea, but the value of victim impact statements has been disparaged by the former Lord Chief Justice, Lord Taylor, who has argued that they are 'an American import we can well do without': 'Voice of the Victim', *The Times*, 25 June 1996.

85 D. Kelly (1984), 'Symposium: Victims' Perceptions of Criminal Justice', *Pepperdine Law Review*, **11**, 15. For citation of a range of other published American material on this matter, see n.135 on p.237. Also A. Ashworth [1993], 'Victim Impact Statements and Sentencing', *Criminal Law Review*, 498; G. Hall (1992), 'Victim Impact Statements: Sentencing on Thin Ice?', *New Zealand Universities Law Review*, **15**, 143; C. Giliberti, 'Evaluation of Victim Impact Statement Projects in Canada' in G. Kaiser, H. Kury and H.-J. Albrecht (eds) (1991), *Victims and Criminal Justice*.

86 482 U.S. 496 (1987).

87 For discussion of these matters, see S. Schulhofer (1974), 'Harm and Punishment: A Critique of Emphasis on the Results of Conduct in the Criminal Law', *University of Pennsylvania Law Review*, **122**, 1497; J. Gobert (1993), 'The Fortuity of Consequence', *Criminal Law Forum*, **3** 1; A. Ashworth, 'Taking the Consequences' in J. Gardner, J. Horder and S. Shute (eds) (1994), *Action and Value in the Criminal Law*.

88 The literature on this topic is vast. See, for example, (1956), 'The Influence of the Defendant's Plea on Judicial Determination of Sentence', *Yale Law Journal*, **66**, 204; W.R. LaFave (1970), 'The Prosecutor's Discretion in the United States', *American Journal of Comparative Law*, **18**, 532; A.W. Alschuler (1975), 'The Defence Attorney's Role in Plea Bargaining', *Yale Law Journal*, **84**, 1179.

89 *Costen* (1989) 11 Cr. App. R. (S.) 182; an example of the exception referred to is *Morris* (1988) 10 Cr. App. R. (S.) 216. A defendant's remorse can be a significant mitigating factor on sentence, but few judges still pretend that they are solely rewarding remorse when they grant the standard discount.

90 See M. Heumann (1978), *Plea Bargaining*, p.157: 'Abolition of plea bargaining is an impossibility. To speak of a plea-bargaining-free criminal justice system is to operate in a land of fantasy. Plea bargaining will remain the bedrock for case disposition in all communities. It will inevitably provide a central means of disposing of cases.'

91 J. Baldwin and M. McConville (1977), *Negotiated Justice*.

92 In England, the decision in *Turner* [1970] 2 Q.B. 321 states that a judge should give advance indication of sentence only in a case where that sentence will be the same (i.e. non-custodial in nature) irrespective of plea. Outside of this exception, any approach made by counsel to the judge for an indication of sentence is wrong: *Coward* (1979) 70 Cr. App. R. 70. When surveyed in 1992, 90 per cent of barristers and two-thirds of judges said that *Turner* should be 'reformed to permit full and realistic discussion between counsel and judge about plea and especially sentence': M. Zander and P. Henderson (1993), *The Crown Court Study*, Royal Commission Research Study No. 19.

93. Since the research was published, changes to the legal framework for police questioning of suspects have been brought about, principally by the Police and Criminal Evidence Act of 1984 and the attendant Codes of Practice. The continuing importance of plea-bargaining is, however, clear. The guilty plea rate remains steady, and the Court of Appeal has endorsed the operation of the sentencing discount on numerous occasions: e.g. *Buffrey* (1992) 14 Cr. App. R. (S.) 511; *Claydon* (1993) 15 Cr. App. R. (S.) 526; *Landy* (1995) 16 Cr. App. R. (S.) 908. The Criminal Justice and Public Order Act 1994 now requires that, whenever a sentencing court reduces punishment on the basis of a guilty plea, it should explain in open court that it has done so.

94 J. Baldwin and M. McConville, 'The Influence of the Sentencing Discount in Inducing Guilty Pleas' in J. Baldwin and A.K. Bottomley (eds) (1978), *Criminal Justice*, p.116, at p.122: 'We would contend that, except in the relatively rare cases in which defendants demonstrate genuine contrition, there is no legal justification for wide differences in sentence according to the plea tendered'.

95 J.K. Bredar [1992], 'Moving Up the Day of Reckoning: Strategies for Attacking the "Cracked Trials" Problem', *Criminal Law Review*, 153.

96 See Royal Commission on Criminal Justice (1993), *Report*, Cm. 2263, pp.110–14.

97 Aside from (i) dismissing lesser counts in return for a plea of guilty to the main charge, (ii) reduction of charge where there is clear evidence of overcharging, or (iii) where there is no longer sufficient evidence to convict.

98 (1982) 4 Cr. App. R. (S.) 388.

99 The substantive law has since been changed by the Criminal Justice and Public Order Act 1994, s.143.
100 *Ahmed* (1984) 6 Cr. App. R. (S.) 391; *Kerrigan* (1993) 14 Cr. App. R. (S.) 179.
101 *Mohun* (1993) 14 Cr. App. R. (S.) 5.
102 *Stevens* (1986) 8 Cr. App. R. (S.) 297; *Jauncey* (1986) 8 Cr. App. R. (S.) 401; *Williams* (1990) 12 Cr. App. R. (S.) 415.
103 *Smith* (1986) 8 Cr. App. R. (S.) 169.
104 *McNulty* (1994) 15 Cr. App. R. (S.) 606.
105 [1996] Crim. L.R. 62.
106 *Gandy* (1989) 11 Cr. App. R. (S.) 564.
107 (1989) 11 Cr. App. R. (S.) 564.
108 [1977] Q. B. 224.
109 An example is *Bent* (1986) 8 Cr. App. R. (S.) 19.
110 *Hawkins* (1985) 7 Cr. App. R. (S.) 351. Such a course should not, however, be taken lightly: *Costley* (1989) 11 Cr. App. R. (S.) 357.
111 *Ogunti* (1987) 9 Cr. App. R. (S.) 325. See also *Broderick* (1993) 15 Cr. App. R. (S.) 476 and *Guppy* [1994] Crim L.R. 614.
112 On hearsay, see A. Keane (1996), *The Modern Law of Evidence*, 4th ed., Chap. 9, and Law Commission (1995), Consultation Paper No. 183, *Hearsay and Related Topics*. Neither source, however, mentions the sentencing context.
113 Criminal Justice and Public Order Act 1994, ss.32 and 33; D.J. Birch [1995], 'Corroboration: Goodbye to All That?', *Criminal Law Review*, 524.
114 See also Law Commission (1996), Consultation Paper No. 141, *Previous Misconduct of a Defendant*.
115 See the references in notes 83–90 on pp. 361–2.
116 Similar points apply in relation to 'imperfect' defences to crime: see M. Wasik [1983], 'Excuses at the Sentencing Stage', *Criminal Law Review*, 450.
117 In England, convictions followed by the grant of an absolute or conditional discharge (or, formerly, a probation order) subsequently count as convictions for certain purposes only. For discussion of comparable laws in Canada, see F.G. Bobiasz (1974), 'Absolute and Conditional Discharge', *Ottawa Law Review*, **6**, 608, and in the US, F.C. Zacharias [1981], 'The Uses and Abuses of Convictions Set Aside Under the Federal Youth Corrections Act', *Duke Law Journal*, 477.
118 M. Wasik (1985), 'The Grant of an Absolute Discharge', *Oxford Journal of Legal Studies*, **5**, 211.
119 This point is made by Thomas in Chapter 2, pp. 60–61. A striking example is *Lester* (1975) 63 Cr. App. R. 144 where the defendant pleaded guilty to strict liability offences under the Trade Descriptions Act 1968 and was sentenced on the assumption that he had *mens rea*. The Court of Appeal said that this assumption should not have been made without the defendant having an opportunity to give evidence on the matter. The sentence was reduced from six months imprisonment to a fine of £280.

Part I
Establishing Facts and Providing Reasons

[1]

UNIVERSITY OF
CINCINNATI LAW REVIEW

VOLUME 41 | 1972 | No. 1

LAWLESSNESS IN SENTENCING *

Marvin E. Frankel **

Sir Winston Churchill was obviously right when he made his frequently quoted observation:

> The mood and temper of the public with regard to the treatment of crime and criminals is one of the most unfailing tests of the civilization of any country.[1]

Consider, then, what it tells about us that in 1970 a high American court could say, correctly, beyond question:

> What happens to an offender after conviction is the least understood, the most fraught with irrational discrepancies, and the most in need of improvement of any phase in our criminal justice system.[2]

The "phase" of our system thus characterized is by and large a bizarre "nonsystem" of extravagant powers confided to variable and essentially unregulated judges, keepers, and parole officials.

I claim no special competence to explain how a nation professing ideals like ours has contrived for so long to impose with such feckless cruelty what may be generally the harshest sentences

* This text was prepared, and used as the basis, for the Marx Lectures given on November 3, 4, and 5, 1971. With the permission of the Editors, I reaffirm here the pleasurable indebtedness of Mrs. Frankel and myself to the Dean, faculty, students, and friends of the Law School for their elegantly gracious hospitality on the days of these lectures.

** United States District Judge for the Southern District of New York. A.B., Queens College, New York City, 1943; LL.B., Columbia, 1948.

1 As quoted in H. BLOCH & G. GEIS, MAN, CRIME, AND SOCIETY 557 (1962).

2 United States v. Waters, 437 F.2d 722, 723 (D.C. Cir. 1970).

in the world.[3] Partly, of course, it reflects familiar vices of old Puritan virtues: the capacity for fierce repressiveness in response to threats against both our outward security and our inner certainty of righteousness.[4] Partly, it illustrates the strong American propensity toward simple denial (in the psychiatrist's sense) of all that is not pretty, favorable, jolly, and young: most of us, most of the time, including those whose duty should dictate otherwise, ignore the subjects of criminal penalties and what lies beyond them. Without pursuing further this amateur beginning of an explanation, I think it plausible to suspect that the time for denial may be passing. In an era of "confrontation," those who have wielded power from sheltered places are being forced to face squarely many practices and many victims formerly kept from view. Still, I prefer to believe that we are free to choose in this and other things. Assuming this, those of us whose profession is the law must not choose any longer to tolerate a regime of unreasoned, unconsidered caprice for exercising the most awful power of organized society, the power to take liberty and (thus far at least) life by process of what purports to be law.

Beginning with such thoughts, it has seemed to me that a trial judge might suitably respond to the honor of the invitation to give these lectures by bearing witness, and tendering some proposals for further study and action, on the subject of sentencing. Perhaps from occupational prejudice but I think on better grounds, the sentencing stage has come to strike me as the key focus of disease in our apparatus of punishment. The disease is insidious; the legal profession, entrusted with the power and responsibility, has tended (in the law school and beyond) to ignore sentencing as an anti-climactic, unruly, doctrinally unalluring area. Nevertheless, the sentence is the primary, if not wholly dispositive, stage of the so-called "correctional" process. The governance of sentencing by rational, intelligible principles could have decisive effects not only upon the length and character of

---

[3] *See, e.g.*, NATIONAL COUNCIL ON CRIME AND DELINQUENCY, MODEL SENTENCING ACT 23 (1963) [hereinafter cited as MODEL SENTENCING ACT]; S. RUBIN, H. WEIHOFEN, G. EDWARDS & S. ROSENZWEIG, THE LAW OF CRIMINAL CORRECTION 268 (1963) [hereinafter cited as LAW OF CRIMINAL CORRECTION]; Helwig, *Reform of the American System of Criminal Justice—Stage Two*, 53 JUDICATURE 52 (1969); Turnbladh, *A Critique of the Model Penal Code Sentencing Proposals*, 23 LAW & CONTEMP. PROB. 544, 545 (1958).

[4] *Cf.* H. WEIHOFEN, THE URGE TO PUNISH 13, 14, 28, 138–41 (1956); G. ZILBOORG, THE PSYCHOLOGY OF THE CRIMINAL ACT AND PUNISHMENT 75–79, 94, 97 (1954).

sentences, but also upon the nature of the institutions and methods for what is in the current euphemism known as "treatment."

In proposing to write about sentencing today, one should in self-defense avoid the appearance of a silly arrogance that would disregard the recent array of substantial efforts of scholarship and proposed law reforms in this area. Most notable among these, and extensively used in this essay, are the Model Penal Code, the proposed new Federal Criminal Code,[5] the Model Sentencing Act promulgated in 1963 by the National Council on Crime and Delinquency, and the work of the American Bar Association Project on Minimum Standards for Criminal Justice.[6] Having acknowledged these major efforts, and intending to use them, I will not attempt to review or summarize them. As will appear, however, in connection with the general idea of indeterminate sentencing, I shall submit the temerarious thought that all these proposals have been insufficiently informed and discriminating.

To chart a little more specifically the matters I mean to discuss, they are:

> *First,* the deeply flawed status quo as I see it, a topic that seems essential even if it includes no novelties;
>
> *second,* some relatively modern improvements, both existing and proposed, and a critique of these; and
>
> *third,* some tentative proposals, few in number but not necessarily modest, for importing rationality into the management of sentencing.

In discussing these matters, I shall tend to have mainly in view the federal establishment, where I have some first-hand experience. I think, however, that most of these observations and suggestions are quite generally applicable.

---

[5] FINAL REPORT OF THE NATIONAL COMM'N ON REFORM OF FEDERAL CRIMINAL LAWS, PROPOSED NEW FEDERAL CRIMINAL CODE (1971), in *Hearings Before the Subcomm. on Criminal Laws and Procedures of the Senate Comm. on the Judiciary,* 92d Cong., 1st Sess., pt. 1, at 129 (1971) [hereinafter cited as PROPOSED FEDERAL CRIMINAL CODE].

[6] AMERICAN BAR ASSOCIATION PROJECT ON MINIMUM STANDARDS FOR CRIMINAL JUSTICE, STANDARDS RELATING TO SENTENCING ALTERNATIVES AND PROCEDURES (Approved Draft 1968) [hereinafter cited as ABA SENTENCING STANDARDS]. The same Project, among its other germinal works, has produced STANDARDS RELATING TO APPELLATE REVIEW OF SENTENCES (Approved Draft 1968), which is also a major source used herein and will be labeled briefly ABA APPELLATE REVIEW STANDARDS.

I. The Evils We Have

A. Poena Sine Lege

The common form of criminal penalty provision confers upon the sentencing judge an enormous range of choice. The scope of what we call "discretion" permits imprisonment for anything from a day to one, five, 10, 20, or more years.[7] All would presumably join in denouncing a statute that said "the judge may impose any sentence he pleases." [8] Given the mortality of men, the power to set a man free or confine him for up to 30 years is not sharply distinguishable.

The statutes granting such powers characteristically say nothing about the factors to be weighed in moving to either end of the spectrum or to some place between.[9] It might be supposed by some stranger arrived in our midst that the criteria for measuring a particular sentence would be discoverable outside the narrow limits of the statutes and would be known to the judicial experts rendering the judgments. But the supposition would lack substantial foundation. Even the most basic sentencing principles are not prescribed or stated with persuasive authority. There is, to be sure, a familiar litany in the literature of sentencing "purposes": retribution, deterrence ("special" and "general"), "denunciation," incapacitation, rehabilitation. Nothing tells us, however, when or whether any of these several goals are to be sought, or how to resolve such evident conflicts as that likely to arise in the effort to punish and rehabilitate all at once.[10] It has for some time been part of our proclaimed virtue that vengeance or retribution is a disfavored motive for punishment.[11] But there is reason to doubt that either judges or the public are effectively

---

[7] *E.g.*, 18 U.S.C. §§ 2032 (up to 30 years), 2231(b) (up to 10 years), 2421 (up to 5 years) (1964).

[8] *Cf.* H. Packer, The Limits of the Criminal Sanction 92–93 (1968).

[9] In a bygone era, for a partial revival of which I will argue (*see* text accompanying notes 138–46 *infra*), such legislative guidance was sometimes attempted. *See* Law of Criminal Correction 112–13 n.20, setting out a since repealed provision of the Iowa Code of 1851.

[10] *See, e.g.*, Law of Criminal Correction 269; President's Comm'n on Law Enforcement and Administration of Justice, The Challenge of Crime in a Free Society 141 (1967); D. Thomas, Principles of Sentencing 3–7 (1970).

[11] *See, e.g.*, Williams v. New York, 337 U.S. 241, 248 (1949); Law of Criminal Correction 692 n.74; N. Walker, Sentencing in a Rational Society 11–12 (1971).

abreast of this advanced position.[12] And there is no law—certainly none that anybody pretends to have enforced—telling the judge he must refrain, expressly or otherwise, from trespassing against higher claims to wreak vengeance.

Moving upward from what should be the philosophical axioms of a rational scheme of sentencing law, we have no structure of rules, or even guidelines, affecting other elements arguably pertinent to the nature or severity of the sentence. Should it be a mitigating factor that the defendant is being sentenced upon a plea of guilty rather than a verdict against him? [13] Should it count in his favor that he spared the public "trouble" and expense by waiving a jury? [14] Should the sentence be more severe because the judge is convinced that the defendant perjured himself on the witness stand? [15] Should churchgoing be considered to reflect favorably? [16] Consistently with the first amendment, should it be considered at all? What factors should be assessed—and where, if anywhere, are comparisons to be sought—in gauging the relative seriousness of the specific offense and offender as against the spectrum of offenses by others in the same legal category? The list of such questions could be lengthened. Each is capable of being answered, and is answered by sentencing judges, in contradictory or conflicting, or at least differing, ways. There is no controlling requirement that any particular view be followed on any such subject by the sentencing judge.[17]

---

[12] *Cf.* H. BARNES, THE STORY OF PUNISHMENT—A RECORD OF MAN'S INHUMANITY TO MAN 186, 196–97 (1930); O. HOLMES, THE COMMON LAW 41–42 (1881); Watson, *A Critique of the Legal Approach to Crime and Correction*, 23 LAW & CONTEMP. PROB. 611, 615–16, 618 (1958).

[13] For differing views on this, *see* D. NEWMAN, CONVICTION: THE DETERMINATION OF GUILT OR INNOCENCE WITHOUT TRIAL 57–66 (1966); Enker, *Perspectives on Plea Bargaining*, in PRESIDENT'S COMM'N ON LAW ENFORCEMENT AND ADMINISTRATION OF JUSTICE, TASK FORCE REPORT: THE COURTS, app. A, at 108 (1967); Note, *The Influence of the Defendant's Plea on Judicial Determination of Sentence*, 66 YALE L.J. 204 (1956). *See generally* Alschuler, *The Prosecutor's Role in Plea Bargaining*, 36 U. CHI. L. REV. 50 (1968).

[14] That judges might answer affirmatively, whether they should or not, *see* United States v. McCoy, 429 F.2d 739, 742–44 (D.C. Cir. 1970); R. DAWSON, SENTENCING: THE DECISION AS TO TYPE, LENGTH AND CONDITIONS OF SENTENCE 187–88 (1969).

[15] *See* LAW OF CRIMINAL CORRECTION 60; D. THOMAS, *supra* note 10, at 53.

[16] *See* ADVISORY COUNCIL OF JUDGES OF THE NATIONAL COUNCIL ON CRIME AND DELINQUENCY, GUIDES FOR SENTENCING 40 (1957) [hereinafter cited as GUIDES FOR SENTENCING].

[17] The statement seems accurate enough as a general proposition. There are cases now and then that may be cited as exceptions. *See, e.g.*, cases cited in note

With the delegation of power so unchanneled, it is surely no overstatement to say that "the new penology has resulted in vesting in judges and parole and probation agencies the greatest degree of uncontrolled power over the liberty of human beings that one can find in the legal system." [18] The process would be totally unruly even if judges were superbly and uniformly trained for the solemn work of sentencing. As everyone knows, however, they are not trained at all.

B. *The Personnel*

Viewed as a group, the people who enter upon service as trial judges are somewhat elderly, more experienced than most lawyers in litigation, almost totally unencumbered by learning or experience relevant to sentencing, and inclined by temperament and circumstance toward the major orthodoxies.[19] Nothing they studied in law school touched our subject more than remotely. Probably a large majority had no contact, or trivial contact, with criminal proceedings of any kind during their years of practice. Those who had such exposure worked preponderantly on the prosecution side. Whether or not this produces a troublesome bias, the best that can be said is that prosecutors tend generally

---

28 *infra*. But such exceptions are trivial at most. Besides, most sentences are passed without articulated reasons, probably without reasons the judge articulates with much precision even to himself. *See* text accompanying notes 28–30 *infra*. It may be doubted, then, how consciously the choices along the way are made, or noticed.

[18] Kadish, *Legal Norm and Discretion in the Police and Sentencing Processes*, 75 Harv. L. Rev. 904, 916 (1962).

[19] To a mind-staggering extent—to an extent that conservatives and liberals alike who are not criminal trial lawyers simply cannot conceive—the entire system of criminal justice below the level of the Supreme Court of the United States is solidly massed against the criminal suspect. Only a few appellate judges can throw off the fetters of their middle-class backgrounds—the dimly remembered, friendly face of the school crossing guard, their fear of a crowd of "toughs," their attitudes engendered as lawyers before their elevation to the bench, by years of service as prosecutors or as private lawyers for honest, respectable business clients—and identify with the criminal suspect instead of with the policeman or with the putative victim of the suspect's theft, mugging, rape or murder. Trial judges still more, and magistrates beyond belief, are functionally and psychologically allied with the police, their co-workers in the unending and scarifying work of bringing criminals to book.

Amsterdam, *The Supreme Court and the Rights of Suspects in Criminal Cases*, 45 N.Y.U.L. Rev. 785, 792 (1970). *See also* President's Comm'n on Law Enforcement and Administration of Justice, The Challenge of Crime in a Free Society 127 (1967).

either to refrain altogether from taking positions on sentencing or to deal with the subject at a bargaining level somewhat removed from the plane of penological ideals.

Thus qualified, the new judge may be discovered within days or weeks fashioning judgments of imprisonment for long years. No training, formal or informal, precedes the first of these awesome pronouncements. Such formal and intentional education, other than from the job itself, as may happen along the way is likely to be fleeting, random, anecdotal, and essentially trivial.[20] Shop talk with fellow judges—at least in my experience on a court where the judges are numerous, convivial, and likely to talk shop in the court lunchroom and other gathering places—rarely lights on problems of sentencing. Because the sentence is not appealable except on rare and extraordinary grounds,[21] there is little occasion for the kind of relatively organized reflection instigated by the reading of advance sheets. The experienced trial judge, then, is one who has imposed many sentences, improving, we would hope, from a course of solitary brooding and conversations with probation officers, consulting in the end himself as the final authority, and perhaps sinking deeper each year the footings of premises that have never been tested by detached scrutiny or by open debate.

Given the sure combination of substantially unbounded discretion and decision-makers unrestrained by shared professional standards, it is not astonishing that the commonplace worry in any discussion of sentencing concerns "disparity." The factual basis for the worry is clear and huge; nobody doubts that essentially similar people in large numbers receive widely divergent sentences for essentially similar or identical crimes. The causes of the problem are equally clear: judges vary widely in their explicit views and "principles" affecting sentencing; they vary, too, in the accidents of birth and biography generating the guilts, the fears, and the rages that affect almost all of us at times and in ways we often cannot know. The judge who reports there is no surge of emotion when he imposes a stiff sentence is likely to

---

[20] *See* text accompanying notes 55–68 *infra*.

[21] Here, as elsewhere, my primary focus is on federal law. The statement is true for a majority of the States, however; only 15 or so allow sentences to be appealed in every serious case. ABA APPELLATE REVIEW STANDARDS § 1.1, comment a, at 13. The State statutes authorizing appellate review of sentences are collected in *id.* app. A, at 67.

be mistaken, unperceptive, or a person of alarmingly flat affect.[22] It is unnecessary, though not irrelevant, to frighten ourselves with the statistical probability and direct personal knowledge that some percentage of judges may be psychotic.[23] It is disturbing enough that a charged encounter like the sentencing proceeding, while it is the gravest of legal matters, should turn so arbitrarily upon the variegated passions and prejudices of individual judges.

These are trite observations. Writers on sentencing never fail to dwell upon the disparities. The writers, including judges, often conclude that the inconsistencies are to a large degree unavoidable.[24] If such resignation were the best we could hope to offer, the case for leaving sentencing to lawyers and judges would be doomed to remain as weak as it is on our record to date. And there are many, again including judges, who are persuaded that the task would be better confided to others. Sometimes the position is expressed with some vehemence. In the words of one earnest scholar:

> The diagnosis and treatment of the criminal is a highly technical medical and sociological problem for which the lawyer is rarely any better fitted than a real estate agent or a plumber. We shall ultimately come to admit that society has been as unfortunate in handing over criminals to lawyers and judges in the past as it once was in entrusting medicine to shamans and astrologers, and surgery to barbers. A hundred years ago we allowed lawyers and judges to have the same control of the insane classes as they still exert over the criminal groups, but we now recognize that insanity is a highly diversified and complex medical problem which we entrust to properly trained experts in the field of neurology and psychiatry. We may hope that in another hundred years the treatment of the criminal will be equally thoroughly and willingly submitted to medical and sociological experts.[25]

---

[22] *See generally* F. ALEXANDER & H. STAUB, THE CRIMINAL, THE JUDGE, AND THE PUBLIC 79, 179, 222–23 (1956); G. ZILBOORG, *supra* note 4, at 74–75; Bennett, *The Sentence—Its Relation to Crime and Rehabilitation*, 1960 U. ILL. L.F. 500, 504–05.

[23] *See* W. GAYLIN, IN THE SERVICE OF THEIR COUNTRY—WAR RESISTERS IN PRISON 325 (1970); Bennett, *supra* note 22, at 505; *cf.* Slayton v. Smith, 404 U.S. 53 (1971).

[24] *See, e.g., Crime and Punishment*, 3 THE CENTER MAGAZINE, May-June 1971, at 6, 32 (proceedings of a conference of the Center for the Study of Democratic Institutions) (remarks of Motley, J.); *cf.* Celler, *An Expression of Congressional Interest in the Federal Sentencing Institute*, in *Pilot Institute on Sentencing*, 26 F.R.D. 231, 241, 243 (1959); Thomsen, *Sentencing in Income Tax Cases*, 26 FED. PROBATION, Mar. 1962, at 10.

[25] H. BARNES, *supra* note 12, at 265–66.

Sometimes we are merely reminded that law training supplies no special talents or competence useful for sentencing.[26]

But at least in one critical respect our training, our habits, and our accomplishments ought to be pertinent: we are taught and qualified to seek and formulate rules—that is, law. We are steeped in a tradition of hostility to unruliness, the condition we condemn when we denounce the arbitrary and the capricious. If we have not followed the tradition in sentencing, it may be because the effort is hopeless. Or it may be that we have not tried hard enough despite all the professions of concern. I join with many others in the belief that a much nearer approach to law and order in sentencing is possible as well as desirable. My eventual hope here, of course, is to offer some suggestions for pursuing that objective. For the moment, however, the account of our existing sorrows should include at least some of the grosser flaws not yet mentioned.

C. *The Failure to Explain or Communicate*

The kadi, unfettered by rules, makes his decrees swiftly and simply. But we learned long ago that the giving of reasons helps the decision-maker himself in the effort to be fair and rational, and makes it possible for others to judge whether he has succeeded. And so we require our federal district judges and many others to explain themselves when they rule whether a postal truck driver was at fault in crumpling a fender and, if so, how much must be paid to right the wrong.[27]

There is no such requirement in the announcement of a prison sentence. Sometimes judges give reasons anyway, or reveal in colloquy the springs of their action. The explanations or revelations sometimes disclose reasoning so perverse or mistaken that the sentence, normally unreviewable, must be invalidated on appeal.[28] Most trial judges (to my impressionistic and conversational knowledge, at least) say little or nothing, certainly far less

[26] *See, e.g.*, R. ENSOR, COURTS AND JUDGES IN FRANCE, GERMANY, AND ENGLAND 22, 87–88 (1933); JUDICIAL CONFERENCE OF THE UNITED STATES, REPORT OF THE COMMITTEE ON PUNISHMENT FOR CRIME 26–27 (1942); N. WALKER, CRIME AND PUNISHMENT IN BRITAIN 232–33 (1965).

[27] *See* FED. R. CIV. P. 52 (a); CAL. CIV. PRO. CODE ANN. § 632 (West Supp. 1970); CONN. GEN. STAT. ANN. §§ 52–226, -231 (Supp. 1971).

[28] *E.g.*, Scott v. United States, 419 F.2d 264, 266–67 (D.C. Cir. 1969); Thomas v. United States, 368 F.2d 941 (5th Cir. 1966); *see* United States v. Malcolm, 432 F.2d 809, 815–19 (2d Cir. 1970).

than a connected "explanation" or rationale of the sentence. Many, aware of their unreviewable powers, and sharing a common aversion to being reversed, are perhaps motivated by the view (not unknown on trial benches) that there is safety in silence.[29] It is likely that the judge, not expected to explain, has never organized a full and coherent explanation even for himself. Some judges use the occasion of sentencing to flaunt or justify themselves by moral pronunciamentos and excoriations of the defendant. This has no relation to the serious and substantial idea that the community's "denunciation" is a—possibly the—chief aim of sentencing.[30] It is, in any event, not kin to the reasoned decisions for which judges are commissioned.

The judge's failure to explain is part of a more pervasive silence that makes sentencing and its sequellae so much a shadowland of doubt, ignorance, and fragmented responsibility. The judge may have opinions or hopes concerning the goals of "treating" the defendant in prison; but he is unlikely to state them, for whatever guidance they might give the jailers.[31] In our federal scheme, we have a provision under which the judge, to assist in sentencing, may send a defendant to a Bureau of Prisons facility for a "complete study" and a report which "may include but shall not be limited to data regarding" the defendant's health, biography, capabilities, "and such other factors as may be considered pertinent." [32] The broad categories of reportable subjects cannot be covered fully within the time (and very possibly the talents) of those entrusted with the task. The judge, I am credibly informed, normally fails to put specific questions that might narrow and focus the study. Responsive to the vague requests, those reporting on the study often supply bland appraisals that add little, if anything, to the presentence reports. The inadequacy is not mitigated by the appending of diagnostic charts and summaries that are sometimes legible and less often intelligible to

---

[29] *See* LAW OF CRIMINAL CORRECTION 122.

[30] *See generally* 2 J. STEPHEN, A HISTORY OF THE CRIMINAL LAW OF ENGLAND 75–93 (1883); Hart, *The Aims of the Criminal Law*, 23 LAW & CONTEMP. PROB. 401, 404–05, 436–37 (1958). *But cf.* H.L.A. HART, PUNISHMENT AND RESPONSIBILITY 169–73 (1968); N. WALKER, *supra* note 11, at 19–21.

[31] Like the other grave flaws in the sentencing process, the lack of communication among judicial and administrative (parole and prison) officials is an old story. *See* R. DAWSON, *supra* note 14, at 239–40, 258–60; R. POUND, CRIMINAL JUSTICE IN AMERICA 178 (1930).

[32] 18 U.S.C. §§ 4208(b), (c) (1964).

the sentencing judge. My own favorite among the grimly amusing reports of this kind concerned an obviously disturbed, inadequate, and troublesome man who had called the F.B.I. to tell them (accurately) the train he was taking to Washington to assassinate the President. Seemingly "competent" legally despite his imprudence, he pled guilty to a charge carrying a maximum possible prison sentence of up to five years.[33] The report I had requested confirmed that he was disturbed and troublesome, told other things I already knew, and concluded that, "giving serious weight to the nature of the offense and primarily for this reason," the defendant should be given the maximum sentence under the statute. Of course, if there was anything for which the sentencing judge would not be looking to psychologists and other experts outside the law, it was guidance as to "the nature of the offense." Undoubtedly, the vagueness of my inquiry merited no more than this useless response. I have tried since to do better. Sometimes, but rarely, the reports are more helpful.

Judges and parole officials rarely communicate with each other, let alone undertake to coordinate what in theory are connected and complementary responsibilities.[34] The stultifying effects of this mutual isolation may be illustrated by the results (or absence of results) of a change intended as beneficent and enacted by Congress in 1958. The amendment empowers a federal district judge to provide in his sentence that the Parole Board may declare a prisoner eligible at any time for parole[35] rather than leave the earliest eligibility date at the normal one-third of the sentence.[36] By this means the lawmakers supposed that "[t]he prisoner's release would be geared more to his readiness for community life, in terms of the public safety, rather than to the completion of a fixed and arbitrary period of imprisonment." [37] At

[33] 18 U.S.C. § 871 (1964).

[34] Prisoners' efforts to have parole decisions reviewed—usually failures thus far, *e.g.*, Thompkins v. United States Bd. of Parole, 427 F.2d 222 (5th Cir. 1970) (per curiam); United States v. Frederick, 405 F.2d 129, 133 (3d Cir. 1968) (per curiam); Brest v. Ciccone, 371 F.2d 981 (8th Cir. 1967) (per curiam); *see* MODEL PENAL CODE § 305.19 (Proposed Official Draft 1962); *but see* United States *ex rel.* Campbell v. Pate, 401 F.2d 55 (7th Cir. 1968); Sobell v. Reed, 327 F. Supp. 1294 (S.D.N.Y. 1971)—are obviously not collaborative exchanges between the parole agency and the court.

[35] Act of Aug. 25, 1958, Pub. L. No. 85-752, § 3, 72 Stat. 845-46 (codified at 18 U.S.C. § 4208(a) (1964)).

[36] 18 U.S.C. § 4202 (1964).

[37] H.R. REP. No. 1946, 85th Cong., 2d Sess. 9 (1958).

least some judges of spacious outlook have reacted enthusiastically, using the new authority liberally and urging others to do so.[38] In this, of course, as in all things, there being no prescribed criteria, the judges vary widely; some employ the statute extensively, some hardly at all or never. More pertinent at the moment, however, is the absence of any provision, or any practice, under which the sentencing judge says what he thinks he is driving at when he authorizes the Parole Board to set an early eligibility date. Is it because of some special promise discerned in the particular defendant? Is it because the defendant uniquely exhibits that rehabilitation is a conceivable objective in his case? Is it a means of showing qualified leniency? Is it simply a way of yielding up responsibility? Whether it should be or not, the authority to allow early parole eligibility is the judge's. But nothing requires him to say, and he normally does not say, why the question is ruled one way or the other.

The Parole Board is nonresponsive in kind. In 13 years or so, we have had no organized account of how the early eligibility statute has worked. We have no sense of what its impact has been, if any. We do not know, to put it simply, whether a provision in the sentence for early eligibility (1) has any effect upon the prisoner's morale or functioning, (2) tends to advance actual release on parole, or (3) has any possible effects on prisoners not granted the putative benefit of eligibility. The Parole Board, where the ultimate burden and responsibility fall, has repaid the silence of the judges by never offering any suggestions as to the kinds of cases peculiarly suited for early eligibility or the factors it would deem material in making the judgment.

Finally, as to the prisoners themselves, my mail from defendants sentenced during some six years reveals an attitude of total cynicism. Without having made a reliable poll, I am inclined to believe, from the reports of other judges as well as defendants writing to me, that the statute is viewed as a farce by its intended beneficiaries. The belief in the prisons seems to be that the Parole Board pays no special attention to cases in which it is authorized to find early eligibility. Some statistics I have obtained, not without difficulty, may tend to support this belief in that they reveal only a minute number of cases in which parole

38 *E.g.*, Devitt, *Setting the Maximum and Minimum Term of Imprisonment*, 26 F.R.D. 312, 317–18 (1959).

is actually granted before one-third of the term has been served.[39] It is not possible, of course, to accept the view that the Parole Board would utterly ignore a power of this sort. Still, the conviction to this effect among prisoners is in itself a fact of depressing moment. And the Parole Board does and says nothing to dispel the conviction.

The silent void in which prisoners live extends through most aspects of sentencing and the so-called corrections process. Going back to the inception, the defendant about to be sentenced is commonly invited to speak in his own behalf. The invitation, the right of "allocution," is meaningful now and then. The Federal Rules of Criminal Procedure preserve the right,[40] recognizing that "[t]he most persuasive counsel may not be able to speak for a defendant as the defendant might, with halting eloquence, speak for himself."[41] But the average defendant, invited to speak for himself, shakes his head, says he has nothing to say, or declares that his lawyer has already said everything there is to say. And how should it be otherwise? Except to beg mercy, which some do with varied effect but most avoid, what is there to say? The situation of counsel, for all the client's professed approval of his thoroughness, is not much better. There being no sure rules or standards, there are no clear issues to define the task. The judge is a target, of course, to be studied for where to aim, but this is a sport for which most lawyers are untrained and modestly equipped. There are exceptions; some lawyers have achieved triumphs by persuasively proposing courses of treatment and sentencing theories. But the usual effort ranges from a quiet, mildly effective marshalling of sympathetic facts to an oratorical assault under which the judge must fight past the poetry and biblical truths to seek a measure of decency for the defendant.

When the sentence is imposed, the darkness deepens for the defendant; there usually is, as I have said, little or nothing to show that a reasoned judgment is being rendered. This is not to imagine that the average defendant, doomed to a term of confinement, is likely to find pleasure or solace in a coherent rationale for the affliction. It is to say that the failure to explain, especially

---

[39] Parole eligibility after one-third of the sentence has been served is routine, 18 U.S.C. § 4202 (1964), apart from the provision allowing the Parole Board to fix a date.

[40] FED. R. CRIM. P. 32(a)(1).

[41] Green v. United States, 365 U.S. 301, 304 (1961).

in light of the ample time for later brooding, lends a quality of baleful mystery rather than open justice. At the least, the absence of an explanation does nothing to quell the disposition to suspect unfairness, fired later by encounters with prisoners who have much lighter sentences based upon circumstances that seem, or are perceived to be (or, simply, are), essentially identical.[42]

It is frequently reported that the prison authorities continue the policy of silence. Among the most common of inmates' complaints is the resentment against being ignored, the feeling that there is no means or opportunity, certainly no right, to be informed about relevant matters either inside or outside the walls. Prisoners have often asserted that they are kept uncertain about how to behave, about what the rules are, about what in general is expected of them, or why.[43] This least bearable aspect of isolation appears often to have included barriers preventing communications with counsel and courts about legal rights and remedies, although this problem, at least according to the law books, seems to be in process of elimination.[44] Feeling that they are kept in the dark, prisoners often complain that their keepers positively deceive and mislead them.[45] This may reflect frequently the paranoia fostered by a regime of secrecy and apparent mystery.[46] It undoubtedly reflects to some considerable extent the actual

---

[42] "It is important . . . that the offender himself understand how his sentence is based on his needs; resentment of what appears to him to be unequal sentencing hinders his adjustment." GUIDES FOR SENTENCING 5; *cf.* G. ZILBOORG, *supra* note 4, at 97-98, 106.

[43] *See, e.g.*, W. GAYLIN, *supra* note 23, at 150-51, 247-48; G. SYKES, THE SOCIETY OF CAPTIVES 74-76 (1958); D. WARD & G. KASSEBAUM, WOMEN'S PRISON: SEX AND SOCIAL STRUCTURE 18-29 (1965).

[44] *See* Johnson v. Avery, 393 U.S. 483 (1969); Burns v. Swenson, 430 F.2d 771, 776-77 (8th Cir. 1970); Nolan v. Scafati, 430 F.2d 548, 550-51 (1st Cir. 1970); Stiltner v. Rhay, 322 F.2d 314, 316 (9th Cir. 1963), *cert. denied*, 376 U.S. 920, *rehearing denied*, 376 U.S. 959 (1964); Gilmore v. Lynch, 319 F. Supp. 105 (N.D. Cal. 1970) (3-judge ct.), *aff'd sub nom.* Younger v. Gilmore, 404 U.S. 15 (1971). For a discussion of some earlier cases dealing with the access of prisoners to counsel and courts, *see* Note, *Constitutional Rights of Prisoners: The Developing Law*, 110 U. PA. L. REV. 985, 987-95 (1962).

[45] *See, e.g.*, W. GAYLIN, *supra* note 23, at 254.

[46] It might go without saying that the wall of silence and distrust has two sides. One need not be a penologist to recognize a chief commandment of the prison community: "Never talk to a screw." *See, e.g.*, Cloward, *Social Control in the Prison*, in SOCIAL SCIENCE RESEARCH COUNCIL, THEORETICAL STUDIES IN SOCIAL ORGANIZATION OF THE PRISON 20, 44-45 (1960); McCleery, *Communication Patterns as Bases of Systems of Authority and Power*, in SOCIAL SCIENCE RESEARCH COUNCIL, *supra*, 49, 57, 59. *Cf.* Goffman, *On the Characteristics of Total Institutions: The Inmate World*, in THE PRISON 15, 18-20 (D. Cressey ed. 1961).

state of affairs wherever petty officials—often frightened, insecure and ignorant themselves—exercise largely unreviewable and irresistible power.[47]

Whatever the qualities of prison life itself—and, obviously, they vary from the most bestial to such relatively civilized conditions as the federal system is generally acknowledged to present [48] —parole officials carry on for the most part the motif of Kafka's nightmares. It has been expressed by the United States Board of Parole almost as a matter of pride that the judgment whether or when a prisoner will be released is inscrutable. Describing itself and its functions, the Board has written:

> Voting is done on an individual basis by each member and the Board does not sit as a group for this purpose. Each member studies the prisoner's file and places his name on the official order form to signify whether he wishes to grant or deny parole. The reasoning and thought which led to his vote are not made a part of the order, and it is therefore impossible to state precisely why a particular prisoner was or was not granted parole.[49]

Viewing this oracular style of unexplained edict as an article of doctrine, parole boards meet demands for explanations with stout resistance, usually successful.[50] The New Jersey Supreme Court has lately denounced and altered for its State this imperious tradition.[51] The change reflects a growing body of thoughtful opinion.[52] As things stand in most jurisdictions, however, and

---

[47] I should acknowledge that the paragraph just ended touches glancingly a minute aspect of an enormous subject. The problems of prison and prison reform are outside the subject of sentencing as it is commonly bounded—*see, e.g.*, MODEL PENAL CODE arts. 6–7, 301–06, 401–03 (Proposed Official Draft 1962); MODEL SENTENCING ACT; PROPOSED FEDERAL CRIMINAL CODE chs. 30–36, at 271–317—and, at least equally, outside my competence. By the same token, the observations here about prisons are the most impressionistic and second-hand of all the factual matters in this paper.

[48] *See, e.g.*, H. BARNES & N. TEETERS, NEW HORIZONS IN CRIMINOLOGY 581-87 (2d ed. 1951); P. TAPPAN, CRIME, JUSTICE, AND CORRECTION 619 (1960).

[49] FUNCTIONS OF THE UNITED STATES BOARD OF PAROLE 4–5 (1964). Compare the text of "demands and grievances" by rioting prisoners in Rahway, New Jersey, who complained, *inter alia*: "Rahway Prison is a place where you never know how to make parole." N.Y. Times, Nov. 27, 1971, at 18, col. 3, 4.

[50] *See, e.g.*, Thompkins v. United States Bd. of Parole, 427 F.2d 222 (5th Cir. 1970) (per curiam); Lewis v. Rockefeller, 305 F. Supp. 258 (S.D.N.Y. 1969), *aff'd*, 431 F.2d 368 (2d Cir. 1970).

[51] Monks v. New Jersey State Parole Bd., 58 N.J. 238, 277 A.2d 193 (1971).

[52] *See* K. DAVIS, DISCRETIONARY JUSTICE 131 (1969); PRESIDENT'S COMM'N ON LAW ENFORCEMENT AND ADMINISTRATION OF JUSTICE, TASK FORCE REPORT: CORRECTIONS 64–65, 86 (1967).

have long stood, parole boards, subject to no precise criteria and offering no explicit clues as to why particular decisions go as they do, exercise secretly the power to decide within broad ranges the actual number of years of confinement.

Not surprisingly, it is widely believed, with the utmost plausibility, that considerations crassly "political" or otherwise unprincipled are weighty in the granting or denial of parole. Everyone should be able with a little thought to recall highly publicized cases in which parole board decisions have spawned pages of rumors, "inside" information, and speculation while the agency maintained its prim and haughty silence. As is true of prison officials, parole boards are often seen by prisoners as tyrannically secret, corrupt, and fraudulent.[53] Decisions based upon secret reasons bear no credentials of care or legitimacy. There is encouraged a feeling that the parole board, like all the other machinery of power, is not to be trusted.[54]

---

[53] *See* K. DAVIS, *supra* note 52, at 132; W. GAYLIN, *supra* note 23, at 150-51; H. GRISWOLD, M. MISENHEIMER, A. POWERS & E. TROMANHAUSER, AN EYE FOR AN EYE 196, 204, 248, 253-54, 276 (1970); Rasmussen, *Prisoner Opinions about Parole,* in CRIMINOLOGY 649-50 (C. Vedder, S. Koenig & R. Clark eds. 1955); *Prisoners' Rights and the Correctional Scheme: The Legal Controversy and Problems of Implementation,* 16 VILL. L. REV. 1088, 1092-93 (1971) (panel discussion) (remarks of Victor Taylor, a former inmate and present member of the Barbwire Society).

[54] The habit of being casual about explanations, and free of any obligation to account, makes it easy to hand out inaccurate or incomplete information even when there is no deliberate purpose to deceive. The United States Parole Board, in a booklet entitled "You and the Parole Board," undertakes to inform prisoners through a series of questions and answers. One passage reads this way:

> Do The Police Or The FBI Make Recommendations To The Parole Board Regarding Parole?
>
> The U.S. Attorney who prosecuted your case *and the Federal judge who sentenced you* are invited to make recommendations regarding parole; these recommendations are submitted to the Board prior to your first hearing and are part of the material the Board considers at this time. [Question No. 26, emphasis added.]

Having consulted judges of my court and my own experience of six years, I can testify this is incorrect information. Most of us have never been consulted about parole. A few of my seniors recall a couple of rare exceptions long ago. One or two have suggested explanations from bygone practices of how the Parole Board's account may once have been accurate though it is not any longer. Nothing justifies, however, the purveying of such misinformation to people in prison. (My copy of the booklet is dated January 1, 1971.) It is not a mitigating factor, though it may be an added irony, that the idea of consulting the sentencing judge is essentially nonsense anyhow. The judge has had no opportunity for the kind of observation that is supposedly for the Parole Board. He knows nothing of the post-sentencing history. He is likely, in a word, to have nothing to contribute.

II. Some Existing Devices and Proposals for Improvement

The two most basic and obvious evils in our sentencing process are (1) the excessive powers of the individual judge and (2) the inadequacies of judges (or anyone) for the fair and acceptable exercise of such powers. Efforts toward reform have concentrated on possible means to abridge and channel the powers of judges. There has been some effort as well to improve the judges' competence for sentencing, but this has not seemed comparably promising or feasible.

I propose now to discuss and comment upon five of these things: first, fairly briefly, the device of sentencing institutes to educate judges; then, also briefly, three measures designed to guide or limit the individual judge—sentencing councils, sentencing tribunals, and appellate review of sentences; and, finally, at greater length, the increasingly favored technique of indeterminate sentences, the effect of which is to transfer power from the sentencing judge to the parole board or some similar agency.

A. *Sentencing Institutes*

By a statute passed on August 25, 1958,[55] adopting a recommendation of the Judicial Conference of the United States, the Congress provided for the conducting of sentencing institutes and joint councils. The action reflected congressional concern with "the existence of widespread disparities in the sentences imposed by Federal courts . . . in different parts of the country, between adjoining districts, and even in the same districts." [56] The new law authorized, "[i]n the interest of uniformity in sentencing procedures," the convening of "institutes and joint councils for the purpose of studying, discussing, and formulating the objectives, policies, standards, and criteria for sentencing." [57] (Nobody stopped, and it would have done no good to stop, over the enormity of explicitly recognizing how, after thousands of years of prison sentences and uncounted executions, even the "objectives" awaited "formulating.") The statute continues in its unaltered terms to provide:

> The agenda of the institutes and joint councils may include but shall not be limited to: (1) The development of standards for

[55] Pub. L. No. 85–752, § 1, 72 Stat. 845 (1958).
[56] H.R. Rep. No. 1946, 85th Cong., 2d Sess. 6 (1958).
[57] 28 U.S.C. § 334(a) (1964).

> the content and utilization of presentence reports; (2) the establishment of factors to be used in selecting cases for special study and observation in prescribed diagnostic clinics; (3) the determination of the importance of psychiatric, emotional, sociological and physiological factors involved in crime and their bearing upon sentences; (4) the discussion of special sentencing problems in unusual cases such as treason, violation of public trust, subversion, or involving abnormal sex behavior, addiction to drugs or alcohol, and mental or physical handicaps; (5) the formulation of sentencing principles and criteria which will assist in promoting the equitable administration of the criminal laws of the United States.[58]

As is our wont, many of us greeted this innovation with unstinting exuberance. For example, the Deputy Attorney General, a former district judge and notably able lawyer, told the first institute the new program is "important because it reconciles the need for judicial independence with the need for consistency" [59] —surely, if he was right, among the grander reconciliations in the law. He stressed that the aim should be "consistency without regimentation of any sort" [60]—meaning, as he proceeded to elaborate, that the individuality of judges must be preserved at all costs because "rules and regulations of a kind needed to control large numbers of people are inappropriate with regard to the Federal judiciary." [61] Finally, he rejoiced:

> The institute program also should eliminate the need for further consideration of legislation giving appellate courts power to modify sentence.[62]

Whatever the enthusiasms of inaugural addresses, sentencing institutes have been, as was foretellable, fairly limited enterprises. They are occasional gatherings for a day or so of judges and, frequently, others (probation officers, parole officials, lawyers, and scholars) from a single Circuit or group of Circuits. Selected topics may include problems of sentencing in particular kinds of cases (tax, auto theft, etc.),[63] general forms of sentence

---

[58] *Id.*

[59] Walsh, *An Expression of Interest on the Part of the Department of Justice*, in *Pilot Institute on Sentencing*, 26 F.R.D. 231, 250 (1959).

[60] *Id.*

[61] *Id.* at 251.

[62] *Id.* For Judge Walsh's further observations on the evils of appellate review, *see* text accompanying note 80 *infra.*

[63] *See Pilot Institute on Sentencing*, 26 F.R.D. 231, 264-321 (1959).

and sentencing procedure (*e.g.*, parole eligibility, commitments for study, motions to reduce sentence),[64] or actual cases in which presentence reports are distributed, the assembled judges formulate tentative sentences, and there is discussion of the predictably divergent views.[65]

The institutes are of some utility. But their worth could easily be overstated. They serve to inform the judges of sentencing options and alternatives that might otherwise be overlooked (at least in the absence of a competent probation officer). They supply occasions for deliberate, connected exchanges of differing premises and attitudes. While that much is worthwhile, it is a small thing after all. The sharp limitations include the infrequency and brevity of these convocations. Without knowing exactly how typical it is, I imagine my own experience cannot be utterly atypical. In six years on the largest of our federal district courts I have spent two afternoons at sentencing institutes, one within my own Circuit, the other at a national seminar for "new" judges to which I was invited after two and one-half years on the bench and some hundreds of years of prison sentences imposed.

The subjects treated in the institutes are somewhat random and disconnected. The results of the discussions are quaintly inconclusive. The goals of the statute providing for the institutes include the hope of achieving "a desirable degree of consensus" among the judges.[66] If this has happened, it is not patent. Sometimes the institutes produce "majority support" for one view or another[67]—supposedly assuring a defendant that something is more likely to happen to him than the opposite if he is sentenced by one of the judges voting. Sometimes it is recorded that there is "no consensus,"[68] which may or may not be less reassuring to a defendant. Some judges may change their views after discussion—perhaps adopting or abandoning positions such as (1) that draft law offenders should all get maximum (five-year) sentences to balance the service of those who comply or (2) that draft law offenders should never be imprisoned if

[64] *See Sentencing Institute* (Ninth Circuit), 27 F.R.D. 287, 303–24 (1960).

[65] *See Seminar and Institute on Disparity of Sentences for Sixth, Seventh and Eighth Judicial Circuits*, 30 F.R.D. 401, 428–57 (1961).

[66] S. Rep. No. 2013, 85th Cong., 2d Sess. 3 (1958). *See also* Celler, *supra* note 24, at 243.

[67] *See Seminar and Institute on Disparity of Sentences*, *supra* note 65, at 459–60.

[68] *See id.* at 460.

their resistance is principled. For the most part the judges tend to record their differences, reassure each other of their independence, and go home to do their disparate things as before.

The imperfections may not be grounds for abandoning the institutes. If they are to be meaningful, however, they must become significantly broader and deeper. Recalling that most federal district judges are more or less thoroughly ignorant of the criminal law when they come to the bench, I would suggest there is need for a serious, carefully planned and organized course of initial study, perhaps for a month or so, devoted to this area, and largely to problems of sentencing. There should be reading, lecturing, and discussion about the fundamental questions of philosophy and penology. Prisons should be visited and studied. Professional scholars should be the main faculty, not older judges too much given to anecdotal wisdom. How much else might be desirable is a question best postponed while we determine the degree to which individual judges are to be left, as they are now, with wide-ranging autonomy.

B. *Sentencing Councils*

Beginning just over a decade ago, the judges of the Eastern District of Michigan (Detroit), concerned about disparities, began to meet weekly to discuss specific cases. The "sentencing councils" thus born have evolved into a regularized procedure. Citing in the margin from the literature on the Michigan practice and its counterparts adopted in 1962 in the Eastern District of New York (Brooklyn) and in 1963 in the Northern District of Illinois (Chicago),[69] I merely sketch here the outlines of the procedure. The judge charged with the case and two or more of his colleagues receive copies of the presentence report; each, after studying the report, notes a tentative sentence; they meet then, together with a probation officer (in Detroit and Brooklyn, at least), and discuss the case; the presiding judge thereafter conducts the sentencing proceeding, with full authority still to

---

[69] ABA SENTENCING STANDARDS 294–98; Doyle, *A Sentencing Council in Operation*, 25 FED. PROBATION, Sept. 1961, at 27; Hosner, *Group Procedures in Sentencing: A Decade of Practice*, 34 FED. PROBATION, Dec. 1970, at 18; Levin, *Toward a More Enlightened Sentencing Procedure*, 45 NEB. L. REV. 499 (1966); Parsons, *Aids in Sentencing*, 35 F.R.D. 423, 431–34 (1964); Smith, *The Sentencing Council and the Problem of Disproportionate Sentences*, 27 FED. PROBATION, June 1963, at 5; Zavatt, *Sentencing Procedure in the United States District Court for the Eastern District of New York*, 41 F.R.D. 469 (1966).

decide and pronounce the actual sentence; and, finally, he records and reports that sentence to the other conferees.

The system supplies material for studying certain obvious kinds of questions. The evidence, not surprisingly, shows:

> (1) The sentencing judge appears in a substantial percentage of cases to move from his tentative stance toward a different sentence reflecting the views of his colleagues;
> (2) the individual extremes in sentencing views, both harsh and lenient, tend to be tempered; and
> (3) despite the tendency towards "averaging," the net overall effect may be a shortening of prison terms and an increasing use of probation.[70]

It appears, in addition, that the participating judges are pleased with the procedure, and that it is of special benefit to the newly appointed judge.

Despite the enthusiasm of the participants, the sentencing council has not spread among the multijudge federal courts. The Ninth Circuit, in a 1964 sentencing institute, adopted a resolution calling for creation of such councils. As of 1966, no district court within the Circuit had followed it.[71] The arguments against the procedure are, first, that it is too time-consuming, and, second, that it is a threat or an affront to the independence of the sentencing judge.[72] These are, with utmost deference to their proponents, not among the most inspiring theses for federal judges. As to the question of time, it is hard to take seriously the matter of a couple of hours a week measured against (a) the hours federal district judges spend deciding copyright claims on plastic flowers or similar objects, questions of "fault" in auto accident cases that should certainly be handled elsewhere, issues as to whether the shipper's or the carrier's insurance company should pay for spoiled vegetables, and other subjects not necessarily momentous; and (b) the possibility that years of people's lives in or out of prison may turn on the time thus invested.

As to the question of "independence," this conception, in this context, is among the most basic confusions afflicting judges and their friends. It is one thing to worry lest extraneous influences or pressures be exerted in ways that might impair judicial integrity by deflecting the decisional process from the course of

---

[70] *See* materials cited in note 69 *supra*.
[71] Zavatt, *supra* note 69, at 471-72.
[72] *See id.* at 471.

law. It is quite another thing, and an error, to suppose that the same subversion might follow from subjecting judges to procedures for study, deliberation, and the exercise of reason.[73] The supporters of sentencing councils have been at pains to emphasize that the sentencing judge remains unfettered in any event.[74] The concern seems excessive; no value worth preserving would be bruised, and solid ends would be furthered, by modifying the absolute authority of the single, unpredictable, possibly unwise district judge. The professed concern about "independence" in sentencing should be compared with the responsible observation of a group by no means revolutionary "that in no other area of our law does one man exercise such unrestricted power. No other country in the free world permits this condition to exist." [75]

What may be the most characteristic, and perhaps the most troublesome, aspect of this subject is the fact that each multi-judge court has been left to decide independently whether its time and its integrity will permit the use of sentencing councils. Perhaps a period of 11 years or so is not long enough to warrant acting, either way, upon the experiment. But this does not appear to be the real reason, or a good one, for inaction. We are back once again to the kind of national indifference to "criminals" that leaves to individual judges a sweeping autonomy lacking rational justification in principle. There has been time enough and evidence enough to know whether sentencing councils are valuable. If the answer is yes, they should be required by law.

C. *Mixed Sentencing Tribunals*

Thirty-five years ago, Professor Sheldon Glueck, pressing, with characteristic vigor, an idea that was not altogether novel even

[73] It has been suggested that the defendant is prejudiced when judges he has no chance to confront participate in discussions leading to the sentence. Apart from its flimsiness as a matter of law, *cf.* Williams v. New York, 337 U.S. 241 (1949), the thought is not substantial. The courtroom ritual is normally (though not always) an empty detail of the sentencing process. Sentencers must and do consider many things, and consult about them outside the courtroom. In those cases where the hearing on sentence raises matters of moment, the judge with the final say is there to hear them, to be influenced by them, and, if need be, to take them back to his council colleagues for further deliberation.

[74] *See, e.g.,* ABA SENTENCING STANDARDS § 7.1, comment e, at 298; Levin, *supra* note 69, at 503.

[75] ABA APPELLATE REVIEW STANDARDS 2.

then, proposed that responsibility for sentencing be given to a three-member panel, still to include the judge, but also to have a psychiatrist or psychologist as a second member and a sociologist or educator as a third.[76] The suggestion has nowhere been adopted. Yet its soundness seems clear to me. Nobody believes judges are expert in the many things relevant to sentencing. It is not seriously questionable that the knowledge of such people as psychiatrists and the others Glueck named is relevant. Knowledge of this kind is not normally supplied to the sentencing judge in anything like sufficient depth through presentence reports or otherwise. And the question is not simply one of knowledge in the dry sense of empirical data. People with such other backgrounds as Glueck proposed would bring to the task attitudes, modes of thought, and values that could usefully broaden and temper the lawyer's view.

Of course, if sentencing councils are an unwelcome assault upon judicial independence, Glueck's idea is unspeakable. Moreover, his proposal presents genuine difficulties of time, personnel, and expense. The objections would not, however, be decisive in my view. If the basic system of sentencing is to continue along existing lines, I think Professor Glueck's form of tribunal would be markedly preferable to either the single judge or the council of three judges. It deserves, at the least, a deliberate legislative judgment, one way or the other, rather than the casual neglect it has thus far enjoyed.

D. *Appellate Review of Sentences*

In the federal system and a majority of the States, the sentence, if within the commonly extravagant bounds of the statute, is unreviewable except for egregious departures from lawful criteria. With all our protests of concern for law and human rights, ours seems to be the only country in the so-called "free world [that] permits this condition to exist." [77] Nevertheless, a great many trial judges, for all their protests about the agonies of the ultimate responsibility for sentencing, oppose the idea of appellate review. Of course, the judges are divided on this, as

---

[76] S. GLUECK, CRIME AND JUSTICE 225–26 (1936).

[77] ABA APPELLATE REVIEW STANDARDS 2. This useful work collects much of the literature, canvasses the arguments pro and con, and proposes a broad scheme of appellate review. I have borrowed from it for the brief account of the subject given here.

on most things, especially issues about sentencing. But it is fair to say that at least a substantial number are opposed to appeals and that one substantial reason, though not the only one, is a common (and recognizably human) aversion to being criticized and countermanded. Most judges seek to follow, within their capacities, what they perceive as the controlling views of higher courts. It is consistent, if not an inescapable corollary, that many at least are not keen to expand the scope of such controls.[78] It is equally clear that this reluctance by itself is no valid reason for barring appellate review of sentences.

On this subject appellate judges, if normally viewed as natural enemies, are numerously allied with the trial bench. The Chief Judge of my own Circuit, a redoubtable force on any subject, becomes almost ruffled at the idea of appeals from sentences. The Chief Justice of the United States is also opposed to such appeals, at least if routed to the standard appellate tribunals.[79] Again, the ranks are not closed; for example, Senior Judge Simon E. Sobeloff, former Chief Judge of the Fourth Circuit, has long argued for review of sentences, lately adding to his writings and talks his services as head of the valuable ABA Advisory Committee on this subject. As is true of the trial judges, those on appellate courts have varying reasons, of varying cogency, for opposing review. One obvious ground is the enormous volume of new work it would entail. This, if better than the concern of trial judges not to be reversed more than they already are, still is not good enough to warrant much discussion. Considering all the things on which appellate judges ponder, the effort to make sentences more rational and just would hardly seem unworthy of their attentions.

It is also argued that the review of sentences might distort the appellate process. Perhaps in slightly inflated and cloudy terms, the thought has been put this way:

> Appellate courts are designed to be students of the law, to consider questions of the law, and to act in a dispassionate and

[78] For a rare illustration of reaction to a rare reversal for what had been held an error of law in sentencing, *see* United States v. Wiley, 184 F. Supp. 679 (N.D. Ill. 1960).

[79] I understand from a recent talk at a Second Circuit Conference (September 1971) that the Chief Justice would favor a form of review by a panel of district judges. Provisions for such review exist in four States. *See* ABA Appellate Review Standards 31–32. For some of the arguments against an attempt to apply that pattern in the federal courts, *see id.* 34–35.

> detached atmosphere. If there were to be appellate review, proceedings in appellate courts would be corrupted by appeals to emotion and sympathy, and the other things that go into sentence. As a result these great institutions would be deteriorated.[80]

More pointedly, the argument has been that appellate judges might stoop to bargaining in the disposition of appeals, trading off votes for affirmance against votes to reduce sentence.

To treat the latter thought separately, it is, I think, overwhelmingly refutable. It may be questioned along the way whether the feared form of negotiated decision would actually be much worse than, or essentially different from, things we have now. We tend with heady logic to think of guilt or innocence as sharply separate from questions of punishment. But is this so in practical fact? It is surely debatable whether a reasonable doubt in the case of an offense punishable by a $100 fine is the same kind or degree of reservation as in a case involving possible imprisonment for a long term of years. Many of us know, and even admit, that the trial judge sitting without a jury, and aware, as the jury would not be,[81] that there is a mandatory minimum sentence, may be unable to determine guilt or innocence wholly free of any logically polluting echoes from the sealed subject of punishment.[82] Similarly, it is an open question whether the judge at sentencing should be, or is, entirely impervious to any thoughts about how clearly the evidence supported the jury's verdict. Once acknowledge that the weight of evidence, the "reasonableness" of a search, the propriety of a discretionary ruling, and a long list of comparable factors are not mathematical integers, and it becomes a complex question

---

80 Walsh, *supra* note 59, at 251.

81 It is routine practice to charge federal juries that punishment is none of their business and to withhold from jurors what the statute says about the possible sentence. *See* 1 E. DEVITT & C. BLACKMAR, FEDERAL JURY PRACTICE AND INSTRUCTIONS 303 (2d ed. 1970). The boiler plate runs about like this:

> The punishment provided by law for the offense . . . charged in the indictment . . . is a matter exclusively within the province of the Court, and should never be considered by the jury in any way, in arriving at an impartial verdict as to the guilt or innocence of the accused.

Id. § 17.08, at 321. Jurors are often told this even when it is literally false, in cases where the statute provides a mandatory minimum sentence so that, to a large extent, punishment actually is not "a matter exclusively within the province of the Court."

82 Beyond its basis in introspection and confessions shared around the robing room, this statement is reported by other observers. *See* Brown & Schwartz, *Sentencing under the Draft Federal Code,* 56 A.B.A.J. 935, 938 (1970).

whether guilt and sentence must never be weighed or debated together. It is, however, a question too large and unnecessary to answer in the present context. For the existing law barring review of sentences is actually known to work covert "bargains" and unpredictable stratagems worse than those feared by the opponents of explicit appealability. All acknowledge that there are cases, often identifiable, where convictions are reversed ostensibly on strained legal grounds touching the trial but in fact because the appellate court (despite the hardiness of our appellate courts in this respect) finds the sentence unbearably harsh.[83] A candid system of known appellate rights should be seen as preferable without a long brief.

Of course, the supposed evil of bargaining is manageable in a variety of ways less crudely excessive than the entire preclusion of appeals. Appeals against sentence could be separate proceedings, as they are in England, perhaps after the appeal from conviction, if any. Or separate appellate tribunals could be constituted. In the end, I agree with the ABA Project on Minimum Standards that the propriety of the sentence should be included generally among the subjects for the single appeal now available in criminal cases.[84]

We come to a final argument against appeals of sentences: sentencing is a matter of discretion, not "law," and hence unsuited for review.[85] Of course, this is an appalling confession of the point I have lingered over at some length: we have been able for so long, with such composure, to use courts of so-called law to execute or lock people away for some or all of the years of their lives while conceding, and, when convenient, insisting, that "our system has yet to develop a rational and consistent approach to the sentencing problem." [86] A slight variation of essentially the same thought is the suggestion—coming with characteristic arrogance from trial judges and rare diffidence from appellate judges—that the trial bench really has the relevant wisdom born of experience and first-hand observation of the defendant, and that, insofar as judges are not qualified for sentencing people, three unqualified second-guessers add nothing worth bothering about.[87]

---

[83] *See* ABA Appellate Review Standards 3.

[84] *Id.* 37-39.

[85] *See, e.g.,* text accompanying note 80 *supra.*

[86] ABA Appellate Review Standards 27.

[87] *Cf.* R. Ensor, *supra* note 26, at 22.

However the point is proposed, it should not prevail. The trial judge's observation of the defendant is a factor, to be sure. It is often a minor and fleeting factor. It is, in the folklore of our judicial system, overdrawn and overweighed.[88] Insofar as it is real, however, it could be acknowledged and respected by appellate judges, as it is in cognate areas where nobody doubts that appeals are perfectly feasible and proper.[89] Similarly, the fact that the subject of sentencing lies in discretion may affect the style and scope of review. It should not preclude review of sentencing any more than it has precluded review of many other discretionary rulings.

That the subject is not now one of "law" should serve to demonstrate the need for review rather than the opposite. The argument in this quarter against appeals is uniquely incongruous in the setting of our common law tradition. It is banal but pertinent to recall how much of our law has been made precisely in the process of reasoned decision by appellate tribunals. That sentencing is susceptible of being ruled by law, at least to some considerable degree, all would presumably admit. Admitted or not, the experience of our legal kin in England is at hand and readily intelligible as demonstration of the point. The English Criminal Division of the Court of Appeal, as it is now known, has evolved over the years a substantial, orderly, meaningful body of sentencing principles which, if its details are open to criticism, is clearly preferable to the anarchy we have been willing to abide.[90]

Apart from the fact that the absence of law is a challenge rather than a barrier, the notion that appellate courts would find themselves at sea in reviewing sentences is overstated. In addition to England and most other civilized countries, many of our own States offer at least the beginnings of a sentencing juris-

---

[88] *See* Blatt, *"He Saw the Witnesses,"* 38 J. AM. JUD. SOC. 86 (1954).

[89] "Findings of fact shall not be set aside unless clearly erroneous, and due regard shall be given to the opportunity of the trial court to judge of the credibility of the witnesses." FED. R. CIV. P. 52(a).

[90] D. THOMAS, *supra* note 10, undertakes to synthesize English Court of Appeal decisions on appeals against sentence during the period between January 1962 and October 1969. The result is a lucid and orderly account that could not fail to guide the efforts of trial counsel and trial judges. My own attendance at a few arguments of such appeals, even as supplemented by the accounts of others similarly impressed, scarcely qualifies as a course of scholarly appraisal. I mention it incidentally and report that it served, if in a modest degree, to bolster the belief that the enterprise is susceptible of rational and fruitful management.

prudence in their practice allowing review. And if there were nothing else, we have the evidence of numerous cases in which, without the articulation of any rule, it is obvious that monstrously excessive punishments have been imposed from whatever access of vice or overweening virtue may prompt judges to do such things. Where there is no review, we have the spectacle of appellate courts wringing their hands and protesting their impotence as they either leave standing some cruel but still excessively usual judgment[91] or seek to cajole or jockey the lower court into reconsidering.[92] Or, as noted earlier, we have the lawlessness, less detectable but well known, of reversal of harsh sentences on other grounds given as pretexts.

While the alternative of candid review seems plainly preferable, nobody suggests that this form of improvement should come as an isolated and exhaustive reform. Closely tied to it is the need—important for its own sake but also to supply the basis for intelligent appeals—that sentencing judges explain what they are doing. Beyond that, concerning the need for *law,* it is late in the day to wait for the slow congealing of principles in the common-law style of more leisurely eras and problems. As I plan to say at greater length, the matter is one peculiarly for broad judgments of policy by the representative agencies of a democratic society.

With these understandings, I would join the powerful current of opinion sweeping now toward provision in the federal system and elsewhere for appellate review of sentences.[93]

---

[91] *See, e.g.,* Jones v. United States, No. 71-1381, at 1200 (2d Cir., Dec. 28, 1971) (Hays, J., concurring); United States v. Jackson, 422 F.2d 975, 978 (6th Cir. 1970); Withrow v. United States, 420 F.2d 1220, 1225 (5th Cir. 1969); United States v. McElreath, 412 F.2d 847 (10th Cir. 1969); Smith v. United States, 407 F.2d 356, 359 (8th Cir.), *cert. denied,* 395 U.S. 966 (1969); United States v. Mitchell, 392 F.2d 214, 217 (2d Cir. 1968) (Kaufman, J., concurring); Smith v. United States, 273 F.2d 462, 467-68 (10th Cir. 1959), *cert. denied,* 363 U.S. 846 (1960). *See also* Gore v. United States, 357 U.S. 386, 393 (1958); Scott v. United States, 419 F.2d 264, 266 n.2 (D.C. Cir. 1969), and cases cited therein.

[92] *See, e.g.,* United States v. Daniels, 429 F.2d 1273, 1274 (6th Cir. 1970); United States v. Ginzburg, 398 F.2d 52 (3d Cir. 1968); United States v. Moody, 371 F.2d 688, 693-94 (6th Cir.), *cert. denied,* 386 U.S. 1003 (1967); United States v. West Coast News Co., 357 F.2d 855, 864-66 (6th Cir. 1966), *rev'd on other grounds sub nom.* Aday v. United States, 388 U.S. 447 (1967).

[93] In addition to ABA APPELLATE REVIEW STANDARDS, and the array of authorities it collects, *see* PROPOSED FEDERAL CRIMINAL CODE 317 (proposed amendment of 28 U.S.C. § 1291). *See also* S. 2228, 92d Cong., 1st Sess. (1971), the latest in a series of federal bills (others of which are collected in ABA APPELLATE REVIEW STANDARDS, app. B, at 86-90) which appear with each Congress to move closer toward passage.

E. *Indeterminate Sentences*

Among the changes in the law of punishments over the last 100 years or so has been the movement toward what may be loosely referred to as "indeterminate sentences." [94] The quoted term is widely used. But it has a somewhat indeterminate meaning.[95] As I use it here, it refers generally to any sentence of confinement in which the actual term to be served is not known on the day of judgment but will be subject, within a substantial range, to the later decision of a board of parole or some comparable agency.[96] In this sense there are varying degrees of indeterminacy, ranging from places like California, where the Adult Authority is empowered to set a maximum term of anywhere from a year to life,[97] to, say, our federal system where, as a general matter, the Board of Parole has discretion to grant parole at any point between completion of one-third and two-thirds of the stated sentence.[98]

The basic premise of the indeterminate sentence is the modern conception that rehabilitation is the paramount goal in sentencing. The idea is to avoid the Procrustean mold of uniform sentences to fit crimes in the abstract and to focus upon the progress over time of the unique individual in order to determine when it may be safe for society and good for him to set him free, at least within the limits of parole supervision. At the same time, the power given to a single parole agency may be expected to mitigate the disparities in sentencing caused by the unregulated vagaries of individual judges. While it has not been advanced as a primary justification for the indeterminate sen-

---

[94] P. TAPPAN, *supra* note 48, at 432–37. The first statute providing for indeterminate sentences was passed for the Elmira Reformatory in New York in 1877. N.Y. LAWS 1877, ch. 173.

[95] *See* ABA SENTENCING STANDARDS 131.

[96] For a different, probably more orthodox usage, *see* S. RUBIN, CRIME AND JUVENILE DELINQUENCY 175–76 (2d ed. 1961).

[97] Under California law, the judge may not "fix the term or duration of the period of imprisonment"; he merely imposes the sentence of imprisonment "prescribed by law." CAL. PENAL CODE § 1168 (West 1970). After service of the prison sentence has begun, the Adult Authority may then "determine and redetermine . . . what length of time, if any, such person shall be imprisoned." *Id.* § 3020. This power to set a term of imprisonment and "redetermine" it is subject to any maximum or minimum prescribed by statute for the particular offense. *Id.* § 3023. If the statute prescribes only a minimum term of imprisonment, as is frequently the case, *e.g.*, *id.* §§ 213 (robbery), 461 (burglary), the "maximum" is life imprisonment. *Id.* § 671.

[98] 18 U.S.C. § 4202 (1964); *see also id.* §§ 4161–64.

tence, this seeming power of equalization appears to be at least one among the conceptions of their functions entertained by parole boards.[99]

The goals of flexibility and even-handedness seem compellingly worthy. While they do not state the whole case, they go far to explain why the movement toward indeterminacy in sentencing is a powerful and continuing one. Recognizing that the shift means a transfer of much power and responsibility from the sentencing judge to the parole board, many judges have warmly endorsed this development.[100] Troubled by the weight of the burden, authoritatively aware of their limited qualifications, and committed to the principle that sentencing is for rehabilitation, concerned judges are often eager to hand the task on to the supposedly more expert and full-time attention of parole officials. The principle of at least substantial indeterminacy has acquired potent support through adoption in such august products as the Model Penal Code,[101] the proposed Federal Criminal Code of the National Commission on Reform of Federal Criminal Laws,[102] and the Model Sentencing Act proposed in 1963 by the National Council on Crime and Delinquency.[103] The impact of these models in State revisions of their

---

99 UNITED STATES BOARD OF PAROLE, BIENNIAL REPORT 13, 22 (1971). *See* Johnson, *Multiple Punishment and Consecutive Sentences: Reflections on the* Neal *Doctrine*, 58 CALIF. L. REV. 357, 381–82 (1970); Wechsler, *Sentencing, Correction, and the Model Penal Code*, 109 U. PA. L. REV. 465, 477 (1961); Note, *Individualized Treatment of Criminal Offenders*, 33 NEB. L. REV. 467, 471 (1954). *See also* Hart, *supra* note 30, at 440.

100 *See, e.g.*, Devitt, *supra* note 38, at 317–18; *Seminar and Institute on Disparity of Sentences*, *supra* note 65, at 459.

101 MODEL PENAL CODE § 6.06 (Proposed Official Draft 1962). Under section 6.06, all sentences of imprisonment for felony are indeterminate. The sentencing court sets a minimum term, ranging from one to ten years for a felony of the first degree to one to two years for a felony of the third degree. But the maximum, ranging from possible life imprisonment for a felony of the first degree to five years for a felony of the third degree, is fixed by the statute. The actual length of the sentence is determined by the Board of Parole. *Id.* § 402.2(1)(a). *See also id.* §§ 6.05(2) (special term for young adult offenders), 6.07 (sentence of imprisonment for extended terms). Alternate section 6.06 would authorize the sentencing court to fix both the minimum and the maximum.

102 *See* PROPOSED FEDERAL CRIMINAL CODE 284–86 (proposed 18 U.S.C. § 3201), which largely follows the Model Penal Code scheme described at note 101 *supra*, except that it would authorize the sentencing judge to fix a maximum below the outside limit set by statute and would not require him to impose a minimum term.

103 Under sections 5, 8, and 9 of the Model Sentencing Act, a defendant sentenced to imprisonment is eligible immediately for parole. The judge is empowered to set only a maximum term of confinement.

criminal codes has been, and continues to be, substantial.[104]

In short, the trend toward indeterminate sentences seems irresistible at the moment. I think, however, that it should be resisted.

Before seeking to justify this reactionary stance, let me state it a bit more precisely: I do not argue that the indeterminate sentence is always and everywhere inappropriate. I believe, however, that its unqualified use rests upon undemonstrated premises; that the premises, even if sound, should not have the sweeping application they are given; and that the excessive extension of indeterminacy has probably resulted in much cruelty and injustice, rather than the great goods its proponents envisage.

1. The case for the indeterminate sentence rests upon what a perceptive scholar has called, and skeptically appraised as, the "rehabilitative ideal."[105] The offender is "sick," runs the humanitarian thought, and/or dangerous. He needs to be treated and cured. Nobody, certainly not the sentencing judge, can know when he will be well or safe. Hence, those charged with treating and observing him must be left to decide the time for release.

The theory is flawed in the vagueness and overbreadth of its first premise, the idea of "sickness" calling for medical or quasi-medical "treatment." Many convicted people are not in need of any known form of therapy or rehabilitation. We sentence large numbers of people who probably fall within the class tagged in a lively, psychoanalytically oriented book as "normal criminals" (in contrast with those driven to crime by neurotic or psychotic drives)—that is, people who have coldly and deliberately appraised the risks and rewards, taken their stand against received morality, but then had the misfortune to be caught.[106] Whatever else such defendants may need or deserve, they are not promising candidates for any sort of useful "treatment" available in either our prisons or our hospitals.

Many defendants, especially among those passing through the federal courts, are clearly outside the reach of the indeterminate sentence theory; they are, that is, neither in need of nor amenable to any known form of rehabilitation. One thinks, for

---

[104] *See, e.g.*, CONN. GEN. STAT. ANN. § 53a-35 (Special Pamphlet 1972); KAN. STAT. ANN. §§ 21-4501 to -4504, 21-4603 (Supp. 1970); N.Y. PENAL LAW § 70.00 (McKinney 1967).

[105] F. ALLEN, THE BORDERLAND OF CRIMINAL JUSTICE 25-41 (1964).

[106] F. ALEXANDER & H. STAUB, *supra* note 22, at 81-82, 96, 107, 139-49, 209-11; *cf.* N. WALKER, *supra* note 11, at 101.

example, of the doctor who evaded taxes, the corrupt public official, the antitrust violator. The sentences of at least many such defendants may be thought to serve the ends of deterrence, of "denunciation," [107] or, if we face what many judges are openly doing, of retribution. Again, however, only a somewhat thoughtless lack of discrimination would subject them to the horror of indeterminacy—to wait while a parole board, with no pertinent criteria for judgment, decides that release should be ordered.[108]

Yet notable advocates of indeterminacy and parole board discretion make no distinctions. The Model Penal Code makes *all* sentences indeterminate,[109] leaving to the parole board in all cases a broad range of discretion to determine the eventual length of the sentence. The distinguished National Commission that has lately proposed a new (and in many respects admirable) Federal Criminal Code [110] and the National Council on Crime and Delinquency, in its Model Sentencing Act,[111] do the same. A number of the States have similar provisions.[112] None of these several codes says what the parole board is supposed to do—what standards it is to follow, what kinds of judgments it is to make—in deciding when to release those who are neither sick nor dangerous.

2. The essentially medical model is employed crudely and simple-mindedly by the proponents of indeterminate sentences—ignoring how little is known about rehabilitation and misconceiving the medical analogy in the process. I have started this attack by taking the burden, by arguing that there are many

---

[107] *See* note 30 *supra*.

[108] To take an example from an area of current anguish, there is evidence and a firm belief among responsible observers that Selective Service violators motivated by hostility to the war in Vietnam are most unlikely to make early parole. *See* Solomon, *Sentences in Selective Service and Income Tax Cases*, 52 F.R.D. 481, 483 (1970). They are at the same time not subjects for any of the available forms of therapy or training in the prison system. *See* W. GAYLIN, *supra* note 23, at 26. The cited passage in Judge Solomon's article does not report detailed documentation. His statement has been disputed by parole officials. I have checked with him, and he has graciously supplied substantial evidence for what he says. My observations, if not systematic, corroborate his. The refutation by the Board of Parole—that it has no parole "policy" for draft resisters, any more than for others—is neither persuasive nor comforting.

[109] *See* note 101 *supra*.

[110] *See* note 102 *supra*.

[111] *See* note 103 *supra*.

[112] *E.g.*, CAL. PENAL CODE §§ 1168, 3020, 3023 (West 1970); ILL. ANN. STAT. ch. 38, § 1-7(d) (Smith-Hurd Supp. 1970); OHIO REV. CODE ANN. §§ 5145.01-.02 (Page 1970).

defendants positively identifiable as not suitable subjects for rehabilitation. But the shoe ought really to be on the other foot. The question has to do with locking people up. That is a fierce, tangible step—and a palpable evil, as the utilitarians highlighted for us long ago. The burden of justification, for the confinement and its duration, is upon the jailers. If we say that the prisoner must stay until the experts declare him "cured"—or cured enough—we ought to start with a theory of the illness and a definition of what the experts are good at. But, with some exceptions, that does not happen. The drug addict, the assaultive sex offender, the youth, the juvenile—some kinds of defendants, in substantial numbers, we may have some hopes of trying to "treat." Even as to these the hopes are modest, not only because knowledge is thin but because our human and material resources are exiguous. Yet the well-intentioned pressure for treatment and confinement of uncertain duration is scarcely abated, and is not limited to special categories of defendants.

Because we commonly do not know for sure what we mean by treatment, it is a corollary that we cannot know how long it will take. It follows for the indeterminate sentencers, on beneficent grounds, that the prisoner must live with the torture of "one year to life" or some similar atrocity.[118] It seems to be assumed that the indeterminacy inheres in the treatment, and there is no doubt some analogous experience from fields like psychotherapy where a precise estimate of total time for treatment is not feasible. But the logic employs bizarre premises. The unthinking use of the medical analogy overlooks that many kinds of medical treatment have reasonably precise timetables. As to chronic ailments, discriminating estimates are possible: some are expected confidently to endure for the patient's life; some are known to require intensive care indefinitely; some may be manageable with only occasional interventions by the physician. Varying with the illness, varying prospects may be

[118] Under the Federal Youth Corrections Act, a young offender may be sent for study and a report within 60 days when the judge believes this will help him to sentence intelligently. 18 U.S.C.A. § 5010(e) (1969). Thereafter (or without requiring such a report), confinement may be ordered until any date when the Youth Correction Division orders the offender released "conditionally," except that the youth must be so released after four years. However, the youth may later be confined again until he is discharged "unconditionally" six years after conviction. *See id.* §§ 5017-20 (Supp. 1972). It is not taught officially, but the young people facing such treatment, and commonly dreading it, have come to call it a sentence of "60 to 6" or "zip-six."

predicted for the patient and for those around him. Analogous judgments do not appear even to be contemplated, let alone required, by the proponents of indeterminate sentencing.

The naive faith in the presumed expertise of penologists and parole officials effectively blots out some of the stark and familiar realities of prisons as they actually function. The notion that the unrehabilitated prisoner should be denied parole because he needs more treatment is not merely unsupported; it runs counter to considerable evidence and opinion concerning the effects of confinement. Taking prisons as they are, and as they are likely to be for some time, it is powerfully arguable that their net achievement is to make their inhabitants worse, not better.[114] It may be bracing doctrine to insist that the prisons must be improved to make rehabilitation a reality.[115] Passing now the question whether we know how to do this, the ideal is worthy beyond question. And I hope nothing said here suggests any cavil about that. My central point, however, entails a firm view about the proper order of things: we have no right to keep people confined ostensibly to rehabilitate them when we lack the means of rehabilitation. Until or unless we have some reasonable hope of effective treatment, it is a cruel fraud to have parole boards solemnly order men back to their cages because cures that do not exist are found not to have been achieved.

This view does not demand certainty or preclude a degree of experimentation conducted with candor and self-awareness. It would allow, for example, for confinements under the Federal Narcotic Addict Rehabilitation Act, despite the frank understanding that our ability to treat addiction is highly doubtful and that treatment may mean the trial-and-error testing of varying hypotheses.[116] But this, after all, is not unlike other kinds of

---

114 *See, e.g.*, ABA Sentencing Standards 63, 72–73; Law of Criminal Correction 268–72; G. Sykes, *supra* note 43, at 34–38.

115 *See, e.g.*, R. Clark, Crime in America 192–218 (paperbound ed. 1971), *reviewed in* Radzinowicz, *The Vision of Ramsey Clark*, 47 Va. Q. Rev. 459 (1971).

116 Under title II of the Act, a court may send an "eligible offender" it suspects of being a narcotics addict to the Attorney General for an examination to determine whether he is an addict and whether he is likely to be rehabilitated through treatment. 18 U.S.C.A. § 4252 (1969). Following the examination, if the court finds that the offender satisfies the two criteria, "it shall commit him to the custody of the Attorney General for treatment" for an indeterminate period not to exceed 10 years or the maximum that could otherwise have been imposed. *Id.* § 4253(a). After receiving six months of treatment, the offender may then be "conditionally released" at the discretion of the Board of Parole. *Id.* § 4254.

strictly medical problems. It differs from the vague credo of "rehabilitation" as a general aim in that it (a) centers upon a defined species of malady, (b) entails rationally limited and prescribed forms of attempted treatment, (c) is subject to reasonably objective measures of achievement, and (d) is an enterprise in which the inmate, like a patient, may be (and, in my own experience, normally is as a condition to applying the Act) enlisted as a willing participant seeking an objective he understands and desires for himself.

Moving to a related but separate category, the "dangerous offender" may perhaps be confined for indeterminate periods upon acceptably principled and defined, if desperately risky, grounds. Existing and proposed measures of this nature [117] raise difficult questions—for example, as to the kinds of dangers warranting such treatment, the availability of reliable tests for dangerousness, the soundness of the hypothesis that a man found "safe" by testing in prison is thereby established as a good risk,[118] and the large prospect that parole officials will play it safe by erring regularly on the side of continued custody for cases of doubt.[119] But these perplexities are suitable for separate handling and discrete judgments, free from foggy pieties about rehabilitation. The dangerous offender, if he can fairly be identified, is a just subject for *incapacitation*. If we are able to "treat" him, usually a dubious hope, so much the better. We may have to hold him for an uncertain and long time, but we ought to be willing to forego certainty and absolute security, remembering that freedom and risk are inseparable. However we handle this distinct and limited category, neither it nor others similarly identifiable justify all-embracing provisions for indeterminate sentencing.

3. The allure of indeterminate sentences, including the prospect of leaning more heavily upon such experts as parole board

[117] *E.g.*, Organized Crime Control Act of 1970, § 1001(a), 18 U.S.C.A. §§ 3575–76 (Supp. 1971); CONN. GEN. STAT. ANN. § 53a–40 (Special Pamphlet 1972); MODEL PENAL CODE §§ 6.07, 6.09, 7.03, 7.04 (Proposed Official Draft 1962); MODEL SENTENCING ACT §§ 5, 6.

[118] There is a considerable body of opinion, which I find persuasive, that a person, "adjusted" after a long term of confinement and minimal autonomy, is likely on that very basis to have become unfitted for effective functioning on the outside. *See, e.g.*, H. GRISWOLD *et al.*, *supra* note 53, at 252–53; Schreiber, *Indeterminate Therapeutic Incarceration of Dangerous Criminals: Perspectives and Problems*, 56 VA. L. REV. 602, 604 (1970).

[119] *See* R. DAWSON, *supra* note 14, at 296–98; Schreiber, *supra* note 118, at 618–24.

members, leads to uncritical transfer of concerns on which the boards have no claim to either expertise or legitimate authority. The therapeutic or penological considerations presumably underlying parole decisions have nothing to do with the sentencing aims of deterrence or denunciation. Nor is the form or timing of the parole decision suited to the service of such ends. Yet the Model Penal Code, followed by the new Federal Code lately proposed by a distinguished National Commission, includes judgments upon such subjects among the things given over wholesale to the parole board.

To explain: for the sentencing court, probation is presumptively preferred to confinement under the Model Penal Code

> unless, having regard to the nature and circumstances of the crime and the history, character and condition of the defendant, it is of the opinion that his imprisonment is necessary for protection of the public because:
>
> (a) there is undue risk that during the period of a suspended sentence or probation the defendant will commit another crime; or
>
> (b) the defendant is in need of correctional treatment that can be provided most effectively by his commitment to an institution; or
>
> (c) *a lesser sentence will depreciate the seriousness of the defendant's crime.*[120]

The words I have italicized sound retributive, but it appears that their authors did not conceive of themselves as acting from any such disfavored motive.[121] Accepting without question that the need not to "depreciate the seriousness of the . . . crime" relates to the assessment of the sentence as a deterrent, this would seem to be peculiarly a matter affecting *the sentence*, when and as it is pronounced, and the court's authoritative voice as the agency for that purpose.[122] But when we turn in the Model Penal Code to the criteria for parole, we find that the identical worry about depreciated seriousness of the crime is included. The parole board is instructed that there is a presumption favoring parole, like that favoring probation in the sentencing court, unless one of four countervailing factors is

---

120 MODEL PENAL CODE § 7.01(1) (Proposed Official Draft 1962) (emphasis added). *See* the similar 18 U.S.C. § 3101 in PROPOSED FEDERAL CRIMINAL CODE 277–78.

121 *See* MODEL PENAL CODE § 7.01, comment 2, at 34 (Tent. Draft No. 2, 1954).

122 *Cf.* T. SZASZ, LAW, LIBERTY, AND PSYCHIATRY 97–98 (1963); Lewis, *The Humanitarian Theory of Punishment*, 6 RES JUDICATAE 224, 225 (1952); Wechsler, *Sentencing Innovations*, 46 F.R.D. 519, 522 (1968).

present. The one of interest here is: "unless . . . release . . . would depreciate the seriousness of [the] crime or promote disrespect for law." [123] At this point, what started out as a device for rehabilitation and reform becomes a means for handing on to the parole board judgments quite outside the field of its supposed competence. The "seriousness of the crime" is a matter of law and policy within the province of judges, best known to the participants in the trial, and properly to be estimated for purposes of voicing the community's condemnation at the time of the pronouncement of sentence. It is, more importantly, not a subject on which there is need to "wait and see" whether the defendant is ready for release. On the contrary, the inclusion of such a criterion in the parole board's domain is, though all inadvertently, an invitation to the illicit, "political" judgments of public opinion of which parole boards are often suspected.[124]

4. What people "suspect" about parole boards obviously cannot be accepted as sufficient grounds for any sort of firm conclusion. But the suspicions are themselves facts, in prison and out. They are born, as suspicions commonly are, of the absence of clear information freely given. The point is worth noting here because parole boards, the powers of which increase with the degree of indeterminacy of sentences, have not been among our most admired and confidence-inspiring agencies.

The qualified esteem has been earned. Parole boards, as I have mentioned, commonly proceed secretly, without explanation, subject to no (or almost no) objective standards, in reaching unreviewable decisions.[125] The proponents of expanded power for parole boards tend to support improved procedures and the promulgation of at least some standards.[126] The Model Penal Code even goes to the extent of having the board make a record, though it is not clear whether the final board decision must be written down.[127] And, as noted earlier, the New Jersey Supreme Court has recently broken new ground and made explanations a requirement for its parole board.[128]

---

[123] MODEL PENAL CODE § 305.9(1)(b) (Proposed Official Draft 1962).

[124] *See, e.g., Invisible Federal Parole,* N.Y. Times, Aug. 30, 1971, at 28, col. 2 (editorial).

[125] *See* K. DAVIS, *supra* note 52, at 126–33.

[126] *See id;* MODEL PENAL CODE §§ 305.6–.10 (Proposed Official Draft 1962).

[127] *See* MODEL PENAL CODE §§ 305.6, 305.8, 305.10 (Proposed Official Draft 1962).

[128] *See* note 51 *supra* and accompanying text.

Apart from such developments, the poor performance record of parole boards is not in itself a decisive reason for opposing indeterminate sentences. The nature of the necessary improvements is known and manageable, given a decent measure of will and public support.[129] I note with concerned skepticism, however, the imposing consensus that would leave parole decisions still final and unreviewable.[130]

This arrangement is favored even by exponents of the growing opinion that the sentencing decision should be reviewable.[131] The contrast, even if logic is not the law's whole life, is striking for its essential illogicality as well as the absence of any clear basis in policy. The idea that the board's decision may not be appealed is not justifiable on grounds of trouble or expense, though both are involved. It may be explained, but it cannot be justified, by an awareness that the reasons for denials of parole have never been articulated so that they have not been subject to effective review. The material considerations affecting the parole decision, if there are valid ones, are not so numerous or mysterious that their statement is impossible.

In sum, to the extent we should maintain provisions for indeterminate sentence with discretionary parole, it should be where the decisions are capable of regulation under explicit standards and thus subject to an effective system of appeals. It may be that the scope of review will be narrow—perhaps a version of the "abuse of discretion" test[132] or the "rational basis" test[133]—but that is equally probable for review of the judicial sentence. At the very least, the case for judicial review of parole decisions stands on an equal footing with the case for review of sentences.

---

129 *See* PRESIDENT'S COMM'N ON LAW ENFORCEMENT AND ADMINISTRATION OF JUSTICE, TASK FORCE REPORT: CORRECTIONS, app. A, 184–90 (1967); E. SUTHERLAND & D. CRESSEY, PRINCIPLES OF CRIMINOLOGY 586–87 (6th ed. 1960); D. TAFT & R. ENGLAND, CRIMINOLOGY 490–91 (4th ed. 1964).

130 *See* MODEL PENAL CODE § 305.19 (Proposed Official Draft 1962); PROPOSED FEDERAL CRIMINAL CODE 303–04 (proposed 18 U.S.C. § 3406). *But see* K. DAVIS, *supra* note 52, at 132–33. The *Proposed Federal Criminal Code* does provide for review of denial by the Parole Board of "constitutional rights or procedural rights conferred by statute, regulation or rule." But this is of small moment. It may well be the law already, without a provision like the one thus proposed. *See* Sobell v. Reed, 327 F. Supp. 1294, 1302 (S.D.N.Y.) 1971).

131 *Compare* PROPOSED FEDERAL CRIMINAL CODE 317 (proposed 28 U.S.C. § 1291) (review of sentence) *with id.* 303-04 (proposed 18 U.S.C. § 3406) (unreviewable parole denial).

132 *See* K. DAVIS, *supra* note 52, at 132–33.

133 *See generally* K. DAVIS, ADMINISTRATIVE LAW TREATISE § 30.05 (Supp. 1970).

The contrary opinion now abroad reflects the fundamental fallacy, widely extirpated lately in other areas, of worshipping Expertise without defining, understanding, or placing salutary limits upon it.

5. My final contention in this brief against indeterminancy is closer to first in importance: the rage and resentment probably bred by indeterminate sentences outweigh in most cases the supposed benefits. This proposition does not rest upon incontrovertible proof. But there is a fair amount of evidence—and introspection and conversation lead me to believe—that the prisoner experiences as cruel and degrading the decision that he must remain in custody for some uncertain period while his fellows study him, grade him, and decide if and when he may be let go. It is remarkable that the supporters of indeterminacy seem not to have consulted much, if at all, with those sentenced to indefinite terms. I have not seen evidence, for example, of such inquiries by the drafters of the Model Penal Code or the recently proposed Federal Criminal Code. The inquiries would be germane. Surely this is so if we mean our profession that we care about convicted persons for themselves. It is true likewise when we consider that the efficacy of any "treatment" is likely to be affected in part by the impact as felt by its beneficiary.

Proceeding first at a more or less *a priori* level, I wonder if, in dealing with convicted persons, we have been guilty of the familiar practice of keeping like things hermetically sealed off from one another as a way of living with flat inconsistencies.[184] In much of our law we quest after predictability as a basic need. The need springs from powerful demands for fairness, equality, and security. We want to be able to gauge in advance the taxes on the deal, the duration of an employment contract, the length of a lease. For the defendant under an indeterminate sentence, however, the need is thought to be less pressing than other supposed values. It has been suggested, in fact, that the possibility of early release on parole is an attractive incentive, to be contrasted with the gray inexorability of a long, fixed term.[185]

[184] "If you think you can think about something which is attached to something else without thinking about what it is attached to, then you have what is called a legal mind." Thomas Reed Powell, in an unpublished manuscript, as quoted in Arnold, *Criminal Attempts—The Rise and Fall of an Abstraction*, 40 YALE L.J. 53, 58 (1930).

[185] R. CLARK, *supra* note 115, at 203.

However that may be, and whether or not that is the apt comparison, prisoners and students of their plight report no joy from the incentive. On the contrary, it appears recurrently in the literature that the uncertainty is a steadily galling affliction. At least in many existing institutions, and probably in any we can foresee for the service of indeterminate sentences by prisoners of all kinds, there is a sense of mystery and bewilderment about what the rules are, about what will "work" toward the tightly focused goal of release.[136] Though the captors, or some of them, perceive the ordeal as "treatment," their charges, closer to the mark, consider that they are being punished, experience the process as hostile, and react with hostility.[137] There is a widespread cynicism that teaches the unsuitability, arbitrariness, and essential corruption of those in power. At least very often, the immediately seen wielders of the power convey to the prisoner that his hope lies in proper "attitudes" and in his demonstration that he can "behave"—a message understood, probably not inaccurately, to counsel a cramped orthodoxy and docility as the stigmata of reformation. There is a sense of helplessness with its concomitants of frustration and rage.

Reactions of this sort seem expectable in a system under which sentences are routinely indefinite and subject to discretionary prolongation without some intelligible prescription of the grounds and goals of "treatment." If we were compelled to choose between such a system and one of rigidly definite sentences across the board, I would prefer the latter. Fortunately, the options are not that limited. Indeterminate sentences, employed with discrimination and under rational criteria, may achieve limited benefits without the monstrous and arbitrarily allocated costs of employing them wholesale.

III. Suggestions for Reform

A. *Some Matters Ripe for Legislative Determination*

The state I have described as lawlessness calls for some immediate, if not immutable, remedies by lawmaking. At least some

---

[136] *See* D. Ward & G. Kassebaum, *supra* note 43, at 18-29; McCleery, *Authoritarianism and the Belief Systems of Incorrigibles,* in The Prison 260, 268-69 (D. Cressey ed. 1961).

[137] *See* Law of Criminal Correction 132; Kirby, *Doubts about the Indeterminate Sentence,* 53 Judicature 63 (1969).

principles of sentencing should by now be attainable. Both by substantive controls and through procedural revisions the unchecked powers of the untutored judge should be subject to a measure of regulation. The vague, indefinite, and uncritical use of indeterminate sentences calls for restriction through meaningful definitions and discriminating judgments. Matters like the "apportionment of punishment" and its "severity . . . are peculiarly questions of legislative policy." [188] Believing it has been time long since to start abhorring the vacuum that exists in this area, I propose here to suggest only some beginnings, leaving for wiser heads and fuller time the continuous task of completion and betterment.

Two kinds of basic prescription should be first principles in a legislative code on sentencing:

(1) A statement of the substantive aims of sentencing—deterrence, reformation, etc.—and an enumeration of relevant factors to be considered in mitigation or aggravation; and
(2) some fundamental procedural directives regulating the steps to be followed in determining the sentence.

Acknowledging the preliminary and incomplete nature of this submission, let me expand somewhat upon these proposals.

1. Substantive Principles

Despite all the philosophizing on this most fundamental of subjects in scholarly works and random judicial opinions, we have virtually no meaningful or specific legislative declarations of the principles justifying criminal sanctions.[189] Thus, we live with seeming unconcern in a world where the intellectual front is almost unbroken in rejecting retribution as an aim while legislatures enact new criminal laws and judges impose sentences that are explicable largely in terms of retributive sentiments. Perhaps there is a tacit view among advanced thinkers that we are better off if the legislatures pay no attention; it may be that the dominant chord in the voice of the people would be shrilly retributive. Without here predicting or desiring any particular

[188] Gore v. United States, 357 U.S. 386, 393 (1958).

[189] The broad statement refers to the contemporary state of affairs in this country. *See* LAW OF CRIMINAL CORRECTION 649-50. *Cf.* McGautha v. California, 402 U.S. 183, 196-208 (1971); Smith v. Follette, 445 F.2d 955, 960-61 (2d Cir. 1971). Statements of fundamental sentencing principles are codified elsewhere. *See* N. WALKER, *supra* note 11, at 10; Mannheim, *Some Aspects of Judicial Sentencing Policy*, 67 YALE L.J. 961, 963-64 (1958).

result, I think it is for the legislature in our system to make the essential judgments underlying the power of the state to impose harsh afflictions as well as unwanted "treatment." [140]

Assuming, then, that the legislature has made such fundamental determinations, we might find an initial section of a sentencing code declaring as objectives general deterrence,[141] retribution, incapacitation, and reformation. The first two are purposes for which the sentence may be measured with finality and substantially implemented by the judge on the day of judgment. For these are purposes that touch other people rather than the defendant himself. As it affects those others, the impact of the sentence is achieved in the fact of its pronouncement. Assuming, of course, that the sentence is carried out—that a man sent to prison for five years actually goes and stays confined for something approaching that term—the effect of the example on other people is achieved and the desire for vengeance is satisfied largely without regard to the kinds of treatment and observation to which the prisoner is thereafter subjected. And everything we need to know to determine the severity of a sentence implementing these purposes—the seriousness of the offense, the probable deterrent impact of the sentence, the potential conflicts with other sentencing purposes—can be known on the day of sentencing with as much (or as little) certainty as is likely to be secured later,

---

140 Because it is not, strictly, within the subject I have chosen, I have tended to refrain in this essay from taking a position on the subject of retribution, as on several others of a difficult and interesting nature. I mention in passing, however, a doubt that retribution can or should be entirely excluded from the grounds of punishment. It is a familiar argument and a social datum that the wreaking of vengeance upon wrongdoers seems necessary, at least sometimes, to assuage the guilt-feelings aroused in the law-abiding by wrongdoing as well as to encourage conformity to law by keeping the promise that others who stray will in fact be visited with the threatened consequences. *See, e.g.*, F. ALEXANDER & H. STAUB, *supra* note 22, at 56, 213–16, 218–20; F. ALLEN, *supra* note 105, at 70, 83–88; Lewis, *supra* note 122. *Cf.* Wechsler, *The Issues of the Nuremberg Trial*, in H. WECHSLER, PRINCIPLES, POLITICS, & FUNDAMENTAL LAW 138, 143–44 (1961). These may not be the loveliest of sentiments. But they appear to exist and to warrant a place in the reckoning. This is not to say, of course, that keeping this factor in check is not a needful and desirable concern.

141 The phrase "general deterrence" is used commonly (and herein) to refer to an impact (or hoped-for impact) upon persons other than the apprehended offender being sentenced. The effect sought upon the defendant himself is commonly distinguished as "special deterrence." *See* F. ZIMRING, PERSPECTIVES ON DETERRENCE 97–107 (1971). That monograph, one of a series entitled *Crime and Delinquency Issues* published by the National Institute of Mental Health, may be consulted generally for some of the complex problems of definition and analysis.

during the period when the sentence is being served. It would seem, therefore, that in the case of a sentence imposed for no purpose other than general deterrence or retribution, none of the usual reasons for indeterminate terms would be applicable.

The situation may be different when the purpose of the sentence is incapacitation, rehabilitation, or both. The essential force of such a sentence for its intended purposes is not spent with its pronouncement; the incidents and consequences of the *service* of sentence are here of fundamental importance. The main concern is not with the effects of the sentence upon others, but with (a) prediction and (b) observation of its effects over time upon the defendant himself. The questions at sentencing may include: When, if ever, is this defendant likely to be less dangerous? How soon may we hope to cure or alleviate the defendant's problems or defects disposing him to violate the criminal law? Being in their nature risky predictions, the answers to these questions must be tentative, and subject to subsequent verification or correction. It is the existence of such questions that supplies grounds for an indeterminate sentence.

It should be obvious, in a word, that the purpose or purposes of a sentence are first premises for the decision as to whether a definite or indefinite term (subject to parole board judgment) is appropriate. While it may be obvious, the point is systematically ignored both in the statutes prescribing penalties and in the judgments of the courts. As mentioned earlier, advanced (and otherwise admirable) efforts like the Model Penal Code and the proposed new Federal Code, among others, make no such distinctions. They simply provide for indeterminacy across the board. There is in such provisions no occasion for the judge imposing sentence even to consider whether some rehabilitative or incapacitating goal is involved. There is likewise no explicit determination whether some legitimate occasion is present for the exercise of wisdom parole officials are supposed to possess and, thus, no determination whether there is any justification at all for giving a parole agency a decisive voice as to length of the sentence.

At least in general terms, the correctives for this situation may be stated briefly. We need (a) a legislative prescription of lawful sentencing purposes and (b) a requirement that the sentencing judge state the purpose or purposes underlying each particular judgment. Measures of this nature could provide at least a start toward rationality in the process.

Some sentences, I have suggested, present no occasion for indeterminacy. A term of imprisonment justified only by the hope that it is needed or useful for general deterrence should be simply and inexorably definite (passing such matters affecting custodial discipline as "good time" or its variants). This does not mean, of course, that a sentence of this (or any) kind should run to the gruesome lengths characteristic generally of American prison terms. It does mean that there is no justification for uncertainty and no pertinent function for the parole board in such a case.

On the other hand, sentences imposed ostensibly for rehabilitation may or may not be suitable for indeterminacy. It is not enough to justify an indeterminate sentence that a judge (perhaps echoing, without deep insight, the views of others) may state there is a need for rehabilitation. Beyond this necessary finding, there ought to be particularized ones as to the nature of the defendant's needs and, of vital importance, the nature and existence of supposed facilities for meeting those needs. It is a familiar kind of mockery for our courts to imagine vaguely, or to say, that psychotherapy or some other form of treatment is the recipe for a defendant, to impose a supposedly rehabilitative sentence for some such dimly perceived purpose, and to ignore that there is no pertinent kind of treatment available among the state's penal resources.

Compelled to focus upon what he means by rehabilitation, the sentencing judge is better able to know whether he really means it at all and to gauge with some measure of precision how long a sentence is suitable.[142] As I have said already, this is the area where indeterminate sentences may continue to be justified. But the judge, with such other wisdom as may be enlisted, should at least be able to set tolerable maximum limits when he faces the concrete meaning of rehabilitation and appraises it in light of the crime for which sentence is being imposed.[143]

---

[142] Identifying the rehabilitative need may also serve to make clear that the relevant treatment facilities are actually outside rather than inside custodial institutions. *See* N. WALKER, *supra* note 11, at 98.

[143] A number of statutes, inspired by sincere concern for the welfare of defendants as well as the public safety, authorize longer periods of confinement for rehabilitation than would be allowed for mere punishment. *See, e.g.*, 18 U.S.C.A. §§ 5005-26 (1969, Supp. 1972), *construed in* Abernathy v. United States, 418 F.2d 288, 290 (5th Cir. 1969); N.Y. PENAL LAW §§ 75.00-.20 (McKinney 1967), *construed*

Beyond dealing with the bedrock subject of sentencing purposes, a new code on sentencing should begin to weigh and decide numerous issues of mitigation or aggravation on which judges are now free to go their disparate ways.[144] It is not acceptable to leave for the normally unspoken and diverse judgments of sentencing courts such questions as: Whether a plea of guilty should be considered in mitigation; whether (what is not the converse) standing trial should be considered aggravating; whether waiving a jury or seemingly lying on the stand should be taken into account; whether disruptive behavior and tactics at trial should be considered aggravating; or whether "cooperation" with the prosecutor (furnishing evidence for other investigations, testifying against codefendants, etc.) should be considered mitigating. In addition to such matters of in-court behavior, there are, of course, more fundamental questions touching the criminal acts and the general character and history of the defendant. Students of the subject recall, and generally scorn these days, the efforts of scholars in times past to catalogue such factors—the relative gravity of the specific offense, the cruelty or stealth or deliberateness of the behavior, defendant's age, prior record, character traits, etc.—and evolve a kind of calculus for computing sentences.[145] The short answer to such

---

in People *ex rel.* Carter v. New York City Reformatory, 62 Misc. 2d 191, 308 N.Y.S.2d 552 (Sup. Ct. 1970). *See also* Schreiber, *supra* note 118, at 616–18. MODEL PENAL CODE § 6.05(2) (Proposed Official Draft 1962) and ABA SENTENCING STANDARDS § 2.6(b), at 110, would forbid such seeming incongruities. Whatever this improved proportionality may say about the underlying sentencing theory, it is confined to the relatively narrow question of upper limits. As a more general proposition, there would be serious question about the seemingly humane position that confinement for rehabilitation should not last longer than confinement for less "helping" purposes. It seems clear, for example, that the end of general deterrence may be served in many situations by a sentence much shorter than might be indicated for incapacitation or reformation of the defendant.

[144] Smith v. Follette, 445 F.2d 955 (2d Cir. 1971); *cf.* McGautha v. California, 402 U.S. 183 (1971).

[145] Perhaps the most notable of such efforts was the REPORT AND PRELIMINARY PROJECT FOR AN ITALIAN PENAL CODE (transl. E. Betts 1921), authored largely by the Italian criminologist Enrico Ferri. Under the provisions of that proposed code, the discretion of the sentencing judge was sharply circumscribed. Punishment was based upon the greater or lesser dangerousness of the offender. Article 21 set forth 17 circumstances of greater dangerousness, which included dissoluteness or dishonesty in prior family or social life, precocity in committing a grave offense, ignoble or trivial motives, deliberate preparation for the offense, acting in prearranged complicity with others, and blameworthy conduct toward the injured party after the offense. *Id.* at 534–35. Article 22 set forth eight circumstances of lesser dangerousness: Honesty of prior family or social life; excusable motives;

proposals for detailed sentencing codes has been the familiar, and weighty, aversion to illusory certainty bought at the cost of inflexible laws that torture disparate people and events into identical molds. But, like other short answers, this one is too short. There has not yet been a sufficient investment of energy and imagination in the attempt to codify precise, detailed factors governing sentences. Until the attempt has been made, with at least a measure of the resources and attention befitting a moon-voyaging society, the vague, futile, helpless wailing about disparity remains hypocrisy. Believing this, and risking the misunderstanding likely to greet a proposition conceded to be rudimentary and tentative, I mean in the next few pages to outline (a) the reasons for a detailed sentencing code and (b) the general nature of the contents and uses of such a code.

(a) The argument for codifying sentencing criteria is, very simply, that they now exist and operate, whether we like this or not, in an arbitrary, random, inconsistent, and unspoken fashion. Factors I have repeatedly mentioned—guilty pleas, prior record, defendant's age and family circumstances—are considered every day by sentencing judges, but in accordance with uncontrolled and divergent individual views of what is, after all, the "law" each time it applies. Every factor of this kind calls for a judgment of policy, suited exactly for legislative action and surely not suited for random variation from case to case. It is not a question, then, of seeking out and attempting to apply artificial criteria. It is a question of making explicit and uniform what is now tacit, capricious, and often decisive.

Making such determinations, a detailed sentencing code would eliminate some of the obscurity and the futility now attending the subject. Counsel would have some basis for knowing what to do and how to argue. The sentencers—the single judge or a group, as well as probation officers—would face a task similarly defined and capable of similarly focused appraisal. The defining

having acted from excusable passion; having yielded to a transitory opportunity or to exceptional and excusable personal or family conditions; unforeseen drunkenness or similar intoxication, transitory ill health, or other similar condition at the time of the offense; having acted through the suggestion of a turbulent crowd; having acted to repair damage done by the offense; and confessing to the offense prior to discovery. *Id.* at 535–36. The weight to be given one or more of these circumstances was governed by articles 75 through 77. *Id.* at 546–47. These and other provisions of Ferri's code are set forth and criticized in Glueck, *Principles of a Rational Penal Code,* 41 HARV. L. REV. 453, 467–75 (1928).

of concrete issues would lead in turn to the possibility of meaningful appellate review.

(b) To posit at least a theoretical ideal, subject to revision of all kinds in the pursuit, I suggest the goal of codification might be conceived as a fairly detailed calculus of sentencing factors, including such use of arithmetical weightings as experimental study might reveal to be feasible. Again, I disclaim anything beyond the crude diagramming of a preliminary hypothesis. The hypothesis begins with the thought that every sentence under the code, as heretofore urged, would be classified in accordance with its basic purpose or purposes—as deterrent, rehabilitative, etc. For each such category, the code might contain some initial or tentative sentencing guides—for example, that a purely deterrent sentence should presumptively fall (subject to aggravating factors) in the lowest quartile of the sentencing range for the particular crime, or that a rehabilitative sentence must be categorized initially in terms of the defined need and proposed form of treatment.

Thereafter, within each broad sentencing category or group of categories, particular factors of mitigation or aggravation would be enumerated in the proposed code. Where possible, as I have suggested, numerical weights or ranges would be assigned—as, for example, for the relative gravity of the offense, the defendant's past criminal record, the favorable or unfavorable character of the defendant's work history and abilities. However unromantic numbers sound, or however misleading they may be in foolish hands, their proper uses may guide and regulate judgment. The physician who speaks of a grade 3 heart murmur may not be reporting a measurement as precise as the number of feet in a yard. But he says a meaningful thing that gives information and guidance to others professionally trained. Similarly, at least over time, a score of 5 on a scale of 1 to 5 for "gravity of particular offense" would help to tell what the sentencing judge thought and to test whether his thoughts made sense for the particular case.

For lack of time and competence, I have not attempted to think through how far a scheme of quantification might be carried. Depending upon the resolution of this basic problem, the aim of the sentencing code would be a sentencing form or chart giving possibly an overall "score" or, more likely, a profile of factors and their weights. The end product thus recorded by the sentencing tribunal could be preceded by proposed forms or charts submitted by counsel, probation officers, and others seeking to affect or determine the sentence. All, as I have urged, would have concrete things to aim at and talk about. All would have bases for comparison in assessing differences of ultimate judgment.

If this sounds crass and mechanical, I press it nonetheless as a goal preferable to the void in which we now operate. Outside the sombre field of sentencing, it has not been our way to make a fetish of vagueness. Whether numbers and scores are useless is a judgment that ought to follow, not precede, earnest study.[146]

2. Procedural Law

As is true of the substantive law, some issues relating to sentencing procedures have, for a long time, been clear and appropriate for legislative resolution. Without pretending to thoroughness, I recall a few of these matters to which reference has been made earlier in this paper. First, I submit that the legislature should face expressly and decide the allocation of sentencing authority or the designation of participants in the sentencing process. The judges, assuming their expertise, are less than entirely detached about such subjects. It seems both appropriate and desirable that the Congress should make and impose some universally applicable judgment, within the limits of feasibility, concerning the requirement of sentencing councils,[147] the more elaborate tribunals of Professor Glueck's model,[148] and the provision of appellate re-

[146] It should not be necessary, but it may not be a bad idea, to note that I do not envision a grading system as mechanically dispositive for sentencing decisions. Some room for judgment must remain during the foreseeable future. The proposal is for a concrete implement to assist what is otherwise a diffuse sort of judgment. An imperfect analogy occurs to me from the less grim, but not uniformly jolly, task of grading examination papers. Many instructors, though the end used to be broad letter grades, have followed the practice of analyzing the essay questions on an examination by assigning numerical values to issues or aspects of what would be expected as thorough answers. The "scores" thus derived are frequently not decisive in themselves. But they help, in my experience and that of others, to rein in erratic departures and to promote a measure of unifom treatment among the diverse papers. Until prisons go the way of examinations and grades, the analogy may be of service.

[147] *See* text accompanying notes 69–75 *supra*. The limits of feasibility may include some obviously necessary modifications in districts that have only one or two judges. Though they may be "details," modifications of this kind would require more attention and ingenuity than are available here and now.

[148] *See* text accompanying note 76 *supra*.

view.[149] Unless they are thought to be matters of utter indifference, decisions to employ or reject such devices should not be left to the varying tastes of the affected judges. If the time and energy required for sentencing councils are soundly invested in Brooklyn, Chicago, and Detroit, there is no principled ground for failing to have council procedures elsewhere. I have stated along the way my own preference for Glueck-style tribunals subject to appellate review. Whatever the ultimate decision may be, the point at this stage is that such matters ought not to go by default. They deserve explicit legislative judgments one way or the other.

Omitting a host of other subjects that merit study for procedural reform in sentencing, I add one suggestion that flows from a thesis advanced earlier. I have argued above that an intelligent sentence, especially if its purported aim is rehabilitation, cannot be formulated without an understanding of the defendant's needs for reform and of the means available for treatment. The standard procedure now followed is largely or wholly inadequate to provide any such fundamental understanding by the sentencing judge. The judge in the usual case has only a vague notion of where the defendant, consigned to "the custody of the Attorney General," will go and what will be done with him. The place of confinement is determined by the Attorney General (through his Bureau of Prisons), not by the judge.[150] The judge may recommend a prison. If he does, the recommendation is likely to be followed. But it need not be. And it is not usual to recommend, or to pretend to be intelligently concerned with, the confinement facility. Despite such basic gaps in his knowledge and power, and without saying anything about it, the sentencing judge may have some vision of reform in mind when he orders a term of confinement.

The cure for this species of absurdity probably requires thoroughgoing modifications of the process as well as the tribunal. I mention here only one change that seems obvious and could be effected even if nothing else were altered. The procedure of "classification," which is the initial step of processing *after* a defendant is sentenced to prison, should be advanced to become part of the presentence study in any case which may come to

---

149 *See* text accompanying notes 77–93 *supra*.

150 18 U.S.C.A. §§ 4001, 4082 (1969, Supp. 1972); *see* Thogmartin v. Moseley, 313 F. Supp. 158, 160 (D. Kan. 1969), *aff'd mem.*, 430 F.2d 1178 (10th Cir.), *cert. denied*, 400 U.S. 910 (1970).

involve confinement. The existing classification procedure, to describe it only briefly, is the work of testing and evaluating the defendant as a basis for charting his treatment in custody.[151] As a result of his first subjection to this procedure, the prisoner may be assigned to course of vocational training, to some form of therapy or counseling, or to a particular kind of disciplinary regime. The classification process may reveal that there is no useful course of treatment in available facilities, or at least that available resources are far from ideal. Such studies and decisions ought patently to be made before there is a decision for or against confinement for rehabilitation.

This suggestion requires relatively minor adjustments. Classification is already a continuing process in orthodox penological theory. The prisoner, the books teach us, is to be reevaluated from time to time both for the duration of his "treatment" and as a prelude to release from confinement.[152] The proposal here would merely advance the process to an earlier and vitally important stage.

B. *A Proposed Commission for Sentencing Studies and Law Revision*

The aspects of sentencing that strike me as most flawed and most urgently in need of law revision have led to the few, somewhat scattered suggestions for legislative reform outlined above. There are needs, however, for action of a more thorough and continuous nature. Ignorance being one of the greatest problems, there is a need to marshal resources and talent for research and experimentation. Because the subject of sentencing is not steadily exhilarating or profitable to political officials,[153] these is a need to fill the gaps in attention between sporadic moments of concern in times of crisis. Another aspect of the same essential point is the lack of political power suffered not only by convicted persons but by their keepers as well. Finally, the need for revision of the law is not a one-time thing: the gross inadequacies of the existing situation require continuing study and reform.

---

[151] *See generally* Loveland, *Classification in the Prison System*, in CONTEMPORARY CORRECTION 91–106 (P. Tappan ed. 1951).

[152] *See id.* at 99–101.

[153] *Cf.* PRESIDENT'S COMM'N ON LAW ENFORCEMENT AND ADMINISTRATION OF JUSTICE, THE CHALLENGE OF CRIME IN A FREE SOCIETY 12, 159 (1967); L. RADZINOWICZ, IN SEARCH OF CRIMINOLOGY 125–30 (1962); Wechsler, *supra* note 122, at 521, 531.

Thoughts along these lines lead to the very possibly impractical but earnest final recommendation of this paper. I propose that there be established a National Commission charged with permanent responsibility for (1) the study of sentencing, corrections, and parole; (2) the formulation of laws and rules to which the results of such study may lead; and (3) the actual enactment of rules subject to congressional veto. To suggest its character and function, I have given the proposed Commission the title heading this final portion of these observations. It is not a sticking-point, however; I would welcome the superior abilities of Madison Avenue or elsewhere for improvements. Similarly, when I suggest details of the Commission's proposed composition and functions, it will be to invite thought rather than to claim anything like certainty or finality. With these *caveats* I sketch the proposal and its rationale.

Starting with the latter, I have mentioned the need for continuous and prestigious attention to problems of sentencing. The Commission, properly launched and populated, could serve in a sense as a lobby within the Government for those sentenced and for those charged with their custody and treatment. Other interests, politically significant, have such representation. Agriculture, labor, business, investors, and others have their spokesmen in various departments and agencies. Lately, reflecting a variety of things we seem to care about as a nation, the Consumer is elbowing his way into the power structure. Prisoners and jailers, like the poor and others who seemed so distant a while ago, are headed for participation unless we mean to deflect sharply the lines of our recent development. But whether or not that is so, the stakes of everyone in a system of rational sentencing are too great for contentment with the disheveled status quo. The improvements needed will not be achieved through fitful bursts of activity. The task requires the continuous attention of a respected agency.

Membership on the Commission would be a matter for discussion. Obvious possibilities suggest themselves—lawyers, judges, criminologists, penologists, more generally based sociologists, psychologists, and, not least but least traditional, former or present prison inmates.[154] This is not to stump for government of

[154] Reacting to tragic events, a judicial selection agency recently named a commission of inquiry to study rioting and over 40 resulting deaths in September, 1971, at the Attica, New York, State Correctional Facility (the name, if little else, of

prisoners by consent. It is to say we have gone too long without paying much attention to the actual impact upon the recipients of our well-intentioned but ineffectual "treatment" programs.

The Commission would not pretend to supersede existing scholarly efforts in universities and elsewhere. Like other agencies of government, the Commission would draw upon such enterprises, generate additional ones, and engage in its own study programs. Early in its career, the Commission would chart a program of inquiry and action and would set priorities. From this would follow decisions on the commissioning of outside studies and the organization of the agency's own projects.

Let me risk a little less abstraction—again, only to invite concrete attention, not to press now for firm choices. I think the whole sentencing procedure, from first to last, could stand a fresh look, with a view to revision. Presentence reports, without which we would all be sunk, are not so efficiently conceived or organized as they should be. There are no agreed criteria for judging in advance when such reports are needed, when they are useless, and when some modified forms would do. The sentencing proceeding is itself a stiff, artificial, often ritualistic encounter. The judge, robed and in a high place, listens to orations and invites comment from a commonly confused, inarticulate, or unconstructively cagey defendant. The pressure of habit and tradition leads in most instances to a decision right then, from the bench, unlike decisions on hosts of trivia that are reserved for later rulings upon reflection and study following oral submissions. All such things merit study and improvement.

Other matters suitable as Commission concerns I have touched upon partially in earlier paragraphs. Assuming the basic principles and purposes of sentencing are for the Congress, they are by no means ripe for final and changeless statutory decisions. These would be among the matters for continuous scrutiny by the Commission. The kind of sentencing "calculus" I have recommended would be a project for at least some years of intensive work. Whether or not that project were deemed worthy, sentencing criteria, now "individualized" judge by judge, would be fit

---

which had been changed in the prior year from Attica State *Prison*). The commission, headed by Dean Robert B. McKay of the New York University School of Law, includes an ex-convict as well as more conventional kinds of experts. N.Y. Times, Oct. 1, 1971, at 1, col. 1. *See also* Taylor, *The Correctional Institution as a Rehabilitation Center—A Former Inmate's View,* 16 VILL. L. REV. 1077 (1971).

for rule-making by the Commission. I have mentioned fleetingly, and now tarry briefly over, the thought that the Commission should be empowered to make rules having the force of law unless countermanded by Congress. The most familiar precedent is, of course, the authority of the Supreme Court to promulgate rules of civil [155] and criminal [156] procedure, effective unless voted down by the Congress. Rules about factors that should be weighed in mitigation or aggravation of prison sentences are different from procedure, to be sure, but there are solid justifications for a similar allocation of authority. As I have said, the subject of sentencing needs ongoing attention, but is unlikely to receive it from the Congress. There is need not only to express but also to implement steady concern.

The Commission's interests would extend inevitably to prisons, other institutions or forms of treatment, and parole. As we have begun lately to sort out the purposes and uses of prisons, it has become evident to everyone that our mostly ancient dungeons are intolerable. There is in the air, and in rudimentary embodiments, a scattered variety of ideas about smaller, different places of confinement, hostels for partial confinement, halfway houses, and other kinds of facilities. The acceptability of confinement as a form of punishment is itself in question. The Commission, after it achieved consensus on basic matters of purpose, would proceed in turn to the inseparable subject of means. It would follow that the whole train of problems through parole and final release would be within the Commission's domain.

I envision a highly prestigious Commission or none at all.[157] The calibre of those to be sought as Commissioners would be a crucial concern. Their roles would be as philospher-statesmen, charged with both basic scholarship and the formulation of rules, but leaving administrative and operating responsibilities to others. It is conceived, however, that the Commission would have significant impact upon the shape and functioning of the affected administrative institutions. It may well be, for example, that the Commission would want to consider whether there is any sound

---

[155] 28 U.S.C.A. § 2072 (Supp. 1972).

[156] 18 U.S.C.A. § 3771 (1969).

[157] The thought may be illustrated negatively by saying that the agency here projected differs *toto caelo* from the part-time *ex officio* "Advisory Corrections Council" created in 1950, in the Federal Youth Corrections Act, ch. 1115, § 4, 64 Stat. 1090, still codified at 18 U.S.C. § 5002 (1964), but evidently deceased some time ago, with its passing as little noticed as had been its inconsequential career.

reason why the Attorney General, the chief prosecutor, should have the Bureau of Prisons and Board of Parole under his jurisdiction. The phrasing here, if it implies a view as to the answer, is accurately revealing, but the Commission might discover two sides to the question. The list of provocative possibilities could be extended, but the result might not be to enhance the palatability of my basic suggestion.

I leave this, then, with the hope that a Commission, better named and more astutely defined, may recommend itself for the fundamental purposes here suggested, and that the service of such purposes may attract the necessary kinds of wisdom and unfettered imagination.

Conclusion

Sentencing is today a wasteland in the law. It calls, above all, for regulation by law. There is an excess of discretion given to officials whose entitlement to such power is established by neither professional credentials nor performance. Some measures already in existence—such as sentencing councils and appellate review—seem desirable because they operate to channel the exercise of discretion. On the other hand, the evil of unbounded discretion is enhanced by the uncritical belief that a beneficent "individualization" is achieved through indeterminate sentencing. Indeterminacy in its most enthusiastic forms takes on its literal dictionary quality of vagueness; it means the conferring of power to extend or terminate confinement where the grounds of the power have been misconceived and the occasions for its exercise are not ascertainable. Some aspects of sentencing and the treatment of convicted persons call for prompt legislative attention—in the choice of basic substantive principles, the prescription of basic procedures, and provisions for appellate review. The entire subject, however, is one for study and a steady process of law revision led by an eminent and permanent federal commission.

[2]

[1970]

Establishing a Factual Basis for Sentencing

By D. A. Thomas
Lecturer in Law, London School of Economics

Discussion of the problem of providing information for sentencers has tended in recent years to centre on the provision of social inquiry reports and other reports dealing with the offender's background and history. Emphasis on this important matter has obscured another aspect of the same problem—that of establishing an accurate version of the facts of the offence itself. The necessity for an accurate account of the offence, and the offender's participation in it where more than one offender is involved, is obvious; the sentencer must be able to form a proper view of the gravity of the offence in order to decide between the tariff and an individualised measure, and, where the tariff is chosen, to determine the appropriate level of sentence. Existing procedures directed to establishing an account of the facts of the offence for the purposes of sentencing are one of the weakest links in our system of criminal procedure; this article examines some aspects of the complex problems involved and makes some suggestions towards their solution.

The Problem

In theory, the law assumes a system of trial by jury. The jury hears the evidence and determines the question of guilt or innocence; if it determines that the accused is guilty the judge passes sentence within the statutory limits applicable to the offence of which the accused is convicted. The crux of the problem of establishing a factual basis for sentencing is that the bare verdict of "guilty" does not always determine the facts at a sufficient level of detail for the sentencer. The verdict itself may be ambiguous, in the sense that it may reflect two or more alternative views of the evidence; in another case it may not imply any determination on a matter which is relevant to sentence. In other situations the crucial evidence may not even have been before the jury at all, and in still others the determining facts may have nothing at all to do with the particular offender. The problems can be more complex where there is a plea of guilty but a dispute over facts which, while not amounting to a defence, would go in the accused's favour to reduce sentence; present procedures provide no satisfactory means of resolving such conflicts.

Interpreting the jury's verdict

Ambiguous verdicts are usually the direct result of defects in the substantive law, particularly the use of loosely defined offences to cover a wide variety of situations. The worst example at the present time is clearly manslaughter, an offence which includes at least six different major sub-categories. It is common for an accused to be charged with murder; evidence is given at the trial which could lead to a verdict of manslaughter on any one of a number of grounds, and the jury returns a verdict simply of "guilty of manslaughter." A good example is *Wheeler*.[1] The appellant was charged with the murder of Tuckermann. The prosecution evidence was that the accused had attacked the deceased in the deceased's flat, striking him several blows on the head with a whisky bottle and kicking him in the face with his bare feet, and had subsequently stolen his watch. Death resulted from asphyxia following inhalation of blood while the deceased was unconscious. The defence admitted the attack on the deceased, but alleged that the deceased had attempted to rape the accused's "common law wife," with whom the accused was sleeping at the time on a mattress in the deceased's flat. Following directions (in subjective terms) on the necessary intent for murder, and the limits of self defence, the jury returned a verdict of guilty of manslaughter without any comment. The jury could have reached this verdict by concluding that the accused's story of the attack on his girl friend (who was not called as a witness) was wholly false, that he had deliberately attacked the deceased to rob him (he admitted stealing his watch), but that he had not sufficient intent to justify a conviction for murder. Alternatively the jury may have decided that the accused's story of the attempted rape on his girl friend was true, that the killing was intentional, or accompanied by an intent to do grievous bodily harm, but that he had used excessive force in her defence. It is not clear whether the possibility of a defence based on provocation was put to the jury, but clearly this would have been a further possible interpretation. It seems reasonable to assume that the difference in the two possible versions would be highly significant for sentencing, but the sentencer gains no assistance from the jury's verdict and is forced in effect to determine all the factual issues over again; the verdict merely provides a legal foundation for the sentence. The same problem arose in *Walker*,[2]

[1] (1967) 52 Cr.App.R. 28. *Church* [1966] 1 Q.B. 59 is another example.
[2] November 14, 1968, No. 4595/68.

where on a charge of murder by stabbing the defences were again lack of intent, self-defence and provocation and the jury returned a bare verdict of " guilty of manslaughter."

In the face of this problem the Court of Appeal has developed the principle that where the factual implication of the jury's verdict is clear, the sentencer is bound to accept it and a sentence which is excessive in the light of the facts implied in the verdict will be reduced. In *Jama* [3] the appellant was convicted of manslaughter on an indictment charging murder in circumstances where it was possible to argue that there was no intent to do grievous bodily harm and an element of provocation: the foreman of the jury in asking for a further direction, indicated that " it is found that there was no intent to murder, but there was intent to do wilful bodily harm under provocation, which unfortunately resulted in death." The Court of Appeal interpreted this statement to mean that the jury found that there was no intent to inflict *grievous* bodily harm, and that on this basis the sentence was excessive; it was not a case of murder reduced to manslaughter by reason of provocation, but an " unlawful act " manslaughter mitigated by provocation. The sentence was reduced from ten years' imprisonment to three. In an earlier case [4] where the jury returned a verdict of manslaughter on an indictment charging murder where the only defence was " a thin case " of provocation, the court reduced the sentence from twelve years' imprisonment to six, saying that the original sentence " cannot be said really to accept the jury's verdict of provocation." This principle can only apply however where the factual implication of the jury's verdict is clear; where (as in the examples discussed earlier) the factual implication is ambiguous, the court has held that the sentencer should not attempt to follow the logical processes of the jury, but may come to his own independent determination of the relevant facts.[5]

Attempts have been made in a number of cases to resolve the problem of ambiguous verdicts by putting questions to the foreman of the jury after the verdict has been returned. This practice was disapproved by the Court of Appeal in 1943,[6] subsequently approved in 1958,[7] and mentioned non-committally in 1967.[8] Questions put after the verdict has been reached can create problems, particularly in manslaughter cases. First there is the practical

[3] (1968) 52 Cr.App.R. 498.

[4] *Paget*, December 19, 1963. The scale of the reductions in these cases indicate the importance of the problem.

[5] *Nuttall* [1968] Crim.L.R. 173.

[6] *Larkin* [1943] K.B. 174.

[7] *Matheson* [1958] 1 W.L.R. 400.

[8] *Warner* [1967] 51 Cr.App.R. 437.

problem that a unanimous verdict of "guilty of manslaughter" does not necessarily mean that there was unanimity in the logical process by which each member of the jury reached that conclusion; apart from the possibility that the verdict is a strictly illogical compromise between some members of the jury favouring a complete acquittal and others wanting to convict of murder, it would clearly be possible in a case such as *Wheeler* (above) for some members to have accepted the prosecution version (an unprovoked attack with a view to theft), some the defence version (excessive force in defence of another) and yet all to have joined in the same verdict. There is also the theoretical problem of onus of proof. Assume in *Wheeler* that all members of the jury are agreed on a verdict of manslaughter, but there is doubt on which of the two versions is the correct one; should not the jury, in accordance with normal principles, find in favour of the version most favourable to the accused unless it is satisfied beyond reasonable doubt that the less favourable version is established? Any other rule would appear to be inconsistent with basic concepts of criminal procedure; but the framing of questions to be put to a foreman after the conviction has been returned, taking account of this principle, would present immense difficulty. The practical problem of obtaining unanimity on the version of the facts accepted could be overcome to some extent by asking the jury, before it retires, to add a finding on the subsidiary issue to its verdict in the event of a conviction, but the problem of directions on the burden of proof as between versions of the facts would remain, and further possible difficulties are opened up—what would the Court of Appeal do on a conviction appeal where the jury returned a unanimous verdict of guilty of manslaughter but stated that they were quite unable to agree on how they had reached that verdict?

Relevant facts not implied in the verdict

The problems discussed above arise in cases where the facts which must be determined for the purpose of sentencing are the same as those determined by the jury in deciding guilt or innocence. Further problems arise where the fact which is relevant for sentence is not one which the jury need consider at all. As Professor J. C. Smith has pointed out,[9] this problem arises most commonly in relation to offences of strict liability. Although the question whether the accused knew the relevant facts does not need to be determined for the purposes of conviction, it is usually crucial for sentence. Drug offences are a problem area; *Warner* [10] is a clear

[9] [1966] Crim.L.R. 505; [1967] Crim.L.R. 530; [1969] Crim.L.R. 374.
[10] (1967) 51 Cr.App.R. 437.

example. The appellant was convicted of unauthorised possession of a large quantity of amphetamine sulphate tablets; his defence was that he did not know the bag in which the tablets were found in fact contained drugs. The jury were directed that this was not a defence to the charge and accordingly their verdict did not imply any finding on that issue. The importance of the matter for sentence is emphasised by the fact that after the conviction had been returned, the chairman invited the jury to retire again and consider the issue of knowledge. The subsequent sentence of two years' imprisonment was upheld on appeal, the court observing that the chairman had obviously come to the same conclusion as the jury which was that the appellant was aware of the nature of the bag's contents, and further that he was involved in distribution. The same problem arises in cases of assaults on police officers; conviction for this offence does not require any knowledge that the victim is a police officer, but such knowledge is clearly highly relevant to sentence. The problem is indirectly illustrated by *Haggas*,[11] where the appellant was convicted of assault occasioning actual harm, the victim being a plain-clothes police officer who suffered minor abrasions. The appellant's defence was that he did not believe that the man was a police officer. The Court of Appeal accepted this claim, and stated that although the sentence of nine months would have been appropriate if the appellant had been aware that the victim was a police officer, it was excessive in the light of the appellant's belief that the victim was an imposter. The sentence was varied from nine months' immediate imprisonment to nine months' imprisonment suspended for two years. Even if the appellant had been charged with assaulting a police officer in the execution of his duty, the vital issue of knowledge would not have been determined by his conviction.

Although cases of strict liability are the most obvious example of this aspect of the problem of establishing a factual basis for the sentence, it appears in many other cases where some issue relevant to sentence is not implied in the determination of guilt. The extent of provocation in a case of wounding, the amount of " contributory negligence " on the part of a rape victim, whether a back-street abortionist accepted payment, are all examples of the kind of issues which may require to be determined for the purpose of sentence but which are not fully examined and determined in the trial proper.

In cases such as these, it seems clear that at the present the sentencer must come to his own view of the facts without regard to any implications which the jury's verdict may have. Questions put to the jury in this type of case may cause even greater difficulty

[11] December 10, 1968, No. 6795/68.

than in cases of the kind mentioned above, as their attention may not have been drawn to the issue at all, and the evidence bearing on the issue may not have been fully explored; there is also the possibility of serious injustice to the accused, who may not have adverted to the issue and whose defence may have been quite properly conducted with complete disregard of the matter.

Pleas of guilty

The problem of establishing an accurate version of the facts can be aggravated in cases where there is a guilty plea, or where a guilty plea is under consideration. The same overriding general principle applies in the case of a guilty plea as in a jury trial, and the sentencer must not pass sentence on a basis inconsistent with the plea; where the accused has pleaded guilty to the lesser of the two charges and the prosecution has accepted the position he must not be sentenced on the basis that he is in fact guilty of the greater offence.[12] This principle does not however go very far. Suppose a youth is charged with the rape of a girl about his own age; he is prepared to admit that he committed the offence and knew that the girl did not consent, but wishes to establish that the girl permitted some degree of familiarity beforehand. This factor will normally have a very substantial effect on sentence.[13] If the prosecution accept this version of the facts, there is no problem, but where the prosecution evidence is that the girl did not act in this way the accused is in a dilemma. If he pleads guilty he risks being sentenced on the basis of the facts presented by the prosecution, with no real opportunity to challenge them. For this reason he may be advised to plead not guilty and contest the trial, in order to provide an opportunity to establish the girl's prior behaviour. If he does this however he risks losing some mitigation which he might otherwise obtain for pleading guilty [14] and additionally will be forced to go further in his evidence than he wishes in order to bring his allegations into issue. The only way in which the girl's prior behaviour could be relevant to the issues before the jury would

[12] See *Kennedy* [1968] Crim.L.R. 566, where the appellant pleaded guilty to manslaughter on the grounds of provocation on an indictment charging murder; reducing the sentence from ten years to five the court stated that "the learned judge . . . was not truly accepting this as a case of manslaughter by provocation"; *Lavender*, December 19, 1967, No. 5222/67 (plea of guilty to unlawful wounding accepted on indictment charging wounding with intent; wrong to sentence appellant on basis that he was really guilty of wounding with intent; three years reduced to two).

[13] See *e.g., Gahan*, April 23, 1968, No. 5379/67, where the girl concerned had gone out with the appellant in a van with a mattress in the back and "given this man a certain amount of encouragement." The sentence was reduced from four years' imprisonment to two on this ground.

[14] See particularly *de Haan* (1967) 52 Cr.App.R. 25.

be as tending to show that she consented to intercourse; if the accused does not make her consent an issue it is likely that evidence of the girl's consent to familiarities would be held inadmissible. The accused is thus forced to make a half-hearted attack on the issue of consent and risk leaving the impression that he has attacked the girl's character and exposed her unnecessarily to the embarrassment of giving evidence, actions which might deprive him of some additional mitigation to which he would otherwise be entitled. In another case the defence may wish only to dispute some allegation made in the depositions which does not bear at all on the issue of guilt of the charge, and the prosecution may well quite properly make no reference to the matter in calling evidence and thus give the defence no chance to refute the allegation without appearing to go completely out of its way. An example of this situation might be a case of unlawful sexual intercourse where the prosecution allege in the deposition that the girl had no previous sexual experience; this allegation is not strictly relevant to the charge and should not be made an issue before the jury, but may have some bearing on sentence. If the defence plead not guilty simply to settle this matter for the purpose of sentence they must raise the issue themselves in order to have the opportunity of refuting it.

It is clearly unsatisfactory that issues of this kind can be resolved only by contesting the allegations of guilt. Apart from the waste of time involved and the other disadvantages as in the hypothetical example of the rape case, the trial of the issue of guilt will itself scarcely provide a better forum for determination of the disputed issue. As has been shown, the determination of guilt will not necessarily involve a determination of the contested issue, and evidence bearing on the disputed issue will be of only marginal relevance to the main focus of the trial; it may not be properly examined and may even be ruled inadmissible. A far simpler solution would be to allow the contested issue to be tried on its own by the judge after the plea has been taken; in the hypothetical example of the rape case given earlier the accused could be allowed to give evidence and if necessary the girl could be examined on the limited issues remaining in dispute.[15] In some cases it would be necessary for the prosecutor to formulate an allegation and call evidence to support it, in other cases the defence could seek to establish a particular fact on their own initiative. The latter pro-

[15] This solution was recommended by the Court of Appeal of Southern Australia in *Maitland* (1963) S.A.R. 332. See also *Underhill* (1955) 14 C.C.C. 320.

cedure is of course not far from that presently used on occasion to support a plea in mitigation.[16]

Extraneous facts involving the accused

A distinction can perhaps be drawn between the kind of facts discussed above—those immediately connected with the commission of the offence—and other facts adverse to the accused which may be relevant to the sentence. In so far as these relate to the accused's character and previous convictions the means of establishing them is governed by well established procedures, whether they are contained in the antecedents statement [17] or the social inquiry report.[18] Where they relate to other matters, such as the general background of the offence, procedures to establish them have not been so fully developed. The kind of allegation involved may be that of professionalism, against a receiver alleged to be receiving from all and sundry or an abortionist said to be performing illegal operations systematically and at a profit. In other cases the scope of a fraudulent scheme involving many individual offences may be in issue. In some cases of this kind the problem of establishing the background can be solved by the prosecution charging a number of different offences as representative counts to show the boundaries of the accused's criminal behaviour; in others the number of offences taken into consideration may be used as an indication of the extent of the accused's involvement. There remain cases where these solutions are not possible. In *Robinson* [19] the appellant was convicted of being in unlawful possession of a very small quantity of cannabis. After conviction, the prosecution asked the Deputy Recorder if he would like to hear the background of the case, and then called two police officers each of whom testified that the appellant was "one of the main distributors of drugs in the Midlands," that he associated with other men who had convictions for unlawful possession of cannabis and that men known to be drug pushers had been seen to visit the appellant's house at night. On the basis of this evidence the trial judge sentenced the appellant to three

[16] See *McLean*, November 4, 1968, No. 3902/68. The appellant pleaded guilty to common act assault on an indictment charging assault occasioning actual bodily harm. Following the appellant's plea, the defence called the complainant who gave an account of the incident more favourable to the appellant than that contained in his original deposition, in support of the speech in mitigation. The court stated that the Recorder was "well within his powers" in rejecting the second version.

[17] The current practice governing antecedents statements is contained in a practice direction at [1966] 1 W.L.R. 1184.

[18] See generally Home Office Circular 138/63. A copy of the report must be given to the accused or his counsel (Criminal Justice Act 1948, s. 43).

[19] [1969] Crim.L.R. 207.

years' imprisonment, a sentence clearly based on the assumption that the appellant, despite the small quantities of cannabis found in his possession, was engaged in distribution. On appeal the Court of Appeal disapproved of the procedure that had been followed. The court accepted that the prosecution could properly introduce evidence relevant to an issue in sentencing after the conviction, but stated that such evidence must be first-hand evidence, not hearsay, and must be sufficiently particularised to make it possible for the accused to challenge it. Additionally, where the prosecution intended to lead evidence after conviction which was not given during the trial it must give notice to the defence of the evidence so that the defence may be prepared to challenge it.

The procedure suggested by the court in this case is one which could clearly be adapted to the other contexts where similar problems arise; the argument will be taken up later.

Extraneous facts not involving the accused

The final category of facts which may be relevant to the sentence are those which have no direct connection with the accused. It is clearly accepted as an aspect of sentencing policy that the sentencer may have regard to the prevalence of a particular form of crime at a particular time or in a particular locality, but the way in which the prevalence of the particular crime, or an increase in its prevalence, is established, leaves a great deal to be desired. In *Lee* [20] the following dialogue took place between the trial judge and a police officer giving evidence after the conviction of the appellant for attacking a man with a knife and injuring his hand:

> *Recorder*: " Am I right in thinking that in Preston for some time you have been experiencing a very considerable outbreak of violence? "
>
> *Officer*: " It is quite true my Lord."
>
> *Recorder*: " And there has been a great deal of the use of knives? "
>
> *Officer*: " Mainly by a foreign element, yes, of knives there has been a lot."

The sentence was increased on appeal from two years to three. In other cases the trial judge has acted on his own impression of the prevalence of the offence; in *Banton* [21] the appellant was sentenced to a total of six years' imprisonment for two offences of wounding with intent partly because there were several similar cases in the lists for the assize and the trial judge assumed for that reason that the offence was becoming more prevalent in the area.

[20] [1962] Crim.L.R. 500.
[21] [1966] Crim.L.R. 400 (the sentence was reduced on appeal).

While it is clear that the prevalence of a particular form of crime is a relevant consideration in sentencing, the practices followed in these cases, which are probably typical, suffer from grave defects. The first concerns the substance of the evidence. Gauging the volume of crime and the variations in levels of particular forms of crime presents very sophisticated problems. If the prevalence of the offence is to have a critical effect on the sentence, it should be established with as much care and particularity as other facts proved at the trial. The second defect of the practice seen in the cases cited is procedural. Typically evidence of this kind will be elicited from the police officer by the trial judge after examination of the officer by counsel has been concluded. This may well mean that the defence is not able to cross examine the officer on this issue, and certainly makes it impossible for the defence to prepare itself to meet the evidence. The fact that the judge, rather than the prosecution, elicits the evidence also means that the judge in effect enters the arena and performs a prosecutorial function. The English practice of limiting the role of the prosecution in the sentencing process is admirable in many ways, but it does leave the danger that the judge will step into the gap left by the withdrawal of the prosecutor and cease to approach the question from a judicial viewpoint. Clearly a procedure analogous to that suggested by the Court of Appeal in *Robinson* (above) would be preferable.

Conclusions

The scale of the reductions in sentence made on appeal in some of the cases cited indicates the practical importance of establishing an accurate factual basis for sentence. Major issues of principle are also involved. It would clearly be considered a gross departure from normal standards to charge and convict a man for common assault and then sentence him for murder, but this is a fair analogy of what can happen in a case like *Warner*. The accused is charged simply with possession—no allegation of knowledge of the nature of the substance, or distribution, is made, and he is convicted simply of possession. The judge then passes sentence on the basis that the accused knew the nature of the substance and was involved in distribution. This amounts in effect to sentencing him without indictment, evidence, cross examination or jury decision. It is clear that present practices can give rise to major injustices both in practice and in theory.

The first line of attack on this problem is the reconstruction of the substantive law. The tendancy of modern criminal legislation, exemplified by the Dangerous Drugs Acts and the Theft Act, is to use broadly defined concepts each covering a wide range of activity.

This type of legislation makes for great convenience in prosecuting and lessens the chance of unjustified acquittals on purely technical grounds. It does have the consequence however of throwing more and more disputed issues of fact into the sentencing stage, whose procedures are not yet sufficiently developed to resolve them in an appropriate manner. It seems essential that the problems of the sentencer as well as those of the prosecutor should be borne in mind during the process of codification of the criminal law, and a reasonable degree of gradation of offences within the same category must be maintained. It would be possible to do this without reproducing the degree of detail found in the more colourful sections of the Offences against the Persons Act 1861, and the greater flexibility in allowing convictions for lesser included offences introduced by the Criminal Law Act 1967 should remove many of the problems which a more detailed system of legislation might pose for the prosecutor. It would not even be necessary for gradations to be tied to gradations in maximum sentences, which are in any event irrelevant to most sentencing practice.

Refinement of the substantive law on the lines suggested would not remove all issues of fact from the sentencing process, and there is clearly a need for a more sophisticated means of determining them than exists at present. The guiding principle must surely be that any significant fact adverse to the accused not implied in the verdict or plea and not accepted by the defence must be established after conviction by proper evidence to a proper level of certainty and subject to the same rights of cross examination as the evidence on which the conviction is founded. The procedure suggested in *Robinson* (above) is clearly a step in this direction. This procedure would involve some extension of the prosecution's present role in the sentencing process, but would clearly be preferable to the present situation where the judge is forced to descend into the arena and fulfil a prosecutorial function, or even decide on an adverse fact without any proper inquiry or opportunity of challenge. A second procedural development would be the recognition of the right of the defence to a separate hearing after conviction (whether by verdict or plea) of any issue relevant to sentence which remains in dispute and has not been determined by the conviction. Finally, the trial judge should state explicitly the facts he assumes as the basis for his sentence.

[3]

Criminal Law: The Missing Element in Sentencing Reform

*Michael H. Tonry**

I. Introduction

Recent developments in sentencing reform have occurred against a background of mounting dissatisfaction with the indeterminate sentencing system that has pervaded the United States for much of the twentieth century.[1] The sentencing reform movement has been underway in earnest since 1976.[2] The Alaska Attorney General banned all forms of plea bargaining in 1975,[3] and the United States Parole Commission's guidelines have been in effect for several years.[4] Denver has adopted the first descriptive sentencing guidelines system.[5] The California legislature enacted the California Uniform Determinate Sentencing Law in 1976.[6] Several

---

* Professor of Law, University of Maryland. B.A., 1966, University of North Carolina; LL.B., 1970, Yale University. Preparation of this Article was supported in part by a grant from the National Institute of Corrections.

1. For comprehensive surveys of recent sentencing reform developments, see von Hirsch & Hanrahan, *Determinate Penalty Systems in America: An Overview*, 27 Crime & Delinq. 289 (1981); 4 Abt Associates, American Prisons and Jails (National Institute of Justice 1980); Criminal Courts Technical Assistance Project, Overview of State and Local Sentencing Guidelines and Sentencing Research Activity (American University Law Institute 1980) [hereinafter cited as Overview].

2. Although the first major institutional developments date from about that time, several influential books appeared some years earlier. *See, e.g.*, American Friends Service Comm., Struggle for Justice (1971); M. Frankel, Criminal Sentences (1973); N. Morris, The Future of Imprisonment (1974).

3. *See* Nat'l Inst. of Justice, U.S. Dep't of Justice, Alaska Bans Plea Bargaining (1980). *See also infra* text accompanying notes 122 & 168.

4. United States Parole Commission Rules, 28 C.F.R. §§ 2.1-2.60 (1981); *see infra* notes 76-77 and accompanying text.

5. *See* L. Wilkins, J. Kress, D. Gottfredson, J. Calpin & A. Gelman, Sentencing Guidelines: Structuring Judicial Discretion (National Institute of Law Enforcement and Criminal Justice 1978) [hereinafter cited as L. Wilkins]; W. Rich, L. Sutton, T. Clear, and M. Saks, Sentencing Guidelines: Their Operation and Impact on the Courts (National Center for State Courts 1980) [hereinafter cited as W. Rich]. *See also infra* text accompanying notes 87-94.

6. 1976 Cal. Stat. ch. 1139 (as amended); *see infra* notes 95-102 and accompanying text.

states, including New York[7] and Massachusetts,[8] have enacted mandatory sentencing laws, and Maine adopted a determinate sentencing statute and abolished its parole board in 1976.[9] By 1981, most states either had considered or planned to consider major changes in sentencing laws, institutions, and procedures.[10]

Although indeterminate sentencing systems vary in significant respects from state to state, the similarities are marked. In the model form of indeterminate sentencing procedures, the legislature sets maximum lawful sentences, the judge sets the maximum—and sometimes minimum—terms, and the parole authorities decide when to release prisoners. The judge and the parole board possess immense discretion to individualize punishment decisions to meet the peculiar needs of each offender. In most jurisdictions, appellate courts lack authority to review the judge's sentencing decision or the parole board's release decision.[11]

Two aspects of indeterminate sentencing—immense discretion[12] and freedom from review[13]—are the targets of many sentencing reform initiatives. The establishment of sentencing standards and review procedures is necessary and laudable, but it is not sufficient to achieve genuine improvement in the justness of sentencing in America. Under indeterminate sentencing laws, the substantive criminal law is not especially important; once the defendant has been convicted of an offense, the sentencing judge is entitled to impose any lawful sentence, and no connection need exist between the defendant's wrongdoing and his punishment. Whether a defendant is convicted of armed robbery, robbery, theft, or assault is unimportant as long as the statutory sentence maximums do not constrain the judge's sentencing choices and his ability to individualize the sentence he imposes.[14]

---

7. *See* Joint Committee on New York Drug Law Evaluation, The Nation's Toughest Drug Law: Evaluating the New York Experience (1977) [hereinafter cited as Joint Committee]. *See also infra* note 117 and accompanying text.

8. Mass. Ann. Laws ch. 269, § 10 (1980). *See* Beha, *"And Nobody Can Get You Out"—The Impact of a Mandatory Prison Sentence for the Illegal Carrying of a Firearm on the Use of Firearms and on the Administration of Criminal Justice in Boston* (pts. 1-2), 57 B.U.L. Rev. 96, 289 (1977); *see also infra* text accompanying notes 110-11.

9. Me. Rev. Stat. Ann. tit. 17-A, §§ 1151-1254 (Supp. 1981). *See* Zarr, *Sentencing*, 28 Me. L. Rev. 117 (Special Issue 1976). Maine's parole board, Me. Rev. Stat. Ann., tit. 34, §§ 1671-79, was abolished in 1975 by 1975 Me. Laws ch. 499, § 71.

10. *See* von Hirsch & Hanrahan, *supra* note 1, at 299 n.27.

11. *Id.* at 289-94.

12. *See* Alschuler, *Sentencing Reform and Prosecutorial Power: A Critique of Recent Proposals for "Fixed" and "Presumptive" Sentencing*, 126 U. Pa. L. Rev. 550 (1978).

13. *See* P. Utz, Settling the Facts: Discretion and Negotiation in Criminal Court (1978).

14. If the maximum authorized sentences for armed robbery, robbery, theft, and assault are twenty-five years, twelve years, six years, and three years respectively, the judge

The thesis of this Article is that the substantive criminal law is the missing element in sentencing reform. If comprehensive sentencing reform strategies are to have lasting effect, legislatures must reintroduce the criminal law to the sentencing process. This step will require a rekindled interest in a moral analysis of the substantive criminal law and the enactment of greatly reduced statutory sentence maximums, along with more conventional institutional changes to structure discretion and increase official accountability.

Objections to American sentencing procedures range from the principled to the practical. Part II of this Article summarizes the basic objections that have influenced recent sentencing initiatives. All concern the unstructured discretion and absence of official accountability that characterize indeterminate sentencing. Part III then outlines the sentencing law reforms that have been proposed or adopted in response to these objections. Part IV asserts and attempts to demonstrate that sentencing in America has been divorced from the criminal law, and that present reform proposals are inadequate because they fail to address this separation. At trial, constitutional rights, the law of evidence, and the criminal burden of proof provide the defendant with important procedural safeguards. In addition, the state must meet all substantive criminal law requirements before the defendant can be convicted. Most convictions, however, result from guilty pleas.[15] In these cases trial rights and protections are unimportant. Under an indeterminate sentencing scheme, defendants have virtually no rights at sentencing except for procedural rights such as the rights to counsel and to present and contest evidence.[16] A court, therefore, can convict and sentence a defendant without ever applying substantive criminal law requirements. The new sentencing reforms have not addressed this systemic flaw. Thus, part V of this Article argues that the logic and effect of sentencing reform proposals require that the criminal law be returned to the sentencing process. Finally, part VI

---

who wishes to impose a five-year sentence would be constrained only if the defendant was convicted of assault.

15. National Criminal Justice Information and Statistics Service, Sourcebook of Criminal Justice Statistics—1978, table 5.19 (guilty plea rates vary from place to place but are typically in the 85%-95% range) & 5.30 (85% of federal convictions in 1977 resulted from guilty pleas).

16. For a comprehensive review of the law, see ABA Task Force on Sentencing Alternative and Procedures, Sentencing Alternatives and Procedures (2d ed. 1979), Pt. VI, Standards 18-6.1 to 18-6.9 and supporting commentary [hereinafter cited as Task Force].

sketches the contours of a comprehensive sentencing reform package that would go a long way towards accomplishing this result.

II. THE HARBINGERS OF REFORM

Indeterminate sentencing was an invention of the early twentieth century.[17] Before 1900 judges set precise terms of incarceration for most defendants. In 1900 only six states provided for probation.[18] A handful of states permitted parole, but generally only for first offenders in reformatories.[19] By 1920, thirty-three states permitted adult probation, and all states permitted juvenile probation.[20] By 1923, approximately half of all persons sentenced to state prisons were under an indeterminate sentence, and slightly more than half of all releases were under parole.[21]

Historians differ in their explanations of the abrupt changes during the early 1900's in the penal sanctioning system.[22] Some suggest that the changes were a reaction to the brutality and ineffectiveness of the prisons, which were themselves a hopeful reform of the first half of the nineteenth century.[23] The more likely answer, however, lies in a series of intellectual developments concerning the causes of crime and methods of crime prevention. First, the early developers of social work and settlement houses offered environmental accounts of crimes and attributed the origins of crime to ghetto poverty and social disruption.[24] Suggested remedies included social programs aimed at improving the moral and economic condition of the ghetto and individualized efforts to provide delinquents with role models, discipline, material resources, and new opportunities.[25] Second, newly influential psychiatrists and psychologists argued that criminal behavior was the result of the personal pathology of the individual.[26] Thus, criminals increasingly began to receive individualized analysis, case work, and treatment

---

17. D. ROTHMAN, CONSCIENCE AND CONVENIENCE: THE ASYLUM AND ITS ALTERNATIVES IN PROGRESSIVE AMERICA 43-81 (1980).

18. *Id.* at 44.

19. *Id.*

20. *Id.*

21. *Id. See also* U.S. ATTORNEY GENERAL, SURVEY OF RELEASE PROCEDURES, vol. 2, Probation; vol. 4, Parole (1939).

22. *See* B. MCKELVEY, AMERICAN PRISONS chs. 4-9 (1977); D. ROTHMAN, THE DISCOVERY OF THE ASYLUM: SOCIAL ORDER AND DISORDER IN THE NEW REPUBLIC chs. 10-11 (1971). *See generally* D. ROTHMAN, *supra* note 17, at 17-40.

23. D. ROTHMAN, *supra* note 17, at 17-18.

24. *Id.* at 50-54.

25. *See id.* at 53.

26. *Id.* at 54-58.

programs.[27] Last, the eugenics movement of the time explained criminal deviance as partly the result of heredity.[28] Since individuals are not responsible for their hereditary traits, the eugenicists questioned the incarceration of criminals for behavior that was based on these traits.[29] According to David Rothman, the leading historian of early twentieth century criminal justice institutions, these conceptual developments and the social movements they precipitated pointed to a single solution to the problems of crime: "[T]he origins of deviancy had to be uncovered through a case-by-case study, an individual approach. Ameliorative action had to be fitted specifically to each individual's special needs, and therefore required a maximum of flexibility and discretion."[30] The resultant indeterminate sentencing system delegated virtually unfettered discretion to judges and parole boards, endured unchallenged into the 1960's,[31] and underwent major changes only in the 1970's.

The history of the sentencing reform movement remains to be written. For reasons that are unclear, indeterminate sentencing retained general acceptablity for three quarters of a century[32] and then lost much of its credibility within a few years.[33] The principal causes of this change presumably included developments such as the prisoners' rights and civil rights movements,[34] loss of faith in the rehabilitative ideal,[35] and demands throughout the legal system for greater accountability in official decisionmaking processes.[36]

Four overriding concerns permeate recent sentencing critiques and reform proposals: disparity in sentencing, discrimination in

---

27. *Id.*

28. *Id.* at 58-59.

29. *See id.*

30. *Id.* at 50.

31. *But see* F. ALLEN, THE BORDERLAND OF CRIMINAL JUSTICE (1964).

32. D. ROTHMAN, *supra* note 17, at 1-13. *See supra* text accompanying notes 17-21. Indeterminate sentencing was the pattern in every American state in 1975 when Maine abolished its parole board and thereby became the first modern "determinate" sentencing jurisdiction. ME. REV. STAT. ANN. tit. 17-A, §§ 1151-1254 (Supp. 1981).

33. *See* von Hirsch & Hanrahan, *supra* note 1, at 289; Crump, *Determinate Sentencing: The Promises and Perils of Sentence Guidelines*, 68 KY. L.J. 1, 3-4 (1979-80).

34. Zimring, *Prisoners, Professors, and Politicians—The Origins of Sentencing Reform*, 2 N. ILL. L. REV. (1982) (forthcoming).

35. *See, e.g.*, AMERICAN FRIENDS SERVICE COMM., *supra* note 2; Martinson, *What Works? Questions and Answers About Prison Reform*, 10 PUB. INTEREST 22 (1974).

36. *See, e.g.*, Goldberg v. Kelly, 397 U.S. 254 (1970) (due process requires notice of accusations and opportunity to respond); *see also* Wolff v. McDonnell, 418 U.S. 539 (1974) (prison disciplinary procedures established); Gagnon v. Scarpelli, 411 U.S. 778 (1973) (minimum procedural requirements for probation revocation); Morrissey v. Brewer, 408 U.S. 471 (1972) (minimum procedural requirements for parole revocation).

sentencing, normlessness, and irresponsibility.[37] A fifth concern is the apparent ineffectiveness of indeterminate sentencing in reducing or controlling crime.[38]

A. Disparity in Sentencing

Compelling evidence suggests that sentencing in America is often unacceptably disparate, and that the identity of the decisionmaker rather than the offender's crime and past criminal conduct is frequently the critical element in sentence determination.[39] For more than a half century, research consistently has demonstrated the existence of significant, unexplained disparities in sentencing.[40] Sophisticated statistical analyses are able to account for only one-third of the variations in sentences.[41] In several well-known experiments researchers asked trial judges to review presentence reports and to indicate the sentences that they would impose. The results demonstrated that for the same defendant, some judges would impose probation and other judges would impose a lengthy prison sentence.[42]

B. Discrimination in Sentencing

Reformers have asserted repeatedly that sentencing is racially discriminatory, and that blacks, Hispanics, and native Americans receive harsher sentences than whites.[43] Numerous social science

---

37. *See, e.g.*, M. FRANKEL, *supra* note 2; N. MORRIS, *supra* note 2; A. VON HIRSCH, DOING JUSTICE: THE CHOICE OF PUNISHMENTS (1976).

38. *See* E. VAN DEN HAAG, PUNISHING CRIMINALS (1975); J. WILSON, THINKING ABOUT CRIME (1975). For a review of the scientific control strategies, see NATIONAL ACADEMY OF SCIENCE, DETERRENCE AND INCAPACITATION: ESTIMATING THE EFFECTS OF CRIMINAL SANCTIONS ON CRIME RATES (1978).

39. *See* Green, *Research on Disparities*, in 2 CRIME AND JUSTICE 529 (L. Badzinowicz & M. Wolfgang eds. 1971).

40. *Id.*; *see also* Gaudet, Harris & St. John, *Individual Differences in the Sentencing Tendencies of Judges*, 23 J. CRIM. L. & CRIMINOLOGY 811 (1933).

41. For a review of the evidence, see NATIONAL ACADEMY OF SCIENCE, RESEARCH ON SENTENCING: THE SEARCH FOR REFORM ch. 2 (1983) (forthcoming) [hereinafter cited as RESEARCH ON SENTENCING].

42. *See, e.g.*, FEDERAL JUDICIAL CENTER, THE SECOND CIRCUIT SENTENCING STUDY (1974); INSTITUTE FOR LAW AND SOCIAL RESEARCH AND YANKELOVICH, SKELLY, AND WHITE, INC., FEDERAL SENTENCING: TOWARD A MORE EXPLICIT POLICY OF CRIMINAL SANCTIONS ch. 3 (1980) (*Sentencing Goals and the Disparity Issue*).

43. *See, e.g.*, AMERICAN FRIENDS SERVICE COMM., *supra* note 2; NATIONAL MINORITY ADVISORY COUNCIL ON CRIMINAL JUSTICE, THE INEQUALITY OF JUSTICE: A REPORT ON CRIME AND THE ADMINISTRATION OF JUSTICE IN THE MINORITY COMMUNITY (Law Enforcement Assistance Administration 1980); Joyner, *Legal Theories for Attacking Racial Disparity in Sentencing*, 18 CRIM. L. BULL. 101 (1982).

researchers have investigated discrimination in sentencing.[44] Research covering periods before 1969 provides compelling evidence of sentencing discrimination—especially in the South—both in capital cases and in cases with black offenders and white victims.[45] The evidence for periods since 1969, however, is inconclusive and inconsistent.[46] Considerable anecdotal evidence suggests that some judges discriminate on the basis of race. The gross disproportion in black/white imprisonment rates—the ratio is approximately nine to one[47]—appears to present a prima facie case of substantial racial discrimination in sentencing. Nevertheless, the black overrepresentation in prison—forty-eight percent of the prison population in 1979,[48] compared with thirteen percent of the general population—is consistent with black overrepresentation both among persons arrested for serious crimes and among persons identified by victims as the perpetrators of crimes.[49] Thus, the evidence does not necessarily support the claim that sentencing is substantially racially discriminatory. Since nearly half the inmates of federal and state prisons are black, however, many people quite naturally believe that sentencing is racially discriminatory.

C. Normlessness in Sentencing

Reformers contend that indeterminate sentencing is normless because the moral distinctions that are discernible in the criminal law bear no necessary relation to punishment.[50] The substantive

---

44. For reviews of the literature, see D. TOMPKINS, SENTENCING THE OFFENDER—A BIBLIOGRAPHY (1971); Green, *Inter- and Intra-Racial Crime Relative to Sentencing*, 55 J. CRIM. L., CRIMINOLOGY & POLICE SCI. 348 (1964); Green, *supra* note 39; Hagan, *Extra-Legal Attributes and Criminal Sentencing: An Assessment of a Sociological Viewpoint*, 8 LAW & SOC'Y REV. 357 (1974); Hagan and Bumiller, *Making Sense of Sentencing: A Review and Critique of Sentencing Research*, in RESEARCH ON SENTENCING, *supra* note 41; Overby, *Discrimination Against Minority Groups*, in CRIME AND JUSTICE, *supra* note 39, at 569.

45. *See* Green, *supra* note 39; Hagan and Bumiller, *supra* note 44.

46. RESEARCH ON SENTENCING, *supra* note 41, ch. 2. *But see* Zeisel, *Race Bias in the Administration of the Death Penalty: The Florida Experience*, 95 HARV. L. REV. 456 (1981). Professor Zeisel sees a clear pattern of continuing discrimination and places the blame on the prosecutor. *Id.* at 468.

47. U.S. DEP'T OF JUSTICE, BUREAU OF JUSTICE STATISTICS, BULLETIN: PRISONS AND PRISONERS (1980).

48. *Id.* In November 1979, the racial distribution of state prisoners was 49.6% white, 47.8% black, and 2.5% "other."

49. Hindelang, *Race and Involvement in Common Law Personal Crimes*, 43 AM. SOC. REV. 93 (1978).

50. *See* G. FLETCHER, RETHINKING CRIMINAL LAW (1978); D. RICHARDS, THE MORAL CRITICISM OF LAW (1977); Richards, *Human Rights and the Moral Foundations of the Substantive Criminal Law*, 13 GA. L. REV. 1395 (1979).

law, for example, scales offenses according to the seriousness of the act.[51] The sentence imposed for robbery, however, need not be less than that imposed for armed robbery. Similarly, the criminal law contains formal mitigations such as the defenses of provocation, extreme emotional disturbance, and diminished capacity that serve to reduce the severity of the offense.[52] The sentence, on the other hand, is not necessarily less severe when the mitigation is present.

In recent years a resurgence of interest has emerged in punishment philosophies that closely relate punishment to blameworthiness.[53] A retributive, "just deserts" approach is widely discussed and firmly supported[54] and attaches high priority to the achievement of equality and proportionality in punishment.[55]

In contrast, the indeterminate sentencing systems were based on utilitarian premises in which blameworthiness was not the primary sentence determinant. A utilitarian punishment philosophy, according to H.L.A. Hart, is "forward looking" to the preventive effects of punishment such as rehabilitation, incapacitation, and deterrence.[56] A retributive punishment scheme, on the other hand, is "backward looking" to the defendant's culpability and, perhaps, to the harm that he caused or threatened.[57] Indeterminate sentencing laws are forward looking in Hart's sense and are not concerned primarily with the sentencing values of equality, proportionality, and moral culpability. Academics and reform activists, as well as legislatures, have criticized this normlessness.[58] Consequently, new sentencing statutes, for example, specify that "the purpose of imprisonment . . . is punishment,"[59] and that "commensurate" deserts[60] should be the primary determinant of sentences.

---

51. *See, e.g.*, MODEL PENAL CODE § 6.01 (Official Draft 1962).

52. *See, e.g.*, *id.* §§ 4.01-4.10 (defenses of mental illness or defect), §§ 210.3(1)(b), .6 (3)-(4) (mental or emotional disturbance reduces severity of homicide offense).

53. *See, e.g.*, A. VON HIRSCH, *supra* note 37.

54. *See, e.g*, N. MORRIS, *supra* note 2, at 59-60; *see also infra* notes 59-60 and accompanying text.

55. A. VON HIRSCH, *supra* note 37, at 66-76.

56. *See* H.L.A. HART, PUNISHMENT AND RESPONSIBILITY 72-83 (1968).

57. *Id.* at 81-82.

58. *See, e.g.*, N. MORRIS, *supra* note 2; A. VON HIRSCH, *supra* note 37. *See generally* Committee Report, *Indeterminate Sentencing*, 35 REC. A.B. CITY N.Y. 61 (1980); Crump, *supra* note 33; Gardner, *The Determinate Sentencing Movement and the Eighth Amendment: Excessive Punishment Before and After* Rummel v. Estelle, 1980 DUKE L.J. 1103; Kennedy, *Introduction, Symposium on Sentencing, Part I*, 7 HOFSTRA L. REV. 1 (1978); Meyerson, *The Board of Prison Terms and Paroles and Indeterminate Sentencing: A Critique*, 51 WASH. L. REV. 617 (1976).

59. CAL. PENAL CODE § 1170(a)(1) (West Supp. 1982).

60. OR. REV. STAT. § 144.780(2) (1981).

D. Irresponsibility in Sentencing

A fourth criticism of indeterminate sentencing is that it is "lawless."[61] Indeterminate sentencing allows judges—often influenced greatly by prosecutors, defense lawyers, and probation officers—to impose any sentence authorized by law. The range of sentence that is legally permitted often extends from probation to a long prison term.[62] Furthermore, statutes seldom require judges to indicate the reasons for the sentences that they impose, and no credible mechanisms exist for review of individual sentences. Thus, judges are not accountable for their sentencing decisions. In contrast, judges in most civil cases routinely indicate the reasons for their holdings. Decisions in civil matters also are subject to review of both the legal analysis and the application of the law to the facts.[63] Moreover, due process requires criminal justice officials in other punishment contexts such as prison disciplinary hearings and parole revocation proceedings to give their reasons for any actions that are contrary to an offender's interests.[64] In sum, traditional indeterminate sentencing procedures have become an anomaly.

E. Crime Control

Critics of traditional sentencing practices argue that indeterminate sentencing and rehabilitative correctional programs have not controlled or reduced crime.[65] For the past decade, increasing attention has been given to deterrent and incapacitative crime control strategies.[66] Millions of federal dollars have been spent on deterrence and incapacitation research. Many jurisdictions have established "career criminal" prosecution units with mandates to identify and prosecute repetitive violent offenders. The goal of such units is to imprison and thereby incapacitate repetitive of-

61. Frankel, *Lawlessness in Sentencing*, 41 U. CIN. L. REV. 1 (1972).

62. For example, the Tennessee Code prescribes a minimum term of five years for robbery. TENN. CODE ANN. § 39-3901 (Supp. 1981). The maximum term is execution. *Id.*

63. For a colorful contrast between the respective opportunities of appellate review of a person sentenced to prison and an unsuccessful party in civil litigation, see M. FRANKEL, *supra* note 2, at 75.

64. Wolff v. McDonnell, 418 U.S. 539 (1974) (prison disciplinary procedures); Gagnon v. Scarpelli, 411 U.S. 778 (1973) (probation revocation); Morrissey v. Brewer, 408 U.S. 471 (1972) (parole revocation).

65. The preventive effects of punishment are too extensive to be addressed in this Article. *See supra* note 38 for several introductory sources.

66. *See* NATIONAL ACADEMY OF SCIENCE, *supra* note 38; E. VAN DEN HAAG, *supra* note 38; J. WILSON, *supra* note 38.

fenders. Mandatory minimum sentence laws represent efforts both to deter prospective offenders—by the threat of certain and severe punishment—and to incapacitate those persons who ignore the law's admonition. These strategies, however, are difficult to implement when judges and parole boards have unfettered discretion in punishment decisions. According to these critics, sentencing can be an effective crime control weapon only if punishments are harsher, more certain, or both.

These five sentencing concerns—disparity, discrimination, normlessness, irresponsibility, and crime control—have coalesced into a compelling case against indeterminate sentencing and have been the harbingers of recent reform. Although indeterminate sentencing has enjoyed almost universal support throughout much of this century, a remarkable coalition of prisoners' groups, reformers, and bureaucrats became convinced by the late 1970's that the indeterminate sentencing era was at its end.[67]

III. The Current Shape of Reform

Current sentencing reform strategies aim in various ways to diminish the scope of officials' discretion, to establish general standards for decisionmaking, and to enhance official accountability. Each of these aims in effect constitutes a repudiation of indeterminate sentencing. Recent sentencing reform initiatives include the Model Penal Code's system of offense classification,[68] the creation of statutory presumptions favoring particular sentencing decisions,[69] requirements that reasons for sentences be stated,[70] sentencing councils,[71] sentencing institutes,[72] and appellate review of sentences.[73] These sentencing initiatives, however, are not inconsistent with indeterminacy and are not discussed at length here. Instead, this part of the Article introduces the major sentencing re-

67. *See, e.g.*, Messinger & Johnson, *California's Determinate Sentencing Statute: History and Issues*, in Strategies for Determinate Sentencing ___ (National Institute of Law Enforcement and Criminal Justice 1978).

68. Model Penal Code §§ 210.0-251.4 (Official Draft 1962). The Model Penal Code has been adopted in more than 30 states.

69. *See, e.g.*, Cal. Penal Code §§ 1170-1170.7 (West Supp. 1982). *See also supra* notes 95-105 and accompanying text.

70. *See, e.g.*, Criminal Code Reform Bill, S. 1630, 97th Cong., 1st Sess. § 2003 (1981).

71. *See generally* von Hirsch & Hanrahan, *supra* note 1.

72. *Id.*

73. *See, e.g.*, 18 U.S.C. § 3575(b) (1976) (sentence limited to a term "not disproportionate" to that for base offense). *See generally* Md. Cts. & Jud. Proc. Code Ann. § 12-302(c) (1980).

form measures that contain structural changes which are designed to remedy the problems described in part II by substantially altering the discretions delegated to prosecutors, judges, and parole boards. These reform measures, which are discussed below in turn, include parole guidelines, descriptive sentencing guidelines, presumptive sentencing, mandatory minimum sentences, parole abolition, and plea bargaining bans.

A. Parole Guidelines

The United States parole guidelines emanated from the Parole Decisionmaking Project of the National Council on Crime and Delinquency Research Center, in collaboration with the United States Board of Parole. One phase of that project was an attempt to identify the weights that decisionmakers gave to various criteria in the parole decision. A study of those criteria showed that decisionmakers' primary concerns were the severity of the offense, the prisoner's parole prognosis, and his institutional behavior, and that "a parole board's decisions could be predicted fairly accurately by knowledge of its ratings on these three factors."[74] The project developed a statistical model that made explicit the Parole Board's implicit policies. Thus, the guidelines were "descriptive" of past practices.[75] The United States Board of Parole initiated the first parole guidelines system in 1972 as part of a pilot project to test the feasibility of regionalizing the parole board's operation. In 1976 the Parole Commission and Reorganization Act[76] modified the parole guidelines that had been developed in the Parole Commission's Northeast Region and then adopted them for use in the entire federal system.[77] Current guidelines are expressed in matrix format, as shown in Table I: the vertical axis contains six offense categories and the horizontal axis contains four parole prognosis categories.

---

74. Gottfredson, Hoffman, Sigler & Wilkins, *Making Paroling Policy Explicit*, 21 Crime & Delinq. 34, 37 (1975).

75. *See generally* D. Gottfredson, L. Wilkins & P. Hoffman, Guidelines for Parole and Sentencing (1978).

76. 5 U.S.C. § 5108 (1976 & Supp. IV 1980); 18 U.S.C. §§ 3655, 4201-4218, 5005-5006, 5010, 5014-5021, 5041 (1976).

77. On the development of the U.S. parole guidelines, see D. Gottfredson, L. Wilkins & P. Hoffman, *supra* note 75.

TABLE 1
U.S. PAROLE GUIDELINES (ADULTS)

	Offender Characteristics			
Offense Severity	Very Good	Good	Fair	Poor
Low	0-6 months	6-9 months	9-12 months	12-16 months
Low moderate	0-8	8-12	12-16	16-22
Moderate	10-14	14-18	18-24	24-32
High	14-20	20-26	26-34	34-44
Very High	24-36	36-48	48-60	60-72
Greatest I	40-52	52-64	64-78	78-100
Greatest II	52+	64+	78+	100+

Source: U.S. Parole Commission, Rules § 2-20 (Eff. Sept. 1, 1981); 28 C.F.R. 2-20.

When setting release dates, hearing examiners determine the category within which the prisoner's criminal conduct falls. The examiners then calculate the prisoner's salient factor score, which is based on the predicted recidivism rates of persons sharing certain characteristics with the prisoner. After consulting the cell at which the applicable offense severity row and parole prognosis column intersect, parole officials in the ordinary case set a release date that is consistent with the range which is identified in this cell.[78]

Florida,[79] Georgia,[80] New York,[81] Oklahoma,[82] Oregon,[83] and Utah[84] have adopted similar parole guidelines. Minnesota and Washington adopted and have since repealed matrix parole guidelines. Minnesota abolished parole release.[85] Washington first adopted a different parole guideline format and later abolished its

78. United States Parole Commission Rules, 28 C.F.R. §§ 2.1-2.60 (1981).

79. FLA. STAT. ANN. §§ 947.16-.18 (1982).

80. GA. CODE ANN. § 77-512.1 (1981).

81. NEW YORK PENAL LAW § 70.40 (Consol. 1981-1982).

82. The Oklahoma Pardon and Parole Board implemented matrix-type parole guidelines without a legislative mandate, on April 1, 1980.

83. 1977 Or. Laws ch. 372.

84. The Utah guidelines were drafted by the research staff of the Utah Department of Corrections.

85. MINN. STAT. ANN. §§ 244.01-11 (West Supp. 1982). For a general review of these developments, see R. SPARKS, A. VON HIRSCH & S. MESSINGER, PROJECT ON STRATEGIES FOR DETERMINATE SENTENCING (a forthcoming federally funded comprehensive review of sentencing reform developments); von Hirsch & Hanrahan, *supra* note 1.

parole board effective July 1, 1988.[86]

B. Descriptive Sentencing Guidelines

Descriptive sentencing guidelines originated in Denver and resulted from an effort to apply the research experience and statistical technology that had been developed in establishing the United States parole guidelines.[87] Researchers collected data on a sample of cases and subjected this data to statistical analyses to identify those offense and offender variables that best "explained" the sentences imposed. The premise of this initial study was that "the gradual build-up of case-by-case decisions results in the incremental development of a sentencing policy."[88] Thus, the Denver guidelines were descriptive because they were purportedly based on the past practices of the Denver courts, as shown by the statistical analyses, and were constructed so approximately eighty-five percent of the sentences in the sample of cases fell within the sentencing ranges contained in the guidelines.[89] The Denver guidelines and most other descriptive sentencing systems, therefore, are in the matrix format of the United States parole guidelines.

Judicial compliance with the resulting empirically informed matrix guidelines is wholly voluntary.[90] The developers postulated that the guidelines' descriptive character would make them inherently credible, and, consequently, that judges would comply with them and "significantly reduce unjustified variation from the norm by making the established policy of the court explicit."[91] The Denver guidelines took effect in 1976. Subsequent generations of federally funded projects have developed descriptive sentencing guidelines in Newark, Chicago, and Phoenix, and, at the state level, in Maryland and Florida.[92] Alaska, Massachusetts, Michigan, New Jersey, and Washington also have developed statewide descriptive sentencing guidelines.[93] According to one recent survey, as of April 1, 1981, twenty-three states had implemented or were developing descriptive sentencing guidelines.[94]

86. *See* WASH. REV. CODE ANN. § 9.95.009 (Supp. 1982).
87. *See supra* note 4.
88. *See* W. RICH, *supra* note 5, at __.
89. *Id.* at 24-25.
90. *Id.* at 31.
91. *Id.*
92. *See* J. KRESS, PRESCRIPTION FOR JUSTICE (1980).
93. *See* von Hirsch & Hanrahan, *supra* note 1.
94. *See* OVERVIEW, *supra* note 1.

C. *Presumptive Sentencing*

California's Uniform Determinate Sentencing Act[95] is an example of a presumptive sentencing scheme. The Act establishes a detailed sentencing scheme that specifies mitigated, normal, and aggravated prison sentences for defendants convicted of particular felonies.[96] The middle term is the presumptive base. The Act directs the judges to impose the middle or normal term in the ordinary case, though the judge may, consistent with criteria established by the California Judicial Council, impose the higher or lower terms to reflect aggravating or mitigating circumstances.[97] In addition, the California Act directs the judge to increase the term variously by one to three years if specific aggravating factors such as weapon possession or use,[98] personal injuries,[99] or great property loss or damage[100] are "charged and admitted or found true."[101] Finally, the Act directs the judge to increase the sentence by specified amounts if the defendant has been incarcerated previously for felony convictions.[102] Alaska, Arizona, Colorado, Connecticut, Illinois, Indiana, New Jersey, New Mexico, and North Carolina have enacted similar presumptive sentencing statutes with much less detailed standards.[103]

Minnesota,[104] Pennsylvania,[105] and Washington[106] have created sentencing commissions and have charged them with establishing presumptive sentencing guidelines. The Minnesota Sentencing Guidelines Commission has promulgated detailed guidelines in the familiar matrix format. These guidelines specify narrow ranges of presumptive sentences—typically five percent on either side of a

95. CAL. PENAL CODE §§ 1170-1170.7 (West Supp. 1982).

96. Three prison terms are specified for every offense. For example, the sentences for robbery are two, three, or five years. *Id.* § 213.

97. *Id.* § 1170.

98. *Id.* § 12022.5.

99. *Id.* § 12022.7.

100. *Id.* § 12022.6.

101. *Id.* § 667.5(d).

102. *Id.* 667.5.

103. ALASKA STAT. §§ 12.55.005-.185 (1968); ARIZ. REV. STAT. ANN. § 13-702 (1978); COLO. REV. STAT. § 16-11-101 (1978 & Supp. 1980); CONN. GEN. STAT. ANN. § 53a-35 (1972 & West Supp. 1981); ILL. ANN. STAT. ch. 38, §§ 1005-5-1 to -5-3 (Smith-Hurd 1973 & Supp. 1981-1982); IND. CODE ANN. § 35-50-1A-7 (Burns 1979); N.J. STAT. ANN. 2C:44-1 (West Supp. 1980); N.M. STAT. ANN. §§ 31-18-12 to -18-21 (1981); N.C. GEN. STAT. § 15A-1340.4 (Supp. 1979).

104. MINN. STAT. ANN. § 244.09 (West Supp. 1982).

105. 42 PA. CONS. STAT. ANN. §§ 2151-2155 (Purdon 1981).

106. WASH. REV. CODE. ANN. §§ 9.94A.010-.94A.910 (Supp. 1982).

midpoint—for various combinations of offense severity and prior criminality and authorize judges to impose other sentences only for "substantial and compelling" reasons.[107] Sentences outside the guidelines can be appealed to the Minnesota Supreme Court.[108] At the present time, sentencing commissions in Pennsylvania and Washington are in the process of developing presumptive sentencing guidelines for their states.[109]

D. *Mandatory Minimum Sentences*

Mandatory minimum sentence laws generally require imposition of a prison sentence that is not less than a specified length. Massachusetts' Bartley-Fox law,[110] for example, requires a mandatory minimum prison sentence of one year without suspension, parole, or furlough for anyone who is convicted of illegally carrying a firearm.[111] Similarly, the Michigan Felony Firearm Statute[112] mandates a two-year prison sentence—in addition to any sentence for the underlying felony—for any defendant who possesses a firearm while engaging in a felony.[113] New York's Rockefeller Drug Law imposes minimum prison sentences of fifteen, six, and one years for persons who are convicted of various heroin trafficking offenses.[114]

Most major law reform bodies have disapproved mandatory minimum sentencing laws.[115] Nevertheless, mandatory minimum sentencing schemes are the single most common recent sentencing innovation.[116] In 1980 the Department of Justice reported that twenty-seven states had adopted mandatory minimum sentence laws between 1977 and 1980, and that fourteen other states were

---

107. Minnesota Sentencing Guidelines Commission, Minnesota Sentencing Guidelines and Commentary, § II. D. [hereinafter cited as Minnesota Guidelines]. *See id.* § II. C.

108. MINN. STAT. ANN. § 244.11 (West Supp. 1982) (authorizes such appellate review of a sentence on request of either the state or the defendant).

109. *See* Pennsylvania Commission on Sentencing, Proposed Sentencing Guidelines, 12 Pa. Admin. Bull. 431 (Jan. 23, 1982) [hereinafter cited as Proposed Pennsylvania Guidelines]; WASH. REV. CODE. ANN. §§ 9.94A.040-.94A.070 (Supp. 1982).

110. MASS. GEN. LAWS ANN. ch. 269, § 10 (West Supp. 1981).

111. *Id.; see* Beha, *supra* note 8.

112. MICH. COMP. LAWS ANN. § 750.227b (Supp. 1982-1983).

113. *Id.;* see Heumann & Loftin, *Mandatory Sentencing and the Abolition of Plea Bargaining: The Michigan Felony Firearm Statute*, 13 LAW & SOC'Y REV. 393 (1979).

114. *See* JOINT COMMITTEE, *supra* note 7.

115. *See, e.g.*, TASK FORCE, *supra* note 16, § 18-2.1 (2d ed. approved Aug. 1979).

116. *See generally* PRESIDENT'S COMMISSION ON LAW ENFORCEMENT AND THE ADMINISTRATION OF JUSTICE, THE CHALLENGE OF CRIME IN A FREE SOCIETY 350-52 (1968).

considering similar action.[117]

E. Parole Abolition

The term "parole abolition" is a misnomer. Most states that have abolished parole release retain short mandatory periods of parole supervision that include the possibility of parole revocation.[118] Many states that have eliminated parole release in general have retained parole systems for small categories of offenders who continue to receive indeterminate sentences.[119] At least nine states have followed Maine's lead and abolished parole release for most prisoners.[120]

F. Plea Bargaining Bans

Plea bargaining provides prosecutors with great influence in the sentencing process, especially under presumptive sentencing laws that determine sentences by the nature of the charges filed or not dismissed.[121] Some localities have attempted to ban some or all forms of plea bargaining.[122] The most dramatic effort to abolish plea bargaining remains the Alaska Attorney General's 1975 directive banning all prosecutorial participation in plea bargaining.[123]

G. Summary

The reform initiatives outlined above address the perceived defects of indeterminate sentencing. Normative standards and limitations on prosecutorial, judicial, and parole board discretion can

117. U.S. Dept. of Justice Press Release (March 23, 1980); *see* Note, *Daring the Courts: Trial and Bargaining Consequences of Minimum Penalties*, 90 YALE L.J. 597 (1981).

118. *See, e.g.*, CAL. PENAL CODE §§ 3000, 3053 (West Supp. 1982) (sets maximum parole supervision periods and creates Board of Prison Terms to administer parole supervision); IND. CODE ANN. § 11-13-3-5 (Burns 1981) (maximum parole supervision periods).

119. California, Illinois, Indiana, Maine and Minnesota have abolished parole, although most have retained a period of parole supervision as a consequence of a prison sentence.

120. Alaska, California, Colorado, Connecticut, Illinois, Indiana, Minnesota, New Mexico, and North Carolina have abolished parole release. *See* NATIONAL INSTITUTE OF LAW ENFORCEMENT AND CRIMINAL JUSTICE, ABOLISH PAROLE? (1978).

121. Under presumptive sentencing procedures the prosecutor can determine the prison sentence by electing which charges to file or dismiss and also by deciding what enhancements and prior prison sentences to charge and prove. *See supra* notes 95-109 and accompanying text.

122. *See* Alschuler, *supra* note 12, at 563-76. *See generally* Church, *Plea Bargains, Concessions, and the Courts: Analysis of a Quasi-Experiment*, 10 LAW & SOC'Y REV. 377 (1976).

123. *See supra* text accompanying note 3.

rationalize sentencing, reduce disparity, enhance accountability, and diminish the likelihood of various forms of invidious discrimination. These sentencing reforms, however, are in an important respect only half-measures. Although purporting to reject the institutional manifestations of the rehabilitative ideology that underlies indeterminate sentencing, the reforms operate within the context of criminal laws that are the product of precisely the same rehabilitative ideology. The Model Penal Code, for example, was avowedly rehabilitative in its premises and provisions and was designed to meet the needs of indeterminate sentencing.[124] Part IV of this Article argues that criminal codes drafted under the influence of indeterminate sentencing are inadequate and suggests that these criminal codes will frustrate modern sentencing reform initiatives unless the sentencing reform movement broadens its focus to include criminal law reform.

IV. The Irrelevance of Criminal Law in Indeterminate Sentencing

A. The Paradox of Sentencing

The defendant at trial stands protected by a formidable array of substantive, procedural, and evidentiary rights. The common law requires strict construction of penal statutes; courts must resolve statutory ambiguities in the defendant's favor.[125] The defendant may be convicted only after a finding of guilt based on proof beyond a reasonable doubt.[126] Prophylactic evidentiary rules limit the evidence that the state may introduce to convict the defendant.[127] In addition, a defendant is entitled to various procedural protections, including the right to counsel,[128] the right to confront accusers,[129] and the right to present evidence in his own behalf.[130] If the defendant is convicted, he may appeal on the grounds that evidentiary rules were inappropriately applied, that the evidence

124. Model Penal Code § 1.02 Commentary (1962). *See generally* Wechsler, *Codification of Criminal Law in the United States: The Model Penal Code*, 68 Colum. L. Rev. 1425 (1968).

125. *See, e.g.*, J. Hall, General Principles of the Criminal Law 35-39 (2d ed. 1960).

126. *In re* Winship, 397 U.S. 358 (1970).

127. *See, e.g.*, Fed. R. Evid. 404, 405. *See* generally Schulhofer, *Due Process of Sentencing*, 128 U. Pa. L. Rev. 733, 760-61 (1980).

128. U.S. Const. amend. VI.

129. *Id.*

130. *Id. See generally* ABA Project on Minimum Standards for Criminal Justice, Standards Relating to Sentencing Alternatives and Procedures § 4.3(a) commentary at 211-12 (1968).

adduced at trial does not support the conviction, or that essential trial or pretrial safeguards were lacking.

Most of these protections are absent during the sentencing stage. Indeed, sentencing in most jurisdictions is a mystery. The judge has immense discretion to impose a wide range of sentences—often ranging from probation to lengthy prison terms—and that discretion is rarely subject to any meaningful constraints. Most statutory maximum sentences are very long—much longer than the prison sentences that typically are imposed or served.[131] The prosecution does not have to meet any burden of proof standard at sentencing proceedings, and the rules of evidence do not apply. The sentencing judge may consider any information that he considers relevant, including allegations of prior criminality that did not result in arrest, that resulted in arrest but no conviction, or even that resulted in a dismissal or an acquittal at trial.[132] Even though a defendant has been charged with armed robbery but convicted only of theft, the judge nevertheless may impose the sentence he would have imposed if the defendant had been convicted of armed robbery. Thus, the substantive law matters only to the extent that it authorizes maximum sentences that often have little practical significance. Finally, in many jurisdictions no right to appeal a sentence exists, and when it does exist, it generally appears to be ineffective.[133]

This litany of distinctions between adjudication and sentencing suggests that adjudication is the important decision and that sentencing is subsidiary. In theory this proposition is true, but the reality is to the contrary. A substantial majority of convictions result from guilty pleas, which often follow plea negotiations.[134] The vast array of evidentiary rules, burdens of proof, and other trial rights are irrelevant to these defendants, although sometimes counsel may tactically invoke these rights during plea negotiations. In these cases the substantive criminal law is substantially attenuated, if not wholly insignificant. If sentence bargaining is preva-

---

131. For example, the maximum sentence for robbery under several federal statutes is 25 years (300 months). In 1976 the average federal prisoners released from prison for the first time had served 44.4 months of an average sentence of 131.3 months. NATIONAL CRIMINAL JUSTICE INFORMATION AND STATISTICS SERVICE, SOURCEBOOK OF CRIMINAL JUSTICE STATISTICS—1978, table 6.61.

132. *See* United States v. Cardi, 519 F.2d 309, 312-13 (7th Cir. 1975). *See generally* Schulhofer, *supra* note 127, at 765.

133. *See* Zeisel & Diamond, *Search for Sentencing Equity: Sentence Review in Massachusetts and Connecticut*, 1977 AM. B. FOUND. RESEARCH J. 881.

134. *See supra* note 15 and accompanying text.

lent, then the conviction offense is of little consequence. If charge bargaining is prevalent, the defendant pleads guilty to an offense less serious than that which was charged originally. The conviction offense, therefore, is at best an uncertain guide to the offender's crime.

B. The Irrelevance of the Criminal Law

Reliance on plea negotiation is a major cause of the diminished importance of adjudication and the resultant deemphasis on the criminal law. The relationship between indeterminate sentencing and the criminal law, however, is more complex and in part explains why plea bargaining has become ubiquitous. This relationship suggests several reasons why the criminal law has become increasingly irrelevant in recent decades.

1. Individualized Sentencing and Rehabilitation

The theoretical premises of indeterminate sentencing require that the sentencing judge tailor sanctions to fit the defendant.[135] A judge, therefore, can legitimately consider during the sentencing process any information—whatever its nature or source—that may be relevant to the sentencing determination. The Supreme Court in *Williams v. New York*[136] held that the determination of evidentiary relevancy at sentencing hearings was solely within the discretion of the sentencing judge.[137] This evidentiary latitude accorded to sentencing judges even extends to the consideration of alleged but unproven prior criminal acts.[138] The Court in *Williams* reasoned that individualized sentencing requires judges to have access to all relevant information.[139] This stance was not remarkable in the rehabilitative penological climate of the 1940's. The effect of *Williams,* however, was to diminish the importance of a defendant's conviction offense. A defendant charged with armed robbery, but convicted by a jury of theft, may later be sentenced as if he had been convicted of armed robbery. The conviction offense, therefore, has little, if any, relevance to sentencing.

---

135. *See supra* notes 11-14 and accompanying text.

136. 337 U.S. 241 (1949).

137. *See also* United States v. Grayson, 438 U.S. 41 (1978) (reaffirming Williams' evidentiary discretion).

138. *Compare* Fed. R. Evid. 608(b) (prior bad acts may not be proved by extrinsic evidence) *with id.* 609 (limitations on admissibility of prior convictions).

139. 337 U.S. at 247.

2. Plea Bargaining and the Law

Since substantive criminal law analysis has few implications for sentencing after *Williams*, lawyers have little reason to argue vigorously over the proper application of the criminal law. The defendant is concerned primarily about whether he will be convicted, and, if so, whether he will be imprisoned. If conviction for some offense appears inevitable, the defense lawyer can best serve a client either by keeping the client out of prison or by attaining the shortest possible sentence. The defendant who makes a sentence bargain knows his punishment when he pleads guilty. The effect of a charge bargain, however, is less predictable. Arrangements with prosecutors over the charge that will be filed can provide real protection, since in most jurisdictions dismissal of felony charges for a misdemeanor plea guarantees that the defendant will not be sentenced to the state penitentiary. Sometimes, of course, charge bargains provide no more than insurance against long sentences. For example, if the defendant pleads guilty to robbery, which often has a ten year maximum sentence, in exchange for the dismissal of an armed robbery charge, which frequently carries a twenty-five year maximum sentence, this arrangement at least provides protection against extremely long sentences.

The prospect or certainty of less severe sentences than would otherwise obtain provides the impetus for guilty pleas. Under indeterminate sentencing procedures, the alternative to a plea bargain is to risk sentencing by a judge, who is subject to no meaningful standards and accorded great statutory latitude. Sentencing by the court entails the risk of an extremely severe sentence relative to sentences received by other defendants for that offense. Thus, the defense lawyer must concern himself with sentencing rather than with either the substantive law or the appropriate conviction offense.

3. Moral Incoherence of the Criminal Law

The theoretical underpinnings of indeterminate sentencing undermine the substantive criminal law in other ways. Professor Zimring implores the "moral incoherence of the criminal law" and refers to the modern tendency of legislatures to draft penal statutes broadly to encompass a wide variety of behaviors.[140] Many

140. Zimring, *Making the Punishment Fit the Crime*, HASTINGS CENTER REP. December, 1976, at 13, 15-16.

statutory robbery definitions and related sanction provisions, for example, include conduct that ranges from professional, violent bank robberies to a fifteen year old's forcible taking of a basketball in a school year.[141] Judges, lawyers, and probation officers distinguish between these acts. The criminal law, however, often fails to address even gross distinctions within a broad statutory offense. This failure creates a shadow criminal law within the sentencing process that distinguishes among cases in ways that the criminal law does not.

Reformers have not addressed this incoherence in the criminal law. Section 1721(1) of the Proposed Federal Criminal Code of the National Commission on Reform of Federal Criminal Laws[142] provides that "[a] person is guilty of robbery if, in the course of committing a theft, he inflicts or attempts to inflict bodily injury upon another, or threatens another with imminent bodily injury." Other subsections grade robberies as Class A, Class B, or Class C offenses for the possession or use of a dangerous weapon,[143] the infliction of serious bodily injury,[144] or the presence of an accomplice.[145] The bulk of robberies, however, fall within the general definition of section 1721(1). This definition, therefore, provides no basis for a judge to distinguish among schoolyard thefts accompanied by threats, muggings, robberies of the elderly, and professional bank robberies. Reasonable people will differ in their assessments of the relative seriousness of these different robberies. Few people, however, would regard all these acts as equally evil and deserving of equal punishment. Thus, the shadow criminal law discriminates among kinds of conduct that the criminal codes fail to distinguish.

This moral incoherence of the criminal law is most acute at the federal level. Under the mail fraud statutes, for example, the prosecution need only prove the existence of a "scheme or artifice to defraud" and the use of the mails in furtherance thereof.[146] Although the statute requires proof of "specific intent,"[147] the factfinder may infer intent from all the surrounding circumstances.[148] The courts have refused to define "scheme to defraud"

141. *See, e.g.*, MODEL PENAL CODE § 222.1 (Official Draft 1962).

142. NATIONAL COMMISSION ON REFORM OF FEDERAL CRIMINAL LAWS, STUDY DRAFT OF A NEW FEDERAL CRIMINAL CODE (1970) [hereinafter cited as STUDY DRAFT].

143. *Id.* § 1721(2).

144. *Id.*

145. *Id.*

146. 18 U.S.C. § 1341 (1976).

147. *Id.*

148. *See, e.g.*, United States v. Mackay, 491 F.2d 616 (10th Cir. 1973), *cert. denied*,

with precision, but instead have

> established that a "scheme to defraud" need not result in actual pecuniary or property loss to any victim nor need the scheme be contrary to state or federal law. Rather, the governing standard seems to be that of fair play, an obviously elusive standard upon which to make the question of criminal liability turn.[149]

The vagueness of the mail fraud statute gives rise to the federal prosecutorial maxim "when in doubt, charge mail fraud"[150] and illustrates the prosecutorial advantages that inhere in a broadly phrased criminal statute. Use of the mails is seldom difficult to prove. Moreover, the elasticity of the "scheme to defraud" language has permitted federal prosecutors to initiate mail fraud prosecutions in response to the temper of the times. Thus, federal prosecutors have invoked the mail fraud statute in many recent political corruption prosecutions.[151] The proverbial visitor from another planet would be surprised to learn that the venal indiscretions of Governor Kerner of Illinois, Governor Mandel of Maryland, and Governor Blanton of Tennessee were all prosecuted under the mail fraud statute.

Arguably, the federal mail fraud statutes and other similar federal statutes such as the Hobbs Act,[152] the Travel Act,[153] the wire fraud statute,[154] and the Racketeer Influenced and Corrupt Organizations Act[155] serve important law enforcement interests. These statutes permit prosecutions in cases that otherwise would fall outside the criminal code. The elements of the crimes are relatively easy to prove, and the statutes can be directed to meet contemporary needs. For example, since no federal statute criminalizes local political corruption and local prosecutors cannot be relied upon to prosecute these cases, mail fraud becomes a useful federal weapon. The mail fraud statute thus permits federal authorities to

---

416 U.S. 972 (1974).

149. Coffee, *From Tort to Crime: Some Reflections on the Criminalization of Fiduciary Breaches and the Problematic Line Between Law and Ethics*, 19 AM. CRIM. L. REV. 117, 127 (1981). *See also* 18 U.S.C. § 1341 (1976).

150. Coffee, *supra* note 149, at 126.

151. Governor Mandel of Maryland, Governor Kerner of Illinois, and Governor Blanton of Tennessee all were convicted under the mail fraud statute. *See* United States v. Mandel, 602 F.2d 652 (4th Cir. 1979) (Mandel); United States v. Isaacs, 493 F.2d 1124 (7th Cir. 1973), *cert. denied*, 417 U.S. 976 (1974) (Kerner); United States v. Blanton, No. 80-30253 (M.D. Tenn. Aug. 14, 1981), *appeal filed*, No. 81-5644 (6th Cir. Aug. 21, 1981) (Blanton).

152. 18 U.S.C. § 1951 (1976).

153. 18 U.S.C. § 1952 (1976).

154. 18 U.S.C. § 1343 (1976).

155. 18 U.S.C. §§ 1961-1968 (1976 & Supp. IV 1980).

proceed without waiting for Congress to enact a federal statute prohibiting local political corruption.

Congress' implicit delegation to federal prosecutors of the power to determine what behavior will constitute federal offenses creates separation of powers and federalism problems. Federal prosecutors may abuse their power to criminalize behavior and to extend federal criminal law into areas that are more appropriately within the province of the states—or into areas that Congress would not have expressly authorized.

The mail fraud statute and other similar federal laws illustrate the same ambivalence toward the criminal law that characterizes sentencing in the state criminal courts. Under indeterminate sentencing procedures, the substantial protections afforded defendants are largely symbolic because most defendants plead guilty. In addition, the rehabilitative sentencing ideology authorizes the sentencing judge to look beyond the defendant's conviction offense to determine the appropriate sentence. Thus, the conviction is a formality; the critical decisionmaking and distinguishing function occurs during the sentencing process. Similarly, the conviction under the mail fraud statute can be a formality that bears no close moral relation to the defendant's wrongdoing. It serves simply to subject the defendant to the court's sentencing authority, under which the judge can assess the moral quality of the defendant's acts and determine the appropriate punitive response.

Informal defenses also contribute to the moral incoherence of the criminal law. The substantive criminal law contains formal defenses that are classified as excuses,[156] justifications,[157] and mitigation.[158] These defenses are formal because they relate to the formal application of the criminal law. Judges, however, often consider informal mitigating defenses when setting sentences. Youth, inexperience, motive, contrition, unemployment, and mental subnormality are examples of the informal considerations that the substantive criminal law does not recognize, but which may be taken into account during sentencing. The Model Penal Code, for example, states that in most contexts the victim's consent to an assault is no defense.[159] Prosecutors and judges, however, routinely dismiss family assault cases if the victim elects to drop the prosecution. Similarly, repayment of stolen or embezzled money is not a

156. *See, e.g.*, Model Penal Code §§ 4.01-4.09 (Official Draft 1962) (insanity excuse).
157. *See, e.g.*, *id.* § 3.04 (self-defense).
158. *See, e.g.*, *id.* § 210.3 (1)(b) (provocation).
159. *Id.* § 2.11.

defense to a criminal charge,[160] but prosecutors and judges often dismiss the charges if repayment is made. These cases require decisionmakers to draw normative and moral distinctions without guidance from the criminal code.

Under an indeterminate sentencing scheme, the criminal law purposely fails to address the moral grading of offenses and informal defenses. Criminal code draftsmen delegated to the judge the authority to take these considerations into account during sentencing. Thus, the moral incoherence of the criminal law enhances the importance of the sentencing stage. Many sentencing initiatives of recent years, however, attempt to establish a closer relation between the offender's wrongdoing and his punishment. Successful sentencing reform, therefore, will require major revisions of the substantive criminal law.

V. The Importance of Criminal Law in Reform

The aspects of the criminal law identified above are responsible for the shift in focus of normative distinctions from the criminal law/adjudication stage of the criminal process to the sentencing stage. The criticisms of indeterminate sentencing—disparity, discrimination, normlessness, irresponsibility, and crime control[161]—relate to the quality and consistency of normative distinctions. Recent sentencing reform initiatives, however, have concerned sanctioning—the back end of the criminal law. Very few sentencing proposals have addressed the substantive criminal law itself. This failure to scrutinize the normative distinctions is an astonishing oversight, since many of the perceived defects in sentencing are the product of the manner in which the criminal law is formulated. If meaningful changes are to result, comprehensive reform efforts must direct their attention to the substantive law.

Three recent developments suggest a need to focus attention on the criminal code. First, most sentencing initiatives that have been implemented under the existing indeterminate sentencing criminal codes have had little effect on the distribution of sentences. Second, since plea bargaining is ubiquitous and can eas-

160. *Id.* § 223.8.

161. *But see* Task Force on Criminal Sentencing, Fair and Certain Punishment—Report of the Twentieth Century Task Force on Criminal Sentencing app. A (1976).

ily frustrate any system of sentencing standards, reformers have made radical and unprincipled proposals for the control of plea bargaining under the guise of sentencing reform. Last, reform efforts, especially sentencing and parole guidelines systems, include attempts to expose the shadow criminal law and to subdivide statutory offenses into categories that draw the moral lines which the criminal codes lack.

A. *Evaluations of Sentencing Reforms*

Evaluations of the effect of recent sentencing reforms consistently point to three broad generalizations about sentencing.[162] First, sentencing officials—judges, parole board hearing examiners, and prosecutors—must comply with the formal requirements of new sentencing procedures only if some mechanisms exist to maintain accountability.[163] When prosecutors or parole boards establish detailed policy guidelines along with managerial arrangements to monitor their employees' decisions, the guidelines are likely to be applied.[164] Conversely, if the sentencing procedures do not contain credible compliance mechanisms, new sentencing standards tend to have little effect.[165]

Second, sentencing reforms that affect only judicial sentencing aspects of the criminal justice process appear to have little effect on sentencing patterns. Mandatory minimum sentence laws, for example, do not increase substantially the likelihood of imprisonment.[166] Defendants who would have been imprisoned before mandatory minimum sentencing are equally likely to be imprisoned under such a scheme. Defendants who clearly would not have been imprisoned before mandatory minimum sentencing remain unlikely to be incarcerated. Mandatory minimum sentencing laws, therefore, increase the likelihood of imprisonment only in marginal categories of defendants—those who might or might not have gone to prison before mandatory minimum sentencing took effect. In addition, an evaluation of California's Uniform Determinate Sen-

162. The body of social science evaluations of recent sentencing reforms remains small. For a critical review of recent studies of the effects of sentencing reforms, see RESEARCH ON SENTENCING, *supra* note 41, ch. 4.

163. *Id.*

164. *Id.*

165. *Id.*

166. *Id.*

tencing Act[167] and Alaska's plea bargaining ban[168] reflects the conclusion that major sentencing reforms have had little effect on sentencing patterns.

Last, sentencing innovations often significantly affect court processes and functionings. The adaptive responses of lawyers and judges have maintained traditional sentencing patterns despite new institutional arrangements. Thus, one common effect of mandatory minimum sentencing laws is that more defendants tend to be diverted or dismissed from the criminal justice process under a mandatory minimum sentencing scheme than under conventional sentencing procedures.[169] Under New York's Rockefeller Drug Law,[170] for example, the percentages of defendants charged with drug offenses who were indicted, indicted defendants who were arrested, and arrested defendants who were convicted all steadily declined.[171] The likelihood of imprisonment among those defendants convicted of drug charges, however, increased substantially.[172]

This minimal effect that sentencing reforms have on sentences is not surprising. Criminal courts, especially urban felony courts, are complex organizations; just sentencing is but one of their many goals. Judges and prosecutors strive to keep cases moving and backlogs down. Prosecutors desire to maintain high conviction rates. Because many defense lawyers operate on a high-volume, low-fee basis, they cannot afford to invest much time or effort into any single case. On the other hand, defense lawyers at the same time need to be perceived as useful and effective. Moreover, lawyers and judges must maintain friendly relations with one another; if the court's daily and seemingly ceaseless work is to be accomplished, judges, prosecutors, and defense counsel must cooperate.[173]

These interests encourage efforts to resolve cases in ways that serve everyone's ends. Amicable disposition of cases through plea negotiations embodies the shared interests of everyone, including the defendant. When sentencing reforms threaten recognized conventions and traditional expectations, lawyers and judges find nu-

---

167. *See supra* notes 95-102 and accompanying text.

168. *See supra* note 3.

169. *See* RESEARCH ON SENTENCING, *supra* note 41, ch. 4.

170. *See supra* note 114 and accompanying text.

171. *See* RESEARCH ON SENTENCING, *supra* note 41, ch. 4.

172. *Id.*

173. *See* J. EISENSTEIN & H. JACOB, FELONY JUSTICE: AN ORGANIZATIONAL ANALYSIS OF CRIMINNAL COURTS 45-52, 60-64 (1977).

merous ways to adapt and to carry on business as usual. This behavior is not necessarily as insidious as it may appear. Judges and counsel may believe that conventions and expectations are right and just, and that sentences mandated by new procedures are unjust. Court functionaries may see avoidance of new sentencing laws as a necessary step toward avoiding injustice, rather than as an improper manipulation of the criminal justice process.

Under indeterminate sentence laws, the criminal codes offer the judge little guidance in sentencing. Statutory maximum sentences are often ten, twenty, twenty-five years, or longer. Generic offense definitions force judges to make their own moral discrimination among crimes. This combination of great power and few standards induces the judge to share the responsibility with plea-bargaining counsel.[174] Moreover, under indeterminate sentencing laws, the alternative to a plea bargain is to risk sentencing by a judge, who possesses great unregulated and unreviewable sentencing power. Defendants accordingly desire assurances either from counsel or through a plea bargain that the range of possible sentences is tolerable. This combination of the judge's great powers, the absence of standards, the functional and psychological benefits of shared responsibility for sentences, and the defendant's need for reassurance fosters a collegial system of case disposition. This tradition, which is firmly rooted in many jurisdictions, explains why many sentencing reforms have had little perceptible effect on sentences and why they instead have caused lawyers and judges to modify their practices to achieve traditional sentencing results. If sentencing innovations are to significantly change existing sentencing patterns, sentencing reforms must address the structural features of the criminal code.

B. Criminal Law Reconstitution

The numerous efforts to recognize normative distinctions in sentencing standards suggest the importance of the criminal law in sentencing. Following the lead of the United States Parole Commission, many jurisdictions have developed guidelines that specify

174. In evaluating the Alaska plea bargaining ban, some judges and lawyers complained that the ban impoverished sentencing by converting what had been a collegial interactive process into an individual and idiosyncratic one. *See* NAT'L INST. OF JUSTICE, *supra* note 3, at 30-32.

a recommended range of sanctions for any combination of offense and offender. The development of guidelines requires that the seriousness of different crimes and the relevance of various offender circumstances be considered. Thus, guideline developers must consider whether the criminal code or the offenses of which defendants are convicted reflect the necessary moral distinctions. If the criminal code fails to distinguish between the professional bank robber and the teenaged basketball thief, then sentencing guidelines must either ignore the obvious differences or create new distinctions. Sentencing reforms have tended to do the latter.

Many sentencing reform efforts reclassify felonies when developing sentencing guidelines, which is a reaction that illustrates even further the criminal law's normative inadequacy. Modern criminal codes either classify all felonies into a small number of classes or implicitly scale severity by specifying maximum lawful sentences.[175] Sentencing guideline drafters, however, often ignore these statutory classes and draft new distinctions. The Minnesota Sentencing Guidelines Commission and the United States Parole Commission, for example, have developed their own offense severity rankings. Drafters developed the severity ratings by conducting exercises in which the commissioners were asked to rate all regularly recurring crimes. The commissioners then negotiated the differences between the ratings. The Commissions subsequently adopted the resultant offense severity scale, notwithstanding the inconsistencies both with applicable criminal statutes and with the ratings implied by the maximum sentences authorized for each crime.[176]

The criminal law's normative inadequacy is also demonstrated by the guidelines developers' efforts to subcategorize the criminal code's substantive offense definitions so that sentencing and parole standards will incorporate gradations of harm and culpability that the substantive law does not recognize. Similarly, the original Denver descriptive guidelines contained a category for unqualified robbery, but provided for sentence enhancement if a weapon was used, if an injury was inflicted, or if death resulted.[177] The Minne-

175. The Model Penal Code, for example, provides for three felony classes. MODEL PENAL CODE § 6.01 (official Draft 1962).

176. *See* MINNESOTA SENTENCING GUIDELINES COMM'N, ESTIMATING THE IMPACT OF SENTENCING POLICIES ON PRISON POPULATIONS 5, 6 fig. 2 (1980); HOFFMAN, BECK & DEGOSTIN, *The Practical Application of a Severity Scale* in PAROLE: LEGAL ISSUES/DECISION-MAKING RESEARCH 169-87 (1975).

177. *See supra* text accompanying notes 66-70; *see also* J. KRESS, *supra* note 92, *pas-*

sota Sentencing Guidelines created four "aggravated forgery" offenses from one statutory offense.[178] The Pennsylvania Commission on Sentencing subcategorized one statutory burglary definition into four different kinds of burglary.[179] These efforts to subclassify categories of conduct demonstrate that criminal statutes draw distinctions that are excessively gross and overly generic. Reform efforts, therefore, must incorporate these reclassifications into the criminal law.

C. *Real Offense Sentencing*

As noted earlier,[180] most convictions are the result of plea negotiation. Under conventional plea bargaining procedures, the defendant is convicted of the offense that he admits to rather than the offense that he committed. This conviction discrepancy presents no difficulty under an indeterminate sentencing scheme because the sentencing judge can disregard the conviction offense and consider the defendant's actual offense. The discrepancy, however, does pose a dilemma under determinate sentencing laws. Sentencing decisions must be based either on the conviction offense, and thus be subject to manipulation by plea bargaining counsel, or be based on the underlying criminal behavior, and thereby make explicit the irrelevance of the defendant's trial rights. After Minnesota abandoned parole release, the Minnesota Sentencing Guidelines Commission debated whether to base its sentencing guidelines on the conviction offense, which could be an artifact of plea bargaining, or on the defendant's real offense. Table 2 sets out the guidelines matrix that the Minnesota Sentencing Guidelines Commission developed. All felonies are divided into ten categories and are shown on the vertical axis.

---

sim; L. WILKINS, *supra* note 5, at 65.

178. Minnesota Guidelines, *supra* note 107, table V; *see* MINN. STAT. ANN. § 609.625 (1964).

179. Proposed Pennsylvania Guidelines, *supra* note 109, at 434; *see* 18 PA. CONS. STAT. ANN. § 3502 (Purdon 1973).

180. *See supra* notes 121-23 & 134 and accompanying text.

TABLE 2
MINNESOTA SENTENCING MATRIX: SENTENCING BY SEVERITY OF OFFENSE AND CRIMINAL HISTORY

		CRIMINAL HISTORY SCORE						
SEVERITY LEVELS OF CONVICTION OFFENSE		0	1	2	3	4	5	6 or more
Unauthorized Use of Motor Vehicle Possession of Marijuana	I	12*	12*	12*	15	18	21	24
Theft-related Crimes ($150-$2500) Sale of Marijuana	II	12*	12*	14	17	20	23	27 25-29
Theft Crimes ($150-$2500)	III	12*	13	16	19	22 21-23	27 25-29	32 30-34
Burglary - Felony Intent Receiving Stolen Goods ($150-$2500)	IV	12*	15	18	21	25 24-26	32 30-34	41 37-45
Simple Robbery	V	18	23	27	30 29-31	38 36-40	46 43-49	54 50-58
Assault, 2nd Degree	VI	21	26	30	34 33-35	44 42-46	54 50-58	65 60-70
Aggravated Robbery	VII	24 23-25	32 30-34	41 38-44	49 45-53	65 60-70	81 75-87	97 90-104
Assault, 1st Degree Criminal Sexual Conduct, 1st Degree	VIII	43 41-45	54 50-58	65 60-70	76 71-81	95 89-101	113 106-120	132 124-140
Murder, 3rd Degree	IX	97 94-100	119 116-122	127 124-130	149 143-155	176 168-184	205 195-215	230 218-242
Murder, 2nd Degree	X	116 111-121	140 133-147	162 153-171	203 192-214	243 231-255	284 270-298	324 309-339

1st Degree Murder is excluded from the guidelines by law and continues to have a mandatory life sentence.

* one year and one day

Source: Minnesota Sentencing Guidelines Commission, Report to the Legislature 14 (1980)

The prior criminal records of defendants are divided into seven groups, which are arrayed on the horizontal axis. To ascertain the applicable guideline sentence, the judge determines the severity level of the conviction offense and the defendant's criminal history source. The cell located at the intersection of the appropriate row and column indicates the number of months that the defendant must serve. The cells below the jagged bold line contain a guideline sentence and a sentencing range. The judge may impose any sentence within this narrow range. Since the conviction offense determines the presumptive sentence, the defense counsel's ability to negotiate the defendant's plea determines the defendant's sentence. Notwithstanding this problem, the Minnesota Sentencing Guidelines Commission decided that to base its guidelines on any offense other than the conviction offense would raise insurmountable problems of fairness: "Offense severity is determined by the offense of conviction . . . . [S]erious legal and ethical problems would be raised if punishment were to be determined on the basis of alleged, but unproven, behavior."[181] The question remains whether the Minnesota guidelines will shift power to lawyers and whether lawyers will use that power to manipulate and circumvent the sentencing guidelines.

Other options were available to the Minnesota Commission. One leading proposal would have acknowledged the pressures that give rise to plea bargaining and would have attempted to confine plea bargaining's scope through "charge reduction guidelines."[182] These guidelines would have specified the amount by which a defendant's sentence could be reduced if he pleaded guilty. The guidelines thus would have authorized judges to award only the prescribed "guilty plea discount."[183]

The Model Sentencing and Corrections Act,[184] which provides for a sentencing commission and a presumptive sentencing guideline system, offers a different solution to the problem of circumventing sentencing guidelines. The Uniform Law Commissioners have attempted to counter charge bargains by basing sentences on "actual offense behavior."[185] The pertinent comment explains: "[T]he language, nature and circumstance of the offense authorizes . . . the sentencing court to consider offense behavior rather than the offense for which the defendant was ultimately convicted. The major purpose of the provision is to reduce disparity resulting from the effect of plea bargaining."[186] Unfortunately, the Model Act tends to trivialize the criminal process and thus is fundamentally flawed. For example, consider three defendants, each of whom has committed and been indicted for armed robbery. The first is convicted at trial of armed robbery, the second pleads guilty to robbery and the armed robbery charge is dismissed, and the third is tried by a jury and convicted only of theft. Under the real offense

---

181. *See* Minnesota Guidelines, *supra* note 107, comment II.A.01.

182. *See* S. Schulhofer, 1 Prosecutorial Discretion and Federal Sentencing Reform 10 (Federal Judicial Center Report 1979); 2 *id.* at 47; Schulhofer, *supra* note 127, at 745. Several federal criminal code reform bills have included this proposal. *See* S. 1722, 96th Cong., 1st Sess. (1979); H.R. 6233, 96th Cong., 1st Sess. (1979).

183. *See* von Hirsch & Hanrahan, *supra* note 1, at 312-15.

184. National Conference of Comm'rs on Uniform State Laws, Model Sentencing and Corrections Act (Approved Draft 1979) [hereinafter cited as Model Act].

185. *Id.* §§ 3-115, -206(d).

186. *Id.* § 3-115(b) comment at 144-45.

provision of the Model Act, all three defendants would be sentenced for armed robbery. This repugnant result trivializes the substantive law, the law of evidence, the defendant's procedural rights, and the criminal burden of proof. At the same time, indeterminate sentencing laws and the practices in most criminal courts today achieve the same regrettable results.

VI. Conclusion

The principal argument of this Article is that sentencing reform efforts have been partially misconceived because they ignore the substantive criminal law—an inattention that is an inherent aspect of indeterminate sentencing. The dilemmas which guideline draftsmen face confirm that determinate sentencing has drawn tighter the relationship between crime and punishment.[187] If sentencing innovations are to diminish sentencing injustices materially, reform must include four elements.

First, reformers must revise criminal codes substantially to reflect the morally salient features of criminal conduct. The Model Penal Code provides the basis of most state criminal codes. The intellectual roots of the Model Penal Code, however, are in the 1950's and reflect the rehabilitative goals of that time. Model Penal Code sentence maximums are long to allow for those whose rehabilitative needs require lengthy detention. Drafters of the Code anticipated that parole boards would shorten sentences routinely. Although offenses are defined in broad generic terms, judges may consider salient offense circumstances and thereby individualize the sentences that they impose. Consequently, developers of sentencing and parole guidelines systems have attempted to specify detailed criteria for decisionmaking and have had to define salient distinctions among crimes in terms that are much more detailed and specific than the offense definitions found in criminal codes.[188] Defining crime, however, is the quintessential legislative function to which guideline developers have been driven by the legislatures' failure to act. Legislatures, therefore, must return the task of drawing moral distinctions to the adjudicative stage where it belongs.

Second, legislatures should shorten to realistic levels the enormously long maximum sentences that are prevalent under inde-

---

187. *See supra* notes 175-86 and accompanying text.
188. *See supra* notes 175-79 and accompanying text.

terminate sentencing laws. Long maximum sentences permit "bark and bite" sentencing—the judge's bark and the parole board's bite. The abandonment of parole release, which has occurred in ten states,[189] makes lengthy maximum sentences unnecessary and invites disparate and aberrant sentences. If criminal statutes authorize judges to impose any sentence from probation to twenty-five years, sentences naturally will span that range. For the same offense, lawful sentences that range from probation to five years would narrow the range of disparity and reduce the likelihood of aberration.

Legislatures can reduce sentence maximums in several ways. The simplest and most honest method, which has been proposed in Great Britain by the Advisory Council on the Penal System and in Canada by the Law Reform Commission, is to amend the criminal code to establish much shorter maximum sentences.[190] The Study Draft of the National Commission on Reform of Federal Criminal Laws reduces statutory maximums through sleight of hand.[191] Although the nominal maximums are conventional—Class A, twenty-five years; Class B, fifteen years; and Class C, seven years—the effective maximum sentences for most offenders are three and four years, since a mandatory parole term—five years, three years, and two years—is included within each maximum sentence. Table 3 sets out the National Commission Proposal. Longer sentences are reserved within each offense class for exceptional cases in which the judge makes a special finding that the defendant "presents an exceptional risk to the safety of the public."[192]

Regardless of the method chosen, reduction of sentence maximums should be a primary goal of sentencing reform. Otherwise, the long sentence maximums of indeterminate sentencing systems will continue to frustrate efforts to reduce disparities in sentencing. Although lengthy sentence maximums occupied a logical position in the era of indeterminate sentencing, they have no place in the current period of reform.

---

189. *See supra* note 120 and accompanying text.

190. ADVISORY COUNCIL ON THE PENAL SYSTEM, SENTENCES OF IMPRISONMENT—A REVIEW OF MAXIMUM PENALTIES 77-88, 147-64 (1978); LAW REFORM COMM'N OF CANADA, STUDIES ON IMPRISONMENT (pt. 2) 21-22 (1975).

191. STUDY DRAFT, *supra* note 142, at §§ 3201-3202.

192. *Id.* § 3202(3)-(5). The "exceptional risk" assessment includes situations in which the defendant is a "persistent felony offender," a "professional criminal," or a "dangerous, mentally abnormal offender." *Id.*

TABLE 3

NATIONAL COMMISSION ON REFORM OF FEDERAL CRIMINAL LAWS: NOMINAL AND ACTUAL MAXIMUM SENTENCES

FELONY CLASS*	NOMINAL	ACTUAL WITHOUT SPECIAL FINDING	ACTUAL WITH SPECIAL FINDING
A	30 years	15 years	25 years
B	15 years	4 years	12 years
C	7 years	3 years	5 years

* The vast majority of felonies, and felons, would fall within Felony classes B and C and thus, ordinarily, be subject to terms of incarceration not longer than 3 or 4 years. An enormous amount of sentencing disparity would disappear.

Source: National Commission on Reform of Federal Criminal Laws, Study Draft §§ 3201-3202 (1970).

Third, reformers must develop detailed sentencing standards that provide clear guidance to judges and permit them to use discretion when appropriate. Minnesota's sentencing guidelines system provides the most hopeful model for reform.[193] The Minnesota system prescribes narrow ranges within which sentences should be imposed in ordinary cases, but permits judges, subject to appellate sentence review, to depart from these ranges if they provide written explanations of the "substantial and compelling circumstances."[194] This sentencing system attaches high priority to equal treatment, but avoids the problems of fixed and mechanical applications.

Last, legislatures should establish appellate review of sentences and provide adequate material support. Although sentencing affects a defendant's most fundamental interests, defendants in most states are unable to obtain review of their sentences.[195] The lack of detailed sentencing criteria, long maximum sentences, and parole board release powers impede effective appellate review under indeterminate sentencing. Appellate review, however, should be more practicable under new sentencing laws. The Minnesota Supreme Court, for example, appears to be monitoring the Minnesota sentencing guidelines with some vigor.

193. *See supra* notes 178 & 180-81 and accompanying text.

194. *See* Minnesota Guidelines, *supra* note 107.

195. *See* ABA PROJECT ON MINIMUM STANDARDS FOR CRIMINAL JUSTICE, STANDARDS RELATING TO APPELLATE REVIEW OF SENTENCES (Approved Draft 1968).

These four changes would make the American criminal process similar to those of other countries. Plea bargaining as the primary form of case disposition, for example, is a uniquely American phenomenon. Similarly, the combination of long sentences with parole discretion for shortening sentences routinely by half is peculiarly American. Parole release, for example, was not established in England until 1967, and West Germany and Scandinavia use parole to reduce prison sentences only by increments that are measurable in months.[196] In addition, the United States is the only major common-law country that lacks a tradition of vigorous appellate review of sentences.[197]

The sentencing reform movement has made major progress in developing decision rules and increasing official accountability. If attention is now refocused to include substantive criminal law in the sentencing process, the result could be a system in which crime and punishment are closely related, and in which the law recognizes the enormity of the issues at stake when depriving citizens of their liberty.

196. *See* R. JACKSON, THE MACHINERY OF JUSTICE IN ENGLAND 280 (6th ed. 1972).

197. The Australian Law Reform Commission recently pointed out that in virtually all common law jurisdictions "with the exception of the United States, appellate review of sentences has been the main method adopted to achieve consistency in, and develop principles for, the imposition of punishment." AUSTRALIAN LAW REFORM COMM'N, SENTENCING OF FEDERAL OFFENDERS 360 (1980).

[4]

Sentencing—The Case For Reasoned Decisions

By D. A. THOMAS, B.A., LL.B.,
Assistant Lecturer in Law, London School of Economics and Political Science

Introduction

The principle that parties to a dispute are entitled to a reasoned decision from the tribunal which tries the issue is one which applies extensively in the English legal system. It is not, however, without exceptions—there is no obligation on a jury, for instance, to state the reasons which have led it to its conclusion on the facts of a case. Indeed, on one occasion the Court of Criminal Appeal strongly disapproved an attempt by an assize judge to discover the reasons which had led the jury to a particular verdict in a case where this information was of vital importance to the question of sentence.[1] This article is concerned with another, and perhaps more important, exception to the principle—the absence of a general requirement that a court passing sentence on an offender should give reasons for its choice of sentence. It is not a new idea that a reasoned decision should be required from a court passing sentence [2]

1 *Larkin* (1943) 29 Cr.App.R. 18. The judge wished to know whether a verdict of manslaughter was based on provocation or gross negligence. The judge may, however, ask the jury whether it has returned such a verdict on grounds of diminished responsibility: *Matheson* [1958] 2 All E.R. 87 at 90; [1958] Crim.L.R. 393.

2 It has been suggested by Dr. Mannheim among others. See his "Penalties to Fit the Crime," *The Times*, November 27, 1957.

but the increased interest in the process of judicial sentencing stimulated by the Report of the Interdepartmental Committee on the Business of the Criminal Courts [3] justifies a detailed examination of the arguments in favour of such a requirement.

Natural justice

There are four principal arguments in favour of the introduction of a requirement that reasons be given for a sentencing decision. The first and probably most obvious derives from the principles of natural justice. This argument can best be illustrated by reference to the development of administrative law in the last thirty years. The rules of natural justice, as developed by the courts, did not include an obligation to give reasons; the decision of a public authority would not generally be quashed for failure to do so. This position was regarded as unsatisfactory by the Committee on Ministers' Powers,[4] who reported:

> "It may well be argued that there is a third principle of natural justice, namely, that a party is entitled to know the reason for the decision, be it judicial or quasi-judicial . . . it cannot be disputed that when further proceedings are open to a disappointed party, it is contrary to natural justice that the silence of the Minister or the Ministerial Tribunal should deprive him of his opportunity. And we think it beyond all doubt that there is from the angle of broad political expediency a real advantage in communicating the grounds of the decision to the parties concerned and, if of general interest, to the public."

The Committee recommended that a party affected by a decision should be entitled to a written statement of the reasons for the decision.[5]

There seems to be no reason why these arguments are not equally applicable to a sentencing decision, which is exactly analogous to a quasi-judicial decision as defined by the committee.[6] The argument that the giving of reasons is essential to fair procedure does not need to be defended—it is already accepted in other parts of the court system. The argument that "broad political expediency" demands the giving of reasons for sentencing decisions

[3] Cmnd. 1289 (1961).

[4] Report, Cmd. 4060 (1932). Section III, para. 3 (3).

[5] s. 3, para. 13.

[6] The essence of a quasi-judicial decision was said to be that the decision-maker "is governed not by a statutory direction to him to apply the law of the land to the facts and act accordingly, but by a statutory permission to use his discretion after he has ascertained the facts and to be guided by considerations of public policy."

is also obvious—it is essential that the substance of criminal law and its administration should be acceptable to the public at large: any appearance of arbitrariness must be avoided. The importance of a statement of reasons where an appeal against sentence is possible will be discussed below.

The recommendation of the Committee on Ministers' Powers that reasons should be given for administrative decisions was not implemented, and it fell to the Committee on Administrative Tribunals and Inquiries [7] to consider the matter again. This committee also recommended that the giving of reasons should be obligatory:

> "It is a fundamental requirement of fair play that the parties concerned in one of these procedures (statutory inquiries leading to a ministerial decision) should know at the end of the day why the particular decision has been taken. Where no reasons are given the individual may be forgiven for concluding that he has been the victim of arbitrary decision." [8]

The committee also pointed out the importance of a reasoned decision where there was a possibility of challenge.

This recommendation was put into effect by the Tribunals and Inquiries Act, 1958, s. 12 (subject to certain qualifications which have no relevance to the present argument) and it is now obligatory for a Minister to give reasons for a decision in any case where a statutory inquiry is or could be held. The same obligation is placed on a large number of tribunals.

The principle has been accepted as of fundamental importance in administrative law. Why then should it not also apply to sentencing decisions? A sentencing decision is likely to have a more serious effect on the person to whom it applies than an administrative decision, which may deprive a man of his property or even his livelihood but not normally of his liberty. It may be said that the convicted offender is not in the same position as the innocent party adversely affected by an administrative decision, in that by offending he has lost his right to be treated in the same manner as an innocent party, but this would be contrary to the whole spirit of English criminal procedure. It is true that the presumption of innocence does not apply to the convicted offender, as he has been proved guilty—but the convicted offender is not generally regarded as being deprived of all his rights. In some cases the courts go to great lengths to avoid even the appearance of denying a convicted offender a possible right to challenge his detention, by hearing on the merits an application for habeas corpus which the

[7] Report, Cmnd. 218 (1957).

[8] Para. 351.

court has no jurisdiction to grant,[9] and procedural formalities relating to the proof of previous convictions are required to be observed strictly.[10] The argument that procedure between conviction and sentence need not reach the high standard of fairness observed before conviction, or even the standard of fairness required of an administrative body, is clearly inconsistent with accepted practice.

Rationalisation

The second argument for a requirement that reasons be given for sentencing decisions is that such a requirement would lead to a rationalisation of sentencing. The choice of sentence in many cases involves the careful consideration of different and often conflicting factors. A judge may be faced with a direct clash between the needs of a particular offender and the necessity to protect the public. An example is the case of a young man with no previous convictions who is guilty of a serious offence of violence, perhaps arising out of domestic difficulty. It is probable that the person will not offend again, particularly if he is placed under the supervision of a probation officer: but on the other hand, the seriousness of the offence demands a heavy sentence.[11] It may be necessary in another case for the judge to bear in mind certain information concerning the probable effects of a particular sentence, which has been obtained on the basis of previous experience of the use of a particular sentence in particular cases. It is accepted, for instance, that a second sentence of Borstal training on a person who has already undergone Borstal training on a previous occasion without response will not serve a useful purpose.[12] In another case, two men may be convicted of participating in the same offence; but there may be proper grounds for awarding widely different sentences to each of them, if perhaps their ages [13] or previous records [14] are different, or if the responsibility of one for the offence is greater.[15] In all such cases, it is essential that the choice of sentence be based on a careful examination of all the factors involved. If the judge is under an obligation to formulate and

[9] See, for instance, *R.* v. *Governor of Parkhurst Prison* [1960] Crim.L.R. 369; *sub nom. Re Philpot* [1960] 1 All E.R. 165; *Re Wring, Re Cook* [1960] 1 All E.R. 536.

[10] *Nicholson* [1962] Crim.L.R. 624; *Dickson* (1949) 34 Cr.App.R. 9; *Evans* [1956] 3 W.L.R. 978; *Scaife* [1959] Crim.L.R. 298; *Long* [1960] 1 Q.B. 681; *Clarkson* [1961] 1 W.L.R. 347.

[11] See *Gill* [1960] Crim.L.R. 440; *Watson* [1962] Crim.L.R. 783.

[12] *Noseda, Field* [1958] 1 W.L.R. 793; [1958] Crim.L.R. 541.

[13] *Freeman, Longstaff, The Times*, September 23, 1961.

[14] *Cuff* [1960] Crim.L.R. 571; *Evans* [1959] Crim.L.R. 61.

[15] *Hammersley* [1958] Crim.L.R. 470; 42 Cr.App.R. 207; *Jawitz, The Times*, May 30, 1962; *Woods* [1962] Crim.L.R. 646.

state the reasons for his decision, it will be necessary for him to arrive at a decision for which proper reasons can be given. As the Franks Committee put it, "a decision is apt to be better if the reasons for it have to be set out in writing because the reasons are then more likely to have been properly thought out." [16]

The immediate effect of an obligatory statement of reasons would be to remove certain obvious risks inherent in the present system. The danger of sentences based on an immediate emotional reaction to some particular feature of the offence would be avoided. The imposition of the intellectual discipline of formulating reasons, a discipline to which the judge is accustomed, would assist the judge to ignore factors which are irrelevant but which might otherwise, perhaps unconsciously, influence the choice of sentence. It is easy to understand the temptation to be influenced by the unco-operative attitude of the offender [17] or his offensive behaviour to the prosecution witnesses [18] or even the judge himself,[19] but these are not factors which should affect the choice of sentence. To require a judge to formulate reasons for a sentencing decision is to do no more than to require him to apply the normal process of judicial decision to the process of sentencing: and where reasons are formulated, there can be no objection to a requirement that they should be stated.

Consistency in sentencing policy

The third argument in favour of an obligation to give reasons is that the rationalisation of sentencing which would follow the imposition of such an obligation would lead in turn to greater consistency of sentencing policy both in the immediate context of a particular court and in the wider context of the system at large. Certain factors would become recognised as valid reasons for the choice of particular sentences. others would be rejected as irrelevant. Differences in practice between various courts would become obvious, and would be removed as a result of decisions of the Court of Criminal Appeal.

This argument could be illustrated by an examination of the sentencing policy of the Court of Criminal Appeal. This is the only court which gives its sentencing decisions in the form of a reasoned

---

[16] All Israeli criminal courts are required to give reasons for the choice of sentence. D. Reifen, an Israeli juvenile court judge, considers this a helpful procedure "because it compels the judge to review for himself the reasons for his decisions." See "The Juvenile Court in Israel," *British Journal of Criminology*," Vol. 3, No. 2, p. 130 at 139.

[17] *Wills* [1958] Crim.L.R. 402.

[18] *Kelly* [1961] Crim.L.R. 564.

[19] *Aston* [1948] W.N. 252.

judgment.[20] It is clearly impossible in a short article to demonstrate the degree of consistency achieved by this court, but reference may be made to some of the better known principles upon which the court acts. In relation to the sentence of preventive detention, for instance, the court works on a number of quite clearly defined principles—the offender must generally be over thirty-five,[21] he must have been convicted of an offence which is neither trivial [22] (in which case preventive detention is excessive) nor too serious [23] (in which case a long term of imprisonment is appropriate); he must have undergone on a previous occasion a sentence of more than three years' imprisonment [24]; he must not have any long periods without conviction, particularly immediately before his present conviction [25]; and he should not be sentenced to a second term of

[20] Even the Court of Criminal Appeal occasionally fails to give reasons for its choice of sentence where the choice arises otherwise than as a result of an appeal against sentence—where for instance a conviction for one offence is substituted for a conviction for another offence, and the court imposes a sentence under s. 5 (1) or 5 (2) of the Criminal Appeal Act, 1907. See for instance *Matheson* [1958] Crim.L.R. 393; 42 Cr.App.R. 145.

[21] *Allen* [1954] Crim.L.R. 554; *Gardiner* [1955] Crim.L.R. 653; *Abbott, The Times*, October 9, 1956; *Oxley* [1957] Crim.L.R. 158; *Swaby* [1957] Crim. L.R. 686; *Slater* [1958] Crim.L.R. 823; *Moody* [1959] Crim.L.R. 300; *Hunt* [1959] Crim.L.R. 530; *Ashworth* [1959] Crim.L.R. 867; *Martin* [1960] Crim.L.R. 713; *Jackson* [1960] Crim.L.R. 373; *Folkard* [1960] Crim.L.R. 372; *Bowler* [1960] Crim.L.R. 572; *Mellor* [1960] Crim.L.R. 845; *Johnson* [1960] Crim.L.R. 846; *Partridge* [1961] Crim.L.R. 838; *Lowe* [1961] Crim.L.R. 563; *Morris* [1961] Crim.L.R. 494; *Miller* [1961] Crim.L.R. 564; *Tucker* [1961] Crim.L.R. 419; *Cairns* [1961] Crim.L.R. 845; *Talbot* [1961] Crim.L.R. 845; *Bannister* [1962] Crim.L.R. 119; *Ondras* [1962] Crim.L.R. 543; *Pritchard* [1962] Crim.L.R. 413; *Turner* [1962] Crim.L.R. 120; *Reed* [1962] Crim.L.R. 573; *Tyler* [1962] Crim. L.R. 499.

[22] *Davies, The Times*, January 1, 1953; *Jenner* [1956] Crim.L.R. 495; *Brown* [1957] Crim.L.R. 457; *Grimwood* [1958] Crim.L.R. 403; *Palmer* [1958] Crim.L.R. 315; *Murphy* [1958] Crim.L.R. 484; *Slater* [1958] Crim.L.R. 823; *Ashwood* [1959] Crim.L.R. 867; *Moulton* [1959] Crim.L.R. 737; *Greenacre* [1959] Crim.L.R. 374; *McCarthy* [1959] Crim.L.R. 220; *Kavanagh* [1959] Crim.L.R. 62; *Shotton, The Times*, January 15, 1960; *Martin* [1960] Crim.L.R. 713; *Brennan* [1961] Crim.L.R. 841; *Naughton* [1961] Crim.L.R. 187.

[23] *Gentry* (1955) 39 Cr.App.R. 195; *Walls* [1956] Crim.L.R. 209.

[24] *Hewitt* (1950) 34 Cr.App.R. 163; *Fordham, The Times*, March 10, 1953; *Maugham* [1956] Crim.L.R. 210; *Jenner* [1956] Crim.L.R. 495; *Oxley* [1957] Crim.L.R. 158; *Murphy* [1958] Crim.L.R. 484; *Moulton* [1959] Crim.L.R. 737; *Hamilton* [1959] Crim.L.R. 531; *Mitchell* [1960] Crim. L.R. 572; *Martin* [1960] Crim.L.R. 713; *Partridge* [1961] Crim.L.R. 838; *Smith* [1961] 1 W.L.R. 1046; *Morris* [1961] Crim.L.R. 494; *Turner* [1962] Crim.L.R. 120.

[25] *Askew* [1949] 2 All E.R. 687; *Hewitt* (1950) 34 Cr.App.R. 163; *Abrahams* (1952) 36 Cr.App.R. 147; *Davies* [1954] Crim.L.R. 222; *Sheldon* [1956] Crim.L.R. 495; *Horn* [1956] Crim.L.R. 343; *Oxley* [1957] Crim.L.R. 158; *Hockey* [1958] Crim.L.R. 555; *Gribben* [1958] Crim.L.R. 555; *Phelan* [1958] Crim.L.R. 483; *Evans* [1958] Crim.L.R. 483; *Brennan, The Times*, May 15, 1958; *Hunt* [1959] Crim.L.R. 530; *Abrahams* [1959] Crim.

preventive detention unless there is absolutely no alternative.[26] The sentence should be for not less than seven years[27] unless the offender is so old that he is likely to die in prison unless a shorter sentence is imposed.[28]

To all of these principles there are exceptions; in some cases the court departs from a principle consistently in a particular kind of case, and it is possible to say that there is a sub-principle. Thus the court may uphold a sentence of preventive detention on a man who has not served a long sentence of imprisonment where he has persistently committed petty larceny,[29] and has accordingly never received a long sentence of imprisonment; or may permit a long sentence of preventive detention on an old man because he would have nowhere to go after his release.[30] The presence in a case of a factor indicating that preventive detention is inappropriate may not lead the court to set aside the sentence entirely, but only to reduce the length of the sentence. These exceptions do not destroy the argument that the policy of the court is consistent; departures from the established practice are not arbitrary, the court invariably giving reasons to justify them.

It would be possible to demonstrate the consistency of the sentencing policy of the Court of Criminal Appeal by reference to topics other than preventive detention. This illustration was chosen because the rules of practice could be formulated briefly, and because it is possible to check the formulation of these rules by the

L.R. 597; *Ashworth* [1959] Crim.L.R. 867; *Mitchell* [1960] Crim.L.R. 572; *Mellor* [1960] Crim.L.R. 845; *Hasemore* [1960] Crim.L.R. 138; *Wright* [1960] Crim.L.R. 440; *Hibbert* [1960] Crim.L.R. 441; *Shotton, The Times*, January 15, 1960; *Jackson* [1960] Crim.L.R. 373; *Whiterod* [1961] Crim.L.R. 125; *Brannan* [1961] Crim.L.R. 61; *Bates* [1961] Crim. L.R. 494; *Cairns* [1961] Crim.L.R. 845; *Brennan* [1961] Crim.L.R. 841; *Doxford* [1961] Crim.L.R. 329; *Barlow* [1961] Crim.L.R. 125; *Farrar* [1961] Crim.L.R. 840; *Horne* [1961] Crim.L.R. 566; *Melia* [1961] Crim. L.R. 62; *Callen* [1962] Crim.L.R. 499; *Pearson* [1962] Crim.L.R. 58; *Turner* [1962] Crim.L.R. 120; *Bayliss* [1962] Crim.L.R. 57.

[26] *Gribben* [1958] Crim.L.R. 555; *Hockey* [1958] Crim.L.R. 555; *Bestford* [1959] Crim.L.R. 140; *Farrar* [1961] Crim.L.R. 840; *Brannan* [1961] Crim. L.R. 61; *Naughton* [1961] Crim.L.R. 187; *Cullen* [1962] Crim.L.R. 499; *Kershaw, The Times*, July 3, 1962; *Rimmer, The Times*, June 5, 1962.

[27] *Hewitt* (1950) 34 Cr.App.R. 163; *Sedgwick* [1950] 2 All E.R. 397; *Churchill* [1952] 2 Q.B. 637; *Lockwood, The Times*, March 3, 1953; *Love* [1954] Crim.L.R. 66; *McKenzie* [1955] Crim.L.R. 269; *Swaby* [1957] Crim.L.R. 686; *Layton* [1961] Crim.L.R. 842; *Turner* [1962] Crim. L.R. 120.

[28] *Howard* [1955] Crim.L.R. 269; *Taylor* [1958] Crim.L.R. 316; *Davies* [1959] Crim.L.R. 868; *Brown* [1960] Crim.L.R. 374; *Astley* [1960] Crim.L.R. 137.

[29] *Ricketts* [1957] Crim.L.R. 458; *Turner* [1962] Crim.L.R. 120; *Fanthorpe* [1961] Crim.L.R. 126.

[30] *Allen* [1960] Crim.L.R. 374.

present writer against that of Dr. James.[31] It may be that this consistency in the sentencing policy of the Court of Criminal Appeal is not produced entirely by the obligation to give reasoned judgments, but the giving of reasons is clearly an essential factor.

The need for consistency in sentencing policy is perhaps too obvious to need elaborate justification: it is an elementary principle of justice that like cases should be treated alike. The giving of reasons would have the secondary advantage of avoiding the appearance of arbitrary departure from practice in those cases where it was necessary to depart from the general pattern. In such cases, the giving of reasons for the unusual sentence chosen would demonstrate that the choice was not a mere whim, but a carefully considered, rational decision. The importance of avoiding the appearance of arbitrary departure from the accepted practice was stressed by Dr. Mannheim[32]; if it is not done "the public will revolt and the prisoner, having been given a grievance, will relapse on discharge."

Right to challenge decision

The fourth argument in favour of reasoned sentencing decisions can also be related to the development of administrative law. It will be remembered that the final argument advanced by both the Donoughmore Committee and the Franks Committee in favour of an obligation to give a reasoned decision in administrative matters was that failure to do so might deprive the party affected of a possible right to challenge the decision. In the particular context of judicial review of administrative decision, this point had a peculiar significance. The Divisional Court can quash on certiorari an order or determination of an inferior tribunal which is erroneous in law, provided that the error of law appears on the face of the record. Where the error does not appear on the record, this remedy is not available. The giving of reasons for a decision may therefore be vital to the right to challenge the decision, as the reasons, if given, form part of the record, and an error of law apparent in the reasoning will be a ground for quashing the decision. If no reasons are given, the decision, though based on reasons which are erroneous in law, will not be subject to this form of challenge.[33]

This point has no direct relevance to the sentencing process, as certiorari is generally not an appropriate remedy, but the giving of

---

[31] "Preventive Detention in 1961 in the Court of Criminal Appeal" [1962] Crim.L.R. 352. See also *Preventive Detention: Report of the Advisory Council on the Treatment of Offenders*, 1963, Chap. 2.

[32] "Penalties to Fit the Crime," above.

[33] See De Smith, *Judicial Review of Administrative Action*, pp. 294-304.

reasons is no less important to the offender who wishes to appeal against sentence than to the party affected by the decision of an administrative tribunal or a Minister. Several cases can be cited where a chance remark made by the judge in passing sentence indicated that he had considered an irrelevant factor, or had been the victim of a misapprehension. In *Regan* [34] a sentence was reduced in the case of a man convicted of receiving certain stolen property where the thief had been given a shorter sentence; although this disparity might be justified in some cases, the recorder in the particular case had taken into consideration the facts that the accused had refused to plead guilty, and had made allegations against the police. In *Roger* [35] a sentence of corrective training was reduced as the recorder had been under the misapprehension that the Prison Commissioners could release the offender at any time. In *Cottrell* [36] a disqualification was varied as the judge who imposed it had had the impression that the disqualification could be removed by another court at a later date. If the judges in these cases had not made remarks in the process of passing sentence it is possible that their errors might have gone uncorrected. If judges were under an obligation to give reasons for their decisions, the possibility of a sentence based on incorrect principles or misapprehensions escaping correction would be greatly reduced.

Statutory obligations

Although there is no general obligation to give reasons for the choice of sentence, such an obligation is imposed by statute in a number of specific cases. These include the imposition of a sentence of imprisonment by a court of quarter session or a magistrates' court on a person under twenty-one years of age [37]; the committal in default of payment of a fine by a magistrates' court of a person under twenty-one who has not been made the subject of a supervision order [38]; and the imposition by a magistrates' court of a sentence of imprisonment on an adult first offender.[39] Where a court has convicted an offender of an offence for which it must disqualify him for holding a driving licence unless there are special reasons for not doing so, and the court decides that there are such special reasons, the court should state the reasons. In this case, the requirement depends on a statement of the Divisional

[34] [1959] Crim.L.R. 529.
[35] [1959] Crim.L.R. 375.
[36] (1956) 40 Cr.App.R. 46. *Rapier* (1963) Crim.L.R. 212.
[37] Criminal Justice Act, 1948, s. 17 (3); Magistrates' Courts Act, 1952, s. 107 (3).
[38] Magistrates' Courts Act, 1952, s. 71 (5).
[39] First Offenders Act, 1958, s. 1 (1).

Court,[40] but it is shortly to be given statutory effect.[41] It has been held by the Court of Criminal Appeal that a statutory obligation to state reasons does not create a condition precedent (at least in the case of a court of quarter session) and that accordingly failure to state reasons does not render the sentence void—but the court emphasised that the requirement should be complied with.[42]

The statutory requirement of a statement of reasons is clearly intended to discourage the use of the kind of sentence in question except in exceptional circumstances, and to restrain the courts from taking a particular course without making proper inquiries and giving the matter careful consideration. But it is essential that all courts should make proper inquiries and give careful consideration to the matter before passing any sentence. It would be ridiculous to argue that in all cases other than those where there is at present a statutory obligation to give reasons the courts may come to an arbitrary decision, or one based on inadequate information. The existing practice admits the validity of the argument that an obligation to give reasons results in a more careful choice of sentence—there can be no justification for restricting this obligation to a small number of specific cases.

The only possible objection to an obligation to give reasons is that it would cast an intolerable burden on the courts and cause excessive delays. In relation to courts of assize and quarter session, this objection can be disregarded. Many judges already give reasons for their choice of sentence, often in the form of a moral homily, and apart from this it has never been the aim of English criminal procedure to sacrifice fairness and accuracy for the sake of speed. In relation to the more trivial of the offences tried by magistrates' courts, it may be that this objection is of more weight. It is perhaps unnecessary to require a carefully reasoned decision where the maximum sentence is a small fine. Such cases may safely be exempted from the principle. It would be sufficient to require a statement of reasons where the court could, in the case of an adult, impose a sentence of imprisonment, or a disqualification. Any case where the sentence is fixed by law would also be excepted. There is, however, a strong argument for imposing the obligation in every case involving a juvenile, irrespective of the offence committed, as failure to take effective steps to prevent further delinquency at the earliest stages may mean the loss of the opportunity to nip a delinquent career in the bud.

The arguments in favour of an obligation to give reasons for

[40] *R.* v. *Recorder of Leicester, ex p. Gabbitas* [1946] 1 All E.R. 615.

[41] Road Traffic Act, 1962, s. 9.

[42] *Tuppin, Taylor, The Times,* April 3, 1959.

sentencing decisions have already been advanced in the context of administrative law by two committees whose reports are regarded as being of the highest constitutional significance. The principle has been accepted and given legislative effect by the present Government in the same context. The obligation could be imposed in the context of sentencing by a single section, for which there are ample precedents in the existing law. Perhaps it is not too much to hope that this reform will not be too long delayed.

[5]

[1988]

Reasons For Sentence: An Empirical Investigation*

By Brian W. Ewart

School of Applied Social Studies Humberside College of Higher Education

and

D. C. Pennington

Department of Social Sciences Sunderland Polytechnic

It is claimed that ". . . society runs on ordinary explanations,"[1] and giving reasons for our behaviour is one way of persuading others of the rightness of our actions. The importance of giving reasons for sentence has been emphasised by judges,[2] legal commentators[3] and the judicial administration.[4] The significance of reasons may be illustrated by reference to Lord Widgery's comments[5] on their role in appeal proceedings. He stated: "One of the matters we look at is the judge's reasons. We consider them part of the material for deciding whether or not the sentence was right."

Although researchers[6] have asked sentencers (usually magistrates) to state their reasons in simulated sentencing tasks, there have been few studies of their behaviour in the courtroom. Those which have taken place suffer from a number of methodological weaknesses. For example, White's study of sentencers' statements was based on a limited range of offences and courts,[7] while Spreutels'[8] survey of reasons neglected the lower courts altogether and the sample was derived from cases which were appealed.

---

* The authors are grateful to Humberside College of Higher Education for funding the research, and to Vivian Moss and Katherine Nicholson for collecting the data. The clerks of the Crown Courts Centres and the clerks to the justices in the magistrates' courts surveyed provided valuable assistance and advice. The comments of Ms Nicholson on earlier drafts of this article were most helpful, although the authors alone are responsible for any errors.

[1] Cantor D. and Brown J., "Explanatory Roles" in *The Psychology of Ordinary Explanations*, edited by Charles Antaki, Academic Press (1981).

[2] Lord Denning, cited by Spreutels (1980), see note 8.

[3] Thomas D. A., "Sentencing—The Case For Reasoned Decisions", [1963] Crim.L.R. pp.243–254.

[4] See p.4, Home Office, *The Sentence Of The Court, A Handbook For Courts On The Treatment Of Offenders*, HMSO, 1986.

[5] Lord Widgery's comments are cited by Spreutels (1980), see note 8.

[6] Two examples of such research are Bond R. A. and Lemon, N. F., "Training, Experience, and Magistrates' Sentencing Philosophies: A Longitudinal Study", (1981) 5 *Law and Human Behaviour*, Nos. 2/3, and Corbett C.L., 1985, "Some Psychological Aspects of Magistrates Sentencing Behaviour in the Adult and Juvenile Courts: Two Experimental Studies," Unpublished Ph.D. Thesis presented to the University of London.

[7] White S., "Homilies in Sentencing," [1971] Crim.L.R. pp.690–699. Minor motoring offences and drunkeness made up almost half of the defendants surveyed (see p.696), and only one PSD was surveyed (see p.697).

[8] Spreutels J.P., "Giving Reasons For Sentence In The Crown Court", [1980] Crim.L.R. pp.486–495. While acknowledging the sampling problems (see p.486) he noted that non-appealed sentences were included, but no information is given on the proportion of the sample they comprise.

The lack of empirical information has not inhibited comments,[9] often directed at magistrates, claiming an absence of reasons accompanying sentences. Even when reasons are given, sentencers are accused[10] of confining themselves to brief stereotyped statements concerning the severity of the offence, instead of providing a fuller description of particular case factors which provide the basis of their decision.

The Present Study

This article reports a study of reasons stated in magistrates' and Crown Courts. Attempts were made to improve upon previous work in terms of the sampling of courts and offences, permitting three important features of sentencers' explanations to be examined. The first concerns the frequency with which at least one reason accompanies a sentence awarded to an offender, and the relationship between reason-giving and the type of offence or sentence awarded is examined. Comparisons between the practices of judges and magistrates are undertaken where it is felt they offer a particular insight into when reasons are stated, or elucidate the role of a factor in the sentencing decision.

The second feature of explanations under investigation is the type of factors cited by sentencers. The claim that they are comprised usually of references to the severity of the offence is evaluated, and there is an opportunity to consider the diversity, or otherwise, of factors which judges and magistrates believe adequately explain their choice of disposal. Statistical studies[11] and sentencers themselves[12] have described how factors such as the gravity of the offence and the offender's previous convictions play an important part in determining sentence. It would be interesting to discover whether those factors which have been *shown* to be important and which judges and magistrates *say* are taken into account, are actually cited by them as reasons.

The third feature of explanations to be addressed is the extent to which a judge or magistrates' reasons provide a full explanation of the sentence chosen; what may be termed the socio-legal function of statements. It has been demonstrated[13] that people's accounts of their attitudes and behaviour may contain considerable variation and even outright contradictions. If

[9] See *e.g.* Andrews J., "Decision Making in the Magistrates Court", *The Magistrate*, June 1985.

[10] Fitzmaurice and Pease suggest that when reasons are given, they are often expressed as a "terse formula—'nature and gravity of offence'—rather than as an explanation of thought-out justification specific to individual cases" (p.36): Fitzmaurice C. and Pease K., *The Psychology of Judicial Sentencing*, Manchester University Press, 1986.

[11] For example Ebbesen E. B. and Konenci V. J. "On the External Validity of Decision-Making Research: What Do We Know About Decisions in The Real World" in *Cognitive Process in Choice Behaviour*, edited by Wallsten T. S., Lawrence Erlbaum Publishers (1980).

[12] For example, the judges in the Oxford study note the importance of previous history of offending. See Ashworth A. J., Genders E., Mansfield G., Peay J., and Player E., *Sentencing in the Crown Court: Report of an Exploratory Study*, Oxford, Centre for Criminological Research (1984).

[13] Potter J. and Weatherall M., *Discourse and Social Psychology; Beyond Attitudes and Behaviour*, Sage Publications (1987).

sentencers' statements lack "internal consistency", it would undermine their validity[14] as an explanation and their usefulness in current proceedings and subsequent appeals. Examination of these features will provide an insight into the extent to which stated reasons are a reflection of the decision making process, the degree to which they explain the sentence and their ability to persuade the offender, victim and the public of the appropriateness of the decision.

Sampling of courts and offences

Magistrates' courts within two petty sessions divisions were surveyed, each being in different Crown Court circuits. The sample of sentences was generated by 20 different lay benches and a stipendiary magistrate. Courts within three Crown Court centres were sampled, two of which were third tier while the third was second tier. The sentences were imposed by 14 judges and recorders. All analyses are based upon the pooled information from individual courts which form the "magistrates' court" and "Crown Court" data respectively. The number of sentences surveyed in the Crown Court (N = 132) is greater than Spreutels (N = 77) or White (N = 27). In comparison to the latter, this study sampled more than one PSD and included a stipendiary court, although the overall sample size of 64 magistrates' cases is less than White's 210 defendants.

A wide range of triable either-way and indictable crimes is included[15] and, to facilitate analysis, offenders are classified into one of two categories on the basis of their principal offence. The "acquisitive offenders" group includes those convicted of a crime of theft, a property offence such as criminal damage or drugs offence,[16] while "violent offenders" is comprised of those convicted of a crime of violence against the person or a sex offence.

The absence of any contemporaneous record of proceedings in magistrates' courts required a researcher (not the authors) to record the data on a pro forma. For all offenders in the sample, details of the sentence awarded were recorded together with any statements by the sentencer.

As far as was practicable, Crown Courts were surveyed in such a way as to avoid the over representation of a particular judge or recorder in the sample. In the lay magistrates' courts, the problem of over sampling was reduced because of the frequent changes of bench. Cases from the higher courts were comprised of contested cases which resulted in a conviction, cases where there was a guilty plea, and those committed by the lower courts for

[14] Fitzmaurice and Pease attack the validity of sentencers' reasons; see note 10 for full reference.

[15] Motoring offences were excluded as they were dealt with in separate motoring courts in the PSDs surveyed, and sentencers' behaviour may differ when dealing with successive similar offences, where sentencing guidelines are formalised, and where defendants are less likely to appear in person. If included in the sample, interpreting differences between practices in the higher and lower courts would be more difficult. A full list of offences surveyed is available from the first author.

[16] The acquisitive offenders group contain the drug offenders because two thirds of the cases involved the supply or manufacture of drugs. Crimes of this nature were considered appropriate to this category.

sentence. In all cases from the stipendiary and lay courts, the offender entered a guilty plea.

Definition of a reason

A reason for sentence is defined as a factor which the sentencer clearly stated to be one which was taken into account in deciding the sentence. Statements which were comments on the offender's behaviour (*e.g.* "what you cannot afford, you should not steal") were not included. In the event of more than one charge, analyses are based upon an offender's principal offence which was determined using the criteria adopted by the Home Office in their "*Criminal Statistics in England and Wales*" publications. Any reason which did not refer to the sentence for that offence was excluded, although statements of this kind were very rare.

How often are reasons given?

A total of 161 cases involving 196 offenders were sampled. The principal offence for each offender was determined, and Table 1 presents the breakdown by type of court and type of offender (according to principal offence) of sentences accompanied by at least one reason for sentence.[17]

In magistrates' courts, at least one reason was given in 66 per cent. of sentences (table 1). While the sample of PSDs in small, it is an indication that claims such as Andrews' that ". . . in practice reasons are not given."[18]

Type of reason	All offenders		Acquisitive offenders		Violent offenders	
	MC N = 64	CC N = 132	MC N = 45	CC N = 100	MC N = 19	CC N = 32
Number of offenders where a reason given	42 (66%)	121 (92%)	28 (62%)	93 (93%)	14 (74%)	28 (88%)
Number of offenders where no reason given	22 (34%)	11 (8%)	17 (38%)	7 (7%)	5 (26%)	4 (12%)

MC; magistrates' courts
CC; Crown Courts

TABLE 1: Table of the number of acquisitive and violent offenders sampled in Crown and magistrates' courts whose sentence for their principal offence was accompanied by at least one reason for sentence.

[17] Four offenders sentenced by Crown Courts (3% of this sample) were subject to the 1982 Criminal Justice Act which requires courts to state their reasons for imposing a period of youth custody. Comparison between the higher and lower courts were conducted with and without these cases of compulsory reason-giving, and conclusions were unaffected.

[18] Andrews p.106, see note 9.

are overstated. The frequency is high considering the very few occasions when magistrates are required by statute to give reasons.[19]

As for Crown Court practice, a significantly[20] greater proportion of offenders' sentences were accompanied by at least one reason in the higher courts (92 per cent. as compared to 66 per cent.). As the Crown and magistrates' courts sentenced roughly equal ratios of acquisitive and violent affenders, the difference is not due to an imbalance between the type of offenders sentenced. The data (see table 2) suggests it is the result of magistrates' courts giving reasons for a non-custodial option less often than Crown Courts, particularly in the case of acquisitive offenders. The relatively high frequency of reasons accompanying non-custodial sentences in the Crown Court may be a consequence of their dealing with more serious cases and with offenders with a substantial prior history of offending. Perhaps the judiciary feel the award of a non-custodial option in relatively serious cases requires explanation, particularly if they assume they operate in a context where a retributive ethos prevails. There is some evidence that compared to severe sentences, lenient decisions are accompanied by a more detailed explanation involving mitigating and aggravating aspects of the case.[21] Interestingly, parole decision makers in the USA exhibit similar behaviour. In comparison to those denied early release, significantly more reasons for the person's current offence and likelihood of further criminal activities are given in cases granted parole.[22]

In terms of the type of offence, the majority of the sentences of violent offenders in both the higher and lower courts were accompanied by reasons (see Tables 1 and 2). The judiciary as a whole appear to feel it is important to explain their sentences in cases involving offences against the person. As Crown Courts deal with the more serious cases, it is the nature rather than the absolute degree of offence seriousness which is important in whether a reason will be given.

---

[19] Magistrates are required to state their reasons when imposing a first prison sentence (s.20 of the Powers of Criminal Courts Act 1973), and when passing a custodial sentence on a young adult offender (s.1(4) of the Criminal Justice Act 1982).

[20] When making comparisons between the data obtained from the higher and lower courts, it is important to ensure that any differences are sufficiently large so as not to represent just a chance variation between the figures. The chi-squared test (see *Nonparametric Statistics for the Behavioural Sciences* by S. Siegel, McGraw-Hill, 1956) calculates the probability of obtaining a difference of the observed magnitude. If the probability is low (the criterion is usually five times in one hundred or less), then it is likely that the result represents a real difference between the courts rather than random variation. The difference between magistrates and crown courts in citing at least one reason would be expected in less than one in a thousand times, and so the conclusion is that a real difference exists between the higher and lower courts surveyed in this respect.

[21] Ewart B. W. and Pennington D. C., "An Attributional Approach To Explaining Sentencing Disparity", in *The Psychology of Sentencing; Approaches to consistency and disparity*, by D. C. Pennington and S. Lloyd-Bostock (Eds.), Centre for Socio-Legal Studies, Oxford, 1987.

[22] Carroll J. S. and Payne J. W., "Judgments About The Crime and the Criminal; A Model and Method For Investigating Parole Decision," in B. D. Sales (ed.) *Perspectives In Law And Psychology, Vol. I, The Criminal Justice System*, New York; Plenum Press, 1977.

	Sentence	Acquisitive Offenders MC N = 45	Acquisitive Offenders CC N = 100	Violent Offenders MC N = 19	Violent Offenders CC N = 32
Reason given	Immediate custody	1 (100%)	47 (96%)	3 (100%)	19 (95%)
	Non custodial	27 (61%)	46 (90%)	11 (69%)	9 (75%)
No reason given	Immediate custody	0 (0%)	2 (4%)	0 (0%)	1 (5%)
	Non custodial	17 (39%)	5 (10%)	5 (31%)	3 (25%)

MC; magistrates' courts
CC; Crown Courts

The percentages represent the proportion of offenders whose custodial or non custodial sentence was or was not accompanied by at least one reason.

TABLE 2: Breakdown by sentence, type of offence and type of Court of the number of offenders whose sentence for their principal offence was or was not accompanied by at least one reason.

Where an explanation was offered, sentencers generally identified between one and three reasons for their decision. Single reasons often referred to the seriousness of the offence or the offender's previous record. An example of the latter is given by one judge's comment that "Looking at your past record—which is atrocious—I simply cannot do anything other than to commit you to a term of imprisonment of six months." More detailed explanations were comprised of a mixture of these generic factors, as well as circumstances specific to the individual case. An extract from one judge's explanation when sentencing an offender convicted of burglary illustrates this combination and how the different factors were weighed to produce the non-custodial sentence passed. He noted that,

> "This was a bad burglary. With your record you were taking a risk with your liberty. However, you have committed no serious crimes since 1981 and were frank and helpful to the police. That you have had jobs and attempted to find work is creditable. You have only just kept out of prison."

In comparison to the stipendiary magistrate or judges and recorders, the lay magistracy tended to cite fewer reasons in their explanations[23] perhaps reflecting the minor nature of the crimes, the relative lack of information available in the event of a guilty plea[24] and the need to maintain a high

[23] The two lay magistrates' courts surveyed produced an average of 1.3 and 1.5 reasons cited per offender. The stipendiary court generated a figure of 2.2, while the three Crown Court centres produced averages of 2.5, 2.9 and 3.2 respectively.

[24] See D. Acres, "Consistently Achieving Our Sentencing Aims", in *The Psychology of Sentencing; Approaches to consistency and disparity*, above, note 21.

throughput of business at each sitting. If magistrates are reluctant to give detailed reasons for fear that their statements may be the basis of appeal, previous writers have emphasised[25] this will not be the case. However, there is evidence that other factors may be important. The saliency of the material, limitations upon people's ability to process information, and the nature of decision making itself are just three influences which are discussed briefly below.

In a simulated sentencing task under conditions of anonymity, an absence of time contraints and the need to state reasons in public, magistrates produced a higher average of 2.6 reasons per case.[26] Yet both lay and full time judiciary rarely use more than three reasons to explain a sentence. One interpretation is that those mentioned are the most memorable[27] or ones recognised as being important in every decision, such as the number of previous convictions. If indeed there is a lack of opportunity for "lengthy deliberation",[28] it is hardly surprising that a few highly salient factors are cited. The brevity of explanations may also be a consequence of a limited capacity to process and remember information, a feature of human performance which has been demonstrated in many psychological studies.[29] Van Duyne claims this is one important reason for the "one-dimensional"[30] nature of the decision process and the surprisingly few pieces of information employed by his sample of Dutch prosecutors and judges when choosing their sentences.

Finally, the number of reasons mentioned may be a product of the nature of sentencer's decision making. If relatively few case factors are actually taken into account, one would not expect a large number of reasons to be stated. One study has shown[31] that even when striving for consensus and processing case information "in depth," only a few items such as the seriousness of offence, previous convictions and previous sentences served were discussed by sentencers. Statistical studies[32] confirm the importance of this small group of factors in determining sentence. This suggests that most decisions are not the product of highly complex cognitive procedures necessitating the processing of large amounts of case specific information. The skill of sentencing is not in considering every detail simultaneously, but to select and weigh the important points, and resolve the legal and human

[25] See notes 7 and 9 for two examples.

[26] This study was conducted by Claire Corbett, see note 6.

[27] For an interesting discussion of this concept, see S. E. Taylor and S.C. Thompson, "Stalking the Elusive 'Vividness' Effect" (1982) 89 *Psychological Review*, pp.155–181.

[28] See comments by Judge Cooke in his paper "The practical problems of the sentencer," in *The Psychology of Sentencing; Approaches to consistency and disparity*, above, note 21.

[29] *e.g.* Baddeley A. D. and Hitch G., "Working Memory", in G. H. Bower (ed.), *The Psychology of Learning and Motivation; Advances in Research and Theory, Vol. 8*, Academic Press, 1974.

[30] For a description of the one-dimensional nature of the decision making process, see Van Duyne P., "Simple Decision Making", in *The Psychology of Sentencing; Approaches to consistency and disparity*, (above note 21), at p.147.

[31] See Van Duyne, p.151, see note 30.

[32] For example Ebbesen and Konenci in the USA (see note 11) and in Britain, the study by Tarling R. and Weatheritt M. J., *Sentencing Practice in Magistrates' Courts*, Home Office Research Study No. 56, London, HMSO (1979).

dilemmas posed by the individual case to arrive at a just award. The task is one of judgment not information processing.

To sum up, it has been shown that the magistrates surveyed offered at least one reason for sentence in the majority of cases. Judges gave reasons more often when sentencing offenders convicted of an acquisitive crime and when awarding a non-custodial disposal. While sentencers as a whole gave reasons in the vast majority of cases involving violent offenders, it was unusual to find explanations of more than three reasons, with lay magistrates being briefest of all.

What kind of reasons are given?

Across all the courts surveyed, four factors account for over half (54%) the reasons cited by judges and magistrates. In one court the figure was as high as 70 per cent., while the lowest proportion was 40 per cent. The factors are;

1. The seriousness of the offence.
2. The offender's previous history of offending.
3. The principle underlying the sentence.
4. The perceived cause of the crime.

One important feature to emerge is that while accounting for a significant proportion of reasons collectively, the frequency with which particular factors are cited is sometimes unexpectedly low. This demonstrates that sentencers do not often use them in combination to form their explanation of the decision. Nonetheless, the judiciary acknowledges the importance of these features (for example see footnote 12), and each is examined in an attempt to understand its role in the decision process. The section concludes with a discussion of other reasons which were mentioned frequently.

The seriousness of the offence

Magistrates mentioned the seriousness[33] of the offence in approximately one quarter of cases surveyed (see Table 3). In acquisitive crimes, it was described usually in terms of the value of the goods taken. For example, in a rare reference to the minor nature of the offence the stipendiary magistrate noted: "This is a blemish on your character. Was it worth it? The article you stole was a mere £1.99, but it is theft and must be punished. I feel a fine will deter you from behaving in such a ridiculous way again." For violent offences, references concerned the injuries sustained by the victim and were sometimes expressed in very dramatic terms given that crimes must be at the lower end of the scale. Expressions such as "You behaved very violently and aggressively . . ." or "You could have easily killed this man . . ." were not uncommon in the magistrates' courts.

[33] The gravity of the offence has been described in terms of 5 elements; social danger, alarm, social disapproval, harm and wickedness. See Cross R., *The English Sentencing System* (3rd ed., 1981). The study employed this definition, and reasons referring to any one of these factors were noted.

Offence seriousness was mentioned in just over a third of offenders sampled at the Crown Courts (see Table 3).[34] Like magistrates, when sentencing acquisitive offenders judges often described seriousness in terms of the amount of money or goods stolen. One judge observed "This is a very serious offence. At a conservative estimate you defrauded the company of some £10,000 at least over two years." Occasionally seriousness was expressed in terms of the fact that disadvantaged or helpless people, usually the elderly, were the victims. In a case where the offender grossly overcharged for repairs the judge noted that the offender's "shameless" crime was ". . . swindling old ladies." In cases of burglary in particular, an implicit reference was sometimes made to the potential for harm to the occupier. One judge commented that ". . . entry of an occupied house in the night must attract a custodial sentence." Another, when sentencing one young offender, noted that ". . . anyone who gets involved in the burglary of a dwelling house deserves to be sent to youth custody or detention centre." The seriousness of a theft was sometimes described in similar terms. A judge commented to two co-defendants: "You stole a large amount of valuable property, an enormous amount of stuff between you and you have caused much anxiety. I am therefore considering a custodial sentence." Even with crimes against property,

Type of reason	All offenders		Acquisitive offenders		Violent offenders	
	MC N = 64	CC N = 132	MC N = 45	CC N = 100	MC N = 19	CC N = 32
Reference to the severity of the crime	16 (25%)	52 (39%)	9 (20%)	31 (31%)	7 (37%)	21 (66%)
Reference to extent of previous offending	12 (19%)	56 (42%)	9 (20%)	49 (49%)	3 (16%)	7 (22%)
Reference to the principle of sentence	24 (38%)	66 (50%)	15 (33%)	48 (48%)	9 (47%)	18 (57%)
Reference to the cause of the crime	10 (16%)	27 (20%)	7 (16%)	15 (15%)	3 (16%)	12 (38%)

TABLE 3: Table of the frequency of reference to the severity of the crime, offender's previous history of offending, the principle underlying the sentence, and the cause of the crime by type of court and type of offender (according to the principal offence).

[34] The frequency is much less than Spreutels observed. One explanation for the different findings is that because his sample included a high proportion of appealed decisions, severe sentences were over-represented. The judges must have considered the offences grave for such awards to be made, and it is not surprising that they cited the gravity of the offence with uncharacteristic frequency.

seriousness is often described in terms of the actual or possible effects upon people.

As in the lower courts, references to the seriousness of violent crimes in the Crown Court were usually in terms of a judgment of the gravity of the attack, for example: "This is a very serious and violent attack upon a relative stranger." Comments were also made on the injuries inflicted, as in the case where the judge emphasised that the ". . . victim will be scarred for life . . . by this senseless attack."

Three important features emerge from this analysis. Firstly, contrary to the claims of some writers[35] reasons for sentence are not comprised only of references to crime seriousness. Indeed, the frequency with which this factor is mentioned is low, particularly in the Crown Court, given it is ". . . perhaps the single most important factor in sentencing."[36] In the magistrates' courts the finding may be attributed to the fact that the serious cases are referred to Crown Court. The lower courts are therefore left with a relatively homogeneous group in terms of the gravity of offence and it is not surprising that this factor is cited infrequently. The exaggerated terms sometimes used by magistrates to describe an offender's violent behaviour may be interpreted as an expression of the court's consternation and disapproval, rather than as a literal description of events. This "socio-legal" function is elaborated in the final section of this article.

Secondly, crime seriousness is expressed in a number of ways including the amount of goods stolen, the injuries suffered in an assault, the actions of the offender and the helplessness or potential risk to the victim. References are not in the form of a "terse formula,"[37] but are comprised of aspects of the specific case which have been selected for comment.

Finally, stressing the minor nature of crimes was unusual,[38] one example being "You (the offender) have never stolen anything worth stealing, this just saves you from prison." Reasons of this sort may be avoided lest the offender believes the court does not view their breach of the law as serious. When stated, they are almost always accompanied by statements emphasising aggravating features such as the offender's "wretched record" or the fact that he was on the brink of a custodial sentence.

Previous history of offending

Magristrates' courts made references to the offender's previous history of offending in only about 19 per cent. of cases (see Table 3). This is an unexpected finding given the frequency with which this factor has been demonstrated to affect the sentencing decision (see note 11). Typically, the reference was brief and used to explain why a custodial or non custodial sentence was being awarded, rather than why a particular disposal was chosen. For example, "You have been before the court on many occasions

[35] For example, Fitzmaurice and Pease; see note 10.
[36] See Rawson S., *Sentencing Theory, Social Enquiry and Probation Practice*, University of East Anglia Norwich in Association with Social Work Today, 1982, p.9.
[37] As Fitzmaurice and Pease claim, see note 10.
[38] In only 12 out of 196 offenders surveyed.

and so we must be thinking in terms of a sentence of imprisonment". Specific details of the number or type of offences were seldom mentioned.

Sometimes the extent of a prior criminal history is used as the basis of inferences about the character or behaviour of the offender, and together they form the explanation of sentence. The statement of one chairman of the bench exemplifies this practice: "You have no history of violence . . . this proves to me that you have not a tendency to get involved in such incidents . . ."

In general, magistrates' references to previous crimes are infrequent. The bench may commit to Crown Court those offenders with a history of offending and for whom the magistrates' powers are thought inadequate,[39] which must leave the lower courts with a relatively homogeneous group in this respect. Just as with the seriousness of the crime, it is not surprising the antecedents are mentioned infrequently. The factor may be more important in determining whether the magistrates will sentence the offender rather than in deciding the most appropriate disposal as Green[40] suggests. This interpretation is consistent with other work[41] which found that previous convictions alone were not a strong predictor of magistrates' choice of disposal.

Judges mentioned the extent of prior offending in under half the cases surveyed. This sizeable proportion is consistent with the importance of the factor as demonstrated by statistical studies (see footnote 11). Like magistrates, judges sometimes used this feature to form judgments concerning the criminality of the offender. For example, on the basis of a "disgraceful record" one judge decided an offender had "turned into a professional criminal working with skill and determination", and the public must be protected by passing a custodial sentence.

Although the proportions of offenders with a previous history of offending were similar in the higher and lower courts surveyed, judges mentioned this factor more often than magistrates. This underlines the need for caution when studying sentencing within the two tier system of England and Wales, as a variable may operate in different ways according to the statutory and procedural framework governing each type of court.

The principle underlying the sentence

The principle underlying the sentence is the sentencer's opportunity to express to the offender, counsel or the public what they hope will be achieved by the disposal. References were classified in terms of one of the classic aims of sentencing, *e.g.* individual deterrence, rehabilitation, or incapacitation.

The frequencies with which judges and magistrates mentioned a principle were similar, although the former tended to cite an aim more often when sentencing those convicted of a crime of violence. Retribution was the aim most frequently expressed by sentencers, followed by individual deterrence

[39] Magistrates' Courts Act 1980.
[40] Green E., *Judicial Attitudes To Sentencing*, Macmillan & Co. (1961).
[41] Tarling and Weatheritt, see note 32.

(33 and 28 offenders respectively). Reformation came next (22 offenders), while incapacitation and general deterrence had an equal frequency of six offenders each.[42]

It has been suggested[43] that retribution is the dominant aim of sentencing, but this study revealed a diversity of aims: sentences aimed at individual deterrence and reformation were together expressed almost twice as often as retribution. It seems that sentencers may be more concerned to reduce offending by changing the behaviour of the criminal through selective punishment or rehabilitation, rather than acting as society's means of demonstrating its disapproval. This is somewhat surprising given the judiciary's scepticism of their ability to influence an offender's actions,[44] no doubt the result of the pessimistic findings of many reconviction studies. However, the tendency for people to favour concrete case specific details over more abstract statistical information is a well documented feature of decision making.[45] Apparently, when faced with individuals and knowing something of their particular circumstances, changing their law breaking behaviour seems a more realistic proposition.

The cause of the crime

It has been suggested[46] that the sentencer's perception of factors which have given rise to the crime affects the sentence chosen. Mitigation speeches are important in this respect and, while sentencers acknowledge their value,[47] evaluative comments are rare in the course of a trial.[48] It is when pronouncing the sentence that the judiciary has the best opportunity to indicate the relevance of the causes which have been suggested.

With the exception of violent offenders in Crown Courts, the cause of the criminal behaviour is cited for only a small proportion of offenders sentenced (see Table 3). Judges consider characteristics of the individual rather than aspects of society to be the principal determinants of crime,[49] and this is reflected in their statements as well as those of magistrates. The effects of alcohol and drugs were the most common causes identified, particularly for violent offences. One judge noted that there ". . . is too much violence occurring in public houses under the influence of alcohol," while another concluded that the crime was the result of the offender being ". . . lost to the drugs habit." Some aspect of personality such as the person's quick temper or their "criminal mind" were the next most frequent, followed by references to

---

[42] These do not sum to 90 as Table 3 suggests, since more than one aim was stated in the case of 3 offenders.

[43] Kapardis A. and Farrington D. P., "An Experimental Study Of Sentencing By Magistrates", (1981) 5 *Law and Human Behaviour*, Nos. 2/3.

[44] For example, Douglas Acres, see note 24.

[45] See for example Kahneman D. and Tversky A., "On the Psychology of Prediction", (1973) 80 *Psychological Review*, pp.237–251.

[46] For example Trivizas E., "Sentencing The Football Hooligan", (1981) 21 B.Jo. Criminology, pp.342–349.

[47] See the Oxford Study, note 12.

[48] For some interesting exceptions see Mackay R. D., "Diminished Responsibility—Some Observations Arising From Three Case Studies", (1986) 26 *Medicine, Science and Law*, pp.60–65.

[49] See the Oxford Study, note 12.

stress or depression. In the case of the latter, the specific circumstances were sometimes described. For example, a chairman of the bench observed that "We realise the stress caused by losing your husband is an important factor . . ." However, it was equally common for a general comment such as "I am aware that you are a depressed and troubled man . . ." to be made. In either event, examining the case material revealed that the stress or depression was usually the result of domestic circumstances rather than being an endogenous psychological condition. Finally, direct references to financial problems and the effect of "bad company" were uncommon. Sentencers' beliefs concerning the validity of the causes of criminal behaviour are rarely made public, although in the lower courts surveyed, magistrates would sometimes admit frankly that they were unable to understand what gave rise to the offender's actions. As people are more likely to generate causal explanations for unexpected events,[50] perhaps sentencers will cite such factors in cases of an adult first offender with a history of law abiding behaviour, or where the current offence differs significantly from previous crimes.

Other factors

Certain factors account for almost all the remaining reasons given. For example, the length of time since the offender's last court appearance was often noted and a relatively long period was interpreted as evidence of an ability to avoid crime and used to explain a more lenient sentence. One chairman of the bench reasoned that deferring sentence for a period was appropriate since ". . . the long time since last conviction shows you have made an effort to work well and settle down . . . to cuild a clean record. Let's see if you [the offender) can continue." Conversely, imprisonment (suspended and immediate) was justified on the ground that the person had just recently been before a court and had "clearly not learned the lesson."

Other recurring reasons were that the offence was committed while on bail or serving a non custodial sentence, and sentencers usually viewed such offending very seriously. A judge noted that one of the circumstances which warranted a "substantial period in custody" was that ". . . these offences were committed while on bail." The offender's involvement in the commission of the crime was also mentioned frequently, as in the case where a judge justified the suspension of a term of imprisonment because the offender had ". . . played a minor part in the conspiracy". The degree of premeditation was often mentioned as a reason. In cases of violence it was usually because the offence was on the "spur of the moment." while for acquisitive offences, in contrast, it was because of their "organised" nature.

Magistrates have been advised of the importance of the plea of guilty in appropriate cases,[51] and that either the type or the amount of a sentence may

[50] Wong P. T. and Weiner B., "When People Ask 'Why' Questions, and the Heuristics of Attributional Search," (1981) 40 *Journal of Personality and Social Psychology*, pp.650–663.

[51] Judge E. F. Jowitt noted that when the issue was addressed at a conference of the Magistrates' Association in 1985, "It obviously came as a surprise to the magistrates. . . . that effect had to be given to a plea of guilty." He describes when and how a guilty plea should operate in the sentencing of the lower courts. See *The Magistrate* (1986), Vol. 42, pp.134–136.

be altered. In the case of the former, they are encouraged to describe to the offender the way in which the factor affected the choice. In the later event, the exact discount is not to be disclosed although the offender should be told of the mitigating effect of the plea. However, the factor was cited very rarely as a reason even though all offenders surveyed in the lower courts pleaded guilty. One suggestion[52] is that the lay judiciary do not consider an admission of guilt as a mitigating factor, and further research is needed to discover the role of this factor in the decision. Similarly, although the majority of offenders pleaded guilty in the cases surveyed at the Crown Court, judges seldom cited this factor and across Crown Court centres the frequency varied between 10 per cent. and 25 per cent. of those sentenced. Perhaps the very prevalence of the factor means that sentencers in both the higher and lower courts discount "automatically". Nonetheless, given the frequency of admissions of guilt and their importance to the decision, the lack of references in explanation of sentence is a puzzling omission.

Concluding Remarks—The Socio-Legal Function of Explanations

Overall, sentencers' reasons relate predominantly to characteristics of the current offence (such as its seriousness), the offender's culpability (such as the degree of involvement in the commission of the crime and the cause of the offence) and criminality (such as the number of previous convictions and whether a non custodial sentence was being served at the time of the current offence). Consistent with simulated studies, decisions were more often explained in terms of these legal factors rather than sociological or psychological explanations of the offender's behaviour. Other decision makers exhibit this characteristic; for example, Van Duyne[53] concludes that Dutch prosecutors, when deciding sentence recommendations to the court, rarely sought information ". . . concerning the personality and social background of the suspect."

This study demonstrates that it was unusual for sentencers to describe how factors of the case were weighed to produce the final sentence.[54] They confine themselves to noting what contributes to the sentence chosen, rather than describing the grounds for rejecting other alternatives. Although not an unreasonable practice, it does not wholly explain the choice of sentence. For only 6 per cent. of offenders sentenced was there a statement of why a sentencing option had been rejected.[55] Even then, arguments concerning specific alternatives were not mentioned and comments referred only to why a category of sentence (*e.g.* non-custodial) was not employed. Yet when seeking consensus,[56] it has been shown that a bench will sometimes debate carefully aspects of the crime and the offender, weigh the merits of particular options and even empathise with the offender. Judges also seek to "match" the sentence[57] to the person and acknowledge the importance of "the impact"

[52] See Kapardis and Farrington note 43.
[53] Van Duyne p.7, see note 30.
[54] The Oxford Study makes a similar point, note 12.
[55] A similar figure emerged from Corbett's simulated study, see note 6.
[56] B.B.C., "The Amateur Justices", produced by B. King, Radio 4, April 24, 1987.
[57] See the Oxford Study, note 12.

the defendant has upon them.[58] In addition to assisting the appeals procedure, if more of the richness of the decision making process were conveyed, the offender, the victim and the public might better understand the justice of some sentences.

In general, sentencers' reasons did not exhibit the contradictions so often observed in everyday explanations.[59] The nature of the decision and characteristics of the legal domain seem to militate against such inconsistency.[60] This internal consistency provides at least tentative support for the validity of reasons as an explanation of the sentence awarded. Further evidence comes from the finding that a systematic relationship exists between the mitigating or aggravating nature of the factors cited by sentencers and the severity of the sentence awarded.[61] While more research is needed, these results suggest it is premature to claim that the judiciary's reasons should be treated with "scepticism" and are ". . . not to be trusted."[62]

Where inconsistences are evident, they may be interpreted as the product of attempting to fulfil simultaneously the "social" function of emphasising the disapproval of the court on behalf of society while explaining a relatively lenient sentence. For example, in a case of assault which was described by the judge as ". . . a very serious and violent assault," he emphasised that the offender ". . . must be punished accordingly" and ". . . the public must be protected from people like you who cause disruption and violence on the streets." Despite asserting that there was no excuse for the behaviour, he then said "I am going to be lenient with you this morning as I believe this is a one-off", and ordered the offender to be bound over in the sum of £100. A number of the statements did not explain the leniency of the sentence in view of the emphasis upon the need to punish the offender and protect the public.

It is unrealistic to believe that the context does not exert an effect upon a sentencer's mode of expression. If they believe their function is to absorb the anger of society[63] or that retribution is more often demanded by the public,[64] their explanations may reflect these beliefs. An indication of this "socio-legal function" of explanations is that the minor nature of a crime is rarely cited. When it is acknowledged, statements emphasising aggravating features of the offender are included. Furthermore, it has been suggested[65] that this retributive ethos may account for the more elaborate explanations associated with awarding sentences perceived as lenient.

In conclusion, this article has discussed a study of the frequency with which sentencers explain their decision and the type of reasons they use. Some of

---

[58] See Cooke, note 28.

[59] This feature of explanations may be contrasted with the processes of reaching a joint decision. Van Duyne observed (p.151) that when discussing what was an appropriate sentence, sometimes judges' ". . . arguments were not worked out or explained, or remained contrary without being noticed". See note 30 for full reference.

[60] For a discussion of these features see Ewart B. W. and Pennington D. C., "The Validity of Reasons for Sentence; a Theoretical and Empirical Investigation", paper in preparation, draft copy available from the first author.

[61] See note 60.

[62] Fitzmaurice and Pease (note 10, above) pp.3 and 137.

[63] A view expressed by Douglas Acres, see note 24.

[64] Cited in the Oxford Study, note 12.

[65] By Ewart and Pennington, see note 21.

the procedures governing the higher and lower courts were examined together with research on human decision making, in an attempt to understand the nature of reason-giving. There is indirect evidence that making reason-giving compulsory in every case may effect how information is processed.[66] In view of the already high frequency with which sentencers attempt to explain their decisions, emphasising the importance of this process and providing guidance on the composition of reasons is likely to enhance their contribution to the operation of the legal system as well as the public's understanding of the decision.

---

[66] Cohen A. R., "Cognitive tuning as a factor affecting impression formation", (1961) 29 *Journal of Personality*, pp.235–245.

Part II
Having a Say on Sentence

[6]

SOCIAL INQUIRY FOR THE COURTS

An examination of the current position in England and Wales

MARTIN DAVIES (*Manchester*) *

THE importance of social inquiry reports in the sentencing process can be gauged both from statistical evidence recording their steady growth during recent years and from the expressions of opinion about their value which are to be found in the penological literature.

Trends

Tables 1–4 present basic data about social inquiry reports in England and Wales for selected years between 1956 and 1971. Table 1 demonstrates the increase in the number of reports being prepared for all courts during the 15-year period: in juvenile courts, the figure has fluctuated slightly since 1963 and fell sharply in 1971 following the implementation of the Children and Young Persons Act 1969 which has led to local authorities taking over the responsibility for some juvenile inquiries; but in both other sectors the total growth has been dramatic with nearly a six-fold increase in inquiries prepared for the higher courts and almost a five-fold increase in magistrates' courts (adults).

TABLE 1

Social inquiries 1956–1971: The growth of inquiry work in all courts (1956 = 100)

Year	Magistrates' Courts Juveniles	Magistrates' Courts Adults	Assizes and Quarter Sessions	Total
1956	100	100	100	100
1961	159	157	229	166
1966	160	294	349	223
1971	140	466	587	292
Numbers in 1971:	62,597	111,338	51,042	224,977

Source: The annual probation and aftercare statistics, Home Office.

Table 2 provides further evidence of the relative decline in inquiry work with juveniles: from 58 per cent. of the total in 1956 to 28 per cent. of the total in 1971. By 1971, inquiry work for the magistrates' courts (adults) accounted for almost half of the total volume.

Table 3 demonstrates that the increase in social inquiry work is not merely a result of the rising crime rate, but also reflects the fact that a higher proportion of offenders appearing before the courts are now likely to be reported on

* Ph.D., Department of Social Administration, University of Manchester. This paper is a revised version of one originally given to the Scandinavian/British Research Seminar in Criminology, 1971.

The author is grateful to two of his former colleagues in the Home Office Research Unit, Miss Joy Mott and Mr. William McWilliams, for valuable discussions about this paper when it was in draft form, and for allowing him to refer to their respective research projects, the reports of which have not yet been published.

SOCIAL INQUIRY FOR THE COURTS

TABLE 2

Social inquiries 1956–1971: Proportionate emphasis in different courts, five-year intervals

Year	Magistrates' Courts Juveniles per cent	Magistrates' Courts Adults per cent	Assizes and Quarter Sessions per cent	Total per cent
1956	58	31	11	100
1961	55	29	16	100
1966	41	41	18	100
1971	28	49	23	100

Source: The annual probation and aftercare statistics, Home Office.

by a probation officer. For all indictable offenders, the proportion on whom reports were prepared rose over the period; the proportionate increase in respect of offenders appearing in higher courts was particularly great—from 39 per cent. in 1956 to 84 per cent. in 1971.

TABLE 3

Proportions of indictable offenders on whom social inquiry reports were prepared: five-year intervals, 1956–1971

Year	Magistrates' Courts Juveniles per cent	Magistrates' Courts Adults per cent	Assizes and Quarter Sessions per cent
1956	66	7	39
1961	66	10	53
1966	74	15	78
1971	67	17	84

Sources: The annual probation and aftercare statistics, Home Office; Criminal Statistics, H.M.S.O. London.

Finally, Table 4 shows how the proportion of full written inquiries also increased. During the 1960s, a consistently high proportion of reports submitted to juvenile and higher courts were the result of full inquiries; in the magistrates' courts (adult), however, the proportion rose from 56 per cent. in 1961 to 84 per cent. in 1971.

Hence the growing importance to the courts of social inquiry work was marked in two ways: the proportion of offenders on whom reports were prepared increased, and the proportion in magistrates' courts for whom brief stand-down inquiries were regarded as sufficient decreased. Partly because of the need to keep pace with this trend, the size of the probation service has grown considerably over the period and, at least until 1966–67, the staffing complement of the service rose in roughly the same proportion to the increases in social inquiry work. (Davies and Knopf, 1973.)

Opinions Expressed

"All probation officers are aware of the great importance of their reports," wrote McLean in 1961, and the representatives of the service (both individually and through their National Association) have consistently campaigned for an extension of court practice in calling for social inquiry reports. Jarvis has listed the rather restricted statutory origins of the requirement for

TABLE 4

Social inquiries 1956–1971: Type of court and type of inquiry at five-year intervals

	Year	Full inquiry N	Full inquiry per cent	Day of hearing inquiry N	Day of hearing inquiry per cent	Total N	Total per cent
(a)	Magistrates' Courts (Juvenile)						
	1956	—		—		44562	100
	1961	69267	98	1458	2	70725	100
	1966	69331	97	2005	3	71336	100
	1971	60844	97	1753	3	62597	100
(b)	Magistrates' Courts (Adults)						
	1956	—	—	—	—	23919	100
	1961	20961	56	16562	44	37523	100
	1966	48824	69	21571	31	70395	100
	1971	94010	84	17328	16	111338	100
(c)	Assizes and Quarter Sessions						
	1956	—		—		8694	100
	1961	18804	95	1095	5	19899	100
	1966	29314	97	989	3	30303	100
	1971	49845	98	1197	2	51042	100
(d)	All courts						
	1956	—		—		77175	100
	1961	109032	85	19115	15	128147	100
	1966	147469	86	24565	14	172034	100
	1971	204699	91	20278	9	224977	100

Source: The annual probation and aftercare statistics, Home Office.

reports in specified circumstances,[1] and this clearly illustrates the precautionary context in which the practice has developed: it was primarily geared to ensuring that every attempt was made to avoid a custodial sentence if possible. The Streatfeild Report's (1961, para. 323) long discussion of the positive value of basing a sentence " on comprehensive and reliable information which is relevant to the objectives in the court's mind " has, however, provided the foundation for much more extravagant claims to be made for the importance of the work of the probation service in the sentencing process; Jarvis (1965, p. 45) has been proved right in his assertion that " such a definite statement from so authoritative a source will strongly influence future practice in the criminal courts." Since then, professional commentators from within probation, magistrates, the press and many criminologists have all tended to argue that the availability of more comprehensive social information in more cases will lead to more appropriate sentencing, not just by keeping the prison population down (as a representative of NAPO recently argued[2]), but by increasing the " effectiveness " of the court's decision.[3]

[1] For example, " When trying a first offender, sentencers in magistrates' courts, before inflicting imprisonment, must satisfy themselves that no other method of dealing with him is appropriate, and in doing this they are required to consider information about the circumstances and take into account information as to his character and physical and mental condition." (First Offenders Act 1958). Other relevant sections are the Children and Young Persons Act 1933: s. 35 (2); the Criminal Justice Act 1948, s. 3 (1), (4), and s. 43. See Jarvis, 1965, p. 44.

[2] D. A. Mathieson, Chairman of the North Western Branch of the National Association of Probation Officers, in a letter to *The Guardian*, July 1971: The probation service can help to alleviate the problem of overcrowding in the prisons " by providing the courts with full social inquiry reports to assist in determining the most appropriate cases for prison sentences."

[3] For example, see the Home Office leaflet on " The Probation Service in England and Wales," H.M.S.O., London 1964: "... The circumstances of the offender are relevant not only to the degree of his culpability but also in the way in which he may be expected to respond to the form of treatment decided upon by the court." Para. 13.

SOCIAL INQUIRY FOR THE COURTS

The Place of Social Inquiry Reports in the Sentencing Process

For a number of reasons it seems to me important that we should look more closely at these developments and try to understand their implications:

(i) First of all, of course, is the simple fact that no researcher can afford to take such a development as this for granted, or assume that it is quite such a straightforward phenomenon as administrators or practitioners might suggest.

(ii) The cost of collecting social inquiry reports is inevitably rising, and according to statistics obtained in a recent Home Office study (Davies and Knopf. 1973), the work now accounts for one-fifth of the total probation budget which itself exceeds £13 million.

(iii) The requirement of a social inquiry report clearly has an effect on the course of justice. Although pre-trial reports are obtained wherever possible, some offenders who plan to plead not guilty may well feel that their case is being pre-judged; on the other hand, if the inquiry is carried out after the trial (still the standard practice in most magistrates' and juvenile courts in Inner London), some delay in the sentencing process is inevitable, and the offender might find himself experiencing a spell in custody even though he eventually receives a community-based disposal.

(iv) Although, because of the difficulties of undertaking adequate research in this area, it is not known precisely how much influence the probation officer exerts on the sentencing decision, there is prima facie evidence that it could be considerable, and that therefore a significant change might be taking place in the penal process; moreover, if this is so, the growing influence of the probation officer as a social worker in the courts is only a reflection of a more widespread trend in the social services as a whole where, usually with fewer legal restraints, other professional social workers are taking decisions or making influential recommendations about clients on the basis of diagnostic and prognostic summaries apparently similar to the probation service's inquiry reports.

Before going any further, let me clear the ground with three negative assertions:

(a) There is no evidence that the growth in the use of social inquiry reports has occurred simultaneously with any significant improvement in the " effectiveness " of sentencing as measured by its success in reducing the level of crime.

(b) As the number of social inquiry reports has risen, there has been no directly related reduction in the number of men received into prison.

(c) Nor does it appear that the growth in the use of social inquiry reports has occurred simultaneously with any lessening in the range of sentencing disparities, the evidence for which " among the judiciary at all levels is overwhelming." (Hood and Sparks, 1970, p. 142.)

But, it is now clear, the increase in the preparation of social inquiry reports has occurred in step with the " growing recognition by the courts of the principle of individualisation of sentence." (Thomas, 1970, p. 3.) Thomas claims that, in the period from 1932 (when " the Departmental

Committee on Persistent Offenders could describe sentencing behaviour almost entirely in terms of a tariff system ") to the present time, a major change has come over the decision-making process of the courts.

> " By 1961, the Streatfeild Committee (paras. 257–262) . . . (suggested that) the courts had increasingly come to consider the offender as an individual, whose needs, rather than whose guilt, would form the basis of the sentence passed. . . . The acceptance of individualism . . . did not mean, however, the disappearance of the tariff: the older order, based primarily on the concepts of retribution and general deterrence, continued to exist parallel to the newer (and still far from comprehensive) pattern of individualised measures. The result is a dual system of sentencing."

Thomas (p. 3) describes how the task of the sentencer is first to decide whether in any particular case the tariff is to apply or whether one of the individualised measures is to be used. " Once the primary decision has been made, the secondary decision follows—where on the tariff is the sentence to be located, or precisely what individualised measure is relevant." Of course, he recognises (pp. 6–7) that such a crude breakdown inevitably over-simplifies a complex pattern of decision-making processes (especially in respect of borderline cases) ; we shall see in the course of this paper that some offenders apparently warranting a tariff sentence might receive individualised treatment because of mitigating factors or even sometimes because of social or personal circumstances, and that an individualised case might nevertheless receive a prison sentence if it was held to be appropriate to his " need ". (The difficulties presented by the inadequacy of the definitions used in this context—especially the concepts of " appropriateness " and " need "—will be considered shortly.)

Social Inquiry and Tariff Sentencing

The primary decision of whether or not an offender is to be sentenced on the basis of the tariff should not in theory be influenced by the social inquiry report, and this is sometimes expressed by the bench in verbal terms: " I don't think we need trouble the probation service in this case. . . . " But even here the pattern has been changing, especially since 1963. Following the publication of the Streatfeild Report, the Home Office issued a series of Circulars[4] which, while not compelling courts to obtain social inquiry reports, have nevertheless greatly influenced them in their practice; and the Court of Appeal will normally give leave to appeal against sentence as a matter of course where a young offender (*i.e.* under 21) has been sentenced without a social inquiry report. Moreover, " the Court is likely to take a similar view in relation to the other categories mentioned in the recommendations of the Streatfeild Committee." (Thomas, 1970, pp. 319–320.)

The groups for whom it is now recommended that reports should be prepared were listed in Home Office Circular, 59/1971, and they cover a wide range of defendants including, for example, all those under 31, all others who have not received a custodial sentence since the age of 17 and all

[4] Home Office Circulars 84/1963, 138/1963, 188/1968, 189/1968, 190/1968, 59/1971.

women. Hence it is by no means uncommon for reports to be available in many cases where the court would previously have had no hesitation in imposing a tariff sentence. If they are available, they are more likely to be read; and, if they are read, it is at least conceivable that they might influence the primary decision of the court.

> " The court should obtain a report in cases of young offenders even when the offence is one for which the offender is likely to receive a sentence of imprisonment, notwithstanding his age, as the report may disclose circumstances which allow the court to depart from its normal approach." (Thomas, 1970, p. 320.)

What is apparently happening in such instances is that the social inquiry report is being used as an additional plea of mitigation; this was certainly the case in the Oz obscenity trial, where the judge obviously made a primary decision in favour of a tariff sentence, but felt obliged by the recommendations of the Home Office to remand the defendants in custody for reports; the probation officer's report referred to the defendant's pride in their work, to their idealistic hopes that the journal might be a vehicle for social change, to the fact that they were all highly intelligent and had no interest in material gain—all factors which were, of course, quite irrelevant so long as the judge stood his ground on the primary decision. But it is easy to see that it is a short step from social inquiry as a means of isolating mitigating factors once the primary decision has been made to social inquiry as a means of helping to determine the primary decision; indeed, in practice, it would be very difficult to distinguish between the two processes.

Social Inquiry and Marginal Cases

Thomas identifies a number of offender-groups " where the primary decision tends to favour individualisation " because of the characteristics of the offender rather than the nature of his offence: young offenders, intermediate and inadequate recidivists, mentally disordered offenders and, to a lesser extent, adult first offenders and women.[5] In respect of the first four groups, he claims (p. 29) that " a tariff sentence will normally be upheld [by the Court of Appeal] only after a careful consideration of the claims of an individualised measure." The implications of this seem to be far-reaching. It does not need a social inquiry report for any of these groups to be identified: all except the mentally disordered can be diagnosed on sight and with access to their record of previous convictions. But if it is accepted in principle by the Court that, even in instances where their behaviour would normally lead to a tariff sentence, the personal and social circumstances that they display render an individualised sentence necessary or at least worthy of consideration, then surely the convention whereby the primary decision is based on offence-behaviour alone is undermined. If that is so, it becomes even more important to consider, both theoretically and empirically, the basis on which individualised sentencing decisions are made, and the developing role of the probation officer in the decision-making process.

[5] Home Office Circular 188/68 (para. 4) particularly emphasises the individualised nature of sentencing women " since it is widely recognised that the social consequences of imprisoning women tend to be more severe and background inquiries are therefore particularly valuable."

MARTIN DAVIES

Social Inquiry Reports and the Individualised Sentence

The social inquiry report, along with other pre-sentence information (from the police, the prison governor, medical personnel, etc.) is intended, according to the Home Office, to enable courts " to select the most appropriate form of treatment for offenders." (Home Office Circular 59/1971, para. 2.) Thomas talks of the court seeking the individualised measure " most suited to the particular offender." And again, with a clearly implied reference to the role of the probation service: " The choice of individualised measure is made empirically in each case on the basis of an assessment of the individual offender's needs." (Thomas, 1970, p. 201.)

Now, there are at least two interpretations of the twin concepts of " need " and " appropriateness of (suitability for) treatment "; and it is because of the confusion which exists between these two interpretations that the notion of individualised sentencing seems to have been inadequately considered, and that the social worker's (probation officer's) role within the penal system remains uneasily ambiguous.

Put in its simplest form, the confusion is between individualised sentencing with a reductivist or reformist aim and individualised sentencing with a rehabilitative and helping aim. Is it the task of the social inquiry report to indicate aspects of the offender's personality and circumstances which, in the officer's judgment, cause him to break the law? And is it then the task of the court to deal with the offender in such a way that the pattern of law-breaking will most probably be reduced? Or, alternatively, does the probation officer in his report draw attention to personal and social problems which appear to indicate a need for support, casework, advice, guidance or what you will, so that the court, in its individualised sentence, can then allocate the offender to that form of treatment most suited to the aim of combating elements of personal and social stress?

It is probably safe to assert that most courts would deny that their primary aim was to provide a social service for offenders no matter what their identified needs, although many sentencers might say that they believed that, by helping his clients, the probation officer was in fact contributing to a reduction in the level of crime; it is almost certain that implicitly the courts hope that individualisation is not only a humane method of dealing with offenders, but that it is also efficient in the sense that it allocates them to those sentences most calculated to reduce the likelihood of their committing further offences. In other words, the courts are attempting to practise a form of social engineering in which their decisions determine, not only the fate, but the future behaviour of individual subjects. If this is so, however, it is in fact no more than a charade in social engineering, for, on present evidence, an individualised sentencing decision can be appropriate to the needs of the offender only in the sense that it should be in some way relevant to the probation officer's description of his background and present circumstances. There are three factors which have to be taken into account in reaching this conclusion.

(1) The first can be dealt with briefly. Probation officers (who are

responsible both unofficially for making recommendations about treatment in general and officially for carrying out the court's decision in a large number of cases) are trained as social workers and not as correctional agents; in so far as there is a body of knowledge and theory behind them, it has more to say about the establishment of a relationship than about the exertion of influence within it. If they contribute to any reduction in criminal behaviour, it is as a by-product of their primary task of serving the client; most officers will hope that, in the course of their work, they do indeed bring about such changes, but most will also remain fully aware of their own limitations in the face of heavy odds.

(2) The second factor is simply that there is, as yet, insufficient evidence to support the notion that differential treatments currently in use vary in their effects on separately diagnosed offender groups. In the light of research carried out during the 1960s, the hope of Streatfeild (para. 278) expressed in 1961 seems almost poignant:

> "It may be hoped that it will eventually be possible, by bringing together the [predictive] formulae for all forms of sentence, to discover to what extent the chances of an offender not being reconvicted depend on the form of sentence imposed, and then to indicate, in respect of individual offenders, whether one form of sentence which the court has in mind is likely to have a different effect from another. These results would be of great importance to sentencers."

As we now know, prediction studies have fallen on lean times (see, *e.g.* Simon, 1971) and some differential treatment experiments, despite limited success among juveniles, have suffered from their own organisational complexity, from a general lack of conceptual clarity and perhaps from an understandable desire to travel a long way in a short time. (Adams, 1961; Palmer, 1969.) The enormous time-scale in researching treatment-effects, and the empirical need to concentrate on clearly focused concepts rather than on generalised treatments for broadly defined problem-groups is only now being recognised: one of the most important treatment studies in England recently was Sinclair's (1971) investigation of probation hostels where a positive but temporary treatment effect was isolated for an identifible group, (also Davies and Sinclair, 1971) but even this finding clearly ought to be replicated before it can legitimately be absorbed into court or probation practice. Streatfeild's enthusiasm for a science-based sentencing system is not only a reflection of where the individualised approach naturally leads, but is a reminder to penologists of the need for immense caution when claiming positive results in their research.[6]

[6] Of course, even when notes of caution are incorporated into the text, the author cannot prevent others from interpreting his results too freely. For example, the argument contained in *The Sentence of the Court* (2nd ed., H.M.S.O., London 1969, pp. 71 *et seq.*) that fines are "more successful" than any other form of sentence is now frequently quoted as an unassailable fact. And yet, despite the reasonable attempts made to make comparisons within different risk-groups for the effectiveness of fines, the limitations of the data and of the research design countenance the need for caution in drawing practical conclusions from the statistics. A recent attempt to check the hypothesis among probationers who were also fined failed to identify any positive effect when financial penalties were imposed. (See Davies, 1970).

(3) The range of treatments available is extremely limited, and new forms tend to be introduced in response to " felt need " rather than because it is known that they will certainly reduce the likelihood of recidivism;[7] moreover, when innovations are made, they are rarely designed so as to facilitate experimental evaluation of their effectiveness in reducing the crime-level. Nevertheless, Thomas (1970, p. 18), having referred to situations where the court had to resort to a tariff sentence because no suitable individualised measure was available, comments: "As new individualised measures become available, it can be expected that the area in which individualisation predominates will expand." One can hardly doubt this in the wake of recent discussion,[8] and it is true that special provisions for the treatment of the alcoholic, the drug abuser and the mentally disturbed offender exist to a limited extent, but if they reflect individualised sentencing practice at all (and most of them are imposed within the flexible framework of the probation order), the most that can be claimed for them is that they appear on the surface to be especially relevant for the needs of some offenders, and that they may or may not prove to be more successful in reducing reconviction rates.

In the present state of knowledge, with the range of treatment tools available, the best we can hope for from individualised sentencing is to match treatment to offender (as distinct from " punishment to crime ") in a commonsense sort of fashion, without making unwarranted assumptions about its probable reformist effect on criminal behaviour.

Decision-making

But who decides what is " commonsense "? Even though we may legitimately doubt to what extent the sentencing process influences an offender's future criminal behaviour, it certainly can affect his immediate position; and it is obviously important to examine the decisions arrived at by both probation officer and court, and in particular to explore the relationship between the two.

Such an assertion is, of course, by no means original, and several research workers have tried to tackle the topic. Hood, in particular, has been concerned with the problem in English magistrates' courts, (Hood 1962; Hood and Taylor 1968 and Joy Mott in the Home Office Research Unit has been engaged for some time on a study of the decision-making processes of magistrates in a juvenile court. The difficulties are enormous, and in the study by Hood and Taylor (p. 433) an attempt to persuade magistrates to explain why they had changed their minds in almost half the cases on which they received reports was largely unsuccessful: " The Bench contented itself with various circumlocutions all meaning that there was nothing to make it

[7] For example, the Reading Report (1966) pinpointed the lack of accommodation for men on release from prison, and since its publication a great deal of effort has been spent on the provision of additional hostel places; no doubt much of this work has fulfilled a specific need but the practical experience of those engaged in the task has taught them that not all homeless offenders can be reformed simply by putting a roof over their heads.

[8] Following the publication of the Wootton Report (1970) and the passing of the Criminal Justice Act 1972.

SOCIAL INQUIRY FOR THE COURTS

change its mind." Other studies have certainly suggested—though not proved—that social inquiry reports influence the Bench in its decisions, and the indications are that, more often than not, the probation officer's recommendation is followed by the court.[9]

If the process by which the magistrates arrive at a decision is difficult to portray, the research based on Wilkins' "decision game" technique (Carter, 1967) would suggest that the probation officer's recommendation is arrived at with a minimum of fuss and on the basis of far less information than eventually goes into the full social inquiry report. Wilkins' technique is neat, attractive and accessible: it identifies one element in the decision-making process and attempts to simulate real-life circumstances. Unfortunately, in spite of widespread appreciation among penologists, its main quality is that it demonstrates again the complexity of the problem in that it illustrates the differences between probation officers in the conclusions they arrive at: for clear-cut cases, non-custodial or custodial recommendations are generally agreed, but when the test is applied to more ambiguous situations (which after all are the ones which create the most interest), probation officers are found to disagree in the conclusions they reach. Moreover, the model does not emulate the mixture of forces which may influence the officer as he arrives at his decision and which may disturb the "commonsense" conclusion arrived at in the simulated situation: for example, the effect on the probation officer of the individual offender; the in-group effect of the officer's colleagues and especially, in some cases, of his senior; the effect of the officer's personal position—his workload, his morale; the effect of the court as a whole and, in particular, of the chairman or judge. The danger of Wilkins' decision game, useful though it undoubtedly is within a limited research sector, is that it implies an over-simplified approach to a complex subject. Hood and Sparks (1970, pp. 168–169) have recognised the complexity in relation to the court as a whole, but for the purpose of our present discussion there is something to be said for aiming at a point midway between the simplicity of a single decision and the complexity of the total situation; in particular, the triangular relationship between probation officer, court and offender has more general relevance at a time when the growing social services juggernaut is involved in thousands of similar decisions every day—in which social worker, administrator or committee and client are similarly related; the only difference is that such decisions are not taken in open court. To what extent then do recommendations to the court reflect the personal attitudes and the social situation of the workers? What is the effect of the relationship between probation officer and decision-maker on determining (a) the recommendation, and (b) the decision?

In the face of such issues, the question-begging nature of phrases such as "the most appropriate sentence," and "treatment according to diagnosed need" is transparent, and the danger of arriving at a glib conclusion about

[9] For example, in her Home Office study, Mott has found both a high level of agreement between probation officers' recommendations and the court's decisions and further evidence of the extent to which magistrates appear to change their minds about the sentence after reading the social inquiry report. See also, White, 1972, pp. 236 *et seq.*

the efficiency and sophistication of modern methods of diagnosis and treatment is highlighted.

The Organisational Context of Social Inquiry

Faced with the unsatisfactory nature of the non-empirical debate in this subject-area and with the shortcomings of research to date, one can either, like Walker (1969, pp. 203 *et seq.*), argue that, if the sentencing system is not efficient at reducing crime levels, then it ought to try to be and accordingly set about the task of producing the simplest possible model of sentencing to satisfy rigorous reductivist criteria; or one can study the existing court situation with a view to identifying the complex factors which determine the eventual decision. One major problem which most research to date has tended to ignore is that the situation almost certainly varies enormously from one court to another, and that therefore merely to describe the influences at work in one court setting is not necessarily to explain the decision-making process in general.

For example:

(i) In one North country court, the probation service was out in the cold. Rarely referred to by the Bench, the relationship was formal and distant; the expression of an opinion in court would have been frowned on had it ever been attempted; sentences tended to be punitive.

(ii) In a Home Counties court, the two probation officers had been in post for over ten years; they were on warm social terms with the Bench, and had a clear understanding of the normal lines of sentencing; recommendations were generally included in reports, and were almost always acted on; case committees were friendly affairs in which three magistrates would visit each officer in the probation office and learn something of his work.

(iii) In one London court, the stipendiary had a regular early morning meeting with " his " probation officer to receive social inquiry reports in advance of the day's business and to reach agreement about the preferred outcome in cases which had been remanded after conviction.

(iv) In a large urban court, the turnover of officers was high, and the Bench frequently made criticisms about the poor quality of some written reports; on the other hand, they knew and respected the work of other more senior men and women, and generally acted on their recommendations.

In order to understand and analyse the decision-making process, it is accordingly necessary first to see it in the context of the relationship between each officer and court (including its local traditions, the role of the chairman, the effect of the presence of different individual magistrates, the role of the clerk, and so on). Moreover, the generally high level of agreement between officers and Bench, already referred to, demands that some attempt be made to disentangle the interacting relationship between the two parties: " probation and other specialists may tailor their recommendations to suit the judge." (Hood and Sparks, 1970, p. 168). This is known as a closed loop system of influence, common enough in economics but not yet sufficiently explored in sociology: " Many influence relations represent closed loop

SOCIAL INQUIRY FOR THE COURTS

systems of this type—either directly or through the operation of the so-called rule of anticipated reactions." (March, 1955, p. 433).

In theory one could find any one of three extreme situations: an entirely static one in which the officer knew precisely what the magistrate would do, and recommended accordingly; one of total influence, where the officer ignored the magistrate's opinion totally but the magistrate sentenced according

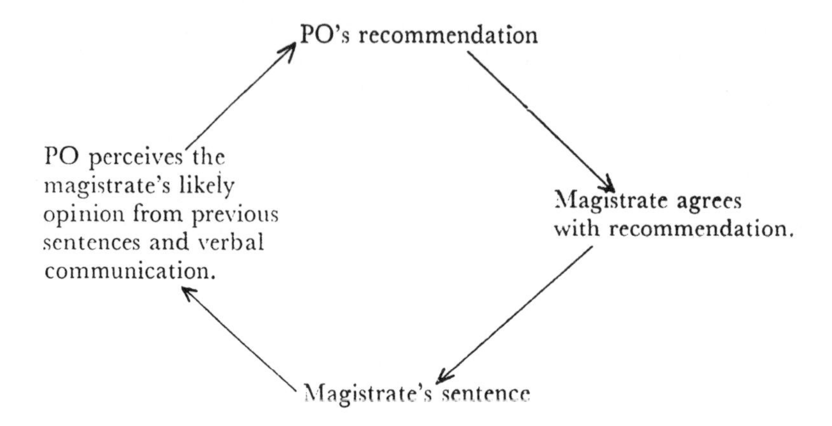

to the recommendation; and one of total conflict in which the PO again ignored the magistrate's opinion, but the magistrate similarly ignored the recommendation. Situations approximating to the first would reflect a process of symbolic communication in which (despite the 100 per cent. agreement) the notion of influence in any single case would be virtually meaningless when seen in the context of the total process. Situations approximating to the second would reflect a process of real influence, in which the PO was seen as a technical expert in an area of limited knowledge and in which the sentencer recognised his own limitations. Situations approximating to the third would indicate a process of non-communication arising from role conflict or open hostility arising from differences of opinion about the purpose of decision-making; in practice, because of the status differences between the two parties, the officer would quickly cease to make recommendations at all.

Although instances might be found of courts approximating to the second and third situations, the probability is that, for most of the time, most courts now tend towards the first situation, but that in any analysis of the decision-making process in such courts, it becomes necessary for the researcher to be able to differentiate between run-of-the-mill decisions in which only symbolic communication occurs and other decisions in which the probation officer attempts to exert influence over the Bench. Depending partly on how committed he appears to be to the recommendation (*i.e.* on how important it is to the officer's own value system) the court might respond either positively or negatively. If positively, this might be either: (a) because they believe his judgment to be more probably right than theirs: *i.e.* they respect his professional skills, and recognise their own limited knowledge; or (b) because they don't like to disappoint him: or (c) because they honestly don't know or because they disagree among themselves.

If they react negatively, this might be either: (a) because they suspect his professional judgment; or (b) because they decide that they have to take other factors into account (this would probably indicate that the PO's symbolic communication had erred); or (c) because they have more information about the case than had the officer.

In situations where symbolic communication characterises the relationship between probation officer and court, a further dimension of the officer's recommendation must be isolated. This is in effect the difference between short-term and long-term tasks. In every decision that has to be made, day-by-day, week-in, week-out, two tasks have to be performed within the social situation: (i) the explicit, specific task of producing a recommendation acceptable to the Bench or capable of influencing the Bench; (ii) the definition, maintenance or development of a structure of interpersonal relations. (March, 1957, p. 268.)

In other words, the steady process of symbolic communication indicates, as we have said, a static situation in which each understands the other's role. But each time a positive reaction is made by the Bench to one of the PO's more radical recommendations, so the officer's influence in the total sentencing process grows; in the event of a negative reaction (and in particular in the event of a whole series of negative reactions) the officer's low status in relation to sentencing is emphasised.

In Conclusion

Two recent papers have concerned themselves with the growing impact of probation officers on sentencing decisions (Ford, 1972; White, 1972), and both provide further evidence of the importance of the relationship between the Bench and the officer. White usefully reviews the question of whether or not it can be shown that any changes in sentencing brought about by the work of probation officers in courts actually lead to reduced reconviction rates. He examines the work of Hood and Taylor (1968) which is still the most relevant of its kind to have been published in Britain but which cannot claim to be more than suggestive in its causal analysis because of methodological limitations; even if intervening variables could be accounted for, the changes noted in reconviction patterns, following an increase in social inquiry work, were relatively slight. Because of the unsatisfactory nature of this and other evaluative evidence regarding the effect of social inquiry reports on reconviction rates, White falls back on the suggestion that the increased use of inquiries might nevertheless be justified if penal results were being achieved " at less cost than formerly, both economically and in terms of the infringement of the liberty of offenders " (pp. 244–245).

Ford points to the way in which the convention has been established whereby recommendations are appended to the social inquiry report, despite the relatively hesitant attitude on the part of officialdom over the years. At the same time, he indicates that the practice presents two distinct dilemmas for the probation service: first, there can be some difficulty in reconciling the officer's social work role as a servant of his client with his responsibility to present an objective report about the offender to the court; secondly, and especially relevant to our present discussion, some officers recognised their own shortcomings as diagnosticians as well as the limitations of the penal remedies available: " they wished that they could write more informed reports on the basis of better methods of diagnosis and personality assessment." (p. 33.)

Thus, however strongly it may be asserted that " increased effectiveness in sentencing [judged by the prevention of recidivism] must be the touchstone of approval for the policy of providing social inquiry reports to the courts " (White, 1972, p. 241), the penologist is faced with the fact that their increased incidence and the general enthusiasm for them have come about in spite of the almost total absence of any such supporting evidence. The situation is a reflection of a much broader phenomenon: that the whole process of planned sentencing achieving intended consequences is largely a mirage. In this context it is not surprising either that there is still ignorance about the most suitable information relevant to sentencing (in a reductivist sense) (White, 1972, p. 246), or that probation officers learn the arts of social inquiry and of making recommendations, not from their academic books or teachers, but from their colleagues and supervisers in the field. (Ford, 1972, p. 32.)

We have argued that the growth of social inquiry work has developed alongside the concept of individualised sentencing: once the primary decision has been taken not to impose a tariff sentence, the Bench and/or the probation officer determine where, on a continuum of need, the offender stands: if the need is minimal, then a residual tariff element is used to determine whether the offence warrants a fine or can be dealt with by a discharge; if problems exist, within a very wide range of circumstances, then a probation order is made and whenever possible the residual tariff is applied again to impose a financial penalty (Davies, 1970, pp. 3–4); where personal or social problems are more severe, or perhaps (though not always) where probation has already failed, a number of alternative measures may be employed—hostel, training, medical treatment or imprisonment. The introduction of intermediate treatment under the Children and Young Persons Act 1969, and of the various experimental schemes offered by the Criminal Justice Act 1972, merely adds to the range of alternatives available along the continuum of social need.

The recent Criminal Justice Act, in particular, lends support to the concept of individualised sentencing by providing new forms of treatment for offenders: it implicitly recognises the probable further growth of social inquiry work and the increased involvement of the probation service in penal decision-making; and the Home Office has lent further emphasis to the scientific connotations of sentencing by providing for the evaluation of each new process by research. The introduction of facilities such as day training centres and community service orders, however cautious official spokesmen may be in committing themselves, nevertheless lead the public to have reductivist expectations; and those who prepare the social inquiry reports are presumed to be able to identify the offenders most likely to be reformed in such specialised treatment settings. But here, as elsewhere in sentencing, we are faced still with the ambiguity of penal aims, and with the sad fact that almost all the reputable evidence leads to pessimistic conclusions concerning our ability to influence future behaviour as a direct result of penal policy: hence the notion of effectively reductivist social inquiry reports is, to say the least, premature. It is important for the probation officer to keep the realities of individualised treatment firmly in perspective. Social inquiry reports are descriptions of circumstances, and they help the sentencer choose a sentence " appropriate " to the offender's apparent circumstances. The recommendations made are unlikely to be able to say anything legitimate about the probable effectiveness of treatment, although they may refer to the probability of reconviction; they will reflect the service's conventional wisdom, backed up by strong in-group support for what is customary (varying, perhaps, from place to place), and tempered by the officer's awareness of what will be acceptable to the Bench. The range of variation is increasingly wide, and conventional wisdom may not always identify the good risks successfully.[10] The use of reports nevertheless represents one of the most important penal developments of the twentieth century, and reflects a crucial change in the balance of sentencing authority. If, during the next decade, treatment research begins to pay dividends (even though the rewards will almost certainly be more modest than Streatfeild envisaged), there seems little doubt that the role of the probation officer as a sentencing adviser will become even more significant than it is now.

References

Adams, Stuart (1961). *Inquiries concerning kinds of treatment for kinds of delinquents.* California Board of Corrections: Monograph Number 2.

Carter, R. M. (1967). " The pre-sentence report and the decision-making process." *J. Res. in Crime and Delinquency*, **4**, 203–211.

Davies, Martin (1970). *Financial penalties and probation.* London: H.M.S.O.

Davies, Martin and Knopf, Andrea (1973). *Social enquiry reports and the probation service.* London: H.M.S.O.

Davies, Martin and Sinclair, I. A. C.: (1971). " Families, Hostels and Delinquents." *Brit. J. Criminol.* **11**, 213–229.

Ford, Peter (1972). *Advising sentencers.* Oxford: Blackwell.

Hood, Roger (1962). *Sentencing in magistrates' courts.* London: Stevens.

[10] For example, in an unpublished study of homeless inadequate recidivists probation was only recommended on the social inquiry report in 29 per cent. of the cases, but the recommendation was almost invariably accepted by the court. However, further analysis showed that the recommendation was usually based on an expressed intention on the part of the offender to put his affairs to rights, although this intention bore no relationship to the likelihood of his succeeding, which was in fact most closely associated with his previous record of vagrancy.

SOCIAL INQUIRY FOR THE COURTS

HOOD, ROGER and SPARKS, RICHARD (1970). *Key issues in criminology.* London: Weidenfeld and Nicholson.

HOOD, ROGER AND TAYLOR, IAN (1968). "The effectiveness of pre-sentence investigations in reducing recidivism." *Brit. J. Criminol.* **8**, 431–434.

JARVIS, F. V. (1965). "Inquiry before sentence" in *Criminology in transition*, edited by T. Grygier *et al.* London: Tavistock. pp. 43–66.

McLEAN, D. S. (1961). "Probation reports." *Probation*, **9**, 176–177.

MARCH, J. G. (1955). "An introduction to the theory and measurement of influence." *American Political Science Review*, **49**, 431–451.

MARCH, J. G. (1957). "Influence measurement in experimental and semi-experimental groups." *Sociometry*, **19**, 260–271.

PALMER, T. *et al.* (1969). *Community treatment project: research report No. 9.* California Youth Authority; Sacramento.

THE READING REPORT (1966). *Residential provision for homeless discharged offenders.* London: H.M.S.O.

SIMON, F. H. (1971). *Prediction methods in criminology.* London: H.M.S.O.

SINCLAIR, I. A. C. (1971). *Hostels for probationers.* London: H.M.S.O.

THE STREATFEILD REPORT (1961). *Report of the interdepartmental committee on the business of the criminal courts.* London: H.M.S.O.

THOMAS, D. A. (1970). *Principles of sentencing.* London: Heinemann.

WALKER, NIGEL (1969). *Sentencing in a rational society.* London: Allen Lane.

WHITE, STEPHEN (1972). "The effect of social inquiry reports on sentencing decisions." *Brit. J. Criminol.* **12**, 230–249.

THE WOOTTON REPORT (1970). *Report of the Penal Advisory Council's sub-committee on non-custodial treatment.* London: H.M.S.O.

Note: Another important review of the literature has appeared since the completion of this manuscript: BOTTOMLEY, A. K. (1973). *Decisions in the penal process.* London: Martin Robertson. Chapter 4 "The sentencing process", is directly relevant to the subject-matter of this paper.

[7]

[1992]

Pre-Sentence Reports, Culpability and the 1991 Act

By Nigel Stone
School of Social Work, University of East Anglia

Defendants are frequently puzzled about the role and legitimacy of the probation service's contribution to sentencing and are reluctant to accept delay in order to obtain a social inquiry report. Such doubts are likely to remain following the implementation of the Criminal Justice Act 1991. Will report writers be substantially clearer about their responsibilities and will offenders be more willing and informed participants?

In the Act's new framework of sentencing there are five decision points at which a pre-sentence report (P.S.R.) will be an essential prerequisite:

1. Is an offence so serious that only a custodial sentence can be justified?
2. If the offence is so serious, what term of custody is commensurate with the seriousness of the offence?
3. In the case of a violent of sexual offence, would only a custodial sentence be adequate to protect the public from serious harm?
4. If a violent or sexual offence satisfies either the seriousness or the public protection criterion, is a longer term required than commensurability would indicate?
5. If an offence is serious enough to warrant a community sentence consisting of a community service order, a combination order or a probation/supervision order with additional requirements, is the offender suitable for such a measure?

(The P.S.R. can be dispensed with at points one to four where the offence is triable only on indictment and the court considers it unnecessary.)

Pre-1991 law and practice has given social inquiry report writers considerable scope to address whatever issues they think fit and relevant. Many practitioners have been inspired by the so-called "justice" model to become much more offence-centred in their reports but this has still left plenty of space for broader biographical detail and assessment. Now that the principles and rules of custodial and community sentencing are to have explicit statutory authority, will P.S.R.s become rather more precise and focused documents?

The Home Office's "near final" draft of *Probation Service National Standards for Pre-Sentence Reports*[1] certainly gives that impression, requiring probation officers to begin by provisionally assessing the seriousness of the offence(s) and then to adapt the style and detail of their P.S.R. accordingly. Annex A of the document seems to be proposing a rationing scheme of approach, loosely linked to the Act's ground rules on factors to be considered. (See Table).

---

[1] Home Office, Draft Probation Service National Standards (CPO 13/1992).

Sentence	CJA Factors	National Standards
Custody (seriousness criterion)	All available information about circumstances of offence (M); any aggravating factors disclosed by circumstances of the offences (D); such matters as the court may consider relevant in mitigation (D)	seriousness of offence; likely consequences of custody
Custody (public protection)	All available information about circumstances of offence (M); any information about the offender (D); such matters as the court may consider relevant in mitigation (D)	as above, plus evidence of risk of serious harm
Community Sentence (seriousness and appropriate degree of restriction on liberty)	All available information about circumstances of offence (M); such matters as the court may consider relevant in mitigation (D)	seriousness of offence
Community Order (suitability)	any information about the offender (D)	information about the offender, especially as relevant to suitability; description of most appropriate community sentence

(M) = Mandatory, (D) = Discretionary

As Curran and Chambers have observed, past guidance in successive Home Office Circulars on social inquiry reports has tended "to concentrate on describing what reports should contain, to the neglect of explaining why such information is relevant".[2] This latest attempt at authoritative guidance still suffers from the same limitations and also has surprising omissions. There is, for instance, absolutely no mention at all about risk of serious harm and how evidence of this should be obtained and assessed. Nor is the report writer assisted in weighing or ignoring previous convictions, in the light of section 29(1) or (2). The draft primarily concentrates on evaluating seriousness of offence but is understandably somewhat circumspect, given the ambiguities of the Act itself. We are simply told that existing Court of Appeal guidance on aggravating and mitigating factors will be of assistance, as will the Court's interpretation of Criminal Justice Act 1982, s.1 (4A)(c). Reporters are given little specific assist-

[2] J. H. Curran and G. A. Chambers, *Social Inquiry Reports in Scotland* (1982).

ance in making their initial judgment. There is no honest acknowledgment of the problematic nature of incorporating social information into logical sentencing calculation. It is upon the interpretation of "seriousness" that this article will concentrate.

The circumstances of the offence

As Thomas has commented in the context of custodial sentences, the Act's leading requirement to take account of "the circumstances of the offence, including any aggravating or mitigating factors" (s.3(3)(a) and s.7(1)), appears to prohibit consideration of information about the offender's background.[3] He suggests that confusion will inevitably arise when sentencers have simultaneously to consider a P.S.R. and yet ignore much of the information likely to be contained therein. Wasik and Taylor have suggested that P.S.R.s "will have to address in a more detailed and thoughtful manner issues relating to seriousness"[4] and the Act clearly expects P.S.R.s to do more than provide sentencers with details of how the offender could be punished in the community with the most constructive or least destructive outcome. Reporters will be party to primary decision-making, i.e. whether the offence is serious enough to require partial restriction on liberty or too serious for anything other than complete deprivation of liberty.

But what particular contribution arises from the report-writer's distinct insights, skills, judgment and opportunities to encounter the defendant? All the draft National Standard can suggest is that:

> "relevant information may include the offender's explanation of the offence, acceptance of responsibility and feelings of guilt or remorse, attitudes, motivation, criminal history, relationships (*e.g.* family, friends and associates), strengths and skills, as well as personal problems such as drug or alcohol misuse, or financial, housing, employment or medical or psychiatric problems".[5]

This somewhat comprehensive shopping list completely fails to acknowledge the Act's purported distinction between offence-centred and offender-centred issues.

It is by no means easy to make such distinction, as Thomas points out, citing as example a 42 year old offender facing sentence for unlawful sexual intercourse with a 14 year old girl. Under the less exacting pre-1991 law, as *Taylor*[6] illustrates, the 42 year old defendant would almost certainly be considered to have, in Lawton L.J.'s phrase, sufficient "degree of guilt" to cross the custody threshold. Lawton L.J. was clearly reflecting the Streatfeild Committee's concern to take proper account of culpability. On this view, evaluation of "serious-

[3] D. A. Thomas, "Criminal Justice Act 1991: Custodial Sentences", [1992] Crim.L.R. 232 at p. 235.
[4] M. Wasik and R. D. Taylor, *Blackstone's Guide to the Criminal Justice Act 1991* (1991) at p. 24.
[5] [1977] 1 W.L.R. 612.
[6] *Ibid.*, para. 15.

ness" should still combine two elements—harm and culpability.[7] Wasik & von Hirsch's suggested statutory clarification of proportionality makes this explicit:

> "The sentence shall be in just proportion to the seriousness of the criminal conduct; that is, the conduct's harmfulness or potential harmfulness and the offender's degree of culpability in committing the conduct."[8]

If in post-1991 law sentencers are to interpret "circumstances of the offence" very narrowly, the P.S.R. writer will make a very modest contribution. Reporters are wary of giving detailed accounts of crimes, conscious of their relative ignorance of what will be stated in court or negotiated between prosecution and defence. The report should not be simply repetitious or a re-statement of the obvious (for example in pointing out the vulnerability of an elderly victim, the breach of trust by an employee, the use of excessive force or gratuitous violence/damage, or the age difference between the perpetrator of unlawful sexual intercourse and the girl concerned). If the report does present new information, will this be an awkward, tangential contribution or a competing view which neither fits readily with the advocates' accounts nor can be easily tested or challenged?

It is possible to envisage the presentation of factual offence details which are not necessarily available to the court by other routes, though this may require a more careful than accustomed line of enquiry and perhaps greater foundation knowledge of criminal behaviour. In the context of the extent of planning, premeditation and skill of execution, examples might include whether the offender used any technical know-how in entering and starting a car taken without consent or in altering a credit card, and how this was acquired. In regard to the defendant's contribution to an offence, the report could address who was influential or played a particular role among a group of co-offenders, *e.g.* in embarking on a burglary or initiating an affray.

The latter example points to the probation officer's principal professional strength, not in tackling factual aspects of a crime's *modus operandi* but in throwing light on the mind, judgment, motives, anticipation/intent, reactions, emotions and mental state of the offender, before, during and after the crime. However, the further we go in exploring this "softer" data, the more unchartered the territory. First, it becomes increasingly difficult to distinguish between what constitutes "the circumstances of the offence" and what is merely "relevant in mitigation" under section 28. Culpability is an expansive concept which can encompass extent of temptation, method of exploitation used, availability of other courses of action, the anticipation of harm, the presence of "diminishing" factors such as provocation or other moral justifications, underlying stress, ignorance of the law, the offender's broader capacity for self-control and the extent to which the offending episode can be regarded as a behavioural aberration. The only obvious limiting boundary in the calculation of culpability is

---

[7] See A. Ashworth, *Sentencing and Penal Policy* (1983) Chap. 4.

[8] M. Wasik and A. von Hirsch, "Statutory Sentencing Principles: The 1990 White Paper", (1990) 53 M.L.R. 508 at p. 510.

that we should not go beyond the offence itself into post-offence realms such as remorse, assisting the police and making restitution, though in practice this may prove a hard line to draw.

Secondly, the Court of Appeal's views on mitigation and aggravation are far less explicit in regard to somewhat shadowy, ephemeral or subjective aspects of the offender's thinking and emotions, in so far as these may have affected behaviour. Thirdly, these ingredients can be very hard to prove and their impact on the defendant's mood or judgment even more so. Without a great deal of extra inquiry we largely have to take the defendant's retrospective word for it. Fourthly, even if these factors are reliably clear, it can be difficult to know if their presence is of aggravating or mitigating effect. The use and impact of alcohol presents a key example of this kind of ambiguity.

Two examples may assist in illustrating the difficulties. The first concerns a 23 year old man with a substantial alcohol problem for which he has been receiving help in a residential recovery project, now convicted of a rather clumsy attempt to rob a petrol station by seizing a customer and pretending to have a knife. The probation report stated:

> "This offence occurred after Mr A had been abstinent for 11 weeks. He had been prompted to drink again because, despite his intentions not to become heavily involved in another relationship until he had re-established his life, he had become infatuated with a female friend and was depressed when she felt unable to respond. He estimates that he consumed alcohol totalling some 42 units or more during that day's binge and thus had difficulty in recalling either the details of his crime or what his intentions were."

Though the defendant's alcohol problem and some degree of intoxication is undoubted, how reliable and relevant is his account of unrequited love and is his culpability diminished because of his distressed and drunken state?

The second extract features the sequence of events, the defendant's role and his frame of mind. A 20 year old man with a difficult upbringing stands convicted of wounding a man whom he had confronted, believing that he had earlier threatened the defendant's younger brother. Another youth was involved in the assault but was not identified or prosecuted.

> "Mr B stated that he did not plan or anticipate the assault. By his account the encounter became violent when his companion unexpectedly swung a dog chain at [the victim]. He said that he then hit [the victim] because 'something snapped' inside him, based on his earlier years in which he had witnessed his brother being hit by their stepfather and had tried to protect him. The two brothers have always felt a strong bond of loyalty and [the victim] appears to have taken some of the brunt of Mr B's revived bad memories of their aggressive stepfather."

This may seem pertinent information but with what impact on culpability for what otherwise seems a relatively serious and unprovoked attack? Also the allegedly leading role of the co-offender in inflicting the more serious of the victim's injuries is virtually impossible to substantiate.

These problematic dilemmas are clearly visible—though not acknowledged—

in the Home Office's recent training pack[9] on the Act for the Probation Service which seeks to differentiate between factors affecting the seriousness of offence and those which mitigate but are unrelated to the offence. The guide characterises "attitude to the offence" ("has the offender shown any signs of guilt, remorse, concern for victim, or desire to make reparation?") as a factor affecting offence seriousness, while the defendant's age (a propos Thomas' USI query) is identified merely as an unrelated mitigating factor. Alcohol or drugs as a feature of the offence is baldly offered as a factor affecting seriousness but without any explanation of their significance either way. We are told that a racial motivation for an offence amplifies seriousness but, whilst this may be a commendable feature of progressive sentencing principles in combatting racism, this may not necessarily accord with the current established sentencing consensus.

Intended or potential harm

The nature of harm intended or risked, as distinct from that caused by the defendant, is a further pertinent factor which can only be grasped either by the sentencer's surmise or the defendant's own admission and thus may become known to the court only through the P.S.R. This is a complex question in culpability and proportionality, not least because it is so intangible or speculative. If the defendant convicted of resisting a police officer tells the probation officer that he was actually trying to kick the officer in the testicles but missed, this somewhat transforms what might otherwise seem merely a truculent incident into an attempted assault of some seriousness. A further illustration arose in a probation report on a man aged 30, convicted of section 20 wounding after inflicting a cut on the victim's elbow with a metal bar in a neighbourhood row:

> "Mr C told me that after the victim swung at him he felt so angry that his intention was to knock him to the ground and inflict serious injury upon him to the extent that 'he'd need an ambulance'. But for the intervention of others he does not know what would have caused him to desist the attack. He still wishes that he had inflicted more grievous injury and claims that if he had his chance again he would 'make a better job of it'."

In addition to the light this extract throws on intent, it is also pertinent to issues of post-offence attitude, to be discussed later in this article.

Criminal history

Thomas has already explored the ambiguity of section 29(2) regarding the extent to which the court may take account of the aggravating circumstances of previous convictions for the purpose of forming an opinion about the seriousness of the current offence. One interpretation of the sub-section is advanced by the Home Office's training guide:

> ". . . s.29(2) can only apply if the circumstances of other offences shed light on aggravating features of the current offence. For example, if the defendant has a history of racially motivated offences, this may help the

[9] *Criminal Justice Act 1991 Training Materials: Practice Issues for the Probation Service* (prepared by NACRO for the Home Office, 1992).

court to realise that an attack on a black person, for which it is now sentencing, was racially motivated and therefore more serious. If someone has a record of stealing from vulnerable victims, this may help the court to conclude that a vulnerable victim was deliberately targeted on this occasion, thereby making the offence more serious."[10]

The P.S.R. may be the most informative source of detail about previous offending and any parallels with or differences from the current crime. Take the instance of a 41 year old man with numerous convictions who has yet again exploited his relationships with women by stealing from them. The probation report, with the benefit of access to an extensive record of past reports and failed attempts to supervise the defendant, recounted:

"Given his record, Mr D is increasingly poorly placed to succeed by legitimate means. He has found it easier once again to trade on his personable charm, optimism, persuasiveness and articulate presentation to form relationships which women initially find convincing and rewarding. Unfortunately, he can also be an unscrupulous parasite and liar and his heavy alcohol habit has been an expensive demand. I am concerned that he always has plausible explanations for his behaviour which suggest that the responsibility lies with others or that he was placed in situations where he had little choice but to offend. Thus in our recent discussions it was noticeable that he placed the blame for his current predicament on the women whom he felt had let him down in various ways. I found little sense of conscience or self-doubt."

Once again we are also drawn into the defendant's *ex post facto* attitude toward the offence. My concern here is the questionable fairness to both defendants and report-writers of placing the responsibility upon the P.S.R. to highlight aggravating factors.

Attitude towards the offence

According to the Green Paper *Punishment and Supervision in the Community*, the P.S.R. "should include information about the offender's attitude towards the offence . . . and willingness to stop committing crimes."[11] This takes us into more uncertain territory. As argued earlier, this seems to fall only within the ambit of section 28(1) and thus be of mitigatory but not aggravatory weight. Nevertheless, it seems reasonable to expect sentencers to be influenced in a pragmatic, commonsense way by such considerations as: is the defendant "facing up to the facts" in a candid or contrite manner? It is commonplace for defence advocates to seek to convey their clients' regrets or remorse and in the good practice examples of P.S.R.s provided in the Home Office's training pack, defendants are characterised throughout as "accepting the dangerous and irresponsible nature of their actions", expressing "shame, remorse and concern for the victim" and "bitterly regretting their actions and severing ties with their co-offenders". The trouble with such reports of remorse, desire to make amends, change habits or lifestyle or seek help with problems is that these are usually

[10] *Ibid.*, Module 3, Part III(2).
[11] Home Office (Cm. 966, 1990) para. 9.6.

matters of unproven future intent. Defendants in my experience have often been advised by the police or their solicitor to avoid contact with their victim prior to sentence and have thus done nothing by way of more tangible action to make good or apologise. There has also to be some doubt whether such expressions of remorse are truly authentic or have been coaxed or prompted in some way, perhaps by the probation officer's line of questioning.

Where does this leave the defendant who takes a less conciliatory line? What, for instance, is the impact upon sentencers of a report which states, in the case of a 17 year old convicted of taking a vehicle without consent, after driving away at speed from a courtyard under the influence of cannabis and knocking down an elderly pedestrian in the process, that the defendant now feels that it was the victim's fault for being in the driveway instead of on the pavement?

Many defendants convicted of routine offences do not necessarily feel much remorse beyond regret that they were caught, and some are very frank about this to the reporter. To cite the example of an 18 year old woman convicted of shop theft, her probation report commented:

> "Ms E rationalised her behaviour as 'just one of those things. I was bored and I had no money. Everybody I know does it. I've always paid before and have contributed to the cost of other people's nicking, so I thought it was my turn to have a share.' With hindsight she regrets getting caught, but feels that lax store security is at fault and, with some frankness, admitted that she could not categorically state that she would never do it again."

In conclusion

The Act's broad intention, that a pre-sentence report should be obtained before a custodial sentence is passed to ensure that potential community sentences can first be properly considered, particularly in borderline cases, is to be welcomed. This is very much in line with sentencers' current perceptions of what constitutes a helpful report: one which conveys something about the defendant as a person, assesses the likely effect of a particular sentence on the individual offender, suggests what might stem their offending and notes the extent of family responsibilities or current efforts to address behaviour problems.[12] Clearly there are other useful and uncontroversial issues which P.S.R.s can readily address, for example the indirect effects of conviction or particular sentence options (has prosecution for this offence ended the defendant's marriage?, will imprisonment terminate the defendant's career or accommodation?), or the effect of same upon innocent dependants of the offender (*e.g.* the consequences of imprisonment for the defendant's children). There is also the potential to achieve greater consistency and clarity in report content and presentation.

This article has attempted to pose more awkward questions about the role of P.S.R.s in the moral evaluation of criminal behaviour. My concern is that the probation officer is requested to interview the defendant in a private, relatively unhurried, in-depth encounter, having some of the ambience of the confessional, encouraging the defendant to be candid, open and trusting. Defend-

[12] See L. Gelsthorpe and P. Raynor, "Report on the Quality and Contents of Reports" in J. Bredar, *Justice Informed: The Pre-Sentence Report Pilot Trials in the Crown Court* (1992) Vol. II, Appendix I.

ants can welcome this opportunity to speak because they can feel listened to, understood and respected in a way that may be missing from their other encounters with criminal justice professionals. Much may depend on skill, time availability, thoroughness, values and perceptions of the reporter who is increasingly trained and encouraged to 'confront' or challenge offending and devise corrective intervention in the community. The written product of the encounter is difficult to challenge and its impact on the sentencer is even more difficult to assess. Little thought appears to have been given to the formidable problems of evidence in establishing factors relevant to seriousness. Should, for instance, the prosecution now be supplied reports in order to anticipate questions about the defendant's role in the offence? This would be a considerable departure from current practice. Will reporters be more routinely expected to attend court to give evidence to support their offence analysis?

Defendants usually conclude or are advised that it is in their interests to participate in enquiries or that the process is, at worst, of neutral weight, but some of the examples provided above suggest that this is not necessarily the case. As I have asked elsewhere, "can it be right for the defendant's culpability to be weighed more heavily as a result of this kind of voluntary self-disclosure, filtered through the judgment of the individual reporter?"[13] What choice does the defendant have to decline to be interviewed? The Act is silent on the question of consent, as is the draft National Standards document. Only the Home Office's training guide refers, in the context of "good practice procedures", to obtaining the defendant's consent. If the defendant declines, a probation officer's written statement of explanation hardly seems to count as a report made "with a view to assisting the court in determining the most suitable method of dealing with an offender", as defined by section 3(5)(c), but the court can doubtless proceed without the benefit of a P.S.R. It is perhaps a regrettable omission that a defendant's participation is taken so much for granted, while the scope to question or challenge P.S.R. writers is likely to remain so limited. The preference to be sentenced on the basis of the advocates' presentations may be a sensible option in some instances. Alternatively, will defendants become more circumspect in what they share with their reporter?

The White Paper indicated:

> "the purpose of requiring courts to consider a report by the probation service where a custodial sentence is contemplated will be to provide the court with detailed information about how the offender could be punished in the community, so that option can be fully considered."[14]

This was reiterated in the Home Office's discussion document prior to the draft National Standards:

> "What a probation officer can most appropriately provide is advice on what form(s) of community supervision would be more or less suitable for an offender, which one is considered most suitable, and what might be the risk

[13] N. Stone "Proportionality and Pre-Sentence Reports" (1991) 155 J.P.N. 439 at p. 455.

[14] Home Office, *Crime, Justice and Protecting the Public* (Cm 965, 1990) para. 3.10.

to the public and the prospects of securing change in the offender from the community supervision that is proposed."[15]

The logic of this would require the P.S.R. to play its part *after* a decision in principle has been taken about the seriousness of the offence and the appropriate "deserts" penalty. As the new law stands, the report is required simultaneously to undertake several burdens which are potentially neither entirely fair nor readily compatible.

[15] Home Office, *Pre-Sentence Reports—Discussion Document* (CPO 46/1991) para. 7.

[8]

"A Balanced Performance" on Sentence– Some Comments on the Modern Role of Defence Counsel in the Sentencing Process

Janet Martin*

Introduction

The modern defence lawyer has the opportunity to play many important roles in the sentencing process. They may range through confessor and adviser (when instructions are first taken), negotiator and conciliator (should plea or charge bargaining be appropriate), problem-solver and truth-seeker (at the fact-finding stage), and eloquent special pleader, historian and social commentator (during the speech in mitigation). At the same time, as a legal practitioner, counsel must discharge professional and ethical duties and obligations to the client who is being represented and to the court before which the sentencing is heard. It goes without saying that the competent lawyer instructed to represent an offender facing sentence must also have an excellent knowledge of the criminal law, evidence and procedure and highly developed communication skills. The defence lawyer must be at ease with and command the confidence and respect of the offender, the prosecution and the sentencer.

In the 1980s, the presence of defence counsel at the sentencing process, especially when the charge is serious, is almost taken for granted. Yet, in Australia there is still no uniform procedure which governs the sentencing hearing and there is not always agreement as to the functions and aims of defence counsel at the sentencing.

The object of this article is not to examine the many and varied tasks, duties and obligations of the defence lawyer representing a convicted person. That subject deserves and demands a long and detailed narrative. What is proposed is simply to draw attention to some legal and ethical dilemmas that have emerged in the last few years and to lament the seeming reluctance of the courts to offer clear guidance and direction to those parties involved in the sentencing process as to what is expected of the offender's legal representative.

To understand how some of these problems have arisen, it is instructive first to review briefly the sentencing process and its participants.

---

* Barrister and Solicitor of the Supreme Court of Western Australia, LL.B. (Hons) (W.A.), Lecturer in Law, University of Western Australia.

The Sentencing Process—Some General Observations

The process of sentencing is generally considered to be quite distinct from the procedure for determining criminal responsibility. At a trial strict rules of procedure and evidence apply and the issues to be decided are well formulated and accepted by the court, the prosecution and the defence. By comparison, the sentencing process tends to be a relatively crude affair. In Australia, it has attracted few procedural or evidential rules and the courts tend to adjust their proceedings to fit the circumstances. That most crucial decision that any sentencer makes in relation to a convicted offender, namely, whether to punish, and if so, the nature and extent of the penalty appropriate to the offender, is sometimes made with scant regard for due inquiry.

Where the sentencing follows a trial[1] the sentencer usually has at least some pertinent information to apply to the sentencing decision. The circumstances of the offence, the offender's role in it and details about the offender usually emerge, especially when the defendant has given sworn evidence relating to the offence. Some small "information base" has been established.[2] But recent research[3] suggests that, in Australia, no more than 10 per cent of all criminal charges culminate in a trial following a plea of not guilty. The remaining 90 per cent are dealt with when an offender is convicted on his or her own plea of guilty. Sentencing on pleas of guilty is therefore the most common exercise for the court. It is also the most difficult. It is not surprising that it is in this area that important questions have arisen as to the duties and obligations of defence counsel in the sentencing process, particularly in the High Court in *Pantorno*[4] and in the Victorian Full Court in *Rumpf*.[5] Both will be examined in detail in this article.

Usually, there are four main parties present for the sentencing—the sentencer, the offender,[6] the prosecutor and the offender's legal representative.

The sentencer takes the most important role and makes the preliminary decision on sentence. The offender awaits the decision and must, of

[1] The word "trial" generally indicates (at least in criminal law) a particular process: the full proof by the prosecution of the charge against the defendant, beyond reasonable doubt, where the defendant has elected to defend the charge against him or her. Below, it will be suggested that the exercise of "fact-finding" which often accompanies the sentencing process is also a trial and should be so treated by all parties.

[2] The Australian Law Reform Commission (A.L.R.C.) adopts this useful description of some of the raw materials that are vital to the sentencing process: "The raw material with which sentencing courts must work is information": *Procedure*, Discussion Paper No. 29 (August 1987), p. 23.

[3] Ibid., p. 25.

[4] *Pantorno v. The Queen* (1989) 63 A.L.J.R. 317 (Full Court).

[5] *R. v. Rumpf* [1988] V.R. 466 (Full Court).

[6] Despite the surprising result of the decision of the High Court in *Coulter v. The Queen* (1988) 62 A.L.J.R. 74 which effectively denied an offender the right to be present during an application for leave or special leave to appeal to the Full Court of South Australia. There was a strong dissent from Deane and Gaudron JJ.

course, be given an opportunity to speak in mitigation.[7] The exact role of prosecuting counsel is still to be finally worked out, but there has been some careful judicial and academic consideration of their function and there is less and less excuse for error on their part.[8]

There is not always agreement on the exact place of defence counsel in the proceedings. It is not easy to explain exactly why this is so, because their presence at the sentencing is virtually taken for granted. Nevertheless, their role is poorly documented, sometimes ignored and occasionally misunderstood. While there is an increasing awareness of the difficulties that they may encounter,[9] no consistent solution has emerged through the case law in the area.

To help appreciate some of these difficulties, consider the phenomenon of sentencing on a plea of guilty.

Sentencing on a Plea of Guilty[10]

Without the benefit of a trial, obtaining information about the offence and the offender can be a haphazard business.[11] Not all jurisdictions in Australia require the court to inquire of the offender as to whether he or she has been subjected to any pressure to admit guilt, and usually the court is forced to rely on the plea as being appropriate to the offender.

In magistrates' courts, sentences are often imposed promptly following a plea of guilty with minimum comment from either prosecution or offender on the circumstances of the charge. This is not to say that the sometimes mechanical sentencing in these courts is inferior or unjust. It is rarely, if ever, necessary to insist on a full-scale plea in mitigation or a pre-sentence report before fixing a penalty suitable to the anti-social

[7] To deny the offender a right to speak in mitigation has always been regarded as a denial of natural justice. There are recent observations from the Full Court of Western Australia confirming the point and referring to the usual authorities in *R. v. Parole Board; Ex parte Birnie* [1988] W.A.R. 249.

[8] For academic comment from the United Kingdom, see G. Zellick, "The Role of Prosecuting Counsel in Sentencing" [1979] Crim.L.R. 493 and A. J. Ashworth, "Prosecution and Procedure in Criminal Justice" [1979] Crim.L.R. 480. For academic assessment in Australia, see I. G. Campbell, "The Role of the Crown Prosecutor on Sentence" (1985) 9 Crim.L.J. 202. The most recent judicial comment in Australia appears in *Rumpf* [1988] V.R. 466, per McGarvie J. on behalf of the Full Court. A practical guide for the lawyers who prosecute for the Director of Public Prosecutions appears in I. D. Temby Q.C., "The Role of the Prosecutor in the Sentencing Process" in *Sentencing in Australia* (Australian Institute of Criminology and Australian Law Reform Commission), p. 109. There are also D.P.P. Prosecution Address Guidelines.

[9] *Rumpf* [1988] V.R. 466.

[10] For a useful work examining the prosecution in New South Wales of indictable charges without trial (the uncontested disposition of criminal charges where the offender pleads guilty), see John B. Bishop, *Prosecution Without Trial* (Butterworths, 1989). It contains some general points relating to Australia as a whole.

[11] Nor should it be accepted that the trial process will necessarily provide the sentencer with a solution to the perpetual problem of obtaining the right information for the sentencing process: see R. G. Fox and B. M. O'Brien, "Fact-finding for Sentencers" (1975-1976) 10 M.U.L.R. 170-178; R. G. Fox and A. Freiberg, *Sentencing—State and Federal Law in Victoria* (Oxford University Press, Melbourne), pp. 47-51.

behaviour of a 19-year-old courier who admits to speeding in a suburban street. It may be useful for the court to be advised of the consequences to the offender of an order which may disqualify him from holding a driver's licence for some period, but little more information would be required. Many matters of a similar nature are dealt with efficiently and fairly and on a daily basis.

More important considerations can arise where, for example, a magistrate comes to impose sentence on a 37-year-old supporting mother of three who has admitted to defrauding the Commonwealth Government of $15,000. Here the court should receive much more information about the offence and the offender. Pity the poor sentencer. It is not unusual for a magistrate to be required to deliver a punishment which is just, but, on present sentencing law and practice, includes prospects for rehabilitation of the offender, and restitution to the victim.[12] He or she should try to avoid any direct reference to general deterrence or incapacitation of the offender and, of course, the approach to imposing sentence must be consistent with the approach taken for similar offences.[13] The decision is expected to be made promptly (for there are many more similar judgments to be made in a busy list) and often with very little information other than the prosecution's brief outline of the circumstances surrounding the offence.[14] Even if the offender is represented, there are problems. For while the court is considering the perfect disposition for this offender, it must continue to function judicially, to ensure that the offender receives natural justice, to conduct the proceedings fairly and without abuse of process and to "administer equal justice to all suitors in open Court".[15] The difficulties are compounded when there are so few formalities to ensure that anything more than the minimum amount of information is before the court.

The sentencing procedure in the higher courts tends to be somewhat more structured,[16] but the practice can and does vary. Just how these variations affect the sentencing process is a fertile area for research, but common sense[17] suggests that serious differences in the quality of information put before a sentencing court must result in seriously inconsistent and probably unfair sentencing decisions. Good decisions flow from a consideration of accurate, balanced and relevant information.

---

12 These are the recommendations of the A.L.R.C., Report No. 44, *Sentencing*, Summary of Recommendations, pars. 1-9.

13 Ibid.

14 In Western Australia, magistrates rarely have the benefit of hearing addresses from prosecution counsel. While the D.P.P. and some State Government prosecutions are presented by lawyers, most police prosecutions are done by police officers. The information accompanying their brief varies from little to none at all. They work under extreme pressure and tend to keep their presentation to the bare minimum. This can work unfairly and have an adverse effect on the sentencing decision.

15 *Scott v. Scott* [1912] P. 241 at 287, per Farwell L.J.: cited with approval by Deane and Gaudron JJ. in *Coulter v. The Queen* (1988) 62 A.L.J.R. 74.

16 The usual procedure is described by Bishop, op. cit., pp. 177-182.

17 Not to mention appellate review.

The sentencer can be placed in serious difficulties when the offender is *not* represented. It is proposed to consider some of these problems.

Sentencing Unrepresented Offenders on a Plea of Guilty

The value to the court, and to the offender, of legal representation is obvious when the problems of dealing with unrepresented offenders are briefly considered.

To echo the warning of Murphy J. in *McInnis*,[18] the assistance of the court is a poor substitute for counsel. The caveat is as valid for some sentencing exercises in magistrates' courts as it is for hearing the so-called more serious offences in the superior courts. It is not the court's role to assist the offender. Attempts to assist an unrepresented party have been described as 'serving to only "gloss over procedural injustice".[19] The function of a sentencing court is judicial.[20] It cannot effectively discharge the obligations of counsel for the defence.

The unrepresented offender is at least as vulnerable in the sentencing process as at trial—some would say more so. Conviction is often a foregone conclusion. The sentence is the dread reckoning. Accepting that some seasoned criminals will be able to look after themselves, to be unrepresented at sentence can seriously disadvantage the offender. The young, the elderly, the mentally incapacitated, the poorly educated and the illiterate are usually in no position to plead their own case in mitigation. Unrepresented offenders rarely have the confidence to challenge the prosecution version of the facts or events surrounding the offence, or to evaluate the seriousness of the offence or their role in it. They cannot realistically remind the court of sentencing options. Their explanations tend to be confusing, conflicting or ill constructed. Sometimes they are unbelievable[21] or patently false.

In dealing with an unrepresented offender, a court can be led into error in at least two ways, both with serious consequences for the criminal justice system. First, the sheer inexperience or incompetence of the offender who attempts to offer his or her own version of a plea in mitigation can lead the court to error through omission of relevant information which has not been brought to its attention. There may be information vital to the sentencing decision which is solely within the knowledge of the offender but never divulged to the court. Secondly, the sentencing decision may be concluded on a totally false understanding.

---

[18] *McInnis v. The Queen* (1979) 54 A.L.J.R. 122 at 128.

[19] Ibid., at 128, per Murphy J.

[20] It has been likened to an administrative decision: R. Jackson, *The Machinery of Justice in England* (7th ed., Cambridge University Press), p. 389. The association appears to have been identified with a view to suggesting that sentencing decisions, like administrative decisions, should be made by those who must take responsibility for carrying out the work involved. With respect, the suggestion is not helpful. Sentencers must, of course, act responsibly, but it is asking far too much to insist that they are responsible for carrying out the sentence. It is enough that a decision is made.

[21] For two recent examples, see *Nekuda* (1988) 12 Crim.L.J. 258 (Supreme Court of New South Wales) and *Mudd* (1988) 10 Cr.App.R. (S.) 22 (C.A.).

The unrepresented offender has no duty to the court. When an explanation is given in mitigation, the offender is rarely if ever sworn. And while a court is not expected to accept a completely unbelievable plea in mitigation,[22] it is bound to give some weight to any explanation offered and it can be misled into imposing a manifestly inappropriate sentence.[23] In either case, the result is serious. In the former, the offender may be sentenced erroneously through having lost an important opportunity to explain his or her conduct. In the latter, the court may be cynically exploited. In both cases, confidence in the sentencing process is eroded.

If the offender is unrepresented, important information relevant to sentence is likely to be poorly presented and may be wrong. This permits a court to make a sentencing decision based on information which is at best unbalanced and at worst erroneous.

Recognition of the Value of Defence Counsel

The High Court endorsed the importance of legal representation during a criminal trial in *McInnes*.[24] All members of the Bench recognised the right to counsel and Barwick C.J. clearly accepted that it was in the best interests of the administration of justice that an offender be represented.[25] The case is not precisely in point as it did not specially deal with the question of legal representation at the sentencing. However, in view of the crucial importance of the sentencing process to the offender, it is difficult to see how the court would not endorse the principle a fortiori when the criminal trial comes to the point of sentencing. As many people no doubt remember, it was in the same case that Murphy J. (who was in dissent on the question of whether an appeal should have been granted) delivered his eloquent plea for the right to legal representation for all offenders whether or not they were able to pay for it.[26] He also expressly adopted the words of Sutherland J. in *Powell v. Alabama*[27] that even the intelligent and educated layman required "the guiding hand of counsel *at every step in the proceedings against him*" (emphasis added).

It is perhaps a matter of some regret that in Australia, a defendant is not obliged to be represented at trial or at sentence,[28] and that there is

22 Ibid.

23 Prosecuting counsel can also be trapped. Relevant points omitted from comment at the sentencing cannot be used to mount an appeal against an inadequate sentence: *Tait* (1979) 46 F.L.R. 386 at 389.

24 *McInnis v. The Queen* (1979) 54 A.L.J.R. 122.

25 Ibid., at 123.

26 It was also responsible for the Western Australian Legal Aid Commission changing its policy on the granting of legal assistance to persons charged with serious criminal charges.

27 (1932) 287 U.S. 45 at 68-69.

28 The position in England is now governed by special legislation. Once convicted, an offender cannot receive a custodial sentence for the *first time* unless he or she is legally represented or has applied for legal aid and been refused on a means test or has had the opportunity of applying for legal aid but has not taken that opportunity: *Powers of Criminal Courts Act* 1973, s. 21; *Criminal Justice Act* 1982, s. 3.

no requirement that the court appoint a member of the Bar to assist, even where the offender is facing a sentence of imprisonment.[29] In theory at least, competent legal representation at the sentencing benefits the offender and the court alike.

What then is the special ingredient that legal representation adds to the dramatic unfolding of the sentencing drama?

Defence Counsel—A Balancing Factor

The finest traditions of the Bar expect defence lawyers to comply strictly with their rules of professional conduct and to display at all times independence, objectivity, diligence and courtesy. Drawing on their knowledge and experience of the law and the courts, it is assumed that they will provide accurate and ethical advice to their client. An offender should be confident of being represented properly and in the manner that is ultimately the most advantageous in all the circumstances.[30]

The presence of defence counsel at court also raises certain expectations for the sentencer. The court does not expect to be deceived or misled[31] and it assumes that counsel appreciates the need to avoid unnecessary expense or waste the court's time.[32] Generally counsel is courteous.[33] Of specific significance to the court is the obligation that falls on all advocates to ensure that the court is advised of any decision or legislation relevant to the issue before it, whether or not it assists the advocate's contention.[34]

With the courts and academic commentators favouring more input from prosecution counsel,[35] it is now arguable that legal representation at sentence should be mandatory in the interests of procedural fairness. Strong and fulsome comments from prosecution counsel on current sentencing law and theories, and appropriate penalty, require balancing comment on behalf of the offender.

But how is this balancing act performed?

The Sentencing Inquiry—A Trial on the Facts

The function of defence counsel is regarded by many lawyers as reasonably straightforward and not particularly onerous: a plea in mitigation is required. Obviously it is an important part of the process, but it is not always the first concern, especially when the sentencing follows a plea of guilty. Sometimes intervention is required immediately after the court has heard the prosecution version of the offender's role in the

---

[29] Although in Western Australia the court does occasionally request the assistance of one of the solicitors who happen to be servicing the Duty Lawyer Scheme on that day.

[30] The Law Society of Western Australia, *Professional Conduct Rules*, rr. 12 and 13.1.

[31] Ibid., r. 13.2.

[32] Ibid., r. 13.4(b).

[33] It is required by all *Professional Conduct Rules*: ibid., r. 13.4(a).

[34] Ibid., r. 13.5.

[35] Supra, n. 8.

charge. More and more, serious differences between the prosecution and defence versions of relevant sentencing facts are being resolved only after the calling of evidence to establish an accurate factual basis on which to ground the sentencing decision.

For several reasons, this process creates difficulties. First, the plea of guilty admits only those facts necessary to prove the charge. It acknowledges no circumstances of aggravation which the prosecution might allege and offers no matters of mitigation arising from knowledge peculiar to the offender alone. If the prosecution asserts aggravated circumstances which are denied by the offender, or if the offender claims mitigating material which the prosecution disputes, sworn evidence should be taken and the facts determined by judicial process.[36] But the court cannot compel an offender to give sworn evidence.[37] It can only seek clarification from the prosecution.[38] So if a dispute arises from unsworn statements on either side, it is usually thought that a sentencer has a duty to act on that version of the facts which is most favourable to the offender within the bounds of reasonable possibility.[39] This raises the second concern: the degree of persuasion required to be discharged. In South Australia and New South Wales *Woolmington*[40] appears to apply so that the criminal standard of proof is required. But in Victoria the courts have adopted a variable degree of persuasion to be adjusted according to the nature and consequences of the relevant circumstances.[41] The position in Western Australia is unclear. Burt C.J. appeared to adopt the *Woolmington* line in *Aloia*,[42] but his observations are, with respect, equivocal to some extent. He asserts that "some" evidence must be led to support mitigating facts which are challenged by the prosecution, but he then retreats.[43] To use his words: "This is not to say that the accused carries the onus of establishing them." He says that a statement from the Bar table alleging an "exculpatory primary fact" but with no evidence capable of supporting it cannot be enough if it is challenged by the prosecution. But, with respect, he fails to explain how and when "enough is enough".

---

36 The English courts have developed the so-called *Newton* hearing to deal with disputed facts on guilty pleas. The procedure was suggested by Lord Lane C.J. in *Newton* (1982) 4 Cr.App.R. (S.) 388, and subsequent decisions have led to the development of a sophisticated series of rules which are now applied to *Newton* hearings. A recent fascinating innovation is the adoption with approval by Lord Lane C.J. of the "Manchester Technique": *Asher Sivan & Ors* (1988) 10 Cr.App.R. (S.) 282. There has been no consistent development along these lines in Australia.

37 *Law v. Deed* [1970] S.A.S.R. 374.

38 *Van Pelz* [1943] K.B. 157; *Butterwasser* [1947] 2 All E.R. 415.

39 *Law v. Deed* [1970] S.A.S.R. 374 at 377; *Martin* [1981] 2 N.S.W.L.R. 640; *Aloia* [1983] W.A.R. 133 at 136.

40 [1935] A.C. 462. See *Saffron* (1988) 39 A.Crim.R. 123.

41 There is an excellent discussion in Fox and Freiberg, op. cit., pp. 51-54.

42 *Aloia* [1983] W.A.R. 133. But see the more recent decision of *Xiao* (1989) 40 A.Crim.R. 468 where the civil standard was applied.

43 *Aloia* [1983] W.A.R. 133 at 136.

Problems of a similar nature may also emerge at the return of a pre-sentence report. A single judge of the Supreme Court of Victoria offered a novel solution in *O'Keefe v. Tankard.*[44] Unfortunately, the decision failed to resolve the difficulties discussed above, but it bears some consideration.

O'Keefe v. Tankard—A Suggested Compromise

The question before the court was whether a magistrate had erred in law in failing to permit an offender to cross-examine the maker of certain statements contained in a pre-sentence report, or to call evidence relating to some of the matters raised in the report. It was claimed in the grounds of appeal that the particular statements under challenge had been taken into account by the magistrate when the sentencing discretion had been exercised.

Nathan J. was very clearly of the view that the offender should have been given the opportunity to test and evaluate the disputed assertion. With respect, he was quite correct. The interests of procedural fairness and natural justice required it. However, when he came to rule on the procedure for testing and evaluating disputed statements, he took an unusual line. He would only permit the statement in dispute to be tested by permitting its maker to be "examined"[45]—a word which, in his own assessment, had been chosen "carefully". This "examination" was not, he said, synonymous with "cross-examination". He offered two reasons for so concluding. The first was that, in his view, the opinions of the maker of the statement were not critical to the issues of proving the charge and were not therefore "evidence-in-chief". The second was based on public policy: the need for people to be fearless and frank in expressing their opinions about offenders in the preparation of pre-sentence reports had to be balanced with the basic requirement that a court should not act on untested or unsubstantiated opinion. He believed these last two principles could be accommodated by permitting "examination", which gave the maker of a disputed claim the opportunity to justify the statement, but not "cross-examination", especially of an "oppressive" or "fishing" nature.

While it is possible to sympathise with his Honour's rationalisation of the granting of a diluted right to "examine" someone whose statement is relevant to sentence *and* disputed, it is just as easy to be critical. To suggest that yet another method of fact-finding should be tolerated within the sentencing process is to invite more confusion. Why shouldn't the maker of a statement contained in a pre-sentence report be subjected to a rigorous cross-examination? The offender's liberty may be at stake. And why should a person be exempted from normal fact-finding techniques merely because his or her statements are not critical to issues *proving the charge*? The sentencing decision has far more impact on the offender than the mere conviction.

---

44 [1989] V.R. 371.
45 Ibid., at 373-374.

Even if the compromise suggested by Nathan J. were to be universally accepted, it would create more uncertainty than it would correct. It offers no protection to the offender whose counsel fails to challenge unacceptable statements in these types of reports, nor does it usefully explain how or when permissible "examination" becomes unacceptable "cross-examination". The defence lawyer is caught in yet another procedural maze. The sentencing process deserves better direction.[46]

In 1987 the Australian Law Reform Commission[47] drew attention to some of the problems caused by the lack of accepted formalities regulating what is, after all, a "trial" on the facts. In the Commission's view, it has not only contributed to unfairness in the sentencing process but it has the clear potential to "wreak havoc with the consistent application of sentencing goals and methods". With the focus of the legal profession then so clearly on these difficulties, it was a great disappointment to see the High Court relinquish an opportunity to offer better guidance in *Pantorno v. The Queen*.[48] This was a case which highlighted concerns arising from some of these areas of difficulty and yielded a somewhat surprising result: the High Court granting an offender special leave to appeal against sentence on the basis that he had been denied natural justice, despite the fact that he was said to have been competently represented at the sentencing hearing.

The case deserves scrutiny both for what it says and what it fails to say on the subject of the role of defence counsel in the sentencing process.

The Pantorno Case

The circumstances in *Pantorno* were, in some respects, unusual and, in others, typical. Problems arose out of what should have been a straightforward sentencing following a plea of guilty to a charge of being in possession of heroin contrary to the *Drugs Poisons and Controlled Substances Act* 1981 (Vic.). Defence counsel had sought a custodial sentence to be served *concurrently* with earlier sentences and urged the County Court to deal with Pantorno on the basis that he had possession of the drug solely for his own use. The relevant legislation prescribed a lesser penalty for unlawful possession where the court was satisfied on the balance of probabilities that the offender was not trafficking in the drug. Nevertheless, the court imposed a sentence of 12 months imprisonment *cumulatively* with prior sentences, the County Court judge

[46] The same sort of problem was dealt with differently by the Supreme Court of Western Australia in *Morse v. The Queen* [1977] W.A.R. 151. The question under discussion was the limits to which the Crown could go in proving the offender's "antecedents". Several statements in the relevant "antecedent report" were under challenge. The Full Court (in a judgment delivered by Burt C.J.) avoided the issue by the simple and popular device of admonishing the original sentencer for permitting the prosecution to lead hearsay evidence and for making findings based on that evidence. The decision is unsatisfactory for the burden it places on the sentencer. No comment is made on the apparent failure of defence counsel to lead any evidence to contradict the prosecution hearsay.

[47] A.L.R.C., op. cit., pp. 28-29.

[48] (1989) 63 A.L.J.R. 317.

announcing that he was not prepared to accept counsel's statement from the Bar table that the offender was not a trafficker.

It transpired that a decision of the Victorian Court of Criminal Appeal (*Bridges*)[49] which should have affected both the way Pantorno was represented at sentence and the method of sentencing, was overlooked by the three main performers: the prosecution and defence lawyers and the judge. *Bridges* was relevant to the initial sentencing because it was authority for the proposition that there was no "jurisdiction" to sentence a person as a trafficker without a positive finding that the drug was possessed for the purpose of trafficking. What was unusual was that *Bridges* was then actually reversed by the Court of Criminal Appeal in Pantorno's own appeal on sentence and before the matter came to the High Court.

Mason C.J. and Brennan J. appeared to have some initial reluctance to grant the appeal. They were somewhat scathing of the claim that defence counsel had not addressed on the relevance of *Bridges* and had not attempted to discharge any onus of proof because it was assumed that the sentencer knew of the decision and of the Crown's practice of averring aggravating circumstances if the prosecution alleged that the offender was a trafficker. But their Honours eventually concluded that the sentencing judge was in error for not giving defence counsel the opportunity to demonstrate the reason why Pantorno was not liable to be sentenced as a trafficker. Deane, Toohey and Gaudron JJ. also found fault with the County Court. They held that in the circumstances it was incumbent on the sentencing judge "to indicate to counsel his lack of acceptance of the underlying assumption upon which the submissions upon sentence had been made".[50] They concluded that Pantorno had lost any opportunity at first instance to call the evidence required because the sentencing judge had inadvertently failed to follow *Bridges* and was therefore effectively denied procedural fairness at the sentencing. For them, even the Court of Criminal Appeal's conclusion that the sentencer's failure to apply *Bridges* had nevertheless led to a situation where the sentencer's decision was correct, did not cure the "essential vice" of the original finding.

The decision seems to herald a healthy obsession with procedural fairness at all costs. It also seems obliquely to overrule *Halden*[51] which indicated that a judge was under no obligation to inform counsel that he was disinclined to accept a version of the facts proposed by counsel from the Bar table, but unsupported by evidence.[52] But at the same time,

---

[49] (1986) 20 A.Crim.R. 271.

[50] *Pantorno* (1989) 63 A.L.J.R. 317 at 324.

[51] (1983) 9 A.Crim.R. 30.

[52] The decision of the Court of Criminal Appeal in *Halden* was not referred to in *Pantorno*. Murphy J., in *Halden* (at 40), had also made it very clear that, when the plea was made, it was "incumbent upon counsel for the prisoner to take objection to such parts of the material which counsel" knew were before the sentencer and were inadmissible against the offender. The sentencer should then make a ruling and permit the calling of further evidence as appropriate.

there are some internal inconsistencies which result in the High Court appearing to both overestimate and underestimate defence counsels' duties and obligations to the court and to the offender at the sentencing inquiry. With the greatest respect to the learned justices, the sentencing judge in the County Court seems to have been made the scapegoat for complacent and presumptuous counsel on either side. An unrealistic burden has been placed on the sentencing court to forgive counsel for failing to bring relevant authority to the court's attention and yet to expect the court to assume full responsibility for a mutual neglect or misapprehension. As Mason C.J. and Brennan J. were quick to note, the County Court did not prevent defence counsel from discharging the onus that the legislation required,[53] and yet the sentencer was said to be in error for denying counsel the opportunity to discharge the onus. It is also hard to reconcile statements such as "a court is under no duty to a party to advise him how to present his case", and "the responsibilities of counsel cannot be assumed by the court", and "we would not hold that there is some general duty . . . to warn a convicted person or his counsel of the onus imposed . . . merely because no attempt is made to discharge it",[54] with the decision to grant leave to appeal based on the court's obligation to ensure that the "accused"[55] was not taken by surprise. The unusual circumstances may well have induced a breach of natural justice, but it seems harsh to lay the blame for the breach at the foot of the court, especially where the offender was represented.

For the sake of consistency, it is hoped that the decision will not be interpreted as a reason to reject the long-standing rule of professional conduct which requires defence counsel to inform the court as soon as practicable of any procedural irregularity of which he or she is aware.[56] Although this requirement is generally directed at matters which arise prior to verdict, there is no reason for it to be so restricted and equally, no reason for it to be rejected simply because the court is dealing with a sentencing process.

On the positive side, the language used by Mason C.J. and Brennan J. in *Pantorno* to describe the sentencing process is significant. They recognise that the proceedings are adversarial and use the terms of criminal trial procedure to describe what occurred at the sentencing in the County Court.[57] It is comforting finally to have High Court acceptance of the importance of the sentencing process and to have such a strong endorsement of the need for procedural fairness. A complaint that a jury trial had miscarried for similar reasons could not have been more carefully analysed. But it is an enormous disappointment to note the omission of any meaningful direction from the court as to how sentencing

53 *Pantorno* (1989) A.L.J.R. 317 at 320.

54 Ibid., at 320.

55 By the use of the word "accused", their Honours appear to be content to equate the sentencing procedure with the trial procedure. See below.

56 See supra, n. 34 and comments of Murphy J. in *Halden* (1983) 9 A.Crim.R. 30.

57 Including referring to the offender as "the accused": supra, n. 55.

trials should be conducted and the appropriate burden of proof to be applied. Perhaps silence indicates a tacit acceptance of the continuing strength of *Woolmington's* golden thread. If it does, how frustrating to find that it is not clearly enunciated.

The decision may also be construed as an indication from the High Court that while the Crown may be estopped from appealing against sentence when it has failed to raise a point at the sentencing, the defence is not so restricted.[58] It would be unfortunate if this were the result as it would tend to permit defence counsel to participate in the sentencing released from the professional responsibility that is so vital to the process as a whole, namely, to draw all significant matters to the attention of the judge or court as soon as practicable. No one has ever seriously suggested that as soon as practicable means "on appeal".

If all sentencing inquiries were given the status of a trial and attracted the strict rules of procedure and evidence that have been formulated expressly for the purpose, the various participants in the process would be far better directed in their role. Their duties and obligations to the offender and to each other would be known. The High Court has given the lead in *Pantorno*. It remains to be seen whether the working courts will take the hint and treat the sentencing as seriously as the trial.

Of course, as was noted earlier, it is not every sentencing which requires the determination of disputed facts. However, when the need does arise, it is embarrassing for all parties, and of particular concern to defence counsel, to have so little consistent authority to guard their performance. There is too much confusion and too little direction.

Arising from the discussion in *Pantorno*, and a topic which presents enormous scope for argument and debate is the question of the delicate balance that defence counsel are expected to maintain between their duty to the court as an advocate and their obligations and responsibilities to their client. The dilemma may arise for defence counsel at any stage in the sentencing process, but it tends to be at its most acute during the plea in mitigation. Why? What is a plea in mitigation?

The Plea in Mitigation

Not all defence counsel share the noble sentiments of Sir David Napley that the purpose of the plea in mitigation is to assist the court "to arrive at what seems to be the least punishment consistent with justice".[59]

---

58 This would be contrary to some serious comments from the Court of Appeal in *Edwards* (1983) 77 Cr.App.R. 5 at 8-9, per Robert Goff L.J. for the court: "We consider it to be inconceivable that counsel for the defence, acting in the best interests of their client, could have failed to draw this serious omission in the summing up to the attention of the judge." The case is not strictly in point as it refers to the conduct of defence counsel at trial, but it is submitted that the same considerations should apply. The case is discussed by Roderick Munday, "The Duties of Defence Counsel" [1983] Crim.L.R. 703.

59 Sir David Napley, *The Technique of Persuasion* (2nd ed., 1975), p. 140.

Counsel usually aim at getting the lightest possible sentence for the offender and it is clearly the view of at least one commentator that the goal of defence counsel is not to strive for a disposition most favourable to society, but one most favourable to the offender.[60] This view, which is shared by many criminal lawyers in Western Australia, requires the channelling of all efforts to the benefit of the offender "though the heavens fall"[61] and is consistent with the adversarial nature of a full criminal trial. As mentioned above, the High Court appears to support that view of the sentencing process in *Pantorno*.[62] Of course, the sentence most favourable to the offender is not necessarily the lightest sentence. But this distinction is usually lost on the client and generally ignored by counsel. Fox and Freiberg[63] also seem to overlook the delicacy of the point by asserting that the aim of defence counsel is to obtain the least punitive measure available for the offence. It is very probable that it is this misconception of the role of defence counsel in delivering the plea in mitigation that has contributed more than anything else to Professor Ashworth's polite lament that the reliability of speeches in mitigation remains "an open question".[64]

That even experienced counsel have misunderstood their obligations to their client and to the court was starkly illustrated in the recent case of *Rumpf*.[65] The case demands a detailed analysis in this context.

The Rumpf Case

The case concerned an appeal by the Director for Public Prosecutions against sentences imposed by Hampel J. at first instance for offences involving the promotion of tax evasion schemes. Rumpf had pleaded guilty to the charges and was effectively sentenced to two years and three months imprisonment. He was also ordered to make reparation to the Commonwealth of nearly half a million dollars. The prosecution appealed and the sentences were increased to three years and six months, plus a fine of $35,000. The reparation order stood. Imagine the surprise of the Full Court when two days after the appeal, Rumpf's defence counsel (senior and junior) blithely advised the Registrar of Criminal Appeal that their client was an undischarged bankrupt. They sought an opportunity to make submissions as to why it was not appropriate to impose a penalty by way of fine. This intelligence prompted a summoning of all parties back to the court to provide some most specific information. Understandably, the court was extremely concerned to know why the sentencing judge was not informed of Rumpf's bankruptcy when the

---

60 E. L. Greenspan, "The Role of the Defence Lawyer in Sentencing", in B. A. Grosman (ed.), *New Directions in Sentencing* (Butterworth & Co. (Canada) Ltd, 1980), p. 265.

61 Ibid.

62 (1989) 63 A.L.J.R. 317.

63 Op. cit., p. 42.

64 A. Ashworth, *Sentencing and Penal Policy* (Weidenfeld and Nicolson, London, 1983), p. 424.

65 *R. v. Rumpf* [1988] V.R. 466 (Full Court).

reparation order had been made. Even more alarm was raised when, shortly after receiving news of Rumpf's prior bankruptcy, the court discovered of its own volition and "as part of the ordinary information which comes to judges as to the work of their own court"[66] that Rumpf had been committed for contempt of court by yet another member of the court and well *before* he had first appeared before Hampel J. for sentence. His imprisonment had apparently been imposed when Rumpf had disposed of significant assets in breach of a Mareva injunction. He remained incarcerated as a direct result of the contempt, both at the first instance sentencing and at the appeal. Thus, at the time of plea and sentence, Rumpf was an undischarged bankrupt and was imprisoned under two orders committing him for contempt of court. What was the justification for the decision on the part of defence counsel to omit this intelligence from the plea in mitigation? It must have been known to Rumpf's legal representatives.

Rumpf's defence counsel presumably felt the omission was warranted by the long-standing recognition by the courts and the legal profession of the rule of professional conduct that relieves defence counsel of any duty to disclose facts which are known to him or her, or to correct any information given by the prosecution, if disclosure or correction would be to the client's detriment. If the prosecution had not raised the issues, defence counsel were not obliged to enlighten the court. The sentencing seems to have been a torrid affair with Rumpf's senior counsel vigorously objecting to all inadmissible evidence advanced by the prosecution. But Rumpf's counsel took two significant extra steps. They first advanced as a mitigating factor the compensatory effect of a reparation order which the court could (and did) make. This suggested Rumpf's ability to discharge it. They then referred to express instructions to call no character evidence; senior counsel then told the sentencing judge that his client had no previous convictions. Did these submissions amount to an ethical breach of the profession's conduct rules and of defence counsels' duty to the court?

McGarvie J., delivering the reasons of the Full Court, pronounced it "beyond question" that, in the circumstances, the sentencing judge should have been fully informed of the bankruptcy and the committal to prison for contempt.[67] He relied on a long-standing rule of professional conduct for counsel: no lawyer shall knowingly deceive or mislead the court.[68] On the bankruptcy issue, the urging of the compensatory effect of a reparation order as a mitigating factor demanded a revelation of Rumpf's solvency, if it were known to counsel. The failure to address on his bankruptcy, however innocently made, was likely to mislead the court. McGarvie J. did not consider the question of any ethical misdemeanour. Rumpf's defence counsel were given the benefit of the doubt as to their knowledge of their client's bankruptcy. They were fortunate. A person's

[66] Ibid., at 469, per McGarvie J.
[67] Ibid., at 470, per McGarvie J.
[68] In Western Australia, this rule appears in the *Professional Conduct Rules*, supra, nn. 30 and 31.

financial circumstances, especially the question of creditworthiness, invariably forms a vital part of instructions relevant to a plea.[69] How could an offer to make reparations have been seriously advanced without first obtaining all instructions on the ability of the offender actually to make the repayments? It is difficult to understand how such vital information could have escaped the attention of the legal advisers on either side.

The contempt issue brought the court closer to a full scrutiny of the ethics of defence counsels' failure fully to advise the sentencing judge of Rumpf's status as an offender "with no prior convictions". But again counsel received gentle treatment from the Full Court. The court was prepared to accept that in the absence of comment by defence counsel on the lack of prior convictions there would have been no duty to disclose the contempt orders. It believed that it was not until the clear record of the offender was offered in mitigation that the duty to the court altered: it was only the reliance on Rumpf's good record which caused the court to be misled as to the offender's antecedents. Only then was full disclosure of the conduct leading to the committal for contempt demanded. The reliance was not diminished or qualified by senior counsel's statement that he was instructed not to call any character evidence, nor was the mention that Rumpf was in custody for contempt on two counts sufficient to inform the sentencing judge about the committals.

Needless to say, the sentence was increased.

The decision is significant for its recognition of the general uncertainty attaching to questions of what should be placed before the court and what should be disclosed by both defence and prosecution in pleas on sentence. It also contains serious concerns for defence lawyers in particular, and for law reformers in general, by its acceptance that defence lawyers may have difficulty in knowing whether, in particular situations, their duty to the court or their duty to the client prevails. But, with respect, it is not entirely clear that the Full Court of Victoria offered anything more than the most general guidance as to *when* the duty to the court prevails. On one reading of the decision, the court has played down the duties of defence counsel and forgiven them their indiscretions by shifting the bulk of the burden—to fully inform the sentencing court and to prevent it being misled—to the prosecution. The prosecution did escape direct criticism, but not a sermon on the importance of an adequate presentation of all of the facts. In the words of McGarvie J.:

> "In my opinion it is beyond question that, in the circumstances of this case, information as to Rumpf's bankruptcy and as to his committal to prison for contempt of court should have been placed in proper form before the sentencing judge and this Court."[69a]

---

[69] It is interesting to observe that this is exactly the type of information that all defence lawyers are urged to obtain during the preparation of a plea in mitigation by G. A. Hampel Q.C. in "Plea Making: Concepts, Preparation and Presentation of Pleas" (1978) 52 *Law Institute Journal* 99. The writer of that article became Rumpf's original sentencing judge.

[69a] [1988] V.R. 466 at 470.

The decision is valuable for the careful analysis of the duties and responsibilities of prosecuting counsel in the sentencing process. Certainty as to the role of the prosecutor creates a firmer basis for certainty as to the role of defence counsel. How disappointing then that the actions of defence counsel at the original sentencing did not receive more critical appraisal. The questions that arose are exactly the points that arise every day for a busy criminal lawyer.

Perhaps even more significant is the very clear warning to all advocates of the serious error of submitting half-truths to support a plea in mitigation. At last there is a recognition of the sin of fraud by omission on the part of the advocate.

The test in *Peek v. Gurney*[70] was applied to identify unethical behaviour and the Full Court's comments were not directed solely at defence counsel. The clear message is that the prosecution's delivery should be similarly constrained. There is nothing in the observations of McGarvie J. to suggest otherwise.

The seriousness of the advocate's dilemma deriving from the dual allegiances to court and client has received recent comment from the High Court in *Gianarelli v. Wraith.*[71] Although the case did not deal specifically with the role of defence counsel at the sentencing, it contains strong dicta from the Chief Justice which cannot be overlooked. The case is significant for the recognition, at the highest level, of the need to reconcile the duties that lawyers owe to their clients with the duties and obligations that are due to the court.

For Mason C.J., the choice is very clear. Counsels' duty to their clients is subject to their "overriding duty to the court".[72] Attendant on the performance of this "overriding duty" is, in his view, a strong element of public interest. And he asserts, no doubt to the surprise of many defence lawyers, that:

> ". . . the performance by counsel of his paramount duty to the court will require him to act in a variety of ways *to the possible disadvantage of his client.*"[73] (Emphasis added.)

It is obvious from the context of this assertion by the Chief Justice of the High Court of Australia that his Honour intended this duty to apply equally to criminal and civil trials. And as it affects the duties of defence lawyers at criminal trials, it is submitted that it must apply a fortiori at the sentencing.

The duties are put even more forcefully in the next paragraph where Mason C.J. describes them as paramount and to be performed "even if the client gives instructions to the contrary".[74] He acknowledges as inevitable that some counsel tend to act as mere "agents" of their clients,

---

70 (1873) L.R. 6 H.L. 377 at 392.
71 (1988) 62 A.L.J.R. 611 (Full Court).
72 Ibid., at 613.
73 Ibid.
74 Ibid.

but proclaims in the clearest terms that these counsel are acting to the "detriment of the interests of the court and the administration of justice generally". It is hard to imagine a better endorsement of the line taken by McGarvie J. in *Rumpf*.

The judicial line in *Rumpf* and *Gianarelli v. Wraith* is consistent to some extent: when there appears to be a conflict between advocates' duties to their clients and to the court, the duties to the court prevail. In the High Court, Mason C.J. also endorsed the rule that counsel are required to draw the court's attention to any irregularity in the conduct of a criminal trial immediately it arises: grounds of appeal are not to be "kept up the sleeve" of counsel. Acceptance of this rule is implied in *Rumpf*.

It is more difficult to reconcile *Rumpf* and *Pantorno*. In both cases defence counsel were spared any direct criticism from the Bench even though, in each instance, it is arguable that they had failed to discharge their duties to the court in complete conformity with accepted standards —in *Rumpf*, through over-zealousness, and in *Pantorno*, through complacency. In both cases, the court was misled by counsel's omissions with significantly different effects. Thus, in *Rumpf* the sentence of the offender was increased while in *Pantorno* it must be assumed that the offender's sentence was eventually reduced. If only more attention had been given to the role played by defence counsel in these two cases.

Conclusion

In the result, we have a series of recent pronouncements from superior and very superior courts which give strong directions to all of the performers in the sentencing process. The tragedy is that they are aimed so inconsistently at one or other of the participants: prosecution, defence or sentencing authority. Defence counsel are poorly guided and are offered little overall certainty as to how they should act, and when.[75] The conduct of the plea in mitigation obviously requires compliance with the directions of the Full Court of Victoria in *Rumpf* and Mason C.J. in *Gianarelli v. Wraith*. But both cases contain only general rules of conduct and each sentencing exercise attracts a range of different considerations. The effects of the *Pantorno* decision are very difficult to predict. Its apparent abrogation of an overriding responsibility attaching to the role played by defence counsel raises serious concerns for the legal profession, not to mention the offender who often gives himself completely into the trust of his legal adviser.

Epilogue

A complete discussion on the modern role of defence counsel in the sentencing process would raise the vexed question of the extent of their

---

[75] The matters raised in the last few years have not been resolved as easily as those raised in, for example, *Tuckiar v. The King* (1934) 52 C.L.R. 335 (Full Court), or *Clyne v. The New South Wales Bar Association* (1960) 104 C.L.R. 186 (Full Court). The current issues are more subtle.

role. The debate as to when the performance begins and when it ends is worthy of several separate papers.

Most experienced lawyers believe that the role of defence counsel should extend to advice on plea[76] but not all accept that this includes plea bargaining or charge bargaining.[77] In any event, early and accurate advice is invaluable. A decision, on good advice and freely made, to plead guilty places the defence lawyer and the offender in a much better position to prepare for the sentencing process. For example, if relevant, reparations can be made to the victim and full character references can be obtained. The offender may be able to commence a rehabilitation programme and present a positive plan for the future to the court. If a gaol sentence is inevitable, the offender's family may start preparing for the incarceration and make adjustments to their own requirements in good time. If a licence disqualification is mandatory, similar contingency plans can be made. A decent interval between the decision to plead guilty and the delivery of sentence also allows counsel the time properly to research sentencing options and trends, locate relevant authorities to assist the court, liaise with the prosecution to confirm the allegations that will be made relevant to the charge and the offender's part in it, and, most importantly, formulate a sensible and appropriate sentencing proposal for the court to consider. The entire sentencing process is enhanced by good preparation, and, if in the course of proceedings, and before the matter has been to court, the prosecution discretion is exercised in favour of the offender, defence counsel should advise and guide their clients.

The role of defence counsel must also extend beyond the task of objecting to inadmissible evidence offered by the prosecution in support of facts relevant to the offence or the offender, beyond the delivery of the plea in mitigation, or beyond the gathering of extra pre-sentence information. *O'Keefe v. Tankard* demonstrated one aspect of the need for continued vigilance even at and beyond the return of a pre-sentence report. Nor does the pronouncement of sentence signal the curtain-call for defence counsel. A complicated sentence may require a translation. Defence counsel should be present in court when sentence is delivered to clarify any unusual points with the sentencer and to explain the effects

---

[76] The importance of having a thorough understanding of the charge and the relevant law cannot be overstated when so advising. There are also ethical problems that can arise: The Law Society of Western Australia, *Professional Conduct Rules*, rr. 14-15; G. A. Hampel Q.C., op. cit.

[77] No attempt has been made to discuss this topic here. The literature is vast and the decided cases are difficult to reconcile. Despite apparent criticism of the practice by the higher courts (see, for example, *Marshall* [1981] V.R. 725) there is no doubt that it exists. The procedure has developed its own set of rules in England from the seminal case of *Turner* [1970] 2 All E.R. 281, and, since 1980, there have been pre-trial reviews in some magisterial jurisdictions, the object being to explore the possibility of streamlining cases for trial by achieving some form of negotiated settlement: Adele Mulvaney, "Pre-trial Reviews: A Study in Six Magistrates' Courts" (1987) *Holdsworth Law Review* 120. For a comment on current thinking in Australia see Paul Byrne, "Plea Bargaining" (1988) 62 A.L.J. 799.

of the sentence to their client. Occasionally, advice on appeal may be necessary.

These, then, are some of the obvious elements of the role of defence counsel. They are functions that can be seen and understood by the offender or by any curious spectators of the sentencing drama. But much more important for the criminal justice system is the hidden role of defence counsel, the effects of which are not documented in legal manuals or taught by lawyers in forensic workshops. The hidden role is played only by competent, experienced and respected counsel, those persons whose very presence seems to have the magical effect of ensuring due process and natural justice. Of course, the presence of any defence counsel assists the regulation of the sentencing process. But it is the advocate in whom a court has confidence, the person who can be relied on to present only fair and accurate information in mitigation, who is more valuable to the sentencing process than all the rules that parliamentary counsel can draft or that parliament can promulgate. Defence counsel can, and should, provide the balance and the background: objectivity and impartiality. They are given every opportunity to draw the court's attention to the relevant law, the recent decisions and the latest trends: legal, criminological, penal, sociological, medical—there are few real limits. They can urge consistency of approach. They are a vital source of information about the offence and the offender. Adversaries to the prosecution, they are the invisible, but audible, friends of the court and supporters of the judicial system.

A common criticism of the current process of sentencing in Australia is that it is basically unregulated, that it has no real formalities or procedural rules. All of the cases discussed in this article demonstrate this phenomenon to some extent. But they also suggest a solution. The path is not yet clearly signposted, but there is some direction. The High Court has recognised the seriousness of the sentencing process in *Pantorno* and has ruled on some difficult ethical problems in *Gianarelli v. Wraith*. If a sentencing is treated as a trial, most of the formalities are already in place. Procedure can be adjusted to suit the seriousness of the offence.

A much graver concern should be to ensure that, whatever the procedure, the sentence is not erroneous. In an effort to correct errors, appeal courts tend to look for blame. Thus the question is: who can be blamed for a sentencing error? The usual scapegoat is the court—the original sentencer. It is an easy target and sometimes, it is an accurate one. The court can make mistakes. But why? The laying of blame will not eliminate error.

It is submitted that the obvious solution is the intelligent development of the role of defence counsel at all stages of the sentencing process. A more formal recognition by the courts of the importance of the part played by defence lawyers representing those offenders who have chosen to admit their guilt should enhance the sentencing process without the need for major reforms, more legislation or upheaval in the criminal justice system. A sentencer who has been thoroughly addressed by responsible and articulate counsel on either side is far less likely to be led into error. And a court is more willing to rely on defence counsel who act carefully in the interests of their clients and in the interests of justice and who are accountable for what is said and for the accuracy of the information placed before the court.

The four cases discussed in detail in this article show some of the trends[78] developing in the sentencing process. They also demonstrate several of the legal and ethical dilemmas facing defence counsel participating in the procedure. Unfortunately, only parts of the trends have been revealed and not all of the dilemmas have been solved. What is emerging, however, is the recognition of the need to develop the role of defence counsel in a more constructive way. With careful direction from the courts and with more concern for the spirit of their own professional conduct rules, lawyers performing the role of defence counsel have the perfect opportunity to improve the quality of the sentencing process. All that should be necessary is for their role to be more finely tuned, and their duties and obligations to the court and their clients properly balanced. They must receive clear direction so that they know their role and carry it out with all of the skill and competence which the legal profession, the public and the criminal justice system expects.

---

[78] It has been assumed that readers of this article are well aware of periodic judicial comment that has been made in most Australian States in such cases as *McIntosh* [1923] St.R.Qd 278, *Piercey* [1971] V.R. 647, *Beresford* (1972) 2 S.A.S.R. 446, *O'Neill* [1979] 2 N.S.W.L.R. 582 on the procedural formalities for ensuring a fair and accurate sentencing process. The case law is not consistent and the A.L.R.C. has recommended formal regulation of sentencing procedure, recognising the unsatisfactory nature of this piecemeal development: Australian Law Reform Commission, *Sentencing*, Report No. 44 (A.G.P.S., 1988), Ch. 6.

[9]

The Role of the Crown Prosecutor on Sentence

By I. G. Campbell, B.A., LL.M. (Syd.)
Senior Lecturer in Law, Queensland Institute of Technology

Summary

There is a gathering momentum in judicial calls for assistance by the Crown Prosecutor upon sentence, and a move away from the traditional reticence. These calls emphasise that the rationale for the active role is the unfairness of a rigorously argued Crown appeal against sentence, when the Crown's representative at trial did not assume responsibility for assisting the court in imposing sentence. The assistance requested goes well beyond the traditional role, and obliges address upon sentencing principles, arguments for or against particular types of sentence, and even address upon severity of punishment. The courts in New South Wales and Victoria have not been so ready to reject the traditional role for the Crown Prosecutor, and have emphasised that the power of the appellate courts is not to be constrained by the conduct of the trial by the Crown Prosecutor. One aspect which has yet to receive attention of the courts is the greater influence in pre-trial charge negotiation which appears to follow a greater sentencing activism by Crown Prosecutors.

Introduction

1. *Past Attitude: Hands Off*

The traditional attitude towards the pageant of the criminal trial is that once the verdict was handed down or plea was taken, the adversarial process was brought to an abrupt halt. For example, the Law Reform Commission of Canada has stated:

> "In most cases, the procedure during sentencing is not, and should not be, strictly adversarial as at trial."[1]

Despite the logical fallacy of presuming what ought to be from what is,[2] this is a view which commands respect in England. In the 1965 *Report of the Interdepartmental Committee on the Court of Criminal Appeal*[3] (the Donovan Committee) it was stated, in support of a conclusion that the Crown should not be given a right of appeal against sentence, that it was a matter of sound tradition that a prosecutor take little, or no, part in the sentencing

---

[1] "Restitution and Compensation", Queens Printer, Ottawa, 19 *Working Paper* No. 5 at 11, cited by Greenspan "The Role of the Defence Lawyer in Sentencing" in *New Directions in Sentencing* edited by Grosman, Butterworths, Toronto, 1980, at p. 264.

[2] Hume, *A Treatise of Human Nature*, 1751, iii, I, i. (Originally published 1739.)

[3] Cmnd 2755, 1965, par. 196.

processes of the courts, and these views were echoed in the later *Report of the Interdepartmental Committee on the Distribution of Criminal Business between the Crown Court and Magistrates Court*, which report was presented in 1976.[4] In particular, it is standard advice to English counsel that it would be wrong for the prosecutor to " . . . attempt by advocacy to influence the court towards a more severe sentence".[5]

Of course, the end of the adversarial contest at verdict or plea of guilty impeded only one of the contestants, the prosecutor, but, it is widely accepted that this monoculous view of sentencing stage of a criminal trial is correct.[6] This is not to say that there are not attempts to urge upon English prosecutors the assumption of a more active role.[7] However, these entreaties appear to have had little persuasive efficacy so far.[8]

Advocates of the traditional approach do concede that there is at least some minor role for prosecutors to address on sentence. Zellick lists several stages of possible involvement and concludes that, in England, prosecutors do not penetrate beyond the first stage. In this first stage:

> " . . . objective remarks about the accused's previous record, . . . invariably form part of prosecution counsel's duty. This may be extended to include the Crown's version of the evidence relied on by defence counsel in mitigation, including clarification and even refutation."[9]

The second stage, submissions on sentencing principles and norms, the third stage, calling for a specific type of sentence, the fourth stage, address on range of sentence, and the fifth stage, recommendation of a particular quantum of sentence, are the further stages which Zellick discusses, and will constitute the substance of this analysis. In fact, Zellick mentions another possibility, a strident or passionate call for severity or leniency, based on emotion, personal opinion or prejudice, but he discards, for purpose of considered analysis, this last mentioned possibility.

The perfunctory nature of the role given to prosecuting counsel in England is familiar to prosecutors in Australia. It is the latter stages which are the focus of recent attitudes on sentencing, and which constitute the call for Australian prosecutors to break away from their English counterparts.

2. *Recent Attitudes: Up to the Elbows*

Despite the attitude of the Canadian Law Reform Commission, Canadian judges do not appear to share the restrictive view of the prosecutor's role on sentence. Houlden J. of the Ontario Court of Appeal has stated that:

---

[4] Cmnd 6323, 1976, pars 39, 66, 184.

[5] Boulton, *Conduct and Etiquette at the Bar*, Butterworths, London, 6th ed., 1975, at p. 75; see also Napley, *The Technique of Persuasion*, Sweet and Maxwell, London, 2nd ed., 1975, at p. 74.

[6] Ashworth, "Prosecution and Procedure in Criminal Justice" [1979] Crim.L.R. 480; Zellick, "The Role of Prosecuting Counsel in Sentencing" [1979] Crim.L.R. 493; King, "The Role of Prosecuting Counsel in Sentencing: What about Magistrates' Courts?" [1979] Crim.L.R. 775; Rinaldi, "Crown Appeals Against Sentence in Australia" (1984) 8 Crim.L.J. 1.

[7] Ashworth, ibid. and Zellick, ibid.

[8] Rinaldi, supra, n. 6 at 2.

[9] Zellick, supra, n. 6 at 493.

"The sentence hearing is as much a part of the trial as the pr ceedings leading to the verdict. It is not an interview or a conference, and it should not be conducted as such."[10]

In a recent commentary on prosecuting counsel's role in sentencing in Australia Rinaldi has stated that:

"An Australian Crown Counsel, like his Canadian counterpart, should not at the sentencing give the appearance of being but a highly paid ornamental dummy adding nothing to the proceedings beyond contributing to the pageantry of the Court. Rather, he is required to display an interest in the sentencing plea submitted by counsel for the defendant and is expected to challenge questions of principle, the weight of objective and subjective facts and inferences that can legitimately be drawn from the facts."[11]

These comments appear to reflect the judicial attitude in utterances from a variety of Australian jurisdictions. In *R. v. McIntosh*, decided in 1923, it was said by McCawley C.J. for the Queensland Court of Criminal Appeal that:

" . . . we think it desirable to emphasise that the circumstances relevant to punishment should be fully placed before the trial judge by Crown Counsel and Counsel for the accused . . .".[12]

Again in *R. v. McKeown*, decided in 1940, it was said by Macrossan C.J. for the Queensland Court of Criminal Appeal that:

" . . . in our opinion, since the Crown now has a right of appeal against sentence it is its duty to take up a positive attitude in assisting the Court to determine sentence."[13]

The occasion for this pronouncement was the first Ministerial appeal against sentence in Queensland, that power having been given by the 1939 amendment to the *Criminal Code* 1899 (Qld). In the unreported Victorian Full Court decision in 1977 in *R. v. Burchielli*, Young C.J. and Lush J. felt obliged to chide prosecutors for the Crown in that State, because " . . . it is desirable that prosecutors should be prepared to take, at their discretion, a more active role in the hearing of pleas".[14]

In *R. v. Cartwright*, decided in 1979, Sangster J. in the South Australian Supreme Court said:

" . . . Crown Counsel should participate in the sentencing processes. At the present time, we hear only the prisoner's argument on sentencing. I for one would welcome the assistance of the prosecutor. At least then I would not have the task of fossicking out the facts and thinking up

---

[10] Cited in Manning, "Sentencing Laws: A Practitioner's View" in Grosman, supra, n. 1 at p. 282.

[11] Rinaldi, supra, n. 6 at 12.

[12] [1923] St. R. Qd. 278 at 282.

[13] [1940] St. R. Qd. 202 at 214.

[14] Unreported, 10 June 1977, Ct Cr. App., Melbourne, cited in *Davies* (1981) 5 Crim.L.J. 64 at 65.

the argument against the prisoner and then have to judge between what I have thought up and what has been argued in favour of the prisoner."[15]

The South Australian Full Court, comprising King C.J., with whom Mitchell and Williams JJ. concurred, said in *R. v. Wilton*, decided in 1981, that:

"It remains true that the Crown is required to make its submissions as to sentence fairly and in an even-handed manner, and that the Crown does not, as an adversary, press the sentencing court for a heavy sentence. The Crown has a duty to the court to assist it in the task of passing sentence by an adequate presentation of the facts, by an appropriate reference to any special principles of sentencing which might reasonably be thought to be relevant to the case in hand, and by a fair testing of the defendant's case so far as it appears to require it."[16]

The recent attitude to the role of the Crown Prosecutors in sentencing certainly allows, even recommends, a more active approach. The features of this approach and the limitations on it remain for consideration, but before turning to them it is necessary to consider why there is this disjunction between the older and the more modern approach to the Crown Prosecutor's role.

Crown Appeals Against Sentence

1. *The Sine Qua Non of the Active Role*

It is fairly obvious that the opinions cited as representative of the "hands off" approach to the Crown's role in sentencing are English and that this approach is conditioned by the absence of power in the Crown to appeal against sentencing.[17] It is equally obvious that the opinions and judgments cited as representative of the "up to the elbows" approach are from jurisdictions where there is power in the Crown to appeal against sentence, albeit that some of these utterances preceded the grant of this power.

It was suggested by the Queensland Court of Criminal Appeal in *R. v. McKeown* that the power in the Crown to appeal against sentence was the spur to the taking of a more active role in sentencing by the Crown Prosecutor. This same link has been noted in Canada by Ruby, who has said:

"One reason for refusing to accept the English practice is the existence of provision in Canada for an appeal by the Crown, with leave, from a sentence imposed by trial court."[18]

---

[15] (1979) 21 S.A.S.R. 564 at 566; see also *R. v. Lamer* (1973) 17 C.C.C. (2d) 411 (Que.C.A.).

[16] (1981) 28 S.A.S.R. 362 at 364. This has been cited with approval by Legoe J. in *R. v. Travers and Davies* (1983) 34 S.A.S.R. 112 at 115, and by the Federal Court of Australia in *Molina* (1983) 13 A.Crim.R. 76.

[17] See Ashworth, supra, n. 6; and Zellick, supra, n. 6.

[18] *Sentencing*, Butterworths, Toronto, 2nd ed., 1980, at p. 44; the same power exists in all Australian jurisdictions. See: s. 5D *Criminal Appeal Act* 1912 (N.S.W.); s. 401(2) *Criminal Code* 1924 (Tas.); s. 669A *Criminal Code* 1899 (Qld); s. 567A *Crimes Act* 1958 (Vic.); s. 688(2) *Criminal Code* 1913 (W.A.); s. 352(2) *Criminal Law Consolidation Act* 1935 (S.A.); for appeals in the A.C.T. and N.T., ss 24 and 25 *Federal Court Act* 1977 (Cth); see also s. 383(2) *Crimes Act* 1969 (N.Z.).

The reason for this link is not hard to find. In a frequently cited opinion of the Federal Court of Australia, Brennan, Deane and Gallop JJ., in *R. v. Tait and Bartley*, stated that:

> "It would be unjust to a defendant to expose him to double jeopardy because of an error affecting his sentence, if the Crown's presentation of the case either contributed to the error or led the defendant to refrain from dealing with some aspect of the case which might have rebutted the suggested error. The Crown has been said not to be concerned with sentence . . . but when a statutory right of appeal is conferred upon the Crown, . . . [the] . . . Crown is under a duty to assist the Court to avoid appealable error . . .".[19]

Failure by the Crown Prosecutor at trial to press upon the trial judge the sentencing arguments presented on appeal has resulted in courts discouraging the presentation of that appellate argument[20] and has even been held in Canada to bind the Crown to prevent or estop the appellate argument.[21] The failure to press, at first instance, the point raised on appeal may result in no alteration to sentence even if the basis of the Crown's appeal is meritorious in principle.[22] Thus, prejudice to the exercise of the right of appeal is a likely consequence of failure by the Crown Prosecutor to take an active role in sentencing.

The Crown's power to appeal against sentence appears to be regarded as the sine qua non of the necessity to assume a more active role in sentencing. This may be well illustrated by reference to the South Australian authorities. The Crown appeal against sentence for major indictable offences in South Australia was not introduced until 1980. Prior to this time, the only reported reference to the Crown's role in sentence was the exhortation by Sangster J. in *R. v. Cartwright*, and it was tied to a judicial plea to the legislature for a general right for the Crown to appeal against sentence. This right having been granted in 1980, the Supreme Court expressed its opinion in 1981, in *R. v. Wilton*, that the Crown has a duty to assist the court in sentencing and went on to endorse the principle in *R. v. Tait and Bartley*. In Queensland, upon the first Ministerial appeal against sentence, in *R. v. McKeown*, the Court of Criminal Appeal accepted the need for prosecutors' activism in sentencing.

The fact that these admonitions for active assistance upon sentence were prompted by Crown appeals against sentence poses the question: Why do Crown appeals dictate a duty on prosecutors to actively assist the trial judge in sentencing?

2. *Crown's Responsibility in Appeals Against Sentence*

In all Australian States and Territories, the representatives of the Crown

[19] (1979) 24 A.L.R. 473 at 476-477; this has been cited with approval in *R. v. Hall* (1979) 28 A.L.R. 107; *R. v. Wilton* (1981) 28 S.A.S.R. 362; *R. v. Bishop* (1982) 45 A.L.R. 331; *R. v. Jones* [1984] W.A.R. 175; *R. v. Boyd* [1984] W.A.R. 236.

[20] See, for example, *R. v. Jacombe*, unreported, 1974, Ct Cr. App. Sydney, cited in *R. v. Tait and Bartley*, ibid.

[21] *R. v. James* (1971) 3 C.C.C. (2d) 1.

[22] *R. v. Sutherland* (1974) 10 N.B.R. (2d) 221; *R. v. Tait and Bartley*, supra, n. 19; *R. v. Wilton*, supra, n. 19; *R. v. Bishop*, supra, n. 19; *R. v. Jones*, supra, n. 19.

have power to appeal against sentence. This power is exercised as of right, except in South Australia where the appeal is instituted with leave.[23] Time and again, the courts have emphasised that the appeal lies from a sentencing discretion and that the obligation assumed by an appellant is to demonstrate error in sentencing principle,[24] albeit that the only specific flaw which can be detected is that the quantum of punishment is so extravagant as to invite the label "gross departure from the norm".[25] This capacity to invoke the appellate jurisdiction in relation to sentence is common to both prisoners' and Ministerial appeals in all jurisdictions,[26] except Queensland, but the distinction drawn there is more illusory than real.[27]

However, the courts have also assigned to Ministerial Appeals another, supposedly less adversarial and more noble function. The Attorney-General, and the representatives of the Crown, have a duty to ensure that there is a principled, just and equitable sentencing system. As Barwick C.J. commented in *Griffiths v. The Queen*:

> " . . . an appeal by the Attorney-General should be a rarity, brought only to establish some matter of principle and to afford an opportunity for the Court of Criminal Appeal to perform its proper function in this respect, namely to lay down principles for the governance and guidance of courts having the duty of sentencing convicted persons."[28]

The same point is implied in the judgment of Jacobs J., with whom Aickin and Stephen JJ. concurred. More will be said of his judgment later. Murphy J. said, tersely:

> " . . . the Attorney-General's appeal . . . is an extraordinary remedy intended to be invoked only rarely . . . and then only for reasons of great public importance . . .".[29]

The point here is not whether Ministerial appeals should or should not be a rarity, but rather is to demonstrate that the purpose of such appeals differs from convicted persons' appeals in that a super-added responsibility is assumed by virtue of the Crown's power to appeal. The purpose of the appeal is said to cause sentencing principle to be articulated.[30]

Since the Federal Court, and the various State courts applying *R. v. Tait and Bartley*, adopt the proposition that the appellate advocacy on Ministerial appeals may, and often will, be constrained by the Crown Prosecutor's sub-

---

[23] See references supra, n. 18.

[24] *Skinner v. The King* (1913) 16 C.L.R. 336 at 339; *Whittaker v. The King* (1928) 41 C.L.R. 230 at 245; *House v. The King* (1936) 55 C.L.R. 499 at 504-505; *Griffiths v. The Queen* (1977) 137 C.L.R. 293 at 310.

[25] *House v. The King*, ibid.; *Griffiths v. The Queen*, ibid.

[26] *Griffiths v. The Queen*, supra, n. 24; *R. v. Thomas* [1975] Tas. S.R. 146; *R. v. Flaherty* (1981) 28 S.A.S.R. 105; *R. v. Holder* [1983] 3 N.S.W.L.R. 245; *R. v. Tait and Bartley* supra, n. 20; *R. v. J.* (1982) 45 A.L.R. 331; *R. v. Town* (1982) 29 S.A.S.R. 199.

[27] See *R. v. Warren* [1979] Qd R. 268 at 270 per Wanstall C.J., and *R. v. Adams* (1979) 2 A.Crim.R. 207 at 208-209 per Andrews J. with Hoare and W. B. Campbell JJ. concurring.

[28] Supra, n. 26 at 310.

[29] Ibid. at 329.

[30] The difference may be more one of rhetoric than reality: presumably, articulation of correct principle will generally follow some error of principle by trial judge or manifest inadequacy in sentence presumptive of error, although this need not always be so.

missions at the sentencing phase of trial, it follows that the Crown Prosecutor is cast in the role of an advocate of principles for the governance and guidance of courts having the duty of sentencing convicted persons. This role on sentencing is consistent with that laid down in the oft-quoted judgment of Newton J. and Morris A.J. in the Victorian Supreme Court decision in *R. v. Lucas* in which they said, albeit in a slightly different context:

> "It is very well established that prosecuting counsel are ministers of justice, who ought not to struggle for a conviction nor be betrayed by feelings of professional rivalry, and that it is their duty to assist the court in the attainment of the purpose of criminal prosecutions, namely, to make certain that justice is done as between the subject and the State."[31]

No doubt, prosecutors in England would also accept this as embodying their duties at trial,[32] so it is necessary to explore the effect which the propositions articulated by Barwick C.J. in *Griffiths v. The Queen* and by the Federal Court in *R. v. Tait and Bartley* have on the Crown Prosecutor's role in sentencing in Australia. The framework employed is Zellick's scheme of depths of penetration into the sentencing process.

The First Stage

1. *Prior Record and Antecedents*

It is commonplace that the Crown Prosecutor should provide the sentencing judge with information about the convicted person's prior criminal convictions, sentences and antecedents.[33] This information is of crucial value to the imposition of sentence. Prior convictions may not, per se, lead to a sentence which is more severe than the circumstances of the offence warrant, but they may suggest a condign punishment for the purposes of special deterrence particularly where the prior convictions indicate a sustained and systematic course of criminal conduct.[34] This has been said to mean that the existence of such a prior record, or even one which indicates a generalised criminality of no particular focus, may outweight or minimise any mitigating factors.[35] Even convictions after the date of commission of the offence may be of relevance and the Crown may present these, again not for the purpose of a more severe sentence than is appropriate to the offence, but to counter-balance any considerations going to leniency.[36] The type of prior sentences received may, of course, be particularly relevant to assist the court in determining the instant sentence. Although there is no general principle that a non-custodial rehabilitative opportunity may not be

---

[31] [1973] V.R. 693 at 705.

[32] See *Dallison v. Caffery* [1965] 1 Q.B. 348.

[33] *R. v. Murphy* [1947] Q.W.N. 4; *Tame v. Fingleton* (1974) 8 S.A.S.R. 507.

[34] *Tame v. Fingleton*, supra, n. 33 at 511 per Walters J.; *D.P.P. v. Ottewell* [1968] 3 All E.R. 153 at 156 per Lord Reid.

[35] *R. v. Cook-Russell* [1976] Qd R. 35 at 39 per Douglas J.; *R. v. Clarke* (1972) 4 S.A.S.R. 30 at 35 per Bright, Walters and Wells JJ.; *Cameron v. Josey* [1970] W.A.R. 66 at 67 per Wickham J.; *R. v. Lemass* (1981) 5 A.Crim.R. 230.

[36] *R. v. Hutchens* (1957) 75 W.N. (N.S.W.) 75 at 76 per Street C.J., Roper J. concurring; cf. *R. v. Adams* (1979) 3 Crim.L.J. 302.

given to a person who has received such a chance in the past, caution is warranted in ordering a second or later opportunity,[37] and the more usual approach is to consider a lost chance for rehabilitation as the last chance.[38] Subsequent sentences may need to be considered in order to ensure that the totality does not destroy any possibility of rehabilitation, or, in terms used by the Victorian judiciary, become a "crushing sentence".[39]

One illustration of the clear necessity for the Crown to inform the court of sentences, and not just of convictions, is furnished by the Victorian Full Court decision in *R. v. Kane.*[40] On an Attorney-General's appeal against sentence, it was noted that the sentencing judge considered that, although the prisoner had a bad prior record, his inclination to reform was manifest by a gap in his convictions between 1965 and 1969. The fact was that a substantial amount of this period was spent in prison under sentence following convictions in 1965. The Full Court observed, however, that his error was not material in the formulation of sentence, and did not thereby have occasion to reprove the Crown for breach of duty of advocacy in relation to this sort of information.

With respect to antecedents, the significance of these for sentencing, and the obligations of the Crown with respect thereto, are well recognised. As long ago as 1911, Lord Alverstone observed, in *Campbell v. The King*,[41] that police officers have the duty of presenting antecedent reports. To this Viscount Cadecote for the Court of Criminal Appeal added, in *R. v. Van Pelz*,[42] that counsel for the prosecution have a duty to control the presentation of antecedent reports and that the prosecutor should confine them to material which they have reason to think will not be disputed or which is capable of proof by the prosecution. This has been subsequently endorsed on numerous occasions in England[43] with the observation that only such information from "first-hand knowledge" should be given, in order that the matters alleged can be proved, if the necessity arises.[44] The decision in *R. v. Van Pelz* has been followed in Canada[45] and Australia.[46]

This admonition against the use of hearsay information in antecedent reports has carried over into pre-sentence reports[47] but since these reports are given for the court rather than for the prosecution, any duties relating thereto attach only to those who prepare the reports and not to the Crown

---

[37] *R. v. McKennarty and Knowles*, Unreported, 107 and 108/1972, Ct Cr. App., Brisbane; *R. v. Walker* (1981) 27 S.A.S.R. 315.

[38] *Nichol v. Brown* (1977) 17 A.L.R. 621.

[39] *R. v. Adams*, supra, n. 27.

[40] [1975] V.R. 759 at 763 per Gowans, Nelson and Anderson JJ.

[41] (1911) 6 Cr.App.R. 131.

[42] [1943] 1 K.B. 160 at 167, Wrottesley and Tucker JJ. concurred.

[43] *R. v. Crabtree* (1952) 36 Cr.App.R. 161; *R. v. Robinson* (1969) 53 Cr.App.R. 315; *R. v. Bibby* [1972] Crim.L.R. 513; *R. v. Sargeant* (1974) 60 Cr.App.R. 74; *R. v. Wilkins* (1977) 66 Cr.App.R. 49.

[44] *R. v. Robinson*, ibid. at 318 per Widgery L.J., Winn L.J. and Lawton J. concurring; *R. v. Wilkins*, ibid. at 53 per Geoffrey Lane L.J., McKenna and Cusack JJ. concurring.

[45] *R. v. Carey* (1952) C.R. 333 (Ont. C.A.).

[46] *R. v. Morse* [1977] W.A.R. 151.

[47] *R. v. Lucky* (1974) 12 S.A.S.R. 136; *R. v. Nuku* [1969] N.Z.L.R. 343; *R. v. Gilder Rose* [1978] Qd R. 61; *R. v. Seres* [1980] Qd R. 29.

Prosecutor. In particular, whilst it has been held that there is a duty on the Crown to disclose to the defence any antecedent reports in order that instructions thereon can be taken,[48] any duty of disclosure of pre-sentence reports was expressed in terms placing the obligation on the court.[49] However, in *R. v. Lucky*, Bray C.J. in the South Australian Court of Criminal Appeal said:

> "Any report of the kind mentioned should always be shown to . . . [the prisoner] . . . and he should be asked whether he admits its contents insofar as it related to matters of fact and what comment he has to make on it. If he disputes any matter of fact alleged in the report, then either that matter must be disregarded by the court, or the question must be resolved by the calling of evidence. Similar remarks apply to the police report and the list of prior convictions."[50]

Although the Crown has duties in relation to the report and list of prior convictions to which Bray C.J. referred, it is difficult to see that he purported to extend these duties to pre-sentence reports, if for no other reason than such reports are not normally within Crown control.

2. *Proof of Facts for Sentencing*

The authorities establish that a trial judge must form his own view of the facts surrounding the commission of the offence, but that he may not form a view which is inconsistent with the jury's verdict.[51] Neither may he consider as circumstances of aggravation, for purpose of sentence, matters which would indicate guilt of an offence more serious than for which the person has been convicted,[52] nor which would indicate guilt of other offences.[53] The formation of his opinion does not oblige the trial judge to accept the convicted person's version, or the most lenient view of the circumstances of the offence,[54] but where a doubt may be genuinely held, and two competing versions are of equal probability, the judge may be obliged to accept the version most favourable to the person convicted.[55]

The obligations in this respect are placed on the trial judge, and do not have commensurate obligations on the Crown. However, duties do arise for

---

[48] *R. v. Sargeant*, supra, n. 43.

[49] *R. v. Seres*, supra, n. 47; *R. v. Nuku*, supra, n. 47.

[50] Supra, n. 47 at 139, Hogarth and Zelling JJ. concurring.

[51] *R. v. Haselich* [1976] Qd R. 183; *R. v. Harris* [1961] V.R. 236; *R. v. Bedington* [1970] Qd R. 353; *R. v. Laporte* [1970] W.A.R. 87; *R. v. Denniston* [1977] Crim.L.R. 46; *R. v. Nuttall* [1968] Crim.L.R. 173.

[52] *Felstead v. Giersch* (1976) 14 S.A.S.R. 27 at 31; *R. v. Boyd* [1975] V.R. 168 at 172; *R. v. Cooksley* [1982] Qd R. 405; *Pecora v. The Queen* [1980] V.R. 499; *R. v. Boyd* [1984] W.A.R. 236 at 243 per Olney J.; cf. *Lane v. Auckland City Council* [1975] 1 N.Z.L.R. 353.

[53] *R. v. Hutchison* [1972] 1 W.L.R. 398; *R. v. Bright* [1916] 2 K.B. 441; *R. v. Hansen* (1962) 79 W.N. (N.S.W.) 148; *R. v. Desimoni* (1981) 35 A.L.R. 205; *R. v. King* [1983] 2 Qd R. 168; *R. v. Hill* [1979] V.R. 311; *R. v. Jackson* [1972] Crim.L.R. 325; *R. v. Foo* [1976] Crim.L.R. 456; cf. *Lane v. Auckland City Council* supra, n. 52; *R. v. Webb* [1971] V.R. 147.

[54] *R. v. Haselich*, supra, n. 51; *R. v. Harris*, supra, n. 51.

[55] *R. v. Murace* (1957) 74 W.N. (N.S.W.) 147; *R. v. Welch* [1983] 1 Qd R. 592; *R. v. West* [1979] Tas. S.R. 1.

the Crown in relation to sentencing when the trial is inadequate to provide full ventilation of the circumstances of the offence, and the offender. This may well be in most instances of a full trial, but the problem becomes acute where the accused pleads guilty. Certainly, in the case of a plea to an indictment, the committal depositions can be read for the facts of the offence[56] but, at least in Western Australia, this does not relieve the Crown Prosecutor of the obligation to restate orally the facts relied upon as grounding the Crown's submissions on sentence.[57]

The depositions may not provide sufficient detail upon which to base a fully considered sentence, and this inadequacy may be particularly apparent in the case where the plea to the indictment is preceded by a "paper committal".[58] It follows, then, that there will frequently be a need to place further material before the court.

In the past decade, detailed and thoughtful commentary has been directed to exposition of the law relating to the factual foundation of sentencing,[59] and no more than a brief summary is warranted here. Essentially, it is that the courts are entitled to act upon allegations, or addresses, from the bar table or the dock, if these matters are not in dispute. If they are disputed, the normal laws of evidence apply at the sentencing stage as they do in the adjudication stage.[60]

Matters arising in address by the Crown which are disputed by the prisoner require proof beyond a reasonable doubt if those matters relate to the circumstances of the offence,[61] but only to the civil standard for all other matters such as prior convictions, antecedents, character and so forth.[62] It appears that the Crown shoulders the burden of disproving any allegations or matters arising in address by the defence, but that this operates only upon the defence satisfying an evidential onus in support of that allegation.[63]

That the burden of proof in sentencing casts a duty on the Crown Prosecutor is clear from comments of several courts. In *R. v. McIntosh*, McCawley C.J. of the Queensland Supreme Court said that:

> " . . . the circumstances relevant to punishment should be placed before the trial judge by Crown counsel and counsel for the accused . . . . The

[56] *R. v. Vecsey* [1962] S.A.S.R. 127; *R. v. Maitland* [1963] S.A.S.R. 332; *R. v. O'Neill* [1979] 2 N.S.W.L.R. 582.

[57] *R. v. Boyd* [1984] W.A.R. 236 at 242 per Olney J.; *R. v. Aloia* [1983] W.A.R. 133 at 137-138 per Pidgeon J.

[58] *R. v. Aloia*, ibid.

[59] Fox and O'Brien, "Fact Finding for Sentencers" (1975) 10 M.U.L.R. 163; Lowenthal, "Some Issues in Fact Finding for Sentences" (1979) 11 U.Q.L.J. 145.

[60] S. 650 *Criminal Code* 1899 (Qld); s. 656 *Criminal Code* 1913 (W.A.); see Lowenthal, ibid., at 196; *R. v. Murphy* [1947] Q.W.N. 4; *West v. Sprinkhuizen* [1961] Qd R. 313; *R. v. Maitland* [1963] S.A.S.R. 332.

[61] *Law v. Deed* [1970] S.A.S.R. 374 at 378; *R. v. Maitland*, ibid. at 335; *R. v. O'Neill*, supra, n. 56 at 588; *R. v. Thompson* (1975) 11 S.A.S.R. 217 at 221; *R. v. Prokopiec* (1982) 7 A.Crim.R. 116 at 120; *R. v. Welch*, supra, n. 55 at 594 per Campbell C.J., Matthews and McPherson JJ., *R. v. Martin* (1983) 32 S.A.S.R. 419 at 440 per Mitchell J.

[62] *Ex parte Kelly; Re Teece* [1966] 2 N.S.W.R. 674 at 677-678; Lowenthal, supra, n. 59 at 148-150; cf. Fox and O'Brien, supra, n. 59 at 190; *R. v. Welsh*, supra, n. 55 at 595 per Campbell C.J., Matthews and McPherson JJ.

[63] *Law v. Deed*, supra, n. 61 at 379.

grave responsibility cast upon the judge cannot be satisfactorily discharged if the necessary data are not placed at his disposal."[64]

Hogarth, Bright and Wells JJ. echoed these observations, in relation to the magnitude of commercial operations in manufacturing, importing or supplying dangerous drugs, in the South Australian Supreme Court decision in *R. v. Beresford.* They said:

> "It seems to us that it is the responsibility of the prosecution, in the first instance, to lead such evidence as is in their possession and will enable the sentencing judge to form an appreciation, not only of the prisoner's conduct, but also of the drug with which the conduct was concerned . . . . It is, in our view, unsatisfactory for a judge to find himself left to perform his own research and formulate his own opinions and conclusions upon such arcane matters. What we can read in books, journals and reports about drugs is no doubt useful as background and as providing the basis for suggestions for further enquiry, but it would, in our view, be entirely wrong if those readings were to take the place of sworn expert testimony, properly presented and tested."[65]

The Court went on to refer to reciprocal duties for defence counsel. A selection of other dicta serve to emphasise the point. In *R. v. Tait and Bartley*, Brennan, Deane and Gallop JJ. said:

> "The Crown has a duty to the court to assist it in the task of passing sentence by an adequate presentation of the facts . . . and by a fair testing of the defendant's case so far as it appears to require it . . . . The Crown is under a duty to assist the court to avoid appealable error."[66]

These comments were subsequently endorsed in the South Australian Supreme Court in *R. v. Travers and Davies.* Legoe J., with whom Millhouse J. concurred, said:

> " . . . the Crown has a duty to the court to assist it in the task of passing sentence . . . I am comforted to know, and I think it worth recording, that the learned Crown prosecutor indicated a tentative view as to the practice of Crown counsel. He told us that Crown counsel normally direct their attention in these circumstances to the following matters (1) to straighten out any factual disputes; (2) to point out to the sentencing judge any error or apparent error in the defence presentation of the facts . . .".[67]

Perhaps the only surprise in this (for Legoe J. went on to claim that he was not adding anything to the views expressed in *R. v. Tait and Bartley* and in *R. v. Wilton*) was that the Crown Prosecutor's view was characterised as "tentative". This may have had something to do with the fact that there were other matters discussed in submissions to the court. These will be considered later.

---

[64] Supra, n. 12 at 282-283.

[65] (1972) 2 S.A.S.R. 446 at 450.

[66] Supra, n. 19 at 477.

[67] Supra, n. 16 at 115-116.

In *R. v. Boyd*, Olney J. in the Court of Criminal Appeal of Western Australia, said:

> "Everything the Crown wishes to say relevant to the question of sentencing should be said to the judge in court before he passes sentence . . . it was incumbent on the Crown to . . . [put its views with respect to the seriousness of the offence for purpose of sentencing] . . . at that time to give the accused the opportunity of answering the case being put against him and to enable the judge to have a full understanding of all the matters which should affect the exercise of his discretion."[68]

Finally, in *R. v. Gamble*, Street C.J. (with whom Lee and Enderby JJ. concurred) said, in the New South Wales Court of Criminal Appeal:

> " . . . the duty of the Crown to assist the court by furnishing of appropriate and relevant material touching upon the determination of a sentence . . . is a duty which the Crown customarily undertakes and is generally expected of the Crown, in the courts of this state. Antecedents reports are expected to be furnished by the Crown showing such of the subjective material elicited in relation to the accused as is necessary to present a fair picture to the judge. The material is also expected to canvass the accused's earlier criminal record, if any. If there is a plea of guilty . . . the Crown would be expected to put before the sentencing judge the broad nature of the factual allegations upon which the Crown relies as constituting the offence to which the accused has pleaded guilty. These are well recognised obligations on the Crown and, indeed, it is difficult to see how the sentencing process could be properly carried through unless the Crown fulfilled them."[69]

The foregoing authorities make it clear that, not only is it fairly well established that the role of the Crown Prosecutor in sentencing includes the presentation of prior record and antecedents, as well as assistance in establishing the factual basis for sentencing, but that the authorities, including the English authorities such as *R. v. Van Pelz*, cast that role in the form of a duty or an obligation to the court.

Interestingly, Brennan, Deane and Gallop JJ. in *R. v. Tait and Bartley* widened the basis of the Crown's duty in this respect beyond the duty to the court, and extend it to the general duty of the Crown to ensure fairness of the trial process, the basis for the imposition of other duties on Crown Prosecutors.[70] They said:

> "The Crown is under a duty to assist the court to avoid appealable error. The performance of that duty to the court ensures that the defendant knows the nature and extent of the case against him, and thus has a fair opportunity of meeting it. A failure by the Crown to discharge that duty may not only contribute to appealable error affecting the sentence, but may tend to deprive the defendant of a fair opportunity of meeting a

---

[68] [1984] W.A.R. 236 at 242-243.

[69] [1983] 3 N.S.W.L.R. 356.

[70] See Campbell, "Discovery in Criminal Trials: Prosecutors' Duties and Judges' Remedies" (1984) 13 U.Q.L.J. (forthcoming).

> case which might ultimately be made on appeal. It would be unjust to a defendant . . . to consider an appeal a case made against him on a new basis—a basis which he might have successfully challenged had the case against him been fully presented before the sentencing court."[71]

The consequence is that an attempt by the Crown to lead fresh evidence on an appeal would probably meet the same fate normally accorded such applications by prisoners. Only in rare circumstances will a prisoner be permitted to put facts before a Court of Criminal Appeal which were not put before the trial judge upon sentence.[72]

In *R. v. Boyd,* Olney J. in the Western Australian Court of Criminal Appeal said, in dealing with a Ministerial appeal against inadequacy seeking to argue a fresh colouration on the offence to show it to be more serious than the trial judge apprehended:

> "Had this been the view of the Crown at the time the accused . . . was about to be sentenced then it was incumbent upon the Crown to say so at that time . . ."[73]

The Second Stage

Zellick's second stage of involvement refers to submissions from Crown Prosecutors on sentencing principles and norms. It is this and later stages which prosecuting counsel in England omit from their repertoire, according to Zellick.

1. *Sentencing Principles and Norms*

The clearest judicial exposition of sentencing principles, which are referred to in the language of philosophy as principles or theories of punishment, comes from Lawton L.J. in his oft-cited remarks in *R. v. Sargeant*:

> " . . . the classical principles of sentencing . . . are summed up in four words: retribution, deterrence, prevention and rehabilitation. Any judge who comes to sentence ought always to have those four classical principles in mind . . ."[74]

and Lawton L.J., with whom Scarman L.J. and Dunn J. concurred, went on to present a brief analysis of each of these principles. In the New Zealand decision in *R. v. Radich*[75] adopted in New South Wales in *R. v. Cooke,*[76] it was asserted that one of the main purposes of punishment was to protect the public, although a close reading of the New Zealand Court of Appeal's decision indicated that it was referring only to deterrence as the factor which

---

[71] Supra, n. 19 at 477.

[72] *R. v. Collins* (1979) 21 S.A.S.R. 38 at 40 per Hogarth, Wells and White JJ.; *R. v. Brett* [1983] 1 Qd R. 38; *R. v. Martin* (1983) 32 S.A.S.R. 419 at 440 per Mitchell J.; see also, on facts not known at the time of sentence, *R. v. Munday* [1981] 2 N.S.W.L.R. 177; *R. v. Campbell (No. 2)* (1981) 6 A.Crim.R. 208; *R. v. O'Shea* (1982) 31 S.A.S.R. 129; *R. v. Duvivier* (1982) 29 S.A.S.R. 217.

[73] Supra, n. 57 at 243.

[74] Supra, n. 43 at 77.

[75] [1954] N.Z.L.R. 86.

[76] (1955) 72 W.N. (N.S.W.) 132.

afforded this protection. This was disapproved in Victoria in *R. v. Williscroft.*[77] In *R. v. Cuthbert*, Herron C.J. for the New South Wales Court of Criminal Appeal said:

> "The sentence should be such as, having regard to all the proved circumstances, seems at the same time to accord with the general moral sense of the community and to be likely to be a sufficient deterrent both to the prisoner and others . . . . Courts have not infrequently attempted further analysis of the several aspects . . . where retribution, deterrence and reformation are said to be its threefold purposes. In reality they are but the means employed by the courts for the attainment of the single purpose of the protection of society."[78]

In Queensland the principles of punishment, of retribution, deterrence and rehabilitation were recognised by Wanstall C.J. for the Court of Criminal Appeal in *R. v. Casey; R. v. Smyth*[79] but no further analysis thereof was attempted, whilst in South Australia, King C.J., with whom Mitchell J. concurred, acknowledged in *Yardley v. Betts*[80] the "fundamental principle" of the protection of the community as being the purpose of criminal law and that this could be brought about by "making the punishment fit the offence and the offender", by deterrence of the offender and others and by rehabilitation.

Given the variety of expressions and the difficulties of reconciling all of these views, it is not, perhaps, surprising that Victorian judges have given up the attempt to have sentencing understood as a rational process of the application of these principles and have resorted to the empty formula, offered in *R. v. Williscroft* that:

> " . . . ultimately every sentence imposed represents the sentencing judge's instinctive synthesis of all the various aspects involved in the punitive process. Moreover, in our view, it is profitless . . . to attempt to allot to the various considerations their proper part in the assessment of the particular punishment presently under examination."[81]

The attitude is iconoclastic and does not appear, at least in reported decisions, to have found favour in other jurisdictions.

It is apparent that whilst prevention, referred to by Lawton L.J. in his lexicon of principles in *R. v. Sargeant*, has been omitted from this selection of the rhetoric of Australian judges, it is not omitted from the reality of their sentencing. The classic instance of this occurs in relation to sentencing principles and norms applicable to mentally ill and potentially dangerous offenders who have been convicted of a serious offence of violence to the person, and the court is faced with the choice of imposing a sentence commensurate with the seriousness of the offence or a sentence to protect the public by incapacitation or prevention of further offences.[82] This refers,

---

[77] [1975] V.R. 292.

[78] (1967) 2 N.S.W. R. 329 at 330.

[79] [1977] Qd R. 132.

[80] (1979) 22 S.A.S.R. 108 at 112.

[81] *R. v. Williscroft*, supra, n. 77 at 300.

[82] See, for example, *R. v. Tutchell* [1979] V.R. 248; *R. v. Kiltie* (1974) 9 S.A.S.R. 452;

of course, to the line of authorities up to, and since, the decision of the High Court in *Veen v. The Queen*[83] decided in 1979. The principles of sentencing involved were of such importance, it is worth noting that this was the first occasion on which the High Court gave special leave to appeal against sentence alone.

The principles for sentencing then, are retribution, deterrence, prevention and rehabilitation, and it is with these that the Crown Prosecutor is expected to wrestle in the second stage of involvement in the sentencing process. It would be an impossibility to deal exhaustively with all principles and norms of sentencing in all situations, but a selection of specific areas in the sentencing process will serve to indicate the nature of the Crown Prosecutors' advocacy in that process.

2. *The Retributive Theory*

Consider the essence of the modern retributive theory of punishment. Professor H. L. A. Hart has expressed this as being that the criminal courts imposing punishment are concerned with the Aristotolean concept of justice in treating like cases alike. This is the focal concern of the retributive theory, for it requires that persons can only be punished for the commission of an offence, which limits who may be punished, and that persons cannot be punished to any greater extent than is proportionate to the gravity of their offence, which limits how much the person may be punished.[84]

Translated into sentencing policies, the retributive principle requires that sentences accord with a set range of penalties (the punishment must fit the crime); and it requires that like offenders be treated alike (sentencing should strive to avoid disparities and endeavour to ensure uniformity).

The set range of penalties for each offence is referred to as the tariff.[85] This is the range of penalties encountered for the usual examples of each particular offence. The judicial attitude towards the concept of the tariff is well represented by the judgment of Darling J. in the Court of Criminal Appeal in *R. v. Woodman* in which he said:

> " . . . while . . . no invariable tariff can ever be fixed . . . the aim of the appellate courts is . . . by the revision of sentences . . . to harmonise the views of those who pass them, and so ensure that varying punishments are not awarded for the same amount of guiltiness."[86]

Occasionally one finds judicial pronouncements to the effect that sentences passed in previous cases are of little guidance to judges about to sentence

---

[82] *contd*
R. v. Masolatti (1976) 14 S.A.S.R. 124; *R. v. Eastham* [1978] W.A.R. 86; *R. v. Gascoigne* [1964] Qd R. 86; *R. v. Murdock* [1980] Qd R. 504; and the High Court decision in *Veen v. The Queen* (1979) 53 A.L.J.R. 305; see also Campbell "Justice and Utility in Sentencing: Gascoigne Revived?" (1981) 12 U.Q.L.J. 43 and on the decision in *Veen v. The Queen*, Tomasic, "Preventative Detention and the High Court", (1981) 55 A.L.J. 259.

[83] Supra, n. 82.

[84] *Punishment and Responsibility*, Clarendon Press, Oxford, 1968, esp. chaps 1 and 9; see also Kleinig, *Punishment and Desert*, Nijhoff, 1973.

[85] For the origin of the term, attributed to Lush J. in 1876, see Thomas *Principles of Sentencing*, Heinemann, London, 2nd ed., 1979 at p. 29.

[86] (1909) 2 Cr.App.R. 67.

in cases before them,[87] but these tend to reflect judicial impatience with either the amount of information about the offences culminating in the prior sentences or with the general insufficiency of the earlier sentences.[88] At the same time, it is recognised that sentencing:

> " . . . is a matter for the exercise of discretionary judgment within wide limits in the particular circumstances of each case and it is not for this court to define or restrict that discretion by attempting to prescribe anything in the nature of a standard punishment to be imposed unless exceptional circumstances are found . . . . It is for the sentencing tribunal to weigh all the varying factors relating to the circumstances of the particular offence and the individual who commits it and to exercise a judicial discretion . . . the choice of the appropriate punishment is not a matter of rule—it is a matter of a wide judicial discretion."[89]

Nonetheless, this discretion must be exercised judicially, and also in accordance with settled principles and policies. One such policy is the retributive necessity to ensure uniformity of sentences. Illustrative of this view is that of Street C.J. in the New South Wales Court of Criminal Appeal decision in *R. v. Oliver*, in which he said:

> "The task of the sentencing judge, no less than the task of an appellate court, is to pursue the ideal of evenhandedness in the matter of sentencing. Full weight is to be given to the collective wisdom of other sentencing judges . . . that collective wisdom is manifested in the general pattern of sentences currently being passed in cases which can be recognised judicially as relevant to the case in hand . . .".[90]

Street C.J. went on to state, however, that this must not lead to sentencing by rote, saying:

> " . . . This is not to suggest that sentences are to be arbitrarily dictated by mathematical application of statistics. There is an enormous difference between recognising and giving weight to the general pattern as manifestation of the collective wisdom of sentencing judges on the one hand, and, on the other hand, forcing sentencing into a strait jacket of computerisation . . .".[91]

That the tariff does not destroy the judicial discretion, nor entail the constriction of a strait jacket, is plain from the comments of Barwick C.J. and Jacobs J. in the High Court in *Griffiths v. The Queen*. Barwick C.J., referring to the power of appellate courts to overturn sentences on Ministerial appeals, said:

---

[87] See, for example, *Reynolds v. Wilkinson* (1948) 51 W.A.L.R. 17; *R. v. Breasley* [1974] 1 N.S.W.L.R. 736; *R. v. James* (1981) 27 S.A.S.R. 348; *R. v. Watson* [1962] Qd R. 418; *R. v. Laporte* [1970] W.A.R. 87.

[88] See, for example, *R. v. James*, ibid. at 350 per Walters, Zelling and Williams JJ., see also *R. v. Stevens* (1975) 13 S.A.S.R. 145; *Yardley v. Betts*, supra, n. 80 at 110 et seq. per King C.J.; *R. v. O'Donnell* (1974) 7 S.A.S.R. 114.

[89] *Lahey v. Edwards* [1967] Tas. S.R. (N.C.) 13.

[90] (1980) 7 A.Crim.R. 174 at 177 per Street C.J.; see also *R. v. Visconti* [1982] 2 N.S.W.L.R. 104 at 107.

[91] Ibid.

> ". . . inadequacy of sentence . . . means, in my opinion, such an inadequacy in the sentence as is indicative of error or departure from principle. No doubt consistency in the sentences imposed by the judges . . is a desirable feature of criminal administration. Gross departure from what might in experience be regarded as the norm, may be held to be error in point of principle."[92]

Thus Barwick C.J. suggested that departure from the norm is a prima facie error in the exercise of sentencing discretion. Jacobs J., to the same effect, said:

> "The best test whether or not [the trial judge was in error] . . . is to ask oneself whether, no matter which judge the matter had come before, the likelihood or probability was that the applicant might have been . . . [given the same sentence]. Disparity of sentencing standards is a very serious deficiency in a system of criminal justice . . . . It is the task of a Court of Criminal Appeal to minimise disparities of sentencing standards yet still recognise that perfect uniformity cannot be attained and that a fair margin of discretion must be left to the sentencing judge."[93]

Thus the tariff is regarded as a yardstick, and a sentence ought, prima facie, to fall within the range of sentences established by the collective wisdom of the judges. This is not to say that exceptions do not exist. Clearly instances occur which merit a sentence greater than the ceiling of the tariff (for example, at the statutory maximum),[94] or which merit a sentence lower than the floor of the tariff (for example, which may entail a non-custodial sentence where the tariff is a prison term).[95] However, Barwick C.J. makes it clear in *Griffiths v. The Queen* that any departure from the tariff requires justification in point of principle if a presumption of error is not to be applied.

The object of the tariff is to bring about consistency in treatment, and the relationship between the ideal, the retributive theory and the concept of justice in sentencing is no better expressed than by Mason J. in *Lowe v. The Queen.* He stated:

> "Just as consistency in punishment—a reflection of the notion of equal justice—is a fundamental element in any rational and fair system of criminal justice, so inconsistency in punishment, because it is regarded as a badge of unfairness and unequal treatment under the law, is calculated to lead to an erosion of public confidence in the integrity of the administration of justice."[96]

The effect of this on sentencing advocacy is to require that material be

---

[92] Supra, n. 24 at 310.

[93] Ibid. at 326.

[94] *R. v. McMahon* (1978) 19 A.L.R. 448; *R. v. Manson* [1974] Qd R. 191; *Bensegger v. The Queen* [1979] W.A.R. 65.

[95] *R. v. Bell* [1982] Qd R. 216; *Duncan v. The Queen* (1983) 47 A.L.R. 746; *Griffiths v. The Queen*, supra, n. 24 at 306 per Barwick C.J.

[96] (1984) 54 A.L.R. 193 at 196.

put before the court on the tariff range, because as Fox J., with whom Kelly and Ellicott JJ., concurred, pointed out in *R. v. Jurkovic*:

> "One of the functions of a court dealing with an appeal against sentence is to endeavour to ensure that there is a measure of consistency or parity between sentences for the same offence. Moreover, the extent of a sentence cannot be worked out a priori; there must be empirical standards of comparison . . .".[97]

The traditional source of empirical standards for comparison has been the reliance upon general judicial information and knowledge of sentences imposed in similar cases, a source approved in the Victorian Full Court decision in *R. v. Piercy.*[98] Becoming more common in most jurisdictions,[99] however, is the citation of comparative sentences in tabular or statistical form, not infrequently with computerised recording of such information. The defects of relying upon general judicial information and knowledge, and the benefit and importance of the capacity of the criminal trial advocate to be able to draw upon comparative statistical data, were discussed by Bray C.J. in *R. v. Barber.* He pointed out that sufficiently comprehensive knowledge from judicial notice or general knowledge may be impossible, at least in jurisdictions with more than one level of court trying indictable offences. He said:

> "We were supplied with a schedule of penalties imposed in other cases of a similar nature. Such information is often incomplete, perhaps usually incomplete, and there is no right of appeal by the Crown on the ground of inadequacy of sentence. These factors limit the reliance that can be placed on this sort of material. But, after all, it is one of the functions of a Court of Criminal Appeal to standardise sentences . . . . Where the sentence is one imposed for a crime commonly dealt with in this Court we can have recourse to our own knowledge and our own records. Where it is one imposed for a crime usually or often dealt with by other Courts, I do not see how we can find out what the tariff is except by use of some such material as was provided in this case, inadequate though it undoubtedly is. It is, of course, always open to the Crown to dispute it and to supplement it."[1]

This decision, in the South Australian Court of Criminal Appeal in 1976, preceded the legislative grant in 1980 of power for the Crown to appeal against sentence. Since then, it is questionable whether the observation of Bray C.J. that the Crown has a discretion to dispute or supplement any material on comparative sentence, is of current relevance. Indeed, the principle in *R. v. Tait and Bartley* has been applicable in South Australia

---

[97] (1981) 6 A.Crim.R. 215 at 220.

[98] [1971] V.R. 647 at 650-651 per Winneke C.J., Adam and Newton JJ.

[99] See, for example, *R. v. Pui* [1978] 2 N.Z.L.R. 193; *Yardley v. Betts*, supra, n. 80 at 115; *R. v. Visconti*, supra, n. 90 at 109-111; *R. v. James*, supra, n. 87 at 350; *R. v. Jurkovic*, supra, n. 97 at 220; *R. v. Aidi* [1970] Q.W.N. 4.

[1] (1976) 14 S.A.S.R. 388 at 390; to the same effect see *R. v. Jurkovic* supra, n. 97 at 220 and *R. v. Sewell and Walsh* (1981) 29 S.A.S.R. 12; for an example of marked disparity between judges of the same Supreme Court, see *Lowe v. The Queen*, supra, n. 96.

since 1980,[2] as it was in all other jurisdictions at the time of pronouncement. This is not to say that citation of comparative sentence material can be characterised as mandatory. Clearly, if defence counsel's material is correct, there would be little point in repetition, even for the sake of completeness if the Crown's information is more comprehensive. However, the principle in *R. v. Tait and Bartley* would seem to preclude any resort, upon Ministerial appeal, to comparative material in support of argument that the sentencing judge erred in principle by imposing an unusually lenient sentence, since the establishment of this proposition would rely upon resort to the yardstick of the tariff range.

One other aspect of retribution is worthy of mention. The treatment of like cases alike in relation to sentencing of co-offenders has occupied a considerable amount of appellate judicial time in recent years.[3] It has also been the subject of a recent High Court judgment, in *Lowe v. The Queen.* The sentencing policy, in accordance with the pre-existing authority, was indicated by Gibbs C.J. when he said:

> "It is obviously desirable that persons who have been parties to the commission of the same offence should if other things are equal, receive the same sentence, but other things are not always equal . . .".[4]

This has certain consequences for the Crown Prosecutor at trial. It is incumbent upon the Crown Prosecutor to point out the other sentence imposed, where an accomplice has been dealt with earlier. Indeed, the decision of Wells J. in the South Australian Supreme Court decision in *Shrubsole v. Rodriguez* takes this even further and suggests it would be desirable to mention quantum of punishment for the instant sentence. He said:

> "No step in the judicial process of sentencing more regularly presents difficulty than the final step in and by which general conclusions are translated into an actual figure—the amount of a fine, the period of disqualification, the term of a sentence . . . . There are exceptional cases where it would be desirable or necessary to mention a figure—for example, if the court was called on to sentence one of two co-offenders whose accomplice had already been sentenced—but, generally speaking, it is, in my opinion, unwise for a prosecutor to mention a figure . . . ."[5]

Indeed, if the earlier sentence were inadequate, but in respect of which no appeal has been brought, it would be incumbent upon the Crown Prosecutor to argue the points of distinction before the sentencing judge

---

[2] *R. v. Wilton*, supra, n. 19; *R. v. Travers and Davies* (1983) 34 S.A.S.R. 112.

[3] See for example *H. v. C.* (1976) 15 S.A.S.R. 251; *R. v. Bloom* [1976] V.R. 642; *Brodie v. The Queen* (1977) 16 A.L.R. 88; *Lovelock v. The Queen* (1978) 33 F.L.R. 132; *R. v. Kennedy* (1979) 37 F.L.R. 356; *R. v. Charles* [1979] V.R. 8; *R. v. Shannon* (1979) 21 S.A.S.R. 442; *R. v. Ruane* (1979) 1 A.Crim.R. 284; *R. v. Wurramarbra* (1979) 1 A.Crim.R. 291; *Millbanks v. Joseph* (1979) 21 S.A.S.R. 310; *Pecora v. The Queen* [1980] V.R. 499; *R. v. Tisalandis* [1982] 2 N.S.W.L.R. 430; *R. v. Dabek* (1980) 24 S.A.S.R. 380; *R. v. Jorgenson* (1981) 25 S.A.S.R. 115; *R. v. Taylor* (1980) 2 A.Crim.R. 202; *Bann v. Frew* (1982) 17 N.T.R. 1; *R. v. Blackmore and Dutoit* (1982) 8 A.Crim.R. 460; *Lowe v. The Queen*, supra, n. 96.

[4] Supra, n. 96 at 194.

[5] (1978) 18 S.A.S.R. 233 at 236-237.

because of the constraint which the decision in *R. v. Tait and Bartley* places upon any subsequent appellate submissions.

So important is the tariff that it has been suggested that the fundamental purpose of Crown appeals against sentence is the proper maintenance of sentencing tariffs. In *R. v. Osenkowski*, King C.J. with White J. concurring, said:

> "The proper role for prosecution appeals in my view, is to enable the courts to establish and maintain adequate standards of punishment for crime, to enable idiosyncratic views of individual judges as to particular crimes or types of crimes to be corrected, and occasionally to correct a sentence which is so disproportionate to the seriousness of a crime as to shock the public conscience."[6]

3. *The Utilitarian Theories: Protection of the Public*

The other major sentencing principles to which Lawton L.J. adverted in *R. v. Sargeant*, deterrence, prevention and rehabilitation, all provide reasons for punishment, or as Hart puts it, general justifying aims of punishing. Under these utilitarian justifications, what is done to the offender is justified if it brings about a greater good.[7] That good may be a reduction in criminality amongst those at whom the punisnment is aimed (whether it be general deterrence aimed at other potential offenders, or special deterrence or prevention aimed at the offender) or, in the case of rehabilitative measures, the reduction of criminality by granting a non-punitive opportunity to refrain from recidivism.

Space does not permit a detailed examination of all the sentencing policies which the courts have built upon these utilitarian principles. However, some areas stand out as being prime examples of the need for active assistance by the Crown Prosecutor upon sentence. This, in turn, is the path to the third, fourth and fifth stages of Zellick's scheme of the Crown's role in sentencing.

The Third, Fourth and Fifth Stages

The third stage is calling for a specific type of sentence and the fourth stage is addressing on a range of sentences. The fifth stage is a recommendation of a specific sentence. These stages may be considered simultaneously, because of the degree of overlap which will become apparent. Indeed, the overlap with the second stage, and even the first stage, is such that these stages ought not really be regarded as exclusive categories.

To begin with, the courts appear to firmly reject any proper role for the Crown Prosecutor in recommending a specific sentence. In the Victorian case of *R. v. Burchielli*, Young C.J. and Lush J., dealt upon appeal with the failure of the prosecution to object to a probation order and indicate the desirability of a more active role in sentencing being taken by the Crown Prosecutor. They added however that:

---

[6] (1982) 30 S.A.S.R. 212 at 213; see also *R. v. Drewitt* (1983) 35 S.A.S.R. 344.

[7] Bentham *Introduction to the Principles of Morals and Legislation*, 1789.

"We certainly do not envisage the development of a practice under which prosecutors make submissions on the extent of the punishment imposed."[8]

Presumably, their Honours were intending to refer to quantum of punishment, although the issue on appeal was the adequacy of a probation order for an offence punishable by a prison term. Thus it appears that what was being proscribed in *R. v. Burchielli* was assistance on the type of punishment, which need not necessarily be the same thing as quantum of punishment.

In *Shrubsole v. Rodriguez*, Wells J. sitting on appeal from a sentence of imprisonment imposed in a Magistrates Court, indicated, in the passage quoted above, that generally speaking, a prosecutor ought not suggest a specific figure.[9] It is clear that he referred to specific quantum of punishment. Wells J. gave one example when mention might be made of a specific figure, namely, in sentencing co-offenders. Another which may merit mention is reference to the statutory maximum, not by way of suggestion as to the sentence to be imposed, but as an indication of relative seriousness with which the offence is to be regarded.

In contrast with these Australian authorities, the Canadian cases suggest that the Crown Prosecutor need not be so reluctant. In *R. v. Simoneau*,[10] the majority of the Manitoba Supreme Court, per Matas J.A., held that English authorities preventing the prosecutor addressing on specific quantum of sentence were not applicable in those jurisdictions where the Crown possessed a right of appeal. It was said, as a consequence, that:

"Once it is accepted that Crown counsel can make a submission on sentence (whether in favour of severity or leniency) it should be possible to permit particularity . . . . In my view, there is no purpose in creating an artificial restraint on what counsel may say to the Court by declaring as a matter of law that counsel should not be permitted to make specific recommendations."[11]

Indeed, in Canada, it may be held to be an error in point of principle for a trial judge to patently ignore any Crown recommendation as to quantum,[12] and appellate courts (on prisoners' appeals) have been minded to increase sentence but declined to do so in deference to Crown submissions on more moderate figures.[13]

The position in Canada has suggested to Zellick that to deny power to a Crown Prosecutor to address generally on quantum is "unreal" and he proceeds to recommend that prosecutors make such an address,[14] but his views are not without opposition, particularly with respect to police

---

[8] Supra, n. 14; see (1981) 5 Crim.L.J. 65; see also *R. v. Jacombe*, unreported, 19 December 1974, Ct Cr. App. Sydney.

[9] Supra, n. 5.

[10] (1978) 40 C.C.C. (2d) 307.

[11] Ibid. at 314-315.

[12] *R. v. Jones* (1974) 17 C.C.C. (2d) 31.

[13] *R. v. Minhas* (1973) 16 Crim.L.Q. 143; *R. v. Weber* (1973) 9 C.C.C. (2d) 49.

[14] Zellick, "The Role of Prosecuting Counsel in Sentencing" [1979] Crim.L.R. 493 at 499.

prosecutors faced with unrepresented defendants.[15] This was the very mischief with which Wells J. was confronted in the appeal in *Shrubsole v. Rodriguez*, and he chose to follow the English practice rather than the Canadian, without adverting to the origins of these practices.

In contrast to recommendations on specific terms of punishment or figures, most Australian courts appear to accept the need for a Crown Prosecutor to address on type of sentence. This is done usually in the case of dispute whether a probation order or a prison term is the proper sentence, although this is generalisable to a dispute with respect to any non-custodial sentence as opposed to a custodial sentence.

It was held in *Kerr v. Matthews*[16] that refusal of a Magistrate to allow a prosecutor to address, in response to submissions for the defendant, on type of sentence was "departure from a fundamental principle of justice". Moreover, the later authorities suggest that courts ought to have the benefit of any such address. In *R. v. Wilton*, King C.J. said:

> " . . . where a submission is made by counsel for a convicted person that a sentence should be suspended or a possible suspension is mentioned by the judge, and this course is regarded by the prosecution as beyond the proper scope of the judge's discretion, a submission to that effect should be made . . ."[17]

and the learned Chief Justice went on to refer to the principle in *R. v. Tait and Bartley*. In *R. v. Aloia*[18] the same principle was employed to dismiss a Ministerial appeal against the inadequacy of a bond imposed after the Crown Prosecutor chose not to dispute the factors in mitigation upon which it was based. In *R. v. Travers and Davies*, Legoe J., after making reference to the duty of Crown Prosecutors to address on principles of sentencing, said:

> "I am comforted to know, and I think it worth recording, that the learned Crown Prosecutor indicated a tentative view as to the practice of Crown Counsel. He told us that Crown Counsel normally direct their attention . . . to the following matters . . . if necessary (or if asked) when the crime can clearly be said to fall within a certain scale of penalties; and in the appropriate case when suspension of the sentence is out of the question."[19]

In a recent decision of the Court of Criminal Appeal of Western Australia, in *R. v. Jones*,[20] the principle of *R. v. Tait and Bartley* was again invoked to dismiss a Ministerial appeal against the inadequacy of a bond, because there had been no attempt by the Crown Prosecutor to urge upon the trial judge the necessity for a custodial sentence.

It seems fairly well established that in appropriate cases the Crown Prosecutor must be heard if her or his view is that a non-custodial sentence is inappropriate to the offence. The inextricable relationship between this

---

[15] King, supra, n. 6 at 776.

[16] (1976) 15 S.A.S.R. 216 at 218 per Walters J.

[17] (1981) 28 S.A.S.R. 362 at 368, Mitchell and Williams JJ. concurring.

[18] [1983] W.A.R. 133 at 136 per Burt C.J., Kennedy J. concurring.

[19] (1983) 34 S.A.S.R. 112 at 116.

[20] *R. v. Jones* [1984] W.A.R. 175.

and the principles of sentencing is readily apparent. A non-custodial sentence will be inappropriate because, for example, the offence is so serious as to warrant a prison sentence (which is merely to say that the tariff range does not encompass non-custodial sentences), or the offence is so serious or so prevalent that there is a need for the deterrent lesson that a custodial sentence will supposedly offer, or that there is some need to specially deter or incapacitate the offender.

In *Kerr v. Matthews*, Walters J. specifically extended the scope of his comments to include any address counsel might wish to make on sentencing principles, and the context in which he did so makes it plain that his Honour envisaged address on the inapplicability of a non-custodial sentence when "preventive and deterrent aspects of punishment assume greater prominence".[21] Again, in *R. v. Wilton* and in *R. v. Travers and Davies*, references to the need for address by Crown Prosecutors on the appropriateness of non-custodial sentences were expressed in the context of the principles of sentencing. Finally, the relationship between the principles of sentencing and the question of whether the sentence should be of a custodial nature was considered in *R. v. Jones*. In connection with the Ministerial appeal against the bond, Pidgeon J. said:

> "The basis of the Crown appeal is that his Honour was in error in giving the weight he did to the rehabilitative aspect, whereas the nature of the distribution . . . [of drugs] . . . required the deterrent aspect to be of primary importance . . . . The Crown's argument in this appeal poses the question whether his Honour fell into error when deciding that the rehabilitative aspect should prevail . . . . Crown Counsel made no comment on this aspect . . . . However, in this case, if counsel for the Crown had strong views on what had been suggested, it would have been open to him to indicate that he wished to comment on sentence . . . . At no time was it suggested that the Crown's view was that the deterrent aspect was paramount . . . . His Honour was therefore forming his conclusions based on actual submissions made by the Crown. In these circumstances, I do not consider it is open for the Crown to submit to this Court that his Honour's discretion miscarried . . .".[22]

Of course, the discussion so far concerns questions of threshold severity of punishment. This refers to an increase (or decrease) in severity by change from one type of punishment to another, such as by a change from a non-custodial sentence to a custodial sentence. In some respects, this terminology may be inappropriate, for many non-custodial dispositions, particularly those for which no conviction is recorded, are not regarded as punishments. By and large, however, the major discussion at appellate level, on crossing this threshold, is of increasing or decreasing severity.

The same relationship with the principles of sentencing can be observed in relation to marginal severity of punishment. Upon the prisoners' appeals

---

[21] Supra, n. 16 at 219; this quotation in fact is from Bray C.J. in *Liddy v. Cobiac* [1969] S.A.S.R. 6 at 10, adopted by Walters J. ibid at 183-184.

[22] Supra, n. 20 at 183-184; see also *R. v. Acerbi* (1983) 11 A.Crim.R. 90.

in *R. v. Travers and Davies*[23] the South Australian Court of Criminal Appeal reduced the sentences from seven years imprisonment to four years (leaving aside orders as to non-parole periods), and in this context Legoe J. decried the lack of assistance on sentencing principles and policies, specifically directed at establishing the tariff range, afforded the trial judge by the Crown Prosecutor. In this respect, his call for assistance to be rendered on "when the crime can clearly be said to fall within a certain scale of penalties" assumes more of the nature of a submission on quantum than does the simple issue of whether the custodial threshold ought to be crossed or not. Again, in the recent Western Australian decision in *R. v. Boyd*[24] concerning a Crown appeal against inadequacy of a three-year prison term for incest, it was argued for the Crown that the trial judge had not given sufficient weight to the need for general deterrence in imposing that sentence. In fact, the Crown Prosecutor at trial, presumably mindful of the Court of Criminal Appeal's admonition in *R. v. Jones*, addressed on sentence and opposed the propriety of a non-custodial sentence. Wallace and Brinsden JJ. dismissed the appeal on the ground that the term was not manifestly inadequate, but Olney J. went further and remonstrated with the Crown for failure to put before the sentencing judge the aggravating factors which, it was submitted on appeal, warranted a prison term of more than three years.[25]

These authorities from South Australia and Western Australia assert the need for address by the Crown Prosecutor upon sentence in matters going not only to threshold severity but also to marginal severity. The Crown, according to these authorities is required, where appropriate, to address on Zellick's third and fourth stages of involvement in the sentencing process and, it is submitted, this necessarily entails consideration of the second stage, address on matters of sentencing principle. In each of these States, the risk that the principle in *R. v. Tait and Bartley* poses to Crown appeals against sentence dictates the assumption of responsibility in the second, third and fourth stages of sentencing advocacy.

In contrast with these States, the Court of Criminal Appeal in New South Wales does not accept that *R. v. Tait and Bartley* refers to anything beyond the traditional first stage, as is the position in England. As Street C.J., with whom Lee J. agreed in substance and Enderby J. concurred, said in *R. v. Gamble*, the Court of Criminal Appeal's power to interfere with a manifestly inadequate sentence was not to be constrained merely by reason of the course followed at the sentencing hearing.[26] Earlier, in his judgment, Street C.J. adverted to the duty of the Crown Prosecutor to participate in the first stage of sentencing advocacy, and continued:

> "The further question arises, however, regarding the existence of a duty on the Crown to press upon the sentencing judge forensic considerations adverse to the person standing for sentence. It has not been the practice in this State to impose upon the Crown such an obligation. I do not read

---

[23] (1983) 34 S.A.S.R. 112.

[24] *R. v. Boyd* [1984] W.A.R. 236.

[25] Ibid. at 243.

[26] *R. v. Gamble* [1983] 3 N.S.W.L.R. 356 at 359.

the passage that has been cited from *R. v. Tait and Bartley* as necessarily differing from what has been regarded as the traditional and proper role of the Crown, that is to say, a role of abstention from forensic urging upon the court of considerations adverse to the person standing before it for sentence."[27]

In issue was the failure of the Crown to argue the inappropriateness of a bond, when it argued on appeal for a prison sentence. This is a question of threshold severity, Zellick's third stage of sentencing advocacy. However, the generality of Street C.J.'s remarks appear to preclude any role for the Crown in relation to the second stage (principles of sentencing) or the fourth stage (marginal severity of punishment) let alone the fifth stage of a recommendation as to specific quantum. Yet it is clear that the obligations of the Crown, referred to by Brennan, Deane and Gallop JJ. in *R. v. Tait and Bartley*, specifically include address on principles of sentencing (the second stage). Moreover, the specific appeals before the Federal Court on that occasion entailed argument that the Crown had not, at trial, addressed on the marginal severity of punishment (the fourth stage). It seems clear that *R. v. Tait and Bartley* goes well beyond the importance which the New South Wales Court of Criminal Appeal has attributed to it.

In contrast with the call for assistance by Crown Prosecutors in relation to threshold and marginal severity of punishment, courts in all jurisdictions reject any role for the Crown in recommendation as to specific quantum of punishment. In *R. v. Tait and Bartley*, Brennan, Deane and Gallop JJ. said:

> " . . . the Crown is required to make its submissions as to sentence fairly and in an even-handed manner, and . . . the Crown does not, as an adversary, press the sentencing court for a heavy sentence . . .".[28]

In *Shrubsole v. Rodriguez*, Wells J. elaborated upon these comments by saying:

> "There are some cases, especially where the facts are within what might be termed the usual range of seriousness, on which no address or even comment is necessary. Where the facts are plainly more or less serious than the usual case, some remarks may well be appropriate—even obligatory. The distinction is, of course, clear between, on the one hand, drawing attention to the prominent features of a case, advancing submissions as to whether or not a particular form of order should be considered, and suggesting, in general terms, the degree of seriousness represented by the facts as a whole (including, it may be, some reference to prevalence or other matter of local concern), and, on the other hand, addressing in terms calculated to influence the emotions of the court against the prisoner, and straining overzealously, to persuade the court to impose a more severe penalty than would otherwise have been imposed. The former class of submissions is entirely proper; the latter would be disapproved of by all courts . . . ."[29]

---

[27] Ibid.

[28] *R. v. Tait and Bartley* (1979) 24 A.L.R. 473 at 477.

[29] *Shrubsole v. Rodriguez* (1978) 18 S.A.S.R. 233 at 236.

These remarks, made in 1978, preceded power to bring Ministerial appeals in South Australia, and the early part of these dicta have, perhaps, been overtaken by subsequent authorities calling for a more emphatic role by Crown Prosecutors in that State. However, the latter part of these dicta raises a point of interest. They appear to equate an address on quantum with an emotive harangue, yet Zellick draws a clear distinction between a recommendation or quantum, and an emotive, personally opinionated or prejudicial call for severity or lenience.

It would seem that there may well be grounds for contending that the Crown ought to address on specific quantum if done without the passion which both Wells J. and Zellick deplore. To return to an example referred to earlier, one of the leading sentencing authorities adopted in Queensland,[30] is that of the Court of Appeal (Criminal Division) in *R. v. Hodgson*,[31] concerned with the circumstances in which a trial judge may (if life is the statutory maximum) impose that sentence on a mentally disordered offender who is likely to be dangerous in future. It would be a patent absurdity to expect an address on sentence, and in particular on the intricacies of the lines of authority in this area, without hearing a Crown Prosecutor employ the words "life imprisonment".

Thus, there may be some merit in Zellick's argument that the proscription on the prosecutor mentioning quantum is "unreal" and, as he says:

> " . . . the words 'more severe' beg the question more severe than what? It cannot be more severe than the judge would otherwise have imposed, since that cannot be known. It can mean only, then, more severe than the defendant would like, which hardly seems a consideration of intrinsic value."[32]

Perhaps there is a third meaning: more severe than would have been imposed if the prosecutor had not addressed. Yet this too is untenable: even an outline of comparative sentences may prompt a more severe sentence than the trial judge might have awarded in response to the urging of rehabilitative considerations by defence counsel. Whilst there may well be objection to address on quantum when defendants are unrepresented, it would be far better to recognise the explicit policy consideration against address in this context, and not to confuse the baby with the bath water.

Consequences of Crown Prosecutors' Activism

Some residual objections to the assumption by Crown Prosecutors of a greater activism in sentencing advocacy remain. These objections centre upon the Crown's proper role in pre-trial sentence negotiations and the influence which these negotiations should have upon the courts.

1. *The Crown View on Sentence*

One apparent objection to the demand for greater activism is that

---

[30] See Campbell, supra, n. 70.

[31] (1967) 52 Cr.App.R. 113.

[32] Zellick, "The Role of Prosecuting Counsel in Sentencing" [1979] Crim.L.R. 493 at 500.

enunciated by the Victorian Full Court, comprising Young C.J., McInerney and McGarvie JJ., in *R. v. Marshall*:

> "The prosecutor before a sentencing judge in accordance with the long tradition of the law invariably refrains from expressing an opinion as to the sentence to be passed. The Solicitor-General explained that it is not possible from a practical point of view, even if it were desirable to depart from the long-standing practice and authorise the Crown Prosecutor in any given case to inform the court what sentence the Crown thought appropriate. The view of the individual prosecutor would be irrelevant and no machinery exists for the submission of, as it were, an ex officio view, nor would it be desirable."[33]

There are several points of response which might be made to this passage. The authorities demanding assistance on sentence from Crown Prosecutors specifically eschew any reference to expressions of opinion on sentence. The authorities call for assistance in determination of facts and in submissions on sentencing principles and policies. In the decision of the Quebec Court of Appeal in *R. v. Lamer*[34] the Crown Prosecutor was criticised for putting submissions on sentence without attempt at citation of any relevant authorities or principles. The mere expression of opinion is irrelevant to the processes of the Court, no matter whose opinion it is.

The old authorities refer to Crown Prosecutors appearing on behalf of, or deputising for, the Attorney-General.[35] Some authorities go so far as to equate the commissioned officer's powers with that of the Minister.[36] The better view seems to be that of Kidston Q.C. of the New South Wales bar, who said that "a Crown Prosecutor has the quality of counsel retained by the Crown, with the functions and discretions of counsel . . .".[37]

This appears to require, therefore, that instructions be sought upon sentence by each Crown Prosecutor appearing in a trial. This may be varied in those jurisdictions which have established Directorates of Public Prosecutions,[38] at least with respect to the instructions of the Attorney-General. However, it is difficult to imagine that the principle in *R. v. Tait and Bartley* is not equally applicable to the Director of Public Prosecution's appeals against sentence as it is to Ministerial appeals.

Nonetheless, the authorities calling for submissions on sentence do not call for expressions of opinion but for addresses upon principles and policies upon types of sentences available and upon tariff ranges. If, as the authorities suggest, the submissions are demanded by duties to the court, then the substance of these duties may well conflict with instructions. Counsel's duty

---

[33] [1981] V.R. 725 at 735.

[34] (1973) 17 C.C.C. (2d) 411.

[35] *R. v. Ellis* (1852) Legge 749; *Re Dakin* (1837) 13 V.L.R. 522.

[36] *Solicitor-General v. Wylde* (1945) 46 S.R. (N.S.W.) 83.

[37] "The Office of Crown Prosecutor (more particularly in New South Wales)" (1958) 32 A.L.J. 148 at 151.

[38] *Director of Public Prosecutors Act* 1982 (Vic.); *Director of Public Prosecutors Act* 1983 (Cth); *Prosecution of Offences Act* 1879 (Imp.).

to the court to assist it to impose a proper sentence would override the duty to ventilate instructions.[39]

Of course, the decision in *R. v. Tait and Bartley* does not deny that it may be necessary to take instructions with respect to sentence. That decision poses the risk that those instructions may not be put on appeal if the Crown Prosecutor does not bother to give voice to them at trial.

2. *Sentence Negotiation*

The principle in *R. v. Tait and Bartley* is the matrix of another group of related issues to do with the influence which Crown Prosecutors have on sentence. Official opprobrium attaches to the involvement of judges in pre-trial sentence bargaining,[40] but not to the involvement of the Crown Prosecutor in this process. For this reason the vast secondary literature on negotiated punishment draws a distinction between sentence bargaining and charge bargaining. The former involves the judge in cloistered conference with counsel, and is disapproved, whereas the latter, albeit subterranean, does not involve the court.[41] Such empirical evidence as there is suggests that charge bargaining is not a rare practice in most Australian jurisdictions.[42] There is an inescapable relationship between charge bargaining and the prosecution role in sentencing,[43] and this suggests that the assumption by Crown Prosecutors of a more active role in sentencing will strengthen their hands in any pre-trial negotiations.

In contrast with the heavy secondary literature on pre-trial negotiation with respect to sentence, there is, in Australia, very little sustained curial analysis of the practice. Rather, the judicial gaze has been focussed on the proper approach which courts ought to take in sentencing those who plead guilty. Certainly, this is not confined solely to those situations where a plea follows pre-trial negotiations, but the principles evolved have a significant impact upon the role of a Crown Prosecutor in sentencing.

A plea of guilty constitutes a solemn confession to the defined elements of the offence.[44] It is fundamental to our criminal jurisprudence that any confession must be voluntary. Thus, pressure by the court upon a defendant to plead is wrong.[45] Similarily, at least in summary proceedings, attempts to procure a plea by a prosecutor's reassurance or promise with respect to

---

[39] *Rondel v. Worsley* [1967] 3 W.L.R. 1666 or 1674 per Lord Reid; *Clyne v. N.S.W. Bar Association* (1966) 104 C.L.R. 186 or 200 per Dixon C.J., McTiernan, Fullagar, Menzies and Windeyer JJ.

[40] *Bruce v. The Queen*, Unreported, 21 May 1976, High Court of Australia; *R. v. Marshall*, supra, n. 33 on p. 228; *R. v. Tait and Bartley*, supra, n. 28.

[41] See, for example, Australian Law Reform Commission, *Sentencing of Federal Offenders* A.G.P.S., Canberra, 1980, par. 112 ff.; Sallman, "The Guilty Plea as an Element in Sentencing" (1980) 54 *Law Institute Journal* 105, 185; Westling, "Plea Bargaining: A Forecast for the Future" (1976) 7 Syd. L.R. 424; McGuire, "Plea Bargaining: Its Significance in the Australian Criminal Justice System" (1981) 6 Q.L. 1 at 47, 102; Davis, "Sentences for Sale" [1971] Crim.L.R. 161, 218.

[42] Australian Law Reform Commission, ibid. at pars 113-119.

[43] Ibid. at par. 122.

[44] *R. v. Tonks and Goss* [1963] V.R. 121; *R. v. Jerome and McMahon* [1964] Qd R. 595; *R. v. Dickens* [1976] 2 N.S.W.L.R. 260.

[45] *R. v. Barnes* (1970) 55 Cr.App.R. 100; *R. v. Clarke* [1972] 1 All E.R. 219; *R. v. Cain* [1976] Crim.L.R. 464.

punishment is soundly disapproved.[46] Even pressure by defence counsel to induce a plea of guilty may be improper if that pressure surpasses informing the defendant of his options in "strong language".[47] As if to remove the incentive for prosecutor's activism in pre-trial negotiations bearing upon punishment, the Australian courts have generally declined to accept a plea of guilty as indicating a lesser, or discounted sentence.[48] This is in contrast with the general practice in England.[49] However, some Australian decisions suggest that a plea of guilty should indicate a lesser sentence[50] and some English authorities suggest that it should not.[51] It is probably safest to say that the decisions on the matter are far from uniform.

Of course, even under the current Australian orthodoxy, courts in this country do not ignore a plea of guilty for sentencing purposes. A plea of guilty may be considered as an indicator of genuine remorse and this may prompt a lesser sentence.[52] The plea may be the culmination of active assistance to the police, and this may prompt a lesser sentence.[53] Or it may manifest a desire to save a complainant from recalling unpleasant experiences in testimony, and this too may prompt a lesser sentence.[54]

The courts have evolved an approach which would suggest that mere willingness to strike a bargain with the prosecutor will not generally, in the absence of more, bring about sentencing credit. This seems inconsistent with the idea of a more active role in sentencing to be undertaken by Crown Prosecutors. If they are to address beyond sentencing principles, if they are to refer to types of available punishments, range of sentences or even quantum of sentence, then Crown Prosecutors might be seen to be endeavouring to influence the trial judge towards a penalty more or less favourable to the convicted person depending upon that person's willingness to participate in a negotiated plea arrangement. In other words, that which is rejected for the public arena is transferred to the privacy of pre-trial negotiation by virtue of the assumption of an active role in sentencing.

Conclusion

The last two decades in the common law world have seen a great increase in attention focussed on punishment. One of the major foci of this gaze has been upon secretive and unscrutinised exercise of discretions by all persons

---

[46] *Heffernan v. Ward* [1959] Qd R. 12; *Salter v. Seibohm* (1972) 4 S.A.S.R. 193; *Tarca v. Price* (1975) 10 S.A.S.R. 604; *Di Camillo v. Wilcox* [1964] W.A.R. 44.

[47] *R. v. Hall* (1968) 52 Cr.App.R. 528.

[48] *R. v. Perry* [1969] Q.W.N. 17; *R. v. Cox* [1972] Q.W.N. 54; *R. v. Tait and Bartley* supra, n. 28; see also *R. v. Harper* (1968) 2 Q.B. 108.

[49] *R. v. De Haan* [1960] 2 Q.B. 108; *R. v. Atkinson* [1978] 1 W.L.R. 425.

[50] *R. v. Gray* [1977] V.R. 225; *R. v. Shannon* (1979) 21 S.A.S.R. 442; *R. v. Schumacher* (1981) 3 A.Crim.R. 441; see also the report of the South Australian Chief Justice, King C.J.'s, call in (1984) 58 A.L.J. 481.

[51] See for example *R. v. Harper* supra, n. 48; *R. v. Plimmer* (1975) 61 Cr.App.R. 264.

[52] *R. v. Cox*, supra, n. 48.

[53] *R. v. Hayes* [1981] W.A.R. 242; *R. v. Perry* supra, n. 48.

[54] See *R. v. Shannon* supra, n. 50 at 446.

associated with the criminal justice system: by police,[55] by prison warders,[56] by parole boards[57] and by prosecutors.[58] The remedy offered to correct undesirable effects of these secret discretions is to bring the matters forward into the public view, frequently in the form of material presented in open court.

At the same time, the sentencing process which is undertaken in open court has undergone change. The number and type of non-custodial dispositions has blossomed. Courts have explicitly recognised the undesirability of imprisonment in many cases. This has manifested itself in bodies of sentencing principle in all jurisdictions. The official law reports have increasingly devoted their pages to sentencing decisions. Specialist law reports and journals have sprung up devoted, entirely in some cases, to sentencing. The pages of academic commentary on sentencing have multiplied.

The courts and commentators in most jurisdictions have called for a more active role in sentencing to be undertaken by Crown Prosecutors. There is explicit recognition that the system of justice we employ necessitates adversarial debate in the sentencing as well as in the adjudicative stages of the criminal trial. Of course, the Crown Prosecutor's role is limited by the duty of fairness, but this is no different from the duty imposed in the adjudicative stage. The visibility of the adversarial debate on sentencing which the Canadian and most recent Australian authorities call for, is in contrast with the concomitant low-visibility of the increased power in pre-trial negotiations. This has yet to be addressed in the cases calling for greater activism on sentence by Crown Prosecutors.

[This paper is a revised version of an address presented at a Seminar on Sentencing held by the Crown Prosecutor's Association of Queensland, 13 December 1984.]

---

[55] Criminal Law and Penal Methods Reform Committee of South Australia, *Sentencing and Corrections* Government Printer, Adelaide, 1973; Australian Law Reform Commission *Criminal Investigation* A.G.P.S., Canberra, 1975; *Report of the Committee of Inquiry into the Enforcement of Criminal Law in Queensland* The Law Reform Commission, Brisbane, 1977.

[56] *Report of the Royal Commission into New South Wales Prisons* Government Printer, Sydney, 1978.

[57] Twentieth Century Task Force on Criminal Sentencing, *Fair and Certain Punishment* McGraw-Hill, N.Y. 1976; Society of Friends, *Struggle for Justice* Hill and Wang, N.Y. 1971; Von Hirsch, *Doing Justice: The Choice of Punishments*, Hill and Wang, N.Y. 1976.

[58] Baldwin and McConville, *Negotiated Justice* Martin Robertson, London, 1977; Wilcox, *The Decision to Prosecute* Butterworths, London, 1972; Moody and Tombs, *Prosecution in the Public Interest* Scottish Academic Press, Edinburgh, 1982.

[10]

VICTIMS' VOICES IN CRIMINAL COURT: THE NEED FOR RESTRAINT

Donald J. Hall*

I. INTRODUCTION AND OVERVIEW

The "victims' rights" phenomenon is now a full-fledged component of the criminal justice system in the United States.[1] This development — in the name of increased sensitivity to and concern for crime victims

---

* Professor of Law, Vanderbilt University School of Law.

I wish to thank Rebecca Brown, Barry Friedman, Susan Kay and Walter Kurtz for taking the time to read and comment upon an initial draft of this article. I also acknowledge the excellent research assistance provided by P. Perry R. Finney and Thomas A. Nicol.

1. *See generally Symposium: Victims' Rights*, 11 PEPPERDINE L. REV. 1 (Symposium 1984), *Follow-Up Issue on Victims' Rights*, 17 PEPPERDINE L. REV. 1-156 (1989); *see also* Carrington & Nicholson, *Victim's Rights: An Idea Whose Time Has Come — Five Years Later: The Maturing of an Idea*, 17 PEPPERDINE L. REV. 1, 17 (1989). Some of the earlier articles on this topic include Hall, *The Role of the Victim in the Prosecution and Disposition of a Criminal Case*, 28 VAND. L. REV. 931 (1975); McDonald, *Towards a Bicentennial Revolution in Criminal Justice: The Return of the Victim*, 13 AM. CRIM. L. REV. 649 (1976); and Goldstein, *Defining the Role of the Victim in Criminal Prosecution*, 52 MISS. L.J. 515 (1982).

— has culminated in a significant number of state and federal statutes.[2] Many of the statutes address the basic concern of compensation to victims of crime.[3] Others, in similar fashion, require that persons convicted of crimes provide financial restitution to victims for the losses they have incurred.[4] Additionally, many jurisdictions require that victims be given information and updates regarding the prosecution of their criminal cases.[5]

A majority of states have gone further with the enactment of "victim participation" statutes.[6] Unlike those laws which provide for financial and informational assistance to victims, these statutes also ensure that a crime victim has the opportunity to be an active participant in at least some phases of the criminal case. Thus, the individual victim has a voice — perhaps even a legal right — to influence the way in which the defendant is treated by prosecutors,[7] judges,[8] juries[9] and parole officials.[10]

---

2. Indeed, some states have amended their constitutions to provide victims greater participatory roles in criminal cases. *See* Roland, *Progress in the Victim Reform Movement: No Longer the "Forgotten Victim,"* 17 PEPPERDINE L. REV. 35, 38-40 (1989) (*citing* CAL. CONST. art I, § 28; R.I. CONST. art I, § 23) (California's amendment provides for victim's right to restitution, safe schools, consideration of public safety when setting bail, and unrestricted admissibility of prior felony convictions. Rhode Island's amendment establishes victim's right to be treated with dignity, to restitution, and to address court regarding impact of crime). *See also Symposium: Perspectives on Proposals for a Constitutional Amendment Proposing Victim Participation in the Criminal Justice System*, 34 WAYNE L. REV. 1 (1987).

3. Certain expenses incurred by a crime victim are reimbursed by the government, irrespective of the defendant's conviction. Approximately 45 states have such plans. NATIONAL ORGANIZATION FOR VICTIM ASSISTANCE, VICTIM RIGHTS AND SERVICES: A LEGISLATIVE DIRECTORY (1987).

4. In contrast to "victim compensation" provided by the government, restitution refers to court-ordered payment by the defendant to directly compensate the victim for his or her loss. Virtually every state grants authority to courts to order restitution. *See* Roland, *supra* note 2, at 41-43 (detailing history and use of restitution in American courts).

5. *See* Roland, *supra* note 2, at 48-50 (forty-three states have enacted laws which require public officials to keep victims informed of criminal proceedings).

6. A 1989 American Bar Association study identified 36 states with legislation providing for victim participation in the criminal justice system. HILLENBRAND & SMITH, VICTIM RIGHTS LEGISLATION: AN ASSESSMENT OF ITS IMPACT ON CRIMINAL JUSTICE PRACTITIONERS AND VICTIMS 4, Appendix A (A.B.A. Crim. Just. Sec. Victim Witness Project 1989). I am appreciative of the helpful assistance provided to me by Ms. Hillenbrand and Ms. Smith, not only in sending documents but in responding to my letters and calls concerning various aspects of their study.

7. The victim sometimes is granted a statutory right to express an opinion regarding plea agreements. *See, e.g.*, FLA. STAT. § 960.001(1)(e) (Supp. 1990) (victim shall be consulted by state attorney to obtain victim's views regarding pretrial release of defendant, pretrial diversion programs, plea agreements, and sentencing); *see also infra* notes 14-34 and accompanying text (discussing types of victim participation statutes); Welling, *Victim Participation in Plea Bargains*, 65 WASH. U.L.Q. 301, 304-05 (1987) (discussing types of involvement victim can have in plea bargaining process).

8. Almost every state allows for victim participation at sentencing. *See* McLeod, *An Examination of the Victim's Role at Sentencing: Results of a Survey of Probation Administrators*, 71

This Article examines those legislative directives that purport to grant victims the power to influence the ultimate disposition of a guilty party's case. More specifically, it addresses processes by and through which the crime victim recommends an appropriate sentence for the defendant, whether in the context of a plea of guilty or sentencing after a finding of guilt. Available data will be examined to determine ways in which victims effectuate this new-found power. An attempt to measure the actual impact of the victims' expressed desires upon case dispositions will also be undertaken. My analysis will examine the fundamental evil associated with victim participation practices: disparate sentencing of similarly-situated defendants. I will conclude by arguing that these specific victim input measures have been pushed too far, and that policymakers should arrive at a better balance between victim involvement and a fair criminal justice system.

II. VICTIM PARTICIPATION SCHEMES: CASE ILLUSTRATIONS

In order to appreciate the significance of victim participation statutes, both as written and as implemented, the stage will be set by presenting hypothetical case illustrations. These incidents, while fictional, cannot be characterized as unrealistic or apocryphal.

A. *The Crime*

The defendant, Jill Schultz, is a single, 22-year-old white female, who has finished two years of college. She has no criminal record and

---

JUDICATURE 162, 164 (1987) (preparation of victim impact statement is authorized or mandated in 42 states). The Hillenbrand & Smith study found that 34 of the 36 states in their study provided for written victim impact statements. As to contents of those statements, seven states authorized or required the victim's opinion of a proposed sentence or sentence recommendation. HILLENBRAND & SMITH, *supra* note 6, at 30. Additionally, 22 of the 36 states have allocution statutes — providing victims the right to make an oral statement at sentencing; five expressly authorize victims to opine relative to sentencing. *Id.* at 30-31.

Victims are expected to convey their opinions to the sentencing authority, which then supposedly incorporates that piece of information into the full mix of factors deemed relevant to sentencing. An extreme example of victim participation in sentencing occurred in Minnesota when a Minneapolis state judge allowed a rape victim to choose her assailant's punishment. "This," he explained, "just seemed to me the right and proper thing to do." Middleton, *Victims of Crime Flexing Muscles*, The Nat'l Law Journal, Mar. 13, 1989, at 26, col. 1.

9. Kentucky, for example, provides for the use of victim impact statements in which a recommendation for an appropriate sentence may be made by the victim. KY. REV. STAT. ANN. § 421.520 (Michie Supp. 1990). This jurisdiction also authorizes jury sentencing in felony cases. KY. REV. STAT. ANN. § 532.055(2) (Michie Supp. 1988).

10. *See* McLeod, *Getting Free*, 4 CRIM. J. 12, 13 (1989) (reporting that 39 states provide for some form of victim participation at parole proceedings). With no VIS, about 50 percent of parole applications are denied; however, "where [VISs] are submitted, the rate of parole denial rises sharply to approximately 80 percent." *Id.* at 43.

is employed as a salesperson in a clothing store. After working on a Wednesday afternoon, she drove to a local bar to meet a friend. Together, each consumed three glasses of wine. Thereafter, she began driving toward her apartment. She turned onto a residential street and accelerated to a speed of forty-two miles an hour, twelve miles over the posted limit of thirty miles per hour. A 10-year-old boy on a bicycle swerved in front of her vehicle. Due to a combination of unlawful speed and inebriation, Schultz was unable to take proper evasive action. The boy was struck and killed, and Schultz has been charged with involuntary manslaughter because of her alleged criminal negligence.

This case is to be heard in a state which affords the parents of the deceased victim an opportunity to consult with the prosecutor regarding a plea of guilty.[11] Moreover, assuming a verdict of guilt after trial, they have the right to submit a victim impact statement (VIS) to the probation officer in which they are allowed to make a sentence recommendation. They also have the privilege to appear at the sentencing hearing and testify in person.[12] Upon receipt of the victim impact statement, and prior to disposition of the sentence, the court is mandated to consider information provided in that statement.[13]

In all of the following case illustrations, the facts above, other than the identity of the manslaughter victim, are identical.

B. *Victim Variables*

Case No. 1. Randall Jones is a 38-year-old black male with a college education who is employed in public relations. His youngest child and only son was struck and killed by Schultz. Jones and his wife are devastated by the loss of their son. After Mr. Jones refuses to concur with a proposed negotiated plea, the case proceeds to a jury verdict of guilty. When later contacted by the probation officer, Jones submits a detailed and forceful statement cataloging his grief and urging articulately that the defendant receive the maximum possible sentence for her offense of involuntary manslaughter. Additionally, Jones appears at the sentencing hearing and gives direct testimony — in very emotional terms — similar to his written victim impact statement. Jill Schultz is sentenced to a term of incarceration of five years.

Case No. 2. Samuel Smith is a 38-year-old white male with an eighth grade education who has worked for various contractors as a day la-

11. *Supra* note 7.

12. *Supra* note 8.

13. *See supra* notes 19-36 and accompanying text (discussing various state statutes).

borer. He and his wife have three children, and his youngest was struck and killed by Schultz. The case proceeds to trial, there having been no serious negotiations attempted by either the prosecutor or defense attorney. When contacted by the probation officer, Smith is very emotional and grief-stricken, but unable to articulate his feelings in a coherent and well-organized way. He nonetheless conveys his sense of loss as best he can, making no comment as to a sentence recommendation. Because of his need to provide income for the family, he does not appear for the sentencing hearing; the pre-sentence investigation report is submitted to the court with a summary of Smith's remarks. Jill Schultz is sentenced to two years' incarceration.

Case No. 3. Wanda Williams is a 38-year-old white woman with a high school diploma. She is a single parent and her only child, who was slightly retarded, was struck and killed by the defendant. Ms. Williams has had a checkered job history, having been fired by several employers. She has sought counseling on many occasions and has been described by friends and neighbors as mentally unstable. She, too, was overwrought over the loss of her child, but responded to the trauma by leaving the state to locate elsewhere. The prosecutor discovered that Ms. Williams had left no forwarding address. After repeated attempts to locate her, the prosecutor concluded that she was unavailable. The criminal court judge accepted a plea of guilty and concurred with the prosecutor's recommendation that Ms. Schultz be sentenced to one year in the county jail.

Case No. 4. John Johnson is a 38-year-old white male with no formal education. Because of illiteracy, his jobs have been limited to menial farm labor. Furthermore, he has had numerous encounters with police and has been convicted of a number of relatively minor offenses over the years. He and his wife, who works as a housekeeper for a local motel, are grief-stricken over the loss of their only son. At the time of his son's death, Johnson was awaiting trial on shoplifting charges. No plea negotiations were attempted, and Schultz' trial resulted in a jury verdict of guilty. When contacted by the probation officer and told that he could submit a victim impact statement, Johnson replied, "No way. It don't matter anyhow. No judge ever believes what I have to say." Accordingly, no victim impact statement was prepared, and Johnson did not appear at the defendant's sentencing hearing. Schultz received a sentence of one year incarceration in the local jail.

Case No. 5. Sharon Alford is a 38-year-old black female who received her bachelor's degree in social work. Her only child was struck and killed by Schultz. When notified by the prosecutor that the defense attorney had initiated plea negotiations, she responded, "My husband and I are at peace with God, as is my little boy. We pray for the woman who did this. Only God sits in judgment. Therefore, we don't see any need for this woman to suffer and we favor placing her on probation. We pray for her soul." Ms. Alford also exercised her right to appear at the sentencing hearing, at which time she reiterated her approval of probation for the defendant. Jill Schultz was placed on probation for a period of two years.

In all of the cases illustrated, the statutory victim participation scheme has been satisfied. In each case, the sentencing judge has complied with the appropriate victim participation statute. The case disposition in each instance — from five years incarceration to probation — is realistic, if not highly likely, even though the criminal event, actual harm to the victim and the defendant's culpability are identical in each scenario. Hence, the sentence for the identical offense and identical offender will have been based upon but one variable: the victim's voice.

III. VICTIM PARTICIPATION STATUTES: OVERVIEW

Almost all states have statutory provisions allowing for victim participation at sentencing.[14] A smaller number expressly allow for victim interaction at the plea-bargaining phase.[15] While victim input is permitted at sentencing, the extent of such involvement varies from one jurisdiction to another, as does the procedure by which that information is conveyed to the court.[16] Also, there is lack of agreement among states as to the question whether the sentencing authority is obligated to consider such information for purposes of imposing sentence.

A sampling of statutes reveals that the crime victim plays what appears to be a significant role in influencing the defendant's sentence. Sometimes these provisions address themselves to prosecutors for implementation. State attorneys in Florida, for example, are under a duty to consult the victim "in order to obtain the views of the victim . . . about the disposition of any criminal case . . ., including the [pre-trial] release of the accused, plea agreements, and participation in pre-trial diversion programs."[17] West Virginia prosecutors have a duty worded in almost identical terms.[18] Contrary to Florida, however (where it is

14. McLeod, *supra* note 8, at 162.

15. Welling, *supra* note 7, at 340-345.

16. HILLENBRAND & SMITH, *supra* note 6, at 26-30.

17. FLA. STAT. §960.001(1)(e) (Supp. 1990).

18. W. VA. CODE §61-11A-6(a)(5) (1989). "[T]he victim of a serious crime . . . shall be consulted by the prosecuting attorney in order to obtain the views of the victim or family about the disposition of any criminal case . . ., including the views of the victim about dismissal, release of the accused pending judicial proceedings, plea negotiations and pre-trail diversion programs." *Id.*

unclear how much weight, if any, must be placed upon this data by the judge), a West Virginia criminal court judge must consider the victim impact statement "as a factor in determining the appropriate sentence."[19] Arizona, in like fashion, affords the victim the right to "express opinions concerning the crime [and] the defendant" which, in turn, must be included by the probation officer in the pre-sentence investigation report.[20] The law then mandates sentencing judges to "consider the . . . opinions presented by the victim."[21] Kentucky,[22] Michigan,[23] and New York[24] also grant to crime victims the right to express personal opinions as to the disposition of the defendant's case.

Two other jurisdictions have enacted provisions ostensibly giving victims participatory roles almost equal to those of defendants. Crime victims in South Carolina have their own "Bill of Rights," which are to be "protected by law enforcement agencies, prosecutors, and judges in a manner no less vigorous than the protections afforded criminal defendants."[25] Among those rights is the right to make recommendations regarding pre-trial release,[26] speedy trial,[27] and to make a victim impact statement (to be considered at sentencing or a disposition hearing, and at any parole hearing).[28] A related section (entitled "Victims . . . Have a Right to Due Process"[29]) affords the victim a right "to participate . . . directly or through representation," which is further defined to mean the right "to retain counsel with standing."[30] These so-called Due

19. *Id.* This legislation was enacted to "enhance and protect the . . . role of crime victims." W. VA. CODE §61.11A-1(b) (1989).

20. ARIZ. REV. STAT. ANN. §13-702(F) (1989).

21. *Id.*

22. KY. REV. STAT. ANN. §421.520(2), (3) (Michie Supp. 1990).

23. MICH. COMP. LAWS ANN. §780.763(3)(d) (West Supp. 1990).

24. N.Y. EXEC. LAW §647(1) (McKinney Supp. 1990).

25. S.C. CODE ANN. §16-3-1510 (Law. Co-op. 1985). Other states have adopted measures frequently characterized as "Victims' Rights" bills. California, for example, amended both its constitution and its statutes in 1982 in the name of a "Victims' Bill of Rights." In that same year, the President's Task Force on Victims of Crime recommended an amendment to the Sixth Amendment of the United States Constitution, providing a crime victim "the right to be present and to be heard at all critical stages of judicial proceedings." For a more detailed discussion of these developments, see Hellerstein, *infra* note 87, at 396-397, and Lamborn, *Victim Participation in the Criminal Justice Process: The Proposals For a Constitutional Amendment*, 34 WAYNE L. REV. 125 (1987).

26. S.C. CODE ANN. §16-3-1530(C)(5) (Law. Co-op 1985).

27. S.C. CODE ANN. §16-3-1530(F) (Law. Co-op. 1985).

28. S.C. CODE ANN. §16-3-1550(B) (Law. Co-op. 1989).

29. S.C. CODE ANN. §16-3-1530(F) (Law. Co-op. 1985).

30. *Id.* This "standing" provision is limited to cases in which the "victim's reputation is involved." It is unclear what kind of criminal matter was intended to be covered by this phrase.

Process guarantees must be protected by "the court, the solicitor, and the defense . . . as diligently as the defendant's right."[31]

In similar fashion, the Washington state legislature has expressed its intention to "grant to victims of crime and the survivors of such victims a significant role in the criminal justice system."[32] Rights explicated include a victim impact statement, right to recommend sentence, right to recommend that no criminal charges be filed (but only if the case is "relatively minor") and — in the context of plea bargaining — the right to approve the prosecutor's exchange of a guilty plea to a charge not fully descriptive of the defendant's actual criminal conduct, but only if the victim's request "is not a result of pressure from the defendant."[33] These rights are to be "honored and protected by law enforcement agencies, prosecutors, and judges in a manner no less vigorous than the protections afforded criminal defendants."[34]

As far-reaching as the laws in these two states appear to be, provisions were enacted by the respective legislative bodies to soften or ameliorate their effects. South Carolina directed that its Sentencing Guidelines Commission develop guidelines for the courts to follow when considering a victim impact statement in determining sentence.[35] Washington, also relying upon a "guidelines" approach, mandates that "standards apply equally to offenders . . . without discrimination as to any element that does not relate to the crime or the previous record of the defendant."[36]

This abbreviated statutory survey demonstrates that some jurisdictions have gone far, indeed, in granting the victim of a crime a significant voice in the sentence given the defendant. Even where the statutory language is silent or ambiguous with respect to a victim's right to recommend sentence, it appears that victims play an important role in shaping criminal case dispositions.[37] Had the case hypotheticals oc-

---

31. *Id.* How, one might ask, is a defense attorney supposed to guarantee those rights without transgressing the duty of allegiance to his or her client? *See* LAFAVE & ISRAEL, CRIMINAL PROCEDURE, §11.9(a) at 514 (1985) (noting that constitutional right to effective assistance of counsel "entitles the defendant to the 'undivided loyalty' of his counsel").

32. WASH. REV. CODE ANN. §7.69.010 (Supp. 1990).

33. WASH. REV. CODE ANN. §§9.94A.110 (1988), 9.94A.440(1)(i) (Supp. 1990), 9.94A.450(21)(c) (1988).

34. WASH. REV. CODE ANN. §7.69.010 (Supp. 1990).

35. S.C. CODE ANN. §16-3-1550(e) (Law. Co-op 1985). This section (Public Act No. 9, section 1) was deleted in 1987; however, the reasons for the deletion are unknown.

36. WASH. REV. CODE ANN. §9.94A.340 (1988).

37. Hillenbrand and Smith have found that statutes have not in fact effectively delimited victim participation practices. *See infra* Part IV(A) (discussing whether victims actually utilize victim participation statutes).

curred in any of these states, it is highly probable that the individual defendant's sentence would have been influenced, if not almost dictated, by the victim's recommendation or absence thereof.

IV. IMPLEMENTATION AND IMPACT

Do victims exercise their participatory rights in criminal cases? If so, do they display vindictiveness through requests for harsh treatment of defendants? Do some victims exhibit merciful attitudes toward their transgressors? Do their voices — either for vengeance or forgiveness — have an effect upon case dispositions? Exhaustive studies are not yet available, but existing empirical data provides preliminary, though sometimes inconsistent, answers to these questions.

A. Utilization Rates

Having demonstrated that crime victims have the right to influence case dispositions, the initial inquiry is whether victims actually utilize these opportunities. For the sheer presence of the victim — at least when the victim offers an opinion as to the appropriate sentence — offers great potential for unequal sentencing.

A number of state statutes are written in such a way as to indicate that victims will almost always be active participants.[38] Yet studies suggest that victims exercise their participatory roles in fewer cases than might have been predicted. Maureen McLeod reported in 1987 that several jurisdictions in her survey had VIS preparations in fifty percent or less felony cases; yet she also found an overall seventy-five percent VIS preparation rate for all felonies.[39] Her study also examined victim allocution, available in all thirty-three states responding to her survey. Overall, fewer than eighteen percent of victims were in attendance when their offenders were sentenced; oral statements were made by less than ten percent of crime victims.[40]

While another study found that a majority of sexual assault victims made sentence recommendations,[41] the most recent assessment by Susan Hillenbrand and Barbara Smith[42] focused on 359 victims from five

38. *See* FLA. STAT. §960.001(1)(e) (Supp. 1990) (requiring victims' opinions regarding sentencing be sought by prosecutor); TENN. CODE ANN. §40-35-207(a)(8) (1990) (requiring victims' opinions regarding sentencing be set forth in presentence investigation report).

39. McLeod, *supra* note 8, at 164.

40. *Id.* at 164-65.

41. In one study, it was found that 248 victims (out of 417 total) — or almost 60 percent — made sentence recommendations regarding their sex assailants. Walsh, *Placebo Justice: Victim Recommendations and Offender Sentences in Sexual Assault Cases*, 77 J. CRIM. L. & CRIMINOLOGY 1126, 1129-30 (1986).

42. HILLENBRAND & SMITH, *supra* note 6, at 128.

states in which victim participation provisions were in effect. Victims were chosen randomly (albeit the majority were from New York City) and they represented robbery, assault, domestic violence and sexual assault victims.[43] The authors found that approximately twenty-five percent of victims in guilty plea cases were consulted about the plea, though about seventy percent had asked to be told if a plea to a lesser crime was being considered.[44] As to sentencing hearings, however, almost fifty percent of the victims reported having been consulted about the sentence.[45] By contrast, very few victims surveyed stated that they had told someone that they desired to make a victim impact statement. Only fifty-nine of 215 victims (twenty-seven percent) reported having actually made such a statement.[46] As to the victim impact statement content, most victims described how the crimes affected them physically and emotionally, with more than fifty-five percent stating that they had expressed an opinion as to how the defendant should be sentenced.[47]

To summarize, the various studies suggest uneven patterns of victim participation in sentencing and disposition phases of criminal cases. Contrary to the notion that victims are actively involved in the overwhelming percentage of cases, surveys suggest that participation rates vary from about one-quarter to three-quarters of felony dispositions.

In one sense, then, victim participation statutes have been muted through lack of full utilization. In another sense, however, victim participation practices have exceeded what appears to be statutorily authorized. Of the thirty-six states surveyed by Hillenbrand and Smith, seven authorized the inclusion of a victim's recommendation of sentence in victim impact statements.[48] Yet, over three-quarters of probation officials surveyed said that they solicited the victim's opinion with respect to the defendant's sentence.[49] Similarly, over fifty-five of victims sur-

---

43. *Id.* at 128.

44. *Id.* at 133; Table 9-4 at 134.

45. *Id.* at 135; Table 9-6 at 135. The authors reported that "almost all victims in cases with separate sentencing hearings said that it was very important . . . to be involved in the sentencing decision." *Id.* at 136.

46. *Id.* at 136; Table 9-7 at 136.

47. *Id.* at 137-138; Table 9-10 at 138. Interestingly, 72 percent of the victims surveyed expressed the opinion that the victim impact statement had either "some" or "a lot" of effect upon whether the defendant was sentenced to jail; 62 percent thought that it had "some" or "a lot" of effect upon length of incarceration. *Id.* at 139, Table 9-11. The study does not indicate whether there is a correlation between victims expressing such opinions and those victims who included a sentence recommendation in their victim impact statement.

48. *Id.* at 30, Tables 3-17 and 3-18. An earlier survey by McLeod found that 11 states authorized sentence recommendations; five states prohibited them from being included in the victim impact statement. McLeod, *supra* note 8, at 166, Table 1.

49. HILLENBRAND & SMITH, *supra* note 6, at 159.

veyed reported that they had included their opinion on how the defendant should be sentenced in their statements.[50] This finding, along with others,[51] led the authors to conclude that, with few exceptions, the specific content of victims' rights legislation had little real effect upon ways in which prosecutors, probation officers, judges and others interacted with victims.[52] Therefore, even though a minority of states specifically authorize victims to express opinions regarding case disposition or sentence, it is quite possible that victim recommendations are more widespread than statutory law would suggest.

B. *Vindictiveness versus Forgiveness*

Specific instances of a victim (or the victim's family) seeking full and harsh application of criminal sanctions are not difficult to find. A recent vivid example is *State v. Huertas*,[53] where Huertas killed a high school friend who had been seeing a young woman with whom Huertas had been having an affair. In the penalty phase of the capital case, the pre-sentence investigation report included an interview with parents of the deceased in which they expressed their opinion that Huertas should be sentenced to death.[54] The father of the murder victim also testified at the sentencing hearing that it was his belief that Huertas should receive the death penalty.[55]

50. *Id.* at 138. Most victims surveyed were from New York, a state which permits victims to express opinions as to the offender's sentence. *See supra* note 24 and accompanying text (discussing New York statute). This figure could be much lower, I suppose, if a more representative sampling of victims had occurred. It should be noted, however, that the authors did not attempt to correlate victims' responses with locale; it is uncertain, therefore, whether any significance should be attached to the "55 percent" figure.

51. Hillenbrand and Smith hypothesized that prosecutors would be more likely to notify victims of final case disposition if the right to such notification were specified in their state's legislation; however, their findings did not support that hypothesis. *Id.* at 162-63.

52. *Id.* at 163.

53. 51 Ohio St. 3d 22, 553 N.E.2d 1058 (1990).

54. *Id.* at 24, 553 N.E.2d at 1062.

55. *Id.* The death penalty was overturned, and the appellate court reduced his sentence to life in prison. The court reasoned that: "[S]tatements by a member of the victim's family recommending a particular punishment . . . have nothing to do with culpability or moral guilt. They are simply opinions . . . given by someone who, though having a great personal interest in the outcome, is not a member of the jury." *Id.* at 27, 553 N.E.2d at 1065.

The United States Supreme Court granted certiorari to consider whether *Booth* and *Gathers* had been properly applied, Ohio v. Huertas, 111 S. Ct. 39 (1990), then dismissed the writ as improvidently granted. 111 S. Ct. 805 (1991). Subsequently, the Court granted certiorari in *Payne v. Tennessee*, 111 S. Ct. 1031 (1991), to consider whether *Booth* and *Gathers* should be overturned. [In June 1991, the Court delivered its opinion in *Payne*, holding that the eight amendment erects no per se bar prohibiting a capital sentencing jury from considering "victim impact" evidence. To the extent that *Booth* and *Gathers* held to the contrary, wrote the Court, they are overruled. Payne v. Tennessee, 111 S. Ct. 2597 (1991)-EDS]

Aside from specific examples of what appear to be vengeance-seeking victims, some studies have suggested that a significant number of victims are prone to vindictive attitudes.[56] The most recent, and perhaps the most comprehensive, is the study of the impact of victims' rights legislation, conducted by Hillenbrand and Smith.[57] While the authors did not identify the kinds of recommendations made by victims in individual cases, the authors surveyed more than 350 victims (in five states), asking, "What, if anything, was least satisfying about the way [your case] was handled?" Responses were received from 254 individuals, some of whom gave more than one answer to that question. Out of 338 individual responses, thirty-six percent of the victims stated that the least satisfying aspect of the case was the "treatment of the defendant."[58] About half of those responding in that category indicated dissatisfaction specifically with respect to the sentence received by the defendant.[59] The authors concluded: "With very few exceptions, such complaints indicated the sentence was too lenient."[60]

While our intuitive sense is likely to be that victims will seek vengeance against their offenders, as is confirmed by the studies above cited, other published studies and reports indicate that victims are not vindictive. One of the earliest studies to have reached this conclusion involved an experiment in which crime victims were allowed to participate in settlement conferences.[61] The victims usually supported the proposed case disposition, and — contrary to what some believed would

56. *See* Davis, Kunreuther & Connick, *Expanding the Victim's Role in the Criminal Court Dispositional Process: The Results of an Experiment*, 75 J. CRIM. L. & CRIMINOLOGY 491, 500 (1984) (indicating that victims are most dissatisfied with case outcomes for reason that defendants are not punished severely enough); *see also* Walsh, *supra* note 41, at 1139 (finding "high level of vindictiveness" based upon fact that almost 90 percent of victims sexually assaulted by non-relatives recommended imprisonment for offender). It has also been reported that two researchers found in 1989 that there is an increased likelihood of incarceration in cases in which victim impact statements are used. Erez and Tontodonato, *The Effect of Victim Participation in Sentencing on Sentence Outcome* (paper presented at annual meeting of American Society of Criminology, Reno, Nevada) (*cited in* DAVIS, HENLEY & SMITH, VICTIM IMPACT STATEMENTS: THEIR EFFECTS ON COURT OUTCOMES AND VICTIM SATISFACTION 32, 38 (New York Victim Services Agency April 1990)). This fact suggests, but certainly does not establish, victim vindictiveness.

57. *Supra* note 6.

58. *Id.* at 146, Table 9-17.

59. *Id.*

60. *Id.* at 146. It is interesting that 38 percent of the victims reported that the *most* satisfying aspect of the case was "treatment of the defendant." In that category, however, only about 20 percent expressed satisfaction specifically with case disposition or sentence. *Id.* at 147, Table 9-18.

61. Heinz & Kerstetter, *Pretrial Settlement Conference: Evaluation of a Reform in Plea Bargaining*, 13 LAW & SOC. REV. 349, 351 (1979). The victims were invited to express their opinions with respect to proposed plea agreements. This group was compared to a control group in which negotiation occurred between prosecutors and defense attorneys and were presented for court approval without victim involvement.

occur — they did not demand the maximum authorized penalty.[62] A later publication, relating to the same study, pointed out that some victims even expressed sympathy for the defendant.[63] While the authors cautioned that their findings should be viewed in the context of that specific experiment,[64] the overall evaluation was clear: "[V]ictim's recommendations did not sound punitive or vindictive."[65]

Other commentators have also suggested that the claims of vindictiveness are ill-founded, albeit with different explanations.[66] Deborah Kelly, for example, reported that crime victims desire better treatment from criminal justice personnel, rather than harsher penalties for the offender.[67] Her interviews of over 100 felony victims disclosed that the victims actually wished (1) to be kept better informed of their case, and (2) to "not be treated as if they were the criminals."[68]

In summary, there are reported instances of victims seeking vengeance and other victims seeking less than harsh enforcement against their offenders.[69] Studies seem almost equally supportive of both vindictiveness and forgiveness claims. At a minimum, in any given criminal case in any jurisdiction allowing active victim participation, the individual victim may express vindictiveness, mercy or neutrality.

---

62. *Id.* at 359.

63. Heinz & Kerstetter, *Victim Participation in Plea Bargaining: A Field Experiment*, in PLEA BARGAINING 167, 172 (1980).

64. *Id.* It was emphasized that the victims may have been intimidated by the professionals present in the hearings. Also, the process occurred over a relatively short period of time; victims were asked to express opinions as to agreements already reached by prosecution and defense counsel.

65. *Id.* at 172.

66. Two researchers found that victims do desire that offenders be incarcerated. But when made aware of other sentencing options, many victims were willing to move away from a position of retribution. Henderson & Gitchoff, *Using Experts and Victims in the Sentencing Process*, 17 CRIM. L. BULL. 226, 229-30 (1981). Another study (in which evidence of vindictiveness was observed) found that in sexual assault cases there was more victim-leniency as the relationship between offender and victim grew closer; indeed, the overall impact of victim recommendations was found to result in "mitigation of the offender's punishment." Walsh, *supra* note 41, at 1137. *See also*, Davis, Kunreuther & Connick, *supra* note 56, at 493 (authors claimed that less than half of victims interviewed desired incarceration of offender); DAVIS, HENLEY & SMITH, *supra* note 56, at 23 (finding that use of victim impact statements did not induce New York officials "to mete out generally harsher sentences").

67. Kelly, *Symposium: Victims' Perceptions of Criminal Justice*, 11 PEPPERDINE. L. REV. 15, 22 (1984).

68. *Id.* at 17. Given the date of this study, it is understandable that she would have asserted that "there is no evidence to support the assumption of victim retribution." *Id.* at 21. I assume that she would concede that there is now credible evidence demonstrating victim vindictiveness.

69. *See* Henderson & Gitchoff, *supra* note 66, at 232 (reporting instances in which "victims offered to testify on behalf of the offender at a sentencing hearing in order to prevent a prison sentence").

No matter what the victim's expressed desire, preference or recommendation may be, it is necessary to address the question of whether those views have any effect on case disposition or sentence. If, in fact, the victim's voice is not heeded by sentencing authorities, the claim of disparate sentencing practices rings hollow. This issue, too, has been the focus of recent studies.

C. *Actual Impact*

Given the widespread availability and use of victim impact statements, one would assume that the statements' contents have at least some effect upon case disposition. While there is substantial empirical evidence that this is true, there is disagreement as to the extent to which the statements actually influence judges' decisions.

The Hillenbrand and Smith study includes an impact assessment gleaned from a survey of seventy-four judges (covering thirty-six states).[70] Judges who received VIS forms prepared by probation officers or victims found them to be effective; indeed, virtually no judges found them to be ineffective.[71] In commenting upon the relative effectiveness of various forms of impact information, a number of judges observed that articulate victims' statements, whether written or oral, were far more effective than those received from inarticulate victims.[72] With regard to actual impact, more than eighty percent of the judges stated that victim impact statements had either "some" or a "substantial" impact upon the length of sentence imposed upon the defendant; almost ninety percent expressed the view that the VIS had a like impact upon the type of sentence (e.g., probation, incarceration, community service, etc.).[73] Yet, there was disagreement among those judges as to the usefulness of specific types of information set forth in the VIS. Overall, the more objective the information, such as the extent of financial or physical loss to the victim, the more useful it was deemed to be.[74] Interestingly, the single least useful piece of information was the individual victim's opinion as to the defendant's appropriate sentence;

70. Of the chief judges in each of 84 jurisdictions in which prosecutors had been interviewed, 74 were interviewed; at least one from each of the 36 states participated. HILLENBRAND & SMITH, *supra* note 6, at 65.

71. *Id.* at 69, Table 5-8. Those terms are not free of ambiguity. The judges were commenting upon VIS effectiveness in the context of making sentencing decisions. Yet, even that assessment does not necessarily mean that a VIS had an actual impact upon a particular sentence.

72. *Id.* at 70.

73. *Id.* at 72, Table 5-10.

74. *Id.* at 70, Table 5-9. Note, though, that almost 90 percent of the judges thought that the crime's psychological impact upon the victim — hardly objectively verifiable — was either "useful" or "very useful." *Id.*

still, thirty-five of seventy-four judges (forty-seven percent) stated that the victims' recommendations were either "useful" or "very useful."[75] Overall, Hillenbrand and Smith concluded that most court personnel (judges, prosecutors, probation officials and victims' advocates) agreed that VIS information has at least some impact on the length and type of sentence received by defendants.[76]

Other commentators have noted that victims have influence over sentencing decisions,[77] including parole release decisions.[78] Many crime victims, however, seem to be less convinced that their impact statements have any effect upon sentencing. Only one-third of the victims interviewed by Hillenbrand and Smith, for example, expressed the view that the VIS had "a lot" of effect on whether the defendant was incarcerated.[79] Over one-third said that such statements had "no effect" on the amount of jail time.[80] Perhaps, this perception is due to the fact that significant numbers of case dispositions result from plea bargaining. Even where the victim plays a participatory role, the bargaining process may encourage acquiescence to the agreement struck between the defense and the prosecution.[81] Additionally, it is possible that some of these victims are attempting to influence sentences in states that do not allow for this participation due to strict sentencing guidelines.[82] Finally, the victim impact statement may do little more than reiterate information already known in the specific case and already accounted for in the grading scheme for that particular crime (e.g., serious bodily injury to a robbery victim may statutorily authorize a harsher sanction).[83]

---

75. *Id.* at 71, Table 5-9. The judges were asked how useful each type of information was "in their sentencing decisions." *Id.* at 70. Again, as discussed in note 71, *supra*, "usefulness" does not necessarily mean that the information had a causal connection to the sentence.

76. *Id.* at 123, Table 8-7.

77. Henderson and Gitchoff, *supra* note 66, at 227-28; Walsh, *supra* note 41, at 1127.

78. McLeod, *supra* note 10, at 13.

79. HILLENBRAND AND SMITH, *supra* note 6, at 139, Table 9-11.

80. *Id.*

81. This has been suggested by one author, who also observed that "some judges simply feel that they receive adequate information about the victim without the victim impact statement." Kennard, *The Victim's Veto: A Way to Increase Victim Impact on Criminal Case Dispositions*, 77 CAL. L. REV. 417, 431 (1989). Other authors have expressed the view that victim participation may have little real effect on case dispositions. Walsh, *supra* note 41, at 1140-41; Davis, Kunreuther & Connick, *supra* note 56, at 504-05; Heinz & Kerstetter, *supra* note 61, at 361-62; Heinz & Kerstetter, *supra* note 63, at 172-73.

82. Hillenbrand and Smith noted that "a considerable number of the minority [of judges] who found no impact [of the VIS upon sentence type or length] commented that applicable sentencing guidelines do not allow variances based on victim impact." HILLENBRAND AND SMITH, *supra* note 6, at 71.

83. Walsh, *supra* note 41, describes this more fully, leading him to comment that "requiring a [VIS] as part of the presentence report is a mere genuflection to ritualistic legalism." *Id.* at 1139.

D. Summary

Full implementation of victim impact statements and allocution statutes has not occurred. Indeed, some jurisdictions have reported a surprisingly small percentage of victims actually preparing a VIS. Yet, it also appears that statutes have not delimited the extent to which some victims have been allowed to influence case dispositions.

When victims participate by expressing views with respect to plea bargains or sentencing, their desires range from conciliatory or forgiving to vindictive. The actual dispositional consequences of those views are difficult to measure or prove, but it is relatively certain that the VIS has a demonstrable effect upon both the length and type of the defendant's sentence. Therefore, it cannot be denied that in some jurisdictions victims' urgings have an impact upon the ultimate sentence received by the defendant.

V. ISSUES AND ANALYSIS

A. Victim Participation in Homicide Cases: How Courts Frame the Issues

The five case illustrations previously presented,[84] coupled with the statutory and empirical data above, underscore the most objectionable yet inevitable feature of victim participation laws: disparate treatment of similarly-situated defendants. Perhaps, Professor Stephen Schulhofer expressed the underlying concern most succinctly: "[L]ike cases ought to be treated alike."[85] Identical sentences for two persons convicted of the same offense are not constitutionally compelled.[86] Yet, notions of fairness militate strongly against explicit victim influence upon criminal case dispositions. Indeed, the United States Congress recognized the goal of uniform sentences for offenders convicted of similar crimes when enacting the Federal Sentencing Guidelines.[87]

He notes, however, that victim participation may have a placebo value (and thus the title to his article) in causing them to think that they had some control over case disposition. *Id.*

84. *Supra* Part II(B).

85. Schulhofer, *Harm and Punishment: A Critique of Emphasis on the Results of Conduct in the Criminal Law*, 122 U. PA. L. REV. 1497, 1601 (1974).

86. Williams v. Illinois, 399 U.S. 235, 243 (1970). *See* Solem v. Helm, 463 U.S. 277, 303 (1983) (examining harshness of defendant's sentence by applying objective criteria which may include comparing sentence to those received by persons who commit more serious crimes in that jurisdiction). In addition, a comparison to sentences received by similar offenders in other jurisdictions may yield the conclusion that a particular sentence is disproportionate to the crime and therefore prohibited by the eighth amendment.

87. Sentencing Reform Act of 1984, Pub. L. No. 98-473, 98 Stat. 1987 (1984), 28 U.S.C. §994(a); S. REP. No. 98-225, 98th Cong., 2d Sess. 37, 42-45 (1984). One author recently summa-

Analysis of this principle, limited principally to homicide cases, culminated in the United States Supreme Court's rulings in *Booth v. Maryland*[88] and *South Carolina v. Gathers.*[89] One of the earliest reported decisions, *Sandvik v. State*[90], involved facts strikingly similar to my basic hypothetical crime. As a result of the defendant's negligence, a 15-year old-girl was fatally injured while riding her bicycle. The presentence investigation report contained information about the girl's life, and described the reaction of her parents to her death. The Alaska Supreme Court ruled that this information was properly before the sentencing judge, observing that data about the crime victim should be a part of the sentencing process.[91] Justice Boochever dissented, complaining that such emotionally-charged information should not be considered: "I cannot comprehend how the victim's social and charitable activities and the extent of the parents' grief can be . . . pertinent to sentencing."[92]

Evidence of bereavement by a manslaughter victim's family was taken into account for sentencing purposes in *People v. Levitt.*[93] Contrary to *Sandvik*, the court in *Levitt* noted the following:

---

rized the legislative objectives as follows: "(1) honesty in sentencing . . .; (2) uniformity in sentencing, by narrowing the wide disparity of sentences imposed by different federal courts for similar criminal conduct by similar offenders; and (3) proportionality in sentencing . . . ." Hellerstein, *The Victim Impact Statement: Reform or Reprisal?*, 27 AM. CRIM. L. REV. 391, 401 (1989).

Hellerstein's article focuses on the interplay between the federal statutes calling for determinate sentencing and victim impact statutes. This article addresses state victim participation statutes. However, Hellerstein's conclusion echoes one theme developed in this Article: "[T]he [federal] victim impact statement . . . has limited relevance in the determinate sentencing scheme." *Id.* at 402.

To the extent that a VIS conveys a sense of the victim's "worth" in his or her community, it is interesting to note a recently published dialogue between United States Sentencing Commissioner Ilene Nagel and an unnamed symposium audience member. The questioner posed hypothetical homicide cases in which one defendant killed a woman who was the mother of five children and head of the P.T.A.; she was shot while walking to morning mass. The second defendant shot and killed a young working-class male (with a lengthy police record) while he was standing outside a pornographic movie theater. Nagel was asked whether sentencing of these two defendants under federal guidelines would result in different sentences presumably because of different victim impact statements. Nagel's response:

> [E]nhancement is appropriate when a defendant targets particularly vulnerable victims — the aged, the infirm, the handicapped, and so on. . . . We would not make a distinction . . . between the sentences for offenders involved in [the hypothetical]. Much as I consider myself very sympathetic to victims' rights, . . . I could not justify a distinction between the penalty for those two offenders.

Symposium, *Equality Versus Discretion in Sentencing*, 26 AM. CRIM. L. REV. 1813, 1835 (1989).

88. 482 U.S. 496 (1987).

89. 490 U.S. 805 (1989).

90. 564 P.2d 20 (Alaska 1977).

91. *Id.* at 23.

92. *Id.* at 27 (Boochever, C.J., dissenting).

93. 156 Cal. App. 3d 500, 203 Cal. Rptr. 276 (1984).

> We agree . . . that this factor [bereavement of the victim's family] could not properly be relied on to aggravate his sentence because it bears no rational relationship to his degree of culpability. . . . We think it obvious that a defendant's level of culpability depends not on fortuitous circumstances such as the composition of his victim's family, but on circumstances over which he has control. . . . [T]he fact that a victim's family is irredeemably bereaved can be attributable to no act of will of the defendant other than his commission of the homicide in the first place. Such bereavement . . . has no relationship to the proper purposes of sentencing in a criminal case.[94]

The most visible litigation in the context of victim involvement in criminal cases relates to the use of victim impact statements in capital cases. In a Maryland homicide case[95] (that would eventually be intertwined with *Booth v. Maryland*[96]), statements by the victim's widow, the victim's mother, and other members of the family were offered at the capital sentencing hearing through victim impact statements. The defendant, sentenced to death, argued that consideration of this information unconstitutionally injected an arbitrary factor into the sentencing decision. Although the case was ultimately reversed on other grounds, the majority had little difficulty in finding the use of such victim impact evidence to be proper. Judge Cole, concurring with the reversal, expressed his concern that this evidence, irrelevant to defendant's record, character or the circumstances of the crime, might constitute a violation of the cruel and unusual punishment clause of the eighth amendment.[97] He observed that when the victim's family pleads for its "pound of flesh," it creates a "frenzied environment" which may "arouse and incite the passions of the sentencing authority."[98]

The *Lodowski* court heard another capital case involving victim impact data the following year.[99] State officials interviewed several members of the victims' family, including children and grandchildren, many of whose statements related to the personal psychological and emotional trauma experienced by each as a result of the murders. The family members gave their impressions of the crime, one person stating

94. *Id.* at 516-17, 203 Cal. Rptr. at 287-288.
95. Lodowski v. State, 302 Md. 691, 490 A.2d 1228 (1985).
96. 482 U.S. 496 (1987).
97. Lodowski v. State, 490 A.2d at 1276-77.
98. *Id.*
99. Booth v. State, 306 Md. 172, 507 A.2d 1098 (1986).

that the killer "could [n]ever be rehabilitated."[100] The defendant appealed his death sentence, and the court affirmed.[101] Judge Cole dissented:

> What can be a more arbitrary factor in the decision to sentence a defendant to death than the words of the victim's family which vary greatly from case to case, depending upon the ability of the family member to express his grief, or even worse depending upon whether the victim has a family at all? A killer of a person with an educated family would be put to death, whereas . . . the killer of a person with an uneducated family or one without a family would be spared.[102]

The United States Supreme Court granted certiorari and reversed, holding that the eighth amendment prohibits a capital sentencing jury from considering victim impact evidence.[103] The Court began its analysis by clarifying that a death sentence requires consideration of factors that bear on the defendant's personal responsibility and moral guilt. The victim impact statement in *Booth* provided two types of information: first, personal characteristics of the victims and emotional impact of the crime on the family: and, second, opinions and characterizations of the crime and the defendant. The Court deemed this information irrelevant to the capital sentencing decision. Therefore, there was an unacceptable risk that the jury imposed the death sentence in an arbitrary and capricious manner. The victim impact statement did not focus on the blameworthiness of the defendant, but rather "on the character and reputation of the victim and the effect on his family."[104] Echoing the concerns articulated by Judge Cole, the Court wrote:

> As evidenced by the full text of the VIS in this case, . . . the family members were articulate and persuasive in expressing their grief and the extent of their loss. But in some cases the victim will not leave behind a family, or the family members may be less articulate in describing their feelings even though their sense of loss is equally severe. The fact that the imposition of the death sentence may turn on such distinctions illustrates the danger of allowing juries to consider this

100. *Id.* at 238, 507 A.2d at 1132 (Cole, J., concurring in part, dissenting in part). This statement is attributed to the victim's daughter, who attended the defendant's trial "because she felt someone should be there to represent her parents." *Id.*

101. *Id.* at 181, 507 A.2d at 1103.

102. *Id.* at 233, 507 A.2d at 1129 (Cole, J., concurring in part, dissenting in part).

103. Booth v. Maryland, 482 U.S. 496 (1987).

104. *Id.* at 504.

> information. Certainly the degree to which a family is willing and able to express its grief is irrelevant to the decision whether a defendant, who may merit the death penalty, should live or die. [Citation to Judge Cole's opinion omitted] Nor is there any justification for permitting such a decision to turn on the perception that the victim was a sterling member of the community rather than someone of questionable character.[105] We are troubled by the implication that defendants whose victims were assets to their community are more deserving of punishment than those whose victims are perceived to be less worthy. Of course, our system of justice does not tolerate such distinctions.[106]

Justice White, writing for the four dissenters,[107] observed that "[t]here is nothing aberrant in a juror's inclination to hold a murderer accountable not only for his internal disposition in committing the crime, but also for the full extent of the harm he caused."[108] Justice White found the question of arbitrariness to be a "makeweight consideration."[109] He explained: "[N]o two prosecutors have exactly the same ability to present their arguments to the jury; no two witnesses have exactly the same ability to communicate the facts; but there is no requirement in capital cases that the evidence and argument be reduced to the lowest common denominator."[110]

Justice Scalia echoed the same theme: "It seems to me . . . that the amount of harm one causes does bear upon the extent of his 'personal responsibility'."[111] Acknowledging that in recent years there has been an outpouring of popular concern for what has come to be known as "victim's rights," he chided the majority for refusing to consider concerns of victims in capital cases.[112]

Notwithstanding the fact that disparate treatment analysis is applicable to all sentencing schemes, the majority suggested that the victim impact statement may be permissible in non-capital cases.[113]

---

105. *Id.* at 506.

106. *Id.* at 506 n.8.

107. He was joined by Chief Justice Rehnquist, Justice O'Connor and Justice Scalia.

108. *Id.* at 516.

109. *Id.* at 518.

110. *Id.*

111. *Id.* at 519.

112. *Id.* at 520. Justice Scalia noted that victims may not "temper justice with mercy, but that is a question to be decided through the democratic process . . . and not by the decrees of this Court." *Id.*

113. *Id.* at 507 n.10 ("[f]acts about the victim and family . . . may be relevant in a non-capital criminal trial"); *see also id.* at 509 n.12 ("[w]e imply no opinion as to the use of [victim impact statements] in noncapital cases").

Two years later, *Booth* was reaffirmed (again by a five-to-four vote) in *South Carolina v. Gathers*.[114] Contrary to *Booth*, no victim impact statement was prepared for use at the capital sentencing phase. Rather, the prosecutor's closing remarks included references to the homicide victim's personal characteristics. The victim was described as a religious person with various mental problems. The prosecutor referred to assorted religious items that had been in the victim's possession at the time of the murder, reading the full text of "The Game Guy's Prayer."[115] The South Carolina Supreme Court reversed the defendant's death sentence on the basis of *Booth* because of the emphasis upon the victim's personal characteristics, and the United States Supreme Court affirmed.[116] Since the remarks, including recitation of the document's contents, related to qualities of the victim — and neither the defendant's moral culpability nor circumstances of the offense — the case was deemed "indistinguishable in any relevant aspect from . . . *Booth*."[117]

Justice O'Connor dissented,[118] arguing that *Booth* should not be interpreted to disallow information which offers a "glimpse of the life" of the victim.[119] This data is a measure of harm, she said, pointing to circumstances in which an offender is punished differently based upon harm actually caused, rather than "any difference in the defendant's mental state."[120] Justice Scalia echoed this sentiment, urging that *Booth* be overruled.[121]

It is important to keep in mind two unique features of both *Booth* and *Gathers*. First, the cases dealt with "victim impact" information arguably related, at least in some ways, to harm suffered by the individual victim or survivors of the victim. Neither case addressed the legitimacy of a specific recommendation by a victim as to the penalty that should be suffered by the defendant, contrary to the statutory schemes described earlier.[122] Second, both cases were decided in the

114. 490 U.S. 805 (1989).

115. The victim had in his possession several bags of articles, which were found at the crime scene. One was the religious tract, in which the virtues of good sport were praised. The prosecutor read this to the jury, notwithstanding the fact that there was no evidence that the defendant had read from this tract. Rather, Gathers appeared to have scattered these papers while looking for something to steal from the victim — which, the majority noted, was a proper subject for comment. *Id.* at 807, 811.

116. *Id.* at 812.

117. *Id.* at 811.

118. She was joined by Chief Justice Rehnquist and Justice Kennedy.

119. South Carolina v. Gathers, 490 U.S. at 816.

120. *Id.* at 819.

121. *Id.* at 823.

122. *See supra* notes 14-34 and accompanying text (discussing victim participation statutes).

context of the special rules utilized in capital cases. While the Supreme Court was careful not to articulate its decisions in terms that would encompass non-capital cases, the rationale of both cases would seem to apply equally convincingly to a non-capital case: arbitrary sentencing practices, based upon the unpredictable "victim participation" factor, are objectionable in both capital and non-capital cases. There is no principled basis upon which an "arbitrary and objectionable-arbitrary but acceptable" line can be drawn.

It might be suggested that the *Booth-Gathers* analysis is strictly limited to capital cases because of the uniquely sensitive way in which the eighth amendment analysis has developed in the context of the ultimate penalty — death. Yet the majority opinion in *Booth* addressed a due process concern which seemingly transcends the capital versus non-capital boundary. Citing to *Gardner v. Florida*,[123] the opinion pointed out that some VIS information — such as emotional trauma suffered by the victim — would not be susceptible to rebuttal. Additionally, allowing the government to cite evidence of a victim's positive qualities would necessitate similarly allowing the defense to offer evidence of a victim's less-than-appealing qualities, resulting in a "mini-trial" on the

---

In a capital case decided four years prior to *Booth*, the defendant, Larry Romine, was convicted of murdering his parents. Romine v. State, 251 Ga. 208, 305 S.E.2d 93 (1983). The father of one victim (Ralph Romine, defendant's grandfather) had been subpoenaed to appear at the trial, but departed because of illness. When the sentencing phase began, defendant's attorney requested a continuance until Ralph Romine could be in attendance. Asked as to what Ralph would testify, counsel responded: "He has expressed a tremendous desire to be able to tell the jury . . . [that] he did not want his grandson electrocuted . . . ." *Id.* at 216, 305 S.E.2d at 100-101. The trial judge denied the motion, ruling that the grandfather's testimony would not be admissible. *Id.* The Supreme Court of Georgia reversed, holding this to be proper mitigation testimony: "Ralph's testimony would have been particularly significant because he was closely related not only to the [defendant] but also to the victims." *Id.* at 217-218, 305 S.E.2d at 101. Assuming that the grandfather is viewed as the "victims' representative," this result is flatly contradictory to both *Booth* and *Gathers*. This was so held in Robison v. Maynard, 829 F.2d 1501, 1505 (10th Cir. 1987), where the defense attorney expressed his desire to call "relatives" of two homicide victims who would urge the capital sentencing jury to reject the death penalty. Affirming the district court's decision to disallow the testimony, the Tenth Circuit found the *Booth* "lesson . . . equally applicable here," noting that "allowing this kind of testimony by the defense would be to permit the State to present witnesses who would testify the penalty should be imposed, thus reducing the trial to a contest of irrelevant opinions." *Id.* at 1504-1505.

It bears repeating that neither *Booth* nor *Gathers* specifically addressed a situation in which the victim (or the victim's survivors) articulated a sentence recommendation. The rationale of both rulings certainly condemns such a practice, but I cannot agree with Hellerstein's reading of *Booth* as a case in which the "entire Supreme Court . . . held [that] sentencing recommendations of victims . . . will not be an appropriate consideration." Hellerstein, *supra* note 87, at 429. Nonetheless, I agree with her conclusion that victim recommendations are irrelevant as a sentencing factor.

123. 430 U.S. 349, 362 (1977) (due process requires that the defendant be given opportunity to rebut information contained in presentence report).

victim's character.[124] To the extent that these concerns are based upon due process considerations, the capital versus non-capital dichotomy collapses.[125]

Another question is whether *Booth* and *Gathers*, both of which involved jury assessments of the death penalty, apply to judge-made sentencing decisions. While there is a lack of uniformity among lower federal and state courts, a significant number have expressed the view that the VIS may have an equal effect on both jurors and judges. As one commentator observed:

> [T]he common strand of thought among the various courts deciding the issue of the application of *Booth* to judge imposed sentences is that the initial introduction of a VIS is error. Judges can be affected as much as juries by powerful victim impact testimony even though they may be accustomed to mentally excluding impermissible evidence.[126]

B. *Victim Participation and Victim Harm*

The arbitrariness condemned by the *Booth* and *Gathers* majorities was defended, however, by the dissenters' notion of "victim harm." That is, many crimes are punished more severely based upon harm to the victim. Some defendants benefit from reduced sanctions through the fortuitous circumstance of less-than-intended harm to the victim (the classic discussion related to completed crimes versus attempted crimes[127]). Indeed, a central question surrounding victim participation statutes is whether the victim's voice is simply a reflection of harm caused by the offender.

Victim participation statutes do not necessarily reflect objective measures of victim harm. Whether they do or do not depends, quite simply, upon the further inquiry into what kind of information is being solicited from the victim and utilized by the sentencing court. Clear distinctions must be made, then, with respect to matters which we invite victims to address. "How much money was stolen?" "What injuries did you suffer?" "What were your medical expenses?" These questions call for answers as to which some objective measure of loss or harm is

124. Booth v. Maryland, 482 U.S. at 507.

125. *See* Hellerstein, *supra* note 87, at 419 (discussing this point further).

126. *Id.* at 415-416.

127. Justice O'Connor referred to this example, asserting that different penalties are permitted not because of any difference in culpability, "but on the notion that one of the legitimate concerns . . . is the harm that the defendant's actions have caused." South Carolina v. Gathers, 490 U.S. at 819.

possible. A second category of matters frequently included in a victim impact statement[128] is arguably "harm-related," but is highly subjective in quantifiable terms. "How has this crime affected your psychological or emotional well being?" "Has this crime affected your relationship with family members and friends?" "How much have you grieved over having been a victim of this crime?" Finally, there are victim impact statements of a recommendatory sort. "How important is it to you that the defendant be incarcerated?" "Do you wish to recommend to the court that the defendant serve the maximum term of incarceration allowed by law for this offense?" "Do you have any objection to a bargained plea, whereby the defendant pleads guilty to a crime less serious than the one he committed, in fact?" "Would you object to a decision placing the defendant on probation?" Only in the most indirect way do answers to these questions reflect any legitimate measure of victim harm.[129] Indeed, they do little more than make available to the victim an opportunity to exhibit forgiveness, vengeance or neutrality, irrespective of the type or degree of harm that may have been experienced by the victim or the victim's family.

A criminal offender's punishment should reflect a proper societal measure of appropriate "blame."[130] This means that the defendant should be held accountable for those harms intended, or those within the realm of reasonably foreseeable consequences to the victim. Within this framework, pieces of VIS "harms" that relate to the circumstances of the crime, itself, are properly before the sentencing authority.[131] Other objectively verifiable harms may be unintended and unexpected

---

128. "Many [VIS] statements . . . mention the impact of the crime on the victim's physical and psychological well-being. The impact on the victim's relationship with family and friends [is] frequently indicated." HILLENBRAND & SMITH, *supra* note 6, at 29-30.

129. It might be argued that the "forgiving" victim probably experienced less loss or harm than the "vindictive" victim. This may be true as between classes of offenses (e.g., property crimes versus assaultive crimes), as indicated by one author: "In larceny cases, victims often press charges as a way of forcing the offender to make restitution; once they have recovered the stolen money or property, they drop charges." C. SILBERMAN, CRIMINAL VIOLENCE, CRIMINAL JUSTICE 266 (1978). As to victims of identical crimes, Silberman suggests that the most probable variable with regard to vindictiveness or forgiveness is whether or not the offender and victim were strangers at the time of the offense. In New York City, for example, "stranger" robbery cases had a conviction rate of 88 percent; "prior relationship" robberies had a conviction rate of 37 percent. *Id.* at 265. Thus, he concluded, "when [victims] know the offender, victims often refuse to press charges, to testify against the offender, or to cooperate with the prosecutor in other ways." *Id.* at 266.

130. *See* White, *Making Sense of the Criminal Law*, 50 U. COLO. L. REV. 1, 16-26 (1978) (discussing practice of "blaming" in criminal law and ways in which punishment may be defined as such).

131. A very similar proposal, with emphasis upon the language in Rule 32 of the Federal Rules of Criminal Procedure, was made by Hellerstein. Hellerstein, *supra* note 87, at 429.

but yet may be legitimately factored in to an award of restitution to the victim. Undoubtedly, there will be categories of harm which will defy easy characterization and as to which reasonably good arguments can be advanced for inclusion in or exclusion from a VIS.[132] Yet, no matter how one decides these problematic "victim harm" issues, we are left with the third category — recommendatory provisions — that are unpredictable, offer an opportunity for vindictiveness and which do not, except in the most tangential way, reflect harm to the victim.

What is the positive value of giving the victim (or victim's family) an opportunity to express an opinion as to the sentence that the defendant should receive? It is difficult to answer this specific question clearly because studies thus far have focused only generally on victim participation measures. To the extent that a victim is given an opportunity to make a sentencing recommendation — and to the further extent that a victim perceives that the opinion expressed has had some actual effect upon case disposition — one can imagine a benefit to the victim.[133] The criminal justice system may also benefit through heightened degrees of victim cooperation at all phases of the case. But at what cost?

C. *Victim Participation and Disparate Treatment*

As discussed in *Booth*, and as illustrated in my case hypotheticals, the use of victim impact statements as to which victim recommendations are invited — at least where judges give them weight[134] — results in uneven sentences for similarly-situated defendants. The crime committed by Jill Schultz deserves appropriate punishment, focusing principally upon her actions and intentions. To set her sanction in response to the victim's relatives's urgings injects an arbitrary and unpredictable element into the sentencing scheme, the result of which may be unduly

132. Some of the "harms" described in the second category are of this variety.

133. Among others, such victims would likely believe that they had been given considerate and compassionate treatment, and they probably would be satisfied with the case disposition or sentence received by the defendant. *See* HILLENBRAND & SMITH, *supra* note 6, at 146-147 (note that these were responses from victims to open-ended questions and there was no attempt to correlate responses to victims who had made disposition/sentence recommendations). Similarly, an earlier study found that where victims were afforded a greater participatory role in the court process they expressed increased levels of satisfaction with the criminal justice system. J. HERNON & B. FORST, THE CRIMINAL JUSTICE RESPONSE TO VICTIM HARM (Nat'l Inst. of Justice 1985). A very recent study in New York, however, calls into question whether any benefits accrue to victims through victim impact statements: "We did not find any indications that impact statements caused greater feelings of involvement, greater satisfaction with the justice process, or greater satisfaction with dispositions." *See* DAVIS, HENLEY & SMITH, *supra* note 56, at 34.

134. Some jurisdictions statutorily require that judges consider those recommendations. *See supra* notes 14-34 and accompanying text (discussing types of victim participation statutes).

harsh or lenient treatment of the offender. This process represents little more than a throw of the dice.

The goal of sentencing evenness certainly cannot be achieved in pristine fashion. Prosecutors, defense lawyers, witnesses and others vary in ability and persuasiveness such that juries and sentencing authorities will respond accordingly, resulting in differing decisions for similar defendants. Nonetheless, our justice system must strive to minimize and mute as many disparity-inducing factors as possible. It cannot be disputed that inviting victim input pushes us further away from the ideal of even-handed sentencing.

Victim participation measures should be carefully evaluated in light of the disparity of treatment phenomenon. But the fact remains that numerous commentators have urged that victims be granted more powerful roles in the critical phases of the criminal case.[135] This fact leads

---

135. Those pushing for greater victim participation include Abrahamson, *Redefining Roles: The Victims' Rights Movement*, 1985 UTAH L. REV. 517, 521-29 (discussing historical role of victim in criminal justice system and impact of victims' rights reforms); Cardenas, *The Crime Victim in the Prosecutorial Process*, 9 HARV. J.L. & PUB. POL'Y 357, 391-92 (1986) (proposing to expand status and role of crime victim by borrowing concepts from restitutionary model); Gifford, *Meaningful Reform of Plea Bargaining: The Control of Prosecutorial Discretion*, 1983 UNIV. ILL. L. REV. 37, 90-92 (proposing that victims of crimes be offered opportunity to participate in guilty hearings to provide a more complete picture of offense); Gittler, *Symposium: Expanding the Role of the Victim in a Criminal Case: An Overview of Issues and Problems*, 11 PEPPERDINE L. REV. 117, 135-49 (1984) (recognizing legitimate and identifiable interests of victims in criminal justice system and suggesting reforms to put victim in more meaningful position in criminal justice system); Goldstein, *supra* note 1, at 520-29 (discussing such victim participation programs as restitution, compensation statutes and witness/victim measures); Hudson, *Symposium: The Crime Victim and the Criminal Justice System: Time for a Change*, 11 PEPPERDINE L. REV. 23, 45-61 (1984) (exploring current reform measures and proposing new programs to increase victims's rights and quality of involvement in criminal justice system); McDonald, *supra* note 1, at 669-72 (discussing programs to help victims such as counseling at the scene of crimes and throughout judicial process and restitution); Welling, *supra* note 7, at 346-48 (advocating implementation of victim participation through court, not prosecutor); and Welling, *Victims in the Criminal Process: A Utilitarian Analysis of Victim Participation in the Charging Decision*, 30 ARIZ. L. REV. 85, 93-94 (1988) (arguing for an extension of victims' rights into charging decision area to aid prosecutor in deciding which cases to pursue and to alleviate feelings of alienation from system).

Those urging caution as to victim participation in matters relating to sentencing include Boudreaux, *Booth v. Maryland and the Individual Vengeance Rationale for Criminal Punishment*, 80 J. CRIM. L. & CRIMINOLOGY 177, 193 (1989) (supporting use of victim impact statements only at sentencing phase of trial, while expressing reservations that use of these statements is useful for crimes less serious than murder). Hellerstein, *supra* note 87, at 422-30 (proposing changes in form and use of victim impact statement); Henderson, *The Wrongs of Victim's Rights*, 37 STAN. L. REV. 937, 1006 (1985) (although victims have limited role to play in determination of restitution, there "appears to be little justification for victim participation in determination of criminal sanction"); Rubel, *Victim Participation in Sentencing Proceedings*, 28 CRIM. L.Q. 226, 248 (1986) ("unofficial party" status of victims in criminal courts provides victim with sufficient involvement in process, such that any additional involvement would provide insufficient benefits to justify risks it would engender for defendant's fair trial); and Talbert, *The Relevance of Victim Impact Statements to the Criminal Sentencing Decision*, 36 UCLA L. REV. 199, 231-32 (1988) (specifically

me to conclude either that these consequences are not viewed as likely to occur or — perhaps more probable — that those effects are deemed offset by the benefits thought to flow from victim participation.[136] Yet, some of the less visible components of the disparity concern deserve closer scrutiny.

Some dimensions of the disparity concern are profoundly disquieting. One of those is the potential for a disparate sentence for the offender based upon the victim's wealth. Some statutes provide that victim input may be presented by the victim or a "representative."[137] To the extent, then, that a privately retained attorney (or other compensated agent) is able to present a more forceful or convincing "case" for the victim, clearly the financial well-being of the victim will determine whether that option is economically feasible. Should a defendant's sentence be based, even in part, upon the fact that the victim is wealthy (perhaps meaning a harsher sentence) or poor (likewise suggesting a more lenient sentence)? I think not.[138]

A second concern is the extent to which a defendant's sentence or case disposition could be affected by the victim's race. It has been forcefully asserted — at least in capital cases[139] — that sentencing of similarly-situated offenders may vary based upon the race of the victim. Specifically, because of selective empathy, more lenient sentences

---

arguing that victim's opinion should not be admitted at sentencing hearing when it would divert attention away from defendant).

136. Schulhofer suggested that laws imposing severe penalties for causing harm (as opposed to gearing penalties to moral blameworthiness) are "largely a holdover from the days of retaliatory justice." Schulhofer, *supra* note 85, at 1602. One wonders whether modern victim participation statutes do not reflect similar retaliatory sentiments.

137. *See* S.C. CODE ANN. §16-3-1530(f) (Law. Co-op. 1986); *see also supra* notes 26, 27 and accompanying text (discussing South Carolina statute).

138. Some might answer by pointing out that the wealth of the defendant is an important factor in numerous respects (private versus appointed counsel, quality of representation, ability to secure pre-trial release, etc.). No one can deny that a wealthy defendant realizes benefits that his or her poor counterpart does not. But this has long been considered a necessary evil, which most people find unsettling and undesirable. We certainly should not exacerbate this injustice through victim participation practices described in this essay.

With respect to the wealthy versus poor victim, it may be very important to know whether the defendant had knowledge of this fact. If, for example, the victim was very poor and emotionally vulnerable, a defendant's sentence could be aggravated if it were shown that the offender preyed upon his victim and purposefully inflicted greater "harm" upon the victim due to those facts. Likewise, knowledge that a well-to-do assault victim was a talented sculptor would be relevant if shown that the defendant intentionally harmed the victim so as to render that person unable to carry on that profession. In this sense, factors personal to the victim give us some measure of the defendant's culpability.

139. McClesky v. Kemp, 481 U.S. 279 (1987) (petitioner sought, and was denied, relief from death sentence based on statistical study purporting to show disparity in imposition of death sentence appearing to correlate with murder victim's race).

may occur in black-victim crimes than in white-victim crimes.[140] One way to at least minimize the potential for race-of-the-victim disparities in sentencing is to implement measures, such as sentencing guidelines, to check the exercise of discretion.[141] Permitting victims to make sentence recommendations, on the other hand, may exacerbate the disparity of sentences by reason of that individual's race.

D. Fundamental Objectives of Criminal Law

The precept of treating like cases alike is compelled both by fairness and the very objectives of criminal law. Professor Stephen Schulhofer years ago advanced the argument that if we punish offenders for reasons usually cited (retribution, deterrence, rehabilitation, and confinement) proper disposition should turn on the defendant's background, past conduct, psychological makeup, nature of the acts committed and motives (among others).[142] While his analysis focused upon the question whether actual harm, in fact, should be an important sentence variable (which it still is), his thesis compels us to think carefully whether victim recommendatory provisions are not, then, antithetical to the basic objectives of criminal punishment. "Differences in punishment," he argued, should "correspond to differences in moral blameworthiness."[143]

The linchpin of our criminal justice system is the notion of measured communal blame, as expressed in the legislature's criminal code. That is, lawbreakers are punished in various ways because they have transgressed standards agreed upon by the community.[144] It is, then, the no-

---

140. One commentator has explained this phenomenon in the context of death penalty cases as follows:

> [R]ace-of-the-victim disparities in sentencing probably reflect racially selective empathy more than racially selective hostility. [There may be more] leniency in black-victim crimes not because of anti-black prejudice but rather because they relate more fully to the suffering of white victims; black victims remain strangers while white victims can be imagined as family or friends.

Kennedy, *McClesky v. Kemp: Race, Capital Punishment, and the Supreme Court*, 101 HARV. L. REV. 1388, 1420 (1988). While it is true that this concern may be more applicable to jury-sentencing, there is little reason to believe that the same biases do not occur — at least sometimes — in judge-sentencing. *See Developments in the Law — Race and the Criminal Process*, 101 HARV. L. REV. 1472, 1477 (1988) (describing continued reality of racial discrimination in sentencing and parole decisions).

141. This approach is suggested in *Developments*, *supra* note 140, at 1634.

142. Schulhofer, *supra* note 85, at 1601-03.

143. *Id.* at 1603.

144. *See* White, *supra* note 130 at 23 (through process of "blaming" defendant held to community standards of conduct, but only those he can meet). Certainly, a forgiving victim should not be permitted to veto criminal sanctions, as was attempted in State v. Burns, 112 Wis.2d 131, 332 N.W.2d 757 (1983). In *Burns*, the victim of a serious crime had apparently attempted to "con-

tion of collective judgment (reflecting blame) that explains why a criminal receives a particular sentence. The individual victim is but a part of that broader society and should not be invited to make an explicit recommendation as to the offender's specific sentence.[145] To permit the victim to do so may bring a sense of satisfaction to the harmed party. But in so doing, we shift focus from the defendant's culpability to the victim's unpredictable desires. In the end, the objectives of even-handed, rational criminal punishments will have been subverted.[146]

E. Victim Participation and Structured Sentencing

Another concern, somewhat related to the disparate treatment discussion, is the issue of whether victim participation statutes are logically or practically consistent with structured or guided sentencing procedures. As discussed earlier in this essay,[147] the states of South Carolina

---

vert" the defendant after having testified against him at his preliminary hearings. Prior to defendant's trial, she maintained that she should not have to testify against the defendant because it was now a private matter between the two. Rejecting this claim (but allowing the use of her preliminary hearing testimony upon a finding of witness unavailability), the Wisconsin Supreme Court pointed out that the defendant's crime is one against society and therefore "punishment of offenders cannot be made contingent on the willingness of their victims to forgive the wrongdoer." *Id.* at 147, 332 N.W.2d at 765. *See also* Clarke, *Crime Begins at Home: Let's Stop Punishing Victims and Perpetuating Violence*, 28 WM. & MARY L. REV. 263, 268 (1987) (urging that prosecutors pursue criminal prosecutions in chronic and severe domestic violence cases "even if the victim does not insist upon, or even request, such action"). In support of that position, she echoes the *Burns* theme: "[T]he state, not the victim, prosecutes criminals." *Id.* at 287.

145. *See* R. ELIAS, THE POLITICS OF VICTIMIZATION 157 (1986) ("we must consider the propriety of allowing victims, who often seek the severest punishment against their attackers, to determine penalties"). The same sentiment has been expressed by Henderson: "[T]here appears to be little justification for victim participation in the determination of the criminal sanction." Henderson, *supra* note 135, at 1006. Where a capital defendant attempted to secure the testimony of his victims' relatives recommending against imposition of the death penalty, the Tenth Circuit characterized such testimony as irrelevant because it related neither to the defendant nor the circumstances of the homicide: "[A]llowing any person to opine whether the death penalty should be invoked would interfere with the jury's performance of its duty to exercise the conscience of the community. . . [T]he offense was committed not against the victim but against the community as a whole." Robison v. Maynard, 829 F.2d 1501, 1505 (10th Cir. 1987).

Obviously, I take strong issue with one writer's argument that "the crime victim's privity of interest in exacting justice for the harm committed ought to be a priority [in our system]." Cardenas, *supra* note 135, at 390. In asserting that the victim should be a party to the criminal proceedings, Cardenas gives no treatment to the question whether this will lead to disparate treatment of similarly-situated defendants.

146. Hellerstein argues that all victim impact evidence must pass a "culpability" standard, focusing on effects of the crime intended or foreseeable at the time of the offense. Hellerstein, *supra* note 87, at 424, 427. Under this standard, victims' sentence recommendations would be inadmissible. *Id.*

147. *See supra* notes 35, 36 and accompanying text (discussing measures to ameliorate impact of "victims' rights" statutes).

and Washington rely upon sentencing guidelines to soften the impact of victim participation statutes. Can this be done? I am very doubtful. Sentencing guidelines, by definition, limit discretion so that gross sentencing disparities will be eliminated. If one remains true to the "guidelines" rationale, victim participation statutes will be rendered largely impotent.[148] On the other hand, if participation statutes are given real meaning — that is, if the victim's expressed recommendations regarding case disposition are given effect by the sentencing judge — principles of guided sentencing decisions will have been sacrificed, if not lost altogether. As discussed below, I predict that in most jurisdictions guidelines statutes will "win out," leaving victim participation laws ineffectual. In this scenario, the ultimate loser is the victim. He or she will have been urged to make a sentence recommendation by a probation officer or prosecutor who knows (or should know) that sentencing guidelines (based upon factors that do not include the victim's recommendation) will essentially negate or veto the victim's voice.[149] This result will lead those victims to a sense of alienation and system distrust — the antithesis of the worthy goals of the "victims' rights" movement.[150]

A brief review of the statutory sentencing structure in Tennessee illustrates this guideline-victim participation schizophrenia.[151] The Tennessee Criminal Sentencing Reform Act of 1989[152] was adopted for the purpose of assuring "fair and consistent treatment of all defendants by eliminating unjustified disparity in sentencing and providing a fair sense of predictability of the criminal law and its sanctions."[153] All criminal offenses, felonies and misdemeanors are categorized in a structured

148. A similar observation was made by Hellerstein with respect to the Federal Sentencing Guidelines and the VIS allowed under Rule 32 of the Federal Rules of Criminal Procedure: "Since the Federal Sentencing Guidelines curtail the flexibility allowed a judge, victim-related information will be relevant only where specified in the Guidelines or possibly within the small amount of permitted judicial discretion. Thus, the [federal VIS] has limited relevance in the determinate sentencing scheme." Hellerstein, *supra* note 87, at 402.

149. Hillenbrand and Smith observed: "A number of [prosecutors] in states with sentencing guidelines pointed out that the guidelines restrict the impact of victim impact statements on sentences." HILLENBRAND & SMITH, *supra* note 6, at 46.

150. The study by Davis, Henley and Smith, *supra* note 56, however, found very little evidence that victim impact statements influenced sentencing decisions, once the charge and defendant's prior records were factored into the analysis. *Id.* at 33. Nonetheless, they reported "on a positive note" that "preparing impact statements [did not cause] greater dissatisfaction by raising victims' expectations to unreasonable levels." *Id.* at 35.

151. I served as an Ad Hoc Member of the Tennessee Sentencing Commission, which successfully recommended a comprehensive sentencing and substantive criminal law reform package to the Tennessee legislature. The views expressed in this essay are mine, of course, and probably do not reflect the views of other Commission members.

152. TENN. CODE ANN. §40-35-101 (1989).

153. TENN. CODE ANN. §40-35-102(2) (1989). Other purposes include: "[punishment] by imposi-

way.[154] Each felony is ascribed a Classification (A through E),[155] and within each class there are ranges,[156] dictating longer or shorter periods of incarceration and later or earlier parole release eligibility dates, based upon whether the defendant has been convicted of felonies in addition to the conviction offense.[157] A special category (entitled "Especially Mitigated Offender") allows for reductions in the minimum sentence and parole release eligibility dates, or both, for defendants (1) with no prior felony convictions, and (2) as to whom there are judicial findings of "mitigating factors but no enhancing factors."[158] Mitigating factors do not include victim-forgiveness,[159] and enhancement factors

---

tion of a sentence justly deserved in relation to the seriousness of the offense; [imposition of punishment] to prevent crime and promote respect for the law . . .; [sentencing decisions in which] all considerations respecting race, gender, and social status [are excluded]; [and giving first priority] regarding sentencing involving incarceration [to] convicted felons committing the most severe offenses, possessing criminal histories evincing a clear disregard for the laws and morals of society, and evincing failure of past efforts at rehabilitation." *Id.* §40-35-102(1), (2-5).

154. Five (5) categories of felonies and three (3) categories of misdemeanors. TENN. CODE ANN. §40-35-110 (1989).

155. *Id.*

156. TENN. CODE ANN. §40-35-112 (1989).

157. A "Multiple Offender" (Range II) has two to four prior convictions. *Id.* §40-35-106. A "Persistent Offender" (Range III) has five or more prior convictions. *Id.* §40-35-107. A "Career Offender" (Range III, but with harsher sentencing rules) has six or more prior convictions of felonies of high classifications. *Id.* §40-35-108.

158. TENN. CODE ANN. §40-35-109 (1989). A "Standard Offender" (Range I) is a defendant who is not deemed "Especially Mitigated" and who does not have the requisite number of prior felony convictions to be considered a "Multiple, Persistent or Career Offender." *Id.* §40-35-105 (1989).

159. TENN. CODE ANN. §40-35-113 provides:

If appropriate for the offense, mitigating factors may include, but are not limited to:

(1) The defendant's criminal conduct neither caused nor threatened serious bodily injury;

(2) The defendant acted under strong provocation;

(3) Substantial grounds exist tending to excuse or justify the defendant's criminal conduct, though failing to establish a defense;

(4) The defendant played a minor role in the commission of the offense;

(5) Before his detection, the defendant compensated or made a good faith attempt to compensate the victim of criminal conduct for the damage or injury the victim sustained;

(6) The defendant, because of his youth or old age, lacked substantial judgment in committing the offense;

(7) The defendant was motivated by a desire to provide necessities for his family or himself;

(8) The defendant was suffering from a mental or physical condition that significantly reduced his culpability for the offense; however, the voluntary use of intoxicants does not fall within the purview of this factor;

(9) The defendant assisted the authorities in uncovering offenses committed by other persons or in detecting or apprehending other persons who had committed the offenses;

(10) The defendant assisted the authorities in locating or recovering any property or person involved in the crime;

(11) The defendant, although guilty of the crime, committed the offense under such unusual

make no reference to a victim's recommendation for a harsh penalty.[160]

This legislative package also contains victim participation provisions relative to sentencing. First, it is mandatory that a victim's statement "relating to sentencing" be set forth in the pre-sentence report.[161] Sec-

---

circumstances that it is unlikely that a sustained intent to violate the law motivated his conduct.

(12) The defendant acted under duress or under the domination of another person, even though the duress or the domination of another person is not sufficient to constitute a defense to the crime; or

(13) Any other factor consistent with the purposes of this chapter.

160. TENN. CODE ANN. §40-35-114 provides:

If appropriate for the offense, enhancement factors, if not themselves essential elements of the offense as charged in the indictment, may include:

(1) The defendant has a previous history of criminal convictions or criminal behavior in addition to those necessary to establish the appropriate range;

(2) The defendant was a leader in the commission of an offense involving two (2) or more criminal actors:

(3) The offense involved more than one (1) victim;

(4) A victim of the offense was particularly vulnerable because of age or physical or mental disability;

(5) The defendant treated or allowed a victim to be treated with exceptional cruelty during the commission of the offense;

(6) The personal injuries inflicted upon or the amount of damage to property sustained by or taken from the victim was particularly great;

(7) The offense involved a victim and was committed to gratify the defendant's desire for pleasure or excitement;

(8) The defendant has a previous history of unwillingness to comply with the conditions of a sentence involving release in the community;

(9) The defendant possessed or employed a firearm, explosive device or other deadly weapon during the commission of the offense;

(10) The defendant had no hesitation about committing a crime when the risk to human life was high;

(11) The felony resulted in death or bodily injury or involved the threat of death or bodily injury to another person and the defendant has previously been convicted of a felony that resulted in death or bodily injury;

(12) During the commission of the felony, the defendant willfully inflicted bodily injury upon another person, or the actions of the defendant resulted in the death of or serious bodily injury to a victim or a person other than the intended victim;

(13) The felony was committed while on any of the following forms of release status if such release is from a prior felony conviction:

(A) Bail, if the defendant is ultimately convicted of such prior felony;

(B) Parole;

(C) Probation;

(D) Work release; or

(E) Any other type of release into the community under the direct or indirect supervision of the department of correction or local governmental authority;

(14) The felony was committed on escape status or while incarcerated for a felony conviction;

(15) The defendant abused a position of public or private trust, or used a special skill in a manner that significantly facilitated the commission or the fulfillment of the offense; or

(16) The crime was committed under circumstances under which the potential for bodily injury to a victim was great.

161. TENN. CODE ANN. §40-35-207(a)(8) (1989).

ond, the victim has the right to offer testimony "relevant to sentencing" at the sentencing hearing.[162]

Given the structure and content of the new sentencing rules, it is clear that the two victim participation provisions can have no effect upon offense classification and no impact on the establishment of the range within a class. It is not unimaginable that an individual judge might give some weight to a victim's forceful and articulate sentence recommendation (either harsh or lenient) within the established class and range, but its actual impact is likely to be small, if not negligible.

VI. CONCLUDING THOUGHTS

Many years ago I,[163] along with a small group of others,[164] urged that victims of crime be given more considerate and compassionate treatment by criminal justice officials. Pleas were made to afford victims opportunities to be more significant actors in the criminal justice system. Many positive and sweeping changes described here and elsewhere[165] have occurred in a relatively short period of time. While we should applaud the general thrust of these efforts, the time has come to signal the call for a proper balance between victim and offender.

It is axiomatic that crime victims are important participants in the criminal justice system and that they must not be the recipients of uncaring or insensitive treatment.[166] However, with regard to criminal case dispositions, we must move cautiously and prudently in deciding the kind of information that we should solicit from victims for consideration by judges in imposing sentence. The victim impact statement is an appropriate conduit through which certain data should flow to court

162. TENN. CODE ANN. §40-35-209(b) (1989): "At the sentencing hearing the court . . . may afford the victim . . . or the family of the victim the opportunity to testify relevant to the sentencing of the defendant."

163. Hall, *supra* note 1, at 982-84.

164. McDonald, *supra* note 1, at 669-72; Goldstein, *supra* note 1, at 560-61.

165. *See supra* notes 1-10 and accompanying text (discussing specific victim participation reforms that have occurred throughout America).

166. Somewhat ironically, a personal friend was the victim of a home burglary during the time in which I was writing this article. After the arrest of two suspects, she was asked to appear in a Nashville criminal court at 9:00 a.m. for a preliminary hearing. Because of court congestion and delay, she was kept until 3:00 p.m., having incurred out-of-pocket expenses for lunch and parking. Needless to say, that experience did not engender enthusiastic victim support for the criminal justice system. Shouldn't our energies and resources be spent in assisting her through prompt scheduling and helping to defray her expenses? Though the two "reforms" are not mutually exclusive, it seems only sensible to me that our efforts to honor "victim's rights" be directed into those arenas far more vigorously than in attempting to implement the victim participation schemes addressed in this article.

officials. The VIS contents, however, should be restricted to factual descriptions of harm suffered by the victim so that a reasonably accurate measure of the defendant's culpability is obtained.[167] Victim participation statutes calling for the victim's opinion or recommendation as to case disposition are ill-conceived measures triggering far more harmful consequences than their meager benefits. They should not be enacted.[168] Where legislatures have already approved such measures, they should be rescinded.

---

167. Clearly, such information is needed for the purpose of measuring an appropriate award of restitution to the aggrieved party. Beyond that, however, problems remain as to a clear definition of "victim harm" and the extent to which certain results which the defendant could not have reasonably foreseen should be factored into the sentencing decision. For a thoughtful and detailed analysis of these issues, see Schulhofer, *supra* note 85, and Hellerstein, *supra* note 87.

168. Interestingly, President Bush recommended to Congress legislation which would amend Fed. R. Crim. P. 32 to provide that "[the court] shall address the victim personally if the victim is present at the sentencing hearing and determine if the victim wishes to make a statement and to present any information in relation to the sentence." Cong. Rec. S.3214, Mar. 13, 1991.

Part III
Issues of Evidence and Process

[11]

SENTENCING PROBLEMS RAISED BY GUILTY PLEAS: AN ANALYSIS OF NEGOTIATED PLEAS IN THE BIRMINGHAM CROWN COURT

Introduction

In recent years, penological theory has increasingly favoured the individualisation of sentencing and this has led to a growing emphasis upon the provision of information for the sentencer about the circumstances of the offender.[1] Thus, it is common today for the sentencing judge to have access to information about the offender's penal history, personality, work record, medical and psychiatric history and his social background. Whilst it is clearly desirable for the sentencer to have detailed information about the defendant before sentence is passed, commentators have until recently tended to lose sight of the importance of providing the sentencer with full information about the circumstances of the offence. Moreover, it is now being realised that current procedures, designed to establish an accurate version of the facts of the offence itself, are one of the most deficient parts of the criminal system in both England and the United States. These deficiencies arise in no small measure from the assumption that, in criminal cases, guilt is determined by means of a formal adversarial process in which prosecution and defence counsel have independent duties to investigate the facts relevant to the charge and to present evidence to an impartial jury. In line with this assumption, the open court adjudicatory stage of the criminal process is surrounded by strict evidentiary and procedural rules which not only offer considerable protection to the defendant from arbitrary or oppressive treatment but also provide a means of ensuring that facts relating to the commission of the offence are accurately established. Even with these safeguards, however, it is clear that a guilty verdict will not necessarily provide sufficient information to ensure that the offender is sentenced on the basis of what he is proved to have done.[2] Having said this, it remains the case that by far the greater source of difficulty in establishing an accurate version of the facts of the offence itself arises not when a defendant is convicted by a jury but when, as is usually the case in criminal trials, the defendant

---

[1] See the excellent discussion of this in Part B of the Report of the Interdepartmental Committee (Chairman Mr. Justice Streatfeild) on *The Business of the Criminal Courts*, Cmnd. 1289 (1961); also Davies, " Social Inquiry for the Courts " (1974) 14 Brit.J.Criminol. 18.

[2] The difficulties inherent in a general verdict of Guilty are explored in Thomas, " Establishing a Factual Basis for Sentencing " [1970] Crim.L.R. 80; McConville, " Sentencing Issues: Judge and Jury " (1974) 11 *University of Western Australia Law Review* 230; Fox and O'Brien, " Fact-Finding for Sentencers " (1975) 10 *Melbourne University Law Review* 163.

tenders a plea of guilty.[3] The main problem is that few rules exist to ensure that the divide between the facts constituting the crime and the facts constituting the plea is not arbitrarily distorted by the exercise of prosecutorial or judicial discretion, negotiated settlements, induced pleas and other similar factors. In this paper we shall describe some sentencing problems encountered in the course of a study conducted in the Birmingham Crown Court involving defendants who had pleaded guilty.[4]

THE METHOD

In the course of conducting research on the outcome of jury trials in Birmingham, we noticed that many cases which we had anticipated would be contested at trial ended instead with the defendant entering a plea of guilty without a jury being empanelled. The decision to plead guilty in many of these cases appeared to have been taken abruptly, often literally minutes before the trial was due to start in court. To find out why changes of plea were occurring in this way, we sought interviews with a sample of defendants whose cases were tried in a 15-month period in 1975 and 1976. The sample consisted of 150 defendants, of whom we succeeded in interviewing 121 (81 per cent). It came as a surprise to find that no more than 35 defendants said that the decision to plead guilty was theirs alone and their plea reflected their admitted involvement in the offence alleged: the remaining defendants (over 70 per cent.) claimed to have pleaded guilty either because of pressure from their own barrister, or else because they had been involved in some form of negotiated settlement of plea. Our interest in this paper focuses on the sentencing difficulties that such unregulated out-of-court discussions tend to produce.

One of the most common complaints voiced by these defendants was that the account of the offence in court frequently bore little relation to the facts. What was said in the courtroom about a particular charge seemed to the defendant concerned to be often dependent not so much upon what he himself had done but rather upon the existence of certain random factors, often not legally

[3] In England, the proportion of defendants pleading guilty in the higher criminal courts is approximately 60 per cent.: Judicial Statistics (1975) Lord Chancellor's Department. The proportion of guilty pleas in the lower courts was almost 90 per cent. in 1976: Home Office Criminal Statistics 1976, Cmnd. 6909. In the United States, it seems that as many as 90 per cent. of all defendants plead guilty: Newman, *Conviction: The Determination of Guilt or Innocence Without Trial* (1966); The President's Commission on Law Enforcement and Administration of Justice, *Task Force Report: The Courts* (1967).

[4] This research, which is described at length in Baldwin and McConville, *Negotiated Justice* (1977), forms part of a more extensive inquiry concerned with the outcome of jury trials in the Birmingham Crown Court. The main results of this research are to be published in *Jury Trials* (1978). We are indebted to Kathlyn Bristow and Ann Keith who were employed as research fellows throughout the study period. The research has been funded by the Home Office. It goes without saying that the views expressed in this article are ours alone and not to be taken as those of the Home Office.

relevant, which happened to favour either the prosecution or the defence. Justice in these cases appeared to be at best fortuitous, at worst arbitrary. Random factors are present in some measure in all criminal cases but it seemed to us that the informal plea negotiations gave an unwarranted importance to such factors. The upshot of this was that sentences often appeared to be imposed on an inaccurate factual basis. Some evidence of these factual distortions comes from the complaints made to us by the defendants we interviewed. Not all defendants were critical, however, and in some of the cases that we shall cite, it is clear that the defendants felt strongly that such distortion had operated in their favour. In this paper, we shall present several verbatim quotes from the defendants in question. Since much of this information was derived from statements volunteered by defendants in the course of a long interview primarily concerned with other issues, it would be inappropriate and misleading to have attempted to subject this material to detailed statistical analysis. The material lends itself rather to qualitative, as opposed to quantitative, analysis. It is our contention that this analysis raises fundamental questions about present procedures adopted by the criminal courts in establishing a factual basis for sentencing.

The Study

Perhaps not surprisingly the defendants in this sample proved to be by and large ignorant of their rights. It was quite clear from the interviews that in general they had little idea of the consequences of a guilty plea, even where they were admitting guilt to, or at least involvement in, the acts constituting the offence charged. Defendants knew what in broad terms the prosecution was alleging but they usually believed that their plea was based, and would be accepted by the court as being based, on the facts as *they* understood them. It therefore came as a shock to many of them to find in court that the prosecution's version of the facts of the offence was quite inconsistent with their own. A frequent complaint was that the prosecution case was too victim-oriented and that the victim's version of the crime was presented to the court as if it were incontrovertible. Defendants involved in offences of violence against the person tended to be especially aggrieved in this respect. These offences were commonly preceded by some heated dispute in which the victim may have precipitated the final assault by striking the first blow or by some other act of aggression. Several defendants complained that the picture presented to the court did not reflect this. In *Case 103*, for example, the defendant pleaded guilty to unlawful wounding, having injured the victim in a pub brawl. According to the defendant, he was one of a group involved in an argument which eventually led to a fight in the course of which he and the victim had struggled together on the floor. He admitted striking the victim a number of blows but said that the victim was also cut by glass as they rolled on the floor, and he pleaded guilty on that basis. The prosecution's case, however, was that the defendant had deliberately struck the victim with a glass. The defendant made the following observation: [5]

> "As soon as I pleaded guilty there was no jury and there was nothing said on my behalf. When I pleaded guilty they weren't interested any more. They just read out what the police and [the victim's friends] said, and my barrister didn't even mention about the circumstances, so it all sounded a lot worse than it really was. What was said in court, well it might have been a different incident entirely; it wasn't like the actual thing that happened."

The defendant was well aware of the implications of this for sentence:

> "If the actual truth had come out, what did happen, I don't think I would have got nearly so much sentence. Judging by what was said in court the sentence [of 2½ years' imprisonment] was probably fair. On the way the judge heard it, he was fair, but he heard a different incident to what happened—even I didn't recognise it as what happened."

By far the greatest source of factual inaccuracy given to the court was, according to defendants, the alleged fabrication of evidence in the form of so-called police "verbals." Some 40 per cent. of defendants said that the police had attributed to them verbal statements they did not make.[6] Although defendants know before they go into court of the existence and nature of these verbal statements, they will usually be advised by their legal representatives, no doubt realistically, that it would be dangerous to challenge police evidence in court, that it is unlikely that their word will be believed, that their previous convictions might be put before the court, and that the judge might well impose a more severe sentence if this line of defence is pursued. The following illustrations show the sort of inaccuracies typically alleged by this group:

Case 109 (a first offender who pleaded guilty to handling and received a suspended sentence.)

> "The various things I was supposed to have said—like 'A load of crap' and 'I don't give a monkey's'—I mean that's not the way I talk. The things they put in like that were character destroying. They tried to make me out a hoodlum. I told my solicitor about it but he said 'I wouldn't push the issue, it's not really anything serious to worry about at this stage.'"

Case 114 (a defendant who pleaded guilty to handling stolen goods and who received a sentence of 18 months' imprisonment.)

---

[5] In quoting defendants in this article, we have disguised details that might identify any individual concerned.

[6] It is interesting to note that this allegation was made more commonly by defendants than allegations that they had been physically assaulted by the police.

"The police were lying and falsifying evidence. I suppose it's just their mentality. They did deals with other criminals and fitted me up with lots more gear [stolen goods] which there was no need for. But I think I was lucky. I was in front of a fair judge. The sentence was fair—it could have been a lot worse. Considering the way it was put over to him, he was fair."

Case 131 (a defendant who pleaded guilty to burglary and was fined.)

"The police were lying from start to finish. Most policemen don't see it as a job, it's a personal vendetta. They must lie, because nobody's going to admit something straight out, not usually, so they must lie here and there otherwise they haven't got a case. But the judge was great. I think he saw through all the police lies."

Far from complaining that they had suffered from inaccuracies given to the court, some defendants claimed to have benefited from them. It might have been expected, particularly where a guilty plea has been entered following some out-of-court discussion with the prosecution, that the professional criminal would be in the best position to extract a favourable deal.[7] A few professional criminals did indeed seem able to secure substantial concessions from the prosecution. Thus, for example, in *Case 121* the defendant, on his own admission a professional "fence" in the city, faced two charges of handling stolen goods valued at £3,500 and one charge of handling 100 motor taxation certificates. The prosecution was in a relatively weak position mainly because he went to the police station with his solicitor and refused to make a statement. His plea of guilty to handling stolen goods valued at £100 and to handling one stolen taxation certificate was accepted by the prosecution. Highly delighted with the outcome, he described the discussions which preceded it as follows:

"My barrister said, 'I'll try and get these charges amended,' and he did do this. It took him about three hours to get the charges dropped down. He was coming backwards and forwards to me saying, 'The prosecution have accepted that, if you'll accept this.' He always kept me right up to date on what was happening. He was a brilliant barrister; I couldn't fault him. I thought I was going to get three years' imprisonment, but I came away with 18 months."

Generally speaking, however, the professional criminals appeared to fare a good deal worse than others in the sample[8] and the people who benefited were those who found themselves, often completely fortuitously, in a strong position to exact leniency from the

[7] See, for instance, Newman, "Pleading Guilty for Considerations: A Study of Bargain Justice" (1956) 46 *Journal of Criminal Law, Criminology and Police Science* 780, and Chambliss, *Crime and the Legal Process* (1969).

[8] See Baldwin and McConville, *op. cit.* pp. 94–98.

prosecution. The defendant in *Case 20,* for example, a young man with previous convictions for sexual offences, was charged initially with rape (the maximum punishment for which is life imprisonment). There was clear medical evidence of sexual intercourse and good evidence that the victim had not consented. However, the prosecution did not want the immature and distraught victim to undergo the ordeal of giving evidence in court and indicated that a plea to a lesser charge of indecent assault (maximum five years' imprisonment) would be accepted. The defendant said he told his barrister that he was willing to plead guilty to the reduced charge so long as he did not have to go to prison, and continued:

> "My barrister disappeared again and came back and said he'd spoken to the judge who intimated that he would fine me. He said, 'Are you agreeable to that?' I said, 'Yes, I am.' I was expecting five or six years' imprisonment before I came to court, so I was very happy with the sentence. I knew I'd done wrong and I've certainly paid the penalty. Had I not been told by the barrister, I might have pleaded guilty to rape."

Similarly, the recidivist in *Case 26* found himself unexpectedly advantaged:

> "I pleaded guilty to two minor offences and they accepted my plea of not guilty to the main charge which carried a severe sentence [up to 14 years' imprisonment]. I was really pleased, I came away with probation. I took the barrister's advice on plea and I was happy to do so. Actually, I would have pleaded guilty to everything but my barrister said he would try and get the main charge dropped. He went away and came back saying, 'I've seen the prosecuting counsel and we had a rather undignified argument, but I've won.' My barrister was excellent. He wangled things so that I'd come up before a lenient judge and it worked. I have been to prison a few times before and I expected to get five years this time. I didn't understand a few things in court, but I'm not complaining."

When pleas are negotiated in this way, there is no doubting the benefits not only to the defendant in question but also to the court system. These benefits have been seen principally by commentators as the avoidance of expensive trials, the elimination of the uncertainties of jury trial, the reduction of sentencing differentials and the mitigation of harsh penalties.[9] On the other hand, the negotiated plea has certain consequences which tend to be detrimental to the proper administration of criminal justice. In the first place, as already indicated, a majority of defendants in our sample remained dissatisfied with the way their cases had been dealt with in court. Some believed they had been punished for a more serious crime than they had in fact committed; others felt that they might well

[9] See, for instance, Newman and NeMoyer, "Issues of Propriety in Negotiated Justice" (1970) 47 *Denver Law Journal* 367; Note, "Plea Bargaining and the Transformation of the Criminal Process (1977) 90 *Harvard Law Review* 564.

have been punished more severely had the judge accepted what they saw as an exaggerated account of their offence given by the prosecution in court; all looked upon the proceedings with a degree of cynicism. Many said they would have more readily accepted their lot if their cases had been more fully ventilated and if they had been more involved in the proceedings and not simply treated as spectators. If the sentencing stage of criminal procedure is conducted almost as though the defendant is not present, one can only expect a bitter reaction. Thus, in *Case 1*, for example: "They were all talking to each other and I just seemed to be watching and listening. I thought I'd have to speak but I didn't. It was like watching a press conference on the television." Also in *Case 102*:

> "It was all one-sided and against me. The depositions were full of lies. Nothing came out in my favour. I could have kicked myself afterwards, I should have pleaded not guilty. If I could have foreseen what would happen, I would have dragged those coppers through the mud. I was doing them all a favour by not going on with the trial; I cut my own throat."

Secondly, we would question whether it is right that certain defendants should have benefited to the extent that they did. Of course there are cases in which, when all the information about the defendant's background and the circumstances of the offence is examined, justice calls for mercy to be extended to the offender. But the practice of plea negotiation can scarcely be said to proceed upon that principle. It proceeds more on the basis of harshness or excessive leniency determined by the strength or weakness of the prosecution case, often irrespective of relevant social or legal considerations. Cases we have cited above illustrate this point and it is worth quoting two others. In *Case 108*, for example, a first offender pleaded guilty to handling a stolen car and was sentenced to 21 months' imprisonment. The severe sentence he received seemed at least partly attributable to his total lack of experience before the courts: he went voluntarily to the police station without a solicitor, made statements of admission, and at court entrusted his case entirely to his barrister. As he put it in the interview:

> "The police took me to the cleaners. They were calling me by my first name, getting me to shop everybody involved with me. When I was taken to court I didn't know what to say, what to do. It was like a kangeroo court; there was no proper trial. There should have been a trial where all the facts and circumstances came out. Telling tales on all my friends, because I didn't know what to do, has done me no good, not a bit. I had never had any tangles with the police before, except for the odd driving offence. I was never asked whether I wanted to say anything in court—it was all over in less than an hour."

The defendant in *Case 81* fared a good deal better. He was a man with a previous history of violence, charged with wounding with intent (maximum life imprisonment) and criminal damage (maximum 10 years). He had been involved in a fight at a dance during which the victim had sustained serious injury after the defendant had hit him with a glass vase. The prosecution eventually accepted his plea of not guilty to the wounding and guilty to the criminal damage, for which he received a small fine. The defendant described what happened:

> " I was expecting five years' imprisonment. I thought that my previous convictions and the [victim's] injuries would have got me five years. I saw my barrister before the trial and he said, ' Will you plead not guilty to the wounding and guilty to the damage?' I said, ' Yes,' and he said, ' Well, that's near enough. Don't build your hopes up too high but I think it'll get thrown out.' He went straight in and saw the judge and they never even called the jury. It was all over in five minutes. My barrister was only with the judge for five or ten minutes but what he did was brilliant. He did a lot behind the scenes. I couldn't believe my luck; I thought I'd have to fight the case in court."

Whatever the aims of sentencing, a minimum requirement in any rational system is that there should be some degree of correspondence between the crime committed, the crime charged and the crime for which the defendant is eventually convicted. As Kuh puts it [10]:

> " Responsibility, if not to be ludicrously regarded, must be for what one has done, not for something so far less serious that it bears hardly more than the vaguest of resemblances to the crime with which the defendant was charged . . . when the two fail to jibe even remotely, scorn and disrespect for the seeming folly of the law is likely to be the harvest, rather than any drive toward the defendant's reform."

Nor is it, as some writers see it, simply a question of the increased likelihood of rehabilitation towards which a plea of guilty is often seen as an important first step.[11] Excessive leniency can bring distress to the victim, weaken the morale of the police and reduce the law's protection of the community. We ourselves have witnessed the shattering effect on victims (not to mention cynicism on the part of the police) caused by the release back into the community of individuals, charged with serious crimes, who had been able to negotiate favourable plea arrangements. Several defendants within our sample of cases found themselves quite fortuitously in a strong bargaining position and were able to turn this to their own advantage. The less favourably placed, the weaker and more compliant can expect no such concessions: only with hindsight do they see that they have failed to benefit. The inexperienced offender in *Case 108,* mentioned above, had this to say after sentence:

[10] " Plea Copping " (1966-67) 24 *New York County Bar Bulletin* 160.

[11] See, for instance, Note, " The Influence of the Defendant's Plea on Judicial Determination of Sentence " (1956) 66 *Yale Law Journal* 204 and Fay, " The ' Bargained For ' Guilty Plea " (1968) 4 *Criminal Law Bulletin* 265.

"I told the solicitor that I was guilty and he gave me the impression that he was going to wash his hands of me. He was a double agent. He wasn't bothered in trying to cut the charge down; he was working hand in glove with the police. Now I realise I could have got away with quite a bit. There were no witnesses or anything to the offence; the police just had my word for it. Without the solicitor I could definitely have got away with half of it. You see it did me no good being honest. I was taken to the cleaners. The solicitor was virtually another branch of the police. He was always trying to make deals with the police—if he pleads guilty to this and that, will you let him out on bail? He was offering them tit-bits at my expense."

Such extreme cases are not, it must be stressed, regular occurrences, but the bargaining system seems to give them a frequency and a legitimacy they do not warrant. This is not to say, however, that the central question is whether sentences in general are too lenient or too severe: our contention is rather that random factors are allowed in negotiated plea cases to give rise to patterns of sentencing which are both haphazard and idiosyncratic.

THE COURTS: POST-CONVICTION PROCEDURES

The English courts, whilst not alive to many of the difficulties raised for the sentencer by guilty pleas, have developed certain rules in an attempt to regulate the determination of the facts for sentencing. Thus, it has long been a basic requirement that the charge brought should match the facts alleged. In consequence, it is the duty of prosecuting counsel, where nothing appears in the depositions which could be said to reduce the crime to some lesser offence than the one charged, to present the offence charged in the indictment, leaving it to the jury, if they see fit, to find a verdict of guilty to the lesser offence only.[12] The rationale for this is that, in the words of Lord Parker C.J.,[13]

". . . There is something more involved than convenience or expedition. Above all, there is the proper administration of criminal justice to be considered, [and] questions such as the protection of society and the stamping out of . . . criminal enterprise, if it is possible."

This rule reduces the frequency with which charges are unduly reduced,[14] although it must be remembered that it cannot eliminate sentences which are excessively lenient since the trial judge's sentencing discretion in England is virtually unfettered.[15] Rules designed to ensure that a defendant is not punished on the basis

[12] *Soanes* (1948) 32 Cr.App.R. 136.

[13] *Coe* (1969) 53 Cr.App.R. 66.

[14] On this, see further, A. Davis, "Sentences for Sale: A New Look at Plea Bargaining in England and America" [1971] Crim.L.R. 218.

[15] Murder is the only offence of significance where the judge has no discretion in sentencing.

of any fact which has not been properly established are at the present time being developed by the court. One interesting example of the courts' concern in this respect was the case of *Gortag.*[16] In that case, the defendants were charged with conspiracy to rob after they had been arrested in the vicinity of a projected wages snatch with an accomplice who had forewarned the police. The only matter in dispute was whether the enterprise had been abandoned at some stage prior to the arrests. This was an issue relating not to conviction but to sentence only. If the prosecution was prepared to accept the defendants' story, there would be a plea of guilty. The prosecution, however, refused and the trial then took a unique turn. Before arraignment, counsel for the defendants invited the judge either to empanel a jury and to hear the evidence up to the issue of abandonment when the pleas would be changed to guilty and the jury directed so to find, leaving the judge to resolve the issue of abandonment; or, alternatively, to accept pleas of guilty and hear evidence without a jury solely on the issue of abandonment. The trial judge adopted the latter course as an unusual but entirely proper solution and, on the issue of abandonment, conformed to all the usual restrictions of a jury trial, including directing himself on the burden of proof and the necessity for corroboration.

Whilst this was an exceptional step to have taken, it is indicative of an increasing willingness on the part of the courts to recognise the severe difficulties the sentencer faces in guilty plea cases. Thus it is now an established principle that a sentencer must not adopt, for the purpose of sentencing, a view of the facts which is inconsistent with the plea. The present position in England is that, where there is an issue of fact (or a possibly adverse inference from established facts) not resolved by the plea, the sentencer should, following the plea, indicate that he considers a particular matter relevant and allow either prosecution or defence to call evidence on the issue.[17] If the prosecution wish to introduce evidence relevant to an issue in sentencing after the plea has been taken, it must give notice to the defence of the evidence so that the defence may prepare to challenge it.[18] The sentencing judge may not adopt a view of the facts which would have justified a conviction for an offence more serious than that of which the defendant was convicted,[19] and any view of the facts adverse to the defendant must be supported by evidence.[20]

It nevertheless remains the case that courts in this country cannot be said to have developed adequate procedures for ensuring that an accurate version of the offence is presented in cases involving a guilty plea. Such safeguards as exist appear largely ineffective and

[16] [1973] Crim.L.R. 648.
[17] *Lester* [1976] Crim.L.R. 389; *Denniston* [1977] Crim.L.R. 46.
[18] *Robinson* (1969) 53 Cr.App.R. 314.
[19] *Foo* [1967] Crim.L.R. 456.
[20] *Hearne* [1976] Crim.L.R. 753.

surprisingly little care is taken in investigating the circumstances relating to the offence. For example, although it might be thought at least desirable that the judge question the defendant about the offence or offer an opportunity to him to make some statement to the court, the practice has grown up that the defendant who pleads guilty is almost never asked if he wishes to say anything before sentence is passed.[21] It is hardly surprising, therefore, that the defendants in our sample commonly felt an acute sense of alienation from the court proceedings and that many complained bitterly that a distorted account of the offence had been presented to the court.

Regulating the Procedures

Although commentators have suggested that many of the problems discussed above would be solved if new rules and procedures were introduced at the plea stage of the criminal process, we do not ourselves believe that this could be more than a partial remedy. It is our contention that a more radical re-appraisal of certain key stages in the criminal process is required. Our belief is very heavily coloured by our experiences in interviewing defendants, and it has been strongly reinforced by interviews we have conducted with police officers and lawyers during the course of our research. There has been a great deal of discussion in recent years on the balance of the criminal trial system, and some have argued that the prosecution is nowadays unfairly hampered and the defence unduly favoured. One influential exponent of this view is Sir Robert Mark, the former Commissioner of the Metropolitan Police, who wrote [22]:

> "It is, of course, right that in a serious criminal case the burden of proof should be upon the prosecution. But in trying to discharge that burden the prosecution has to act within a complicated framework of rules which were designed to give every advantage to the defence. The prosecution has to give the defence advance notice of the whole of its case, but the accused, unless he wants to raise an alibi, can keep his secret until the actual trial. When the police interrogate a suspect or charge him they have to keep reminding him that he need not say anything. . . ."

This view, at least as far as guilty plea cases are concerned, is not one that we share. Defendants may be subjected to intense pressures at various stages of the criminal process to plead guilty

[21] There used to be a requirement that a person convicted of felony be asked formally whether he had anything to say why sentence should not be passed. This requirement lapsed in 1967 with the abolition (by the Criminal Law Act 1967) of the distinction between felonies and misdemeanours, and defendants are now rarely invited to address the court in guilty plea cases despite the fact that the Criminal Law Revision Committee, on whose seventh report the 1967 Act was based, stated that it was " desirable that the accused should be invited to add anything to his counsel's address in mitigation if he wishes . . .": Criminal Law Revision Committee, *Felonies and Misdemeanours, Seventh Report* 1965, Cmnd. 2659.

[22] Sir Robert Mark, *Minority Verdict* (1973).

and, in this sense, the system often appears heavily weighted in favour of the prosecution.[23] The principal causes of this imbalance, as we see it, are, *first*, the largely unregulated system of interrogating suspects whilst in police custody and, *secondly*, the practice of allowing a substantial discount in sentence for a plea of guilty. Thus, in many of the cases within our sample, some of the most damaging evidence in the prosecution case consisted of allegedly fabricated verbal admissions attributed to the defendant by police officers. In no less than 57 per cent. of cases, no written statement had been made to the police by the defendant. Many of the allegations of fabricated "verbal" admissions were convincingly put forward to us by defendants and frequently made with no real sense of grievance. Some complaints, on the other hand, were doubtless untrue or grossly exaggerated. We had, of course, no way of verifying any allegations but the important point is that neither the defence barrister nor the court were in any better position to do so.[24] Furthermore, it is undeniable (as often defence counsel told defendants) that a police officer's evidence will almost invariably be preferred to that of the defendant. The point is that, since disputes about what took place whilst the defendant was being interrogated in police custody cannot be satisfactorily resolved, it makes good sense for a barrister to advise his client that it is foolish to attempt to challenge police evidence in court. Similarly, it may well be prudent for a barrister, working within the constraints of the existing system, to advise a defendant to plead guilty in the hope of a more lenient sentence, if the alternative is probable conviction and a much more severe sentence. Viewed in this way, the largely unregulated interrogation of suspects in police custody, coupled with the very considerable reduction in sentence offered virtually automatically to those defendants who plead guilty,[25] demonstrates why defence counsel may often, quite properly, bring pressure upon his client to plead guilty. Indeed it has been put to us that any barrister would be obliged to give this advice once a written statement has been made, and that he would be failing in his duty to do otherwise. These considerations also suggest that mere tinkering with pre-trial plea procedures (as for instance by

[23] This has led to one recent writer to observe: ". . . although . . . great weight is traditionally attached to the principle of the 'presumption of innocence,' yet . . . once a person has appeared in court facing a criminal charge many of the subsequent decisions taken by the various parties concerned . . . often seem to be influenced rather by a principle of 'assumption of guilt,'" Bottomley, *Decisions in the Penal Process* (1973), p. 84.

[24] A Home Office Steering Committee reported in October 1976 that it would be feasible to conduct a limited experiment in tape recording police interrogations: *The Feasibility of an Experiment in the Tape-Recording of Police Interrogation*, Cmnd. 6630 (1976). According to newspaper reports, the Police Federation has expressed its total opposition to even this limited experiment: *The Times*, October 20, 1976. See also Price and Caplan, *The Confait Confessions* (1977).

[25] The extent of sentence discounts for pleading guilty is discussed in detail in Baldwin and McConville, "The Influence of the Sentencing Discount in Inducing Guilty Pleas" in Baldwin and Bottomley (ed.), *Criminal Justice* (1978), pp. 116–128.

amending the code of professional ethics which control counsel's conduct and the advice he can give) is likely to leave the *de facto* position substantially unaltered since, in most cases, advice to plead guilty *is* probably prudent, or at least expedient.

Moreover, viewed from the defendant's side, it is apparent that procedural amendments alone are not likely to assist the search for the truth. The available research evidence[26] suggests that defendants commonly feel themselves outside the network of those intimate relationships which comprise the court. Many within our own sample found it difficult to decide whose side their barrister was on,[27] and almost a half said that it was not they but their barrister who took the final decision on plea. The sorts of comment we encountered commonly in the course of the research are indicated by the three following cases:

Case 9

> " My barrister didn't ask me, he told me to plead guilty."

Case 42

> " They [the pre-trial discussions on plea] were all going on in the judge's chambers, so how could I understand what was happening? All this talking and arranging was done in secret, I hadn't a clue what was happening."

Case 75

> " The barrister and solicitor took the decisions. I was in a sticky position but they told me I had no alternative. They spoke to me for about 20 minutes. I was saying that I hadn't done three [counts in the indictment] and the barrister kept saying 'Yes, but the statement.' I said the statements weren't true but he said, 'You'll know better next time' meaning next time you'll be careful, but this time you've got no chance. So they just kept on about these depositions and getting me to plead guilty to all. I was supposed to tell them, but they were directing me."

Once the decision on plea was made, most defendants felt even more estranged and powerless. Sometimes a defendant made an attempt to advance his own account of the offence to the court but this was rare and, where it did happen, it was apparently without effect. For instance,

Case 4

> " My barrister kept talking about the verbals. The police said they'd chased me for 200 yards but I'd just come out of hospital

[26] See Blumberg, " The Practice of Law as a Confidence Game: Organisational Cooptation of a Profession " (1967) 1 *Law and Society Review* 15; Bottoms and McClean, *Defendants in the Criminal Process* (1976), and Carlen, *Magistrates' Justice* (1976).

[27] As one American writer aptly puts it: " When a defendant thinks of [his legal representative] as one of 'them' rather than as someone on 'his' side he is, in an organisational sense, probably right." Casper, *American Criminal Justice: The Defendant's Perspective*, Prentice Hall (1972), p. 105.

and I couldn't have run if I'd wanted to. I kept trying to interrupt in court but my barrister wouldn't let me. My barrister said afterwards, 'I didn't want you to commit yourself—I *knew* you'd get a suspended sentence.' But what I want to know is how he knew; there must have been something funny going on."

In general defendants said nothing in court, perhaps aggrieved by what was being said but resignedly accepting their lot, as in *Case 102*:

"From the day you get nicked to the day you are sentenced, you've got no say in the matter. You don't get a chance to say the things you want. I'd defend myself in future: I might not be able to use the long words but in my own simple way I could put my points better. You just don't get any say at any stage in what is happening to you."

Another defendant, who was a first offender, in *Case 122* gave a more graphic description of his experience:

"I was quite bewildered really because it was the first time I'd been in court. I thought it was like a different world, like a big game. It's like a ritual. You have got to stand up and you have got to sit down, and there's one side going on and then there's another side going on. They're like speaking in riddles. You are a pawn in a chess game; you are just sitting there and there are people throwing your life about."

It might be thought that these kinds of problem could be alleviated if the trial judge questioned the defendant in court after the guilty plea has been entered. In the view of many commentators, however, where such questioning does take place, as in the United States, the proceedings are for the most part no more than an empty ritual in which the defendant assures the court that no bargain has been made and that no pressure has been brought to bear when almost everyone present knows that this is manifestly not the case.[28] The reason for the ineffectiveness of such procedures is that, at the stage when these safeguards are introduced, the defendant is already a consenting party to the courtroom charade because he has been led to believe, as is indeed often the case, that a guilty plea is his best or only course of action. He has in effect been co-opted into a system which encourages the passive, rewards the compliant, and elevates empty ceremony above strict observance of due process of law. American courts may be criticised for trying to solve fundamental problems by engaging in empty ritual: English courts appear unwilling even to recognise that such problems exist. There can be little doubt, in our view, that existing procedures for establishing the factual basis for sentencing in

[28] On this, see particularly White, "A Proposal for Reform of the Plea Bargaining Process" (1971) 119 *University of Pennsylvania Law Review* 439 and Katz, Litwin and Bamberger, *Justice is the Crime: Pre-trial Delay in Felony Cases* (1972).

England are inadequate. In some cases, the account of the offence in court appears to bear an uncertain relation to the crime committed. In such cases the factual distortions are likely to be sufficiently serious to raise questions about the just disposition of the case. Sometimes the distortion operates to the defendant's benefit, sometimes to his detriment, but distortion can never operate in favour of justice. No system of criminal justice can for all cases accurately reflect in court what happened in the street, but the English system which allows considerable scope for, but inadequate supervision of, the negotiation of guilty pleas, appears to make such an objective the more difficult to achieve. It is only when the problems created by this kind of informal settlement are tackled and resolved that the sentencer can claim that the defendant is being sentenced on the basis of what he is proved to have done.

JOHN BALDWIN *
MICHAEL MCCONVILLE †

* Lecturer in Judicial Administration, Faculty of Law, University of Birmingham.
† Lecturer in Law, Faculty of Law, University of Birmingham.

VOLUME 97 MARCH 1984 NUMBER 5

HARVARD LAW REVIEW

IS PLEA BARGAINING INEVITABLE?

*Stephen J. Schulhofer**

In the past decade, the notion that plea bargaining is a permanent component of our criminal justice system has gained near-unanimous acceptance among the system's defenders and critics alike. The twin evils of caseload pressure and an irrepressible tendency toward cooperation among members of the courtroom "work group" are said to render plea bargaining unavoidable. Professor Schulhofer challenges this dogma; he offers, in place of plea bargaining, a bench trial system that is based on one actually used in Philadelphia today. Drawing on his own close study of the Philadelphia system, Professor Schulhofer argues that bench trials can be — and in Philadelphia are — genuine adversary proceedings in which defendants retain many of the constitutional protections that plea bargaining sacrifices. Moreover, he demonstrates that such a system could be instituted— even to the total exclusion of plea bargaining — with only a minimal increase in the resources needed to handle modern criminal dockets. Against this background, Professor Schulhofer considers how bargaining came to be seen as an inevitability. He concludes that plea bargaining has won widespread acceptance not because it is a necessary concession to immutable "realities," but rather because it serves a seductive but highly problematic normative conception of justice.

IN most criminal cases, plea bargaining is necessary and inevitable — at any rate, that is the view of nearly all knowledgeable scholars and practitioners and much of the public at large. In this Article, I suggest that this pervasively important assumption is erroneous. I shall argue that effective containment of plea bargaining is realistically possible for American criminal courts, and that in fact this goal has already been achieved in one large, heterogeneous, crime-conscious urban jurisdiction. By plea bargaining I mean any process in which inducements are offered in exchange for a defendant's cooperation in not fully contesting the charges against him. Thus, I am

* Professor of Law, University of Pennsylvania. Princeton University, A.B., 1964; Harvard University, LL.B., 1967.

This Article grows out of empirical research supported by grants from the Rutledge, White, and Temin Funds at the University of Pennsylvania Law School. Though I cannot adequately acknowledge all those who aided the project, special thanks are due to my four resourceful student assistants — Alice Beck, Scott Bok, Maribel Figueredo, and Sharon Gornstein; to officials who facilitated the research — Philadelphia Court of Common Pleas President Judge Edward J. Bradley, District Attorney Edward Rendell, Assistant District Attorney Arnold Gordon, Philadelphia Defender Benjamin Lerner, and First Assistant Defender Louis Natali; and to colleagues who commented on the manuscript — C. Edwin Baker, Edward Becker, William Evan, Alvin Klevorick, David Rudovsky, Joan Saltzman, Louis Schwartz, Marvin Wolfgang, and especially the late Edward Sparer.

asserting the feasibility of restricting or even eliminating not only formal, officially sanctioned plea bargaining, but also the wide variety of informal, sub rosa behavior patterns in which indirect inducements, unspoken commitments, and covert cooperation create the functional equivalent of explicit bargaining. The mechanism for realizing this ostensibly utopian vision is the Philadelphia bench trial, an institution I will undertake to describe and then assess.

In offering the Philadelphia bench trial as a model, I am claiming not only that it is feasible in the narrow administrative sense, but also that it is compatible with the complex of values that should inform the choice of procedural arrangements for ascertaining guilt. The normative argument for the bench trial model includes both an appeal to adjudication over negotiation and an appeal to judicial adjudication over lay participation. In both respects, the normative argument poses a challenge to widely accepted procedural traditions. The descriptive argument for the bench trial model is at least equally problematic. In claiming that bargaining can be and *has been* successfully restricted, I am denying the deeply held belief that plea bargaining in one form or another is universal and inevitable. I will therefore be obliged to examine the conceptual and empirical foundations of that belief and to present the evidence supporting a contrary conclusion — an empirical study of Philadelphia bargaining and trial practice — in enough detail to satisfy readers who will be and should be extremely skeptical of my claim.

Part I of this Article locates the issues treated here within the wider debate over plea bargaining and provides an overview of the important bodies of theory and research suggesting that bargaining and cooperation are inevitable. Part II describes the Philadelphia empirical study and considers the extent to which this jurisdiction may be said to afford its defendants a genuine adversary trial. Part III considers the implications of the empirical findings for the immediate questions of plea bargaining reform. Part IV examines the implications for two more general sets of concerns — first, for the further development of behavioral theories of criminal litigation, and second, for an understanding of the conceptions of justice that give those theories their strong attraction for students of the criminal process.

I. The Plea Bargaining Debate

The debate over plea bargaining has centered on two major issues. First, is resolution of criminal cases by bargaining better in principle than resolution by trial? Second, whether or not plea bargaining is superior in principle, is it inevitable in practice?

The first issue is perhaps the more fundamental. Nonetheless, I propose to restrict my attention to the second issue exclusively. Although a large number of criminal justice scholars and practitioners accept as more or less obvious the notion that plea bargaining is in principle less desirable than disposition by trial,[1] both supporters and detractors assume that bargaining is in any event inevitable.[2] In some quarters, in fact, any attempt to advocate the abolition of plea bargaining will simply be dismissed as a theoretical exercise.[3] The inevitability of bargaining is thought to be so well understood by every intelligent, well-informed person that serious consideration of its desirability is often difficult to sustain

Putting to one side, then, the possibility of debate over the desirability of bargaining, I assume rather wide agreement that, in an ideal world, plea bargaining would be infrequent or nonexistent. The question remains whether this ideal can be attained in the context of the heavily burdened criminal justice systems that exist in most American cities today.

A. *Theoretical Perspectives: Case Pressure and Cooperation*

Defenders of plea bargaining usually argue that bargaining is unavoidable for either of two reasons. First, a prohibition of plea bar-

---

[1] To be sure, the Supreme Court asserted in Santobello v. New York, 404 U.S. 257, 261 (1971), that plea bargaining "is not only an essential part of the process ***but a highly desirable part***" (emphasis added). As one commentator has noted, however, "each of the reasons cited as making the practice desirable related at least partly to the reason the Court claimed it was essential [that is, speed and efficiency]." Note, *Constitutional Alternatives to Plea Bargaining: A New Waive*, 132 U. PA. L. REV. (forthcoming 1984) [hereinafter cited as Note, *A New Waive*].

For other commentary suggesting that plea bargaining is or could become an intrinsically desirable method of disposition (without regard to the alleged infeasibility of trial), see, for example, Enker, *Perspectives on Plea Bargaining*, in PRESIDENT'S COMM'N ON LAW ENFORCEMENT & ADMIN. OF JUSTICE, TASK FORCE REPORT: THE COURTS 112 (1967); P. UTZ, SETTLING THE FACTS (1978); Church, *In Defense of "Bargain Justice,"* 13 LAW & SOC'Y REV. 509 (1979). Discussion in that vein bears a close affinity to the extensive body of analysis suggesting the potential advantages of dispute settlement through negotiation and relatively informal procedure. *See, e.g.*, THE DISPUTING PROCESS — LAW IN TEN SOCIETIES (L. Nader & H. Todd eds. 1978); P. GULLIVER, DISPUTES AND NEGOTIATIONS (1979); P. GULLIVER, SOCIAL CONTROL IN AN AFRICAN SOCIETY (1963); Abel, *A Comparative Theory of Dispute Institutions in Society*, 8 LAW & SOC'Y REV. 217 (1973); Eisenberg, *Private Ordering Through Negotiation: Dispute-Settlement and Rulemaking*, 89 HARV. L. REV. 637 (1976). For criticism of such approaches, see THE POLITICS OF INFORMAL JUSTICE (R. Abel ed. 1982); Cain & Kulcsar, *Thinking Disputes: An Essay on the Origins of the Dispute Industry*, 16 LAW & SOC'Y REV. 375 (1982); Note, *Dispute Resolution*, 88 YALE L.J. 905 (1979).

[2] *See, e.g.*, Barzilay, *The D.A.'s Right Arms*, N.Y. Times, Nov. 27, 1983, § 6 (Magazine), at 118, 124 ("[Plea bargain] compromises are inevitable in an overburdened criminal-justice system . . . ."). The principal exceptions are NATIONAL ADVISORY COMM'N ON CRIMINAL JUSTICE STANDARDS & GOALS, REPORT ON COURTS 46–49 (1973); Alschuler, *Implementing the Criminal Defendant's Right to Trial: Alternatives to the Plea Bargaining System*, 50 U. CHI. L. REV. 931 (1983).

[3] As political scientist Milton Heumann puts it, "abolition [of plea bargaining] is an impossibility. . . . [T]o speak of a plea bargaining-free criminal justice system is to operate in a land of fantasy. . . . Plea bargaining . . . will remain the bedrock for case disposition in all communities . . . . It will inevitably provide a central means of disposing of cases . . . ." M. HEUMANN, PLEA BARGAINING 157, 162, 170 (1978).

gaining, it is said, would generate enormous costs and monumental delays; plea bargaining is essential for handling massive criminal caseloads. Second, a prohibition of plea bargaining would be subverted by counsel and other participants in the system; thus, bargaining would continue and the courts would not collapse, but the resulting process would be less visible and would afford even fewer safeguards than the present one.

Illustrative of the first theme are the influential comments of Chief Justice Burger in a 1970 speech to the American Bar Association:

> The consequence of what might seem on its face a small percentage change in the rate of guilty pleas can be tremendous. A reduction from 90 per cent to 80 per cent in guilty pleas requires the assignment of twice the judicial manpower and facilities — judges, court reporters, bailiffs, clerks, jurors and courtrooms. A reduction to 70 per cent trebles this demand.[4]

The assumed relationship between bargaining and judicial resources requires two qualifications. First, Chief Justice Burger was concerned not with bargaining but with the "guilty plea rate," and it is far from clear that an elimination of bargaining (in all its forms) would result in the elimination of all guilty pleas.[5] Second, and perhaps more importantly, the analysis appears to assume that the existing stock of judicial resources is used exclusively for trials — that no "judges, court reporters, bailiffs, clerks, jurors and courtrooms" are needed to process the convictions currently obtained by plea. This is plainly something of an exaggeration. Yet nearly all discussion of the practical necessity for bargaining appears to assume that the time and effort expended in guilty plea dispositions are trivial compared to the time and effort required for trials.[6]

The second line of argument asserts that we need not fear a collapse of the courts, but only because there can never be a genuinely

---

[4] Burger, *The State of the Judiciary — 1970*, 56 A.B.A. J. 929, 931 (1970). Ironically, when the Chief Justice observed that court administration is based on the premise of a very high guilty plea rate, he added the caveat that "[t]hat premise may no longer be a reliable yardstick of our needs." *Id.* His main purpose apparently was to urge expansion of judicial capacity in order to reduce the courts' vulnerability to increases in the trial rate. Nonetheless, the Chief Justice's vivid analysis only served to highlight the futility of attempts to reduce bargaining. *See, e.g.*, Santobello v. New York, 404 U.S. 257, 260 (1971) (Burger, C.J.) ("'[P]lea bargaining' is an essential component of the administration of justice. . . . If every criminal charge were subjected to a full-scale trial, the States and the Federal Government would need to multiply by many times the number of judges and court facilities.").

[5] In less serious cases, the incidental "process" costs of going to trial appear to induce large numbers of guilty pleas even in the absence of sentencing concessions of any kind. *See* M. FEELEY, THE PROCESS IS THE PUNISHMENT 186–87, 241 (1979). Where felony guilty plea rates approach the 90% level, it seems fair to assume that a significant proportion of the pleas could not be obtained without concessions of some sort.

[6] As Professor Hans Zeisel writes, "[t]ime spent on cases that are pleaded guilty is measured in fractions of an hour; time spent on preparing and conducting a trial is measured in days and weeks." Zeisel, *The Offer That Cannot Be Refused*, in F. ZIMRING & R. FRASE, THE CRIMINAL JUSTICE SYSTEM 558, 558 (1980).

effective prohibition of bargaining. For many observers, this conclusion follows from the caseload problems just discussed: lawyers and judges are forced to bargain (explicitly or covertly) because any other behavior would bring the judicial system to a halt. In this theory the inevitability of bargaining depends on the assumed need for bargaining, and the theory thus can be questioned to the extent that the "administrative need" can be shown to be illusory.[7]

Some social scientists, including many who question the case pressure hypothesis, have advanced a different explanation for the inevitability of bargaining. For these scholars, plea bargaining is not the result of anything so transitory or (in theory) controllable as case pressure; rather, it is produced by much more complex factors that are deeply rooted in social dynamics and perhaps no more subject to change than is human nature itself. Thus, whether or not case pressure contributes to bargaining, these other factors ensure that bargaining will continue even if caseloads should slacken. This much stronger version of the inevitability hypothesis guides a now-substantial body of research organized around two separable, though not entirely distinct, theoretical perspectives — organizational analysis and socialization (or adaptation) analysis.

Building on studies of behavior in ordinary commercial enterprises and large public agencies,[8] organizational theorists view the criminal process in terms of the structure of roles and relationships among workers in the courtroom setting.[9] Because courtroom work groups

---

[7] The case pressure hypothesis has also been questioned on the basis of empirical data said to show no significant correlation between heavy caseloads and heavy plea bargaining rates. *See* M. HEUMANN, *supra* note 3, at 27–33; Heumann, *A Note on Plea Bargaining and Case Pressure*, 9 LAW & SOC'Y REV. 515 (1975). This kind of empirical evidence, however, appears much too weak to be even suggestive. For a detailed critique, see Nardulli, *The Caseload Controversy and the Study of Criminal Courts*, 70 J. CRIM. L. & CRIMINOLOGY 89, 91–93 (1979). Nardulli developed a more sophisticated test of the case pressure hypothesis, and with one exception he found no significant correlation between case pressure variables and either guilty plea rates, dismissal rates, or sentences in guilty plea cases. He attributed the apparent insignificance of case pressure changes to an astonishing excess capacity in the Chicago courts: most judges spent only two to three hours on the bench per day and were not occupied with other duties thereafter; over a two-year period, the 16 courtrooms studied averaged only one disposition per working day, even though 70% of these dispositions were guilty pleas or dismissals. *Id.* at 96–97. For an interesting empirical study casting doubt on the case pressure hypothesis in the context of misdemeanor prosecutions, see M. FEELEY, *supra* note 5, at 247–61.

[8] The seminal work is H. SIMON, ADMINISTRATIVE BEHAVIOR (1945). Other representative studies include A. ETZIONI, COMPLEX ORGANIZATIONS (2d ed. 1961); C. PERROW, ORGANIZATIONAL ANALYSIS: A SOCIOLOGICAL VIEW (1970); J. THOMPSON, ORGANIZATIONS IN ACTION (1967); Parsons, *Suggestions for a Sociological Approach to the Study of Organizations* (pts. 1 & 2), 1 AD. SCI. Q. 63, 225 (1956); Selznick, *Foundations of the Theory of Organizations*, 13 AM. SOC. REV. 25 (1948).

[9] Important works that self-consciously adopt an organizational perspective include J. EISENSTEIN & H. JACOB, FELONY JUSTICE: AN ORGANIZATIONAL ANALYSIS OF CRIMINAL COURTS (1977); P. NARDULLI, THE COURTROOM ELITE: AN ORGANIZATIONAL PERSPECTIVE ON CRIM-

display no formal hierarchical relationships, organizational theorists do not conceive of such groups as bureaucracies.[10] Rather, the judge has a limited formal authority over attorneys and other participants, but all workers can influence one another. Although each worker has a specialized role, all share certain goals and have a mutual interest in avoiding conflict and maintaining group cohesion.[11] The character of the work group is also influenced by outside groups — most immediately, the workers' "sponsoring organizations" (for example, the public defender's and district attorney's offices), but also police, the media, appellate courts, the public, and so on. As elaborated by James Eisenstein and Herbert Jacob, this perspective suggests four general goals that courtroom work groups seek to achieve: the internally generated goals of maintaining group cohesion and reducing uncertainty, and the externally inspired goals of doing justice and disposing of the caseload.[12]

This analysis does not by itself imply the inevitability of bargaining. On the contrary, it posits the existence of one goal ("doing justice") that requires adherence to formal, adversary roles, and it draws explicit attention to factors that may affect the relative priorities of conflicting goals. In fact, Eisenstein and Jacob emphasize the way that different internal and external environments in the three cities they studied influenced the strength of particular goals and thus the behavior and output of particular courtroom work groups.[13]

Organizational analysis of this sort provides a useful conceptual framework that — on its face — is sufficiently open textured to accommodate a great variety of messy empirical facts. Nevertheless, implicit and often explicit in the work of organizational theorists is a strong commitment to the importance of internal group dynamics and an assumption that the desire to minimize uncertainty and conflict is virtually inherent in human nature.[14] These postulates suggest that, whatever changes may occur in caseload pressure (or, for that matter,

---

INAL JUSTICE (1978); Feeley, *Two Models of the Criminal Justice System: An Organizational Perspective*, 7 LAW & SOC'Y REV. 407 (1973); Mohr, *Organizations, Decisions, and Courts*, 10 LAW & SOC'Y REV. 621 (1976); Skolnick, *Social Control in the Adversary System*, 11 J. CONFLICT RESOLUTION 52 (1967).

[10] *But cf.* A. BLUMBERG, CRIMINAL JUSTICE 178–203 (2d ed. 1979) (analyzing courtroom work groups as bureaucratic organizations). The Weberian concept of bureaucracy, which implies a highly centralized, hierarchical system with close supervision and effective control of subordinate actors, does not provide a useful tool for analysis of behavior in courtroom work groups. *See* Feeley, *supra* note 9, at 422.

[11] *See* J. EISENSTEIN & H. JACOB, *supra* note 9, at 24–28; P. NARDULLI, *supra* note 9, at 66–81; Cole, *The Decision to Prosecute*, 4 LAW & SOC'Y REV. 331 (1970); Feeley, *supra* note 9, at 413–16; Skolnick, *supra* note 9, at 53–55.

[12] *See* J. EISENSTEIN & H. JACOB, *supra* note 9, at 25.

[13] *See id.* at 244–51.

[14]

> Pervasive conflict is not only unpleasant; it also makes work more difficult. Cohesion produces a sense of identification and belonging that satisfies human needs. . . . [S]ome

in demands to "do justice"), the crucial internal considerations that drive the bargaining process will remain unaffected. Thus, cities may display marginally different bargaining rates, but this analysis anticipates no radical discontinuities in the extent of bargaining.

Adaptation analysis proceeds from much simpler premises. Although it treats courtrooms as work groups with internally generated norms and objectives, adaptation analysis views courtroom behavior primarily as the product of a socialization process.[15] As developed by Milton Heumann, moreover, this approach attributes crucial importance to socialization through "learning" rather than through "teaching." Heumann acknowledges that a newcomer to the courts "may be taught that rewards and penalties are attached to certain actions."[16] He stresses, however, that this "teaching" is not the paramount element in the process of socialization: "newcomers simply learn," he argues, that the "reality of the local criminal court differs from what [they] expected. . . . [M]uch of the variance in newcomer adaptation is a function of the newcomer's learning about his role and about the associated constraints that the 'realities' of the case characteristics impose upon him."[17]

The "reality" Heumann has in mind is, above all, the hopelessness of defendants' cases. On the basis of extended interviews with defenders and other court personnel, he concludes that "[t]he most important thing the new defense attorney learns is that most of his clients are factually guilty":[18]

> [Newcomers] begin their jobs with a vague notion that "many" defendants are innocent. After several months in the system, they offer estimates that about 50 percent are guilty. The figure contrasts with the 90 percent estimate given by almost all experienced defense attorneys. . . .
>
> . . . .
>
> . . . [E]xperienced defense attorneys agree that of the approximately 90 percent of the defendants who are factually guilty, most have cases devoid of any legally disputable issue. These cases, as one defense attorney phrased it, are "born dead."[19]

For Heumann, plea bargaining results neither from case pressure nor from group needs to avoid either conflict or, a fortiori, uncertainty.

---

workgroups value cohesion less than others because they find conflict less threatening to their survival. But in general we believe that the variation is not great.

Id. at 27–28.

[15] *See* M. HEUMANN, *supra* note 3. For other versions of adaptation and socialization analysis, see, for example, J. SKOLNICK, JUSTICE WITHOUT TRIAL (1966); Feeley, *supra* note 9, at 413, 416; Skolnick, *supra* note 9, at 55.

[16] M. HEUMANN, *supra* note 3, at 3.

[17] *Id.* at 2–3 (citation omitted).

[18] *Id.* at 58.

[19] *Id.* at 58, 60.

(Indeed, in Heumann's world, uncertainty does not appear to be much of a problem.) Rather, given "the defendant's factual culpability coupled with the absence of contestable legal and factual issues," counsel choose bargaining because there is simply no issue to take to trial.[20]

Curiously, Heumann — a political scientist — does not appear to doubt either the intrinsic possibility of a "reality" such as the one his interview subjects described or the ability of individuals immersed in complex social relationships to provide accurate descriptions of their world.[21] Although Heumann's conclusions therefore must be approached with great caution, they suggest questions that cannot simply be dismissed. What proportion of criminal cases filed (or adjudicated) are devoid of disputable issues of fact and law? To what extent do such cases prompt or impel bargaining? To what extent would effective barriers to bargaining influence the plea rate in such cases? The Philadelphia study discussed in Part II suggests answers to these questions that diverge sharply from those offered by Heumann.

I have thus far attempted to present the diverse hypotheses offered to explain the alleged inevitability of plea bargaining. Two bodies of empirical material lend further support to the contention that bargaining is unavoidable. One set of studies compares guilty plea rates

---

[20] *Id.* at 91. The attorney's feelings of certainty extend not only to the question of guilt, but also to the question of "what the case is worth" in terms of sentencing: "Once an attorney has a feel for cases, he knows whether to try or plea bargain a case; if he chooses plea bargaining, he knows how to weigh [diverse sentencing] factors. . . . He is confident that he can predict early what disposition is obtainable." *Id.* at 76. Heumann appreciates that perceptions about "what the case is worth" vary from attorney to attorney, *see id.* at 78, but he devotes primary attention to perceptions of legal and factual guilt — perceptions that he treats as reflecting an objective reality. *See also* Heumann, *Author's Reply*, 13 LAW & SOC'Y REV. 650, 651 (1979) ("[M]ost court personnel (regardless of ideological persuasion) will readily admit that in many cases there are simply no contestable factual or legal issues . . . ."). For a sharply contrasting assessment that stresses the "malleable" quality of facts in Connecticut plea bargaining, see M. FEELEY, *supra* note 5, at 168–75.

[21] Heumann did not have an experienced defense attorney independently review any of the "hopeless" files. Heumann did look at some of these files himself, however, and his appraisal is revealing:

> [M]y overall impression of these files comported with what the [defense attorneys] indicated. In many of the cases, [1] the defendant was simply caught red-handed, or [2] a codefendant was prepared to testify against him, or [3] the defendant had sold heroin to an undercover agent without any evidence of entrapment in the record, and so on.

M. HEUMANN, *supra* note 3, at 60–61.

It is of course understandable that a conscientious social scientist might overlook specialized legal tactics and defenses: example [1] might involve a questionable arrest or search; in example [2], the codefendant's testimony might be vulnerable to impeachment, or the need for a fully informed waiver of the codefendant's fifth amendment privilege might keep him from testifying at all. More surprising, however, is that Heumann's attempt to verify appearances remains largely within the confines of the file. In example [2], the codefendant's apparent willingness to testify is accepted as hard fact. In example [3], defense counsel's defeatism becomes self-verifying: entrapment is ruled out because no evidence of it is found in the record. For reasons to doubt the accuracy of the impressions reported by these Connecticut defenders, see *infra* note 201.

during different periods of time within particular jurisdictions; the other compares plea rates in different jurisdictions.

B. Comparative Studies: Changes over Time

A number of highly touted studies grow out of attempts to "abolish" plea bargaining in one jurisdiction or another. Some of these studies purport to prove the feasibility of a bargaining ban, but in nearly every case either the study or the abolition attempt itself has major shortcomings that undermine the experiment's relevance to that question. In several cases, for example, a ban on "bargaining" did not increase the trial rate, but the ban covered only one form of bargaining, and the researchers either knew that bargaining in other forms continued or never investigated this possibility.[22] In a few cases, the trial rate did increase, but not unmanageably; in many of these cases, some varieties of bargaining could have continued, and in others, the ban failed to reach major segments of the criminal caseload.[23]

The most serious study casting doubt on the inevitability of bargaining grew out of the prohibition instituted by Alaska's Attorney General in 1975. The 1975 ban covered all forms of prosecutorial bargaining; in 1977, the Alaska Supreme Court barred judges from bargaining over charges or sentences.[24] Despite this comprehensive prohibition, the courts were not overwhelmed with trials.[25] Researchers concluded, therefore, that "the incidence of plea bargaining *can* be substantially reduced without wrecking a criminal justice system."[26] Unfortunately, even this relatively careful study did not actually support that conclusion: the "before-and-after" comparison was made prior to the 1977 ban on judicial bargaining, and some judges thus were offering explicit concessions during the study period.[27]

---

[22] These criticisms apply to a number of studies. *E.g.*, Berger, *The Case against Plea Bargaining*, 62 A.B.A. J. 621 (1976) (report of Maricopa County (Phoenix) District Attorney that after plea bargaining prohibition, trial rate actually declined; prosecutorial bargaining had been barred, but tacit judicial concessions may have continued); Parnas & Atkins, *Abolishing Plea Bargaining: A Proposal*, 14 CRIM. L. BULL. 101, 109–10 (1978) (United States Attorney for the Southern District of California abolished sentence bargaining without increase in trial rate; neither charge bargaining nor tacit concessions were eliminated); Note, *The Elimination of Plea Bargaining in Black Hawk County: A Case Study*, 60 IOWA L. REV. 1053, 1063–64 (1975) (no increase in trial rate after explicit bargaining was banned; tacit concessions were known to continue).

[23] *See, e.g.*, Callan, *An Experience in Justice Without Plea Negotiation*, 13 LAW & SOC'Y REV. 327, 338–39 (1979) (reporting effects of plea bargaining ban in El Paso County, Texas); Parnas & Atkins, *supra* note 22, at 112–13 (data on Portland, Oregon, experience).

[24] State v. Buckalew, 561 P.2d 289 (Alaska 1977).

[25] *See* Rubinstein & White, *Alaska's Ban on Plea Bargaining*, 13 LAW & SOC'Y REV. 367, 373–74 (1979).

[26] *Id.* at 382.

[27] *See id.* at 372.

Moreover, some defense attorneys continued to recommend pleas because they feared that judges might penalize clients who insisted on trial,[28] and analysis of sentencing data showed that in fact some groups of defendants who went to trial did receive much more severe sentences than did similarly situated defendants who pleaded guilty.[29] The study would not in any event shed much light on the question whether a bargaining ban is feasible for a large urban jurisdiction, but it seems inconclusive even for Alaska.

In contrast to these uniformly unsuccessful attempts to demonstrate the feasibility of a plea bargaining ban, a number of studies have found clear evidence of covert tactical adaptations that substantially diminished or even nullified the effect of prohibition attempts in various jurisdictions.[30] These studies do not suggest any particular explanation for the seemingly stubborn persistence of bargaining, but they do reinforce the notion that the process is indeed inevitable for one reason or another.

C. Comparative Studies: Differences Among Jurisdictions and the "Slow Plea" Hypothesis

Comparisons among different jurisdictions seem to lend further support to the inevitability notion. Along with a high guilty plea rate, researchers have found covert, largely illicit bargaining in England.[31] Germany, according to John Langbein, is a "land without plea bargaining,"[32] but other scholars have pointed to possible functional equivalents of pleas and concessions there.[33] Ironically, even if Langbein is correct, his case may bolster the inevitability notion for most immediate purposes. Langbein stands solidly with theorists of the case pressure persuasion, for he sees our problems as rooted in cumbersome, costly adversary trial processes that *force* us to bargain;[34]

---

[28] *See id.* at 380 n.18.

[29] *See id.* at 382. For crimes of violence, the trial/plea sentencing differential was 445%. *Id.* n.22.

[30] *See, e.g.*, Church, *Plea Bargains, Concessions and the Courts: Analysis of a Quasi-Experiment*, 10 LAW & SOC'Y REV. 377 (1976); Heumann & Loftin, *Mandatory Sentencing and the Abolition of Plea Bargaining: The Michigan Felony Firearm Statute*, 13 LAW & SOC'Y REV. 393 (1979).

[31] J. BALDWIN & M. MCCONVILLE, NEGOTIATED JUSTICE (1977); Baldwin & McConville, *Plea Bargaining and the Court of Appeal*, 6 BRIT. J.L. & SOC'Y 200 (1979). In addition to the covert practices described by Baldwin and McConville, English defendants face a system of formally approved guilty plea inducements, because English judges are now *required* to treat a guilty plea as a mitigating factor in sentencing. *See* Regina v. Ross, 1984 CRIM. L. REV. 53 (C.A. Sept. 7, 1983).

[32] Langbein, *Land Without Plea Bargaining: How the Germans Do It*, 78 MICH. L. REV. 204 (1979).

[33] Goldstein & Marcus, *The Myth of Judicial Supervision in Three "Inquisitorial" Systems: France, Italy, and Germany*, 87 YALE L.J. 240, 259–65, 272–76 (1977).

[34] *See* Langbein, *supra* note 32, at 205–06.

Germany escapes these problems through streamlined nonadversarial procedures that for the present we are not free to adopt.[35]

Turning to practice in the United States, many commentators appear to assume that American jurisdictions uniformly suffer from heavy dependence on guilty pleas.[36] A closer look, however, reveals sharp differences in guilty plea rates among major American cities. In a 1970 article, Donald McIntyre and David Lippman compared several large urban jurisdictions and estimated that, while guilty plea rates fell within the 80%–90% range for Brooklyn, Detroit, and Houston, only 47% of all cases in Los Angeles and only 17% in Baltimore were disposed of by plea.[37] Pittsburgh and Philadelphia also have long been identified as "exceptions" to the rule. In 1972, for example, guilty pleas accounted for only 36% of felony dispositions in Philadelphia; in 1966, the guilty plea rate in Pittsburgh was only 35%.[38] More recent studies have suggested that such "exceptions" are not uncommon. An extensive survey by the Georgetown University Law Center in the late 1970's revealed widespread differences in guilty plea rates among different jurisdictions.[39]

How can this pattern of widely varying plea rates be reconciled with assumptions about the inevitability of plea bargaining? Researchers have not, to my knowledge, studied the small jurisdictions with heavy trial rates, but they have examined all the major cities that rely on trials — Philadelphia, Pittsburgh, Los Angeles, and Baltimore. Scholars found that each of these cities made extensive use of bench trials that were not fully adversary proceedings. In a 1971

---

[35] If we could reinterpret our Constitution and, like the Germans, escape the problems of case pressure, the question would remain whether other forces would generate bargaining anyway. Indeed, organizational analysts presumably would seek to read Langbein's data differently from the way Langbein himself does. They might well contend that to the extent that Germany has avoided bargaining, the explanation lies not only in the lack of case pressure, but also in the hierarchical organization of prosecutorial and judicial functions. *See* Damaška, *Structures of Authority and Comparative Criminal Procedure*, 84 YALE L.J. 480 (1975). These organizational arrangements tend to enforce loyalty to societal norms and to an external professional structure rather than to colleagues in the courtroom work group. From the perspective of various organizational theories, the institutional and cultural basis of Germany's success would appear even harder to emulate than that country's freedom from burdensome procedural requirements. For a contrasting perspective, however, see *infra* pp. 1099–100.

[36] *See, e.g.*, Note, *The Unconstitutionality of Plea Bargaining*, 83 HARV. L. REV. 1387, 1387 & n.1 (1970).

[37] *See* McIntyre & Lippman, *Prosecutors and Early Disposition of Felony Cases*, 56 A.B.A. J. 1154, 1156 (1970). These figures give the guilty plea rate as a percentage of all dispositions on the merits. If dismissals and nol pros cases were included in the total number of all dispositions, the guilty plea rates would be even lower.

[38] *See* M. LEVIN, URBAN POLITICS AND THE CRIMINAL COURTS 80 (1977); 1972 ANNUAL REPORT OF THE PHILADELPHIA COMMON PLEAS & MUNICIPAL COURTS (1973) [hereinafter cited as 1972 REPORT]. Again, these percentages are based on adjudications and thus do not include dismissals and nol pros cases. *See supra* note 37.

[39] H. MILLER, W. MCDONALD & J. CRAMER, PLEA BARGAINING IN THE UNITED STATES — PHASE I REPORT 16–24 (1978).

article, Professor Welsh White — himself a former prosecutor in New York and Philadelphia — wrote that, although only 35% of all Philadelphia cases were disposed of by guilty plea, this figure was somewhat misleading:

> [M]any cases recorded as "waivers" (trials before a judge without a jury) can be more accurately characterized as "slow pleas of guilty." That is, the defendant's counsel facilitates the presentation of evidence and implicitly or explicitly admits that the defendant is guilty of some offense, but does not enter a formal plea. Were all of these cases classified as guilty pleas, the figure would probably rise to above fifty percent.[40]

Studies of each of the other exceptional cities have produced similar reports. Political scientist Martin Levin studied Pittsburgh in the late 1960's. At the time of his study, only 28% of the Pittsburgh cases ended in guilty pleas, while 50% went to nonjury trials.[41] Levin found that "[a]lmost all the nonjury trials were 'slow pleas,' a 'slower,' more drawn-out manner of pleading guilty."[42] Social scientist Lynn Mather studied Los Angeles in 1970, when 48% of the felony cases ended in guilty pleas and 40% were disposed of by bench trial.[43] Mather found some variation in the nature of these bench trials but concluded that most of them were "really 'slow pleas' of guilty."[44]

---

[40] White, *A Proposal for Reform of the Plea Bargaining Process*, 119 U. PA. L. REV. 439, 441–42 (1971). White's impressions about "slow pleas" in Philadelphia accord with those of Charles Silberman. *See* C. SILBERMAN, CRIMINAL VIOLENCE, CRIMINAL JUSTICE 279–80 (1978). In contrast, however, are Albert Alschuler's observations of Philadelphia bench trials in 1968 and in 1977; in Alschuler's view, many of the trials were genuinely contested. *See* Alschuler, *The Changing Plea-Bargaining Debate*, 69 CALIF. L. REV. 652, 725 (1981); Alschuler, *supra* note 2, at 1034–42.

[41] Nineteen percent were dismissed or "nol prossed" by the district attorney. A total of 53% went to trial, but only 3% of all cases were jury trials. *See* M. LEVIN, *supra* note 38, at 80.

sp[42] *Id.* Levin further noted that

> [s]low pleas are informal and abbreviated, and consist largely of the defense's presentation of statements concerning the defendant's allegedly favorable personal characteristics. . . . Such "trials" usually take less than fifteen minutes, though they may take thirty minutes. The defense presentation is not concerned with guilt or innocence since it usually is implicitly assumed by all parties involved in the process that the defendant is guilty of at least some wrongdoing.

Id. Levin caytioned that there is "no precise method of ascertaining the exact proportion of nonjury trials that were 'slow pleas.'" *Id.* at 293 n.25. His rough estimate was that only 4% of the bench trials were "full-length" trials; 96% were "slow pleas." *Id.*

[43] Only 8.5% of the felony cases were dismissed; 44% were tried, but only 4% of the dispositions were by jury trial. Mather, *Some Determinants of the Method of Case Disposition: Decision-Making by Public Defenders in Los Angeles*, 8 LAW & SOC'Y REV. 187, 195 (1973).

[44] Although 40% of the dispositions were by bench trial, 80% of these (32% of total dispositions) were by an unusual type of bench trial known as a "[s]ubmission on the transcript (S.O.T.)." *Id.* at 195. In these S.O.T. trials, formally authorized under California procedure, both sides agreed to be bound by the testimony recorded in the transcript of the preliminary hearing. Mather explained:

> Most S.O.T. proceedings substitute for guilty plea dispositions, often including discussion or bargaining beforehand. . . . In [some] cases, S.O.T. is a semi-adversary proceeding where the defense concedes certain points in the case but wishes to contest others . . .

James Eisenstein and Herbert Jacob studied Baltimore in the early 1970's. Thirty-five percent of the felony cases in their sample were disposed of by guilty plea and 34% by bench trial.[45] Analyzing the latter cases, they reported that "bench trials became the functional equivalent to the guilty plea; they were sometimes called a 'slow plea.'"[46] Milton Heumann and Colin Loftin studied Detroit in 1977 and similarly found that bench trials in that city "resemble[d] slow pleas of guilty far more than any standard conception of a trial."[47] Summarizing their own findings and those of the earlier studies, Heumann and Loftin commented on the inherent nature of the bench trial in Detroit and other cities:

> The waiver, or bench, trial is simply a "trial" in which the defendant waives his right to a jury and elects to go to "trial" before a judge alone . . . .
>
> . . . .
>
> . . . Call these procedures trials, if you like, but the functions they serve and the manner in which they are held resemble our plea bargaining processes (or the [uncontested] European trial) far more closely than they do a full-fledged trial.[48]

The "slow plea" concept developed in these studies plainly occupies a central position in the case for the inevitability of plea bargaining. The relatively low guilty plea rate observed in several large cities would raise serious doubts about the inevitability notion if the trials that these jurisdictions held in large numbers were in fact genuine adversary proceedings. For the substantial group of social scientists, legal scholars, and practitioners committed to the view that bargaining in some form is universal and unavoidable, the "slow plea" hypothesis provides a way to reconcile theoretical commitments with the diversity of observed patterns of disposition.

How good is the evidence for the "slow plea" hypothesis? Researchers do not always make clear whether the proceedings disparaged as "slow pleas" lacked all elements of adversary behavior or only some (and if the latter, how many of the essentials). Nor do they always make clear whether the "slow pleas" observed were character-

> However, most S.O.T. trials are really "slow pleas" of guilty, with the advantages that the defendant reserves his right to appeal and does not have to admit guilt . . . .

Id.

[45] Twenty-two percent of the cases were dismissed; 43% were tried, but only 9% of all cases were jury trials. J. EISENSTEIN & H. JACOB, *supra* note 9, at 233.

[46] *Id.* at 250.

[47] Heumann & Loftin, *supra* note 30, at 420. Detroit has traditionally relied on guilty pleas rather than bench trials, but beginning in 1977 a new felony firearm statute mandated a two-year minimum prison sentence for any defendant convicted of possessing a firearm while committing a felony. Studying the effects of the new statute, Heumann and Loftin found that the proportion of bench trials increased sharply for some types of offenses and that judges (with the cooperation of counsel) used these trials to limit conviction to lesser charges; the result was to nullify the effect of the statutory minimum sentence. *See id.* at 411–21.

[48] *Id.* at 417, 426.

istic of all bench trials or only some (and again, if the latter, what proportion). Those who do recognize these complexities — Mather and White, for example — provide only rough, intuitive estimates of the proportions involved.[49] More basically, nearly all the researchers draw their "slow plea" conclusions almost entirely from subjective impressions of particular trials; except for Mather's formally designated "submission on the transcript" proceedings,[50] we are given no tangible measures of "adversariness" against which to test the researchers' perceptions about actual cases.[51] Yet whatever their imperfections, nearly all these studies suggest that where bench trial is a major means of case disposition, the device becomes the functional equivalent of the guilty plea.[52]

The study described in the next Part was designed to provide a closer look at bench trials, in order to put the "slow plea" hypothesis on a firmer foundation or to specify more clearly its limitations. We found that the "slow plea" concept was largely inapplicable to Philadelphia procedure in 1982. The basis for this conclusion, and its implications for the supposed inevitability of plea bargaining, are traced in Parts II, III, and IV.

II. FELONY DISPOSITIONS IN PHILADELPHIA

A. *The Research Setting*

The Philadelphia trial court system has two levels: the Municipal Court and the Court of Common Pleas. The Municipal Court processes arraignments and initial bail applications and conducts all preliminary hearings. In addition, the Municipal Court conducts trials for all cases in which the maximum potential imprisonment is five years or less.[53] There is no right to a jury in Municipal Court trials, but the defendant may, by filing an appeal, obtain a trial de novo in the Court of Common Pleas. Appeals are rarely filed, however, because prison sentences are uncommon.[54]

---

[49] *See supra* p. 1048 & notes 40 & 44.

[50] *See supra* note 44.

[51] For further discussion of shortcomings in these studies, see *infra* pp. 1100–02 & notes 203–13.

[52] The only significant impressions to the contrary appear to be Professor Alschuler's, which are nevertheless equally subjective. *See supra* note 40. For other reports relating specifically to Philadelphia, see *infra* note 199.

[53] The 22 Municipal Court judges confront a heavy caseload. Along with minor civil matters handled by this court, 45,222 new criminal cases were filed in 1981. The court conducted 15,892 preliminary hearings, took 4259 guilty pleas, and held 3536 trials. With an additional 19,031 cases disposed of by dismissals, nol pros motions, and pretrial diversion programs, total dispositions amounted to 42,718 cases. *See* STATISTICAL REPORT OF THE COMMON PLEAS AND MUNICIPAL COURTS OF PHILADELPHIA: DECEMBER TERM 1981, at 32, 39 (Bull. No. 82-32, 1982).

[54] Only 14% of the defendants convicted in 1981 received any term of incarceration, *id.* at 40, and fewer than 500 appeals were filed from all Municipal Court convictions, *id.* at 31.

The Court of Common Pleas, consisting of roughly seventy-five judges, handles appeals from the Municipal Court and initial trials in cases involving more than five years' potential imprisonment. The court also handles all significant civil matters, including juvenile prosecutions and other family court cases. The caseload is large and growing. On the criminal side alone (the discussion throughout will refer to adult prosecutions only), there were 10,539 new filings[55] and 9458 dispositions in 1981.[56] Because nearly all these cases had been screened by preliminary hearing or trial in Municipal Court, relatively few cases (21%) were diverted or dismissed at the Common Pleas stage. Of the remaining 7510 cases, 45% were disposed of by guilty plea, 49% by bench trial, and 6% by jury trial.[57]

For administrative purposes, the criminal docket of the Court of Common Pleas is divided into three "programs" — the homicide program, the "Calendar" program (major or complex cases other than homicide), and the "List" program (all other cases). At the time of our study, thirty-five courtrooms were allocated for conducting criminal trials and taking pleas — ten in the homicide program, seventeen in the Calendar program, and eight in the List program.[58] The implications of this structure become apparent when one considers that in 1981, 307 case dispositions were recorded in the homicide program, 2397 in the Calendar program, and 6771 in the List program. In other words, each homicide courtroom processed an average of 31 cases (2.6 per month), each Calendar courtroom processed 141 (12 per month), and each List courtroom processed 846 (70 per month). The Calendar and List programs are aptly named. In the Calendar program, judges normally must think in terms of days per case. In the List program it is a question of cases per day: each judge begins the morning with eight to ten cases and must "get through the list."

[55] Except as otherwise indicated, all Common Pleas statistics in this Article were calculated from data appearing in the appropriate annual edition of the Philadelphia Court of Common Pleas' *Annual Report*, published by the Office of Court Administrator, and from the *Statistical Report of the Common Pleas and Municipal Courts of Philadephia*, issued by the Common Pleas Planning Unit, for December Term 1981 (Bull. No. 82-32); June Term 1982 (Bull. No. 82-148); December Term 1982 (Bull. No. 83-18); and June Term 1983 (Bull. No. 83-146). Working papers are on file with the author.

[56] In contrast to the heavy volume of dispositions in 1981, dispositions totalled 7161 in 1978, 6200 in 1979, and 7498 in 1980. In 1982, there were 7042 dispositions in the first six months alone. Several new judgeships, along with the institution of Saturday court sessions, helped account for the sharp rise in the court's output. Changes in the guilty plea rate apparently did not play a role in facilitating the higher volume of dispositions achieved in the most recent years. *See infra* note 57.

[57] The guilty plea rate has not jumped sharply as dispositions have grown. The plea rate (as a percentage of dispositions on the merits) was 40% in 1978, 38% in 1979, 45% in 1980, and 45% again in 1981, and the rate actually dropped to 43% for the first half of 1982. Thus, an increase in the plea rate may have helped to achieve the increase in dispositions from 1979 to 1980, but the plea rate remained roughly constant during the rapid growth in dispositions after 1980.

[58] Five other courtrooms handled criminal matters, primarily case assignment and miscellaneous motions.

A staff of paralegals in the District Attorney's Office assigns cases to either the List or the Calendar program. In general, the decision is based on the complexity of the case (the number of codefendants and witnesses) and the expected duration of the trial, rather than on the seriousness of the offense. But cases involving rape, serious arson, or "career criminals"[59] are assigned to the Calendar program automatically. Cases assigned to the List program are assumed to be headed for either a guilty plea or a relatively uncomplicated bench trial.[60] Because jury trials are not available in List courtrooms, defense counsel can always veto an assignment to the List program by demanding a jury trial. But counsel do not exercise this veto very often;[61] the reason lies in the way that judicial assignments are managed.

President Judge Edward Bradley assigns judges to the various trial programs. Because many judges do not desire the List room assignments, he generally gives those assignments to the judges with the least seniority. If, however, defense counsel consider a judge's attitude unfavorable, especially with respect to either the reasonable doubt standard or leniency in sentencing, they will be unwilling to waive a jury in cases scheduled before that judge. In that event, a portion of the judge's list will repeatedly require reassignment to the Calendar program, his courtroom will not generate its share of dispositions, and in time Judge Bradley will replace him with a judge who can successfully elicit jury waivers. Thus, List program judges unacceptable to the defense tend to be culled out by a process of natural selection.

The District Attorney's Office employs roughly 180 full-time attorneys. Within the office, List cases are handled by the "Felony Waiver" unit, which assigns a trial attorney to each of the List courtrooms, usually for a full week. Calendar cases (both bench and jury trial) are normally handled by the "Felony Jury" unit, which also assigns an attorney to all cases scheduled for a given courtroom.[62]

---

[59] "Career criminals" are defined by the District Attorney's Office as defendants with at least three prior convictions involving serious robberies or burglaries similar to the crime with which they are charged.

[60] Although all jury trials are channeled into the Calendar program or the homicide program, cases headed for bench trials and guilty pleas are not uniformly allocated to the List program. Once a serious or complex case is assigned to the Calendar or the homicide program, it will normally remain there, and any bench trial or guilty plea will be handled in a Calendar or homicide courtroom. In 1981 only 31% of the homicide dispositions were by jury trial; 22% were by guilty plea and 47% were by bench trial. Similarly, in rape cases (all assigned to the Calendar program), only 27% of the dispositions were by jury trial; 32% were by guilty plea and 41% were by bench trial.

[61] After the completion of our study, demands for jury trial became somewhat more frequent as a result of certain changes in Pennsylvania law. *See infra* note 166.

[62] Career criminal and sex offense cases are channeled into separate units in which attorneys are assigned to particular cases that they handle through all stages of the process. Homicide cases are likewise channeled into a separate unit and treated in case-by-case fashion.

The Defender Association of Philadelphia, which represents roughly seventy percent of all criminal defendants in the Philadelphia courts, employs 104 attorneys, 12 paralegals, 24 investigators, and 14 social workers. Office procedures for handling cases generally parallel those of the District Attorney's Office. List program cases are assigned to a "Felony Waiver" unit, in which one attorney handles all public defender cases listed for a given courtroom in a particular week. Calendar cases are assigned to a "Majors" unit, in which attorneys are likewise responsible for given courtrooms.[63]

B. The Research Design

How were the Philadelphia courts able to process a massive and rapidly rising criminal caseload, without heavy reliance on guilty pleas? Were the bench trials recorded in court statistics simply "slow pleas of guilty"? Were forces at work to induce other forms of cooperation by the defense bar? These questions were the principal focus of a study I carried out, with the assistance of four student researchers, in the spring and summer of 1982. We decided to devote our primary attention to the List program in the Court of Common Pleas. Although bench trial procedure and bargaining possibilities at the Municipal Court level are not unimportant, our interest centered on pressures for plea bargaining or "slow plea" behavior in serious felony cases. We excluded homicide cases and deemphasized Calendar program cases, because it seemed evident that the court structure facilitated relatively careful processing of these matters. In contrast, the List program, which in 1981 accounted for seventy-one percent of all Common Pleas dispositions, had been consciously designed and administered with a view toward processing large numbers of cases as expeditiously as possible. If there were "slow pleas" to be found in the Philadelphia courts, we thought that the List program would be the place to find them.

We sought to gather information from four sources. First, we interviewed President Judge Bradley, administrative personnel at the court, four experienced public defenders assigned to the List program, and the chief of the Felony Waiver unit at the District Attorney's Office. Second, we observed proceedings in court. The researchers, all law students who had studied criminal law and procedure, each visited at least four List program courtrooms and spent a full week in each. After six weeks, each List room had been observed for separate week-long periods by at least two and sometimes three re-

[63] Whenever the District Attorney assigns a case to the sex offense unit or the career criminal unit, each of which handles matters on a case-by-case basis, the Defender Association normally transfers the case to its "Special Defense" unit, in which case-by-case treatment is likewise afforded. Homicide cases are not handled by the Defender Association; indigents in these cases are always represented by appointed private practitioners.

searchers.[64] We devoted two additional weeks to Calendar room proceedings; during this period we observed most of the Calendar judges known to hear bench trials (though for shorter periods of two to three days each), and we also observed several jury trials. Third, we conducted informal interviews with nearly all prosecutors and public defenders in the courtrooms under observation. Many judges and private counsel also agreed to be interviewed or made a point of volunteering their thoughts. Fourth, we noted and ultimately analyzed details of the plea and trial dispositions in all the cases we observed.[65]

The research generated a sample of 340 cases (277 List cases and 63 Calendar cases) disposed of by plea or bench trial during June and July of 1982. Though technically nonrandom, the sample is substantial and essentially unbiased; it includes roughly half of all List program dispositions during our observation period.[66]

---

[64] The only courtroom not observed to this extent was Room 704. The Defender Association did not have sufficient staff to assign an attorney to this room, and because only private counsel appeared there, scheduling was more than normally unpredictable. We were unable to observe more than the equivalent of about one week's worth of proceedings in Room 704, and we therefore lost an opportunity to analyze the behavior of private attorneys in a distinct setting. We were able, however, to observe large numbers of cases involving private attorneys in the other seven List courtrooms.

[65] The case numbers and initials of participants that will be reported here have been modified to prevent unnecessary identification of individuals. Actual docket numbers and full names corresponding to these case numbers and initials are on file with the author.

[66] Although the observations were carried out over a relatively short interval, the use of four full-time researchers made possible a data base that compares favorably — in terms of both sample size and sampling procedure — with that of related observational studies. *See, e.g.*, J. EISENSTEIN & H. JACOB, *supra* note 9, at 175–80 (in study of Baltimore system, statistical analysis was performed on a sample of 1127 cases, but the observational sample contained only 152 cases).

The short observation period does raise a question about the possibility of seasonal bias. *Cf. id.* at 177–78 (possibility of seasonal bias in Chicago observations over two-month period). The Philadelphia courts operated more-or-less normally during June, but in July many courtrooms heard cases only three days per week, and in other courtrooms we observed some pressure to end early and head for "the shore." Had we been studying continuances or speedy-trial issues, the limited research period would have raised serious problems. The time period did not appear atypical, however, with respect to litigation styles and the vigor of the adversary process. At worst, the summertime tempo conceivably could have rendered cooperative, nonadversary behavior somewhat more frequent in June and July than in wintertime, and thus could have exaggerated the perceived incidence of "slow pleas." In the absence of a year-long study, unfortunately, one cannot be certain about the impact of this factor, but interviews and comparisons with observations made in early June suggested no such effect. In any event, one can be fairly confident that the level of "adversariness" observed was not *greater* than that present at other times of the year.

For commentary on problems of observer bias, distortion of observed behavior, and related methodological difficulties in "participant observer" studies of this kind, see G. MCCALL & J. SIMMONS, ISSUES IN PARTICIPANT OBSERVATION (1969); Schwartz & Schwartz, *Problems in Participant Observation*, 60 AM. J. SOC. 343 (1955); Vidich, *Participant Observation and the Collection and Interpretation of Data*, 60 AM. J. SOC. 354 (1955); Zelditch, *Some Methodological Problems of Field Studies*, 67 AM. J. SOC. 566 (1962).

C. Guilty Pleas in Philadelphia

1. The Procedure in Court. — The typical guilty plea disposition in Philadelphia lasts about twenty minutes, from the time the defendant approaches the bar to the time the judge accepts the defendant's plea. The bulk of that time is spent on the colloquy. In some courtrooms, the judge conducts the colloquy; in others the judge delegates this responsibility to the district attorney or defense counsel. The person who conducts the colloquy usually follows an established checklist of items to be discussed with the defendant. The checklist covers the three constitutionally mandated areas: the elements of the offenses charged and the maximum sentence for each, the rights the defendant waives by pleading guilty, and the voluntariness of the plea.[67] Defendants are always asked whether they are satisfied with their attorney. All told, the colloquy covers nineteen general issues, with three or four subquestions for most of these.

In our List program sample, the average guilty plea colloquy lasted twelve minutes, but the time consumed varied widely. Even excluding a few extreme instances (four minutes in two cases and forty-three minutes in another),[68] typical colloquies ranged from eight to fifteen minutes, depending primarily on the extent to which particular rights were discussed and illustrated.[69] After completion of the colloquy, the district attorney would recite into the record the evidence she would have presented at trial, including the names of witnesses and a summary of their anticipated testimony. This portion of the proceeding usually required several minutes. The judge would then ask the defendant whether the prosecutor had accurately described the basic facts to which the defendant was pleading guilty; once satisfied that the defendant agreed with the prosecution's summary of the evidence, the judge would accept the plea.[70]

---

[67] In each instance the checklist calls for somewhat more detail than state and federal case law strictly requires. The rights waived are enumerated in detail. On the issue of voluntariness, questions cover not only threats and promises, but also the defendant's age, schooling, history of mental illness, and use of drugs or alcohol.

[68] On one occasion Judge WO called four unrelated cases (Nos. 0369, 1441, 1617, 2964) at the same time, and with all of the defendants standing before the bench, he conducted a single waiver colloquy in which he simply paused after each item to ask each defendant in turn whether he or she understood the matter. Afterwards, the judge asked our researcher whether she thought that this had been a case of "assembly-line justice."

[69] Sometimes several examples would be used to explain concepts like reasonable doubt or the peremptory challenge; at other times the defendant would merely be given a legal definition of the term.

[70] Occasionally a judge rejected the plea. For example, in No. 0951, a perjury case, the defendant attempted to plead nolo contendere, but Judge PF stated that the allegedly false testimony might not satisfy the materiality requirement, and he therefore refused to accept the plea. When the defendant, persisting in his desire to plead, stated that he wanted to get the matter over quickly, the judge told him that a trial would take no longer than a nolo plea. The defendant then agreed to withdraw his plea, and the case was transferred to another judge for trial. In No. 2650, an arson case, Judge PF again refused a plea, this time because the defendant

In most cases the judge then proceeded to consider the sentence. Usually, defense counsel spoke quite briefly at this stage, and prosecutors — if they spoke at all — took even less time. From the colloquy through the imposition of sentence, the entire proceeding consumed about twenty to twenty-two minutes.[71] Often, however, the judge decided to defer sentencing and order a presentence report. Deferred sentencing, which occurred in 43% of the guilty pleas in our sample, required an additional ten to twenty minutes of court time at a subsequent hearing.

Our observations appear to be consistent with standard assumptions about processing time for guilty plea cases. Yet they suggest some unexpected conclusions. The average court time (about twenty minutes) seems short, but of course this figure excludes all the time consumed in court and out of court at both earlier and later stages. Every case required a preliminary hearing, and many cases involved earlier listings, presentence investigations, and deferred sentencing hearings.[72] Obviously, the system invests much greater time and many more resources in guilty plea cases than the brevity of the conviction proceeding itself suggests.

Even as a measure of courtroom time spent at the conviction stage, the twenty-minute figure can be quite misleading. Participants spend much of the courtroom day waiting for something to happen. Some of this time is simply wasted, but many delays are essentially unavoidable. Before the judge can accept any pleas, he must call the list and identify cases ready for disposition. Later, a defense attorney or prosecutor may be called to another courtroom, and others must wait if the case is reached before that person can return. Time is always lost while participants wait for defendants in custody to be brought from the holding cell; delay necessitated by custody procedures is often quite substantial.[73] Nearly all of these delays, moreover, are independent of whether the disposition, when it finally occurs, is by trial or by plea.

We estimated that in a typical courtroom day, the average case involved about thirty-five minutes of waiting time,[74] so that the av-

---

sought to plead guilty but refused to admit to the facts charged. Although defender PR pointed to case law permitting such pleas (for example, North Carolina v. Alford, 400 U.S. 25 (1970)), the judge stated that he personally disagreed with that approach. The plea ultimately was accepted only because the defendant acquiesced and admitted committing one of the alleged offenses.

[71] For the List room guilty pleas in our sample, the median disposition time was 19 minutes; the mean was 22 minutes.

[72] *See infra* note 157.

[73] Union work rules mandated that each prisoner be accompanied by two sheriff's deputies. Prisoners therefore could not be brought to the courtroom until the necessary personnel were available, and this often meant long delays until a pair of deputies returned a prisoner from some other courtroom and prepared to take a new prisoner from the holding cell.

[74] Judges normally heard trials and took pleas from 10:00 a.m. until 3:30 p.m.; sentencing

erage guilty plea proceeding in fact required about fifty-five minutes of courtroom time for the conviction stage alone. Whether this period appears long or short depends, of course, on one's perspective. The figure of fifty-five minutes hardly seems to square with the supposedly typical American courtroom scene in which "the observer will hear one case after another called and disposed of within a few seconds or minutes. Over a hundred [felony] cases may be handled in this fashion during the course of a day . . . ."[75] The significance of guilty plea disposition time will become clearer, however, when we explore questions of disposition time in connection with contested trials. We leave these questions for the time being and turn to a consideration of the factors that prompt defendants to reject the trial route and to plead guilty instead.

2. *Bargaining and Concessions for the Plea.* — In 1981, guilty pleas accounted for only 36% of all Common Pleas dispositions and only 45% of all dispositions on the merits. Why were pleas not obtained in most cases? Conversely, what led some defendants to plead guilty?

The Philadelphia District Attorney's Office has not attempted to "abolish" plea bargaining or even to condemn it in principle. District Attorney Edward Rendell and his staff supervisors believe, however, that in practice defense attorneys demand unreasonable concessions. To prevent acquiescence in such demands and to ensure a measure of uniformity in actions taken by individual prosecutors, each unit in the District Attorney's Office has developed guidelines governing the kinds of agreements trial attorneys may make.

In the Felony Waiver unit, which processes List program cases, a trial attorney ordinarily has discretion to dismiss lesser counts in return for a defendant's plea to the most serious charge against him.[76] Defenders and prosecutors alike indicated that dismissals of lesser counts were virtually automatic in guilty plea cases and did not really need

---

and probation revocation hearings were held thereafter. With about one hour out for lunch, there were thus approximately 4 1/2 hours available for trials and pleas. The average day involved a little over three actual dispositions; for convenience, and to provide a conservative estimate of waiting time, we may assume a typical day to involve four dispositions — two trials averaging 45 minutes each, *see infra* p. 1066 & note 108, and two pleas averaging 20 minutes each, *see supra* p. 1056 & note 71. Thus, 130 minutes were spent actually hearing trials and pleas, and the waiting time not attributable to any actual disposition totalled 140 minutes, or 35 minutes for each disposition.

[75] J. Eisenstein & H. Jacob, *supra* note 9, at 19. The dispositions to which the authors refer presumably include many continuances, but even a disposition on the merits apparently required only a few minutes. In contrast, a Philadelphia List courtroom handles at most only eight to ten cases per day, including cases that are simply continued. In accord with our findings for Philadelphia, Peter Nardulli found that the Chicago felony courts also completed very few cases per day. *See supra* note 7.

[76] When the lesser count is a weapons charge, a conviction would influence sentencing in the event of a later conviction for a subsequent offense; accordingly, trial prosecutors have been denied authority to dismiss the weapons count in return for a plea agreement.

to be negotiated. Nearly all the attorneys agreed, moreover, that these dismissals had no sentencing impact whatsoever. Sentences near the top of the range for a single serious charge (for example, twenty years for robbery or burglary, or seven years for a serious theft) are unheard of in the List program; consecutive sentences exceeding the authorized range for a single serious offense are considered unthinkable. Under these conditions, we were told, an offer to dismiss lesser charges would be of no value to the defense and would not in itself induce a plea.[77]

Agreements to drop serious charges or to recommend a sentence are considered potentially attractive to the defense. These kinds of agreements require the specific approval of unit chief Arnold Gordon or his deputy. Gordon told us that normally he will approve these more significant concessions only when the police have overcharged or when, because of changed circumstances, there is no longer sufficient evidence to convict. In such instances, the offer, again, is not really very valuable, because the defense usually realizes in such cases that its prospects will be even better at trial.

Both prosecutors and defenders indicated dissatisfaction with the inflexibility of the District Attorney's policy guidelines. But they uniformly agreed that the policy did in effect foreclose bargaining in most cases and that prosecutors genuinely adhered to the policy in practice.[78]

Observations in court largely confirmed what we had been told. Our sample of 340 dispositions included 149 guilty pleas, 44% of the total.[79] In the List program, as Table I indicates, 15% of the guilty pleas were "open" pleas — that is, pleas made without any commitment by the prosecution — and an additional 44% involved only a promise to dismiss unimportant counts. Agreements to recommend disposition were involved in only 15% of the guilty plea cases.[80]

---

[77] Only one defender gave us a different assessment on this point. HT maintained that the defendant benefits from an agreement to drop lesser counts because it precludes the possibility of consecutive sentences on multiple charges. We do not know whether HT really believed this (some of the other defenders considered the idea preposterous), but we do know that HT told it to his clients.

We wondered why prosecutors bothered to suggest the dismissal of lesser counts if this standard offer was indeed known to be valueless. Defender SP suggested that the dismissal of lesser counts was primarily a matter of convenience for the prosecution and the court. At the guilty plea colloquy these dismissals save time and reduce the risk of reversible error, by making it unnecessary to explain to the defendant each element of four or five inconsequential lesser charges.

[78] A few defenders said that in certain kinds of cases they nevertheless contact an assistant district attorney before trial to sound out the possibility of some concession. Defender HI stated that he never bothers to do so because he knows that the assistant district attorney either will not consider any concessions or will offer a sentence much higher than any judge would give.

[79] The observed guilty plea rate closely approximates the overall rates reported in the court's statistics: 45% for 1981 and 43% for the first half of 1982.

[80] Even in cases involving significant charge reduction (10% of the List program pleas) or an explicit prosecutorial recommendation (15%), the practical value of the concession could be

TABLE I

DISTRIBUTION OF GUILTY PLEAS BY KIND OF AGREEMENT[81]

	List		Calendar	
	N	%	N	%
Open plea to all counts	17	15	12	35
Agreement to nol pros:				
Lesser counts only	51	44	16	47
Any significant charge	11	10	1	3
Agreement not to recommend disposition	8	7	-	-
Agreement to nol pros and not to recommend	11	10	1	3
Agreement to recommend disposition	2	2	-	-
Agreement to nol pros and to recommend	15	13	4	12
Total	115	100	34	100

We had been told that judges generally did not get involved in bargaining but that agreements occasionally could be negotiated with certain judges. None of our guilty plea dispositions involved an actual agreement with the judge, but two cloakroom episodes in Judge DC's courtroom — one in a bench trial case and the other at a deferred sentencing hearing — lent credibility to the claim that Judge DC did occasionally bargain directly with counsel.[82]

quite small, as when the prosecutor agreed to drop a charge that was obviously unwinnable. There were, nonetheless, a few clearly significant compromises in cases that could have gone either way — for example, in No. 2650, an arson case, and in No. 4047, which involved a felony charge of risking catastrophe.

Defense attorneys disagreed about whether a pledge not to make any sentencing recommendation had substantial value. Some thought it did, because the prosecutor's silence might encourage the judge to impose a lenient sentence. Others thought the prosecutor's silence insignificant, especially given the fact that many prosecutors made no recommendation in any event. But whatever the impact of promises not to recommend, Table I indicates that they were unusual.

[81] The figures include pleas of nolo contendere. Although most nolo pleas were in effect full guilty pleas, some of the nolo pleas occurred in cases in which the defendant admitted the basic facts but challenged the legal characterization or grading of the offense — for example, Nos. 0132, 0328, 0488, 0956, 3146. These instances are recorded here as "open pleas," but they were in effect the "functional equivalent" of partially contested proceedings; they might more accurately be described as "fast trials."

[82] *See infra* p. 1074. For a more detailed study of participation in plea bargaining by Pennsylvania judges, see Ryan & Alfini, *Trial Judges' Participation in Plea Bargaining: An Empirical Perspective*, 13 LAW & SOC'Y REV. 479, 488–91 (1979).

If plea agreements seldom involved significant concessions, why did defendants plead guilty? We suspected that tacit inducements of some sort might have been at work. Some defenders did report that defendants could win minor sentencing concessions by pleading guilty,[83] but the majority of defenders insisted that generally no concessions could be obtained in return for a plea.[84] Part of the disagreement among defenders appeared to stem from differing assumptions about whether a defendant electing trial will choose to testify. When defenders claimed (or told their clients) that judges reward "remorse" or penalize defendants who go to trial, they seemed to be thinking primarily about the situation in which a judge will punish defendants for giving perjured testimony. Defendants can, however, demand trial without testifying, and in our sample many such defendants won acquittals.[85] When the perjury problem is put to one side, as it must be,[86] the evidence suggests that Philadelphia defenders do not often expect a judicial concession in return for the guilty plea decision as such.

Defenders' perceptions are difficult to test empirically against actual sentencing patterns. Our own sample was too small to permit rigorous comparisons among cases with similar offense and offender characteristics. In a much larger empirical study, Thomas Uhlman and Darlene Walker analyzed sentencing for over 29,000 defendants convicted in Philadelphia between 1968 and 1974.[87] Their data lend

[83] Defenders DE, VN, TS, and OT all believed that the defendant who pleaded guilty generally did get some sentencing break in exchange for saving the court's time, showing "remorse," or simply "putting the judge in a better mood." Defenders HI and VO told us that most judges treated guilty plea cases more leniently but that a few did not. Calendar Judge CF stated that he sentenced more leniently after a guilty plea because he gave great weight to the contrition factor.

[84] Defenders WD, TA, and TH believed that judges usually did not give any break in guilty plea cases, and asserted that judges who did seem to give a slight break (such as Judge WO) were the exceptions. These defenders nonetheless generally told their clients that a guilty plea might help make a favorable impression on the judge. Defenders CE, SH, RO, CR, and FT, however, claimed that List program judges did not give a break for pleading guilty, and in talking to their clients, these defenders generally stressed that the defendant would not be penalized for asserting the right to trial.

[85] *See infra* p. 1079; Table V, *infra* p. 1080.

[86] In United States v. Grayson, 438 U.S. 41 (1978), the Supreme Court held that a trial judge may impose a more severe sentence on the basis of his belief that the defendant committed perjury at trial. Even those who consider this result problematic will recognize that penalties imposed to deter or punish the commission of perjury are not equivalent to penalties imposed to deter or punish the exercise of the constitutional right to trial.

[87] Uhlman & Walker, *"He Takes Some of My Time; I Take Some of His": An Analysis of Judicial Sentencing Patterns in Jury Cases*, 14 LAW & SOC'Y REV. 323 (1980). The authors identify their research site only as an anonymous Eastern urban jurisdiction that they dub "Metro City." The court structure and case disposition patterns of "Metro City," however, are identical to those of Philadelphia. Any lingering doubt about the identity of the locale is removed by statements that the authors attribute to the "Metro City" courts' 1972 annual report. *See id.* at 325. The identical statements may be found in 1972 REPORT, *supra* note 38, at iv, ix.

strong support to the prevailing perception that Philadelphia judges rarely, if ever, grant more lenient sentences in return for guilty pleas.[88]

If both tacit and explicit inducements were weak or nonexistent, the question remains: why were guilty pleas tendered? In virtually all cases not involving direct prosecutorial concessions, the apparent answer was simply the absolute futility of taking the case to trial.[89] Nearly all the defenders made clear that, given the general lack of concessions in guilty plea cases, they would recommend a plea only when no conceivable defense existed or when the prosecutor offered one of the exceptional "significant" concessions. Even defenders who expected judges to be somewhat more lenient in guilty plea cases indicated that the chance of leniency was much too slight to justify abandoning any significant defense.[90] Unlike their attorneys, most defendants who pleaded guilty probably did think they had gained some advantage.[91] But even the defendants' decision to plead often seemed prompted by the futility of any other course.[92]

Our findings support the frequently made claim that most guilty pleas occur in utterly hopeless ("dead bang") cases. Some of the cases in which defense counsel failed to obtain a significant concession (59%

---

[88] The authors found the average guilty plea sentence to be very close to the average bench trial sentence — on their scale, 24.9 units versus 25.1 units, figures that correspond roughly to probationary sentences of 77 and 78 months, respectively. Uhlman & Walker, *supra* note 87, at 328, 340 app. Controlling for prior criminal record and seriousness of the present offense, Uhlman and Walker found bench trial sentences to be 10%–20% more severe than guilty plea sentences in comparable cases. *Id.* at 332–33. The study unfortunately relied only on crude surrogates to estimate prior record and seriousness of the offense, and it did not control for the possibility of perjury at trial.

A more recent study similarly reports that in a sample of over 400 Philadelphia rape, robbery, and burglary cases commenced in 1976, the choice of plea had no significant impact on the sentence imposed. *See* D. Lebor, Differentials in Attrition by Race and by Plea in the Philadelphia Criminal Justice System 11–12, 32–33 (Oct. 1981) (unpublished paper on file with University of Pennsylvania Department of Sociology).

[89] Our conclusion on this point differs from that of Uhlman and Walker, who report that although the benefits of pleading guilty in Philadelphia are in fact minimal, "the consensus among court personnel in [Philadelphia] is that those who plead receive sentencing bargains." Uhlman & Walker, *A Plea Is No Bargain: The Impact of Case Disposition on Sentencing*, 60 Soc. Sci. Q. 218, 232 (1979).

[90] A few defenders indicated that they would recommend a plea not only in open-and-shut cases, but also when there was a conceivable defense but little reason to believe that the judge would find reasonable doubt. In such cases the defendant might get some break in sentencing, and as long as a sentence other than probation or time served seemed unlikely, the defendant in any event "would not get hurt" by pleading guilty.

[91] In many cases, defenders themselves probably generated or reinforced this belief among their clients. *See supra* notes 83–84.

[92] Defender VO had a unique tactic for dealing with clients who resisted his recommendation to plead. VO would hand the reluctant defendant the transcript from the preliminary hearing and tell him to read it thoroughly. If the defendant did not apprehend the uselessness of contesting the charges, VO would proceed to trial, but usually the defendant was persuaded.

of the List room pleas[93]) might not have been truly hopeless; conversely, there may have been some essentially hopeless cases among those in which a potentially significant concession was obtained. On balance, the 59% figure probably gives a good approximation of the proportion of "dead bang" cases among the guilty pleas in the List program sample. This estimate is nonetheless much lower than earlier studies would lead one to expect. Because guilty plea cases accounted for only 42% of our sample of List program dispositions on the merits, the hopeless cases identified so far amounted to only 25% of the List program sample.[94]

Drawing together all the various forms of plea bargaining, one finds a somewhat ambiguous picture. Both explicit plea negotiations and tacit, "structurally induced" pleas occur in the Philadelphia court system.[95] Nevertheless, our conclusion is that no significant concessions are available to induce a guilty plea in the majority of Philadelphia felony cases. Skeptics may, of course, prefer to believe that hidden concessions of some sort continue to operate in ways we were unable to detect. Although we can never entirely exclude this possibility, it is of only incidental relevance for present purposes, because any such concessions could not, in any event, have been very effective. Only 45% of the 1981 Common Pleas defendants did plead guilty. The remaining 55% (and 58% of the defendants in our List program sample) chose to go to trial. The next Section considers whether the processing of the bench trial cases differed in substance from straightforward dispositions by guilty plea.

D. The Philadelphia Bench Trial

1. The Decision to Waive a Jury. — Defenders uniformly pointed to sentencing expectations as the overriding consideration in the decision whether to waive the right to a jury. In general, they believe that defendants convicted in jury trials receive sentences substantially more severe than those imposed in bench trials.[96] Although we did not attempt to verify their perceptions statistically, previous research tends to confirm the impression that sentencing differentials between

---

[93] This figure reflects the first two categories in Table I, *supra* p. 1059.

[94] The overall incidence of "dead bang" cases is actually higher than this, because some hopeless cases are taken to trial. *See infra* pp. 1081–82.

[95] For development of the concept of the structurally induced plea, see A. GOLDSTEIN, THE PASSIVE JUDICIARY 33 (1981).

[96] Defender WD indicated that a List room judge might impose a sentence of probation or three months' county jail time in a case that would probably draw one to three years in state prison after conviction by a jury. Defender CE asserted that jury trial sentences are about four times greater than bench trial sentences in comparable cases. Certain changes in Pennsylvania sentencing law, which took effect after the completion of our study, have probably reduced the extent of these sentencing differentials between bench and jury trial. *See infra* note 166.

Defenders mentioned a few situations in which they might choose a bench trial for tactical

jury and bench trials are marked.[97] Because defenders also believe that juries are often more favorable to the defense on reasonable doubt questions,[98] a bench trial is seen as an option that reduces the chances for acquittal but substantially increases the prospects for leniency in sentencing. Most defenders fully explained to their clients the alternative dispositions (guilty plea, bench trial, or jury trial) and then made a recommendation.[99] In discussing the pros and cons, most defenders left the distinct impression that only one alternative was reasonable. Their advice was almost always followed.[100]

Because expectations of leniency usually prompt the decision to waive a jury, and because the system of judicial assignments actually encourages and reinforces such expectations,[101] a kind of structural "bargaining" for jury waivers clearly does take place. Defendants do not, however, waive their other adversarial trial rights. The question, therefore, is whether this structural jury-waiver bargaining has effects similar to the effects of guilty plea bargaining in other American cities.

---

reasons unrelated to any possible sentencing differential. Some defenders believe that judges may be more likely than juries to acquit in cases arising out of fights among acquaintances or to doubt the credibility of police testimony in certain unusual situations. Other tactical considerations favoring the choice of a bench trial were mentioned by defender CE: a defendant in custody may have to wait less time for a bench trial; a district attorney has less time to prepare for a bench trial, and the defender therefore may have a better chance to exploit inconsistencies in the complainant's testimony; and bench trial judges tend to be less suspicious than do juries of the defendant who chooses not to testify or who makes a poor impression on the stand. Some private attorneys probably also take into consideration the fact that the client may not be able to afford the fee for a jury trial.

[97] After controlling for prior record and seriousness of charge, the study by Uhlman and Walker found that the average jury trial sentence was nearly three times greater than the average bench trial sentence (on their scale, 35.5 units versus 11.9 units). Uhlman & Walker, *supra* note 87, at 332. The average sentence units correspond roughly to sentences of one year's minimum imprisonment and one year's probation, respectively. *See id.* at 340.

[98] The published court statistics indicate a higher acquittal rate in bench trials than in jury trials (for example, 31.6% compared to 27.5% in 1981). But these figures are deceptive, because defenders are likely to elect a jury trial in very serious cases in which the prospects for acquittal are remote. Other things being equal, defenders believe that the prospects for acquittal are higher in a jury trial. For other factors bearing on the validity of the acquittal rates suggested by published statistics, see *infra* note 142.

Because they perceive that juries are somewhat more likely than judges to acquit, defenders do recommend jury trial in some cases despite the sharp sentencing differential. They may do so, for example, when it is especially important for the defendant to preserve a clean record and therefore to maximize his chances for acquittal. Defenders also tend to recommend jury trial in the opposite situation — when a client with a long prior record faces very strong evidence with little hope of acquittal. In such a case, the defendant is likely to draw a very severe sentence even after a bench trial; the slightly better chances for acquittal or for reversal after a jury trial offer the only possible hope for a defendant who will otherwise be facing a very long prison term regardless of the kind of trial he chooses.

[99] Defender VN was an exception. When he thought that a bench trial was preferable, he never mentioned jury trial unless the defendant asked about it.

[100] There were a few exceptions. For example, in No. 1034 — an arson case — the defendant rejected defender WD's recommendation and insisted on a jury trial.

[101] *See supra* p. 1052.

2. Preparation for Trial. — The District Attorney's Office usually assigns a prosecutor to each List courtroom for at least a week. Although prosecutors are not allowed any free days out of court to prepare their cases, the prosecution's case is ordinarily well developed by the preliminary hearing stage. In addition, two prosecutors sometimes share the list of cases for a single courtroom, so that each has some free time during the day to prepare her cases. List program prosecutors nonetheless have to rely heavily on the files developed by their predecessors. Witness preparation often consists simply of handing the preliminary hearing transcript to the witnesses and telling them to read their prior testimony carefully to refresh their recollection.

The Defender Association organizes trial preparation somewhat differently. A single attorney is assigned to all cases scheduled for a given courtroom in a given week. Of the roughly forty to fifty cases scheduled in each List courtroom weekly, about thirty to forty will be the responsibility of the public defender. Unlike the District Attorney's Office, the Defender Association normally allows the attorney a full week out of court to prepare for the following week's trials. The week of preparation time usually proves adequate, even for such a heavy caseload, as a result of three factors. First, the defender need not prepare cases that he or the prosecutor will continue. Continuances can account for up to half the list, and usually the defender knows about these in advance. Second, in the typical case another defender has already interviewed the defendant and ordered any necessary investigation; by the week before trial, therefore, many cases demand little preparation or require only some additional investigation by other personnel in the office. Third, during the week in court the defender often has several hours per day available for preparation while the court is in recess or while a private attorney is defending a case.

A defender's preparation begins with an analysis of the preliminary hearing transcript and any police reports. The defender then makes a preliminary determination of what defenses are available. During the preparation week, the defender also attempts to find and interview witnesses. If laboratory work, photography, or other investigative efforts are needed, the defender may obtain assistance from an investigator in the office. Some time before the preparation week, a defendant not in custody will have received a letter asking him to telephone or visit the defender during the preparation week, but few defendants take this opportunity to confer with their appointed counsel. The defender is, however, able to visit and interview most defendants who are in custody.[102]

[102] Even under these circumstances, some defendants do not respond when called to the room where the attorney is waiting.

Any remaining preparation takes place on the day of trial. With one exception, every defender we observed made good use of the available time. During periods when the court was not in session, defenders interviewed the defendant (often for the first time), interviewed prosecution witnesses, and prepared any defense witnesses. The fact that defendants often did not meet their attorneys until the day of trial usually did not seem to impair their defenses. If the defendant pointed out a possible defense or witness that the defender had not considered, the defender ordinarily could secure a continuance.[103]

3. The Procedure in Court. — Bench trials always began with a colloquy designed to ensure that the defendant's waiver of his jury trial right was knowing and voluntary.[104] The colloquy usually followed the standard format for the guilty plea colloquy: discussion focused on the elements of the offense and the maximum sentence, the defendant's state of mind, and the rights being waived.[105] A few judges and prosecutors conducted virtually identical colloquies for bench trials and for guilty pleas. More often, however, rights unaffected by the jury waiver were not discussed.[106] For the List cases in our sample, the waiver colloquy lasted an average of five minutes; some colloquies took as long as ten or fifteen minutes, but several others lasted only one or two minutes.

After the colloquy and acceptance of the jury waiver,[107] the prosecution immediately called its first witness; we never observed an opening statement. Trial procedure followed the usual course, with cross-examination (if any), demurrers at the close of the Commonwealth's case, and testimony by defense witnesses (if any). Attorneys presented closing arguments in virtually every case, though the judge sometimes limited argument to one or two issues or heard argument only from the defense. The judge then announced a decision and — sometimes — a brief reason for it.

---

[103] Because of speedy-trial rules, judges were often reluctant to grant continuances. Judge LD was especially strict in this regard. But in the situation mentioned in text, a continuance normally would be granted.

[104] Pretrial motions were normally heard at a prior listing or in a separate motions courtroom. For case law considering the prerequisites to a valid waiver of a jury and to the valid entry of factual stipulations, see, for example, United States v. Strother, 578 F.2d 397, 402–05 (D.C. Cir. 1978); Sutton v. State, 289 Md. 359, 366–67 & n.2, 424 A.2d 755, 758–59 & n.2 (1981); Annot., 17 A.L.R.4TH 61 (1982).

[105] *See supra* p. 1055 & note 67.

[106] In addition, most judges and prosecutors did not discuss the standard of reasonable doubt as thoroughly as they did in the guilty plea colloquy, but all discussed the possible difference between the prosecution's having to convince one judge and its having instead to convince all 12 jurors of guilt beyond a reasonable doubt.

[107] In No. 0811, a robbery case, the defendant answered hesitantly during the colloquy. Although the defendant ultimately did state unequivocally his desire to waive, Judge EE (a Calendar judge) refused to accept the waiver and summoned a jury.

Consideration of sentencing followed. Apart from the infrequent cases in which the defendant's prior record had been introduced at trial, the judge saw the "rap sheet" for the first time at this point. Brief pleas in mitigation, often including statements by members of the defendant's family or church, were also made at this time. Sentences were imposed immediately after trial in 58 of the 128 List room convictions, and these sentences tended to be light: only 14 of the 58 defendants (24%) drew any term of incarceration beyond time served awaiting trial. In the remaining 70 cases (55% of the 128 convictions), the judge deferred sentencing and ordered a presentence report; these were the problem dispositions likely to involve a mandatory drug program or a substantial prison term.

The time consumed by such proceedings was typically rather short. As Table II indicates, 64% of the Calendar trials in our sample were completed in less than two hours. List program trials tended to be even shorter; the typical List room trial lasted about forty-five minutes,[108] and 69% were completed in less than one hour. Allowing for the waiting time attributable to each disposition,[109] the total courtroom time consumed by the typical List program bench trial was approximately one hour and twenty minutes, compared to the fifty-five minutes of total courtroom time spent on a typical guilty plea.

TABLE II
TIME FOR TRIAL[110]

	List		Calendar	
	N	%	N	%
Less than 30 minutes	27	18	1	4
30–59 minutes	78	51	5	20
1–2 hours	43	28	10	40
2–3 hours	2	1	5	20
Over 3 hours	3	2	4	16
Total	153	100	25	100

To what extent were these trials genuine adversary proceedings? Analysis of the procedures followed and of the time consumed points in two directions. The traditional procedural requisites of a contested trial were normally present, and in many instances they required

108 The median trial lasted 45 minutes, and the median time per disposition (allowing for joint trials) was 44 minutes. The mean disposition time was 51 minutes.

109 *See supra* pp. 1056–57 & note 74.

110 The times shown are net of recesses. Totals reflect the number of trials rather than dispositions of individual defendants. Eleven of the trials involved two defendants each: one

considerable courtroom time. On the other hand, 18% of the List room trials were completed in about the same amount of time as was a typical guilty plea case, and most of the List cases required only a little more time — just twenty to thirty minutes more than a guilty plea. Were these "trials" really the functional equivalent of guilty pleas? The following subsections present qualitative and quantitative material bearing on that question.

4. "Adversariness": Behavior of the Attorneys. — In their trial preparation and their advice to their clients on the jury waiver decision, defenders generally seemed to assume that bench trials would be genuinely contested. Nearly all defenders directly confirmed this impression by stressing that they press hard for acquittals, that their relationship with the prosecutor is quite adversarial, and that the judges decide cases on the basis of the evidence.[111] But there were exceptions. Three defenders told us that in all but a few cases, the List room trial is nothing but a slow guilty plea. Defender HI explained that the system is geared toward sentencing and not toward determining guilt or innocence. RO said that the bench trial is "just a charade . . . . The parties go through the motions." VO claimed that the List program is not designed to give fair verdicts, but only to dispose of cases quickly; because of lenient sentencing, defendants are not really hurt, but "it has nothing to do with justice."

We observed wide differences in the style and demeanor of the public defenders. We were able to make extended observations of two of the three defenders who saw the process as simply a "slow plea," and the courtroom performance of these lawyers was particularly revealing. When interviewed, HI had been the epitome of worldly cynicism, and the researchers had been grateful to learn from this experienced and articulate practitioner what the "real world" was actually like. In court, however, HI was extremely vigorous. On cross-examination, he often asked rhetorical questions and stressed his incredulity at what the witness had said. He used exaggerated hand gestures and often paced across the floor. HI said that he reserved his vehemence for cases in which he felt that the Commonwealth's witnesses were lying or mistaken, and that he behaved with more restraint when he saw little room for reasonable doubt. He felt that this approach would lead the judge to take him more seriously when he made strenuous arguments. HI always demurred to some, if not all, of the charges, and he always chose to make a closing statement.

VO's approach, in contrast, seemed more consistent with his own portrayal of defenders' behavior. He was by far the most "low key"

List case at 30 to 59 minutes, six List and two Calendar cases at one to two hours, and two cases (one List, one Calendar) that lasted more than three hours. Two trials included for other purposes are not recorded here, because accurate time figures were not available.

[111] Many defenders, such as WD, CE, SH, CR, and FT, rejected the "slow plea" characterization explicitly.

attorney we observed. He often declined to cross-examine, and when he did ask questions, he kept them to a minimum. Although we did once see VO put some energy into a cross-examination,[112] on every other occasion he asked his questions in a monotone and showed no sign of emotion. VO said that he never varied his low-key style and that he believed doing so would be unethical because it would favor some clients over others. Similarly, VO never demurred to any charges; he seemed to consider this procedure a waste of time on the theory that it would make no difference whether there was a dismissal at the demurrer stage or an acquittal at the end of the trial. VO made either a very brief closing statement or none at all; he felt that he should give the judge credit for being able to remember the evidence. When VO did offer a closing statement, he sometimes admitted that the prosecution had made its case on some charges, and then confined his remarks to the others.

For all this, VO was not really ineffective. Of course, we did not necessarily admire his style or believe that his explanations for it were always sound, legally or tactically. VO was plainly not a man to waste words, but he did not cooperate with the prosecutor either. In his own way, he did oppose the Commonwealth's case whenever possible, and he did achieve results: he won acquittals on at least the major charge in several cases that had been strongly pressed by the prosecution.[113]

However one chooses to regard the performance of VO, he was a distinct exception among the attorneys we observed. Many other defenders might also be described as "low key," but they were far less cynical. These lawyers[114] were calm and unemotional, unintimidating to witnesses, and generally respectful toward the judge. Nonetheless, they cross-examined thoroughly and pressed available points firmly. Their somewhat understated style enhanced the impression that their arguments were sincere and reasonable, just as it would have in a jury trial. These were very capable attorneys, thoroughly adversarial in their approach to trial.

When defense tactics seemed to us unwise or ineffective, the problem most often was not that the attorney was too "low key," but rather that he went to the opposite extreme. Whether by temperament or by choice, several defenders[115] were highly assertive, flamboyant in style, and frequently emotional. Defender TH, though by no means

---

[112] No. 2827 (a robbery case).

[113] In two robbery cases, Nos. 1635 and 2827, VO won acquittals on the major charge, and his clients were convicted only on related misdemeanor counts. In the latter case, he apparently felt that he had made his point in a brief cross-examination, and he did not even bother to give a closing statement. In No. 1567, an auto theft case, VO asked the arresting officer only three short but pointed questions, and in a very brief closing statement he challenged the circumstantial evidence of the defendant's guilty knowledge; the judge granted an acquittal on all counts.

[114] The group included WD, TL, DE, PR, and FT.

[115] Examples were SH, OT, and HI.

the most aggressive attorney, routinely demurred to at least some of the charges, even when such a motion was utterly frivolous.[116] Many defenders made closing arguments that were too long, argumentative, or repetitive.[117] Private defense attorneys were even more likely to "go overboard" by pursuing unproductive cross-examination that only tended to reinforce the witness' story, using the closing argument for a speech about the reasonable doubt requirement, or making the same point repeatedly until the judge asked them to sit down. Although there were notable exceptions, private attorneys generally seemed less capable and less seasoned than the public defenders, and these factors may explain the private attorneys' frequent use of such counterproductive tactics. Possibly the private attorneys were more interested in impressing their clients than in persuading the judge (especially if the case was hopeless). A perceptive observer of attorney behavior would find much to question or criticize, but an insufficiently adversarial stance was seldom the problem.

Much of the argumentative behavior we observed would have been counterproductive even in a jury trial, but some tactics seemed especially unnecessary in the particular setting of a bench trial. In most cases, judges quickly caught the point of a cross-examination, and they certainly did not need a long speech about the importance of reasonable doubt. Attorneys may have stayed with the style that they used in jury cases, whether through force of habit or as a result of trial advocacy training based on the jury trial model. One other explanation was suggested during the trial of an aggravated assault case.[118] The prosecutor cross-examined forcefully, pacing back and forth. His voice rose and fell with dramatic intonations. Finally the judge interrupted: "Counsel, there's no jury here." The prosecutor replied, "Sorry, your Honor, I was just practicing."

A lapse of "adversariness" may occur when the defense stipulates to all or part of the prosecution's case. We recorded stipulations in twenty-one cases, nearly thirteen percent of the List program bench trials we observed. In twelve of these cases, the defense stipulated only to peripheral, incontrovertible issues such as the owner's testimony in an auto theft case that he owned the car and had not given the defendant permission to use it.[119] Other issues in such cases —

---

[116] An example was No. 1763, a burglary case.

[117] For instance, in No. 2379, an aggravated assault case, defender SF spent nearly 30 minutes making one simple argument — that the blood-stained shirt allegedly worn by the assailant did not fit the defendant. The argument was valid, but a more experienced defender probably would have made the point in less than five minutes.

[118] No. 3566 (prosecutor CH; Judge RT).

[119] Because of an ambiguity in the data sheet, several stipulations on seemingly technical issues were not recorded at all. The totals recorded therefore include only some of the stipulations on such matters as laboratory analysis of the character or quantity of drugs, prior criminal record (stipulations that would extend to the existence but not to the admissibility of

identification of the defendant, his control of the car, or guilty knowledge — were contested vigorously. But even when stipulations are limited to unimportant issues, the defense might appear to be cooperating in a limited way with the prosecution, for the defendant always has a right to put the Commonwealth to its proof and may win a dismissal if any essential witness fails to appear. Of course, when the defense stipulates to all the alleged facts (as happened in nine cases), the inference of cooperation is strong.

Despite appearances, most stipulations had persuasive tactical justifications. Sometimes a defender concluded that factual arguments would be futile but that there was a fatal legal weakness in the prosecution's case. A stipulation helped focus the judge's attention on the winning claim. In one burglary case,[120] the defender stipulated to the facts established at the preliminary hearing, because he felt that the prosecution might, if given another chance, fill a critical gap in its case; the tactic proved successful.

The more limited stipulations usually had tactical justifications as well. Sometimes a stipulation had occurred at an earlier listing; the judge was more likely to grant a defense request for a continuance if minor witnesses did not have to return for another hearing. In other cases a defender might stipulate to routine testimony (such as that of a car owner) in order to get the victim out of the courtroom. Once the victim had appeared and was prepared to wait for the case to be called, the defender lost nothing by letting the witness go home immediately, and he might gain something if, as some defenders believe, a judge is more likely to show leniency when the victim is not present at sentencing.

In a few of the cases, stipulations did not seem justified on tactical grounds. These instances of "cooperation" are described in more detail below.[121] In general, though, lapses of adversary behavior were extremely rare. If anything, defense attorneys seemed much more adversarial than the circumstances strictly required.

5. "Adversariness": Judicial Behavior. — Judges typically played an active role at trial. Nearly all the judges questioned witnesses at least occasionally. A few[122] questioned witnesses in virtually every case. Sometimes a judge sought to clear up an important point after direct and cross-examination had been completed; in No. 3087,[123] a burglary case, Judge WO even recalled two witnesses to the stand after both sides had rested. Some of the judges also interrupted direct

the record), or the owner's testimony in auto theft cases. All together, roughly 10 to 20 stipulations of this nature were overlooked. The totals do, however, include every potentially significant stipulation and every fully stipulated trial.

120 No. 0164 (defender WD).

121 *See infra* pp. 1073–75.

122 These judges included DC, TG, and WO, and Calendar Judges EE and VT.

123 Case numbers are based upon court docket numbers. *See supra* note 65.

or cross-examination to put their own questions to the witnesses. Judge VT frequently intervened to ask even the most routine questions ("What happened next?"); he seemed to prefer to conduct direct examination himself. The judges also freely interrupted questioning that they considered irrelevant or repetitive. Attorneys were sometimes forcefully told to stop wasting time or to hurry up; Judges DC and RT and Calendar Judge LL gave such commands in nearly every trial. In No. 2592, an aggravated assault case, Judge DC cut short a lengthy cross-examination by telling private attorney TG that he (the judge) would convict if questioning continued. TG sat down and won an acquittal. Given the lengthy and repetitive questioning that seemed a habit with some attorneys, judicial badgering of this kind was not always unwarranted.

Closing statements were almost always a time for active participation by the judge. Judge DC usually began by summarizing his own analysis and asking the attorneys to refute it. List Judge WO and Calendar Judge VT directed the attorneys to the issues they found most troublesome. Many judges would from the very beginning rule out issues that they considered unnecessary to discuss. ("This boils down to credibility. Confine yourselves to that.") Although Judges LD and RT were rather formal and tended to sit through closing arguments in silence, most judges quickly became involved in lively dialogues with counsel.

Interchanges with the judge usually covered the main points very rapidly. The parties used a great deal of verbal shorthand that would no doubt mystify a casual observer (or first offender), and judges seldom seemed to ponder or agonize over an issue. On the other hand, most of the judges did appear to focus conscientiously on the law and the evidence. Though they made up their minds in short order, most of them took the decision seriously and showed concern to "get it right."[124] When credibility issues were paramount, for example, judges and counsel might trade rapid comments on testimony (or personal theories of human nature) that cast doubt on the plausibility of a witness' story. At other times, cases turned on quite technical issues: Was the defendant trying to steal the car (seven-year maximum sentence) or only its contents (five-year maximum)?[125] Did the victim's injuries satisfy the strict requirements for aggravated assault (ten-year maximum) or only those for simple assault (two-year maximum)?[126] In a weapons case, was the offense "PIC" (five-year

---

[124] Defenders felt that many judges, especially in the List program, lacked either the patience or the ability to focus on particularly complex legal issues that sometimes arose — for example, issues of intent, problems in forgery and other "paper" cases, and some of the search and seizure questions.

[125] *See* 18 PA. CONS. STAT. ANN. § 3903(a)–(b) (Purdon 1983).

[126] *See id.* §§ 2301, 2701–2702. To establish an aggravated assault at the felony level (10-year maximum), the prosecution must show that the defendant caused or attempted to cause

maximum), "POW" (also a five-year maximum), or neither one?[127] These issues arose over and over, and judges usually could make up their minds after asking one or two questions.[128]

Following oral argument, judgment was rendered immediately; we never saw a case taken under advisement.[129] The judges often gave no explicit reasons for their rulings, but many times they briefly referred to a critical weakness in the prosecution's or defense's theory of the case. Not all the decisions seemed completely logical. Particularly in cases arising out of fights among neighbors or acquaintances, judges sometimes seemed to find fault on both sides; under these circumstances a decision might be something of a compromise. In several cases, Calendar Judge VT explained his decision by stating simply, "This is a 'jury verdict.'"[130]

Apart from the situations in which equities intruded (much as they might in a jury case), the decisions almost uniformly seemed to be

"serious bodily injury," defined in § 2301 as "injury which creates a substantial risk of death or which causes serious, permanent disfigurement, or protracted loss or impairment of the function of any bodily member or organ."

[127] The "PIC" charge, "possessing instruments of crime," requires proof that the defendant possessed an "instrument of crime" (for example, "[a]nything . . . specially adapted for criminal use") with intent to employ it criminally. *Id.* § 907. The "POW" charge, "prohibited offensive weapons," requires proof that the defendant made, sold, used, or possessed any offensive weapon (defined to include bombs, firearms specially made for concealment, and switchblade knives). *Id.* § 908. Thus, the latter charge applies only to a more limited category of "instruments of crime," but it does not require proof of intent to use.

[128] No. 1485, though not a typical case, provides a clear illustration of the hazards inherent in assuming that arguments and decisions are perfunctory simply because they are brief. No. 1485 was an unusually serious case that involved charges of burglary, attempted rape, aggravated assault, and indecent assault, and the hotly contested trial was one of the longest in our sample — four hours and 16 minutes (net of recesses). At the close of the prosecution's case, the defendant demurred to several charges. Judge EE quickly sustained the demurrer to the burglary count; he noted only that there was no evidence that the decision to commit an offense had been made before the defendant had entered the house. With respect to the aggravated assault count, testimony and photographic evidence showed that the victim had sustained major bruises and bite injuries and had been severely beaten just above the right eye. The issue was whether the strict definition of "serious bodily injury," *see supra* note 126, was satisfied on these facts. The judge simply indicated that he thought the evidence failed to establish the requisite kind of injury, and prosecutor LN's response consisted of pointing to the photograph and stating, "But Judge, look at her eye." Judge EE sustained the demurrer nonetheless; the decision surprised some observers at the time, but later reference to the statute showed that the decision, though a close one, was correct. Argument and rulings at the demurrer stage consumed no more than 10 minutes in this case, but the parties were clearly adversarial, and the brief interval afforded the judge time to sort out some subtle issues of fact and law. (The speed of the judge's ruling did not reflect simply a general sympathy for the defense; at the end of the case, the judge convicted on both the indecent assault and attempted rape charges.)

[129] In two cases the verdict was "deferred." The defendant in such an arrangement is in effect placed on probation, on the understanding that when the terms of probation are satisfactorily completed, an acquittal will be entered. The arrangement thus amounts to a posttrial version of "pretrial" diversion.

[130] No. 1692 (an aggravated assault case); No. 2582 (rape). In No. 2377 (burglary and assault), Judge VT rendered what he termed a "compromise verdict."

based on the law and the evidence.[131] This does not mean that the judge's ruling would invariably coincide with an observer's personal judgment or with a guess about how a jury might rule in an identical case. On questions of reasonable doubt in particular, there is almost always room for disagreement among participants and observers.[132] Defenders were often disappointed by the outcome.

To describe the judges' behavior as "adversarial" would risk confusion, because the adversary model is often identified with a system in which the parties assume absolute control over facts and issues while the judge remains wholly passive.[133] The Philadelphia judges certainly were not "adversarial" in this sense.[134] Our central concern, however, was to determine the extent to which the bench trials were genuinely contested, with vigorous efforts by opposing counsel and decisions based on applicable law and the testimony given in court. These features (which are said to be characteristic not only of jury cases, but also of trials within the nonadversary systems of continental Europe) seemed fully present in the Philadelphia bench trials we observed. In their relative activism, the judges may have taken a step toward the nonadversary role of the continental judge, but in no relevant sense could the proceedings be described as the functional equivalent of a guilty plea. With rare exceptions that will now be described, these trials were not "slow pleas."

6. Exceptions: The "Slow Plea" Cases. — In the course of eight weeks of observation by four full-time researchers, we found seven trials that might be considered candidates for the "slow plea" designation. In No. 2803, a shoplifting case, public defender CR told the judge at sidebar that his client should plead guilty but was "too stupid to get through the colloquy." After some discussion (which participants called a "whisper trial"), Judge LD told the defender to enter a plea of not guilty and accept a bench trial, which led to conviction in short order.[135] In No. 2919, a defendant charged with possession

---

[131] A few judges indicated that when a defendant would get no more than probation upon conviction, they occasionally acquitted as a gesture to the defense attorney. In No. 2942, the judge stated that he felt the public defender "deserved [to win] one a week." For other situations in which the judge's decision might not be based strictly on the facts, see *infra* note 142.

[132] Of the List room judges, we found that Judge VY was consistently difficult to persuade on reasonable doubt and that Judge DC was unpredictable; the others seemed to us rather fair (and perhaps even too easy to persuade), though we know that many defenders would not share this assessment.

[133] *See* Damaška, *Evidentiary Barriers to Conviction and Two Models of Criminal Procedure: A Comparative Study*, 121 U. PA. L. REV. 506, 563–64 (1973).

[134] To be sure, the American trial system tolerates departures from this pure conception of "adversariness," even in jury trial cases. *See* Quercia v. United States, 289 U.S. 466, 469 (1933) (dictum); Goldstein, *Reflections on Two Models: Inquisitorial Themes in American Criminal Procedure*, 26 STAN. L. REV. 1009 (1974). But the judges' active participation in cross-examination would have been unusual in a jury case, and their intervention in closing arguments would of course be unheard of in a jury trial.

[135] Even in this case, defender CR did cross-examine, and in a brief closing statement he

of stolen credit cards stipulated to the preliminary hearing testimony, raised no issues, and was promptly convicted. We were told that the defendant should have pleaded guilty but that defense counsel CD, who was the uncle of prosecutor VD, wanted "to avoid any indication of collusion" and therefore took the case to trial. We were left to ponder this problem and its remarkable "solution." In three other very perfunctory trials,[136] we were unable to learn what — if anything — motivated defense counsel's cooperative behavior.

The sixth case of this kind was No. 2439. The defendant, having chased and attacked a person who had just robbed his mother, found himself charged with aggravated assault. The attorneys asked Judge DC to meet them in the cloakroom for an off-the-record discussion, and when they emerged, defender SK reported that the case was "wired" for acquittal. The judge apparently agreed that the accused had taken reasonable action in defense of property. At trial, the complainant testified that the defendant had attacked him with a meat cleaver, a detail that appeared to surprise and trouble the judge. Still, defender SK stipulated to the testimony of the arresting officer, offered no defense, and proceeded directly to his closing argument. When Judge DC interrupted the argument to say that using a meat cleaver seemed to go beyond defense of property, the defender asked permission to reopen the defense and call his client to the stand. Judge DC granted the request but eventually convicted, stating that the defendant had taken "street justice" too far. Cloakroom sessions like this one were infrequent, and No. 2439 was the only case in which such a session seemed responsible for material shortcuts at trial.[137] The defender, of course, was being completely adversarial, and had it not been for the surprise testimony, the case might have ended as the functional equivalent of a nol pros — in effect, a "slow dismissal." As it turned out, however, the courtroom proceedings even in this case were far from a sham. The charges were contested, and ultimately the case was resolved on the testimony given in open court.

The final example is No. 0821, a burglary case. EY, a retained attorney, sought to withdraw from the case. After the judge denied the motion, EY proceeded to trial but attempted no cross-examination and made no closing argument. Although Judge PF convicted, he

argued that there was a reasonable doubt about whether his client had attempted to pay for the goods.

[136] The cases were No. 3474, an auto theft case before Judge SB; No. 2578, a burglary case before Judge WF; and Nos. 2807 and 2810, a burglary trial involving two defendants before Judge WO.

[137] Defender VN spoke privately with judges, at sidebar or in chambers, somewhat more often than did the other defenders. He explained that these sessions might cover normal sidebar matters (for example, information that a witness should not hear), but he also indicated that sometimes the sessions were designed either to lay the foundation for a dismissal (in effect a "slow dismissal," *see infra* note 142), to clarify what the issues "boiled down to," or to "agree on the facts."

immediately appointed a public defender to file a motion for new trial on the ground of ineffective assistance of counsel. The judge's irritation probably stemmed in part from counsel's attempt to withdraw from the case, but it was clear that he considered her lack of vigor unusual and, as he put it privately, "extremely unprofessional." Beyond the infrequency of attorney behavior of this kind, the reaction of the judge when such behavior did occur spoke volumes about the extent to which perfunctory performance and easygoing attitudes toward defense work are alien to the prevailing "courtroom norm" or "work group ethic" in the Philadelphia courts.

7. *"Adversariness": The Data.* — Our observations led us to conclude that a very few trials were perfunctory but that most were vigorously contested. Previous studies have almost uniformly asserted the opposite proposition — that a few bench trials may be contested but that most are not.[138] Plainly, the choice between these two views depends critically on assessments of the relative frequency of "slow pleas." Under these conditions, one may too easily conclude that such assessments are simply a matter of subjective impression and that the "other side" has not carried its burden of proof.[139] The qualitative information we have developed for Philadelphia provides such a clear, unequivocal picture that this problem should not arise. Nonetheless, quantitative material less dependent on evaluation and impression would furnish a useful supplementary perspective. Can we therefore develop an "objective," quantitative measure of "adversariness" and use it to gauge the vigor of the Philadelphia trials?

The difficulties of such an endeavor are not small. The elements of vigorous trial advocacy do not come in measurable units of intensity. A short, pointed cross-examination may be more effective than a long one; sometimes defense counsel may wisely prefer none at all. Even stipulations, which seem on their face the essence of cooperation rather than challenge, may be chosen as part of a carefully considered, vigorous defense strategy.[140] One could, of course, compare the incidence of cross-examination, stipulations, or other defense tactics in bench trials and in jury trials, on the assumption that the latter provides a workable benchmark of genuine adversariness. But the two groups of cases differ systematically, in part because the very tactical concerns we want to study will affect the threshold decision whether to demand a jury. And even in otherwise "identical" cases, the tactics of vigorous defense differ when the trier of fact is a judge.

Despite these obstacles, we can develop useful "objective" indications of adversariness, provided that we recognize their limitations

[138] *See supra* pp. 1047–50.

[139] Witness the reaction of some scholars to differing characterizations of the European trial. *See, e.g.*, Arenella, *Reforming the Federal Grand Jury and the State Preliminary Hearing to Prevent Conviction Without Adjudication*, 78 MICH. L. REV. 463, 527–28 (1980).

[140] *See supra* pp. 1069–70.

and do not forget their role as a supplement to the essential qualitative material. We may begin by examining the outcome of the trials. According to published court statistics, approximately 30% of all Philadelphia bench trials end in acquittal.[141] Because this acquittal rate is somewhat higher than the one for jury trials, one might conclude that bench trials are the more effectively contested. Such a comparison, however, is quite misleading. Not only are the bench and jury cases dissimilar, but the published 30% acquittal rate for bench trials may be inflated by factors that are not relevant to adversariness.[142] In our own sample, the bench trial acquittal rate was only 20% for List cases and 24% for Calendar cases, figures that by themselves say very little about whether the trials were perfunctory or genuine.

A clearer picture emerges when we examine the outcomes of cases in terms of the various charges at issue in each case. Table III indicates that in addition to the acquittals, many bench trials ended in conviction only on charges significantly less serious than the principal counts. In the List program sample, significant charge reduction occurred in only 20% of the guilty plea cases but in 25% of the bench trial cases; moreover, significant charge reduction was present in 31% of the 128 bench trial *convictions* — 55% more often than in guilty plea cases.[143] Of course, the guilty plea and bench trial cases are not strictly comparable, because the former group presumably contains many more open-and-shut cases. But this is, in part, the point. When a case involves debatable issues, the defendant goes to trial and often wins significant charge reduction, a result normally unobtainable in

---

[141] The figures were 32% for 1980, 31.6% for 1981, and 29.8% for the first half of 1982.

[142] This was particularly true in earlier years. The published court statistics indicate bench trial acquittal rates of well over 40% for the years 1972–1977, with an acquittal rate of over 50% in 1975. Although it is not possible to be certain about the explanation for such figures, we believe that some acquittals may have been recorded for cases in which the defendant was convicted on other related charges; today, in contrast, all related bills of information against a single defendant are treated as one "case," and if there is a conviction on any count the result is recorded as a conviction. We also believe that in the earlier period many acquittals occurred in poorly screened cases that the prosecutor did not seriously press for conviction. Instead of moving to drop the charges, an action that would attract the attention of his superiors, the prosecutor could simply submit the case to the judge for acquittal. This procedure would amount in effect to a "slow dismissal," and the outcome could not necessarily be taken to reflect vigorous advocacy by the defense. With better screening procedures and better trial preparation by prosecutors, such "slow dismissals" have become much less common, but even in the latest court statistics, some of the recorded acquittals may have been of this type. In our own sample, with only a 20% acquittal rate, virtually none of the acquittals were "slow dismissals."

A final factor that cannot be ignored is the possibility that some acquittals result not from vigorous adversarial behavior, but rather from close personal relationships between some private attorneys and particular judges. District Attorney Edward Rendell has made this charge publicly. Interview and public lecture in Philadelphia, Pennsylvania (Apr. 14, 1983). Again, in our own sample, with only a 20% acquittal rate and with some underrepresentation of private attorney cases, *see supra* note 64, this factor seems unlikely to have played a major role.

[143] This difference is statistically significant at the .05 level.

TABLE III

CASE OUTCOME BY TYPE OF DISPOSITION

Outcome Code	Outcome Description	Bench Trials				Guilty Pleas			
		List		Calendar		List		Calendar	
		N	%	N	%	N	%	N	%
1	Conviction on all charges	46	28	4	14	21	18	10	29
2	Conviction on all principal charges	39	24	11	38	67	58	19	56
3	Conviction on some principal charges	3	2	1	3	3	3	2	6
4	Conviction on lesser charges only	40	25	6	21	23	20	2	6
5	Acquittal on all charges	32	20	7	24	-	-	-	-
6	Verdict deferred	2	1	-	-	1	1	1	3
	Total	162	100	29	100	115	100	34	100

Philadelphia plea bargaining. Thus, even the relatively simple criterion of case outcome suggests that a bench trial is not the functional equivalent of a guilty plea.

The outcome criterion cannot tell us whether the bench trials resulting in major convictions were genuinely contested. Fifty-two percent of the List cases ended in conviction on all the principal charges — the same outcome as in the typical guilty plea case. Many of these cases conceivably could have been "slow pleas." To refine the analysis further, we need to measure adversariness in terms of effort as well as result.

For the great bulk of the cases, stipulations alone do not provide an adequate measure of the vigor of the defense.[144] Demurrers and reasonable doubt arguments also are unsatisfactory, because one or the other is almost always present and because there is no strictly objective way to distinguish serious from perfunctory efforts in these areas. We therefore chose to focus on the extent to which a factual defense was developed. We recorded for each case the nature of any cross-examination and the use of witnesses in defense. As Table IV indicates, only 11% of the List cases lacked any apparent challenge to the prosecution's factual allegations,[145] and in only 30% of the List trials was the defense confined to cross-examination. Sixty percent involved both substantial cross-examination and an affirmative defense case, and the defense called witnesses other than the defendant

TABLE IV

CHARACTERISTICS OF DEFENSE

Defense Code	Defense Description	List		Calendar	
		N	%	N	%
A	No substantial cross-examination; no defense witnesses	18	11	1	3
B	Cross-examination; no defense witnesses	48	30	6	21
C	Cross-examination; defendant testifies	56	35	3	10
D	Cross-examination; third-party defense witnesses	13	8	4	14
E	Cross-examination; defendant and other defense witnesses testify	27	17	15	52
	Total	162	100	29	100

[144] *See supra* pp. 1069–70.

[145] This figure includes the nine fully stipulated trials.

in 25% of the List room trials.[146] Still, a skeptic might stress that 41% of the List cases involved no affirmative defense case. By contrast, in only 24% of the Calendar program cases did the defense fail to present an affirmative case, and 66% of the Calendar cases involved third-party defense witnesses. Do these contrasts simply reflect the deliberate channeling of complex, multiwitness cases into the Calendar program, or do they instead suggest the existence of time pressures and less serious attitudes among defenders in the List courtrooms?

In order to assess the extent to which relatively limited defense efforts were tactically justified, we cross-tabulated the measures of defense effort against the measures of case outcome. The results for the List program appear in Table V. Complete acquittals occurred in 33% of the cases involving the most fully developed defense, compared to an average acquittal rate of only 20% in the cases as a whole, but the acquittal rate was also much higher than average (33%) in the cases involving no factual defense at all. Conversely, conviction on all counts occurred with lower-than-average frequency when the defense was most fully developed (19% as opposed to an average of 28%), but the rate of complete conviction was actually lowest of all (11%) in the cases involving no factual defense.[147] These patterns are counterintuitive only if one assumes that when attorneys forego a vigorous factual defense, they must be cooperating with the prosecutor in order to facilitate conviction (possibly in return for a lighter sentence). If instead one believes that the attorneys adopt an adversary stance and pass up opportunities for challenge only when it is tactically advantageous to do so, the very high success rate in the "undefended" cases makes perfect sense.[148]

---

[146] Of the 59 cases in which third-party witnesses were called by the defense, eight cases (two of the 17 in level D and six of the 42 in level E as shown in Table IV) involved witnesses who testified only to the defendant's good character.

[147] A similar pattern is evident if one compares the relatively successful results (acquittals and substantial charge reductions) with the relatively unsuccessful results (complete convictions and convictions on the top count). Successful results occurred more often than average (about 55% versus 45%) in the most fully defended cases, but they also occurred very often (55%) in cases involving no factual defense at all. Unsuccessful results occurred less often than average (about 45% versus 54%) in the most fully defended cases, but they occurred least often (33%) in the cases that seemingly were not defended at all.

[148] To permit a test of statistical significance, we collapsed the five-by-six cross-tabulation in text into a three-by-two table, with unsuccessful outcomes (1, 2, and 3) and successful outcomes (4 and 5) cross-tabulated against three defense levels: A; B and C together; and D and E together. For this simplified table, chi-square = 4.196, the contingency coefficient = 0.160, and p = 0.1227. Thus, there is no statistically significant correlation between outcome and the observable measures of defense effort. In other words, as indicated in text, the distribution of successful results seemingly could have occurred at random. As long as one believes that a failure of vigorous advocacy will in fact significantly increase the probability of conviction, one must conclude that the objective benchmarks of defense effort do not adequately indicate the actual vigor of defense effort, and that effective advocacy did occur even in some cases that, gauged by purely "objective" criteria, appeared to involve minimal effort.

TABLE V

CASE OUTCOME BY CHARACTERISTICS OF DEFENSE (LIST PROGRAM)

		Defense Code and Description											
		A		B		C		D		E			
				Cross-Examination									
Outcome Code	Outcome Description	No cross-examination or defense witnesses		No defense witnesses		Defendant testifies		3rd-party defense witnesses testify		Defendant & other defense witnesses testify		Total	
		N	%	N	%	N	%	N	%	N	%	N	%
1	Conviction on all charges	2	11	15	31	18	32	6	46	5	19	46	28
2	Conviction on all principal charges	4	22	13	27	14	25	1	8	7	26	39	24
3	Conviction on some principal charges	-	-	1	2	2	4	-	-	-	-	3	2
4	Conviction on lesser charges only	4	22	12	25	17	30	1	8	6	22	40	25
5	Acquittal on all charges	6	33	7	15	5	9	5	38	9	33	32	20
6	Verdict deferred	2	11	-	-	-	-	-	-	-	-	2	1
	Total	18	100	48	100	56	100	13	100	27	100	162	100

Data concerning the intermediate levels of defense effort suggest a similar interpretation. As one moves from cross-examination only (level B) through testimony by the defendant (level C) and by third-party witnesses (level D), the frequency of successful results does tend to rise, but the various outcomes are distributed throughout all the categories of defense effort, and the differences in success rates are not great.[149] Again the suggestion is strong that in nearly all instances the attorneys probably were doing the best they could, given whatever opportunities the cases themselves may have provided.

Although the defense attorneys, almost without exception, did make genuine efforts to test the Commonwealth's case and to defend whenever possible, it is nevertheless fair to say that much of the time these efforts were hopeless. We saw a good deal of utterly futile cross-examination, and even when the defendant took the stand to deny participation in the crime, the claim sometimes sounded hollow indeed. Under such circumstances there appeared to be little doubt that a "dead bang" case had been taken to trial.

Because proponents of plea bargaining often assert that nearly all criminal cases (up to 90%) are devoid of triable issues, it seems important to try to assess that claim empirically. Any attempt to gauge the frequency of such cases quantitatively and "objectively" is of course fraught with difficulty, but Tables III and V provide a useful perspective on the problem. The cases ending in acquittal or significant charge reduction (45% of the List program total) can safely be treated as triable ones. I believe that the same is true of the nineteen cases (an additional 12% of the total) in which unsuccessful defense efforts included testimony from third-party defense witnesses. Thus, roughly speaking, at least 57% of the List program cases involved legitimately triable issues.

Cases in which the defense neither called third-party witnesses nor won acquittal or any significant charge reduction are at least potential candidates for "dead bang" characterization. Among the unsuccessful defense efforts were thirty-five List program cases (22% of the 162 dispositions) in which no affirmative defense testimony was offered, and thirty-four cases (an additional 21%) involving testimony by the defendant but no defense testimony from third-party witnesses. In these two groups of cases, defense efforts rested largely or entirely upon the cross-examination of Commonwealth witnesses. Did any of these cases (43% of the total) contain genuinely triable issues? One might suspect that much of the cross-examination in these cases was inherently futile, but it would certainly be an exaggeration to disparage all such defense efforts simply because they proved unsuccessful. This qualification applies even more strongly to cases in which defense

[149] Thus, relatively successful results occur 40% of the time for level B and 39% of the time for level C; the mean for all cases is only 45%.

counsel both cross-examined the prosecution's witnesses and placed the defendant on the stand. These two groups of unsuccessful defense cases therefore suggest only rough outer limits for the proportion of "dead bang" cases. Such cases represented only 22% or, if both groups are combined, 43% of the List room trials we observed.

E. Summary and Evaluation of Philadelphia Felony Dispositions

It is perhaps obvious, but worth stressing, that the Philadelphia court system is by no means a perfect one. Attorneys and other court personnel are not always above criticism. Among the judges, inefficiency and unfairness sometimes occur, just as they would in any large human institution — or, in particular, in any large, elected city judiciary. Although local observers are justifiably preoccupied with these sorts of problems, we can for present purposes focus our primary attention on the especially distinctive features of Philadelphia's case processing system.

1. Plea Bargaining and "Dead Bang" Cases. — Philadelphia officials do not claim to have "abolished" plea bargaining, and a visitor to the courts will hear of a good many plea "agreements." Yet there is, in effect, much less plea bargaining than meets the eye. The available concessions are generally quite limited, and in the majority of cases, no concessions for pleading guilty are available at all. In the List program, we found concessions (mostly modest ones) in roughly 41% of the guilty plea cases — that is, 17% of the dispositions on the merits.[150]

In the absence of significant concessions, most cases — including many quite hopeless ones — were taken to trial. We concluded that within the List program, about 59% of the guilty pleas (sixty-eight cases) and roughly 22% to 43% of the bench trial cases (thirty-five to sixty-nine cases) were devoid of triable issues.[151] When the two groups are combined, one finds approximately 103 to 137 "dead bang" cases, and in roughly one-half to two-thirds of them, guilty pleas were obtained without any concessions.[152]

The roughly 103 to 137 "hopeless" cases represent only 37% to 49% of the 277 List program cases we observed. Although these figures are crude approximations from a data base that is itself imperfect, they nonetheless raise doubts about the view, held by many

[150] *See supra* pp. 1058–62.

[151] *See supra* pp. 1061–62, 1081–82.

[152] On the basis of the estimate of 137 "dead bang" cases, the 68 guilty pleas represent 50% of the total; on the basis of the lower estimate of 103 such cases, the 68 guilty pleas represent 66% of the total. Putting the matter the other way around, one-third to one-half of the "hopeless" cases were taken to trial. This observation tends to support our claim that defenders generally did not expect significant sentencing concessions in return for a plea; they took cases to trial even when there was apparently nothing to be gained by doing so.

plea bargaining proponents, that up to 90% of all criminal cases are devoid of triable issues of fact or law.[153] The much lower figures suggested for Philadelphia are particularly striking in view of our focus on the Common Pleas List program, a segment of the caseload that might be expected to display an unusually heavy proportion of open-and-shut cases.[154] Roughly speaking, only one-third to one-half of the List cases fit that description, with the latter figure representing a rather generous upper limit.

2. *The "Slow Plea" Question.* — Most Philadelphia dispositions are by trial rather than by plea, and these trials are not "slow pleas of guilty." By waiving a jury, the defendant may in many cases reduce the probability of an acquittal on grounds of reasonable doubt, and such waivers may be induced by the prospect of a more lenient sentence in the event of conviction. In these two respects, there is a functional resemblance between the jury waiver and traditional forms of plea bargaining. But any assumption that the judge is always a less favorable trier of fact would prove invalid with respect to many cases and many judges; moreover, the defense can often successfully steer litigation away from unfavorable judges. Thus, by no means do all bench trials involve the waiver of a meaningful defense privilege.

Even when the jury waiver does deprive the defendant of a valuable procedural right, it does not deprive him of *all* valuable procedural rights. For this reason, it would be thoroughly misleading to picture the typical Philadelphia bench trial as the functional equivalent of the guilty plea. The defendant retains the rights to confront the witnesses against him, to object on constitutional or other grounds to the admissibility of evidence, to cross-examine witnesses, to develop factual defenses, to have his guilt determined on the basis of the testimony presented in open court, to have that testimony evaluated under applicable substantive law, and to test by appeal any of the trial judge's rulings on matters of admissibility, legal interpretation, or evidentiary weight. We found that, apart from isolated aberrations, all the bench trials we observed were genuinely contested proceedings. The lawyers remained within their traditional adversary roles, and the judges took seriously their obligation to adjudicate. Participants were (normally) courteous to one another, but they did not cooperate at the expense of their separate institutional responsibilities. Cases

---

[153] *See supra* pp. 1043–44.

[154] Cases reaching the Common Pleas level are subjected to serious screening in Municipal Court proceedings that weed out many weak cases. In 1981, for example, the Municipal Court conducted preliminary hearings in 15,892 cases. Defendants were held for trial in only 69% of these cases, whereas in the remaining 31% the defendants were discharged. Among the cases thus screened, relatively simple cases that can be tried quickly are systematically channeled into the List courtrooms. Of course, the more complicated Calendar cases do not all involve genuinely debatable issues, but there is little doubt that "hopeless" cases will be more common in List than in Calendar courtrooms.

were not compromised but were decided on the governing law and the evidence. In short, most of the Philadelphia cases were tried, and these trials were fully contested adversary proceedings.

3. The Problem of Case Pressure. — How do the Philadelphia courts manage to provide most felony defendants a genuine trial? Matters of resource allocation may account for part of the answer[155] — but only part. Even if Philadelphia has assigned an unusually high priority to conducting trials in felony cases, the question remains: how do the courts actually manage to do this — how is it *possible*?

The most important and perhaps most unexpected part of the answer is that a genuine trial does not require many more resources than a guilty plea does. This conclusion diverges from most previous assessments of both the resources needed to process guilty pleas and the resources needed to conduct trials.

Guilty plea cases typically involve not only preliminary investigation and preparation, but also formal preliminary hearings and, in many cases, one or more abortive listings resulting in continuances. Many guilty plea cases also entail presentence reports, followed by a hearing for imposition of sentence a month or so after conviction. All in all, guilty plea cases represent a considerable investment of effort by court personnel, wholly apart from what happens when the plea itself is taken. Finally — on the day of disposition — the waiver colloquy and the showing of a factual basis, together with waiting time (much of it unavoidable), add up to nearly an hour of courtroom time for each guilty plea conviction.[156]

A jurisdiction might choose to resolve its guilty plea cases with less effort. Pleas could be settled even before preliminary hearing; sentences, even in serious cases, could be fixed by negotiation, without benefit of a presentence report. The waiver and factual basis inquiries could be completed more expeditiously, and waiting time could, to some extent, be reduced. An efficiency-minded jurisdiction could thus choose to make the guilty plea a greater timesaver by accepting the additional sacrifice of process values that such measures would entail. Whether or not particular jurisdictions might wish to make these sacrifices, the fact remains that Philadelphia and probably many other

[155] It would be worthwhile to attempt a comparison of Philadelphia and other cities in terms of total judicial personnel and the allocation of personnel among such functions as misdemeanor and felony trials, juvenile matters, the civil calendar, and so on. It seems doubtful, however, that Philadelphia would prove to be very different from most major urban jurisdictions. *See* Jacob, Swank, Beecher & Rich, *Keeping pace: court resources and crime in ten U.S. cities*, 66 JUDICATURE 73 (1982). The authors report that during the period 1948–1978, court resources in 10 cities (including Philadelphia) expanded somewhat but did not keep pace with the rising crime rate. The Philadelphia pattern was not markedly different from that in the other jurisdictions. Among the cities for which data were available, Philadelphia ranked sixth of nine in growth in the number of assistant prosecutors and fourth of eight in growth in the number of felony judges. *Id.* at 82.

[156] *See supra* pp. 1056–57.

cities have been able to commit significant resources to the processing of guilty pleas.

Once time and effort of this kind have been devoted to a guilty plea case, what additional resources must be expended to afford the defendant a trial? The great bulk of the investment in a case, particularly for prosecutors and the court, occurs at the pretrial and posttrial stages and is completely independent of whether disposition is by trial or by plea.[157] Preoccupation with differences in court time at the disposition stage thus greatly exaggerates the overall difference between the resource requirements for trials and those for pleas.

Even at the disposition stage, we found the differences between trials and pleas to be quite small. The typical bench trial lasted about forty-five minutes — roughly twice as long as the typical plea. This is an appreciable difference, to be sure, but by no means one that puts the goal of trials utterly out of reach. On these figures, reducing a 90% guilty plea rate to an 80% rate would require not a doubling of judicial capacity, but only an 11% increase; a reduction to 70% would require not a tripling of judicial capacity, but only a 22% increase.[158]

For several reasons, the above figures, which compare a forty-five-minute average for bench trials with a twenty-minute average for pleas, actually exaggerate the time differences between the two methods of disposition. The figures suggest, for example, that a courtroom could process twice as many pleas as trials on a given day, but this suggestion is quite misleading because of the considerable waiting time attributable to both trial and plea cases. With waiting time included, pleas required an average of fifty-five minutes and trials lasted eighty minutes, only 45% longer. On the basis of these figures, the move from a 90% to an 80% plea rate would require only a 4% increase in judicial capacity; a reduction to 70% would require only a 9% increase.[159] Moreover, when one allows for the resources already de-

[157] This is not the case when a defendant pleads guilty before the preliminary hearing, but such pleas appear to be quite rare in serious felony cases in Philadelphia. With respect to posttrial effort, we found that in our List program sample, sentencing was deferred in 43% of the guilty plea cases and in 55% of the bench trial cases ending in conviction. Although the samples are not large enough to control systematically for differences between cases in the two categories, the expected probability of presentence investigation does not appear to vary radically according to whether disposition is by trial or by plea.

[158] This calculation assumes that among 100 cases, the 90 resolved by plea would require 1800 minutes (20 minutes each) and the 10 resolved by bench trial would require 450 minutes (45 minutes each). On this basis the total court time required would be 2250 minutes at a 90% plea rate; it would rise by 11% to 2500 minutes (1600 minutes for 80 pleas and 900 minutes for 20 trials) at an 80% plea rate. Using the mean disposition times of 51 minutes for a bench trial and 22 minutes for a guilty plea, *see supra* notes 71 & 108, the shift from a 90% to an 80% plea rate would increase total court time by 12%.

[159] This calculation assumes that among 100 cases, the 90 resolved by plea would require 4950 minutes (55 minutes each) and the 10 resolved by trial would require 800 minutes (80

voted to the small number of jury trials, the proportional impact of a shift from guilty pleas to bench trials appears even less significant. Assuming that 5% of all cases are resolved by jury trial and that this figure would remain constant as bench trials increased, the move from a 90% to an 80% plea rate would require only a 3% increase in judicial capacity; a reduction to 70% would require only a 6% increase.[160]

It is worth stressing that these rough calculations are based entirely upon changes in resources required at the disposition stage. If judicial effort in the pretrial and posttrial phases were considered, the increase in overall judicial capacity needed to process greater numbers of trials would be considerably smaller than even the above figures suggest.[161]

To summarize, genuine trials were possible because even in rather complicated cases, an hour or so often afforded ample time for a formal trial, and most cases were quite straightforward, requiring even less time. For the simplest cases, testimony, cross-examination, and closing arguments could be completed in little more time than it would have taken to conduct a guilty plea colloquy and read the facts into the record. In short, case pressure does not make bargaining necessary, because in the great majority of cases a contested trial simply does not make unmanageable demands on court resources.

F. Implications

In America's fourth-largest city, there are relatively few inducements to plead guilty, most felony defendants do in fact claim a trial,

---

minutes each). On this basis the total court time required would be 5750 minutes at a 90% plea rate; it would rise by 4.3% to 6000 minutes (4400 minutes for 80 pleas and 1600 minutes for 20 trials) at an 80% plea rate. Using mean disposition times, *see supra* note 158, the required court time would rise by 4.8%.

[160] This calculation assumes that among 100 cases, the 90 resolved by plea would require 4950 minutes (55 minutes each), the five resolved by bench trial would require 400 minutes (80 minutes each), and the five resolved by jury trial would require 3600 minutes (an average of two days or 12 hours of trial time each). On this basis the total court time required would be 8950 minutes at a 90% rate; it would rise by 2.8% to 9200 minutes (4400 minutes for the 80 pleas, 1200 minutes for the 15 bench trials, and 3600 minutes for the five jury trials) at an 80% rate. Using mean disposition times, *see supra* note 158, the required court time would rise by 3.2%. The assumption of two days for the average jury trial is an arbitrary but possibly conservative estimate. One study showed that in Los Angeles the average felony jury trial lasted 7.2 days. *See* Langbein, *Torture and Plea Bargaining*, 46 U. CHI. L. REV. 3, 10 & n.18 (1978).

[161] One further qualification is necessary because of differences between cases in the plea and trial groups. Again, this qualification is one that most discussions of the resource problem seem to overlook. When trials average three days each and often take a week or more, the cases must be relatively complicated, even for jury trials. The move from a 10% to a 20% trial rate presumably would reduce the average time spent on contested trials, unless many complicated and debatable cases previously had been settled by plea. Because most Philadelphia guilty pleas occur in relatively simple cases that could be tried in less than 30 minutes, the 45-minute average for bench trials probably overstates the time that would be needed to try all cases in

and their cases are resolved in genuinely contested adversary proceedings. These findings cast some doubt on the widespread belief that case pressure or the behavioral dynamics of criminal litigation make plea bargaining inevitable. The next two Parts explore some of the important questions raised by these findings. Part III considers the possibility of transferring the Philadelphia approach to other jurisdictions and examines implications for the issues of practical plea bargaining reform. Part IV returns to broader questions about cooperation and other behavioral adaptations to the environment and institutions of criminal justice; it suggests the need to rework some of the theories that shape our understanding of litigation behavior, and it concludes by considering the relationship of those descriptive theories to society's normative conception of a just criminal process.

III. The Problem of Reform

Can plea bargaining be restricted or even eliminated? If so, how? Although the jury waiver system appears effective for one city, we cannot simply assume that this approach, which developed naturally in Philadelphia, can be successfully transferred, in all its particulars, to jurisdictions with different indigenous traditions. In this Part, I consider legal changes that other cities could adopt in order to become less dependent on plea bargaining.[162] Two questions must be faced. First, how can a system of jury waiver concessions be successfully structured in different legal settings? Second, within a system of inducements to elect bench trial, should a guilty plea earn a further concession, or can guilty plea concessions be abolished completely?

A. The Jury Waiver Concession

1. Some Alternative Mechanisms. — If bench trials are to be made attractive to defendants, the system must offer concessions in exchange for waiver of the right to a jury. The concessions could be either tacit or explicit and could be offered primarily by either the court or the prosecution. In Philadelphia, simple cases are channeled to a separate court program staffed by judges who are viewed as acceptable triers of fact (and as lenient sentencers).[163] Defendants opting for bench trial accept a higher likelihood of conviction in anticipation of a more lenient sentence. This system would likely work well in

---

the guilty plea group. The same would be true for any other city in which guilty pleas occur predominantly in straightforward or "dead bang" cases.

[162] I postpone until Part IV a discussion of the cultural and environmental considerations that can affect behavior within the framework of new legal rules. *See infra* pp. 1096–100, 1102–05.

[163] *See supra* pp. 1052, 1062–63.

many cities, but it might be unacceptable to courts that attempt to preserve for each judge a varied or individually managed calendar.

An alternative for such courts would be to allow individual judges to impose more lenient sentences after conviction in a bench trial. Tacit sentencing differentials of this kind are already thought to exist in some jurisdictions.[164] If restrictions on plea bargaining began to generate sharp increases in demands for jury trial, such differentials probably would become more common and would be much more effectively communicated to the defense bar. Sentencing concessions could also be extended at the initiative of prosecutors, who could use jury waiver agreements analogous to the now-familiar guilty plea agreement.[165]

Jurisdictions with mandatory or presumptive sentencing systems would face somewhat different problems. In some of these jurisdictions, however, the formal sentencing structures continue to allow significant variation in actual sentences: authorized sentencing ranges may be rather wide, aggravating and mitigating factors may be loosely defined, judges may retain some freedom to depart from the "presumptive" sentence, and control of sentencing through appellate review may be weak or nonexistent. These relatively flexible sentencing structures do not pose any obstacle to a practice of tacit jury waiver concessions.[166]

---

[164] *See, e.g.*, R. DAWSON, SENTENCING 181–82, 187–88 (1969); Tiffany, Avichai & Peters, *A Statistical Analysis of Sentencing in Federal Courts: Defendants Convicted After Trial, 1967–1968*, 4 J. LEGAL STUD. 369, 379–86 (1975). *But see* J. EISENSTEIN & H. JACOB, *supra* note 9, at 282–83 (after one controls for other variables, disposition mode explains very little of variance among sentences).

[165] A significant charge reduction before trial might complicate the prosecution's efforts to present an effective case on the lesser charges; conversely, dismissal of *lesser* charges would pose a problem if the higher counts could not be sustained at trial or on appeal. Accordingly, dismissal of lesser charges should be accomplished by an agreement that any sentence on such charges would run concurrently. A jury waiver agreement for dismissal of higher counts presumably should not take effect until after conviction on the lesser counts; if the judge convicted on the higher counts, the prosecution would be obliged to obtain the postconviction dismissal of those counts in order to sustain the validity of the jury waiver. *Cf.* Santobello v. New York, 404 U.S. 257 (1971) (holding that prosecution must honor terms of plea agreement or permit defendant to withdraw plea).

[166] For discussion of this point in connection with the related problem of preserving tacit guilty plea concessions under a regime of sentencing guidelines, see 1 S. SCHULHOFER, PROSECUTORIAL DISCRETION AND FEDERAL SENTENCING REFORM 44–46 (1979); 2 *id.* at 49–57.

Philadelphia's experience suggests that a system of jury waiver concessions can survive the introduction of a mandatory or guidelines sentencing system. Sentencing guidelines calling for more severe sentences (and not differentiating between bench and jury trials) have recently been adopted in Pennsylvania. *See* 42 PA. CONS. STAT. ANN. §§ 2151–2155 (Purdon 1981); 12 Pa. Admin. Bull. 431, 432 § 303.1(d) (1982). The guidelines, applicable to offenses committed after July 22, 1982, began to influence the processing of cases shortly after the completion of our study. In addition, a mandatory enhancement of at least 12 months for use of a deadly weapon took effect at the same time. *Id.* Because the guidelines and the enhancement together had the effect of raising the sentencing stakes in most cases while nominally obliterating the sen-

A more tightly restricted regime of presumptive or even mandatory sentencing would foreclose tacit sentencing concessions, but comparable results could be achieved by prosecutors who extended charging concessions or by bench trial judges who followed a practice of convicting only on certain lesser included offenses.[167] Alternatively, the legislature or its sentencing commission could authorize an explicit jury waiver concession as part of the official computation of the mandatory or presumptive sentence.[168] The candor of the latter approach would make it unconventional and even, for many, unpalatable; in my view it represents the most coherent solution.[169] Where unattainable ideals and unstated realities are preferred to coherence (that is, virtually everywhere in criminal justice), various forms of tacit inducement may be more likely to emerge and to function successfully.[170]

2. Constitutional Questions. — Whether tacit or express, are jury waiver concessions of any kind constitutionally permissible? Questions of constitutional doctrine in this area call for analysis of at least three elusive lines of decisions. First, the "unconstitutional condition" cases have involved situations in which the government offers some benefit on condition that the recipient forego the exercise of a constitutional

---

tencing differential between bench and jury trials, some Philadelphia court personnel predicted that the courts would be swamped with jury trial demands. To date, this has not happened, and changes in the basic patterns of disposition have been modest. The proportion of jury trials among all adjudications on the merits rose from 4.8% in the first half of 1982 and 4.6% in the second half to 6.9% in the first half of 1983. Over the same three periods, the bench trial rate held relatively steady (51.8%, 51.9%, and 51.3%), while the guilty plea rate declined slightly (43.3%, 43.6%, and 41.8%).

These modest changes in disposition patterns can be contrasted with the dramatic change in sentencing practice effected by the new laws. Over the same three six-month periods, there were steady increases in the percentage of convicted offenders sentenced to prison (48%, 52%, and 61%) and in the percentage receiving sentences in excess of two years (18%, 22%, and 25%). The persistence of a large number of jury waivers in the face of these substantial increases in sentence severity suggests that some significant inducements for choosing the bench trial route must have remained under the new sentencing regime.

[167] *See* 1 S. SCHULHOFER, *supra* note 166, at 31–33; Heumann & Loftin, *supra* note 30, at 425–27.

[168] *Cf., e.g.*, S. REP. No. 553, 96th Cong., 2d Sess. 1235–37 (1980) (proposing a comparable approach to provide incentives for pleading guilty in the context of a sentencing guidelines system).

[169] *See* Schulhofer, *Due Process of Sentencing*, 128 U. PA. L. REV. 733, 778–90, 800–13 (1980).

[170] Tacit inducements also tend to disguise the opportunities for punishment that society must relinquish in order to keep its procedural system functioning smoothly. In practice, however, no American jurisdiction provides prison facilities adequate to permit imposing the customary jury trial sentence on more than a small minority of offenders. In a sense, therefore, the level of sentencing severity that society actually "wants" may be best indicated by the lower penalties imposed on the more typical offender who waives his procedural rights. For a discussion of this question in connection with guilty plea concessions, see *id.* at 803–04, 810–11.

right. The trend has been to hold such conditions unconstitutional,[171] but the recent decisions are by no means uniform.[172] Second, the "vindictiveness" cases have held it impermissible for prosecutors or judges to deploy their charging and sentencing authority to "punish" defendants for exercising procedural rights.[173] The vindictiveness cases are problematic not only because they have ignored the apparent relevance of unconstitutional-condition principles, but also because the Supreme Court has not made clear the precise ingredients of "punishment" or "vindictiveness."[174] Third, the "plea bargaining" cases have upheld the use of sentencing concessions to induce pleas of guilty.[175] The plea bargaining cases appear consistent with one another, but commentators have found it difficult or impossible to reconcile them with the unconstitutional-condition cases and the vindictiveness cases.[176]

Given the current state of the case law in this area, the task of rationalizing the relevant decisions and bringing them to bear on the specific problem of jury waivers is a rather large one, and it might be pursued on many different levels of doctrinal or institutional analysis. Because my present purpose is limited to determining whether a jury waiver system is a viable reform option, I must confine my attention to the question whether, in light of the current state of the law, the courts would or should hold jury waiver concessions impermissible. Do such concessions involve "punishment" or an "unconstitutional condition," or are they analogous to guilty plea concessions and sustainable on that basis?

Although some scholars have treated the guilty plea cases as sui generis, the Court itself has sought a principled theory for distinguishing "vindictiveness" from plea bargaining and other permissible gov-

---

[171] *See, e.g.*, Lefkowitz v. Turley, 414 U.S. 70, 82–83 (1973); Sherbert v. Verner, 374 U.S. 398, 404–05 (1963); Speiser v. Randall, 357 U.S. 513, 528–29 (1958); Frost & Frost Trucking Co. v. Railroad Comm'n, 271 U.S. 583, 594 (1926).

[172] *See, e.g.*, Wyman v. James, 400 U.S. 309, 324 (1971) (upholding warrantless home visits by welfare caseworkers, in part on the ground that welfare recipients could legitimately be required to accept such intrusions as a condition of receiving government largesse).

[173] *See, e.g.*, Blackledge v. Perry, 417 U.S. 21, 27–29 (1974); North Carolina v. Pearce, 395 U.S. 711, 725 (1969).

[174] In several cases the Court has offered only elusive explanations for finding an absence of "vindictiveness" and thus upholding the imposition of heavier penalties that were a direct result of a defendant's decision to exercise constitutional rights. *See, e.g.*, United States v. Goodwin, 457 U.S. 368, 384 (1982); Chaffin v. Stynchcombe, 412 U.S. 17, 26–28 (1973); Colten v. Kentucky, 407 U.S. 104, 116 (1972).

[175] *See* Corbitt v. New Jersey, 439 U.S. 212, 219 (1978); Bordenkircher v. Hayes, 434 U.S. 357, 363 (1978); Blackledge v. Allison, 431 U.S. 63, 71 (1977); Brady v. United States, 397 U.S. 742, 750 (1970).

[176] *See* Halberstam, *Towards Neutral Principles in the Administration of Criminal Justice: A Critique of Supreme Court Decisions Sanctioning the Plea Bargaining Process*, 73 J. CRIM. L. & CRIMINOLOGY 1, 5–25 (1982); Schwartz, *The Limits of Prosecutorial Vindictiveness*, 69 IOWA L. REV. 127, 164–74 (1983).

ernmental responses to the exercise of constitutional rights. The distinctions that emerge from the Court's recent attempts all tend to support the legitimacy of jury waiver concessions.[177] Nonetheless, each of these potential distinctions poses enough problems of logic and precedent[178] to make dependence on a single analytical touchstone seem unwise.

---

[177] One justification for plea concessions that would not extend to jury waiver concessions was advanced in Brady v. United States, 397 U.S. 742, 753 (1970): the Court suggested that the defendant who pleads guilty demonstrates remorse and thus shows himself to be a more promising candidate for rehabilitation. But shortly after *Brady*, the Court made clear that guilty plea concessions remain permissible even when the defendant refuses to admit or affirmatively denies his guilt. North Carolina v. Alford, 400 U.S. 25, 37 (1970). The remorse factor, therefore, can no longer be considered essential to the legitimacy of these kinds of concessions. Other factors that the Court has found to distinguish plea bargaining from "vindictiveness" situations are discussed at *infra* note 178.

[178] The problem requires more extended analysis than I can attempt here. Four factors have been said to distinguish plea bargaining from vindictiveness:

(1) Advance Warning. — In Bordenkircher v. Hayes, 434 U.S. 357, 362–63 (1978), the Court distinguished its leading vindictiveness case, North Carolina v. Pearce, 395 U.S. 711 (1969), on the ground that in *Pearce* the increased sentence had not been announced in advance; "there is no such element of punishment or retaliation so long as the accused is free to accept or reject the prosecution's offer." From this perspective, jury waiver concessions announced in advance would likewise present "no such element of punishment or retaliation." This "take it or leave it" approach, however, is flatly inconsistent with the unconstitutional-condition cases, and it even fails to account for *Pearce* itself. *See* 395 U.S. at 723 ("[I]t would be a flagrant violation of the Fourteenth Amendment for a state trial court to follow an announced practice . . . .").

(2) Impersonal Motivations. — An important element in assessing the likelihood of vindictiveness has been the danger of what the Court has called personal "self-vindication" by the official who imposes the harsher sentence. *See* Chaffin v. Stynchcombe, 412 U.S. 17, 27 (1973). This danger would be absent in a jury waiver system. But the Court has also referred to broader "institutional" factors that would give rise to a presumption of impermissible vindictiveness. *See* United States v. Goodwin, 457 U.S. 368, 383 (1982); Schwartz, *supra* note 176, at 151, 157. The distinction between the vindictiveness cases and the plea bargaining cases therefore appears to turn on the perceived legitimacy of particular institutional motivations.

(3) Legitimate Institutional Interests. — The vindictiveness cases are prominently concerned with an "institutional bias against the retrial of a decided question," *Goodwin*, 457 U.S. at 383, an interest the Court plainly regards as illicit. The institutional interest in conserving resources is mentioned with disapproval in Blackledge v. Perry, 417 U.S. 21, 27–28 (1974); the Court there was concerned that a prosecutor might seek economies by deterring retrials that the system had otherwise committed itself to provide. If the Court was holding that efficiency objectives are illicit in general, its approach appears irreconcilable with the guilty plea cases. Presumably, the Court meant that the objective was illicit in the context of *Blackledge*, either because there was no systemic commitment to economizing by deterring retrials or because cutting costs in that fashion is especially suspect. On either rationale, a jury waiver system would be sustained.

(4) The Pretrial Context. — In *Goodwin*, 357 U.S. at 380–81, the Court distinguished *Bordenkircher* from the vindictiveness cases on the ground that the latter involved *posttrial* decisions, which the Court found "much more likely to be improperly motivated than . . . a pretrial decision." *Id.* at 381. *Goodwin* technically held only that there is no *presumption* of vindictiveness when a prosecutor files additional charges after a defendant scheduled for a bench trial elects a jury trial instead; a defendant can still prevail by "prov[ing] objectively that the prosecutor's charging decision was motivated by a desire to punish him." *Id.* at 384. *Goodwin* therefore appears to leave the jury waiver problem where it was before, tied to the uncertainties of determining when a response to the exercise of rights constitutes "punishment." Yet because

One recent commentator has suggested that the decisions approving plea bargaining ultimately rest on three premises: that the waiver of trial rights is truly voluntary, that the defendant's interests are protected by counsel, and that a defendant will not plead guilty unless he is guilty.[179] The Court appears to have embraced these highly debatable premises because it views efficient case processing as a valid state interest and plea bargaining as an essential means of pursuing that interest.[180] In any event, jury waiver concessions appear to satisfy even these more complex conditions of constitutional legitimacy. The waiver of a jury, made after proper inquiries in a formal colloquy, would satisfy the same voluntariness standard that a guilty plea does, and counsel would advise and protect the defendant. The reliability of the guilt-determining process would be even less suspect than in a guilty plea proceeding, because the conviction would rest on formal proof in open court. As in the guilty plea cases, the concessions system would not involve "punishment," because it would have both the purpose and the effect of furthering the state's legitimate interest in efficient processing of criminal charges.[181]

Beyond this kind of doctrinal analysis lie concerns about whether a system of jury waiver concessions would be unfair to defendants in its actual administration. Jury waiver concessions differ from guilty plea concessions in three striking ways. First, and most importantly, the defendant who waives a jury retains most of his significant adversary trial rights. Thus, although from the state's perspective the jury waiver concession has the same justification and most of the same advantages as does a guilty plea concession, the jury waiver concession entails far fewer dangers for the accused. Second, because the defendant who waives a jury gives up much less than does one who pleads guilty, the concession needed to induce the jury waiver will necessarily be smaller than that needed to induce a guilty plea in the same case.

Bordenkircher itself was not a presumptions case, but one involving proof of an explicit motive to deter the exercise of rights, the Court's stress on the pretrial context of *Bordenkircher* seems to imply not only a rejection of presumptions in that context, but also a different substantive conclusion, one that recognizes the legitimacy of the state's resource conservation interests in the area of pretrial procedure.

179 *See* Halberstam, *supra* note 176, at 25–35.

180 *Id.* at 35–36; *see supra* p. 1040.

181 In Commonwealth v. Siers, No. 7804-1869 (Philadelphia, Pa., Ct. C.P. Mar. 21, 1982), the court found as a fact that under the Philadelphia case assignment system, defendants are "much more likely to get a stiffer sentence from a jury judge than from a waiver [List program] judge," slip op. at 8, and that such "sentencing disparity is *used as a tool* to encourage defendants to waive their right to a jury trial," *id.* at 9 n.2 (emphasis added). Relying on the guilty plea cases, the court held that the Philadelphia system was constitutionally permissible. Commentary on the constitutional issues has seldom focused specifically on the jury waiver problem. The only recent discussion concludes not only that jury waiver concessions are constitutional, but also that the very availability of this approach renders guilty plea concessions constitutionally suspect even within the framework of the Court's own plea bargaining decisions. Note, *A New Waive*, *supra* note 1.

Third, jury waiver concessions are much less likely than guilty plea concessions to vary in attractiveness as the probability of acquittal changes from case to case; thus, the risk that excessive concessions may elude judicial control and endanger the innocent defendant is in practice much less serious than in the case of plea bargaining. Under these circumstances, a court willing to permit plea bargaining will be impelled a fortiori to sustain a system of jury waiver concessions designed to encourage disposition by bench trial rather than by guilty plea.[182]

To summarize, a system of jury waiver concessions would be feasible and constitutionally permissible. Once a jurisdiction has instituted such a system, should it permit any form of plea bargaining to survive?

B. The Future of Plea Bargaining

Although Philadelphia has not abolished plea bargaining completely, its experience supports in several ways the potential feasibility of total abolition. First, the data indicate that bargaining by trial prosecutors is not inevitable. The Philadelphia prosecutors complied with office policy that prevented bargaining in nearly all cases.[183] Our observations strongly suggest, moreover, that office policy could have effectively foreclosed the few areas remaining for negotiation. Second, tacit judicial sentencing concessions in exchange for guilty pleas are likewise not inevitable. The Philadelphia judges generally did not extend such concessions, and the criminal defense bar was fully aware of this.[184] Third, failures of adversariness are not inevitable on the defense side. In the absence of incentives to cooperate, Philadelphia defense counsel made the bench trial a genuinely contested proceeding.[185] Finally, contested trials will not inevitably create unmanageable case pressure; the study showed that large numbers of contested cases did not overwhelm the trial capacity of the system.[186]

---

[182] If the Supreme Court attempted to confine the principles of the plea bargaining cases to that context exclusively, it would have to confront the intermediate problem of a genuine "slow plea" — that is, a case in which a defendant, in return for sentencing concessions, waives his right to a jury and accepts a bench trial in which he facilitates the introduction of evidence and implicitly concedes his guilt. Because such a proceeding is the "functional equivalent" of a guilty plea, the induced waiver presumably falls within the *Brady* line of cases, *see supra* note 177, and the sentencing concessions are permissible. Should the sentencing concessions be regarded as impermissible, however, if the bench trial is not a sham but rather a genuinely contested proceeding? Can the state induce the defendant to accept a sham proceeding but not a genuine one? The Supreme Court would be hard pressed to rationalize an affirmative answer to these questions.

[183] *See supra* pp. 1057–60.

[184] *See supra* pp. 1060–61.

[185] *See supra* pp. 1083–84.

[186] *See supra* pp. 1084–86. The present study does not permit a direct estimate of the time required for trial in the relatively few "triable" cases in which concessions were deployed to

Thus, although Philadelphia itself does not provide a direct model for total abolition, its experience indicates that the conditions necessary for the successful abolition of plea bargaining are achievable. Bargaining by trial prosecutors and defenders can be stopped, tacit judicial concessions need not emerge to take its place, and contested trials can be provided within available resource constraints.

Even if jury waiver concessions and plea bargaining prohibitions are legally and administratively feasible, however, the particularities of courthouse culture remain to be reckoned with. Will attorneys actually adopt an adversarial stance in a bench trial system? Or will they simply find new ways to cooperate so that the functional equivalents of plea bargaining will reappear? Philadelphia defenders seem committed to an adversarial posture — but what accounts for that attitude, and under what conditions could it be expected to emerge elsewhere? The next Part explores these questions in light of the various organizational theories of the criminal process.[187]

IV. Some Problems for Theory

Why did the Philadelphia lawyers and judges choose not to mute their adversary behavior or to cooperate in disposing of the daily workload? Adversary behavior increases personal conflict among lawyers and judges and makes case outcomes less predictable. For these reasons alone, organizational theories of litigation predict an emphasis on cooperation.[188] Moreover, one might expect lawyers and judges to cooperate simply for the purpose of completing their work on time (or even ahead of time). Finally, cooperation tends to ease the burden on judges, who otherwise must resolve delicate reasonable doubt questions or assess witness credibility under circumstances that sometimes pose very difficult choices.

Behavioral theories do allow for variations in the extent of cooperation. For example, the model proposed by Eisenstein and Jacob[189]

obtain pleas. *See supra* pp. 1058–59, 1061–62. In addition, because of our focus on List program cases, we have no direct evidence of the potential trial time involved in the presumably more complicated cases resolved by guilty plea in the homicide and Calendar programs. Everything we learned about trial time suggests, however, that truly complex cases are rather infrequent and that even these cases can be resolved in a few hours in a bench trial. Further research undoubtedly would help put such impressions on a firmer footing, but there is no reason to assume that a total abolition of bargaining would drastically increase the need for judicial resources.

[187] If there are differences of "legal culture" and behavioral attitudes between Philadelphia and other cities, such differences could conceivably stem from factors other than those of organizational structure examined here. One might wish, for example, to compare different cities in terms of indicators of the education, social status, and economic class of judges, prosecutors, and defense attorneys.

[188] *See supra* pp. 1042–43.

[189] *See* J. Eisenstein & H. Jacob, *supra* note 9, at 24–28.

posits that degrees of adversariness and patterns of case disposition reflect the interaction of four general goals, two of them internally generated (reducing conflict and avoiding uncertainty) and two externally imposed (processing cases and doing justice). One might conclude that adversary behavior persists in Philadelphia because the goal of doing justice is so strong that it trumps all the others. But such an interpretation is simply a postulate that reconciles observations with the theoretical model. If the model is to be verifiable or to have any predictive value, then "doing justice" and other goals must be conceived as independent variables that reflect structural or cultural givens, and not simply as residual concepts devised to explain patterns of disposition that are already known. Can we therefore independently predict the circumstances under which "doing justice" will outweigh other goals?

Organizational theories suggest that the structure of the courtroom work group is likely to affect the relative priorities that participants ascribe to such internal goals as reducing conflict and avoiding uncertainty. When attorneys are assigned to individual cases and seldom confront the same opponent or judge from one case to the next, relationships are slow to develop and less important for participants to preserve. Cooperative behavior is therefore said to be less likely than in stable courtroom work groups in which the same team — prosecutor, defender, and judge — processes a flow of cases all day or all week.[190] Again, however, theory is confounded by observation, because Philadelphia prosecutors and defenders are assigned to a given courtroom for an entire week or longer.[191] Why were internally generated goals relatively weak, even in these stable courtroom work groups? Why were adversarial attitudes and the notion of "doing justice" so strong?

To see whether such questions can be explored in terms of a more refined behavioral analysis, I will consider first the general framework of organizational theory employed by criminal justice scholars. I will then examine adversariness and cooperation as they have developed in Philadelphia and as they have been portrayed in the other cities where "slow pleas" are said to predominate. Finally, I will turn from the attitudes of courtroom participants and consider instead some problems of perspective and attitude in the behavioral studies themselves.

---

[190] *See id.* at 35–37, 61, 244–51.

[191] *See supra* pp. 1052–53. Private attorneys do move in and out of courtrooms without developing stable work group relationships, and we found such attorneys to be more adversarial in their courtroom style than the typical public defender. What struck us, however, was that the demeanor of the private attorneys often seemed unnecessarily adversarial in the context of a bench trial. Factors other than the unstable work group relationships appeared to be responsible for this phenomenon. *See supra* p. 1069.

A. *The Framework of Organizational Analysis*

Most organizational analyses of criminal justice draw on a well-developed body of industrial and public administration theory in which cooperation has been treated in relatively qualified, contingent terms. Within industrial firms, the importance of such goals as stability and certainty (and in turn the importance of cooperation) varies widely; in high-technology industries that depend on constant innovation, for example, firms are likely to value change and to deemphasize stability.[192] Relationships among firms display similar diversity. Although competing firms frequently attempt to cooperate, organizational analysts also find many instances in which the traditional norms of vigorous competition prevail. Indeed, public or charitable agencies, though in one sense free of the profit motive, often prove to be vigorous "competitors"; these organizations, no less than profit-oriented firms, may strive ruthlessly to control scarce resources and power.[193]

The persistent tension between the norms of cooperation and competition and the continuing importance of the latter in both public agencies and private sector firms appear to have receded from sight when organizational theories have been transposed to the criminal justice setting.[194] Organizational analysts typically have assumed that the members of a criminal justice "work group" share goals that can be pursued cooperatively, and do not value goals that can be realized only at the expense of other participants.

The general body of organizational theory does not compel this view. Indeed, it suggests the contrary possibility — that the conventional competitive (or "adversarial") norm may strongly affect behavior in many diverse settings. In the next Sections, I wish to explore factors that may explain the apparent ascendancy of the adversarial norm in Philadelphia's courtrooms, and to consider why organizational theorists working specifically in criminal justice seem to have given so little attention to this sort of phenomenon.

B. *The Philadelphia Background*

Resistance to bargaining and reliance on bench trial have a long history in Philadelphia. Since at least the 1960's, the disposition pattern has remained relatively stable: 30% to 40% guilty pleas, 1% to 6% jury trials, and 50% to 60% bench trials. Under District Attorney Arlen Specter (1965–1973), plea bargaining was very unusual

---

192 *See* C. PERROW, *supra* note 8, at 42–47, 89–91.

193 *See id.* at 127–30. For a provocative effort to unpack some of the elements conducive to cooperative and competitive modes of behavior, see M. SHERIF, O. HARVEY, B. WHITE, W. HOOD & C. SHERIF, INTERGROUP CONFLICT AND COOPERATION: THE ROBBERS CAVE EXPERIMENT (1961).

194 *See supra* pp. 1042–43.

except in homicide cases.[195] When District Attorney F. Emmett Fitzpatrick assumed office in 1974, changes were instituted. Fitzpatrick apparently favored bargaining as a way to increase efficiency and the conviction rate. He also faced a sudden caseload "crisis" because a new speedy trial rule, effective in 1974,[196] mandated prompt disposition of a large inventory of pending cases. Under Fitzpatrick's explicit encouragement, bargaining became more common in the Philadelphia courts, and the guilty plea rate jumped sharply. From a level of 33% in 1973, the rate rose to 49% in 1974 and continued to rise thereafter. By 1977, the last year of the Fitzpatrick administration, the guilty plea rate had reached what, for Philadelphia, seemed an astronomically high figure — 52% of all dispositions on the merits.[197]

The "wheeling and dealing" of the Fitzpatrick era drew much criticism and became an issue in Fitzpatrick's 1977 reelection campaign. Opponents charged both favoritism toward well-connected defendants and undue leniency by assistant district attorneys, who were free to "give away the store" in "routine" burglaries and robberies. When a new district attorney, Edward Rendell, assumed office in 1978, efforts to restrict bargaining again became an explicit priority. The guilty plea rate dropped from 52% in 1977 to 40% in 1978, and it has since remained in the 40%–45% range.

What happened to the bench trial during this period? We know that bench trials were genuinely contested proceedings as of 1982.[198] Were earlier perceptions of these trials as "slow pleas" simply inaccurate, or did the character of the trials change? A precise picture of the earlier period is difficult to reconstruct, but our interviews, together with impressions reported by previous observers, suggest that in all likelihood some significant changes did take place. Even in the 1960's, a majority of bench trials probably were contested, but cooperative behavior and "slow pleas" sometimes occurred.[199] The fif-

---

[195] *See* Specter, Book Review, 76 YALE L.J. 604, 605 (1967) (reviewing D. NEWMAN, CONVICTION: THE DETERMINATION OF GUILT OR INNOCENCE WITHOUT TRIAL (1966)).

[196] PA. R. CRIM. P. 1100.

[197] The figures indicate guilty pleas as a percentage of all Common Pleas dispositions by plea, jury trial, or bench trial. If dismissals and nol pros decisions are included, the guilty plea rate is lower — 40% at its peak in 1977 and only 27% in 1973.

[198] *See supra* pp. 1083–84 .

[199] Four sources provide subjective but useful impressions concerning the tone of the earlier Philadelphia bench trials. All four tend to support the view that adversarial behavior has always been common:

(1) Professor Welsh White's observations suggested that, as of the late 1960's, at least 15% of the Philadelphia dispositions — or 25%–30% of the bench trials — were "slow pleas." *See supra* p. 1048. Because White's discussion referred to misdemeanors as well as felonies, the incidence of "slow pleas" in the latter category might have been even lower.

(2) Observations by Albert Alschuler in 1968 and in 1977 corroborate White's impressions of significant numbers of "slow pleas" but a heavy predominance of adversary trials. *See* Alschuler, *supra* note 2, at 1034–42.

(3) A student study carried out during the summer of 1967, though not focused on the "slow

teen-year period before 1982 appears to have been marked by an overall increase in preparedness and professionalism among counsel, growing formality in the courtroom, and increasingly adversarial relationships.[200]

The Fitzpatrick years, 1974 to 1977, are of special interest because of the deliberate change in plea bargaining policy during this period. Prevailing assumptions about the inevitability of bargaining suggest that when plea rates are low, bench trials are not likely to be genuinely contested. When plea rates rise sharply and trial rates correspondingly decline, as happened in 1974, one might expect sham proceedings to become less common among the remaining bench trials. Conversely, when plea rates drop sharply, as happened in 1978, one might expect "slow pleas" to become common again in ostensibly contested trials.

Although an accurate empirical estimate of trends in cooperation between 1974 and 1978 is scarcely possible, impressions reported to us suggest that the expected changes did not occur. In fact, the general perception is that the changes were almost exactly the opposite of those one might have predicted. Defenders remember the Fitzpatrick period as a time of relatively harmonious relationships with prosecutors, and cooperation in various forms was not uncommon. In contrast, the firm antibargaining policies instituted in 1978 became a source of irritation and frustration for defenders. Assistant district attorneys no longer had anything to give them, and the defenders became much less cooperative as a result. Defenders' relationships with the District Attorney's Office currently are said to be at an alltime

---

plea" issue, also suggests that most trials were vigorously contested. The researchers reported: "[E]ven attorneys assigned not by case but by courtroom are willing to press matters as hard as necessary when the situation warrants. Particularly common, for example, is the sight of a Defender attorney . . . doggedly making a record for appeal despite obvious judicial impatience." Comment, *Client Service in a Defender Organization: The Philadelphia Experience*, 117 U. PA. L. REV. 448, 469 (1969).

(4) Uhlman and Walker's research on "Metro City" (that is, Philadelphia — *see supra* notes 87 & 89) focused primarily on statistical analysis, but the authors also conducted interviews with "Metro City" attorneys and court personnel. Though the date of research is not given, the interviews presumably took place after 1974. Uhlman and Walker report:

> [W]hile "slow pleas" may have been more prevalent in the past and may still arise with some frequency in misdemeanor courts, few, if any, felony bench trials are nonadversarial. . . . A public defender noted, "After the fact, if the defendant is found guilty it may look like a slow plea, but the defense is doing the best it can with limited legal tools."

Uhlman & Walker, *supra* note 89, at 222.

[200] Just before Gideon v. Wainwright, 372 U.S. 335 (1963), the Defender Association's professional staff consisted of six attorneys. By July 1967, 36 attorneys were employed, along with 10 investigators and a social worker. *See* Comment, *supra* note 199, at 448 & n.3. These attorneys had responsibility for a caseload not significantly smaller than that of today. (Total filings have increased somewhat, but more minor cases are diverted to Municipal Court because of an expansion of that court's jurisdiction.) Defenders normally received 10 to 20 files the night before trial, and opportunities for preparation were minimal. Following resolution of a funding crisis and reorganization of the Defender Association in 1969, its staff expanded dramatically, and preparation time was explicitly built into the defenders' work schedules beginning in the mid-1970's.

low. Understandably, the "tough," aggressive stance of the prosecutors has elicited corresponding attitudes from defense counsel. In short, it seems probable that tight restrictions on bargaining and a sharp drop in the guilty plea rate have actually sharpened the adversarial tone and content of the rising numbers of trials.

Against this background we may identify several factors that have contributed to an environment conducive to genuinely adversarial trials:

(1) Overt prosecutorial plea bargaining has long been discouraged and, to an extent, viewed with suspicion. Specific political developments and a general public demand for greater consistency and severity in punishment have combined to reinforce that tradition.

(2) Because trials are expeditious, judges do not feel strong pressure to induce pleas through overt or tacit concessions. At the same time, penalties for unduly adversarial trial behavior are inhibited by two circumstances: sentences are subject to appellate review; and before imposing significant prison terms, judges traditionally order presentence investigations, which delay sentencing for many weeks and thus give time for any feelings about irritating trial tactics to recede into the background.

(3) Aggressive prosecutorial policies and refusals to compromise have engendered equally uncooperative attitudes among defense counsel.

(4) A well-run public defender's office affords trial attorneys an opportunity to consider and prepare possible defenses and thereby alleviates cognitive pressure to see cases as hopeless.[201]

(5) Partly as a result of the foregoing factors and partly for independent reasons, trial attorneys cannot win respect or professional advancement primarily on the strength of their ability to be easygoing, cooperative, or nice to work with. Within both the District Attorney's Office and the Defender Association, promotion to the most respected and challenging assignments — felony jury trials — requires demonstrated competence in traditional adversarial trial skills. Like-

[201] The attorneys who described to Milton Heumann the utter hopelessness of most criminal cases, *see supra* pp. 1043–44, were themselves hopelessly overburdened. The Connecticut state caseload reported by Heumann was roughly one-third to one-half of the Philadelphia totals for serious felony cases (processed in the Connecticut Superior Court) and roughly twice the Philadelphia totals for misdemeanors and less serious felonies (processed in the Connecticut Circuit Court). To handle these cases there were, at the time of Heumann's study, only 39 defenders (15 part-time) assigned to the Circuit Court and only 17 defenders (12 part-time) assigned to the Superior Court. Thus, for the serious felony cases processed in the Superior Court, there were only five full-time defenders for the entire state of Connecticut. *See* M. HEUMANN, *supra* note 3, at 8–9, 27, 34. To process two to three times as many serious felony cases (but only half the number of less serious cases), Philadelphia had 104 full-time defenders, together with a substantial professional support staff. *See supra* pp. 1051, 1053. For recommendations concerning maximum caseloads per attorney in public defender systems, see NATIONAL STUDY COMM'N ON DEFENSE SERVS., NAT'L LEGAL AID & DEFENDER ASS'N, GUIDELINES FOR LEGAL DEFENSE SYSTEMS IN THE UNITED STATES 286–88 (1976).

wise, to move successfully into private practice, and particularly into lucrative civil litigation, an attorney needs to establish a reputation for forceful, effective trial advocacy. Neither professional success nor self-respect can be built on a reputation as a well-liked "pushover."

Is this array of factors unique and unreproducible? To be sure, certain elements seem distinctive and historically fortuitous. But what is most striking about the list is simply its comfortable, almost banal conformity with the assumptions, attitudes, and incentive structures of legal professionalism within the conventional adversary model. Most of the factors mentioned might have been thought pervasive and virtually inescapable rather than unique to Philadelphia. Organizational theorists of criminal justice have so forcefully propounded the inevitability of cooperation that it can seem surprising to encounter the most ordinary components of the adversary tradition.[202]

Even if Philadelphia is an aberration, its experience nonetheless suggests the great vulnerability of theories that assume the inevitability of cooperation. There are grounds for suspecting, moreover, that Philadelphia may not be unique. When earlier "slow plea" studies are reexamined in light of the Philadelphia material, doubts about the strength of their findings emerge. Just as, in the theoretical models of criminal justice, qualifications concerning the importance of competitive norms have been pushed aside, so in the empirical studies, qualifications and exceptions to the "slow plea" hypothesis seem gradually to have dropped from sight.

C. The "Slow Plea" Studies

Professor Welsh White, one of the first scholars to explore the "slow plea" concept, suggested cautiously in a 1971 article that a significant portion of the Philadelphia bench trials were "slow pleas."[203] Professor Lynn Mather's analysis of Los Angeles builds on White's article and preserves its cautious tone. Describing the prior studies, Professor Mather states only that "many" of the Philadelphia trials were "slow pleas." Her own conclusions for Los Angeles indicate that pretrial suppression hearings were "quite adversarial," that many bench trials were fully adversary proceedings, and that even some of the stipulated "S.O.T." trials were "semi-adversary" proceedings.[204] Thus, although Mather does conclude that "most S.O.T. trials [were]

[202] *See also* Rubinstein & White, *supra* note 25, at 371–72 (noting that after Alaska's plea bargaining ban, prosecutors worked much harder but enjoyed their jobs more).

[203] White, *supra* note 40, at 441–42; *see supra* p. 1048. In an earlier and even more cautious discussion, Jerome Skolnick observed, in the California city of "Westville," a "fixed" trial or "slow plea of guilty" in which "the presumed antagonists merely put on a show." Skolnick, *supra* note 9, at 53, 66. But Skolnick warned that "[r]eliable statistics on 'fixed' trials are, of course, impossible to obtain, and prudence prevents an observer from even speculating on the proportions of such trials." *Id.*

[204] *See* Mather, *supra* note 43, at 190–93, 195–96.

really 'slow pleas' of guilty,"[205] she does not attempt to quantify the exact proportion, and she makes clear that adversarial behavior persisted to a considerable degree.

Martin Levin's 1977 discussion of Pittsburgh trials makes stronger claims. Levin still allows for possible exceptions, but he finds "[a]lmost all" the bench trials to be "slow pleas."[206] Levin does not explain how he estimated the frequency of such dispositions, but in the examples he gives, the "slow plea" characterization for Pittsburgh bench trials does seem relatively apt.

The Baltimore study, by Eisenstein and Jacob, raises many more questions. Going one step beyond Levin, Eisenstein and Jacob seem to drop any qualification to the "slow plea" characterization: "In Baltimore, bench trials became a functional equivalent to the guilty plea . . . ."[207] Once again, there are no quantitative estimates of frequency to buttress the strong "slow plea" claim. In this instance, moreover, even the internal evidence fails to support fully the "slow plea" characterization. The only trial described is a hypothetical composite in which an unsuccessful suppression motion is followed by brief presentation of evidence (including alibi testimony by the defendant) and brief closing arguments in a proceeding that lasts a total of fifty minutes.[208] The authors report frequent judicial questioning of witnesses but do not evaluate or even mention the nature of any cross-examination by defense counsel. In addition, their account seems to ignore the possible implications of the suppression motion, which the trial option presumably served to preserve for appeal.[209] One cannot by any means dismiss Eisenstein and Jacob's impressions as irrelevant, but from the evidence they themselves present, it seems far from certain that the Baltimore trials were nothing more than "slow pleas."

The most recent of the "slow plea" studies, Heumann and Loftin's 1979 discussion of Detroit bench trials, displays similar problems. From the initial, cautious presentation by Professor White, the "slow plea" hypothesis seems to have grown in the telling; in Heumann and Loftin's article, it assumes a status approaching that of scientific law: "The waiver, or bench, trial is simply a 'trial' in which the defendant waives his right to a jury and elects to go to 'trial' before a judge alone. . . . These 'trials' resemble slow pleas of guilty far more than any standard conception of a trial."[210] The authors conclude that

---

[205] *Id.* at 195; *see supra* note 44.

[206] M. LEVIN, *supra* note 38, at 80; *see supra* p. 1048 & note 42.

[207] J. EISENSTEIN & H. JACOB, *supra* note 9, at 250.

[208] *See id.* at 68, 71–72.

[209] Even the reported length of trial suggests, in light of Philadelphia practice, that these may not have been sham proceedings. The authors estimated that the average Baltimore bench trial (a "slow plea" in their view) lasted roughly one to two hours. *Id.* at 250.

[210] Heumann & Loftin, *supra* note 30, at 417, 420; *see supra* p. 1049. In support of their description, Heumann and Loftin refer to the earlier studies by Levin, Eisenstein & Jacob, and

Detroit bench trials fit this pattern, but once again, the evidence they offer seems equivocal in light of the Philadelphia findings. Heumann and Loftin quote one prosecutor who describes a waiver trial as "just one of those walk-through numbers. . . . [I]t's all arranged really between the judge and the defense attorney beforehand."[211] If this cynical account can be accepted at face value, the "slow plea" label is of course entirely apt. In support of the same hypothesis, however, the authors cite a quite different interview with a judge. They stress his response to questions about the time factor (jury trial takes about a day, a guilty plea fifteen minutes, and a waiver trial half an hour) and quote his description of truncated procedures: "Both sides waive opening arguments, examination of witnesses is very brief, no tricks are done because there's no jury there. . . . [H]alf the time they don't make any closing arguments . . . and there's no time spent for jury selection."[212] From this report it is much less clear that the proceeding has diverged from "any standard conception of a trial"; only the waiver of closing argument suggests a failure of vigorous advocacy.[213] Once again, we cannot say that the authors' impressions are necessarily mistaken, but much more evidence seems needed to support the strong "slow plea" assertions that they make. The degree and frequency of cooperation cannot really be determined from the material they present, and in fact some of the material suggests that certain essentials of a genuine contest may have been preserved.

D. Perspectives on Cooperation and Its Literature

The evidence on Detroit, Baltimore, Pittsburgh, and Los Angeles not only leaves room for doubt about the pervasiveness of cooperation in those cities; it also suggests some problems with the "slow plea" studies themselves. The seeming tendency to exaggerate cooperation may stem in part from a lack of legal training among some of the researchers — the implications of attorney behavior that preserved points for appeal or understated a point for tactical advantage were not always appreciated.[214] More significant and more revealing, how-

Mather, and then explain: "Mather argues that 'trials' on submission of the preliminary hearing transcript in Los Angeles are really nothing other than 'slow pleas of guilty.'" Heumann & Loftin, *supra* note 30, at 420 n.40. Mather's actual discussion is more nuanced. *See supra* pp. 1100–01. In an earlier study, Heumann's own analysis allowed more room for the existence of the "nonconformist attorney" who, though distinctly in the minority, might nevertheless survive and persist in his desire to try cases rather than systematically settle them. *See* M. HEUMANN, *supra* note 3, at 164–65.

[211] Heumann & Loftin, *supra* note 30, at 418.

[212] *Id.* at 417.

[213] Several courts, for example, have held that it is permissible to deny defense counsel the opportunity to make an opening statement, even in a jury trial. *See, e.g.*, United States v. Salovitz, 701 F.2d 17, 18–20 (2d Cir. 1983).

[214] Interestingly, social scientist Lynn Mather noted some of these qualifications in one of

ever, is the way in which the jury trial model seems to color the entire analysis. When a proceeding lacks the paraphernalia and imagery that our legal mythology associates with "Trial" (elaborate jury selection, dramatic opening and closing statements, artful cross-examination, "tricks"), and when the proceeding consumes little more time than that required for a guilty plea, observers have difficulty treating the proceeding as a trial at all. In effect, we become trapped by the powerful imagery of jury trial: the full-fledged version seems much too time consuming for everyday use, but any streamlining appears to sacrifice the very essence of trial. Indeed, the inefficiency of jury trial may *be* its essence in common understanding; an efficient proceeding of any kind is automatically seen, in this conception, as the "functional equivalent" of a guilty plea.

One other factor may have been at work in the building and testing of many of the criminal litigation theories. We have seen that important qualifications and exceptions were clearly recognized in the early literature on cooperation and in early work on "slow pleas." Over time these limitations received less and less attention until they virtually disappeared from the literature. We have also seen that the empirical evidence did not compel this disregard of possible qualifications, and that researchers even tended to deemphasize evidence suggesting exceptions to the perceived pattern. Of course, the flaws of earlier studies may suggest nothing more than the inevitable imperfections of any body of research (the present study included). Still, one must wonder whether any more fundamental considerations account for the apparent tendency of researchers to accept incomplete evidence and to deemphasize exceptions and qualifications that had once been stressed.

On the surface, plea bargaining and cooperation between prosecution and defense appear sharply at odds with American legal ideals.[215] It was only natural that courts long sought ways to disre-

the earlier studies. *See* Mather, *supra* note 43, at 195. We must not overlook the possibility that legally trained observers may in turn *over*estimate the practical import of ritualized legal maneuvering. *Cf.* Goldstein, Book Review, 1 LAW & SOC'Y REV. 148, 151 (1966) (reviewing H. KALVEN & H. ZEISEL, THE AMERICAN JURY (1966)) (noting that when judges characterize the thinking of jurors, "it is impossible to tell whether the judges are doing any more than attributing to jurors the feelings and sentiments that judges expect jurors to have," and that, "[a]s a result, the risk is very great that the entire research design is confined by a stereotype borrowed by the judges from the lawyer-culture"). With respect to the present study, the attempt to check measures of legal "effort" against actual results, *see supra* pp. 1076–81, provides a partial safeguard against bias of this kind.

[215] The association of plea bargaining with cooperation requires some qualification. Just as a formal trial can involve cooperative behavior (a "slow plea"), so plea negotiators may on occasion engage in relatively aggressive, adversarial bargaining tactics. *See, e.g.*, P. UTZ, *supra* note 1, at 41–87 (describing highly adversarial behavior of San Diego plea bargainers). We are therefore impelled to recognize varying degrees of cooperativeness within the diverse behavior patterns that pass for "plea bargaining." Even at its most "adversarial" extreme, however, bargaining necessarily entails a search for a mutually acceptable outcome, and this effort to find

gard the existence of these practices. When they could no longer do so, it might have seemed equally natural for courts, practitioners, and scholars to look very skeptically at alleged justifications for the deviation from tradition and to work tirelessly to bring practice back into conformity with prevailing ideals. That this did not happen is undoubtedly explained in part by problems of case pressure that are by no means imaginary; from the evidence available, some observers understandably viewed bargaining as inevitable and accordingly came to see "legitimization of bargaining through standards and judicial oversight"[216] as an essential strategy for containing the damage to our aspirations. More puzzling is the fact that the legitimation of bargaining seems to have proceeded in the face of doubts about the extent of case pressure and the inevitability of cooperation; strong claims for the necessity of bargaining have even tended to suppress awareness of those doubts. Do plea bargaining and cooperation hold some more basic attraction, beyond their value as adaptations to the real problems of case pressure?

Though on one level plea bargaining has always seemed unnatural, at odds with our ideals, in a more fundamental sense the opposite is probably the case. Our ideals include, of course, the norms of the adversary system. But "[t]he essence of the adversary system is challenge[,] . . . a constant, searching, and creative questioning of official decisions and assertions of authority at all stages."[217] Such a system cannot — should not — be a very pleasant one for officials seeking to exercise authority. We assume that an adversary system will nonetheless command the allegiance of society at large, but we also know that this assumption is based more on hope than on experience. Vigorous, unrelenting challenge to authority can only be viewed with ambivalence, if not hostility, by the communities for whom those in authority are attempting to act; the essentials of the adversary system have needed constitutional protection precisely for this reason.[218]

Under these circumstances, it is the adversary system itself that may seem unattractive and even unnatural, not simply for members of a courtroom "work group," but for much of the community at large. In its constant probing and questioning, adversary behavior deliberately seeks to sow doubt — doubt about the facts, doubt about the law, doubt about the propriety and legitimacy of punishment, doubt about the probity and fairness of constituted authority at every level. These doubts must, in the nature of things, prove unfounded

common ground sets bargaining behavior apart from the noncooperative behavior of adversaries in a fully contested trial.

[216] H. MILLER, W. MCDONALD & J. CRAMER, *supra* note 39, at vi.

[217] U.S. ATTORNEY GENERAL'S COMM., POVERTY AND THE ADMINISTRATION OF FEDERAL CRIMINAL JUSTICE 11 (1963).

[218] The recent history of fading public support for legal services on the civil side provides one of many possible illustrations of this phenomenon.

a good deal of the time. Thus, the impulse to disapprove conflict and to embrace cooperative modes of dispute resolution develops strength not only within the courtroom, but also on a much broader social and political front.[219] Even the detached, scholarly observer can record, with all accuracy, that adversary behavior is irritating, inefficacious, and even, in important senses, unnecessary.[220]

Is it not better for society to encourage opponents to negotiate in a spirit of shared interests and values? Is it not better if the defendant admits his guilt so that we need not doubt it ourselves? Is it not better if he accepts the punishment, or actually welcomes it as a "good deal"?

Even if one is prepared, as plea bargaining proponents are, to defend the particulars of the process that generates the defendant's acceptance of punishment, the essential point is that once defended and legitimated, the process no longer commands specific attention case by case. What remains — highly visible and directly experienced every day — is the fact that both sides see eye to eye, know "what the case is worth," and come to terms that all accept. Bargaining, from this perspective, is functional not only for the immediate participants, but also for an entire community that no longer needs to justify, on any substantive ground, its decisions to inflict suffering on individual citizens. The legitimation of bargaining in turn legitimates, at one stroke, every individual instance of criminal punishment.

In this move from adversariness, only one thing is lost — the vigorous probing and questioning that, in their very unpleasantness, have been thought to serve a crucial function in the preservation of freedom. One can, of course, question that view; many civilized nations have rejected it. But within the American constitutional tradition, the assumption remains:

> [A] system of justice that provides inadequate opportunities to challenge official decisions is not only productive of injuries to individuals, but is itself a threat to the state's security and the larger interests of the community. . . . [T]he loss in vitality of the adversary system . . . significantly endangers the basic interests of a free community.[221]

---

[219] The movement to promote "informal" methods of dispute resolution reflects the impact of such impulses across a wide range of diverse legal matters. *See supra* note 1. These attitudes about potential "disputes" have a place within wider trends in contemporary social theory. The rejection of adversarial conflict and the tendency to embrace informality and cooperation should be compared to the attention paid to sources of stability and cohesion in, for example, the work of Talcott Parsons, *e.g.*, T. PARSONS, SOCIOLOGICAL THEORY AND MODERN SOCIETY (1967), and should be contrasted with the emphasis on conflict in, for example, the work of C. Wright Mills, *e.g.*, C. MILLS, THE POWER ELITE (1956). *See* P. BACHRACH & M. BARATZ, POWER AND POVERTY 3–16, 39–51 (1970); A. GOULDNER, THE COMING CRISIS OF WESTERN SOCIOLOGY 210–337 (1970).

[220] *See, e.g.*, P. UTZ, *supra* note 1, at 137–48.

[221] U.S. ATTORNEY GENERAL'S COMM., *supra* note 217, at 11.

If one accepts the importance of vigorous challenge within an overall scheme of limited government, then the attractions of cooperation and bargaining, though understandable, must be resisted. The questions facing the various bodies of cooperation theory may therefore be something like the following. First, if cooperation is not inevitable, does the case for legitimating it actually rest on an unspoken premise that cooperation is desirable? Second, if the case for cooperation is to be put in terms of desirability, from what societal perspective is that case to be made? Is the claim simply the plausible but unremarkable one that muted adversariness serves the interests of the community's prevailing social and political coalitions? Or can the claim address the more problematic but essential question whether the loss of vigorous adversary behavior in the long run threatens the foundations of legal control over organized governmental power? Finally, if a vigorous adversary system is worth preserving, under what conditions can the impulses toward cooperation be defeated — in the courtroom and, more importantly, in the wider political community?[222]

V. Conclusion

From repeated pronouncements of the Supreme Court and a near-unanimity of scholarly opinion, we have learned that most felony cases are devoid of triable issues of fact or law; that a contested trial in such cases is therefore a needless waste of resources; that affording most defendants a contested trial is in any event wholly beyond the capacity of any American urban jurisdiction; and finally that even if we could somehow, heroically, make genuine trials available, opposing attorneys would nonetheless find ways to cooperate and would settle cases by negotiation anyway. It follows from all this that plea bargaining need not clash with due process values, that it is in any event inevitable, and that one had best accept this reality, make one's peace with it, and work to legitimate the plea bargaining process and to ameliorate its harshest effects.

The present study throws each of these assumptions into question. It shows that in America's fourth-largest city, no concessions of any kind are offered for guilty pleas in the great majority of felony cases. In the absence of concessions, most felony defendants do in fact demand a trial, and their cases are resolved in genuinely contested adversary proceedings. Many of these cases turn out to involve difficult, debatable questions of fact or law, and many defendants win

---

[222] The effort to situate bargaining and discretionary justice within the entirety of criminal justice institutions, legal and political, raises related questions that I have tentatively explored elsewhere. Schulhofer, *supra* note 169, at 757–90, 798–820; Schulhofer, Book Review, 68 Calif. L. Rev. 181, 196–201 (1980) (reviewing G. Fletcher, Rethinking Criminal Law (1978)).

acquittal or substantial charge reduction — results that in nearly all cases reflect not intuitive or off-the-cuff compromise, but the considered application of law to facts proved in open court.

Plea bargaining is not inevitable. In most American cities, judges and attorneys have *chosen* to process cases that way. The Supreme Court has chosen to tolerate, to legitimate, and finally to encourage the plea bargaining system. We can instead choose, if we wish, to afford criminal defendants a day in court. We can cease imposing a price, in months or years of incarceration, upon defendants who exercise that privilege, and can instead permit or even encourage defendants to ask for a hearing in which they may put the prosecution to its proof. We can make available a formal bench trial that permits the expeditious but fair and accurate resolution of criminal cases on the basis of public testimony, tested and challenged with the traditional tools of American adversary procedure. If we nevertheless continue to tolerate plea bargaining, that choice will not tell us that resources are too scarce or that *other* lawyers, those over there in court, are impatient with zealous advocacy and uncontrollably drawn to more comfortable modes of work. A choice to prefer plea bargaining to an inexpensive, feasible adversary trial will instead tell us a great deal about ourselves.

[13]

Rules of Evidence in the Sentencing Process

MARTIN WASIK

Both in criminal justice practice and traditional academic writing, a sharp line is drawn between the trial and sentencing stages in an enquiry into criminal guilt.[1] The evidential and procedural constraints which apply at the former stage are well known—they constitute the normal rules of criminal evidence and procedure. This stage, which is characterised by an adversarial trial before a bench of magistrates or a judge and jury, and which is governed by strict rules of relevance, admissibility and proof of evidence, ends with the finding of guilty or not guilty. If guilt is established then the court moves on to the sentencing stage, where very different considerations are said to apply. The jury has, by and large, no further role to play,[2] the enquiry about the defendant becomes far more general, wide-ranging and inquisitorial in tone and the rules of evidence and procedure are substantially relaxed.

This sharp distinction, while convenient for exposition and reflective of practice, is intellectually unsatisfying for a number of reasons. First, the division of issues between those to be considered at trial and those to be looked at on sentence is not fixed immutably but represents a balance between different considerations which may alter over time. Thus, such questions as whether ignorance or mistake of the criminal law should be recognised as a general defence to liability, or whether provocation should be made available in cases of attempted murder or serious assault[3] are really questions about the more appropriate stage—trial or sentence—at which to consider mistake of law or provocation.[4] On the one hand the moral claim of a particular consideration may be so strong that it is regarded as wrong to return a conviction without giving the tribunal of fact a chance to consider it,[5] but on the other hand there may be policy considerations militating against this, not least the danger of the jury becoming confused or overburdened by too many issues. What is clear, however, is that the relegation of an issue such as mistake of law to the sentencing stage does not entail that it thereby loses significance, and there will be cases where its relevance is so great as to make an absolute discharge the appropriate sentence.[6] A second point is that there are in English law partial excuses, such as provocation and diminished responsibility, which straddle the supposed divide between the trial and sentencing stages. The merit of each defence is assessed by the jury, but they have their effect on sentence rather than directly upon liability.[7] The third reason is that the overwhelming bulk of defendants plead guilty. The first stage, the criminal trial, is therefore absent, and any enquiry into the circumstances of the admitted offence(s) and the defendant's culpability must emerge, if at all, at the sentencing stage. The bare bones of the indictment and plea may provide insufficient information to form the basis for a reasoned sentencing decision and may hide stark disputes between the prosecution and defence over what actually happened. Two examples may be given to illustrate the point.

In *Lester*,[8] the defendant pleaded guilty to strict liability offences involving the sale of second-hand motor cars on which the milometers had been turned back. The defendant claimed in mitigation that he had not known of the falsification of the mileages but the judge, on passing sentence of six months' imprisonment, observed that in his view Lester had known what was going on. On appeal against sentence the Court of Appeal observed that there was clearly a difference between the prosecution and defence versions of the facts, the plea of guilty being consistent with either version. If the judge was minded to draw an adverse inference then he should offer the defendant a chance to call evidence on the point. Since the judge had not done that, a fine of £280 was substituted. This is a sentencing decision of the first importance, because it reminds the courts that a plea of guilty may not settle all outstanding issues affecting culpability. On a charge which involves strict liability, the issue of *mens rea* itself is relegated to the sentencing stage. A more recent example is *Newton*,[9] where the defendant pleaded guilty to a charge of buggery committed on his wife. By his plea he clearly admitted the deed, but the prosecution and defence versions of what happened could hardly have been more different. In particular, the prosecution asserted that the wife had not consented to the act, whereas the defendant claimed that she had. Both versions were consistent with the plea,[10] but the question of the wife's consent was clearly a crucial matter to be settled on sentence. The judge adopted the prosecution version and imposed an eight-year prison term. The Court of Appeal reduced this sentence to one of 10 months, observing that the judge had failed to hear evidence on the disputed point and that in the absence of the prosecution establishing the aggravating feature the judge was bound to sentence on the version advanced by the defendant. The importance of the issues arising in these two cases is well illustrated by the scale of alteration of sentence thought appropriate by the Court of Appeal.

Although most of the cases giving rise to problems of this sort follow pleas of guilty, comparable situations can sometimes arise even after a full trial of the issues. This may be because a question affecting the defendant's culpability was not strictly relevant at the trial stage, or because the jury's verdict is on the face of it consistent with the versions advanced by the prosecution and by the defence. Of particular difficulty here are broadly defined criminal offences such as manslaughter, where the verdict of guilty may not indicate to the judge the basis on which the verdict was reached.[11] A number of important questions are raised here, such as the desirability of the modern trend of drafting offences in broad bands, which tends to worsen problems of fact-finding for sentencers,[12] the proper division of issues between judge and jury, and the case for allowing the judge to enquire of the jury the factual basis for their verdict.[13] These questions will be left on one side, however, because we are to concentrate here on the means for resolving such factual disputes which is currently being advocated by the Court of Appeal in an important series of appeals against sentence. The preferred solution is for the judge to embark on a post-conviction enquiry, hearing evidence from the defendant and others as necessary, and listening to representations from counsel, to determine the factual basis for sentence. Our special concern is to consider to what extent traditional rules of evidence and procedure should be taken to apply at this stage. It is essential to view this in the context of the sentencing process generally.

Developing Clearer Procedures

That part of the criminal justice process which deals with the reception and use of information on sentence has, until recently, received very little attention from Parliament, the appellate courts or legal writers.[14] According to the Streatfeild Committee Report in 1961, the only comprehensive official investigation of this area, sentencing procedure has "developed empirically and piecemeal and difficulties and anomalies have naturally arisen."[15] There is a dearth of relevant legal rules.

It is the task of prosecuting counsel to summarise the facts of the offence. This is partly to assist the judge, partly to set out the prosecution's view of the facts and partly to inform the public.[16] At the sentencing stage there is a very strong tradition in England that the prosecution should take a neutral stance towards the case, neither underestimating the seriousness of the offence nor necessarily agreeing with the defendant's version. In particular, the prosecutor does not ask for any particular sentence to be passed, or urge the judge to pass a severe sentence.[17] After this summary, counsel will call a police officer dealing with the case to tell the court what is known about the defendant. This testimony consists of his reading out a document which contains the defendant's antecedents. This procedure is not governed by any statutory requirements, but the principles to be observed have been outlined in appellate cases. It has been held that the antecedents should be given publicly so that the defendant has a chance to deal with any matter he disagrees with.[18] The witness should not be permitted to make general allegations prejudicial to the defendant which are clearly incapable of proof.[19] A copy of the antecedents should be given to the defence in good time before their presentation to the court. Next, counsel will ask the officer to inform the court of the defendant's previous convictions. Sometimes all the record is read out,[20] sometimes only the last four or five if the list is a lengthy one. If the defence wishes to challenge any of the information contained in the antecedents or previous convictions there is now a chance to do so. If the evidence is challenged, the onus is on the prosecution to satisfy the judge of the truth of the assertions made.[21] After the antecedents evidence, the judge reads any reports which have been prepared on the offender. The most frequently encountered document is a social enquiry report, which is prepared by a probation officer. The report contains an expanded version of the antecedents, describing the offender's background, circumstances, income and any relevant social problems that he might have. At the end of the report the probation officer may make a recommendation as to sentence.[22] Guidance in the preparation of such reports is given in Home Office Circulars. Defence counsel should know as soon as possible whether a report is being prepared and be able to obtain a copy.[23] The probation officer may be called to give oral evidence.[24] Once the reports have been presented, defence counsel puts forward mitigation on behalf of the offender, much of which material may have been foreshadowed in the reports. The sentencer must listen patiently to the mitigation.[25] During mitigation the defendant or other witnesses may be called to give oral evidence and documentary evidence, perhaps relating to the character of the offender, may be introduced.[26] Counsel will place emphasis upon the immediate circumstances of the offence, stressing any aspects which tend to lessen its gravity or upon any special circumstances of the offender such as domestic or financial difficulties which, it may be argued, contributed to the commission of the offence.

It will be appreciated from this bare sketch that sentencing procedure is very different from trial procedure. Shapland has suggested that it can best be understood in the context of the requirement of further information about the offence and the offender to achieve a more individualised approach to sentencing[27]:

> "At the beginning of the century the process between conviction and sentence began to develop out of the adversary model exemplified by the system during a trial. At that stage there was no doubt as to on which side each of the limited number of participants, the prosecution, the police and the defence, could be placed. We have moved from an adversary model, through a model combining adversary processes between prosecution and defence with expert testimony by independent outsiders, towards what may be called a problem-solving model. In this each participant may be regarded as a provider of particular information required to solve the problem—the sentence."

There is much in this, but the decisions of the Court of Appeal in *Lester* and *Newton*, already referred to, and numerous others, indicate that at least where disputes occur over the facts of the offence, the defendant disputing an aggravating feature of the case alleged by the prosecution, the adversarial model remains entirely appropriate at the sentencing stage. Perhaps the most difficult question in this complex area is to determine at what point in the sentencing process the adversarial approach may safely be relaxed.

Determining the Factual Basis

In several appeals against sentence the Court of Appeal has suggested that an appropriate way to resolve a factual dispute between the parties is to try the whole matter on a plea of not guilty.[28] This is rarely an appropriate course, however. First, the trial may not resolve the factual matter in dispute for, as we have seen, some issues crucial to sentence are in principle irrelevant at trial. Secondly, the defendant will be deprived of whatever discount he may have received for saving the court's time by pleading guilty. The Court of Appeal now seems to have recognised that it is more appropriate for the judge to make a clear ruling on such disputed matters at the sentencing stage and that this is best achieved by way of a post-conviction enquiry.[29] In *Newton*,[30] where the factual dispute was over the wife's consent to a sexual offence, the Court of Appeal indicated that there were two approaches which the sentencer could adopt. The first would be for the judge himself "to hear evidence on one side and another and come to his own conclusion acting so to speak as his own jury on the matter."[31] From observations made in other appeal cases, it seems that the defendant himself, or any other person, may give evidence and be cross-examined at this stage, whether or not they have given evidence at any earlier trial. The recent case of *McGrath and Casey*[32] elaborates further on the procedure to be followed. The Court of Appeal commented that the post-conviction hearing[33]:

> "... is not the same as an investigation on the voir dire—it is the investigation of the facts of a case in order that the judge may be properly apprised of the factual basis upon which he should sentence. The investigation ... should be conducted by counsel appearing for the defendant on one hand and for the Crown on the other. It is not an investigation on which the judge should embark on a cross-examination of the accused person."

The second approach, indicated in *Newton* would be for the sentencer to hear no evidence as such but to listen to the submissions of counsel and then come to a conclusion. The Court said, however, that if the judge adopted that course, where there was a conflict between the two sides, he must come down on the side of the defendant, in so far as this version was not inconsistent with the plea already made. If the judge's provisional view favours the version adduced by the prosecution, he should give the parties the opportunity to call evidence.

The guidance in *Newton* is appropriate where there is a "sharp divergence"[34] between prosecution and defence on the factual basis of the offence. It follows from this that the procedure is inappropriate where, whichever version of the facts was adopted, the sentence would be the same.[35] It also seems that *Newton* does not apply in the situation where the defendant advances particular mitigation which the prosecution does not accept but is not in a position to refute.[36] Here it seems that the sentencer can form his own view of the credibility of the mitigation without embarking on a formal enquiry or hearing evidence. An example of this type of case is *Kerr*,[37] where the defendant pleaded guilty to the importation of a controlled drug, cannabis. He claimed in mitigation that he had not been aware that the packages he had been carrying contained cannabis until he recovered his baggage at London Airport, when his suitcase was found to be open. The prosecution was not in a position to disprove this story, but made it clear that they did not accept it as the basis for the guilty plea. The judge allowed the defendant to mitigate on the point, including giving evidence on oath. He was not cross-examined. The judge decided that the story was a fabrication.

The Court of Appeal held that the judge's approach to the case was correct and that he was clearly entitled to disbelieve the defendant. Similarly, in *Connell*,[38] the defendant pleaded guilty to blackmail but claimed in mitigation that he was acting under some degree of duress from one "Belfast Johnny," though such duress as was suggested could not have formed the basis for a not guilty plea.[39] The judge sought information from the defendant about this claim and then said that in his view the story was most unlikely to be true. On appeal it was urged by counsel for the defendant that the judge should have held a post-conviction enquiry. The Court of Appeal rejected this claim, saying that the judge had gone through the defendant's story carefully and that there was a limit to his credulity. This was not the kind of case, it was added, where the mitigation advanced would "fundamentally and basically"[40] affect the gravity of the crime charged. It is suggested that the central point, however, was that the prosecution was not in a position to refute the claim, and hence a post-conviction enquiry would not have assisted matters.[41]

The importance of observing proper procedure at the sentencing stage has been commented upon by May L.J. in *McGrath and Casey*[42]:

> "Everybody should realise that the rules that there are for the conduct of proceedings and about the admissibility of evidence, although they may seem complex to the layman and on occasions too restrictive, have grown up in the course of time in order that justice should be done between society on the one hand and defendants charged with criminal offences on the other. In our view it is essential that the proper and recognised procedures should always be followed, so that courts, counsel and prosecutors do not get themselves into the sort of muddle that they did in this case."

The basic procedure to be followed in resolving factual disputes between the parties is now somewhat clearer after a spate of recent Court of Appeal decisions.[43] But there are still a number of unresolved issues. One of the most important of these is the extent to which the various rules of evidence, familiar at trial, should be taken to apply to the post-conviction hearing, and to the sentencing process more generally. It is easy to find comments in the books to the effect that the rules of evidence are relaxed at the sentencing stage,[44] but no further debate is embarked upon. It is appropriate to deal first with the fundamental matters of burden and standard of proof.

Burden and Standard of Proof

There have been several judicial pronouncements in England that in the post-conviction hearing the defendant is entitled to be given the benefit of any doubt,[45] but two recent cases have now apparently established that the standard to be satisfied by the prosecution is the criminal rather than the civil one. In *Ball*,[46] the Court of Appeal approved the course taken by the sentencer which included hearing evidence from both sides as to a factual matter in dispute, and then directing himself that he was satisfied so that he was sure that the prosecution version was the correct one. In *McGrath and Casey*, May L.J. specifically observed that[47]:

> "In coming to a conclusion about the facts the judge should, in our view, direct himself in accordance with the normal criminal burden of proof."

This latter statement seems, remarkably enough, to be the first direct reported reference to the issue. Its context is such that it should be taken as being confined to matters raised in the post-conviction enquiry, as opposed to being relevant to sentencing issues generally.[48]

Although the basic position in English law now seems clearer after *McGrath and Casey*, a far more impressive discussion of the issues has been provided by the Supreme Court of Canada in *Gardiner*.[49] In this case, the defendant had been sentenced to four and a half-years' imprisonment following a plea of guilty to a charge of assault occasioning actual bodily harm. The sentencer accepted a number of aggravating features of this offence advanced by the prosecution after conviction. The Ontario Court of Appeal held that the judge had erred in adopting the standard of a balance of probabilities, and that the burden of proof was on the prosecution to prove the disputed facts beyond reasonable doubt.[50] The prosecution's appeal to the Supreme Court was dismissed. The Crown, relying on American authorities,[51] argued that there was a sharp demarcation between the trial and sentencing stages. Once guilt is established, it was said, the presumption of innocence no longer applies. Since sentencing is a discretionary and highly subjective exercise on the part of the judge, the strict rules on admissibility of evidence are relaxed to allow the judge access to the maximum information in the task of fitting the punishment to the person convicted. To require proof beyond reasonable doubt, it was argued, would complicate and extend sentencing hearings, with a resultant loss of economy. These arguments were decisively rejected by the Supreme Court, Dickson J. saying[52]:

"To my mind, the facts which justify the sanction are no less important than the facts which justify the conviction; both should be subject to the same burden of proof. Crime and punishment are inextricably linked.... Upon conviction the accused is not abruptly deprived of all procedural rights existing at trial: he has a right to counsel, a right to call witnesses and cross examine prosecution witnesses, a right to give evidence himself and to address the court.... In my view both the informality of the sentencing and procedure as to the admissibility of evidence and the wide discretion given to the trial judge in imposing sentence are factors militating *in favour* of the retention of the criminal standard of proof beyond reasonable doubt at sentencing.... The *rationale* of the argument for the Crown for the acceptance of a lesser standard of proof is administrative efficacy. In my view, however, the administrative efficacy argument is not sufficient to overcome such a basic tenet suffusing our entire criminal justice system as the standard of proof beyond a reasonable doubt." (emphasis added.)

The breadth of these remarks suggests that the ruling on the standard of proof may not be confined solely to factual issues arising in a post-conviction hearing, but can be applied more generally throughout the sentencing process, where the defendant disputes information given about him. At least one subsequent Canadian case appears to support a broad interpretation of *Gardiner*.[53]

In an important article published 10 years ago, Fox and O'Brien[54] showed that in a series of decisions handed down by the Supreme Court of South Australia a comprehensive set of propositions had been developed by the judges in relation to determination of the factual basis for sentence. In particular, the decisions established that "the golden thread of *Woolmington*[55] applies to the dispositional as well as the adjudicatory stage of the criminal trial.[56] As Bray C.J., the chief architect of this area of law, observed in the case of *Weaver* v. *Samuels*[57]:

"The defendant must be given the benefit of any reasonable doubt on matters of penalty, as well as on matters of guilt or innocence, in the absence of any statutory provisions to the contrary. The plea of guilty admits no more than the bare legal ingredients of the crime. Any dispute as to anything beyond this must be resolved on ordinary legal priciples, including the presumption of innocence."

More recently, however, Judge Lowenthal[58] has expressed doubt on the universal application of this rule in sentencing proceedings in Australia.[59] He argues that proof beyond reasonable doubt at the sentencing stage is confined to matters relating to "the exact details of the offence."[60] If the factual dispute between the parties is not so confined, his view is that it can be decided on a balance of probabilities. He cites a number of decisions of the Court of Appeal in Queensland in support of this claim.[61] This is not the place for a detailed analysis of the merits of the Australian cases. What the judge's criticisms should do, however, is alert us to the possibility that in English law the criminal standard advocated in *McGrath and Casey* may be applicable in some circumstances at the sentencing stage of a criminal trial, but not in others.

A determination of the appropriate burden and standard of proof operative in any judicial proceedings is regarded as being of great importance. This is because each party should in fairness know what facts he or she is required to establish in order to succeed, and the fact-finder should have a proper and consistent means of determining disputed facts in the absence of convincing evidence either way.[62] It was argued, in the early part of this discussion, that it is often unhelpful to draw a sharp distinction between trial and sentencing stages because crucial aggravating features of the case may be urged against the defendant at the latter stage. Consistency should therefore require proof of the relevant prosecution assertions beyond reasonable doubt.[63] Such a clear rule on the prosecution's standard of proof should serve to remind judges that allegations of an aggravating feature of the defendant's conduct may be just as damaging to him when adduced on sentence. A number of appellate decisions in England, as well as other sources, strongly suggest that sentencers are too ready to swallow without further question associated allegations about a defendant's behaviour once his guilt on the offence charged has been established or admitted.[64] In the appellate cases, the Court of Appeal has emphasised that a sentencer should not take into account aggravating features of the case unless these have been admitted by the defendant or clearly proved by the prosecution. This important principle of sentencing has been applied in cases where the sentencer has proceeded on the basis of admissions allegedly made by the defendant to the police on another occasion but since retracted,[65] or where allegations have been made by another defendant which suggest that the defendant is guilty of offences other than the ones with which he has been convicted.[66] It has not, however, been applied consistently to specimen counts, where the Court of Appeal has been prepared to countenance the fixing of sentence on the basis of a background of alleged offending where the prosecution has chosen to proceed with sample instances. In *Price*[67] and *Singh and Singh*,[68] prosecution allegations of systematic wrongdoing were adopted as the basis for sentence even though the defendant in the former case had been convicted in relation to only one sample count and the defendants in the latter case had been acquitted on one count but convicted on another. It is thought that these cases represent an unconvincing exception to the general principle.[69] The great importance of the principle, of course, is that to sentence on the basis of unproved and disputed assumptions about further offending bypasses the defendant's rights with regard to trial on those issues, not least the normal incidence of burden and standard of proof.

A further consideration here is that a clear understanding that the standard of proof at sentencing is a high one would tend to encourage the presentation of better evidence at the post-conviction enquiry. To the extent that "the tariff" represents the dominant influence in English sentencing practice, accuracy of information regarding the nature of the offence and the offender's culpability must be regarded as crucial.[70] Research observations make it clear, however, that evidence adduced at the sentencing stage is often sketchy and unsatisfactory.[71] It will be appreciated that selection of a high standard of proof would affect the comparative frequency of erroneous outcomes on sentence whereby more would be made in favour of defendants than against them. This would reflect an acceptance of the view that on sentence, as at trial, the rights of the individual defendant not to be dealt with on the basis of a mistaken factual inference should prevail over an alternative increase in the efficiency of crime control.[72]

The writers suggest that in determining questions of burden and standard of proof, a balance has to be struck between fairness to the parties, public policy considerations and the interests of judicial economy.[73] It was suggested by Crown counsel in *Gardiner* that an intermediate standard such as proof by "clear and convincing" evidence was appropriate on sentence, rather than proof beyond reasonable doubt. This was said to offer a compromise position whereby a heavy burden would still rest on the prosecution but the lower standard would fall short of making "sentencing proceedings the equivalent of trials."[74] The convincing objections to adopting this as the general rule, however, are that the existence of different standards of proof at trial and at sentence would be confusing and also indefensible in a system such as ours which reserves important matters of culpability to the sentencer's discretion. There appears, then, to be much to be said in favour of requiring the prosecution to establish disputed sentencing facts beyond reasonable doubt. To what extent, however, may this rule admit of exceptions in sentencing? Three possible exceptions are now considered.

The first situation is that which was encountered in cases like *Kerr* and *Connell*, discussed earlier, where the defendant advances particular mitigation and the prosecution, while not accepting this as the basis for sentence, is not in a position to refute it. Should the defendant have to prove that his version is the correct one, or is it sufficient for him to raise a reasonable doubt in the mind of the sentencer, or is some other standard appropriate? The cases suggest that procedures advocated in *Newton* are inappropriate to this type of case,[75] but they give no guidance on the issue of proof. *Kerr* certainly makes it clear that the sentencer is not bound to accept the truth of the mitigation, so that the defendant must in practice adduce some evidence in support of his story. In the South Australian case of *Law* v. *Deed*,[76] Bray C.J. appeared to suggest that in such a case the defendant had to discharge an evidential burden with regard to that issue[77]:

> "I do not mean to suggest that it is for the prosecution to rebut in advance any matters of mitigation before they are raised by the defence . . . but once they become issues in the case, in the sense that there is some evidence about them from some quarter, then the onus is on the prosecution to disprove them beyond reasonable doubt."

Some may wish to place a heavier onus on the defendant in a case where the prosecution is not in a position to refute the mitigation. Judge Lowenthal, for instance, suggests proof on a balance of probabilities.[78] Clearly, placing a burden of proof on the defendant is geared towards reducing frivolous mitigation, but the sentencer could surely be relied upon to rule this out anyway.[79] Further, to place a civil burden of proof on the defendant would create inconsistencies between the trial and sentencing stages. On the facts of *Connell*, where the defendant was urging that he had committed the criminal acts under duress from one "Belfast Johnny," had this been put forward at trial the burden of proof beyond reasonable doubt would have rested on the prosecution once the defendant had discharged his evidential burden on the issue of duress.[80] Why should the position be different when the same matter is raised on sentence? It is submitted that the better view is that the defendant does *not* bear a burden of proof in such cases, but rather has the task of adducing evidence in mitigation. While the defendant should therefore be given the benefit of a reasonable doubt, he is most unlikely to succeed by making a bare assertion to the sentencer.[81]

A second possibility, as yet unexplored by the courts, is the extent to which statutory or other exceptions may be found to exist to the general principles of burden and standard of proof suggested. It has to be conceded that the "golden thread" of *Woolmington* is somewhat tarnished as far as the trial stage is concerned.[82] To what extent should the inroads into the *Woolmington* principle, such as the specific statutory exceptions[83] and the rule in *Edwards*[84] be adopted in sentencing? Some of these, of course, will have no direct application on sentence, but for one clear example where the burden of proof has been held to rest on the defendant on sentence we need look no further than *Jones* v. *English*,[85] where it was held that by virtue of the Road Traffic Act 1972, the defendant bears the burden of establishing the existence of special reasons for not disqualifying from driving, on a balance of probabilities. The burden of proof with regard to mental disorder defences is placed on the defendant at trial. What is the position if the defendant seeks to establish some lesser form of mental disorder on sentence with a view to securing, say, a probation order with a condition of psychiatric treatment, rather than a punitive disposal? The relevant section of the Powers of the Criminal Courts Act 1973 requires that the court be "...satisfied, on the evidence of a duly qualified medical practitioner...."[86] What burden, if any, does this place on counsel arguing for such a sentence for his client? It is not thought that the issues relating to burden and standard of proof, discussed above, or the legal precedents on the meaning of "satisfied" in the context of a criminal case,[87] would be directly relevant to the interpretation of this provision. This is because at the stage when the provision becomes relevant the court will have moved from its "adversarial" model to its "problem-solving" model,[88] where insistence upon legal standards of proof becomes less appropriate. It seems that it is this shift in the court's emphasis in fulfilling two rather distinct functions in sentencing which may help to determine the proper ambit of the rules of evidence at the sentencing stage, rather than Judge Lowenthal's limitation of such rules to the "exact facts of the offence."[89]

A third problem which has not yet received the attention of the appellate courts is the extent to which the evidential rules for settling disputes over the factual basis for sentence apply to disputes over the extent of the victim's loss. In *Vivian*,[90] the Court of Appeal said that before a compensation order could be made the amount of the loss had to be formally admitted by the defendant or proved by the prosecution. It is unclear to what extent such burden of proof on the prosecution has been affected by later cases[91] or by section 67 of the Criminal Justice Act 1982. If compensation orders are seen as positive instruments of penal policy, securing reparation for the offence, then establishing the facts concerning the extent of the loss should be done to the criminal standard, but on the view that compensation orders are collateral to sentence and simply provide the victim with the means of short-circuiting civil action, a civil standard of proof might seem quite appropriate.[92] It is submitted that the latter view is to be preferred. A clear ruling from the Court of Appeal on this matter is required.

Other Rules of Evidence in Sentencing

It seems to be universally agreed that the strict rules of evidence applied at trial are relaxed at the sentencing stage, though it is significant that Dickson J., in *Gardiner*,[93] regarded "the informality of the sentencing procedure as to the admissibility of evidence" as being an additional reason for requiring a high standard of proof of the prosecution. There appears to be virtually no discussion, however, of which rules apply to their full extent on sentence, which to a lesser extent, and which do not apply at all. The present writer has suggested, above, that the relevance of such rules is of much greater importance when the court is engaged upon the determination of the factual basis for sentence rather than considering the wide range of collateral matters relevant to selection of the appropriate disposal. This is not to say, however, that evidential rules are irrelevant in the latter context, particularly where such rules preserve the defendant's rights to see and to challenge the accuracy of information (*e.g.* in social enquiry reports), help to ensure that such information is conscientiously compiled and presented from reliable sources, and preserve the defendant's rights to cross-examine his accusers. It is not possible here to examine a large number of the rules of evidence applicable at trial and to discuss the extent to which they should be applicable in the sentencing process. Some attempt will be made, however, to sketch out a few groundrules.

(i) *Hearsay*

The reasons for the operation of a general rule excluding hearsay evidence at criminal trials are numerous, though few would defend the rather capricious operation of the rules at present. Essentially, such evidence is excluded because it may be unreliable and because there is a danger that the jury or magistrates will place too much weight on evidence the source of which is not available for cross-examination.[94] At the sentencing stage the position is different at least to the extent that there is no jury and it is arguable that, as with civil cases, a judge is perfectly capable of according proper weight to hearsay evidence. On the other hand, it has been suggested that there is a tendency for sentencers to accept too readily further allegations made against a defendant in relation to whom some reprehensible conduct has already been proved or admitted. A defendant may be taken by surprise by broad and unspecific allegations and find it difficult to refute them. Effective denial of the right to cross-examine the original maker of the statement undermines a fundamental right of the defendant in criminal proceedings[95] and, as Lawton L.J. said in *Sargeant*[96]:

> "Nothing gives a bigger sense of injustice to a convicted man than false statements being made about him after the verdict."

There are very few authorities on the relevance of hearsay evidence in the post-conviction enquiry. In *Robinson*,[97] it was held by the Court of Appeal that evidence given by a police officer called by the prosecution after conviction should not be admitted unless the police officer could speak from first hand knowledge without reliance on hearsay. The evidence should also be sufficiently particularised so that the defendant has a chance to refute it. In that case the sentencer had allowed the police officer to assert that the defendant was much more heavily involved in the drug scene than was indicated by the offence with which he had been convicted, and he had relied on this information in imposing a substantial prison term. Acceptance of this information was said by the Court of Appeal to be "a clear and obvious injustice."[98] A similar finding was made in the later case of *Wilkins*,[99] where after conviction a police officer put in evidence a two-page document casting imputations of a wide-ranging nature against the defendant, based very substantially on hearsay evidence. On the other hand, there is authority that hearsay evidence is acceptable so long as the defendant does not dispute its content and is given adequate opportunity to object.[1] This seems to be the rule of practice currently operating for social enquiry reports and other reports which often contain substantial passages of hearsay information.[2] A leading guide for the probation officer on the presentation of social enquiry reports states[3] that an officer is not bound by the rules of evidence with regard to hearsay.

The legal position at present is unclear. It is arguable that hearsay evidence, whether oral or documentary,[4] should in principle be inadmissible, though with exceptions, broadly as at trial. This ought to improve the quality and reliability of the information received at the sentencing stage. It would, however, make the presentation of evidence after conviction more time-consuming, perhaps requiring the presentation of witnesses to testify to facts which, in the event, the defendant does not dispute. An alternative approach would be to adopt a rule of practice that hearsay evidence should not be proffered where the defendant is known or expected to dispute the matter, unless the prosecution is fully intending to prove it. If the hearsay evidence is given, and the defendant does dispute it, the sentencer should put the prosecution to proof. If the prosecution is then unable to establish the matter beyond reasonable doubt the sentencer must, preferably by express statement, ignore any unproven assertion made against the defendant.[5]

(ii) *Corroboration*

To what extent do rules relating to corroboration apply at the sentencing stage? At least one case, *Long*,[6] suggests that the rules have some formal significance. In that case the defendant pleaded guilty to two counts of indecent assault on a girl aged 12. There was a significant discrepancy between the victim's version of what happened and the defendant's admissions to the police. In the Court of Appeal, Bridge L.J. pointed out that in so far as the two accounts differed, the girl's version was uncorroborated. In fact the only corroboration of her story was provided by what the defendant had admitted. The court decided that it was therefore appropriate to sentence the defendant on the basis of his admissions rather than the girl's allegations. There have been one or two other cases in which corroboration has been specifically mentioned as a factor significant on sentence,[7] but there have also been many cases on similar facts to *Long* where corroboration has not been mentioned.[8] We should not, therefore, make too much of this case.

The reasons advanced for requiring corroboration or for warning the jury of the danger of convicting without such evidence at a criminal trial are many and varied. The justifications differ from one form of corroboration to another, but essentially corroboration is looked for where there is reason to think that the witness, as a member of a particular class of witness, may be unreliable, either through error or through malice. Corroboration requirements at trial have recently been subjected to searching criticism[9] and there is no doubt that there is inconsistency, illogicality and prejudice in their current operation. On the facts of *Long*, for instance, if the defendant had entirely rejected the girl's version and had pleaded not guilty, the corroboration issue would have turned on whether the girl gave evidence on oath. A child witness may be sworn provided that he or she understands the nature and consequences of the oath.[10] If not, unsworn evidence may be given if the child is of sufficient intelligence to justify the reception of the evidence and understands the duty of speaking the truth.[11] If the oath is taken, the judge must direct the jury that it is dangerous to convict on this evidence unless it is corroborated. If, however, the jury believes the child, a conviction may be returned in the absence of corroboration. If the evidence is unsworn, then there must be corroboration from an independent source. The distinction between sworn and unsworn evidence in this context is now largely one without a difference, however, since recent cases have meant that the test to be applied by the judge for allowing a child to take the oath, or allowing unsworn evidence to be given, is virtually the same.[12] There is also the further complication that on a charge of a sexual offence, the judge should direct the jury that it is dangerous to convict on the uncorroborated testimony of the complainant. Enough has been said, it is suggested, to show that the full complexity of the corroboration rules should not reach into the sentencing stage.

The absence of the jury at the sentencing stage removes a principle plank of argument for incorporating precisely formulated rules of corroboration into sentencing. It may be assumed, perhaps, that a judge is capable of assigning proper weight to evidence on sentence which at trial would require independent support, though this assumption may not be so justifiable in relation to summary proceedings before lay magistrates. It is suggested, however, that there is no good reason for adopting technical rules of corroboration into the sentencing process, because the matter can be dealt with perfectly adequately by references to established principles of sentencing and the burden and standard of proof. Clearly, it is wrong to sentence the defendant on the basis of the girl's version of the facts if this is disputed by him,[13] but to put this in terms of "corroboration" adds nothing to the general requirements just mentioned. Defence counsel should be entitled to cross-examine any witness alleging an aggravating feature of the case against the defendant. In the case of the child witness a further important consideration would be whether it was on balance desirable to put the child through the ordeal of giving evidence and being cross-examined. If this is thought inappropriate, then the defendant can surely only be sentenced on the facts clearly proved against him, to the requisite standard of beyond reasonable doubt, or have been admitted.

(iii) *Other rules*

The Court of Appeal has considered on several occasions to what extent a sentencer may rely on allegations about the defendant made by a co-defendant tried separately or together with the defendant. *Wishart*[14] is a clear case, where in the course of a joint trial the co-defendant made allegations that the defendant was implicated in an offence with which he had not been charged. The Court of Appeal criticised the sentencer for dealing with the defendant on the basis of this evidence[15]:

> "It has long been accepted in the courts that a man should only be sentenced for the offences of which he has been convicted. Indeed the courts . . . have made it clear that the trial judge should disregard any information which might be available to him after conviction which may aggravate the sentence if that information is not accepted by the convicted man . . . ."

Later cases[16] have held that whether evidence is given by other witnesses, or by the co-defendant tried separately or together with the defendant is immaterial.

The continuance into the sentencing stage of a number of familiar rules of evidence may perhaps be assumed, though authority is very thin. The normal rules of competence and compellability presumably apply, particularly in relation to the defendant and his spouse.[17] This would be important in a case like *Newton*,[18] with regard to the wife's evidence at the sentencing stage as to her consent to the sexual offence. Since the defendant's criminal record is revealed at the sentencing stage, this tends to undermine the justification for a number of rules of evidence protecting the defendant at trial, but presumably the privilege against self-incrimination remains intact. Perhaps evidence excluded at trial on the ground that its prejudicial effect outweighs its probative value can nevertheless be relied on at sentence.[19] The rule that the defendant's silence should not normally be construed against him apparently extends to sentencing.[20]

Notes

[1] See, for instance Glueck, "Principles of a rational penal code" (1928) 41 Harv.L.Rev. 453 at p. 475: "The treatment (sentence-imposing) feature of the proceedings must be sharply differentiated from the guilt-finding phase." Also Wootton, *Crime and Penal Policy* (1978) p. 19.

[2] *Stosiek,* (1982) 4 Cr.App.R.(S) 205; *Solomon and Triumph* (1984) 6 Cr.App.R.(S) 120.

[3] See Criminal Law Revision Committee, *Working Paper on Offences Against the Person* (1976) para. 109. The idea was dropped in their Report in 1980.

[4] Wasik, "Excuses at the sentencing stage" [1983] Crim.L.R. 450.

[5] This argument was advanced in relation to the defence of duress by the Law Commission, Report No. 83, *Defences of General Application* (1977) para. 2.17.

[6] Wasik, "The grant of an absolute discharge" (1985) 5 *Oxford Journal of Legal Studies* 211.

[7] Wasik, "Partial excuses in the criminal law" (1982) 45 M.L.R. 516.

[8] (1975) 63 Cr.App.R. 144.

[9] (1982) 4 Cr.App.R.(S) 388.

[10] Smith and Hogan, *Criminal Law* (5th ed., 1983) p. 443. Compare *Courtie* [1984] 1 All E.R. 740.

[11] Thomas, "Establishing a factual basis for sentence" [1970] Crim.L.R. 80; *Solomon and Triumph* (1984) 6 Cr.App.R.(S) 120.

[12] Thomas, "Form and function in the criminal law" in Glazebrook (ed.), *Reshaping the Criminal Law* (1978) p. 21 and Thomas, "The law of sentencing—some unresolved issues" in Oxner (ed.), *Criminal Justice* (1982).

[13] Discussed in Fox and O'Brien, "Fact finding for sentencers" (1975) 10 *Melbourne University Law Review* 163 at pp. 170–178.

[14] An important contribution, however, is provided by Shapland, *Between Conviction and Sentence* (1981).

[15] *Report of the Interdepartmental Committee on the Business of the Criminal Courts* (1961) Cmnd. 1289, para. 265.

[16] Practice Direction, Court of Appeal [1968] 2 All. E.R. 144.

[17] For discussion of the implications of expanding the role of the prosecutor in sentencing see Ashworth, "Prosecution and procedure in criminal justice" [1979] Crim.L.R. 480 and Zellick, "The role of prosecuting counsel in sentencing" [1979] Crim.L.R. 493. And see below.

[18] *Hastings* v. *Ostle* (1930) 94 J.P. 209. Many courts are now staffed by Court Liaison Officers who have not prepared the antecedents themselves. This has sometimes led to misleading or insufficient information: *Phillips, The Times*, March 3, 1973.

[19] *Van Pelz* (1942) 29 Cr.App.R. 10; *Wilkins* (1978) 66 Cr.App.R. 49.

[20] Normally, no reference should be made to "spent" convictions: Practice Direction, Court of Appeal (1975) 61 Cr.App.R. 260.

[21] Previous convictions should be admitted by the defendant or proved. If the defendant challenges other statements in the antecedents, the judge should ask for proof to be given or expressly disregard the statement: *Campbell* (1911) 6 Cr.App.R. 131. If the defendant admits facts, he should still be allowed to qualify or explain them: *Metcalfe* (1913) 9 Cr.App.R. 7.

[22] See Harris, "Recommendations in social enquiry reports" [1979] Crim.L.R. 73.

[23] *Dewitt* (1969) 113 S.J. 507. See also *Adams* [1970] Crim.L.R. 693.

[24] *Kirkham* [1968] Crim.L.R. 151.

[25] *Billericay Justices, Ex p. Rumsey* [1978] Crim.L.R. 305.

[26] *Roche* (1944) 30 Cr.App.R. 29; *Marquis* (1951) 35 Cr.App.R. 33; *Cross* [1975] Crim.L.R. 591.

[27] Shapland, *Between Conviction and Sentence* (1981) pp. 143–144.

[28] *Taggart* (1979) 1 Cr.App.R.(S) 144; *Depledge* (1979) 1 Cr.App.R.(S) 183.

[29] *Milligan* (1982) 4 Cr.App.R.(S) 2. See commentary on *Newton* by Dr. Thomas at [1983] Crim.L.R. 199–200.

[30] (1982) 4 Cr.App.R.(S) 388.

[31] *Per* Lord Lane J., *ibid.* at p. 390.

[32] (1984) 5 Cr.App.R.(S) 460.

[33] *Ibid.* at p. 463, *per* May L.J.

[34] (1982) 4 Cr.App.R.(S) 388 at p. 390, *per* Lord Lane C.J.

[35] *Hall* [1985] Crim.L.R. 54.

[36] See commentary on *Newton* and *Odey* by Dr. Thomas at [1983] Crim.L.R. 199 and [1985] Crim.L.R. 55 respectively. See also *Connors* [1984] Crim.L.R. 507 and Emmins, *A Practical Approach to Criminal Procedure* (2nd ed., 1983) p. 182.

[37] (1980) 2 Cr.App.R.(S) 54.

[38] (1984) 5 Cr.App.R.(S) 360.

[39] See also *Taonis* (1974) 59 Cr.App.R. 160.

[40] *Supra*, note 38, at p. 362, *per* Drake J.

[41] See *Odey* [1985] Crim.L.R. 55.

[42] (1984) 5 Cr.App.R.(S) 460 at p. 462.

[43] Apart from those cited in the text, see *Solomon and Triumph* (1984) 6 Cr.App.R.(S) 120; *Connell* (1984) 5 Cr.App.R.(S) 360; *Ball* (1982) 4 Cr.App.R.(S) 351; *Milligan* (1982) 4 Cr.App.R.(S) 2.

[44] Shapland (1981) p. 1: "Unlike a trial, there are no rules to exclude particular kinds of evidence—anything may be introduced at the discretion of the judge." Emmins, *op. cit. supra*, note 36, p. 183: "The normal rules of evidence are relaxed at this stage."

[45] *Campbell* [1980] Crim.L.R. 248; *Taggart* (1979) 1 Cr.App.R.(S) 144; *Stosiek* (1982) 4 Cr.App.R.(S) 205.

[46] (1982) 4 Cr.App.R.(S) 351.

[47] (1984) 5 Cr.App.R.(S) 460 at p. 463.

[48] See below. Also *Ahmed* [1985] Crim. L.R. 250.

[49] (1983) 140 D.L.R.(3d) 612.

[50] The trial judge had regarded himself as bound by the earlier decision of the Ontario Court of Appeal in *Cieslak* (1977) 37 C.C.C.(2d) 7.

[51] In particular *Williams* v. *New York* 337 U.S. 241, 69 S.Ct. 1079 (1949). For comment on American developments since that case see Note, "Procedural due process at judicial sentencing for felony" (1968) 81 Harv.L.Rev. 821 and Note, "Constitutional rights during the sentencing proceeding" (1978) 69 *Journal of Criminal Law and Criminology* 362.

[52] *Supra*, note 49, at p. 649.

[53] *Petrovic* (1984) 13 C.C.C.(3d) 416 (Crown required to prove aggrevating feature of absence of remorse beyond reasonable doubt).

[54] (1975) 10 M.U.L.R. 163.

[55] [1935] A.C. 462.

[56] *Samuels* v. *Festa* [1968] S.A.S.R. 118; *Law* v. *Deed* [1970] S.A.S.R. 374; *Beresford* (1972) 2 S.A.S.R. 446.

[57] [1971] S.A.S.R. 116 at pp. 119–120.

[58] Lowenthal, "Some issues in fact finding for sentences" (1980) 10 *University of Queensland Law Journal* 145.

[59] See also Heydon, *Evidence; Cases and Materials* (2nd ed., 1984) p. 34: "The standards of proof beyond reasonable doubt in criminal cases does not extend to facts relevant to sentence: *Welsh* [1983] Qd.R. 592." And see below.

[60] *Loc. cit. supra*, note 58, at p. 148.

[61] Three unreported cases in 1979. For a more recent example see Welsh, *loc. cit. supra*, note 59, also reported at [1982] 7 A.Crim.R. 249. See also *Halden* [1983] 9 A.Crim.R. 30, approving *Chamberlain* (unreported 1982) and the judgment of Dixon J. in *Briginshaw* v. *Briginshaw* (1938) 60 C.L.R. 336 (proof on a balance of probabilities).

[62] See Morgan, "Some observations concerning presumptions" (1931) 44 Harv.L.Rev. 906; McBaine, "Burden of proof: degrees of belief" (1944) 32 Cal.L.Rev. 242; an important modern discussion is provided by Dworkin, "Easy cases, bad law and burdens of proof" (1972) 25 Vanderbilt L.Rev. 1151.

[63] See commentary on *Campbell* [1980] Crim.L.R. 248, by Dr. Thomas at p. 249: "... it seems to follow from general principle that an offender should not be held accountable for facts unless they have been established against him to the same standard of evidence, irrespective of whether those facts are technically elements of the offence with which he is charged."

[64] *Foo* [1976] Crim.L.R. 456; *Chadderton* (1980) 2 Cr.App.R.(S) 272; *Fisher* [1982] Crim.L.R. 191. See Frankel, *Criminal Sentences; Law without Order* (1972), Chap. 3; Wilkins, *Consumerist Criminology* (1983).

[65] *Connor* [1981] Crim.L.R. 791; *Ayensu* [1982] Crim.L.R. 764; *contra, Russen* [1981] Crim.L.R. 573.

[66] *Wishart* (1979) 1 Cr.App.R.(S) 322; *Craine* [1981] Crim.L.R. 727.

[67] [1979] Crim.L.R. 468.

[68] (1981) 3 Cr.App.R.(S) 90.

[69] See *Huchison* [1972] 1 W.L.R. 398 and *D.P.P.* v. *Anderson* [1978] A.C. 964. See the comments of Dr. Thomas [1979] Crim.L.R. 468 and those of the present writer, [1984] Crim.L.R. 708 at p. 720.

[70] Galligan, "The return to retribution" in Tapper (ed.), *Crime, Proof and Punishment* (1981); Von Hirsch, *Doing Justice* (1976); Goldman and Mullenix, "A hidden issue in sentencing: burdens of proof for disputed allegations in pre-sentence reports" (1978) 66 Georgetown L.J. 1515.

[71] See Shapland, *Between Conviction and Sentence* (1981), Chap. 6; Bottoms and McLean, *Defendants in the Criminal Process* (1976) especially p. 131.

[72] See Ashworth, "Concepts of criminal justice" [1979] Crim.L.R. 412.

[73] Dworkin, "Easy cases, bad law and burdens of proof" (1972) 25 Vanderbilt L.Rev. 1151; Goldman and Mullenix, "A hidden issue in sentencing: burdens of proof for disputed allegations in pre-sentence reports" (1978) 66 Georgetown L.Rev. 1515; Criminal Law Revision Committee, 11th Report, *Evidence* (1972), Cmnd. 4491, pp. 87–91.

[74] Goldman and Mullenix, *loc. cit. supra*, note 73, at p. 1543.

[75] See also *Odey* [1985] Crim.L.R. 55, and commentary. Compare *Petrovic* (1984) 13 C.C.C.(3d) 416.

[76] [1970] S.A.S.R. 374.

[77] *Ibid.* at p. 379.

[78] Lowenthal, *loc. cit. supra*, note 58, at p. 150.

[79] See the observations of the Criminal Law Revision Committee, 11th Report, *Evidence* (1972), Cmnd. 4991, p. 88: "We are strongly of the opinion that, both on principle and for the sake of clarity and convenience in practice, burdens of the defence should be evidential only."

[80] *Gill* [1963] 1 W.L.R. 841. Compare *Taonis* (1974) 59 Cr.App.R. 160 and see Wasik, "Excuses at the sentencing stage" [1983] Crim.L.R. 450.

[81] This seems to have been the view adopted by the judge in *Gortat and Pirog* [1973] Crim.L.R. 648. Goldman and Mullenix, *loc. cit. supra*, note 73, at p. 1531 are of the view that in the situation where the defendant disputes an allegation about him in a pre-sentence report, he should be required to produce "some evidence" to show this allegation to be incorrect. This is preferred to "raising a reasonable doubt" (too strict) and producing a "scintilla of evidence" (too lax): "This standard recognises the need for judicial economy by preventing frivolous claims, but does not endanger the defendant's right to be sentenced only on the basis of accurate information."

[82] See [1978] Crim.L.R. 385.

[83] *e.g.* Homicide Act 1957, s. 2 (diminished responsibility).

[84] [1975] Q.B. 27.

[85] [1951] 2 All E.R. 853. See also *Flewitt* v. *Horvath* (1972) 136 J.P. 164; *Pugsley* v. *Hunter* [1973] R.T.R. 284.

[86] s. 3(1).

[87] *Ewing* [1983] Q.B. 1039, disapproving *Angeli* [1979] 1 W.L.R. 26. Also *Yacoob* (1981) 72 Cr.App.R. 313.

[88] See above.

[89] See above.

[90] [1979] 1 W.L.R. 291.

[91] *Swann* [1984] Crim.L.R. 300. The *Vivian* rule does not apply to simple cases involving small sums: *Bond* v. *Chief Constable of Kent* (1982) 4 Cr.App.R.(S) 314 and

Welch [1984] Crim.L.R. 242. See also *Horsham Justices, ex p. Richards, The Times*, May 25, 1985.

[92] See *Inwood* (1974) 60 Cr.App.R. 70 and the comments of the *Hodgson Committee on the Profits of Crime and Their Recovery* (1984), Chap. 5, and the criticisms by the present writer at [1984] Crim.L.R. 708. *Chappell* (1985) 80 Cr. App. R. 31 at p. 35.

[93] (1983) 140 D.L.R.(3d) 612 at p. 649.

[94] See Criminal Law Revision Committee, 11th Report, *Evidence* (1972), Cmnd. 4991, pp. 132–154; Heydon, *Evidence; Cases and Materials* (2nd ed., 1984), Pt. 4.

[95] In *Hilton* [1972] 1 Q.B. 421, a conviction was quashed where the trial judge refused to permit the defendant to cross-examine a co-defendant, even though the latter was only testifying in his own defence and had not given evidence against the defendant.

[96] (1974) 60 Cr.App.R. 74.

[97] (1969) 53 Cr.App.R. 314.

[98] *Ibid.* at p. 318. It is clear that even had the evidence been original and reliable it should not have been admitted because it was adduced post-conviction to tend to show the defendant to be guilty of offences other than those with which he had been convicted. See the cases cited *supra*, note 65 and note 66 and the text, above.

[99] (1977) 66 Cr.App.R. 49.

[1] *Campbell* (1911) 6 Cr.App.R. 131 at p. 132: "If the prisoner wishes to say anything he can. . . . If the prisoner does not challenge the statements, and the court takes them into consideration, no injustice is likely to be done." This remark probably underestimates the opportunity available for a defendant to make such objections, or the defendant's perceptions of such opportunity, and is less convincing in relation to unrepresented defendants. See on this Shapland, *Between Conviction and Sentence* (1981) particularly pp. 145–146.

[2] See Yates, "When reporting restrictions will not be lifted" [1980] J.S.W.L. 413; Rae, "Welfare reports on children" (1978) L.A.G. Bull. 232.

[3] Jarvis, *Probation Officer's Manual* (3rd ed., 1980) p. 126.

[4] Though see now Police and Criminal Evidence Act 1984, s. 68.

[5] In a recent report of the Government of Canada, *Sentencing* (1984), it is suggested that hearsay evidence should be admitted in sentencing proceedings "subject to the proviso that persons with personal knowledge of a matter may be required to testify if the best interests of justice are thereby served" (at p. 40).

[6] (1980) 2 Cr.App.R.(S) 8.

[7] *Rogers* (unreported, 1979), where on similar facts the Court of Appeal observed that "it would not be right to base any sentence on the girl's uncorroborated evidence." See also *Gortat and Pirog* [1973] Crim.L.R. 648.

[8] *e.g. Huchison* [1972] 1 All E.R. 936.

[9] Dennis, "Corroboration requirements reconsidered" [1984] Crim.L.R. 316, and references to reform proposals cited therein.

[10] *Brasier* (1779) 1 Leach. 199.

[11] Children and Young Persons Act 1933, s. 38.

[12] *Hayes* [1977] 1 W.L.R. 234 and *Campbell* [1983] Crim.L.R. 174, and commentary by Professor Smith.

[13] See above.

[14] (1979) 1 Cr.App.R.(S) 322.

[15] *Ibid.* at p. 324, *per* Lawton L.J.

[16] *Michaels and Skoblo* (1981) 3 Cr.App.R.(S) 188; *Craine* [1981] Crim.L.R. 727.

[17] See now Police and Criminal Evidence Act 1984, s. 80, and Government of Canada, *Sentencing* (1984) p. 40.

[18] (1980) 2 Cr.App.R.(S) 272, and see the text, above.

[19] This is suggested by Lowenthal *loc. cit. supra*, note 58, at p. 147: "In dangerous driving trials evidence of consumption of alcohol given on committal is often excluded at trial on the basis of its prejudicial effect outweighing its evidentiary value. It is submitted that such evidence could be used by the sentencing judge after verdict."

[20] *Kerr* (1980) 2 Cr.App.R.(S) 54 at p. 56, *per* Eveleigh L.J.: "... he claimed the right to remain silent, as indeed he was entitled to do. This Court draws no inference from that one way or the other...."

[14]

How Unreliable Factfinding Can Undermine Sentencing Guidelines

Peter B. Pope†

Over the last decade, forces from across the political spectrum have been attacking sentence disparity—the sentencing of like cases differently.[1] Most frequently, disparity is attributed to the enormous discretion that judges have enjoyed in imposing sentences.[2] With little statutory guidance[3] and virtually no appellate review,[4] sentencing judges in most jurisdictions have been left to themselves to decide what facts about a crime or a criminal are at all relevant to a sentence, and how those facts ought to affect

---

† I would like to thank the Daniel and Florence Guggenheim Criminal Justice Program at the Yale Law School for graciously permitting me to use the data gathered by the Sentencing Project. I would also like to thank those who organized and participated in the project, but particularly Professors Daniel J. Freed and Milton Heumann and Justice Harold J. Rothwax.

1. PANEL ON SENTENCING RESEARCH, NATIONAL RESEARCH COUNCIL, 1 RESEARCH ON SENTENCING: THE SEARCH FOR REFORM 72 (1983) [hereinafter cited as SENTENCING RESEARCH]. Society's concern with sentence disparity is reflected in the legislative history that accompanied the Sentencing Reform Act of 1984, Pub. L. No. 98-473, §§ 211-39, 98 Stat. 1987 (codified in scattered sections of U.S.C.): "The shameful disparity in criminal sentences is a major flaw in the existing criminal justice system, and makes it clear that the system is ripe for reform." S. REP. NO. 225, 98th Cong., 2d Sess. 65, *reprinted in* 1984 U.S. CODE CONG. & AD. NEWS 3182, 3248 (Senate Committee on the Judiciary) (discussing S. 1762, from which Congress drew much of Sentencing Reform Act of 1984). State legislatures have echoed the sentiment, *see* 1983 N.Y. Laws ch. 711, § 2(1) ("Similar crimes committed under similar circumstances by similar offenders should receive similar sanctions"), as have judges, *see* M. FRANKEL, CRIMINAL SENTENCES: LAW WITHOUT ORDER (1972) [hereinafter cited as CRIMINAL SENTENCES], and academicians, *see* P. O'DONNELL, M. CHURGIN, & D. CURTIS, TOWARD A JUST AND EFFECTIVE SENTENCING SYSTEM: AGENDA FOR LEGISLATIVE REFORM (1977) [hereinafter cited as LEGISLATIVE AGENDA]. For a discussion of the breadth of concern with sentencing reform, see SENTENCING RESEARCH, *supra*, at 65 (By late 1970's "a broad consensus in favor of change had formed among the political left and right, law enforcement agencies and prisoners' groups, and reformers and criminal justice systems officials.").

2. *See, e.g.*, CRIMINAL SENTENCES, *supra* note 1, at 69 ("It is far from a novelty to contend . . . that the sweeping power of a single judge to determine the sentence, as a matter of largely unreviewable 'discretion,' is a—perhaps 'the'—central evil in the system."); LEGISLATIVE AGENDA, *supra* note 1, at 10 ("Substantial disparities are the inevitable result of judicial discretion exercised by 378 federal district judges across the country . . . .").

3. Legislatures typically have provided judges with enormous statutory ranges within which they may sentence. For instance, in the District of Columbia, a judge may sentence a convicted robber to anywhere from 2 to 15 years. D.C. CODE ANN. § 22-2901 (1981). Although this range allows judges to sentence one robber to a term seven times as long as another, the statute gives no guidance as to who deserves the fifteen years and who the two. *See id.*

4. *See* United States v. Tucker, 404 U.S. 443, 447 (1972) ("[A] sentence imposed by a federal district judge, if within statutory limits, is generally not subject to review."). *See also* Symposium, Appellate Review of Sentences, 32 F.R.D. 257, 260-61 (1962) (Remarks of Kaufman, J.) ("At present the United States is the only nation in the free world where one judge can determine, conclusively, decisively and finally the minimum period of time a defendant must remain in prison, without being subject to any review of his determination."), *quoted in*, Dorszynski v. United States, 418 U.S. 424, 440 n.14 (1974).

Unreliable Factfinding and Sentencing

sentence length. As a consequence, judges have been able—indeed they have virtually been forced—to sentence on the basis of their own philosophy of criminal law. This has created a situation in which one judge might grant probation for the same case that, in the next courtroom, another might impose ten years. As former Judge Marvin Frankel has said: "[S]weeping penalty statutes allow sentences to be 'individualized' not so much in terms of defendants but mainly in terms of the wide spectrums of character, bias, neurosis, and daily vagary encountered among occupants of the trial bench."[5]

Accordingly, reformers have sought to curtail disparity by limiting judicial discretion. For instance, between 1975 and 1982 more than 30 states passed mandatory minimum sentencing laws.[6] Today a legislatively fashionable way of controlling discretion is through "Sentencing Guidelines," rules that direct sentencers how sentence length should change as salient facts in a case vary.[7]

---

5. CRIMINAL SENTENCES, *supra* note 1, at 21.
6. SENTENCING RESEARCH, *supra* note 1, at 61.
7. The nation's first sentencing guideline commission was established in Minnesota in 1978. D. PARENT, THE MINNESOTA SENTENCING GUIDELINE PROCESS ch.1, at 1 (forthcoming 1986). In 1980, the first version of the Minnesota Guidelines went into effect, *id.*, and the updated version still is, *see* MINN. STAT. ANN. ch. 244-app. (West Supp. 1985) (Minnesota Sentencing Guidelines & Commentary). Widely viewed as successful in achieving its objectives, the Minnesota system has served as a model for other jurisdictions considering guidelines. Since Minnesota broke the ground, the states of Washington, WASH. REV. CODE. ANN. § 9.94A.310 (Supp. 1985) (Washington Sentencing Grid), and Pennsylvania, 204 PA. ADMIN. CODE §§ 303.1-03.9 (Fry 1986) (Pennsylvania Sentencing Guidelines), have enacted guidelines as well.

More recently, the New York State legislature established a sentencing committee to draft guidelines for the legislatûre to consider. 1983 N.Y. Laws ch. 711. The New York Committee chose to follow the grid form, *see* Minutes of the Meeting of New York State Committee on Sentencing Guidelines 6-7 (Mar. 30, 1984), and, as a result, their product looks much like Minnesota's grid—offense severity on the vertical axis, offender history on the horizontal. *See* NEW YORK STATE COMMITTEE ON SENTENCING GUIDELINES, DETERMINATE SENTENCING REPORT AND RECOMMENDATIONS 56 (Mar. 29, 1985) (reproduction of grid) [hereinafter cited as N.Y. GUIDELINE REPORT]. Unlike the Minnesota Guidelines, which in the absence of legislative action automatically went into effect after promulgation and a lay-over period, MINN. STAT. ANN. § 244.09, Subd. 12 (West Supp. 1985), the New York Guidelines "have no force and effect unless enacted [by the legislature] into law." 1983 N.Y. Laws ch. 711 §3(1). Published by the New York Guidelines Committee in March 1985, the New York Guidelines have gathered scant support, and the chances of their enactment into law seem slim.

In Washington, D.C., the Chief Judge of the District of Columbia Superior Court has established a committee of judges and non-judges to develop guidelines. Judge Frederick H. Weisberg, Remarks to Guggenheim Sentencing Project Seminar, Yale University (Mar. 1, 1985) (tape on file with Guggenheim Project). Their proposal has not yet been made public.

For years, the federal government has used a shadow sentencing guideline system in the guise of parole guidelines. *See* 28 C.F.R. § 2.20 (1985) (parole guidelines); 44 Fed. Reg. 26,549 (1979) (arguing that parole guidelines mitigate sentence disparity). Thinking it politically infeasible to impose sentencing guidelines on district court judges, Congress attacked sentence disparity through the parole board. It set up a guideline system for the U.S. Parole Commission which was analytically identical to sentencing guidelines. Thus the Parole Commission became the *de facto* sentencer in federal crimes. *See* United States v. Addonizio, 442 U.S. 178, 188-9 (1979) ("Whether wisely or not, Congress has decided that the [Parole] Commission is in the best position to determine when release is appropriate, and in doing so, to moderate the disparities in the sentencing practices of individual judges."). This

In this essay, I will argue that, in the war against disparity, the tacticians of the guidelines movement have paid insufficient attention to the procedures that develop the facts to which guidelines are applied. Tacking shiny, new sentencing guidelines onto the tail end of a system of criminal procedure which does an unreliable job of developing the facts (as so many of the nation's criminal justice systems do) is a lot like putting a new coat of paint on an old clunker. The car looks good, but it still doesn't run much better. Ironically, sentencing guidelines may entrench a different kind of disparity—factual disparity.

I. The Minnesota Guidelines As Model

The archetypical sentencing guideline system is the Minnesota Guidelines, which have been in effect since 1980.[8] The Minnesota system has become a model for reform in other jurisdictions,[9] and exhibits the four traits which best characterize modern sentencing grids: 1) it identifies the set of facts relevant to sentencing;[10] 2) it determines how these relevant facts will affect a sentence;[11] 3) it allows the sentencer to depart from the indicated sentence by stating reasons;[12] 4) it provides review by a higher body to bring into compliance sentences impermissibly outside the guideline range.[13]

The Minnesota Guidelines divide facts into two categories, facts about the crime and facts about the criminal, and establish scales for each set. One scale ranks the seriousness of the crime;[14] the other ranks the criminal history of the offender.[15] Each serves as one of the two axes of the sentencing grid.[16]

---

has been changed by the Sentencing Reform Act of 1984, Pub. L. No. 98-473, §§ 211-39, 98 Stat. 1987 (codified in scattered sections of U.S.C.). The Act eliminates parole and sets up a federal sentencing commission charged with developing and promulgating a set of federal sentencing guidelines which federal judges must apply.

8. *See* Minn. Stat. Ann. § 244.09 (West Supp. 1985) (establishing sentencing commission); *id.* at Subd. 12 (providing for adoption of guidelines in absence of legislative action); *id.* at Ch. 244-app. (guidelines and commentary).

9. *See supra* note 6.

10. Minn. Stat. Ann. § 244.09, Subd. 5(2) (West Supp. 1985) (sentence grid to be based on "appropriate combination of reasonable offense and offender characteristics").

11. *Id.*

12. *Id.* at § 244.10, Subd. 2.

13. *Id.* at § 244.11.

14. *Id.* at Ch. 244-app. (West Supp. 1985) (guidelines and commentary) (Offense Severity).

15. *Id.* (Criminal History).

16. *Id.* (reproduced on facing page).

Unreliable Factfinding and Sentencing

IV. SENTENCING GUIDELINES GRID

Presumptive Sentence Lengths in Months

Italicized numbers within the grid denote the range within which a judge may sentence without the sentence being deemed a departure.

SEVERITY LEVELS OF CONVICTION OFFENSE	CRIMINAL HISTORY SCORE 0	1	2	3	4	5	6 or more
Unauthorized Use of Motor Vehicle Possession of Marijuana I	12*	12*	12*	15	18	21	24
Theft Related Crimes ($150-$2500) Sale of Marijuana II	12*	12*	14	17	20	23	27 *25-29*
Theft Crimes ($150-$2500) III	12*	13	16	19	22 *21-23*	27 *25-29*	32 *30-34*
Burglary - Felony Intent Receiving Stolen Goods ($150-$2500) IV	12*	15	18	21	25 *24-26*	32 *30-34*	41 *37-45*
Simple Robbery V	18	23	27	30 *29-31*	38 *36-40*	46 *43-49*	54 *50-58*
Assault, 2nd Degree VI	21	26	30	34 *33-35*	44 *42-46*	54 *50-58*	65 *60-70*
Aggravated Robbery VII	24 *23-25*	32 *30-34*	41 *38-44*	49 *45-53*	65 *60-70*	81 *75-87*	97 *90-104*
Assault, 1st Degree Criminal Sexual Conduct, 1st Degree VIII	43 *41-45*	54 *50-58*	65 *60-70*	76 *71-81*	95 *89-101*	113 *106-120*	132 *124-140*
Murder, 3rd Degree IX	97 *94-100*	119 *116-122*	127 *124-130*	149 *143-155*	176 *168-184*	205 *195-215*	230 *218-242*
Murder, 2nd Degree X	116 *111-121*	140 *133-147*	162 *153-171*	203 *192-214*	243 *231-255*	284 *270-298*	324 *309-339*

1st Degree Murder is excluded from the guidelines by law and continues to have a mandatory life sentence.

*one year and one day

The Yale Law Journal Vol. 95: 1258, 1986

In devising the "Offense Severity" scale, the Minnesota Guideline Commission ranked crimes from most to least serious, divided the list into a series of categories (or "bands"), and assigned a number to each band.[17] This ranking and categorization in effect defined the facts about the offense that are relevant to the sentence.[18]

Similarly, the Commission created a "Criminal History" scale. It was not the aim of sentencing guidelines to eliminate the individualization of sentences, but to ensure that the individualization is consistent from judge to judge. (That is, facts about the *offender* ought to matter in individualization, not facts about the *judge*.) Accordingly, the Minnesota Guidelines established a numerical scale to quantify the offender's criminal past. To calculate an offender's criminal history "score," the sentencer adds one point for each prior felony conviction,[19] one point if the offender was on probation or parole at the time of the offense,[20] one-half point for each prior gross misdemeanor conviction,[21] and one-quarter point for each prior misdemeanor conviction.[22] Theoretically, an offender score could include a much broader range of facts. For instance, the United States Parole Guidelines—which work on the same general principle as the Minnesota grid—include factors such as the offender's age at the time of the offense and any history of heroin or opiate dependency.[23]

After determining the crime's Severity Category (a factual determination) and the offender's Criminal History Score (another factual determination), the sentencer draws a line across from the vertical axis and down from the horizontal axis to the box in which the two lines intersect. That

17. *See* D. PARENT, *supra* note 7, at ch. 4, pp. 8-16.

18. These facts do not always track the statutory definitions of crimes. For instance, the Minnesota Guidelines place kidnapping when a victim suffers great bodily harm in a higher severity band than kidnapping when the victim is released unharmed, but in an unsafe place, MINN. STAT. ANN. Ch. 244-app. (West Supp. 1985) (Minnesota Sentencing Guidelines & Commentary) (felonies), even though an offender who does either of these things meets the elements of being legally guilty of the single crime of kidnapping, MINN. STAT. ANN. § 609.25(1) (West. 1964 & Supp. 1986) (acts constituting kidnapping), and even though the legislature has authorized the same maximum sentence in both circumstances, *id.* at § 609.25(2)(2). Similarly, the U.S. Parole Guidelines place those who use the mails to *retail* child pornography in a lower offense severity band than those who *wholesale*, 28 C.F.R. § 2.20 ch. 11(D) (1984) (Severity Index), although the wholesale/retail distinction is irrelevant to guilt, *see* 18 U.S.C. § 2252 (1982). The New York Guideline Committee also divided crimes into finer bands than current law provides, and recommended to the legislature that it amend the penal law to match the newly drawn bands. *See* N.Y. GUIDELINE REPORT, *supra* note 7, at 6-7, 37-38.

19. MINN. STAT. ANN. Ch. 244-app. (West Supp. 1985) (Sentencing Guidelines & Commentary) (Criminal History).

20. *Id.*

21. *Id.*

22. *Id.* Under certain circumstances, juvenile convictions are scored as well. *Id.*

23. *See* 28 C.F.R. § 2.20, at 101 (1985) (Salient Factor Score chart).

Unreliable Factfinding and Sentencing

box contains a narrow range of months, and the statute directs the judge to impose a sentence within that range.[24]

To allow flexibility in unusual cases, Minnesota permits a judge to depart from the range in the box. To do so, the judge either must find that a "departure factor" listed by the guidelines exists,[25] or must identify an unlisted factor that demonstrates that the sentence in the box is inappropriate or inequitable.[26] In either event, the finding must be placed on the record.[27] Any system of departures, however, would threaten to undermine the system unless policed to ensure that the departures, like the presumptive sentences, were regular. Thus, in a pronounced break with sentencing practices of the past, the Minnesota Guidelines allow appellate review of sentences,[28] which enables the higher courts to develop a common law of departures. All sentences have thus become standardized—those that do not depart by statute, and those that do by emerging case law. No longer can one judge apply a different, unwritten sentencing code than a brother or sister judge across the corridor.

The guiding principle of sentencing grids, then, is that they yield a specific sentence when applied to a specific factual situation. Indeed, this must be true of any reform seeking to curtail judges' sentencing discretion by making them follow rules. As Arthur Leff has said, "it is a fundamental tenet of most systems of justice that identical things be treated identically; that is what 'following a rule' *means*."[29] Although guidelines still might allow some disparity—because they put a small range instead of a single number in a box—the notion of equal treatment of factually identical cases is at their core.[30]

---

24. MINN. STAT. ANN. Ch. 244-app. (West Supp. 1985) (Departures from the Guidelines) ("The judge shall utilize the presumptive sentence provided in the sentencing guidelines unless the individual case involves substantial and compelling circumstances.").

25. For instance, the Guidelines explicitly allow a judge to depart from the box upon finding: "The offender played a minor or passive role in the crime . . . ." *Id.*

26. *Id.*

27. *Id.*

28. MINN. STAT. ANN. § 244.11. (West Supp. 1985).

29. Leff, *The Leff Dictionary of Law: A Fragment*, 94 YALE L. J. 1855, 2016 (1985) (emphasis in original) (from definition of "analogy"). Of course, before they can apply this rule, decisionmakers need to answer the difficult question, "*When* is something so like something else that it should be treated the same, or so unlike that it should not[?]" *Id.* (emphasis in original). One of the main points of sentencing guidelines is that they make this decision for judges, unlike traditional schemes where each judge decides for himself.

30. Providing a small range instead of a single number actually can even promote the principle of consistency. Because "it is in fact never the case that *all* other things are equal," *id.* at 2235 (from definition of "caeteris paribus") (emphasis in original), it might be counter-productive to require a single number. By providing a small range, the grid allows judges to impose slightly different sentences in cases which are slightly different.

The Yale Law Journal Vol. 95: 1258, 1986

II. The Jerome Frank Problem of Slippery Facts

To truly eliminate disparity, sentencing reformers must standardize not only substantive sentencing law, but also the procedures that bring to the sentencer the facts to which that law will be applied. Jerome Frank pointed out over a half century ago that judicial decisions (D) are a function of substantive rules of law (R) as applied to the facts of individual cases (F).[31] Frank expressed the relationship in an equation:[32]

$$F \times R = D$$

In striving to eliminate disparity, guideline authors have standardized the R, the substantive rules of sentencing. Decisions will not, however, be regular or predictable unless the F's are being established through reliable procedures, procedures which will ensure that cases that are factually similar are being described as similar to whomever is applying the R.[33]

In the rest of this essay, I will use examples from the literature and from the ongoing Guggenheim Sentencing Project at Yale[34] to demonstrate that the procedures that develop the facts for sentencers are often unreliable and erratic.[35]

31. Frank, *What Courts Do In Fact*, 26 Ill. L. Rev. 645, 649 (1932).

32. *Id.* at 649; J. Frank, Courts on Trial 14 (1950).

33. That sentencing guidelines are sometimes characterized as "computerized sentencing" helps demonstrate this point. There is an acronym among computer programers: GIGO. It stands for "Garbage In, Garbage Out," which means that it makes no difference how good a computer program is if you feed bad data into it. *See* Computer Science & Eng'g Bd., Nat'l Academy of Sciences, Databanks in a Free Society: Computers, Record-Keeping and Privacy 300 (1972). Professor John Coffee has made this observation with regard to sentencing in two articles. Coffee, *Repressed Issues of Sentencing: Accountability, Predictability, and Equality in the Era of the Sentencing Commission*, 66 Geo. L. J. 975, 986-87 (1978); Coffee, *The Future of Sentencing Reform: Emerging Legal Issues in the Individualization of Justice*, 73 Mich. L. Rev. 1361, 1374 (1975). Coffee seems particularly concerned with probation officers including in the Presentence Investigation Report (PSI) unverified information about the offender gleaned from databanks: computerized educational records, juvenile records, arrest records, conviction records, police intelligence reports, and the like. Alone, these problems pose formidible difficulties for sentencing guidelines. *Id.* at 1376-91. The problem of bad information, though, is not only that bad information can make its way into a PSI from computerized files elsewhere, but that the procedures and customs at nearly every stage of the criminal process are so lax that they virtually ensure that like cases will not be described to the sentencer as alike.

34. For the last three years, the Daniel and Florence Guggenheim Criminal Justice Program at the Yale Law School has been examining the problems of sentencing through close study of a small number of trial judges from different jurisdictions. The judges have undergone extensive interviews by members of the Yale Project, have been observed by students and faculty members while plea bargaining and sentencing in their home jurisdictions, and have participated in seminars with each other. Among its other data, the Project has so far produced a number of unpublished studies of different judges from Connecticut, Ohio, Massachusetts, New Jersey, New York, and Washington, D.C., from which I will draw examples.

35. The rest of the essay is not meant to catalogue every step in the criminal process that bears on factfinding at sentencing (because virtually every step will), but only to discuss a few topics which demonstrate the kinds of factfinding issues that commissions framing sentencing guidelines must face.

Unreliable Factfinding and Sentencing

A. *Developing the Facts at Trials and at Guilty Pleas*

The overriding reality of today's criminal justice system is that the trial—society's model for getting at the truth[36]—is used in only a fraction of criminal cases; the overwhelming majority of criminal convictions nationwide are entered by an offender's guilty plea.[37] One of the characteristics of a trial is that it often fleshes out the particulars of an offense in the way that a plea allocution does not. At a trial, the prosecution must prove the defendant's guilt through real evidence and testimony. In the normal course of telling their stories, witnesses will relate their version of the incident in exacting detail, because a witness in a trial needs to demonstrate a command of the minute to prove the accuracy of his or her memory.[38] In contrast, when pleading guilty, an offender need admit only the broad elements of the crime, and no witnesses rehearse the details of the offense for the court.[39]

---

36. Tehan v. United States *ex rel.* Shott, 382 U.S. 406, 416 (1966) ("The basic purpose of a trial is the determination of truth . . . ."); Louisell, *Criminal Discovery: Dilemma Real or Apparent?*, 49 CALIF. L. REV. 56, 97 (1961) (The "objective" of a criminal trial is "accurate fact ascertainment"). Of course, the trial also serves much wider purposes in our system of government, which may conflict with simple factfinding. For instance, factual accuracy at trial is sacrificed in the service of the Bill of Rights when the 4th Amendment excludes evidence seized without a valid warrant. And even the nature of the adversary system itself can impede the search for truth. "[T]ruth and victory are mutually incompatible for some considerable percentage of attorneys trying cases at any given time." Frankel, *The Search for Truth: An Umpireal View*, 123 U. PA. L. REV. 1031, 1037 (1975).

37. BUREAU OF JUSTICE STATISTICS, U.S. DEP'T OF JUSTICE, REPORT TO THE NATION ON CRIME AND JUSTICE 65 (1983) [hereinafter cited as REPORT TO THE NATION] (in selected jurisdictions in 1979, guilty pleas ranged from a low in one jurisdiction of 81% to a high in another of 97% of all convictions) (citing unpublished study). *See also* N.Y. GUIDELINE REPORT, *supra* note 7, at 26–27 (in 1983, guilty pleas accounted for 92% of felony convictions in New York State).

38. Despite the relatively great amount of information considered during the course of a trial, the trial, of course, is by no means a *perfect* factfinding mechanism. Probably, there is no imaginable type of legal hearing that could always be objectively, historically accurate. As Jerome Frank has pointed out:

> The facts themselves do not walk into court. The court has to guess what actually happened, basing its own fallible guess on fallible inferences made while listening to and watching fallible witnesses—sometimes lying, often mistaken, who frequently disagree with one another about what actually occurred outside the court-room—what happened, mind you, weeks or months or years before the case began.

Frank, *supra* note 31, at 650. *See also* J. FRANK, *supra* note 32, at 14–16. But acknowleding that some uncertainty will persist no matter how thorough the factfinding procedures is not to say that all factfinding procedures are equal. It seems self-evident that the judge's "guess" at the truth will be a better educated guess after a hearing in which he has heard and seen witnesses telling their stories in detail (as in a trial) than after a hearing at which he has heard only a quick summary of the relevant events (as in a guilty plea).

39. *See* Newman & NeMoyer, *Issues of Propriety in Negotiated Justice*, 47 DEN. L.J. 367, 398–99 (1970) (discussing gap between "formal words of charge" and rich variation of conduct which may underlie any given charge).

"[A]n express admission of guilt" is not the only way that an offender is permitted to enter a guilty plea. North Carolina v. Alford, 400 U.S. 25, 37 (1970). On the theory that the standard of legal guilt is sometimes "uncertain and elusive," *id.* at 33 (quoting McCoy v. United States, 124 U.S. App. D.C. 177, 179, 363 F.2d 306, 308 (1966)), it is sufficient that an offender concede that there is a likelihood of conviction, *see id.* at 28 n.2, 37, and that the court conclude that there is a "strong factual basis for the plea," *id.* at 38. Though it may be disturbing for other reasons that an offender is allowed to

Of course, both after a trial and after a guilty plea, the sentencer will probably gather additional information relevant to sentencing, perhaps through a presentence report or counsel's submissions.[40] But it is likely that some of the facts about the offense that would come out at trial will never reach the sentencer, and, even if they do, they will not always present themselves with the same vividness.

The extra information that a trial elicits can cut either way. In some cases the facts look better and in others they look worse. One of the judges studied by the Guggenheim Project gave a hypothetical (based on a real case of his) to demonstrate how a trial can change the picture of a case that a judge develops during plea negotiations:

> The defendant is accused of coming upon a 65 or 70-year-old woman. . . . The [prosecutor's] write-up reads, "He grabbed her pocketbook, he yanked it from her, she fell to the ground, broke her hip, injured her arm and he fled." Okay? And your immediate assumption in [trying to negotiate a plea bargain] is, "What a mean little rat to knock down that nice old lady and steal a pocketbook." . . . The defense counsel is usually at a loss at that point. He has not seen the old lady. He doesn't really have a great understanding of the event. His client gives him a particular version [which] he finds hard to believe, so he's not terribly convincing in persuading you . . . . When you get to trial, what you discover is that he reached out to this woman, who indeed is 70 but looks 50, and grabbed her pocketbook, and she said, "Hey you son-of-a-bitch, what are you doing," and she grabbed it back. He then pulled her pocketbook again and she tripped over a crack in the sidewalk and fell down, and as she fell she hit a fire hydrant and broke her hip. Your entire perspective with respect to that defendant has changed . . . .[41]

During this hypothetical plea negotiation, the judge had made two implicit "findings" of fact: first, that the victim was frail; second, that the offender gratuitously threw her to the ground.[42] At trial, both "findings" are proven false. The victim is vigorous, and she was not viciously

plead guilty while simultaneously maintaining innocence, it makes little difference to the argument here. Under *Alford*, the offender need concede that only those facts which establish the elements of the offense would likely be proved. So there is neither admission to "sentencing facts" nor a judgment that there is a likelihood that they would be proved.

40. *See infra* text accompanying notes 74-102.

41. Justice Jeffrey Atlas, Remarks to Guggenheim Sentencing Project, in New Haven (Oct. 12, 1984).

42. Under a guideline system, either of these findings could justify a departure from a presumptive sentence. For instance, the proposed New York Guidelines allow an upward departure either when, "The defendant's conduct during the commission of the offense manifested deliberate cruelty to the victim," N.Y. GUIDELINE REPORT, *supra* note 7, at 88 (Aggravating Factors), or when, "The defendant knew, or should have known, that the victim was particularly vulnerable because of age [or] infirmity . . . ," *id.*

Unreliable Factfinding and Sentencing

knocked down, but she tripped during a struggle. To this judge, the difference in the two descriptions of the same event would probably have meant the difference between brief incarceration and probation.[43]

On the other hand, trials can bring home the brutality of some cases in a way that no plea discussion ever could. When witnesses detail the brutal circumstances of the crime and when the victim testifies about the terror he suffered, new "facts" about the gravity of the offense are put before the sentencer.[44]

B. *Factfinding Accompanying Guilty Pleas*

When there is a trial, the trial itself is not the only source of information that the judge has before sentencing. A number of other channels—such as plea conferences, presentence reports, and various hearings—supplement the judge's knowledge of the facts. When there is no

---

43. Remarks of Justice Atlas, *supra* note 41. Justice Atlas also told the project that differences in the ways that cases looked before and after trial would, when he was a trial lawyer, sometimes dictate defense strategy: "There were times when I tried cases because . . . although I knew my client was going to be convicted that the judge would be persuaded not to send him to jail after the trial. . . ." *Id. Accord* Kuh, *Trial Techniques: Defense Counsel's Role in Sentencing*, 14 CRIM. L. BULL. 433, 436 n.5 (1978) [hereinafter cited as *Defense Counsel's Role*]. Kuh says:

> Sometimes, a trial can be helpful, even if there is little chance of acquittal, in constituting a full dramatic living presentence report of sorts; it may assist the court in recognizing that the defendant's intent was not as heinous as the mere existence of the plea of guilty—in isolation—may indicate.

44. *See, e.g.*, O. Sohmer, Portrait in Profile: A Study of the Sentencing Practice of Judge Robert J. Callahan 44 (Mar. 22, 1985) [hereinafter cited as "Callahan Profile"] (unpublished manuscript available from Guggenheim Sentencing Project):

> When sentencing on a plea, the Judge is basing his decision on the statements of the lawyers, the cold legal dissection of the elements of a criminal statute, and sometimes the reaction of the victim as related in the PSI. But after a trial, the Judge has seen the people involved. He has watched the defendant for several days or even weeks and has heard him speak, perhaps. He has seen the victim and heard testimony of the trauma and terror of the crime. That does not come from the file.

See also Comment, *The Influence of the Defendant's Plea on Judicial Determination of Sentence*, 66 YALE L.J. 204, 218-19 (1956) (guilty plea "may contribute" to shorter sentence because "brutal circumstances" may neither be emphasized by prosecutor nor "vividly recounted" at trial). Some defense attorneys will use the guilty plea as a technique for avoiding damaging facts:

> Under the pressure of a heavy, time-consuming caseload, the prosecutor may easily be seduced at an early stage of the proceedings, before such facts are more fully developed, by the offer of a quick guilty plea in exchange for a light sentence, only to discover too late that the offense, or the offender, was far more serious than originally thought.

Enker, *Perspectives on Plea Bargaining*, in TASK FORCE ON THE ADMINISTRATION OF JUSTICE, PRESIDENT'S COMMISSION ON LAW ENFORCEMENT AND ADMINISTRATION OF JUSTICE, TASK FORCE REPORT: THE COURTS app. A, at 108, 110-11 (1967). Although it would be difficult to fill in facts that are absolutely missing from the case during plea negotiations, some judges try to compensate for the lack of vividness: " 'When I look at a defendant,' says Judge Rothwax, 'I try not to think of him as he looks in court, well-dressed, polite. I try to picture him as he threw the old lady down the stairway.' " P. Pope, Sentencing Profile of [Justice] Harold J. Rothwax 29 (Sept. 1984) [hereinafter cited as "Rothwax Profile"] (unpublished manuscript available from Guggenheim Sentencing Project).

trial, however, these "supplementary" sources become the *only* procedures bringing the facts to the sentencer.

1. *Pre-Negotiation Factual Development*

In the absence of a trial, even those procedures far removed from the adjudication of guilt take on heightened importance. For instance, in jurisdictions in which a case is passed from lawyer to lawyer as it progresses through the various stages (both prosecutors' and public defenders' offices sometimes follow this pattern),[45] it can make an enormous difference who conducts the original interviews of the witnesses, victims, and police officers. If the interviewer—who, depending on the place and the crime, may be a junior attorney, a senior attorney, or a layperson[46]—fails to elicit a salient piece of information or forgets to write it in the file, it may never reach the sentencer.[47]

The extraordinary lack of diligence that some attorneys demonstrate can make the problem of information development and communication even more acute. The literature reports, for instance, that many public defenders interview their clients for the first time with an eye not toward developing the facts of the case, but toward trying to figure out what charge the defendant is willing to "cop out" (plead guilty) to.[48] Because

45. Graham & Letwin, *The Preliminary Hearings in Los Angeles: Some Field Findings and Legal-Policy Observations*, 18 U.C.L.A. L. Rev. 635, 645 (1971) (case passed from prosecutor to prosecutor like baton in relay race); Rothwax Profile, *supra* note 44, at 31 (prosecutor who investigates case usually does not negotiate plea); Sudnow, *Normal Crimes: Sociological Features of the Penal Code in a Public Defender Office*, 12 Social Problems 255, 265-66 (1965) ("Over the course of his proceedings, a defendant will have several attorneys . . . . [T]he file is relied upon to furnish all the [essential] information . . . .").

46. In Manhattan, rookie prosecutors are broken in on misdemeanors while the more seasoned work in the Supreme Court on felonies. Rothwax Profile, *supra* note 44, at 98 n.17. In the Bronx, particularly experienced prosecutors are assigned to "major offenses." Merola, *The Major Offense Bureau: A Blueprint for Effective Prosecution of Career Criminals*, 11 The Prosecutor 8, 9 (1975). In Nashville, Tennessee, non-legal clerks tutored by the D.A.'s office have conducted the initial examination of the arresting officer, and usually the D.A. has no further discussion with the officer about the case. *See* Domash, Stromatt, Carr, Schnelle, Kirchner & Shriver, *Criminal Case Preparation: A Police-Prosecution Cooperative Effort*, 14 The Prosecutor 417, 418 (1979).

47. "[I]f [the deputy prosecutor conducting the original interview] fails to record the existence of a piece of evidence, another deputy will not be able to use it in the prosecution and may in good faith reply to the defense attorney either in discovery or in negotiations that such evidence does not exist. As a result the defendant may choose a course of conduct, such as a guilty plea or a demand for a jury trial, in ignorance of the true facts. The same may be true of bail motions, motions to suppress and even sentencing." Graham & Letwin, *supra* note 45, at 645.

48. J. Casper, American Criminal Justice: The Defendant's Perspective 106-07 (1972). Some public defenders suffer such enormous caseloads that they may spend less than 10 minutes total with a client before pleading him guilty. *Id.* at 106. Casper reports: "among the first words uttered by [the public defender when meeting a client] were: 'I can get you ——— if you plead guilty.' " *Id.* at 106. *Accord* Sudnow, *supra* note 45, at 266-70 (1965) (P.D.s' interviews of defendants not conducted to establish detailed facts or to wage a defense, but to determine that case is suitable for rapid guilty plea disposition). This approach to criminal "defense" work obviously precludes any possibility of an independent investigation of the facts. And where a lawyer solely relies on an initial interview with a client for the facts, he is unlikely to get even the client's complete version; in the best of

Unreliable Factfinding and Sentencing

"factfinding" at a guilty plea often relies heavily on investigation and representation by counsel, such a cursory development of the case virtually assures that cases will not be described accurately to the sentencer, and, therefore, that like cases will not be perceived and treated by the sentencer as alike.

After the initial interviews, attorneys engage in discovery about the case. This stage may constitute the most crucial "factfinding" of the process, because the information developed here will be the grist for the plea discussions. Facts never discovered will never be discussed and cannot figure into the plea bargain. Thus the procedures under which discovery takes place can bear directly on the final sentence imposed.

Pretrial criminal discovery laws vary enormously from state to state. For instance, whereas Louisiana explicitly does *not* authorize defense discovery of statements by prospective witnesses,[49] Alaska requires the prosecutor to disclose statements made by anyone "known by the government to have knowledge of relevant facts,"[50] and Florida not only requires prosecutors to disclose statements, but also allows the defendant to depose potential witnesses.[51] Each of these procedures will put different facts in the hands of the defense for the plea negotiations, or, put another way, each will produce different descriptions of the same case. If guidelines are to reduce sentence disparity, they must be supported by discovery procedures that find facts fully, accurately, and consistently.

But one does not learn the full story about pre-plea discovery simply by looking at statutory provisions; local custom may "rewrite" the rules on the books. For instance, in some towns in Connecticut, the defense counsel gets only a quick look at the prosecutor's file when he and the prosecutor go over it briefly together in the prosecutor's office.[52] In other towns, defense counsel are actually permitted to take the files home overnight.[53] There are even discovery variations from lawyer to lawyer. Some prosecutors are more willing to open their files than others,[54] and some prosecu-

---

circumstances, "A lawyer cannot accept a client's first account as complete or accurate." H. FREEMAN & H. WEIHOFEN, CLINICAL LAW TRAINING: INTERVIEWING AND COUNSELING 30 (1972).

Private defense lawyers can be in even worse positions, as their "professional livelihood depends on . . . *not* trying many cases." L. WEINREB, DENIAL OF JUSTICE 73 (1977) (emphasis in original). *See also* Alschuler, *The Defense Attorney's Role in Plea Bargaining*, 84 YALE L.J. 1179, 1180 (1975) (even conscientious attorneys are led by plea bargaining to work against clients' interest); Comment, *In Search of the Adversary System—The Cooperative Practices of Private Criminal Defense Attorneys*, 50 TEX. L. REV. 60, 61 (1971) [hereinafter cited as *Private Lawyers*] ("Fee limitations necessitate abbreviated defenses, just as do inadequate budgets for a public agency.").

49. LA. CODE CRIM. PROC. ANN. art. 723 (West 1981).

50. ALASKA R. CRIM. P. 16(b)(1)(i).

51. FLA. R. CRIM. P. 3.220(a)(1)(ii), (d).

52. M. HEUMANN, PLEA BARGAINING 35 (1978) (discussing courts of limited felony jurisdiction).

53. *Id.*

54. *See Private Lawyers*, *supra* note 48, at 70.

tors play favorites with defense counsel, opening files only to those with whom they have good relationships.[55] All in all, different attorneys, even operating under the same formal discovery rules, will get different pictures of a case.

2. *Factual Development at the Plea Negotiation*

The paradigm of the plea bargain is that a defendant pleads guilty in exchange for a "break" on the sentence. For instance, one of the Guggenheim judges gives a plea discount by awarding one-third off the sentence expected for an offender who is convicted at trial.[56] Dispensed this way, the plea discount is a part of Jerome Frank's R, and the fact of the guilty plea part of the F: *If* guilty plea *then* award discount. Putting aside whether this kind of "break" is wise or just (either under a traditional sentencing scheme or a guideline regime), it creates no disparity as long as it is awarded even-handedly.[57]

---

55. *See id.* at 68–70; M. HEUMANN, *supra* note 52, at 63 (prosecutor punishes lawyer who files pretrial motions in case by denying access to files in other cases). *See also id.* at 183 n.36 ("the state's attorney might be more willing to share his files with the cooperative attorney . . .").

56. M. Berkman, Profile of Judge Frank J. Kinney, Jr. 23 (May 5, 1986) [hereinafter cited as "Kinney Profile"] (unpublished manuscript on file with Guggenheim Sentencing Project). Plea discounts are not always given so forthrightly, and, in some places, judges do not grant them at all; prosecutors do by dismissing or reducing charges. This "charge bargaining" lowers the ceiling on the judge's sentencing range, reducing the offender's "exposure." Whether a sentence is cut through the exercise of sentencing discretion (by a judge) or the exercise of charging discretion (by a prosecutor) is analytically irrelevant. The point is that both judges and prosecutors grant discounts off of what they believe to be the real, historical offense. One of the *rules* of sentencing is that the offender's sentence is reduced when a *fact* of the case is that it was disposed of by guilty plea.

57. Ensuring even-handed award of discounts becomes a technical issue. For instance, where judges themselves offer the discount, it could be mandated that the discount be a specific proportion of the sentence. *See* Note, *Restructuring the Plea Bargain*, 82 YALE L.J. 286, 301 (1972) (proposing fixed-rate plea discount). It is also technically possible to vary the size of the discount to serve any special concerns of judicial administration. For instance, one of the Guggenheim judges consciously gives bigger plea discounts when he has a particularly heavy case backlog. Another gives bigger discounts when there are provability problems with the case. If society decides to retain these practices, it is easy enough to make provability and caseload relevant factors in the size of the guideline's plea discount.

When prosecutors grant the discount instead of judges, there must likewise be regularization, lest judicial sentencing discretion simply be passed backwards. *See* Alschuler, *Sentencing Reform and Prosecutorial Power: A Critique of Recent Proposals for "Fixed" and "Presumptive" Sentencing*, 126 U. PA. L. REV. 550, 563–72 (1978). One way of preventing the mere relocation of disparity-causing discretion is to create prosecutorial guidelines to go with sentencing guidelines. *See* Schulhofer, *Due Process of Sentencing*, 128 U. PA. L. REV. 733, 787–98 (1980) (advocating guidelines for plea bargaining). For example, Washington has already accompanied its sentencing grid with nonbinding prosecutorial guidelines. WASH. REV. CODE ANN. §§ 9.94A.430–.460 (West Supp. 1986) (Recommended Prosecuting Standards for Charging and Plea Dispositions).

In addition, the very enactment of sentencing guidelines—even without explicit prosecutorial guidelines—can be read as an empowerment of and mandate to judges to police prosecutorial charge bargaining. Although the prosecutor has generally been thought to have a monopoly in charging decisions, the charge bargain is the frontier at which the prosecutor's decision to charge meets the judge's decision to sentence. United States v. Miller, 722 F.2d 562, 564 (9th Cir. 1983) ("When a plea bargain is placed before court, the necessary interplay between charging and sentencing decisions becomes manifest."). Several circuits have, under traditional sentencing schemes, already adopted a

Unreliable Factfinding and Sentencing

The plea bargain can, however, affect sentence disparity in another way. The process of the plea negotiation itself may tend to misdescribe the facts from which the discount will be taken. To avoid disparity, the "break" must be applied to an accurate factual predicate.

a. *The Sentence Bargain*

One variety of the plea bargain is the sentence bargain, in which an offender pleads guilty in exchange for a promise that a particular sentence will be imposed. At the time of the guilty plea, the judge puts the promised sentence on the record, and that promise must be kept subject to the same restriction that applies to all promises put on the record when a defendant tenders a guilty plea: if the state does not keep the promise, the defendant may withdraw the plea.[58] Because a sentence bargain requires a judge to ratify the number that opposing counsel have worked out, the crucial question is how much the judge knows about the facts of the case when he approves the bargain, because, for all practical purposes, approval is the imposition of a sentence.

The way that judges learn of the facts varies greatly. For instance, one judge studied by the Guggenheim Project conducts all of his sentence negotiations at the bench, off the record.[59] The prosecutor—generally not the prosecutor who investigated the case[60]—hands the judge a sheet from a yellow legal pad on which, in a few paragraphs, the prosecutor who did do the investigation has written out the state's version of the offense.[61] In the course of the next few minutes, the judge, the defense counsel, and the prosecutor try to agree on the appropriate sentence based on the description on the yellow sheet, the defendant's prior record, and any information

---

rule which allows a judge to reject a charge bargain when the bargain intrudes too deeply on the sentencing authority of the trial judge. *See, e.g.*, United States v. Ammidown, 497 F.2d 615, 622 (D.C. Cir. 1973) ("protection of the sentencing authority reserved to the judge" may sometimes justify refusing plea bargain); United States v. Bean, 564 F.2d 700, 704 (5th Cir. 1977) (that bargain would result in "too light a sentence" is "sound reason" to reject agreement); United States v. Ocanas, 628 F.2d 353, 358 (5th Cir. 1980), *cert. denied*, 451 U.S. 984 (1981) (same) (dicta). In a system in which statutory punishment ranges are broad and overlapping, a judge's scope will only infrequently be significantly infringed. In *Ammidown*, for example, the court ruled that the difference in possible sentences was too slight to warrant upsetting the bargain. In a guideline system, however, reducing charges will actually change the box on the grid. Thus, to protect their roles as authoritative sentencers, United States v. Escobar Noble, 653 F.2d 34, 36-37 (1st Cir. 1981) ("It is the peculiar function of the court, not the prosecutor, to say the last word about the justice of a sentence."), courts can read the very enactment of guidelines as a command to ensure that the discounts granted by prosecutors are regular. *See also* A. GOLDSTEIN, THE PASSIVE JUDICIARY: PROSECUTORIAL DISCRETION AND THE GUILTY PLEA (1981) (advocating judicial fashioning of common law of prosecutorial discretion).

58. Santobello v. New York, 404 U.S. 257 (1971).

59. Rothwax Profile, *supra* note 44, at 33.

60. *Id.* at 31.

61. *Id.* at 28, 33.

that defense counsel might add.[62] The entire negotiation takes place out of earshot of the defendant, who is seated at the defense table some 20 feet away. When the negotiation is complete, defense counsel steps over to the defendant to relay the terms of the deal. If the deal is acceptable, the defendant pleads guilty on the spot. The judge puts the negotiated sentence on the record as part of the plea, orders the probation department to prepare a PSI (which is fairly inconsequential at this stage), and sets a date at which the sentence will actually be imposed. In the course of a routine day, the judge will try to negotiate sentences in 40 to 80 felony cases, roughly a defendant every six minutes.[63]

Another of the judges studied by the Guggenheim Project also deals in sentence bargains, but the negotiating customs in his jurisdiction are very different.[64] The negotiating is done in the judge's chambers with a group of attorneys present, but no defendants.[65] A defense counsel or state's attorney may sit through several other lawyers' quasi-public negotiations before the judge gets to his cases. The judge listens to the lawyers' versions of the case, and then gives his estimate of its "worth," sometimes pointing to facts in the case which demonstrate his "going rates," thus using negotiations to school less experienced lawyers.[66]

A third judge studied by the Project conducted plea negotiations more casually, sometimes discussing plea dispositions in chambers when only one of the attorneys was present, and piecing together a version of the events from the attorneys' separate accounts.[67] This judge tried to take special care to make sure that he repeated to each attorney everything that the other had told him, and, unlike the first two judges, put every fact of importance on the record at the sentencing.[68]

None of the differences in these practices are dictated by the law of the jurisdiction. Each is a result of habit, local custom, or the style of the judge. And it is easy to see how the differences can lead to deeper or shallower discussion of the facts and leave more or less room for poor communication and mistakes.

b. *The Charge Bargain*

Another variety of the plea bargain is the charge bargain. In a charge bargain, the judge does not commit himself to a specific sentence before

62. *Id.* at 33-35. Usually, the D.A.'s request for a particular sentence will also be in the file. *Id.* at 29-30, 33.
63. *Id.* at 16.
64. Kinney Profile, *supra* note 56, at 25.
65. *Id.* at 25-28.
66. *Id.*
67. Proceedings of Guggenheim Sentencing Project, in New Haven (Mar. 30, 1985).
68. *Id.*

Unreliable Factfinding and Sentencing

the plea is entered. Instead of dealing with the judge, the defense deals with the prosecutor. If the prosecutor agrees to drop some charges, the total number of years that the judge can impose—the defendant's "exposure"—is reduced.[69] The judge may not participate in negotiations at all,[70] and, therefore, may be largely ignorant of the facts of the case before going into the plea hearing.

At the plea hearing, the judge must develop at least some of the facts of the case.[71] However, the set of facts necessary to support a conviction (guilt facts) is much smaller than the set which the judge may use to impose sentence (sentencing facts).[72] For instance, if three offenders plead guilty to conspiracy to import heroin into the country, it is enough, for the purpose of their guilty plea, that each admits to agreeing to carry out the importation. Yet in order to assess culpability and levy sentence, the judge would want to know that one was the financier, the other the captain of the freighter that would carry the drugs, and the third merely a deckhand. Therefore, to impose a sentence after a guilty plea has been induced by a charge bargain, most judges will turn to various post-conviction factfinding tools.

---

69. Charge bargaining will have one of two effects. It may actually cut into the sentence that the judge would impose. For instance, consider a case where the top charge carries 25 years, and the prosecutor allows the defendant to plead out to a charge which carries a maximum of 15 years. If, after learning the facts, the judge wishes to impose a 20-year sentence, his sentence has actually been affected by the charge bargain; it has been reduced by 5 years. On the other hand, if he wishes to impose a 10-year sentence, then the bargain has not affected the sentence at all; it is irrelevant whether the maximum is 25 or 15 years. *See* M. Heumann, *supra* note 52, at 42 ("Charges can be dropped without reducing the realistic range of years within which the defendant will be sentenced."). If there is a problem here it is not that the plea bargain has upset regularity in sentencing, but that the defendant may have been duped into thinking that he was getting something for his guilty plea that, in fact, he already had. *See* W. Rhodes, Plea Bargaining: Who Gains? Who Loses? 57 (1978) ("Contrary to expectations, sentence concessions were not routinely awarded to suspects entering guilty pleas").

70. Some jurisdictions unequivocally forbid judges to participate in negotiations. *See, e.g.*, United States v. Werker, 535 F.2d 198, 205 (2d Cir. 1976) ("[W]e conclude that fair and expeditious disposition of criminal cases is best achieved by the [federal] trial judge completely abstaining from any participation in any discussions or communications regarding sentence . . . ."); Fed. R. Crim. P. 11(e)(1) ("The court shall not participate in any such discussions").

71. *See, e.g.*, Fed. R. Crim. P. 11(f) ("[T]he court should not enter a judgment upon [a guilty] plea without making such inquiry as shall satisfy it that there is a factual basis for the plea."); Conn. R. Crim. P. § 713 ("The judicial authority shall not accept a plea of guilty unless he is satisfied that there is a factual basis for the plea."); Tenn. R. Crim. P. 11(f) (same as federal rule); Vt. R. Crim. P. 11(f) (same); Wash. R. Crim. P. 4.2(d) ("The court shall not enter a judgment upon a plea of guilty unless it is satisfied that there is a factual basis for the plea."). One of the Guggenheim judges carefully reviews the notes he took at the guilty plea before going into the sentencing hearing, and mentions on the record that he has done so. E. Liebman, Sentencing Profile of Judge Frederick H. Weisberg 31 (Jan. 23, 1985) [hereinafter cited as "Weisberg Profile"] (unpublished manuscript on file with Guggenheim Project).

72. Almost 40 years ago, Williams v. New York, 337 U.S. 241 (1949), established that a sentencing judge could—indeed ought to—use information far beyond that which established the requisite elements of the offense. The "modern penological procedural policies" of individualizing punishment created a need for greater information about both the offense and the offender to impose a thoughtful sentence. *Id.* at 250. Hence the gap between guilt facts and sentencing facts.

3. *Factual Development After the Plea*

As should be plain from earlier discussions, after a *sentence* bargain, any post-conviction factfinding will largely be for naught. Unless the judge learns something important enough to upset the plea and start from scratch,[73] the sentence negotiated is the sentence imposed. After a *charge* bargain, on the other hand, the judge must still arrive at a sentence; thus understanding the post-conviction procedures is vital to understanding factfinding at sentencing.

a. *The Presentence Investigation Report*

The first of these post-plea procedures is the Presentence Investigation Report (PSI), the document that the judge commissions after a guilty plea has been entered to inform the court about facts relevant to sentencing.[74] Normally researched and written by a probation officer acting as an arm of the court,[75] the PSI is likely to be the most complete written version of the offense that a judge will see.[76]

Like pre-plea discovery laws, state laws on the preparation of PSI's vary dramatically. Statutes range from forbidding a judge to sentence until a PSI has been prepared and delivered to court,[77] to requiring a PSI on defendant's motion,[78] to not providing for a PSI at all.[79] But as with dis-

---

73. For instance, after a sentence bargain has been accepted by the court, Connecticut rules provide:

> If the case is continued for sentencing, the judicial authority shall inform the defendant that a different sentence from that embodied in the plea agreement may be imposed on the receipt of new information . . ., but that if such a sentence is imposed, the defendant will be allowed to withdraw his plea . . . .

CONN. R. CRIM. P. § 697.

74. *See* Williams v. New York, 337 U.S. 241, 249-50 (1949) (discussing value to sentencing judge of information contained in PSI). For statutory authority for PSI's and what they may include, see, e.g., FED. R. CRIM. P. 32(c); N.Y. CRIM. PROC. LAW §§ 390.20-.30 (McKinney 1983 & Supp. 1986); MASS. R. CRIM. P. 28(d); CONN. GEN. STAT. § 54-91a(a), (c) (1985).

75. *See, e.g.*, FED. R. CRIM. P. 32(c)(1) ("The probation service . . . shall make a presentence investigation . . . ."); CONN. GEN. STAT. § 54-91a(a) (1985) (probation officer writes report); MASS. R. CRIM. P. 28(d)(1) ("The probation officer shall inquire . . ."). *But see* IOWA CODE ANN. § 901.2 (West Supp. 1985) (investigation conducted by branch of correctional services). For a historical explanation of why this task has fallen to probation officers—at least in the federal system—see Note, *The Presentence Report: An Empirical Study of its Use in the Federal Criminal Process*, 58 GEO. L.J. 451, 454-55 (1970) [hereinafter cited as "Note, *Presentence Report*"]; Fennell & Hall, *Due Process at Sentencing: An Empirical and Legal Analysis of the Disclosure of Presentence Reports in Federal Courts*, 93 HARV. L. REV. 1615, 1623 (1980).

76. "[B]ecause an overwhelming majority of defendants plead guilty and therefore forego trial, the report often substitutes for the trial itself as a mechanism through which facts are found in a criminal case." Fennell & Hall, *supra* note 75, at 1627 (footnote omitted). *See also* Note, *Procedural Due Process at Judicial Sentencing For Felony*, 81 HARV. L. REV. 821, 836-37 (1968).

77. *See* N.Y. CRIM. PROC. LAW § 390.20(1) (McKinney 1983) (after felony conviction, "the court must order a pre-sentence investigation of the defendant and it may not pronounce sentence until it has received a written report of such investigation").

78. *See* VA. CODE § 19.2-299 (1983) (court "shall" order report "on the motion of the defendant").

covery, the laws as written do not necessarily dictate the practices that are followed. For instance, one of the Guggenheim judges reported that in his jurisdiction, PSI's were usually prepared for cases that were tried, but were often dispensed with in cases that pled out.[80] The statute that provides for PSI's in his state does not make this distinction (if it did, you might expect it to command just the opposite of the practice), and, indeed, seems not even to admit of the possibility of waiver at all.[81] Thus local practice can undo even legislative provision for a PSI.

The literature has shown that those PSI's that *are* prepared often omit information,[82] contain erroneous information,[83] or are slanted because of

---

79. Georgia does not have a presentence report. Jackson v. State, 248 Ga. 480, 484, 284 S.E.2d 267, 270–71 (1981). The closest it has is a "probation report," *id.*, 284 S.E.2d at 270–71; *see* GA. CODE ANN. § 42-8-34(b) (1985) (formerly § 27-2709(b)), which is designed solely to determine whether an offender is suitable for probation, and "cannot be used in *fixing* the length of a sentence," McDuffie v. Jones, 248 Ga. 544, 549, 283 S.E.2d 601, 606 (1981) (emphasis in original). It is prepared at the discretion of the sentencing judge. *Jackson*, 248 Ga. at 484, 284 S.E.2d at 271.

80. While he was still on the bench, former Judge Rudolph F. Pierce from Massachusetts reported to the Guggenheim Project:

> We have not had a tradition in our court of presentence reports, which I think is unfortunate. . . . In our court now, I use a presentence report in every case that's tried. I do not use presentence reports in every case that's pled. If the lawyers agree on the numbers and the numbers seem reasonable to me, I just don't get involved in a presentence report. If the lawyers are disagreeing on the numbers but they're fairly close (and I don't see any problems with those numbers), I don't get involved in a presentence report on a plea. If there is a wide divergence of numbers and I don't know what seems appropriate, I'll order a presentence report on a plea. But I don't as a matter of rule in every plea order a presentence report.

Remarks to Guggenheim Project, in New Haven (Dec. 15, 1984).

81. *See* MASS. R. CRIM. P. 28(d) (no mention of any distinction between guilty pleas or trials for preparation of PSI). Rule 28 appears to speak in mandatory terms: "The probation officer *shall* inquire . . .," *id.* at (d)(1) (emphasis added); "The report of the presentence investigation *shall* contain any prior criminal . . . record of the defendant . . .," *id.* at (d)(2) (emphasis added); "[T]he report *shall* include such other available information as may be helpful to the court . . .," *id.* (emphasis added). However, because there is no explicit provision which requires these reports to be *in writing*, Massachusetts judges apparently let oral presentations or case intake information suffice. *See* Standards of Judicial Practice: Sentencing and Other Dispositions, Admin. Reg. No. 3-84 (Sept. 1984) (Admin. Off. of Dist. Ct.), *reprinted in* 43C MASS. GEN. LAWS ANN. (West Supp. 1986) (annotation to Rule 28).

82. A 1979 study of New Haven PSI's showed that "certain items of information were frequently missing from the PSI's, even when [probation] officers were instructed to include them or [were] made aware of their importance." J. England, Presentation and Use of Presentence Information in New Haven 91 (Jun. 1, 1979) (unpublished manuscript available at Yale Law Library). For instance, about offender employment the study found:

> 36 per cent of the time it was impossible to tell how the defendant was employed at the time of the offense, or even whether s/he was employed at all; if the defendant were not shown to be unemployed, it was impossible to tell how long s/he may have been employed when the offense was committed over 60 per cent of the time; alternatively, length of time unemployed at the time of the offense was not shown in 25 of the 35 cases where the defendant was shown to have been other than unemployed, or about 71 per cent of the time. It was more often possible to determine a defendant's employment status at disposition, but only because a large number of defendants were unemployed as a result of pre-trial detention or a loss of job after arrest. Even then, it was not reported in 40 per cent of the cases (or about 56 per cent of the cases with defendants shown to be other than unemployed) how long the defendant had been unemployed.

Id. at 46–47 (footnotes omitted). *See also id.* at app. C.

83. *See* Fennell & Hall, *supra* note 75, at 1628–30; Note, *A Proposal to Ensure Accuracy in*

the bias of the probation officer.[84] The reasons for this are straightforward enough. Because of limited resources and worries about intruding on the privacy of those who will eventually be found innocent,[85] the probation officer generally does not begin the investigation until after guilt has been established, which is weeks, months, or years after the offense has taken place.[86] Evidence is now stale. Witnesses may no longer be available. And if there are disputes over the details of the offense, they will get harder to resolve as the crime fades further into history.

Moreover, the professional ethic of a probation officer is that he is not supposed merely to report the facts, but also to interpret them.[87] In an office which "combines the role of therapist with that of peace officer,"[88] it is easy to see how the facts might take on a pro-state slant, a phenomenon which has been reported often.[89]

Presentence Investigation Reports 91 YALE L.J. 1225, 1226 (1982) [hereinafter cited as *Accuracy Proposal*]; Project, *Parole Release Decisionmaking and the Sentencing Process*, 84 YALE L.J. 810, 878 & n.333 (1975). For specific examples of errors in descriptions of offenses, see, *e.g.*, D. NEWMAN, CONVICTION: THE DETERMINATION OF GUILT OR INNOCENCE WITHOUT TRIAL 223 (1966) ("knife" that PSI reported offender had carried during commission of crime turned out to be pocketknife offender always carried which was folded and in pocket at time of offense); Portman, *The Defense Lawyer's New Role in the Sentencing Process*, FED. PROBATION, March 1970, at 3, 6 (PSI omitted provocation that immediately preceded assault); Lehrich, *The Use and Disclosure of Presentence Reports in the United States*, 47 F.R.D. 225, 242-44 (1969) (listing several examples of erroneous information in PSI's).

84. *See* P. KEVE, THE PROBATION OFFICER INVESTIGATES 45-46 (1960) (examples of probation officer bias); Fennell & Hall, *supra* note 75, at 1667 n.214 (reports of lapses in probation officer neutrality); Justice Jeffrey M. Atlas, Remarks to Guggenheim Sentencing Project, in New Haven (Oct. 12, 1984) ("[I]n our county . . . the probation officers have a bias when they start. So you're looking for the bias and then you've got to try to offset it.") (tape recording on file with Guggenheim Project).

85. *See* Note, *Presentence Report*, *supra* note 75, at 465-69 (discussing disadvantages of beginning presentence investigation before determination of guilt).

86. H. ABADINSKY, PROBATION & PAROLE: THEORY & PRACTICE 71 (2d ed. 1982) (PSI "usually made after the conviction of a defendant"). In general, a rule of investigations "that is self-evident and universally recognized and yet which is too often neglected is to make the investigation just as quickly after the fact has occurred as possible . . . ." Hornaday, *Some Suggestions on the Investigation of Facts*, 15 IND. L.J. 498, 499 (1940) (author former FBI agent).

87. A. SMITH & L. BERLIN, INTRODUCTION TO PROBATION & PAROLE 35 (1976) ("A compilation of facts and descriptions of behavior is meaningless without analysis and interpretation in the light of psychiatric, psychological and sociological concepts."); P. KEVE, *supra* note 84, at 67 ("the probation officer is looking at that offense not for its own sake but as one facet of his client's personality, one symptom of his inner maladjustment").

88. A. SMITH & L. BERLIN, *supra* note 87, at 93. The roots of the probation officer as peace officer reach back to 1878, when the very first paid probation officer in the United States was directed by the supervisor of police. R. HENNINGSEN, PROBATION AND PAROLE 14 (1981).

89. As observed about New Haven PSI's: "It is an unavoidable observation that the evaluative sections of the PSI's frequently appear for all the world as if they had been lifted from a prosecuting attorney's sentencing argument." J. England, *supra* note 82, at 91. A federal Assistant Chief of Probation wrote in the 1960's: "Here are some examples of bias I have found in reports: 'He is a cheap, crooked swindler.' 'Never have I dealt with such a liar.' " Evjen, *Some Guidelines in Preparing Presentence Reports*, 37 F.R.D. 177, 179 (1964) (paper delivered at Institutes on Sentencing, U.S. Judicial Conference). *See also Fennell & Hall*, *supra* note 75, at 1667 n.214; Justice Jeffrey M. Atlas, Remarks to Guggenheim Sentencing Project, in New Haven (Oct. 12, 1984) (discussing probation officer "antagonism" toward some defendants) (tape on file with Guggenheim Project).

Unreliable Factfinding and Sentencing

Even when the probation officer himself has no such bias, the pressure of caseload, ever-present in the criminal justice system, may impose a slant on the PSI. Because of overwork,[90] the probation officer may rely excessively on the prosecutor's files for information, files filled with facts which, though collected by an adversarial party, have never been tested through adversarial means.[91] Similar information from the defense counsel may not be forthcoming, either because of caseload, custom, or a lack of diligence.[92]

Recognizing the problem of inaccuracies and misrepresentations in PSI's, a number of jurisdictions have enacted provisions designed to correct their errors.[93] These reforms have focused largely on disclosing the PSI's before sentencing so that defendants can dispute any erroneous information. Disclosure laws now range from making the PSI available to defense counsel and allowing him to cross-examine the probation officer who wrote the report, to allowing the court to withhold crucial parts of the report.[94] Again, the extent to which different counsel avail themselves of these statutory protections will affect the accuracy with which the facts are developed. For instance, when the federal rules were first amended to require PSI disclosure upon an attorney's request, sizeable portions of the defense bar never bothered to exercise their new privilege.[95] Similarly,

90. *See* J. WILLIAMS, THE LAW OF SENTENCING AND CORRECTION 15 (1974) ("Probation officers are overworked and rushed because they have to produce reports at the convenience of the court."); Taparauskas, *An Argument for Confrontation at Sentencing: Bringing the Offender into the Sentencing Process*, 8 CUM. L. REV. 403, 421 (1977) ("Presentence reports are produced, for the most part, by underpaid, overworked members of the probation department.")

91. Note, *Procedural Due Process at Judicial Sentencing for Felony*, *supra* note 76, at 837 (probation officers "are likely to rely uncritically on reports supplied by the prosecutor, who cannot be expected to be disinterested") (footnote omitted). *See also* J. WILLIAMS, *supra* note 90, at 15–16 (information obtained from prosecutor has "inevitable tendency to prejudice the defendant").

92. *See supra* note 48 for discussion of the failure of many defense attorneys to be strong advocates.

93. For the history of the law of PSI disclosure and its development in the federal courts, see Fennell & Hall, *supra* note 75, at 1630–40. For discussion of the different procedures district courts may employ when facts in the PSI are disputed, see United States v. Charmer Indus., 711 F.2d 1164, 1172 (2d Cir. 1983); United States v. Stephens, 699 F.2d 534, 537–38 (11th Cir. 1983). For a critique of the correction process, see *Accuracy Proposal*, *supra* note 83.

94. In Virginia, the probation officer must present his report to the sentencer in the presence of the accused in open court, having furnished a copy of the report to defense counsel at least five days earlier. VA. CODE § 19.2-299 (1983). The defendant has a right to cross-examine the probation officer on any matter in the report, and also to present any additional relevant information. *Id.*

On the other hand, subject to appellate review, New York courts may withhold from disclosure "a diagnostic opinion which might seriously disrupt a program of rehabilitation, or sources of information which have been obtained on a promise of confidentiality, or any other portion [of the PSI], disclosure of which would not be in the interest of justice." N.Y. CRIM. PROC. LAW § 390.50(2) (McKinney Supp. 1986). And although the defendant does have the right to make written submissions to the court, *id.* at § 390.40, he has no right to cross-examine the officer who prepared the report. Indeed, the question of whether even to hold a pre-sentence conference to resolve factual issues is within the discretion of the judge. *Id.* at § 400.10.

95. Fennell & Hall, *supra* note 75, at 1640–43. Fennell and Hall partly attribute this attorney inaction to judges' discouraging attitudes toward disclosure, partly to the fact that defense counsel

The Yale Law Journal Vol. 95: 1258, 1986

although New York law requires disclosure of the PSI one day before sentencing,[96] in the courtrooms of the Guggenheim judges from New York, the PSI's sometimes were not delivered to the judge until the day of the sentencing, and counsel would not pick them up—if they did so at all—until minutes before the sentencing.[97]

b. *The Sentencing Hearing*

At the sentencing hearing itself, there is wide room for procedural variation. At the most basic level, a single constitutionally required standard of proof at sentencing has never been required.[98] Thus different federal district court judges may apply different standards of proof.[99] Likewise, the choice of what procedures are used at the sentencing hearing itself has been left largely within the discretion of the sentencing judge.[100]

Judges have used this license to fashion very different sentencing procedures. For instance, in the jurisdiction of one of the Guggenheim judges, it is not customary for the prosecutor even to appear in court at the sentencing hearing.[101] In another, not only was the prosecutor always present, but if doubt was cast on parts of the PSI during the course of the hearing, the judge would call in the probation officer who wrote it to quiz him

---

were not always notified of the right to see the PSI, and partly to the lack of an activist defense bar in certain localities. *Id. See also* Dickey, *The Lawyer and the Accuracy of the Presentence Report*, FED. PROBATION, June 1979, at 28, 38 (significant number of Wisconsin lawyers did not bother to read PSI).

96. N.Y. CRIM. PROC. LAW § 390.50(2) (McKinney Supp. 1986).

97. Field observations of Justice Harold J. Rothwax's courtroom, in New York City (Feb.-Mar. 1984); Interview with Justice Jeffrey M. Atlas, in New Haven (Mar. 28, 1986). Justice Atlas reported an astonishing lack of attention to a PSI by counsel: "I sentenced a guy in a murder case last week. The defense lawyer never bothered to read the probation report—we watched him. The D.A.'s frequently don't read them either."

98. *See* United States v. Fatico, 603 F.2d 1053, 1057 n.9 (2d Cir. 1979), *cert. denied*, 444 U.S. 1073 (1980) (declining to adopt specific standard of proof at sentencing).

99. Indeed, in United States v. Fatico, 458 F. Supp. 388, 409 (E.D.N.Y. 1978), *aff'd*, 603 F.2d 1053 (2d Cir. 1979), *cert. denied*, 444 U.S. 1073 (1980), Judge Weinstein suggested that the same judge might properly apply different standards of proof in different cases or for different kinds of facts.

100. *See* United States v. Needles, 472 F.2d 652, 658 (2d Cir. 1973) ("[T]his court has generally left the decision as to the appropriateness in any particular case of these procedures largely to the discretion of the sentencing judge."); United States v. Charmer Indus., 711 F.2d 1164, 1172 (2d Cir. 1983) (listing different allowable procedures). *Cf.* Williams v. New York, 337 U.S. 241, 251 (1949) ("The due process clause should not be treated as a device for freezing the evidential procedure of sentencing into the mold of trial procedure.").

101. In the Cuyahoga County Court of Common Pleas in Cleveland, Ohio, the prosecutor usually does not appear at the sentencing hearing. Judge Burt W. Griffin, Remarks to Guggenheim Sentencing Project, in New Haven (Jan. 27-28, 1984). In addition, Ohio judges are discouraged from participating in the plea negotiation or making a promise to induce a plea. *Id.* While the sentencing judge reads the state's version of the offense in the PSI, the prosecutor's absence at the sentencing hearing means the judge may never hear adversaries present their versions of the facts and rebut their opposition's.

about where he got the information and would sometimes even ask to see his notes.[102]

A method that these two judges share, however, is close personal questioning of defendants. Both engaged in extensive colloquys with the defendants at the sentencing hearing—hashing out the offense once again, delving into every circumstance that might bear on the sentence. Another of the Guggenheim judges followed a sharply contrasting practice. He would not commit himself to a sentence before the guilty plea, but after the plea had been entered, he would usually impose a sentence that both attorneys could agree on.[103] If counsel both recommended a certain sentence—or if they recommended sentences which were very close—the judge would dispense with the PSI and with any detailed inquisition of the defendant at the sentencing hearing and impose the recommended sentence.[104]

The enormous flexibility in the procedures allowed at a sentencing hearing thus magnifies the temperament of the sentencing judge. And because it is part of the lore of every courtroom that some judges take more time and care in conducting factfinding than do others,[105] this flexibility allows the development of varying factual descriptions for similar crimes.

III. Striving for Accuracy

From the initial interviews in a case to the hearing at which the judge imposes the sentence, the criminal justice system presents occasions for misdescription of sentencing facts. In this essay, I have argued that the flexibility of procedures—both as established by rule or statute and as "amended" by local custom—allows an unwarranted degree of error. My evidence, however, has been largely anecdotal. Further work needs to be done to try to discover just how great and how regular factual errors are. If closer study confirms my hypothesis, then lawmakers will need to reform factfinding procedures if they are truly to curtail disparity.

In framing the reforms, legislatures and sentencing commissions will be forced to make unpleasant choices. Many of the procedures that can reduce factfinding errors take time and money. Lawmakers should be

102. Justice Jeffrey M. Atlas, Remarks to Guggenheim Sentencing Project, in New Haven (Oct. 12, 1984) (tape on file with Guggenheim Project).

103. Judge Rudolph F. Pierce, Remarks to Guggenheim Sentencing Project, in New Haven (Dec. 15, 1984) (tape on file with Guggenheim Project).

104. *Id.* The judge reports he would go behind the numbers only if something "smelled wrong."

105. The varying care with which different judges examine the facts of a case are known even by the defendant population. A probation officer interviewed by a Guggenheim researcher told a story of a defendant who had been uncooperative with the officer in a previous case. This time the defendant was to be sentenced by Judge Frederick Weisberg (the judge being studied by the researcher), and cooperated because of the Judge's reputation for fully considering the information in the PSI. Weisberg Profile, *supra* note 71, at 32.

guided by a simple principle: if they have chosen to make a given fact substantively relevant to a sentence, then they should ensure that the procedural machinery exists to describe that fact accurately to the sentencer. It makes little sense to engineer a substantive sentencing law refined enough to take into account detailed information unless the procedures can withstand the stress of being asked to describe those details accurately in the daily operation of the criminal justice system. Without this fit between substance and procedure, sentencing reform presents a nasty paradox: we care enough about a fact to change a sentence when we know the fact exists, but we don't care enough about the same fact to put in place procedures that tell us accurately when it exists and when it doesn't. This is a clear recipe for disparity.

In adjusting the fit, lawmakers can work both sides of the equation; they can tinker either with the substantive law or with the procedure. That is, one way of dealing with the problem is to decide how much procedure we are willing to pay for and then match the substantively relevant facts to those procedures. The other is first to decide what facts are substantively relevant, and then to pay whatever it costs to develop those facts accurately. From the point of view of disparity, either approach is acceptable.

It will take time, however, for lawmakers to close the gap between the substance and the procedure of sentencing. In the meantime, the very existence of guidelines provides various actors with tools to coax more accurate facts out of the current system.

A. *Better Identification of Relevant Facts*

In a way never done before, the existence of sentencing guidelines will identify for litigants the issues important to the sentence. Because prosecutors boast such high conviction rates,[106] the critical question for a majority of defendants is not "guilty or not guilty?" but "how long?"[107] In a non-guideline system, an attorney trying to litigate the "how-long?" question is in a quandary. He may not know what facts matter to the judge, or how the facts that do matter will affect the sentence,[108] and thus does not even know exactly what facts to investigate. It is as if he were trying to

106. In New York State in 1983, convictions accounted for 85% of all felony dispositions. N.Y. GUIDELINE REPORT, *supra* note 7, at 26.

107. *See* Kuh, *Defense Counsel's Role*, *supra* note 43, at 433 ("Recognizing that the majority of seriously charged defendants are guilty of something, and that prospective sentencing is a prime concern of theirs, their attorneys should be pointing toward the day of sentence from the first client meeting . . . ."); Lehrich, *supra* note 83, at 225 ("[T]he crucial determination for most criminal defendants is not that of guilt or innocence, but that of the sentence to be imposed.").

108. *See supra* text accompanying note 2-5.

Unreliable Factfinding and Sentencing

prepare to try a burglary case without knowing the statutory elements of burglary.

By telling lawyers what facts will affect sentences, guideline systems can make lawyers' investigation and preparation for sentencing litigation more intelligent. It will be possible to sit down with a guideline manual and the case law on permissible and impermissible departures and write a kind of sentencing checklist,[109] a litigation outline for sentencing. Focusing the lawyers' attention on the salient facts should raise the quality of sentencing litigation and bring more information to the judge.

B. *Generating Accuracy through Habeas Corpus*

Prisoners can exert pressure for early accuracy in the system through habeas corpus actions. Since the 1940's, defendants have enjoyed a constitutional right to be sentenced on the basis of accurate facts.[110] However, offenders have gotten little mileage out of this constitutional guarantee because of two doctrines of traditional sentencing law. First, nobody defines for judges what facts are or are not relevant to a sentence.[111] Second, judges are not required to state for the record which facts they are relying on or how far those facts move the sentence up or down.[112] Put together, the doctrines make it difficult indeed to show that erroneous information

---

109. Minnesota judges and Federal Parole Hearing Examiners already use various checklists to help apply the guidelines. *See* MINN. STAT. ANN. ch. 244–app. (Supp. 1985) (Minnesota Sentencing Guidelines & Commentary) (Forms) (reproduction of "Sentencing Worksheet"); 28 C.F.R. § 2.20 (1985) (reproduction of "Salient Factor Score" worksheet). Neither of these checklists thoroughly covers the full range of factors which the guidelines and departure policy allow the sentencer to take into account, however.

110. *See* Townsend v. Burke, 334 U.S. 736, 741 (1948) ("[T]his prisoner was sentenced on the basis of assumptions concerning his criminal record which were materially untrue. Such a result, whether caused by carelessness or design, is inconsistent with due process of law. . . ."). *See also* Roberts v. United States, 445 U.S. 552, 556 (1980) ("We have . . . sustained due process objections to sentences imposed on the basis of 'misinformation of constitutional magnitude.' "); United States v. Tucker, 404 U.S. 443, 447–48 (1972) (affirming circuit court's remand for resentencing because original sentence was predicated on inaccurate information); United States v. Jones, 640 F.2d 284, 286 (10th Cir. 1981) ("[Supreme Court] cases recognize a due process right to be sentenced only on information which is accurate."); United States v. Tobias, 662 F.2d 381, 388 (5th Cir. 1981) ("Sentences based upon erroneous and material information or assumptions violate due process."), *cert. denied*, 457 U.S. 1108 (1982).

111. *See* Dobbert v. Strickland, 718 F.2d 1518, 1524 (11th Cir. 1983) ("Whether particular evidence . . . is mitigating depends on the evidence in the case as a whole and the views of the sentencing and reviewing judges. What one person may view as mitigating, another may not."), *cert. denied*, 104 S.Ct. 3591 (1984); LEGISLATIVE AGENDA, *supra* note 1, at 3 ("Sentencing judges are thus left free to formulate and apply their own personal theories of punishment.") (footnote omitted).

112. United States v. Garcia, 617 F.2d 1176, 1178 (5th Cir. 1980) (no requirement that courts announce reasons for sentences); United States v. Inmon, 594 F.2d 352, 354 (3d Cir. 1979) ("Enunciating reasons for a sentence has never been held to be a constitutional requirement."). In fact, current incentives push trial courts to omit reasons, because, once given, reasons can be considered as a basis for vacating sentences. *See* United States v. Vasquez, 638 F.2d 507, 534 (2d Cir. 1980) (once reasons given, basis for sentence can be scrutinized), *cert. denied*, 450 U.S. 970, 454 U.S. 847, and Vasquez v. United States, 454 U.S. 975 (1981).

affected the length of a sentence.[113] Yet in order to have a sentence vacated because it is predicated on erroneous information, an offender must show that the court did, in fact, rely on a specific piece of mistaken information.[114]

Sentencing guidelines cast new light on facts used in sentencing. By the very act of choosing a specific box in a sentencing grid, a judge is making certain implicit findings of fact. And to depart from the range in a box, a judge must explicitly state the reasons for doing so. Thus, one way or another, the guidelines bring into the open the facts that a sentencing judge is relying on, and explain exactly how those facts affect the sentence. As the problems of showing reliance and harm consequently diminish, post-conviction attacks on the accuracy of the factual predicate of sentences should develop new muscle, and prosecutors and judges will be encouraged to pay more attention to the accuracy of the facts at earlier stages of the process in order to ensure the finality of sentencing decisions.

Conclusion

When the issue of factfinding came up in the New York Committee on Sentencing Guidelines, the minutes of the meeting report that Robert Morgenthau, District Attorney for Manhattan "said that the bottom line was that the system could not include a lot of fact-finding."[115] But as Jerome Frank has said: "No matter . . . how excellent the 'substantive' legal rules (the R's) and the social policies they embody, specific decisions will go astray, absent competent fact-finding."[116]

113. "A Sphinx-like silence on the court's part precludes anyone (including the parties, the judge, and an appellate tribunal) from learning whether he acted in error." United States v. Brown, 479 F.2d 1170, 1173 (2d Cir. 1973); United States v. Green, 680 F.2d 183, 204 (D.C. Cir. 1982) (Bazelon J., dissenting) (the majority's rule "adopts a mechanistic view of sentencing that challenges the defendant to find that one special fact that would push a lever marked 'leniency' in the sentencing judge's mind"), *cert. denied*, 459 U.S. 1210 (1983).

114. United States *ex rel.* Welch v. Lane, 738 F.2d 863, 865 (7th Cir. 1984) (defendant must show that "sentencing court relied on the misinformation in passing sentence"); United States v. Cimino, 659 F.2d 535, 537 (5th Cir. 1981) ("To prevail on a claim that a sentence was based on materially inaccurate information, an appellant must demonstrate that a court *relied* on that information.") (emphasis in original) (footnote omitted). *But see* United States v. Baylin, 696 F.2d 1030, 1042 (3d Cir. 1982) (remanding for resentencing because unreliable information *may* have added to sentence).

115. Minutes of the Meeting of New York State Committee on Sentencing Guidelines 3 (Apr. 27, 1984).

116. *In re* Fried, 161 F.2d 453, 464 (2d Cir.), *cert. granted*, United States v. Fried, 331 U.S. 804, *cert. dismissed*, 332 U.S. 807, *cert. denied*, 331 U.S. 858 (1947).

[15]

FACT-FINDING AT FEDERAL SENTENCING: WHY THE GUIDELINES SHOULD MEET THE RULES

Deborah Young†

TABLE OF CONTENTS

---

† Associate Professor of Law, Emory University School of Law; Assistant United States Attorney for the District of Columbia 1983-1990; J.D. 1982, University of Michigan. The author thanks Barry Adler, Ian Ayres, Jennifer Brown, Barry Friedman, Michael Gerhardt, Andrew Kull, Janet McAdams, Marc Miller, Ellen Podgor, Gary Smith, and Ron Wright for helpful comments and Margaret Chriss, Soma Simon, Karen Ann Ballotta and Scott Bertschi for excellent research assistance. The author gratefully acknowledges the financial support of the David Gershon Endowment of Emory University School of Law.

Introduction

The quest to sentence defendants fairly and effectively has led countries and communities continually to reform their sentencing systems. In a recent example of such reform, the United States Congress established the United States Sentencing Commission to draft federal sentencing guidelines.[1] Deep concerns about unwarranted disparity of sentences fueled the transformation to guidelines sentencing, from the previous system of discretionary sentencing aimed at rehabilitation.[2] Under the previous system, defendants who had committed the same crime and had the same prior criminal record could receive dramatically different sentences. Congress directed the Commission to develop guidelines that would reduce this disparity.[3]

Given this broad mandate, the Commission developed detailed presumptive guidelines that require federal judges to make specific factual determinations at sentencing about the nature of the offense and the defendant's criminal history.[4] The guidelines then translate these factual determinations into fines or months of probation or incarceration. The core principle—that specific factual determinations by the court directly produce identifiable consequences—was intended to reduce disparity in outcomes for similar defendants. To accomplish this goal, factual determinations must be accurate.

---

1 Sentencing Reform Act of 1984, Pub. L. No. 98-473, 98 Stat. 1987 (1984) (codified as amended at 18 U.S.C. §§ 3551-3742 (1988), 28 U.S.C. §§ 991-98 (1988)).

2 During the 1970s judges and scholars paid great attention to the problem of sentencing. Judge Marvin E. Frankel was a leading critic of unfettered sentencing discretion and a proponent of sentencing reform. MARVIN E. FRANKEL, CRIMINAL SENTENCES: LAW WITHOUT ORDER (1972). His call for reform was supported by other thoughtful literature about sentencing disparity and its causes. *E.g.*, ROBERT O. DAWSON, SENTENCING: THE DECISION AS TO TYPE, LENGTH, AND CONDITIONS OF SENTENCE (1969); WILLARD GAYLIN, PARTIAL JUSTICE: A STUDY OF BIAS IN SENTENCING (1974); JOHN HOGARTH, SENTENCING AS A HUMAN PROCESS (1971); PIERCE O'DONNELL ET AL., TOWARD A JUST AND EFFECTIVE SENTENCING SYSTEM: AGENDA FOR LEGISLATIVE REFORM (1977); RESEARCH ON SENTENCING: THE SEARCH FOR REFORM (Alfred Blumstein et al. eds., 1983); ANDREW VON HIRSCH, DOING JUSTICE: THE CHOICE OF PUNISHMENTS (1976).

3 In establishing the United States Sentencing Commission, Congress stated that one of its purposes was to establish policies and practices that:

> provide certainty and fairness in meeting the purposes of sentencing, *avoiding unwarranted sentencing disparities among defendants with similar records who have been found guilty of similar criminal conduct* while maintaining sufficient flexibility to permit individualized sentences when warranted by mitigating or aggravating factors not taken into account in the establishment of general sentencing practices.

28 U.S.C. § 991(b)(1)(B) (1988) (emphasis added). For a discussion of the importance of considering the purposes of sentencing, see Marc Miller, *Purposes at Sentencing*, 66 S. CAL. L. REV. 413 (1992).

4 For a discussion of the reasoning and compromises of the Commission, see Stephen Breyer, *The Federal Sentencing Guidelines and the Key Compromises Upon Which They Rest*, 17 HOFSTRA L. REV. 1 (1988).

Concurrent with reducing disparity, Congress wanted the Commission to develop a system that would assure sentences were fair, both in the individual case and in the overall pattern of sentences.[5] Congress directed that a defendant should receive an appropriate sentence, but not more than that. This means that the imposition of fact-finding standards should not unfairly burden individual defendants. Despite the goal of fair sentencing, Congress, the Sentencing Commission, and the courts have failed to impose the necessary standards to ensure fair and reliable fact-finding.[6]

The accuracy of fact-finding is determined by the burden of proof, the reliability of the underlying evidence, and the opportunity for review of the decision. The burden of proof for questions of fact at pre-guidelines sentencing was low—a mere preponderance of the evidence.[7] Moreover, courts could consider virtually any evidence without regard to its admissibility under the Federal Rules of Evidence.[8] The Supreme Court held that these standards met the requirements of the Constitution.[9]

In establishing sentencing guidelines, neither Congress nor the Commission adjusted the burden of proof at sentencing[10] or the standards for the reliability of evidence, although Congress did provide the safeguard of appellate review.[11] Courts have held generally that sentencing under the guidelines is not so different from pre-guidelines sentencing that higher standards are constitutionally mandated.[12]

---

5 S. Rep. No. 225, 98th Cong., 2d Sess. 52-56 (1984), *reprinted in* 1984 U.S.C.C.A.N. 3182, 3235-39.

6 One commentator, writing before the federal guidelines were adopted, foresaw that "[t]o truly eliminate disparity, sentencing reformers must standardize not only substantive sentencing law, but also the procedures that bring to the sentencer the facts to which that law will be applied." Peter B. Pope, *How Unreliable Factfinding Can Undermine Sentencing Guidelines*, 95 Yale L.J. 1258, 1264 (1986). Pope reviewed the Minnesota guidelines sentencing model and pointed out the importance of fact determinations at each stage of the criminal case.

7 *See* discussion *infra* part I.A.3.

8 *See* discussion *infra* part I.A.

9 *See* discussion *infra* part I.A.2.

10 Neither Congress nor the Commission initially specified what burden of proof should apply at sentencing, leaving the matter for the courts to resolve. The Commission has not subsequently issued a guideline or policy statement on this issue. However, in an amendment that became effective on November 1, 1991, the Commission indicated in the commentary to § 6A1.3 that the preponderance standard is appropriate. United States Sentencing Comm'n, Guidelines Manual: Appendix C 216 (1991) (amending the Commentary to § 6A1.3) [hereinafter U.S.S.G.].

11 The statute provides that the defendant as well as the government may appeal a sentence. 18 U.S.C. § 3742(a),(b).

12 *See* discussion *infra* parts I.A.2 and I.A.3. There have been strong dissents to these rulings, including a dissent by Justice White to a denial of certiorari by the Supreme Court. Kinder v. United States, 112 S. Ct. 2290 (1992); *see* discussion *infra* note 217.

The reliance by the Commission and courts on pre-guidelines cases to decide constitutional standards for guidelines sentencing is unsatisfactory for two reasons. First, the Commission and courts have failed to question the original reasoning of the cases establishing the constitutional standards. This article contends that even under pre-guidelines sentencing evidentiary standards were inadequate. Second, the inadequacy of these standards is even greater with guidelines sentencing.[13] Discretion in pre-guidelines sentencing permitted judges to vary their reliance on evidence depending on its level of reliability. Restricting judges' ability to exercise discretion and directly basing sentences on factual determinations, when combined with a failure to raise the reliability standards, has created an unjust sentencing scheme.

A constitutional requirement identified by the Commission or the courts is not the only possible mandate for stricter evidentiary standards at sentencing. There is an alternative solution. The federal judiciary and Congress have the authority to adopt stricter evidentiary standards through rules. This article presents an affirmative analysis of why applying the Federal Rules of Evidence at sentencing would improve fact-finding.

Two key harms to be avoided in fact-finding at guidelines sentencing are inaccuracy in fact-finding and having defendants unfairly bear the burden of errors in fact-finding. In light of these potential harms, this Article analyzes the potential impact of raising the burden of proof at sentencing and of increasing the standards for admissibility of evidence at sentencing. Adjusting the burden of proof clearly affects who will benefit if the evidence is inadequate, but does not necessarily improve the accuracy of fact-finding. Assessing how higher reliability standards for the admissibility of evidence, such as those required by the Federal Rules of Evidence, would affect sentencing involves a more complex analysis.

Who bears the burden of proof at sentencing, the likelihood that evidence offered will be inculpatory, and the probability that evidence that would be inadmissible at trial is more likely to be false than admissible evidence—all these affect the calculation of the impact of evidence at sentencing. At best, the use at sentencing of evidence generally inadmissible at trial, such as hearsay, may increase accuracy while also increasing the number of errors being borne by defendants. However, as the analysis demonstrates, limiting evidence at sentencing to that which meets the Federal Rules of Evidence will ensure that defendants do not unfairly bear the burden of errors and is likely to

13 Judge Bright of the Eighth Circuit recently noted that "[w]hen it comes to proof of facts undergirding guideline sentences, the principle courts often apply is . . . 'Anything Goes.'" United States v. Smiley, 997 F.2d 475, 483 (8th Cir. 1993) (Bright J., dissenting).

also increase accuracy of fact-finding.[14] The Federal Rules of Evidence, which are generally neutral to both the defendant and the government, provide the most effective method for improving fact-finding at sentencing.

Congress or the federal judiciary can extend application of the Federal Rules of Evidence beyond the culpability phase of trials to govern sentencing.[15] The evidence rules could efficiently be incorporated into the existing sentencing scheme, where both parties are represented by counsel familiar with the rules. Application of evidence rules at sentencing may even be preferable to finding a constitutional requirement for heightened evidentiary standards. Application of the rules would ensure comprehensive reform, rather than piecemeal solutions to specific problems, while still permitting refinement through amendments.

Part I of this Article traces the development of current procedural protections from early American sentencing through the recent adoption of guidelines sentencing. Part II examines how federal courts are currently wrestling with guidelines sentencing under the pre-existing procedural standards. This section discusses how courts have considered increasing sentencing reliability by finding a constitutional requirement for a heightened burden of proof, finding a right of confrontation at sentencing, or adopting specialized rules for fact-finding at sentencing.

Part III presents a new argument for heightened procedural protections. This section applies theories of evidence to fact-finding at sentencing to demonstrate what errors in fact-finding exist under the guidelines, who should bear the consequences of errors, and what choices are available for reducing errors. Part III concludes that improved reliability is best accomplished by applying the Federal Rules of Evidence.

Part IV reviews the issues that arise at sentencing in light of the proposed application of evidentiary rules. This section demonstrates that the Federal Rules of Evidence governing reliability of evidence could readily be applied at sentencing. The Article concludes by explaining how the existing rules could be extended to sentencing.

Judges, academics, and practicing lawyers continue to debate the extent to which specific factual determinations should mandate specific sentences.[16] As long as judges are required to make such fact

---

14 *See* discussion *infra* part III.

15 *See* discussion *infra* part IV.C.

16 Judges, academics, and practicing lawyers continue to criticize the Federal Sentencing Guidelines and the United States Sentencing Commission for a variety of reasons including failure to reduce disparity, failure to respond to judicial suggestions for amendments, excessive curtailment of judicial discretion, and continued use of an overly broad definition of relevant conduct. *E.g.*, United States v. Concepcion, 983 F.2d 369, 393

determinations at sentencing and to presumptively rely on them, however, defendants should be protected from unreliable and unfair fact-finding. Applying the Federal Rules of Evidence to guidelines sentencing would be a significant step toward this goal.

I
SENTENCING WITHOUT EVIDENTIARY STANDARDS: PAST AND PRESENT

The heightened importance of fact-finding at guidelines sentencing is inherent in the guidelines' structure. The court is required to make factual determinations at sentencing.[17] These specific fact determinations have identifiable consequences because they determine the prescribed sentencing range. Nothing in the Sentencing Reform Act,[18] the guidelines, or other federal law imposes any substantial procedural protections for this fact-finding.[19] If Congress or the Commission had been drafting sentencing procedures on a clean slate, either might have developed higher standards for evidence at sentencing. Both Congress and the Commission deferred to courts, locating procedural rules as judicial matters. The courts, in turn, relied on pre-guidelines sentencing procedures, despite questions about their original validity and their appropriateness for guidelines sentencing.

(2d Cir. 1992) (Newman, J., concurring) (noting "the bizarre results that occasionally occur from a combination of the Sentencing Guidelines and the sentencing jurisprudence that was developed prior to the Guidelines and is now applied to the Guidelines regime"); United States v. Galloway, 976 F.2d 414, 436 (8th Cir. 1992) (Bright J., dissenting) (arguing that in establishing constitutionality of the guidelines, pre-guidelines case law is inapposite); United States v. Davern, 970 F.2d 1490, 1501 (6th Cir. 1992) (Merritt, C.J., dissenting) (protesting the overbroad reach of the relevant conduct guideline); United States v. Harrington, 947 F.2d 956, 964 (D.C. Cir. 1991) (Edwards, J., concurring) (referring to the guidelines as "a bit of a farce"); *see* Albert W. Alschuler, *The Failure of Sentencing Guidelines: A Plea for Less Aggregation*, 58 U. CHI. L. REV. 901 (1991); Daniel J. Freed, *Federal Sentencing in the Wake of Guidelines: Unacceptable Limits on the Discretion of Sentencers*, 101 YALE L.J. 1681 (1992); Gerald W. Heaney, *The Reality of Guidelines Sentencing: No End to Disparity*, 28 AM. CRIM. L. REV. 161 (1991); Ilene H. Nagel & Stephen J. Schulhofer, *A Tale of Three Cities: An Empirical Study of Charging and Bargaining Practices Under the Federal Sentencing Guidelines*, 66 S. CAL. L. REV. 501 (1992); Deborah Young, *Untested Evidence: A Weak Foundation for Sentencing*, 5 FED. SENTENCING REP. 63 (1992); *The Four Year U.S.S.C. & G.A.O. Impact Reports*, 5 FED. SENTENCING REP. 122-83 (1992); Richard Husseini, Comment, *The Federal Sentencing Guidelines: Adopting Clear and Convincing Evidence as the Burden of Proof*, 57 U. CHI. L. REV. 1387 (1990); Steve Y. Koh, Note, *Reestablishing the Federal Judge's Role in Sentencing*, 101 YALE L.J. 1109 (1992).

17 U.S.S.G., *supra* note 10, § 6A1.3.

18 Sentencing Reform Act of 1984, Pub. L. No. 98-473, 98 Stat. 1987 (1984) (codified as amended at 18 U.S.C. §§ 3551-3742 (1988), 28 U.S.C. §§ 991-98 (1988)).

19 *See, e.g.*, U.S.S.G., *supra* note 10, § 6A1.3 (policy statement specifying that in resolving disputes, sentencing court may consider any relevant information so long as there are "sufficient indicia of reliability to support its probable accuracy"); *see also* FED. R. CRIM. P. 32(a)(1) (noting that sentencing should not take place until factors in dispute are resolved, but failing to specify how to resolve these factors).

The section first examines the history of sentencing in the United States to discern why pre-guidelines sentencing employed such low evidentiary standards. The section then describes guidelines sentencing and its lack of evidentiary standards.

A. The Evolution of Sentencing Without Evidence Standards

Initially, sentencing in the United States was determinate,[20] so there was no fact-finding at sentencing and consequently no need for procedural standards for fact-finding.[21] Even when sentencing evolved into indeterminate sentencing focused on rehabilitation, only the most minimal standards were developed.[22] Because of the vast discretion afforded judges under indeterminate sentencing, few defendants could identify the impact of particular evidence or discern the significance of low evidentiary standards. Consequently, such standards could only be evaluated by assessing the validity of the reasons given for those standards and theorizing about the importance of low standards in the context of indeterminate sentencing.

The Supreme Court evaluated a sentence based on evidence that would have been inadmissible at trial in *Williams v. New York*.[23] The Court affirmed the trial court's right to consider any evidence without regard to rules of evidence.[24] Despite weak analysis,[25] the *Williams* case became the landmark decision on evidentiary standards at sentencing. After determinate sentencing was reintroduced, the Court revisited the issue. In *McMillan v. Pennsylvania*,[26] the Court concluded that preponderance of the evidence was an adequate burden of proof for establishing a fact that invoked a mandatory minimum penalty.[27]

This section reviews how sentencing without significant evidentiary standards evolved, and argues that the reasons given for low standards for evidence at pre-guidelines sentencing were ill-founded. However, the vast discretion afforded judges, which made determining consequences difficult, did permit courts to ameliorate any ad-

20 Although the first colonies operated under criminal justice systems that gave judges more discretion, as laws and penalties were codified the colonies adopted a more rigid, determinate system of sentencing. BRADLEY CHAPIN, CRIMINAL JUSTICE IN COLONIAL AMERICA 1606-1660 15-22 (1983).

21 Note, *Procedural Due Process at Judicial Sentencing for Felony*, 81 HARV. L. REV. 821, 822 (1968) [hereinafter *Procedural Due Process*] (stating that once a defendant was found guilty, "[n]o further proceedings were necessary on the issue of quantum of punishment").

22 Sanford H. Kadish, *Legal Norm and Discretion in the Police and Sentencing Processes*, 75 HARV. L. REV. 904 (1962), *reprinted in* SANFORD H. KADISH, BLAME AND PUNISHMENT 243, 252 (1987).

23 337 U.S. 241 (1949).

24 *Id.* at 251-52.

25 *See* discussion *infra* part I.A.2.

26 477 U.S. 79 (1986).

27 *Id.* at 91.

verse impact on defendants from unreliable fact-finding. Because the sentencing guidelines do not allow similar flexibility, the impact of low evidentiary standards on defendants under guidelines sentencing is harsher. The section concludes with a discussion of the procedural law of sentencing under the guidelines.

1. *Early American Sentencing and Procedure*

The initial lack of procedural protection in sentencing is easy to comprehend when one considers American sentencing history. When the United States was colonized, sentences were definite and harsh.[28] If a defendant was convicted of a felony, the statutorily mandated penalty was often death, unless the defendant could offer a legal reason, such as insanity or pregnancy,[29] against the imposition of that penalty.[30] Thus, technically the court imposed the sentence, but the court had no meaningful discretion once a defendant was convicted of a felony. Neither the defendant's character nor prior criminal conduct was an issue.[31] The legal reasons that excused punishment were defined, and the court only had to make the factual determination of whether the defendant fit one of the excused categories.

Despite the harshness of the prescribed penalties, the system contained some opportunities for leniency. A jury might find a defendant guilty of a lesser crime in order to avoid the penalty of death.[32] Pardons were also possible.[33] Depending on the colony, the power to pardon was vested in the executive, legislature or the court.[34] Colonies also adopted determined penalties other than death, such as branding, whipping and the stocks,[35] for many felonies. In 1682, William Penn introduced the concept of imprisonment at hard labor as the punishment for many serious crimes.[36] By the end of the seventeenth century the penitentiary had become an accepted, significant part of criminal punishment.[37]

In contrast to felony statutes, statutes governing misdemeanor offenses usually granted the court sentencing discretion, often allowing a choice of either a fine or corporal punishment.[38] Gradually, crimi-

---

28 *Procedural Due Process*, *supra* note 21, at 821-22.

29 *Id.* at 832-33.

30 *Id.*

31 *Id.*

32 SOL RUBIN, THE LAW OF CRIMINAL CORRECTION 31 (2d ed. 1973).

33 *Procedural Due Process*, *supra* note 21, at 822. One study of the period between 1631 and 1660 indicates that Massachusetts carried out fifteen death sentences. CHAPIN, *supra* note 20, at 58.

34 CHAPIN, *supra* note 20, at 60.

35 RUBIN, *supra* note 32, at 26, 28.

36 *Id.* at 27-28.

37 *Id.* at 27-30.

38 *Id.* at 26.

nal laws shifted toward providing more discretion to the sentencing authority for all types of crimes. When Congress first legislated federal criminal laws, beginning in 1789, judges were often given discretion in sentencing individuals convicted of misdemeanors and non-capital felonies.[39]

In the early twentieth century, the concept of punishment as retribution was criticized, and the focus was shifted from the gravity of the particular criminal act to the dangerousness of the offender.[40] Commentators argued that because the assessment of dangerousness was beyond the ken of law alone, the establishment of boards of psychologists or psychiatrists, sociologists, and lawyers should be established to determine the correct treatment for a convicted criminal, with the courts retaining opportunity to modify any sentence imposed.[41] But the role of imposing an initial sentence, however indeterminate that sentence might be,[42] was never transferred to boards of experts.[43] Instead, the concept was followed in the establishment of parole boards and, accordingly, a "board of experts" did ultimately determine the actual length of time served.[44]

---

39 Kate Stith & Steve Y. Koh, *The Politics of Sentencing Reform: The Legislative History of the Federal Sentencing Guidelines*, 28 WAKE FOREST L. REV. 223, 225 n.7 (1993).

40 *Procedural Due Process*, *supra* note 21, at 823-24.

41 Sheldon Glueck, *Principles of a Rational Penal Code*, 41 HARV. L. REV. 453, 462-63 (1928) ("Psychiatry, psychology, and social case work—not to mention those disciplines more remotely connected with the problems of human motivation and behavior—must be drawn into the program for administering criminal justice."); Matthew F. McGuire & Alexander Holtzoff, *The Problem of Sentence in the Criminal Law*, 20 B.U. L. REV. 423, 432 (1940) ("[T]he imposition of sentence is . . . a matter for administrative consideration by experts, who by their peculiar training and experience are best able to reach a conclusion as to the type and degree of treatment that is most likely to result successfully in respect to the individual immediately concerned."); Comment, *Reform in Federal Penal Procedure: The Federal Corrections and Parole Improvement Bills*, 53 YALE L.J. 773, 775 (1944) (hereinafter *Reform in Federal Penal Procedure*) ("Because of the opportunity for error afforded by such broad discretion . . . pre-sentence investigations were made available to trial judges under the Federal Probation system, established in 1925.").

42 Some scholars believed that the sentencing reforms did not go far enough in their reliance on experts instead of judges. *Reform in Federal Penal Procedure*, *supra* note 41, at 786-87. These scholars argued that parole boards, not judges, should impose sentences or prescribe the appropriate corrective treatments because such boards would make decisions based "on scientific analysis of individual therapeutic needs." *Id.* at 786.

43 Although the majority of states today have initial sentences imposed by judges, a few states have jury sentencing even in non-capital cases. ARTHUR W. CAMPBELL, LAW OF SENTENCING 258 (2d ed. 1991). States that have jury sentencing in non-capital cases include Kentucky, Missouri, Oklahoma, Tennessee, and Texas. *Id.* at 258 n.32.

44 Chapter One of the guidelines notes that, "the pre-guidelines sentencing system . . . required the court to impose an indeterminate sentence . . . and empowered the parole commission to determine how much of the sentence an offender actually would serve in prison." U.S.S.G., *supra* note 10, § 1A.3. Under this system, defendants generally only served about one-third of the court-imposed sentence. *Id.*

With discretionary, indeterminate sentencing, the courts tried to tailor sentences to meet the goals of treatment and rehabilitation.[45] They increasingly considered a defendant's character, personal relationships, and individual abilities or disabilities in determining sentences. Courts obtained information about defendants from prosecutors, defense attorneys, and probation officers. By the early 1900s, all states had indeterminate sentencing schemes[46] and by 1944 all states had parole boards.[47]

During the rise of indeterminate sentencing, little discussion occurred about the procedural protections afforded defendants at sentencing proceedings.[48] Instead, discussion focused on the substantive transition to determinations of appropriate sentences for rehabilitation.[49] Notably, even as procedural protections for criminal defendants increased, both pretrial and during trial, the lack of protection at sentencing remained.[50]

2. *The Landmark Case on Evidence Standards at Sentencing:* Williams v. New York

In 1948 the Supreme Court held in *Townsend v. Burke*[51] that the due process clause guaranteed a defendant the right to be sentenced based on accurate information.[52] Any hope that this decision would lead to increased procedural protections for sentencing was diminished the following year, however, when the Court decided *Williams v. New York*.[53] New York law provided that before imposing sentence a court had to consider the defendant's previous criminal record, any reports of mental, psychiatric, or physical examinations, and any other information that could aid the court in determining the proper treat-

---

45 The theory of indeterminate sentencing was that the criminal was morally sick and could be rehabilitated. The time required for this rehabilitation, however, varied with the individual. RICHARD G. SINGER, JUST DESERTS: SENTENCING BASED ON EQUALITY AND DESERT 1-2 (1979).

46 David J. Rothman, *Sentencing Reforms in Historical Perspective*, 29 CRIME & DELINQ. 631, 637 (1983).

47 RUBIN, *supra* note 32, at 622.

48 The 1957 edition of WHARTON'S CRIMINAL LAW AND PROCEDURE recognized that in most capital cases the court had to allow the defendant to make any statement. RONALD A. ANDERSON, WHARTON'S CRIMINAL LAW AND PROCEDURE § 2181 (1957). Some courts also imposed this rule in non-capital felonies, but the author deemed it unnecessary in misdemeanors. *Id.*

49 McGuire & Holtzoff, *supra* note 41, at 423 (observing that in order to fashion an appropriate sentence, the court should conduct a "thorough study . . . of [the defendant's] background, environment, training, education, and experience").

50 *See infra* notes 94-96.

51 334 U.S. 736 (1948).

52 *Id.* In *Townsend*, the Court overturned a sentence for failure to comply with due process because at sentencing the lower court failed to distinguish prior arrests from prior convictions and because the defendant was not represented by counsel.

53 337 U.S. 241 (1949).

ment of the defendant.[54] The court sentenced Williams to death, despite a jury's recommendation of life imprisonment.[55] At the sentencing, the trial court commented on information from the presentence report, which it considered in determining the sentence, including information that the appellant had committed thirty other burglaries, possessed "a morbid sexuality," and was a "menace to society."[56] The defendant argued on appeal that use of the presentence report under the New York statute conflicted with the right of an individual to be given reasonable notice of charges against him and an opportunity to examine adverse witnesses, as guaranteed by the Due Process Clause of the Fourteenth Amendment.[57]

The Court rejected this argument, emphasizing that historically, different evidentiary rules had been applied at trial and sentencing.[58] The Court then considered practical reasons for the different procedures at trial and sentencing. First, the Court stated that rules of evidence at trial were designed to prevent consideration of collateral issues and to avoid the possibility of a conviction resting on misconduct other than that charged.[59] In contrast, the judge at sentencing needed a broad spectrum of information, particularly for individualized sentencing with a goal of rehabilitation.[60] Second, the judge needed to be able to rely on the presentence report.[61] The Court concluded that requiring the presentence report's information be presented by testimony would cause undue delay.[62]

The Court decided that full access to information was necessary for a judge's selection of the appropriate penalty because fashioning appropriate individualized, indeterminate sentences required consideration of an offender's past life and habits.[63] The Court approached the problem as an all-or-nothing choice between the existing system, permitting consideration of anything by the court, and the imposition of complete trial procedures with all evidence at sentencing presented by live witnesses subject to cross-examination. Fearing that formalized trial-like procedures would exclude most of the information judges

---

54 *Id.* at 243.

55 *Id.* at 242.

56 *Id.* at 244.

57 *Id.* at 245.

58 *Id.* at 246.

59 *Id.* at 247.

60 *Id.*

61 *Id.* at 246.

62 *Id.* at 250.

63 "Modern changes in the treatment of offenders make it more necessary now than a century ago for observance of the distinctions in the evidential procedure in the trial and sentencing processes. For indeterminate sentences and probation have resulted in an increase in the discretionary powers exercised in fixing punishments." *Id.* at 248-49.

relied on at sentencing,[64] the Court concluded that the Due Process Clause should not be applied to require that evidentiary procedure at sentencing match trial procedure.[65]

The Court justified its decision, in part, by pointing out that discretionary sentencing had not made "the lot of offenders harder."[66] Despite its unwillingness to impose any procedural requirements, the Court stated, without further explanation, that this opinion "is not to be accepted as a holding that the sentencing procedure is immune from scrutiny under the due process clause."[67]

Williams has been criticized recently for failing to meet current constitutional standards.[68] A close examination of *Williams* on its own merits, however, reveals that the Court's assertions about sentencing did not necessarily establish that evidentiary standards were inappropriate or unnecessary at sentencing. The Court relied heavily on the long tradition of applying different standards of evidence at trial and sentencing, without discussing how these different standards originated.[69] The Court then asserted that the sentencing court needed a broad range of information for rehabilitative sentencing, should be able to rely on experts such as the presentence investiga-

64 *Id.* at 250.

65 *Id.* In dissent, Justice Murphy wrote that "[d]ue process of law includes at least the idea that a person accused of crime shall be accorded a fair hearing through *all* the stages of the proceedings against him." *Id.* at 253 (Murphy, J., dissenting) (emphasis added). Justice Murphy also noted that the sentencing judge changed Williams' jury sentence of life imprisonment to death based on "a probation report, consisting almost entirely of evidence that would have been inadmissible at . . . trial." *Id.* According to Justice Murphy, the sentencing judge's consideration of whether to increase Williams' sentence should have involved "the most scrupulous regard for the rights of the defendant." *Id.*

66 *Id.* at 249.

67 *Id.* at 252 n.18 (citing Townsend v. Burke, 334 U.S. 736 (1948)).

68 *See, e.g.*, Susan N. Herman, *Procedural Due Process in Guidelines Sentencing*, 4 FED. SENTENCING REP. 295, 296 (1992). Herman argues that changes in the analysis of procedural due process suggest that *Williams* should not apply today and that subsequent decisions about the right to counsel at sentencing and the right to disclosure of the presentence report undercut *Williams*. *Id.*

69 *Williams*, 337 U.S. at 246. For example, the Court failed to discuss the historical reasons for not requiring evidentiary standards at sentencing. Once sentencing evolved beyond determinate sentencing, such procedural protections might have been expected. One historical explanation offered for the lack of procedural protections and evidentiary standards at sentencing was the belief that any penalty less than the maximum was an act of leniency, not an entitlement. Kadish, *supra* note 22, at 252. The force of this leniency argument when the sentence imposed was branding rather than the death penalty is obvious, but even determinations of leniency may be more valid if founded on reliable evidence. Furthermore, in *Williams* the Court was not moving toward a penalty less than the maximum.

With the advent of the federal sentencing guidelines this leniency notion has been unequivocally abandoned. Sentences are determined by the nature and seriousness of the event, the defendant's criminal history, and other articulated sentencing factors. Unarticulated leniency is not a basis for a reduction in sentence under the Guidelines. *See infra* note 153 and accompanying text.

tors, could not apply evidentiary standards without great delay, and that the loose sentencing scheme generally benefitted defendants. Reexamining these reasons suggests that the Court's conclusion that heightened evidentiary standards would be an impediment was ill-founded.

The Court correctly stated that the imposition of a discretionary sentence aimed at rehabilitation was premised both on knowing the defendant's character and background and on predicting the defendant's future behavior. In analyzing the need for particular evidence at sentencing, however, the *Williams* Court did not distinguish between the *kind* of information a court needed for indeterminate sentencing and the *reliability* of the form of the evidence. The information the Court believed necessary for rehabilitative sentencing included character evidence and prior crimes evidence. This *kind* of information was generally excluded from trials because the evidence was deemed unduly prejudicial in the decision of guilt or innocence,[70] not because the information was in a form deemed *unreliable*.

The *Williams* Court did not consider the different role of evidence rules that excluded trial evidence because it was unreliable, such as hearsay evidence. While a broad range of information was critical for discretionary sentencing, and rightfully encompassed information excluded in the guilt phase, such as prior crimes, the need for such information did not mandate that every form of evidence be accepted.

Applying rules of evidence based on the reliability of evidence, such as the hearsay rules, would not limit the subject matter of the information available to the sentencing court.[71] Evidence of a defendant's character and other attributes that might affect a determination of sentence under the rehabilitative model was not so unusual as to make the application of evidentiary rules inappropriate. For example, a defendant might want to present a letter attesting to the defendant's good character from a former teacher or minister. Such evidence would be objectionable on hearsay grounds. Any such objection could be easily overcome, however. First, the defendant could try to obtain the government's agreement to admit the evidence.[72] If that

---

70 FED. R. EVID. 404 advisory committee's note. The two risks of prejudice to the defendant are that the fact-finder might accord undue weight to evidence of the defendant's bad character in the determination of guilt, and that the fact-finder might de-emphasize the risk of erroneously convicting the defendant because the character evidence demonstrates that the defendant deserves to be punished. GRAHAM C. LILLY, AN INTRODUCTION TO THE LAW OF EVIDENCE 109 (1978).

71 *See* discussion *infra* part IV.B.

72 Stipulations of evidence occur in two key ways. First, the parties may stipulate to facts, thus agreeing the facts as stated are correct. Alternatively, the parties may stipulate to expected testimony, thus agreeing only to what that person's testimony would be. EDWARD

were unsuccessful, the defendant could have the witness come to court.

The *Williams* Court identified the importance of the probation officer's presentence report as another reason not to have evidentiary rules.[73] The Court first pointed out that probation officers were trying to aid offenders, not to prosecute.[74] The Court reasoned that these reports were the best available information and without them the courts would rely on guesswork and inadequate information.[75] However, the Court's reasoning was founded on the mistaken premise of its earlier argument, that is, that the alternative to the presentence report is *no* information. As with character evidence, it would be possible to obtain admissible evidence, relating to information in the presentence report, that would be *better* evidence.

The Court voiced the concern that if trial courts could not rely on presentence reports, sentencing hearings would become mini-trials.[76] As the hearsay example above recognizes, prohibiting the use of

---

J. Imwinkelried, Evidentiary Foundations 235 (1980). The exact procedure to be followed, such as whether the stipulation may be oral, varies among courts. *Id.*

73 A similar argument offered in support of not requiring evidence standards at discretionary sentencing was the need for social science evidence, particularly to assist the court in predicting behavior. Glueck, *supra* note 41, at 462-63. The criminal justice system viewed the use of psychological information as not susceptible to legal standards of prbof. *Id.* The imposition of a discretionary sentence was considered a diagnostic judgment by experts, and therefore not appropriately subject to substantive and procedural restraints. *Id.* Although this need for expert judgment is often cited as the reason for not imposing procedural standards in discretionary sentencing, upon closer inspection the argument seems invalid.

The difficulty in sentencing aimed at rehabilitation and treatment did not lay in finding evidence that would meet common evidentiary standards. The difficulty was in evaluating and predicting human behavior. Attempts were made to determine how long someone should be incarcerated in order to be rehabilitated. There never has been a consensus, even among experts, about how to make such a decision. In sum, no evidence could clearly identify an appropriate sentence. This certainly does not, however, lead to the conclusion that less reliable evidence should be admitted for consideration.

Psychological or behavioral information considered at sentencing is no more or less susceptible to legal conclusions than other evidence, which is susceptible to different interpretations and conclusions. At trial the rules of evidence impose evidentiary standards on many types of scientific evidence, such as pathology reports. Fed. R. Evid. 803(6). When we believe that the evidence may not be readily interpreted by the fact finder, an expert witness aids in the interpretation. Fed. R. Evid. 702-705. Courts do not abandon the standards of evidence because the nature of the evidence is scientific. *See, e.g.*, Daubert v. Merrell Dow Pharmaceuticals, 113 S. Ct. 2786, 2795 (1993) ("[T]he trial judge must ensure that any and all scientific testimony or evidence admitted is not only relevant, but reliable").

74 *Williams*, 337 U.S. at 249.

75 *Id.*

76 Under the guidelines, when an issue of the degree of guilt is deferred from the trial phase to the sentencing phase, such as in determining relevant conduct, a "mini-trial" may be appropriate. However, in most cases the imposition of evidentiary standards would not make the sentencing proceeding less efficient. *See* discussion *infra* part IV. Moreover, under the guidelines an increase in time for the sentencing proceeding seems warranted

evidence that is inadmissible at trial could result in witnesses being called at sentencing. Alternatively, courts could ignore second-hand or unsubstantiated reports in determining sentences. Most likely, however, higher evidentiary standards at discretionary sentencing would have increased the expense of the proceeding, in terms of effort, time, and money. Accordingly, under a cost-benefit analysis, there appeared to be systemic costs associated with adopting heightened evidentiary standards and no way to measure the benefit of such evidence.[77]

Although the *Williams* Court cited the trial court's discretion in sentencing as a justification for a lack of procedural standards,[78] the Court did not articulate why this discretion reduced the problems of unfairness and inconsistency generated by low standards for reliability of evidence. Generally, sentencing discretion refers to a court's right to impose any sentence within the statutory parameters. For most federal offenses, the parameters ranged from probation to a maximum sentence of five years incarceration;[79] for more serious offenses the range was from probation to ten years incarceration, or even to life imprisonment.[80] Under this sentencing system, there was no identifiable impact of any specific factor, such as the amount of money embezzled, on the actual sentence. Whether the defendant embezzled $500 or $500,000 a judge could sentence the defendant to probation or to any period of imprisonment up to ten years.[81]

Judges had discretion to decide the goal for sentencing a particular defendant, the facts relevant to that goal, and the ultimate sentence.[82] This vast discretion meant that judges could take into

---

by Congress' goal of increasing the fairness and consistency of sentences. With discretionary sentencing, because there was no requirement that a given fact have a certain consequence, the need for accurate fact-finding was less compelling.

77 Current due process analysis incorporates consideration of increased administrative burdens from new procedural protections into the balancing test. *See infra* note 126 and accompanying text.

78 *Williams*, 337 U.S. at 247.

79 *See, e.g.*, 18 U.S.C. § 1341 (1988 & Supp. 1992) (mail fraud).

80 *See, e.g.*, 18 U.S.C. § 2113 (1988) (bank robbery).

81 The only distinction in penalty for most federal crimes was between a misdemeanor and a felony. For example, in the case of embezzlement of public funds, embezzlement of $100 or less would have constituted a misdemeanor, punishable by a maximum of one year in jail and $1,000 fine. 18 U.S.C. § 641 (1988) (embezzlement of public money, property, or records).

82 Stanton Wheeler, Kenneth Mann, and Austin Sarat conducted extensive interviews of federal judges in 1978-1980 to learn how they sentenced white-collar criminals. Deborah Young, *Federal Sentencing: Looking Back to Move Forward*, 60 U. CIN. L. REV. 135 (1991) (reviewing STANTON WHEELER ET AL., SITTING IN JUDGMENT: THE SENTENCING OF WHITE-COLLAR CRIMINALS (1988)) [hereinafter Young, *Looking Back to Move Forward*]. Wheeler and his colleagues concluded that sentencing occurred in two stages. First, judges evaluated the seriousness of the offense; then they translated that determination into an actual sentence. *Id.* at 169-70. The first stage entailed evaluating the harm caused, deter-

account characteristics of the offense, the defendant's personal characteristics, the victim's characteristics, and even community sentiment.[83] Consequently, all sorts of evidence might be relevant. Courts could evaluate speculative issues such as the defendant's character and the likelihood of recurrent criminal behavior. Courts could consider the impact of a particular sentence on the community as a whole, or on the defendant's immediate family.

A defendant might present past achievements in education and employment, relationship to the community, and relationship to family. Evidence of these factors often was simply an oral summary by defense counsel at sentencing. Letters of support for the defendant from family, employers, or neighbors were common. Ongoing responsibilities of the defendant that would be impeded by incarceration were also brought to the attention of the court, particularly the need to support a family by continued employment. Because there were no limits on what a court could choose to consider as a basis for sentencing, anecdotal evidence on any topic could be presented.

The prosecution also relied on anecdotal evidence, commonly to show the defendant's other past transgressions, including previously uncharged conduct. The prosecution might also describe the terrible crime or drug or fraud problem in America and the outrageous part this defendant had played in the great crime wave. Because the judge could seize on any aspect of information presented, without even acknowledging it, and adjust a sentence, prosecutors and defendants brought in a wide array of evidence hoping something would favorably influence the judge.

Although the vast discretion exercised by courts did not obviate the need for procedural protections, it did allow courts to avoid some of the most unjust consequences that now occur under guidelines sentencing. At pre-guidelines sentencing a court could ameliorate any lack of reliability by weighting the trustworthiness of the evidence. When a court "judged" a sentence in the traditional sense of authoritatively deciding the sentence, the court was not required to make any factual determinations. When the court did receive factual information, the court could weight that information as it chose.[84] Assessing

mining the blameworthiness of the defendant, and predicting the consequence of a sentence. *Id.* at 169. Wheeler and his colleagues found that judges substantially agreed on the relative seriousness of offenses. *Id.* at 173-74. Disparity in discretionary sentencing arose in the second stage, translating the assessment of seriousness into the actual sentence.

83 WHEELER ET AL., *supra* note 82, at 54.

84 This analysis was stimulated by Wheeler, Mann and Sarat's discussion of how judges weight different sentencing factors. By weighting the authors mean determining a factor's significance in deciding the sentence. For example, the authors make a distinction between measuring the amount of harm—such as the amount of money embezzled—and determining how much that amount of harm should count in the pre-guidelines sentencing decision. *Id.* at 168-70.

the facts and assigning their relative weights was fundamental to the sentencing judge's discretionary authority. Critics of the system, however, charged that different judges weighted different items of information differently, so that like individuals could receive unlike sentences.[85] The sentencing guidelines remove this discretion and weight individual factors by determining how many points each factor should receive.[86]

One of the generally unacknowledged merits of the discretionary sentencing system was that it permitted judges to weight evidence based on its reliability. For example, a judge might have two cases in which there was an allegation of substantial drug sales over a period of time. In one case, the evidence of this might be direct testimony by an eyewitness. In the other case, the evidence of this might be hearsay testimony by a government agent of what an unidentified informer had said. The judge could impose a harsher sentence in the first case because of the degree of certainty of the alleged conduct. In the second case, with much less reliable evidence, the court could impose a more lenient sentence, to reflect the much lower probability that the information was correct. Despite this vast discretion to weight evidence, courts rarely mentioned it, because there was no requirement that they justify particular sentences.

The *Williams* Court did not explicitly state why it believed that discretion at sentencing required the use of evidence that did not meet admissibility standards. But the Court implied that the need for a broad range of information, rather than a court's ability to adjust a sentence according to the reliability of the evidence, mandated the Court's holding.[87]

A final reason the *Williams* Court gave for not imposing stricter procedural standards was that the indeterminate sentencing scheme without evidentiary standards generally benefitted offenders.[88] This must have seemed ironic to Williams, whose sentence was changed from the jury's recommendation of life imprisonment to the judge's determination of the death penalty. But the Court's argument does highlight one reason that there was not a louder call for procedural reform of sentencing: there was no clear constituency for change. Defendants were as likely to obtain an advantage as prosecutors in presenting "highly colored" statements of fact.[89] With the inability to

---

85 *Id.* at 10.

86 The Federal Sentencing Guidelines delineate the presumptive impact of a given factor, such as the type of crime, the degree of harm, and the characteristics of the victim. U.S.S.G., *supra* note 10, §§ 2A1.1-3A1.3.

87 Williams v. New York, 337 U.S. 241, 247, 251-52 (1949).

88 *Id.* at 249.

89 In the mid-1940s, a Sixth Circuit judge observed that a sentencing court "had few real facts before it upon which to base its judgment." McGuire & Holtzoff, *supra* note 41,

determine what the judge might consider important, both defendants and prosecutors took a "kitchen sink" approach to sentencing, trying to mention every possible favorable fact or issue in the hope that the judge would be moved by one of them. Because courts could consider any aspect of the defendant's personal life at sentencing, defendants could be the beneficiaries of open evidence standards.[90]

Another key reason why the issue of low evidentiary standards at discretionary sentencing was not raised more frequently was that the impact of a specific item of evidence was rarely apparent. The reasoning behind discretionary sentencing was usually done privately. Although the prosecutor, defense attorney, and defendant had an opportunity to speak at a sentencing hearing, the court was not required to respond in any way. The court could simply pronounce the sentence. When the court gave no explanation, it was impossible to demonstrate the specific effect on sentencing of the use of informal, unreliable evidence. Moreover, there was no basis for appeal, other than imposition of an illegal sentence.[91]

Despite its weak foundation, the *Williams* ruling has been consistently followed. *Williams* has been cited repeatedly for the proposition that sentencing courts should be allowed to consider any information in any evidentiary form.[92] The principle of *Williams* was subsequently codified in 1970 in 18 U.S.C. § 3577 with the language:

> No limitation shall be placed on the information concerning the background, character, and conduct of a person convicted of an offense which a court of the United States may receive and consider for the purpose of imposing an appropriate sentence.[93]

The durability of *Williams* stands out amidst the significant development of increased procedural protections for criminal suspects and defendants, which began during the mid-twentieth century. Many of the basic procedural protections, such as the right to counsel, were promulgated in the Federal Rules of Criminal Procedure in 1946.[94] Some of these rights, such as the right to counsel, were subsequently

---

at 424 (quoting Judge Florence Allen). Judge Allen also noted that the court routinely received "highly colored" statements of fact from both the government and the defense counsel. *Id.*

90 In contrast, under the guidelines personal history characteristics have much less impact on a sentence. *See* discussion *infra* part I.B.

91 *See, e.g.*, United States v. Fessler, 453 F.2d 953, 954 (3d Cir. 1972).

92 *See, e.g.*, United States v. Wise, 976 F.2d 393, 399 (8th Cir. 1992).

93 This was originally codified as 18 U.S.C. § 3577 in 1970. The Sentencing Reform Act of 1984, 98 Stat. 1987, renumbered the provision as 18 U.S.C. § 3661.

94 The Federal Rules of Criminal Procedure, as enacted in 1946, contained wide-ranging provisions governing warrants for arrests and searches, joinder of defendants, pre-trial motions practice, venue, presentence reports and appeals. U.S. CODE CONG. SERV. 2275 (West 1946).

recognized as constitutionally required.[95] Other protections were established by both statute and case law in the ensuing decades.[96] In 1976, the Federal Rules of Evidence were adopted to codify the evidentiary rules to be applied at all federal trials, both jury and nonjury.[97] These rules were not extended to sentencing, however.[98]

Wide acceptance of *Williams* effectively closed the door to court challenges to the reliability of evidence at sentencing. As long as a judge had discretion to sentence within statutory parameters, there was no restriction on the type of evidence the judge could consider. In the 1959 case of *Williams v. Oklahoma*,[99] the Court again permitted the use of hearsay evidence at sentencing, this time provided orally by the prosecutor rather than in a written presentence report.[100] Because the defendant had conceded that the prosecutor's statements were correct, there was no question of reliability.[101]

Circuit courts eventually addressed the question of the reliability of hearsay used at sentencing. In *United States v. Weston*,[102] the Ninth Circuit reviewed a sentence in which the court had relied on the opinions of unidentified bureau personnel and the unsubstantiated statements made by federal drug agents to the probation officer that the defendant was a large scale heroin dealer.[103] The court concluded that the probative value of this evidence was "almost nil"[104] and that "a sentence cannot be predicated on information of so little value as that here involved."[105] Other courts subsequently interpreted the holding in *Weston* to require some minimal indicia of reliability for hearsay evidence considered at sentencing.[106] "Minimal indicia of reliability" thus became the standard for assessing hearsay evidence at pre-guidelines discretionary sentencing.[107]

---

95 Mempha v. Rhay, 389 U.S. 128 (1967).

96 For example, the timing of criminal prosecutions was governed by the Speedy Trial Act, 88 Stat. 2076 (1974) (codified as amended at 18 U.S.C. §§ 3152-56, 3161-74; 28 U.S.C. § 604); the disclosure of exculpatory information was controlled by Brady v. United States, 397 U.S. 742 (1970); the disclosure of statements by government witnesses was limited by the Jencks Act, 84 Stat. 926 (1970) (current version at 18 U.S.C. § 3500), and the eliciting of confessions was circumscribed by Miranda v. Arizona, 384 U.S. 436 (1966), and its progeny.

97 FED. R. EVID. 1101.

98 FED. R. EVID. 1101(d)(3).

99 358 U.S. 576 (1959).

100 *Id.* at 576.

101 *Id.* at 584.

102 448 F.2d 626 (9th Cir. 1971), *cert. denied*, 404 U.S. 1061 (1972).

103 *Id.* at 628.

104 *Id.* at 633.

105 *Id.* at 634.

106 *See, e.g.*, United States v. Baylin, 696 F.2d 1030, 1039-40 (3d Cir. 1982).

107 As discussed *infra* part II.A, this standard remains in effect under guidelines sentencing.

In 1967, the Supreme Court considered the application of the due process clause to fact-finding at sentencing. In *Specht v. Patterson*,[108] the Court reviewed a Colorado statute which provided that a defendant convicted for indecent liberties, with a penalty maximum of ten years, could be sentenced under a sex offenders act.[109] The sex offenders act provided for an indeterminate prison term of one day to life if the court found that the defendant constituted a threat of bodily harm, or was an habitual offender and mentally ill.[110] The statute permitted the court to reach that conclusion after reviewing a psychiatric report, without any hearing or confrontation by the defendant.[111] The Court held that the requirements of due process were not satisfied because the sentencing involved making a new finding of fact that was not an ingredient of the offense charged.[112] Due process required that this defendant have an opportunity to be heard, to confront and cross-examine witnesses, and to offer evidence.[113] The Court did not discuss what burden of proof should apply.

3. *The Landmark Case for Preponderance of the Evidence at Sentencing:* McMillan v. Pennsylvania

Even as indeterminate sentencing became entrenched in the American legal system, some judges and scholars began to question the wisdom of such vast discretion in sentencing, probation, and parole decisions.[114] Even before indeterminate sentencing had been adopted nationwide, critics argued that there was unfair disparity among similar defendants in different courts.[115] Concerns about disparity led to calls for reform of sentencing through the creation of guidelines.[116] Congress and some state legislatures responded with determinate sentencing statutes.[117]

---

108 386 U.S. 605 (1967).

109 *Id.* at 607.

110 *Id.*

111 *Id.* at 608.

112 *Id.* at 608-11.

113 *Id.* at 610.

114 *See, e.g.*, Kadish, *supra* note 22, at 250 ("[T]he new penology has resulted in vesting in judges and parole and probation agencies the greatest degree of uncontrolled power over the liberty of human beings that one can find in the legal system.").

115 For a list of articles expressing concerns about sentencing disparity, see *supra* note 2.

116 Other sentencing reforms were also suggested, such as the use of appellate review of sentences. The Supreme Court disapproved of this suggestion in Dorszynski v. United States, 418 U.S. 424 (1974).

117 For a summary of the history of mandatory minimum penalties in the United States, see UNITED STATES SENTENCING COMM'N, SPECIAL REPORT TO THE CONGRESS: MANDATORY MINIMUM PENALTIES IN THE FEDERAL CRIMINAL JUSTICE SYSTEM (1991) [hereinafter MANDATORY MINIMUM PENALTIES]. Determinate sentences had previously existed in the United States, beginning with mandatory capital punishment for specified crimes in the late eighteenth century. *Id.* at 5. Determinate sentences for drug offenses were adopted by

In 1984, Congress began adopting numerous statutes with mandatory minimum sentences for drug and weapons offenses.[118] Mandatory minimum sentences require a judge to sentence a defendant to a period of incarceration based on the quantity of drugs or the possession of a weapon despite any other characteristics of the crime, the defendant's degree of involvement, or the likelihood of rehabilitation.[119]

Although these mandatory minimums generated a great deal of controversy, the concern focused on the appropriateness of non-discretionary sentencing according to quantity or a single offense characteristic, in lieu of a totality of the circumstances view of sentencing.[120] Mandatory minimum legislation imposed a more ministerial role on federal judges in sentencing. Once the government established the quantity or other controlling factor, the judge identified the mandatory minimum and then was limited to exercising traditional sentencing discretion by increasing the sentence.

The quantity of the drug or presence of a weapon could be charged in the indictment and either proved at trial, as demonstrated by the jury verdict, or admitted in a guilty plea.[121] In such cases, because the judge did not assume a new fact-finding role, concerns

Congress in 1956, but repealed in 1970 when they did not appear to decrease criminal activity. *Id.* at 6. In 1984, Congress again began adopting mandatory minimum penalties. *Id.* at 8. For a comprehensive compilation of state sentencing reform as of 1985, see NATIONAL INSTITUTE OF JUSTICE, SENTENCING REFORM IN THE UNITED STATES: HISTORY, CONTENT, AND EFFECT (1985).

118 From 1984, the year Congress authorized the Federal Sentencing Guidelines, through 1990, additional mandatory minimum penalties were adopted every two years. MANDATORY MINIMUM PENALTIES, *supra* note 117, at 8.

119 For example, current federal mandatory minimum sentences are imposed for, *inter alia*, distribution or possession with intent to distribute certain quantities of drugs and for the use of a weapon in the commission of a crime of violence or drug trafficking. 21 U.S.C. § 841 (1992); 18 U.S.C. § 924 (1992).

120 *See, e.g.*, United States v. Klein, 860 F.2d 1489, 1501 (9th Cir. 1988) (upholding constitutionality of defendant's mandatory minimum sentence but observing that mandatory minimums gave less attention to judicial gradation and discretion). Under sentencing guidelines, courts continue to express dismay over their inability to adjust sentences for factors other than the quantity of drugs. In the course of one sentencing proceeding involving a defendant who had been employed for twenty-four years and never been involved in crime before, Judge Schwarzer of the Northern District of California noted that the evidence clearly established that defendant was found with a bag of crack cocaine in his vehicle. United States v. Anderson, Cr. No. 88-804 (N.D. Cal. Sept. 15, 1989), Excerpt from Transcript reprinted in 2 FED. SENTENCING REP. 185, 186 (1990). Due to the mandatory minimum for this offense, Judge Schwarzer stated that he was compelled to give a ten year sentence but complained that this sentence "did anything but serve justice." *Id.* at 186. Judge Schwarzer described mandatory minimums as "computers automatically imposing sentences without regard to what is just and right, and when that is allowed to happen, the rule of law is drained of the semblance of justice." *Id.*

121 FED. R. CRIM. P. 11.

about procedural safeguards ensuring that the defendant had in fact sold the quantity alleged in the charge did not arise.[122]

When a court did have to determine facts at the sentencing phase that would invoke a mandatory sentence, concerns about both the reliability of evidence and the burden of proof arose. In the 1986 case of *McMillan v. Pennsylvania*,[123] the Supreme Court addressed the issue of burden of proof at a state mandatory minimum sentencing proceeding. McMillan challenged the constitutionality of a Pennsylvania law that provided a minimum sentence of five years of imprisonment for specified felonies if the sentencing judge found, by a preponderance of the evidence, that the defendant visibly possessed a firearm during the commission of the felony.[124] The trial court found the act unconstitutional, but the Pennsylvania Supreme Court reversed.[125]

McMillan argued that visible possession of a firearm was an element of the offense and thus should be proved beyond a reasonable doubt and, in the alternative, that even if visible possession was not an element of the offense, due process required a higher burden of proof than a preponderance of the evidence.[126] In *McMillan*, the majority held that Pennsylvania's delineation of "visible possession of a firearm" as a sentencing factor subject to the preponderance of evidence standard did not violate the due process clause.[127] The Court emphasized that under *Patterson v. New York*[128] states had discretion, although not unlimited, to designate factors as sentencing factors rather than elements of the offense.[129] The Pennsylvania statute only

---

122 Even when there were no fact determinations to be made by the judge, mandatory minimum sentencing dramatically changed sentencing hearings. In many cases, mandatory sentencing left nothing to be said. The defense attorney often was aware that the mandatory minimum penalty was substantially more than the particular judge would have given a similar defendant in the past, so there was no fear of a higher sentence. Because of the mandatory minimum there was no chance of a lower sentence, so there was no incentive to expound on the rehabilitative potential of the defendant. Likewise, the prosecutor did not expect the judge to give more than the mandatory minimum, and may even have thought less was appropriate. Hearings often were perfunctory, ending with the judge explaining to the defendant, sometimes with apologies, why the particular sentence had to be imposed. *See supra* note 120.

123 477 U.S. 79 (1986).

124 *Id.* at 81.

125 *Id.* at 82-83.

126 By 1986 the Supreme Court was using a two-stage analysis for due process. *Id.* at 83. This test was first delineated in Matthews v. Eldridge, 424 U.S. 319 (1976). In the first part of the test, the court would determine whether the claimant had a property or liberty interest protected by the Due Process clause. *Id.* If so, in the second part of the analysis, the court would balance the private interest that would be affected by official action, the risk of erroneous deprivation of the interest and the probable value of any additional safeguards, and the government interest, including the administrative burdens associated with additional safeguards. *Id.* at 335.

127 *McMillan*, 477 U.S. at 91.

128 432 U.S. 197 (1977).

129 477 U.S. at 85.

limited the court's discretion in selecting a penalty within the existing range. In the Court's estimation, the statute was not a case of a "tail which wags the dog."[130]

After concluding that visible possession of a firearm could be designated as a sentencing consideration, the majority perfunctorily concluded that the preponderance of the evidence standard satisfied due process. The Court relied on the tradition of sentencing "without any prescribed burden of proof at all," citing *Williams v. New York*, although the *Williams* opinion never mentioned burden of proof.[131]

Justice Stevens, in dissent, strongly disagreed with the wide discretion given to states in the majority opinion.[132] He argued that because the Pennsylvania statute prohibited conduct for which conviction mandated a special punishment, proof beyond a reasonable doubt should be required.[133] He found the conduct of visibly possessing a firearm to be an element of the offense, despite the Pennsylvania nomenclature of a sentencing factor.[134]

Mandatory minimum statutes, such as the one at issue in *McMillan*, previewed the sentencing guidelines in three key respects. First, the mandatory minimums were a harbinger of sentencing decisions focused on harm—or the easiest indicator of harm—rather than on *mens rea* or rehabilitative potential. With mandatory minimums, the extent of the offense was the single controlling factor in most sentencing decisions.[135] Despite the judiciary's growing concerns about the subjective fairness of mandatory minimums,[136] harsher sentences for drug offenders were popular politically as evidence of the war on drugs.[137] Second, the guidelines were drafted to reflect existing mandatory minimum sentences.[138] For example, the guideline for distributing half a kilogram of cocaine encompassed the mandatory minimum of sixty months for distributing half a kilogram of cocaine.[139] Finally, this intermediate stage of quantity based sentencing without adequate procedures for fact-finding provided a transition to fact determined sentencing without improved procedural protections.

---

130 *Id.* at 88.

131 *Id.* at 91 (*citing* Williams v. New York, 337 U.S. 241 (1949)).

132 *Id.* at 95-104 (Stevens, J., dissenting).

133 *Id.* at 96.

134 *Id.*

135 For drug offenses, for example, the quantity of drugs was the controlling factor. U.S.S.G., *supra* note 10, § 2D1.

136 *See supra* note 120.

137 *See, e.g.*, Voters' Unrest Overrode Doubts About Sentencing Law, WASH. POST, May 11, 1986, at A14 (reporting voter approval of mandatory minimum laws in response to growing public unrest over drug sales).

138 MANDATORY MINIMUM PENALTIES, *supra* note 117, at 20, 29.

139 U.S.S.G., *supra* note 10, § 2D1.1(8).

The federal sentencing guidelines were being drafted when *McMillan* was decided. In passing the Sentencing Reform Act, Congress had given little attention to the procedural aspects of sentencing other than the right of appellate review.[140] The only reference to evidentiary standards was the recodification of 18 U.S.C. § 3577.[141] The act does not mention the burden of proof. In drafting the guidelines, the Sentencing Commission did not mandate either the appropriate standard of proof or who would have that burden.[142] The Commission left these matters for the courts.[143]

B. The Lack of Evidentiary Standards in the Guidelines

The guidelines present as radical a change from discretionary sentencing as did the emergence of rehabilitative sentencing at the end of the nineteenth century. This change is not necessarily demonstrated by outcomes in individual cases, however. A defendant may receive the same sentence under the guidelines as at pre-guidelines sentencing.[144] The radical change of the guidelines is demonstrated by what functions judges *must* carry out to impose sentences and by what factors now determine a sentence.[145]

When judges sentenced under discretionary sentencing, they were only required to decide sentences, as an exercise of pure discretion, within the statutorily permissible range. Judges did not have to make factual determinations or to convert factual determinations into months in jail. Judges were not required to assess explicitly the reliability of any evidence or rule on its admissibility. Judges could weight evidence according to its reliability or choose to ignore it. They had discretion in both what the final sentence would be and how to determine that sentence.[146] The sentencing function matched the classic definition of judging: authoritatively deciding the issue.[147]

---

140 18 U.S.C. § 3742 (1985 & Supp. 1993).

141 This provision was recodified as 18 U.S.C. § 3661 in the 1984 Sentencing Reform Act.

142 *See supra* note 10.

143 *See infra* notes 193-97 and accompanying text.

144 The United States Sentencing Commission said it designed the guidelines to result in defendants' receiving, on average, substantially the same sentences they would have received under pre-guidelines sentencing. Breyer, *supra* note 4, at 7. However, studies indicate that sentences have increased for many types of crimes. Theresa W. Karle & Thomas Sager, *Are the Federal Sentencing Guidelines Meeting Congressional Goals?: Empirical and Case Law Analysis*, 40 EMORY L.J. 393, 415-16 (1991).

145 The guidelines are phrased as affirmative directives, such as considering specific factors in determining the level of an offense. By stating what judges must do in passing sentence and limiting discretion, the guidelines also effectively dictate what judges may not do, such as determining the weight of factors as they could under pre-guidelines sentencing.

146 *See supra* notes 82-86 and accompanying text.

147 THE RANDOM HOUSE COLLEGE DICTIONARY 724 (rev. ed. 1980).

The sentencing guidelines now require a judge to perform three distinct functions. First, the judge must make factual determinations.[148] Even when the defendant has been convicted by a jury, the judge is not bound by the jury's factual determinations.[149] The judge must independently decide the defendant's culpability and role in the offense. Second, after deciding the facts required by the guidelines, the judge must perform the ministerial function of calculating the sentencing range based on the factual determinations.[150] Third, once the judge identifies the appropriate guidelines range, the judge assumes the traditional function of actually determining the sentence.[151] At this point, the guidelines impose an additional, significant constraint.[152] If the sentence chosen is not within the guideline range, the judge must justify the departure from that range.[153]

In addition to prescribing a judge's sentencing functions, the second fundamental change of the guidelines is the establishment of two basic determinants of a sentence: the offense level and the criminal history category. Once a defendant's offense level and criminal history category are established, the court must consider whether any factors exist that warrant adjustments or departures. With each of these determinations the court must make specific findings of fact. Each of these determinations of fact is then calculated into the equation that defines the parameters of the judge's limited discretion. Considering the factors to be assessed in evaluating offense levels, criminal history

---

148 U.S.S.G., *supra* note 10, § 6A1.3.

149 For examples of cases in which the judge sentenced based on a different set of facts than the jury had found, see *infra* note 251.

150 The guidelines provide a step-by-step overview of how to determine the proper sentencing range. First, the judge selects the applicable offense guideline section from Chapter Two, Offense Conduct. U.S.S.G., *supra* note 10, § 1B1.1(a). Second, after determining the base offense level, any applicable specific offense characteristics are added. *Id.* at § 1B1.1(b). Third, the offense level is adjusted in accordance with Chapter Three, Adjustments. *Id.* at § 1B1.1(c). These three steps are repeated if there are multiple counts of conviction. *Id.* at § 1B1.1(d). The base offense level then is adjusted if the defendant accepted responsibility as defined by § 3E. *Id.* at § 1B1.1(e). Next, the defendant's criminal history category is determined along with any applicable adjustments mandated by § 4B. *Id.* at § 1B1.1(f). Section 5A then supplies the correct guideline range based on the defendant's offense level and criminal history category. *Id.* at § 1B1.1(g).

151 *Id.* at § 1B1.4.

152 This outline of guidelines sentencing is consistent with the application instructions in the guidelines. *Id.* at § 1B1.1. Marc Miller and Daniel J. Freed have argued that this sequence is inconsistent with the authorizing legislation. Marc Miller & Daniel J. Freed, *Honoring Judicial Discretion Under the Sentencing Reform Act*, 3 FED. SENTENCING REP. 235 (1991). They suggest that judges should fact-find, identify purposes for the sentence, consider sentencing options, and only then consider the range recommended by the guidelines.

153 In the introduction to the guidelines, the Commission states that a sentencing court may depart only in an "atypical case . . . where conduct significantly differs from the norm. . . ." U.S.S.G., *supra* note 10, § 1A4(b) (policy statement).

categories, and adjustments and departures highlights the importance of accurate fact-finding.

The initial basic determinant is the offense level. An offense level is established by the category of the crime[154] and the amount of harm inflicted.[155] The elements of the offense identify the appropriate category of the crime. Within each category, specified factors determine the degree of harm or severity of offense. To a large extent the guidelines have adopted easily quantifiable measurements of harm. For drug distribution crimes, the primary factors delineating the offense level are the type and quantity of the drug.[156] For crimes involving theft of money, the primary determinant of the offense level is the quantity of money stolen.[157] For example, if a business employee embezzles $15,000, the base offense level will be four out of a possible forty-three levels for embezzlement plus five levels for the "specific offense characteristic" of taking an amount over $10,000. Thus, the total offense level is nine. If more money is embezzled, the offense level will be higher, directly representing the increased harm. These specific factual determinations of degree of harm have a direct impact on the sentence imposed. A determination of a larger quantity of drugs in a distribution case or money in an embezzlement case raises the parameters of the potential legal sentence. Thus, in sharp contrast to pre-guidelines sentencing, the importance of a single factual finding at guidelines sentencing is readily ascertained and directly influences the sentence.[158]

A critical component of the offense level determination is the concept of sentencing the defendant based on all relevant conduct.[159] At the sentencing phase the court must make factual findings about all of the defendant's known criminal conduct. The court is not

---

[154] There is not a separate guideline for each federal crime. For example, a variety of crimes concerning theft and other property offenses under 18 U.S.C. §§ 641, 656, 657, 659, 1702, 1708, 2113(b), 2312, and 2317 are sentenced according to one guideline, U.S.S.G., *supra* note 10, § 2B1.1.

[155] For further discussion of how the guidelines incorporate the traditional assessment of harm at sentencing, see Young, *Looking Back to Move Forward, supra* note 82, at 145-46.

[156] U.S.S.G., *supra* note 10, § 2D1.1.

[157] U.S.S.G., *supra* note 10, § 2B1.1.

[158] At pre-guidelines sentencing, a judge could impose a sentence because of a specific fact and the judge could identify that specific factor as the basis of the sentence, but neither was required. *See* discussion *supra* part I.A.

[159] U.S.S.G., *supra* note 10, § 1B1.3. For a thorough explanation of the relevant conduct guideline, see William W. Wilkins, Jr. & John R. Steer, *Relevant Conduct: The Cornerstone of the Federal Sentencing Guidelines*, S.C. L. Rev. 495 (1990). The relevant conduct guideline has been the subject of extensive criticism. *See, e.g.*, United States v. Galloway, 976 F.2d 414, 428 (8th Cir. 1992) (Bright, J., dissenting), *cert. denied*, 113 S. Ct. 1420 (1993); United States v. Silverman, 976 F.2d 1502, 1519 (6th Cir. 1991) (Merritt, C.J., dissenting), *cert. denied*, 113 S. Ct. 1595 (1993); Freed, *supra* note 16, at 1712-14.

bound by what the defendant admitted in a plea of guilty[160] or by what a jury found at trial.[161] For example, a prosecutor may have chosen to try an individual for distributing two kilograms of cocaine because that was readily provable. Before, during, or after trial, the prosecutor may have discovered additional evidence of drug distribution by the defendant. If this evidence was not admissible at trial because the source was hearsay, the defendant may nevertheless be sentenced based on that evidence.

Factual determinations made under the relevant conduct inquiry can dramatically increase a defendant's sentence. Consider the case of a defendant who has pleaded guilty or been convicted of distributing two kilograms of cocaine. At the sentencing phase, the prosecution may contend that the defendant in fact distributed twenty kilograms of cocaine. The court must make this factual determination.[162] If the court determines that the defendant probably did distribute twenty kilograms of cocaine, then the defendant's offense level

---

160 Courts routinely consider counts dismissed as part of a plea agreement in calculating the defendant's sentence if the counts are part of the same course of conduct to which the defendant pleaded guilty. *See* United States v. Frierson, 945 F.2d 650, 653-55 (3d Cir. 1991), *cert. denied*, 112 S. Ct. 1515 (1992); United States v. Smallwood, 920 F.2d 1231, 1239 (5th Cir. 1991), *cert. denied*, 111 S. Ct. 2870 (1991); United States v. Rodriguez-Nuez, 919 F.2d 461, 464-65 (7th Cir. 1990); United States v. Williams, 880 F.2d 804, 805-06 (4th Cir. 1989); United States v. Scroggins, 880 F.2d 1204, 1213-14 (11th Cir. 1989), *cert. denied*, 494 U.S. 1083 (1990); United States v. Wright, 873 F.2d 437, 440-41 (1st Cir. 1989); United States v. Sailes, 872 F.2d 735, 738-39 (6th Cir. 1989).

The policy statement in the guidelines states that the court is not bound by the parties' stipulation contained in the plea agreement. U.S.S.G., *supra* note 10, § 6B1.4(d); *see* United States v. Mason, 961 F.2d 1460 (9th Cir. 1992) (district court may base sentencing upon drug quantity asserted by the presentence report rather than the lesser quantity the parties had stipulated); United States v. Russell, 913 F.2d 1288, 1293 (8th Cir. 1990), *cert. denied*, Moore v. United States, 111 S. Ct. 1687 (1991) (defendant's mistaken belief that facts contained in the presentence report would mirror those in the stipulation did not obligate the sentencing court to follow the stipulation). However, the Guidelines mandate that if the defendant pleaded guilty to one offense but stipulated to a more serious offense as part of a formal plea agreement, the court *must* sentence the defendant based on that more serious offense. U.S.S.G., *supra* note 10, § 1B1.2(a); *see* United States v. Gardner, 940 F.2d 587, 590-92 (10th Cir. 1991) (defendant was sentenced for bank robbery, which he had orally stipulated to at sentencing, rather than the less serious offense of bank larceny to which he had plead guilty); United States v. Martin, 893 F.2d 73, 74-76 (5th Cir. 1990) (defendant pleaded guilty to using a communication facility to distribute drugs but stipulated to negotiating for five pounds of methamphetamine; reviewing court found error because district court failed to sentence for the more serious stipulated offense). See *infra* note 179 for an explanation of the effect of policy statements.

161 Courts may consider conduct for which the defendant was acquitted, illegally seized evidence suppressed at trial, and evidence from the trial of codefendants. *See infra* note 251.

162 In a policy statement, the guidelines state that "the court shall resolve disputed sentencing factors. . . ." U.S.S.G., *supra* note 10, § 6A1.3(b). A second reason that a court must resolve disputed factors is that either side may appeal a sentence. 18 U.S.C. § 3742 (1992). If the government did not have the right to appeal, a court might decide in favor of a defendant to avoid reversal.

will be adjusted accordingly. The difference in the sentence is dramatic. The sentencing range for the distribution of two kilograms of cocaine is 78 to 97 months; for twenty kilograms it is 151 to 188 months.[163]

Once a defendant's offense level is initially calculated, it may be adjusted either upward or downward depending on additional factors. Again, consideration of any of these potential adjustments requires additional factual determinations by the court. Adjustments that may raise a defendant's offense level include: the status of the victim,[164] a defendant's aggravating role in an offense,[165] obstructing justice,[166] and multiple counts.[167] Adjustments that may lower a defendant's offense level include: a defendant's mitigating role in an offense[168] and acceptance of responsibility.[169]

The second basic determinant, the defendant's criminal history category, is usually a straightforward determination based on the type and number of the defendant's prior convictions.[170] However, the guidelines provide that a court may consider prior adult criminal conduct that did not result in a conviction.[171] The criminal history category has essentially replaced the traditional assessment at sentencing of the defendant's character and personal history.[172] Policy statements to the guidelines provide that age, education, mental and emotional conditions, physical condition, previous employment, family ties and responsibilities, and community ties are matters "not ordinarily relevant in determining whether a sentence should be outside the guideline range."[173]

---

163 U.S.S.G., *supra* note 10, § 5A.

164 *Id.* at § 3A1.

165 An upward adjustment for an aggravating role in the offense is limited to four levels. *Id.* at § 3B1.1 The downward adjustment for a mitigating role in the offense also is limited to four levels. *Id.* at § 3B1.2. In drug cases, where base offense levels are often high, this limited adjustment seems inadequate to differentiate sentences between key players and minor figures in distribution networks. Deborah Young, *Rethinking the Commission's Drug Guidelines*, 3 FED. SENTENCING REP. 63-66 (1990).

166 U.S.S.G., *supra* note 10, § 3C1.1.

167 *Id.* at § 3D1.

168 *Id.* at § 3B1.2.

169 *Id.* at § 3E1.1. A downward adjustment for acceptance of responsibility has been described as "a thinly disguised reduction for pleading guilty." United States v. Escobar-Mejia, 915 F.2d 1152, 1153 (7th Cir. 1990). However, as an application note to this guideline makes clear, a defendant's guilty plea does not guarantee such a reduction. U.S.S.G., *supra* note 10, § 3E1.1 (application note 3).

170 U.S.S.G., *supra* note 10, § 4A1.1.

171 *Id.* at § 4A1.3.

172 Young, *Looking Back to Move Forward*, *supra* note 82, at 147.

173 U.S.S.G., *supra* note 10, §§ 5H1.1-1.6 (policy statements). Such factors may be relevant in determining where, within a particular sentencing range, the defendant should be sentenced. In exceptional cases, courts may also consider these factors with departures.

Military, civic, charitable or public service is also designated "not ordinarily relevant." *Id.* at § 5H1.11 (policy statement). A defendant's race, sex, national origin, creed, religion,

Under the guidelines, factual determinations that affect the offense level or the criminal history category influence both the maximum and minimum penalty that a defendant may receive. Despite the appellation "guidelines," which suggests a guide that courts are free to follow or ignore, the guidelines as applied define the appropriate sentence for conduct for which there is a strong presumption. If a court chooses to sentence outside that prescribed range, the sentence is deemed a "departure" and the court must give reasons to justify it.[174]

A hypothetical example demonstrates the importance of fact-finding at guidelines sentencing. Assume that, after apprehension, a drug dealer agrees to provide information about the drug supplier. The informant tells the government that the supplier has been regularly providing two kilograms of cocaine a month for six months. The government arranges for an undercover agent to purchase two kilograms of cocaine from the supplier. The undercover agent also negotiates with the supplier to buy ten kilograms of cocaine, but the supplier is tipped off before that sale occurs.

The supplier is indicted for the two kilogram sale to the undercover agent and for conspiracy to sell the ten kilograms that were not delivered. Because the government wants to use the informant for future investigations, it does not indict the defendant for the alleged sale of twelve kilograms to the informant. At trial, the defendant is convicted of the two kilogram sale to the agent but acquitted of the conspiracy count. At sentencing an agent tells the court about the informant's statement that the defendant had sold twelve kilograms of cocaine to the informant over a six month period. The government declines to name the informant.[175]

The judge now must decide whether the government has shown by a preponderance of the evidence that the defendant distributed the twelve kilograms of cocaine to the informant and whether the defendant conspired to distribute the ten additional kilograms of cocaine. Thus, the defendant may be sentenced for distributing two kilograms of cocaine, twelve kilograms of cocaine, fourteen kilograms

---

and socio-economic status are factors deemed "not relevant" in determining a sentence, inside or outside the guideline range. *Id.* at § 5H1.10 (policy statement). Lack of guidance as a youth is "not relevant" for imposing a sentence outside the guideline range. *Id.* at § 5H1.12 (policy statement).

See infra note 179 for an explanation of the effect of policy statements.

174 *See, e.g.*, U.S.S.G., *supra* note 10, § 5K1.1(a).

175 The commentary to section 6A1.3 addresses the general facts set out in this hypothetical. The commentary provides that "[o]ut-of-court declarations by an unidentified informant may be considered 'where there is good cause for nondisclosure of his identity and there is sufficient corroboration by other means.'" U.S.S.G., *supra* note 10, § 6A1.3, comment., *citing* United States v. Fatico, 579 F.2d 707, 713 (2d Cir. 1978), *cert. denied*, 444 U.S. 1073 (1980).

of cocaine, or twenty-four kilograms of cocaine. Assuming all other sentencing factors are constant, and assuming no criminal history, the sentence could range from 78 months to 188 months. The court does not have the discretion to choose between these limits, however. The court must make factual determinations about whether the defendant has committed the alleged relevant conduct and sentence accordingly.

As with any factual determination, accuracy can be regulated in more than one way. Three parameters generally determine the outcome of legal fact-finding: the burden of proof, the reliability of the underlying evidence, and the standards for review of the decision. Where the chance of an erroneous decision harming an individual is high, such as conviction of an individual for a crime, a high burden of proof, a high standard of reliability for the evidence, and a guaranteed opportunity for review should be imposed.

As discussed earlier, traditional sentencing imposed none of these protections. All evidence not demonstrated to be unreliable was accepted, no formal burden of proof was imposed, and there was virtually no opportunity for review. The Supreme Court held that these standards met the requirements of the Constitution.[176]

With the adoption of the guidelines, Congress changed only the opportunity for appellate review. Under the guidelines a defendant may appeal a sentence on the basis that the court improperly applied the guidelines.[177] Many of these appeals are, essentially, arguments about the sufficiency of the evidence. Defendants contend that there was insufficient evidence for the initial offense level determination, an adjustment, or a departure.[178]

The guidelines do suggest[179] that the determination of the appropriate sentence is to be made by the court after resolving any factual

---

176 *See* discussion *supra* part I.A.

177 18 U.S.C. § 3742(a). The government also has rights to appeal under 18 U.S.C. § 3742(b).

178 The statute specifies that a district court's factual findings and its assessments of a witness' credibility may not be overturned unless the appellate court finds them "clearly erroneous." 18 U.S.C. § 3742(d).

179 The provisions setting forth sentencing procedures were originally issued as guidelines. U.S.S.G., *supra* note 10, §§ 6A1.1-6A1.3. They were subsequently amended to be policy statements. *Id.* Section 6A1.2 was amended to be a policy statement effective June 15, 1988. *Id.* at App. C., amend, 59. Sections 6A1.1 and 6A1.3 were amended effective November 1, 1989. *Id.* at App. C., amends. 293 and 294.

The extent to which policy statements are binding on courts is unclear. Initially, leading commentators interpreted policy statements to be nonbinding on courts. THOMAS HUTCHISON & DAVID YELLEN, FEDERAL SENTENCING LAW AND PRACTICE 46 (1989). However, in Williams v. United States, 112 S. Ct. 1112 (1992), the Supreme Court held that "[w]here . . . a policy statement prohibits a district court from taking a specified action, the statement is an authoritative guide to the meaning of the applicable guidelines." *Id.* at 1119. The *Williams* holding does not necessarily mean that any policy statement is binding. One

disputes in a hearing.[180] This limited prescription acknowledges three aspects of guidelines sentencing: first, the final determination of the appropriate sentence is to be made by the court; second, the sentencing determination may only be reached after any disputes over facts are resolved by the court or determined to be insignificant to the sentence; and third, disputes over factual issues are to be resolved publicly.

The first of these, determination of the sentence by the court, is, in one sense, not a change from pre-guidelines sentencing. Although the probation officer played an important role in advising the court, judges have consistently assumed the responsibility for sentencing. However, in pre-guidelines sentencing, the court essentially established the maximum and minimum potential sentence. Subsequent parole and probation decisions determined the actual time of the sentence.[181] When Congress established the United States Sentencing Commission, it phased out parole.[182] Thus, under the guidelines, the defendant must actually serve the sentence imposed by the trial court,[183] unless that court's judgment is reversed by an appellate court.

---

commentator has argued that "[w]here the policy statement is not an authoritative guide to the intended meaning of a particular guideline, the sentencing court should remain free—consistent with the *Williams* opinion—to reject the policy statement after giving it due consideration." Ronald F. Wright, *The Law of Federal Sentencing in the Supreme Court's 1991-92 Term*, 5 FED. SENTENCING REP. 108, 109 (1992). In Stinson v. United States, 113 S. Ct. 1913 (1993), the Supreme Court in dicta suggested that policy statements generally are binding on federal courts. *Id.* at 1917. Professor Wright described this dicta as "seriously overstat[ing] the authority of policy statements." Ronald F. Wright, *Federal Sentencing Law in the Supreme Court's 1992-93 Term*, 6 FED. SENTENCING REP. 39, 41 n.8 (1993).

[180] The guidelines do not explicitly state that a court must hold a sentencing hearing or describe what such a hearing should entail. The first reference to a hearing appears in a policy statement:

> Courts should adopt procedures to provide for the timely disclosure of the presentence report; the narrowing and resolution, where feasible, of issues in dispute in advance of the sentencing hearing; and the identification for the court of issues remaining in dispute.

U.S.S.G., *supra* note 10, § 6A1.2 (policy statement). The following policy statement refers to Federal Rule of Criminal Procedure 32(a)(1), which provides that there should be a sentencing hearing at which attorneys for the defendant and for the government should have an opportunity to comment on the presentence report and other matters relating to the sentence. The commentary to policy statement 6A1.3 suggests that although factors at pre-guidelines sentencing were determined in an informal fashion, "[m]ore formality is . . . unavoidable if the sentencing process is to be accurate and fair" under guidelines sentencing. *Id.* at § 6A1.3 (commentary).

[181] The theory of parole was that parole officials would determine when a prisoner was rehabilitated and ready to rejoin society. Freed, *supra* note 16, at 1689 n.34.

[182] Sentencing Reform Act of 1984, Pub. L. No. 98-473, 98 Stat. 1987 (1984) (codified and amended at 18 U.S.C. §§ 3551-3742 (1988); 28 U.S.C. §§ 991-98 (1988).

[183] However, as with pre-guidelines sentencing, federal statutes provide that a defendant's sentence may be administratively reduced by a statutorily specified amount of time for good behavior in prison. 18 U.S.C. § 3624 (1988). Currently, a prisoner may receive up to fifty-four days per year in good time credit. *Id.*

The second factor, the requirement of resolution of disputed facts, is a more significant change. Although the Federal Rules of Criminal Procedure previously required a sentencing hearing, that hearing merely required that the defendant, the defendant's counsel, and the attorney for the government each be given an opportunity to speak.[184] The rules did not require resolution of disputed factual issues. Judge Eisele has written that under discretionary sentencing judges would usually omit from consideration facts in the presentence report that the defendant denied.[185] This clearly was not required, however, by statute or case law. At a minimum, under discretionary sentencing a judge could give evidence less weight if it seemed less reliable. Chapter Six of the guidelines, governing sentencing procedures, provides little guidance for how fact-finding should be accomplished.[186] Consequently, the standards for fact-finding at guidelines sentencing have evolved in the courts.

The requirement that factual disputes be resolved publicly highlights the importance of each factor in sentencing. Moreover, the creation of a record provides both a basis for appellate review of an individual case and for evaluation of the sentencing process. Despite the public record and the specifically delineated right to appeal, appeals based on evidence issues do little to raise evidentiary standards. As with review of alleged evidentiary errors from trial, appellate courts give the trial court great deference, applying a clearly erroneous standard of review.[187]

In practice, specific facts used in sentencing may be determined at various stages of the process. The facts of the case may be first outlined in an arrest warrant,[188] an indictment, or an information.[189] For a mandatory minimum narcotics offense, the quantity of narcotics will be alleged in the indictment. For other offenses, the indictment may be more general. For example, a fraud indictment may or may not allege a specific quantity of money was fraudulently obtained.

Once a trial court admits evidence about the details of an offense, which it then relies on in determining the appropriate sentence, a defendant has little hope for subsequently challenging the use of such

184 FED. R. CRIM. P. 32(a)(1).

185 United States v. Clark, 792 F. Supp. 637, 649-50 (E.D. Ark. 1992).

186 Policy statement § 6A1.3 merely provides that "[i]n resolving any reasonable dispute concerning a factor important to the sentencing determination, the court may consider relevant information without regard to its admissibility under the rules of evidence applicable at trial, provided that the information has sufficient indicia of reliability to support its probable accuracy." U.S.S.G., *supra* note 10, § 6A1.3 (policy statement).

187 18 U.S.C. § 3742(a).

188 The contents of an arrest warrant are governed by Federal Rule of Criminal Procedure 4(c)(1). FED. R. CRIM. P. 4(c)(1).

189 The contents of an information or indictment are governed by Federal Rule of Criminal Procedure 7(c)(1). FED. R. CRIM. P. 7(c)(1).

evidence. The district court's factual findings are protected by the clearly erroneous rule,[190] even when the court relied on uncorroborated hearsay statements of an unidentified declarant.[191]

The Sentencing Reform Act does not specify the burden of proof that should be imposed at sentencing or establish new evidentiary standards for sentencing under the guidelines.[192] Congress left these matters for the Sentencing Commission or the courts to resolve.

The Sentencing Commission acknowledged the need for higher evidentiary standards under the guidelines, but simply adopted the pre-guidelines standard. Policy statement 6A1.3[193] states that at sentencing a court may "consider relevant information without regard to its admissibility under the rules of evidence applicable at trial, provided that the information has sufficient indicia of reliability to support its probable accuracy."[194] Circuit courts developed the "sufficient indicia" standard as a minimal limitation on the expansive information that could be considered by courts at pre-guidelines sentencing.[195] The Commission left to the courts the responsibility to "determine the appropriate procedure" for resolving factual disputes.[196] However, the Commission did state in commentary that "the use of a preponderance of the evidence standard is appropriate to meet due process requirements and policy concerns in resolving disputes regarding application of the guidelines to the facts of a case."[197]

---

190 18 U.S.C. § 3742(e); *see* United States v. Cetina-Gomez, 951 F.2d 432, 434 (1st Cir. 1991); United States v. Poole, 929 F.2d 1476, 1483 (10th Cir. 1991); United States v. Alfaro, 919 F.2d 962, 966-68 (5th Cir. 1990); United States v. Thomas, 870 F.2d 174, 176 (5th Cir. 1989).

191 United States v. Manthei, 913 F.2d 1130, 1138 (5th Cir. 1990).

192 The Act alludes to evidentiary standards only where it recodifies 18 U.S.C. § 3577 into 18 U.S.C. § 3661. This section provides that "[n]o limitation shall be placed on the information concerning the background, character, and conduct of a person" who is being sentenced. 18 U.S.C. § 3661 (1987). The Supreme Court established this standard in Williams v. New York, 337 U.S. 241 (1949). *See supra* part I.A.2.

193 The Commission originally issued § 6A1.3 as a guideline. It was amended, to convert it to a policy statement, effective November 1, 1989. U.S.S.G., *supra* note 10, App. C, amend. 294. The Commission stated, without further explanation, that "[d]esignation of this section as a policy statement is more consistent with the nature of the subject matter." *Id.* For an explanation of the impact of policy statements, see discussion *supra* note 179.

194 U.S.S.G., *supra* note 10, § 6A1.3.

195 The actual standard developed by the circuit courts was one requiring "minimal indicia" of reliability. *E.g.*, United States v. Baylin, 696 F.2d 1030, 1039-40 (3d Cir. 1982). Because the minimal indicia standard and the sufficient indicia standard have been interpreted as imposing approximately the same reliability constraints on courts, this article uses the terms interchangeably. For an example of a case that also uses these terms interchangeably, see United States v. Silverman, 976 F.2d 1502, 1504 (6th Cir. 1992), *cert. denied*, 113 S. Ct. 1595 (1993). At least one court has stated that the sufficient indicia standard is the more stringent standard. *See* United States v. Paulino, 996 F.2d 1541 (3d Cir. 1993), *cert. denied*, 114 S. Ct. 449 (1993).

196 U.S.S.G., *supra* note 10, § 6A1.3 commentary.

197 *Id.* at § 6A1.3 commentary.

II
Wrestling with the Guidelines: Judicial Approaches to the Lack of Evidentiary Standards

Once the guidelines were enacted, defendants soon began challenging the low standards for fact-finding at sentencing.[198] The focal points of guidelines sentencing are the offense level and the defendant's criminal history, which the government need establish only by the low evidentiary standards. In contrast, evidence that defendants introduced at discretionary sentencing now has minimal impact on sentencing decisions because, in most instances, the guidelines limit consideration of the defendant's age, education, mental and emotional condition, physical condition, previous employment, family ties and responsibilities and community ties.[199] Thus, the prosecution primarily benefits from loose evidentiary standards. Also, unlike with discretionary sentencing, guidelines sentencing enables a defendant to directly trace the length of the sentence imposed to specific evidence. These factors have created among defendants a constituency for changing evidentiary standards at sentencing.[200]

Defendants' challenges to the lack of procedural protections for fact-finding under the guidelines have often involved sentences based on information in the form of hearsay.[201] The hearsay may appear in the presentence report[202] or in testimony by a government

198 *See, e.g.*, United States v. Sciarrino, 884 F.2d 95, 96-97 (3d Cir. 1989), *cert. denied*, 493 U.S. 997 (1989) (defendant's assertion that sentencing guidelines precluded use of hearsay rejected by reviewing court which reasoned that because hearsay was permitted before the guidelines, it should therefore be allowed under the guidelines). Defendants have continued to challenge the low fact-finding standard at sentencing. *See, e.g.*, United States v. Mergerson, 995 F.2d 1285, 1291-93 (5th Cir. 1993) (appellate court rejected defendant's assertion that the district court should have applied a beyond the reasonable doubt standard at sentencing; reviewing court confirmed that the preponderance standard was proper).

199 Policy statements to the guidelines provide that age, education, mental and emotional conditions, physical condition, previous employment, family ties and responsibilities, and community ties are "not ordinarily relevant in determining whether a sentence should be outside the guidelines." U.S.S.G., *supra* note 10, §§ 5H1.1-5H1.6. For an explanation of the impact of policy statements, see *supra* note 179. Professor Marc Miller has argued that Congress' purposes for sentencing require an assessment of a defendant's history and characteristics. Miller, *supra* note 3, at 464.

200 The constituency for changing the evidentiary standards for guidelines sentencing in the courts is defendants and their counsel. Many scholars and judges have joined in this constituency.

201 *See, e.g.*, United States v. Miele, 989 F.2d 659, 664 (3d Cir. 1993); United States v. Silverman, 976 F.2d 1502 (6th Cir. 1992), *cert. denied*, 113 S. Ct. 1595 (1993).

202 The presentence report includes information about the history and characteristics of the defendant (including financial status and criminal record); classification of the offense and of the defendant; the kinds of sentence and sentence ranges; explanation of factors that may indicate a departure from the guidelines may be warranted; information regarding impact (*e.g.*, financial, social, medical) upon victim(s); and information con-

agent.[203] This use of hearsay may occur with any fact that must be determined at sentencing, but has proved particularly troubling when the defendant is being sentenced for relevant conduct after conviction for a "base offense."[204]

In addressing these problems, courts have considered three avenues for raising the standards at sentencing: first, a due process requirement that the burden of proof be higher than a preponderance of the evidence, particularly with respect to sentencing for relevant conduct that could have been the basis of separate charges;[205] second, a limit on hearsay evidence required by the Confrontation Clause or Due Process Clause;[206] and third, specialized, judicially created rules to regulate fact-finding procedures at sentencing.[207]

Analysis of these avenues is complicated because judges who appear to share the same basic concern about the lack of procedural protections may propose different solutions predicated on different rationales. One judge may propose a different burden of proof while another proposes not relying on hearsay. The first judge may argue the Due Process Clause requires the higher burden; the second judge may make the same claim or rely on the confrontation clause. Also, relying on pre-guidelines case law necessarily involves applying old rules and analyses to a fundamentally different sentencing system.[208] A review of post-guidelines case law indicates that the degree of thought courts have given to applying old rules to new sentencing varies dramatically.[209]

---

cerning nature and extent of non-prison programs and resources available to the defendant. FED. R. CRIM. P. 32(c)(2).

203 *See, e.g.*, United States v. Sherbak, 950 F.2d 1095, 1100-01 (5th Cir. 1992) (district court credited Drug Enforcement Agency officer's unsworn statements over the defendant's counter-assertions).

204 *See* discussion *supra* note 159.

205 *See* discussion *infra* part II.A.

206 U.S. CONST. amends V & VI. *See* discussion *infra* part II.B.

207 *See* discussion *infra* part II.C.

208 Judge Heaney of the Eighth Circuit makes this point. *See* Heaney, *supra* note 16, at 166.

209 *Compare* United States v. Concepcion, 983 F.2d 369, 393 (2d Cir. 1992), *cert. denied*, 114 S. Ct. 163 (1993) (Newman, J., concurring) (noting the "bizarre results" that can be created by applying pre-guidelines case law to guidelines sentencing); United States v. Mobley, 956 F.2d 450, 465-66 (3d Cir. 1992) (Mansmanu, J., dissenting) (describing differences between pre-guidelines and guidelines sentencing schemes and why those differences matter) *with* United States v. Sciarrino, 884 F.2d 95, 96-97 (3d Cir. 1989), *cert. denied*, 493 U.S. 997 (1989) (stating without explanation that because hearsay statements were admissible under pre-guidelines sentencing, they should continue to be admissible under guidelines sentencing).

A. The Burden of Proof

Burdens of proof[210] establish the standard of proof and allocate which party bears the responsibility for providing the proof on a particular issue. The burden of proof theoretically determines outcomes in cases depending on who has the burden of proof and what level of proof is required. In addition to allocating the risk of error, the burden of proof instructs the fact-finder about the degree of confidence society deems appropriate for a particular decision.[211] Absent a statute specifying the burden of proof, defendants have looked to the Due Process Clause as the foundation for that right.

The Supreme Court never ruled that due process required a particular burden of proof under general pre-guidelines discretionary sentencing.[212] Under that sentencing scheme, courts were not required to make any factual findings before imposing a sentence, so there was no clear need for standards establishing facts or direct consequences for failing to do so. In *McMillan*, the Court explicitly did find a preponderance of the evidence standard adequate for mandatory minimum sentencing.[213]

Cases questioning the standard of proof for guidelines sentencing first reached the federal courts of appeal three years after *McMillan*. In *United States v. Wright*,[214] the defendant argued that the preponderance of the evidence standard was inadequate for evaluating evidence of relevant conduct at sentencing.[215] Writing for a First Circuit panel, Judge Breyer, a member of the United States Sentencing Commission, dismissed this challenge with the conclusion from *McMillan* that, "[t]he Supreme Court has held that the 'preponderance standard satisfies due process.' "[216] Judge Breyer's opinion did

210 "Burden of proof" is a term used to refer to either the "burden of persuasion" or the "burden of production." LILLY, *supra* note 70, at 41 n.2. In the context of evaluating standards for fact-finding at guidelines sentencing, courts have fairly consistently used "burden of proof" to mean "burden of persuasion." To avoid confusion, this article follows the courts' convention. The burden of persuasion regulates the decision of close cases by the fact-finder and the burden of production specifies the result when evidence on an issue is inadequate to satisfy the threshold requirement. Barbara D. Underwood, *The Thumb on the Scales of Justice: Burdens of Persuasion in Criminal Cases*, 86 YALE L.J. 1299, 1300 (1977).

211 Addington v. Texas, 441 U.S. 418, 423 (1978) (citing *In re* Winship, 397 U.S. 358, 370 (1970)) (Harlan, J., concurring).

212 In *Williams v. New York*, the Court concluded that the "due process clause should not be treated as a device for freezing the evidential procedure of sentencing in the mold of trial procedure," but did not explicitly discuss the burden of proof. 337 U.S. 241. 251 (1949).

213 *See* discussion *supra* part I.A.3.

214 873 F.2d 437 (1st Cir. 1989).

215 *Id.* at 441.

216 *Id.* (citing McMillan v. Pennsylvania, 477 U.S. 79, 91 (1986)).

not discuss whether guidelines sentencing warranted reconsideration of the standards used for discretionary sentencing.

Although the Supreme Court has not addressed the issue,[217] each of the federal courts of appeals has concluded that, in most instances, the appropriate standard of proof for resolving factual disputes at guidelines sentencing is a preponderance of the evidence.[218] Some courts have followed the lead of *Wright* and reached this conclusion with little analysis.[219] Other courts have looked beyond *McMillan* and pointed to the Sentencing Commission's declination to adopt any standard of proof,[220] to the fact that the defendant was already deprived of the right to liberty at the point of conviction so that the

---

217 The Supreme Court recently denied certiorari on the issue of burden of proof at sentencing in Kinder v. United States, 112 S. Ct. 2290 (1992). Justice White dissented, noting that, "[t]he Sentencing Guidelines do not explicitly adopt a standard of proof required for relevant conduct, and we have not visited this issue since its new procedures took effect in November 1987." *Id.* at 2292. Justice White observed that, "[t]he burden of proof at sentencing proceedings is an issue of daily importance to the district courts, with implications for all sentencing findings." *Id.* The justice recognized that the importance of this issue rests on the fact that, "[t]he resolution of disputed matters at sentencing . . . controls the length of the sentence actually to be imposed." *Id.*

218 United States v. Wilson, 900 F.2d 1350, 1353-54 (9th Cir. 1990); United States v. Frederick, 897 F.2d 490, 492-93 (10th Cir. 1990), *cert. denied*, 498 U.S. 863 (1990); United States v. Alston, 895 F.2d 1362, 1372-73 (11th Cir. 1990); United States v. Gooden, 892 F.2d 725, 727-28 (8th Cir. 1989), *cert. denied*, 496 U.S. 908 (1990); United States v. Casto, 889 F.2d 567, 570 (5th Cir. 1989); United States v. Silverman, 889 F.2d 1531, 1535 (6th Cir. 1989), *cert. denied*, 113 S. Ct. 1595 (1993); United States v. Guerra, 888 F.2d 247, 249-51 (2d Cir. 1989), *cert. denied*, 494 U.S. 1090 (1990); United States v. Burke, 888 F.2d 862, 869 (D.C. Cir. 1989); United States v. McDowell, 888 F.2d 285, 290-91 (3d Cir. 1989); United States v. Urrego-Linares, 879 F.2d 1234, 1237-38 (4th Cir.), *cert. denied*, 493 U.S. 943 (1989); United States v. Wright, 873 F.2d 437, 441-42 (1st Cir. 1989); United States v. White, 888 F.2d 490, 499 (7th Cir. 1989).

219 *See, e.g.*, United States v. Urrego-Linares, 879 F.2d 1234, 1237-38 (4th Cir.), *cert. denied*, 493 U.S. 943 (1989). The court's opinion, which was written by Judge Wilkins (who served as a member of the Federal Sentencing Commission) relied on *McMillan*, stating that it saw no reason to apply a higher standard. *Id.* at 1238. The court added that:

> Fairness to a defendant is substantially increased under guideline sentencing with application of a preponderance of the evidence standard, for if a court is considering applying an aggravating factor which will have the effect of increasing the sentence, the court must afford a defendant the opportunity to oppose and specifically address its application.

Id. *See also* United States v. White, 888 F.2d 490, 499 (7th Cir. 1989), in which the court noted the potential conflict between respecting a jury's verdict and sentencing for all relevant conduct if a defendant was acquitted of a charge but found the evidence persuasive by a preponderance of the evidence. The court concluded that the issue was not ripe for decision. *Id.* For another case in which the court arrived at this conclusion, see United States v. Alston, 895 F.2d 1362, 1372-73 (11th Cir. 1990).

220 United States v. Gooden 892 F.2d 725, 727-28 (8th Cir. 1989), *cert. denied*, 496 U.S. 908 (1990); United States v. Guerra, 888 F.2d 247, 250-51 (2d Cir. 1989), *cert. denied*, 494 U.S. 1090 (1990).

A preliminary draft of the guidelines required that judges apply a preponderance of the evidence standard. Harvey M. Silets & Susan W. Brenner, *Commentary on the Preliminary Draft of the Sentencing Guidelines Issued by the United States Sentencing Commission in September, 1986*, 77 J. CRIM. L. & CRIMINOLOGY 1069, 1079 (1986). Ironically, this requirement was

sentencing proceeding was not as critical as the finding of guilt,[221] or to the courts' concern with judicial economy.[222] These are essentially the same justifications that were offered for not providing procedural protections at pre-guidelines discretionary sentencing.[223]

The Tenth Circuit explicitly considered the appropriateness of continuing the pre-guidelines standards in *United States v. Frederick.*[224] In addition to relying on *McMillan*, the court found support in the Sentencing Reform Act's continuation of the *Williams* standard that no limits should be placed on the information a court could consider at sentencing.[225] The Tenth Circuit reasoned that because Congress did not modify this rule, the pre-guidelines sentencing procedures were presumptively correct.[226]

In upholding the preponderance standard, some courts also pointed to the appellate courts' previous refusal to raise the standard of proof at sentencings where an increased penalty resulted from a finding that the defendant was a dangerous special offender.[227] Although primarily relying on *McMillan* to find that the government did not have to prove sentencing factors beyond a reasonable doubt, the Ninth Circuit considered the impact of requiring only a preponderance of the evidence. In *United States v. Wilson*,[228] the court recognized that the standard was simply "that the relevant fact is deemed more likely true than not on the basis of the available information—no matter how limited or unreliable."[229]

In discussing their concern with the low burden of proof, judges and scholars have often focused on the Supreme Court's analysis in *McMillan* that a sentencing factor may be determined by a lower burden of proof when that factor is one traditionally associated with sen-

---

not enacted because of the realization that the pre-guidelines system differed too greatly to provide an effective model for the new sentencing scheme. *Id.*

221 United States v. McDowell, 888 F.2d 285 (3d Cir. 1989). The *McDowell* court observed that "[o]nce criminal proceedings reach the sentencing stage, the decision has already been made that the defendant can be deprived of his liberty." *Id.* at 290.

222 *Id.* "The long history of judicial sentencing and strong policy reasons, including judicial economy, persuade us . . . that a defendant's rights in sentencing are met by a preponderance of evidence standard." *Id.* at 291. The *McDowell* court limited its holding to cases involving simple enhancement. *Id.* at 290-91. The court did not consider cases where the adjustment was "a new and separate offense." *Id.* at 291.

223 *See* discussion *supra* Part I.

224 897 F.2d 490 (10th Cir.), *cert. denied*, 498 U.S. 863 (1990).

225 *Id.* at 492.

226 *Id.*

227 United States v. Silverman, 889 F.2d 1531, 1535 (6th Cir. 1989), *cert. denied*, 113 S. Ct. 1595 (1993) (citing United States v. Davis, 710 F.2d 104 (3d Cir.), *cert. denied*, 464 U.S. 1001 (1983)).

228 900 F.2d 1350 (9th Cir. 1990).

229 *Id.* at 1354 (citing United States v. Davis, 715 F. Supp. 1473, 1481 (C.D. Cal. 1989), *cert. denied*, 113 S. Ct. 210 (1992).

tencing, rather than traditionally deemed to be a separate crime.[230] Accordingly, some judges concluded that the sentencing factor involved in calculating the relevant conduct of a drug offense which included separate drug sales went beyond the *McMillan* principle and warranted a higher burden of proof.[231]

In *United States v. Restrepo*,[232] the Ninth Circuit, sitting *en banc*, reconsidered the question of standard of proof in the context of a significant increase in sentence based on relevant conduct. The *Restrepo* court found the preponderance of the evidence standard adequate but defined it to require that a court be convinced "by a preponderance of the evidence that the fact in question exists."[233] This definition contrasts with the literal interpretation that courts need only weigh the evidence and find that the evidence tipped the scales.[234]

Despite the uniformity in outcome among the circuits in upholding the preponderance of the evidence standard, there was great dissension among the Ninth Circuit judges in *Restrepo*.[235] The dissenters distinguished between the guidelines sentencing for relevant conduct and the *McMillan* finding of a sentencing factor.[236] Because separate sales of illegal substances can be charged as separate crimes, some dissenters found that relevant conduct sentencing under the guidelines crossed the constitutional line, drawn in *McMillan*, between elements of a crime and traditional sentencing factors.[237]

Judges opposed to continuing the preponderance of the evidence standard have condoned low evidentiary standards at pre-guidelines sentencing but have argued that prior case law, such as *Williams*,

---

230 Generally, judges cite *McMillan* for the proposition that guidelines sentencing may employ the preponderance of the evidence standard without provoking any due process concerns. *See, e.g.*, United States v. Galloway, 976 F.2d 414, 422-26 (8th Cir.) *cert. denied*, 113 S. Ct. 1420 (1992); United States v. Mobley, 956 F.2d 450, 454-459 (3d Cir. 1992); United States v. Richards, 936 F.2d 575 (7th Cir. 1991). In relying upon *McMillan*, courts seek to allay any worry about the overlapping of current guidelines practice onto pre-guidelines case law by explaining that "[t]he Sentencing Guidelines do not differ from the Pennsylvania statute [at issue in *McMillan*] in any manner material to a constitutional inquiry." *Galloway*, 976 F.2d at 423 (citing United States v. Restrepo, 946 F.2d 654, 657 (9th Cir. 1991) (en banc) *cert. denied*, 112 S. Ct. 1564 (1992)).

231 *See infra* note 243 and accompanying text.

232 946 F.2d 654 (9th Cir. 1991) (en banc), *cert. denied*, 112 S. Ct. 1564 (1992).

233 *Id.* at 661 (citing United States v. Streeter, 907 F.2d 781, 792 (8th Cir. 1990), *overruled on other grounds*, by United States v. Wise, 976 F.2d 393 (8th Cir. 1992)).

234 United States v. Restrepo, 903 F.2d 648, 654 (9th Cir. 1990) (panel opinion), *modified*, United States v. Restrepo, 946 F.2d 654 (9th Cir. 1991) (en banc), *cert. denied*, 112 S. Ct. 1564 (1992).

235 United States v. Restrepo, 946 F.2d at 663-78.

236 *Id.* at 665 (Norris, J., dissenting).

237 *Id.* at 664-65 (Norris, J., dissenting).

has little relevance in evaluating the guidelines' constitutionality.[238] Some have also contended that sentencing under the guidelines is analogous to the sentencing scheme discussed in *Specht v. Patterson*[239] because the maximum penalty available to the court is raised by a finding of relevant conduct.[240] The Court in *McMillan* distinguished *Specht* because *McMillan* did not raise the maximum potential sentence.[241]

Five courts of appeals have suggested that an increase in penalty due to information presented at the sentencing phase might be so great in relation to the sentence for the original crime of conviction that the standard of proof should be higher than a preponderance of the evidence.[242] In *United States v. Kikumura*,[243] the Third Circuit concluded that due process required fact-finding by clear and convincing evidence when the consequence was an increase in sentence from thirty months to thirty years. The court observed that this was a case of "a tail which wags the dog of the substantive offense."[244] *Kikumura* presented an easier case than usual because the district court had noted that although a preponderance was sufficient, its findings were supported by clear and convincing evidence.[245] Accordingly, reversal was not required.

The problem with *Kikumura* was subsequently illustrated in *United States v. Townley*,[246] in which the Eighth Circuit acknowledged that at some point the disparity might be so great as to require a higher level

238 United States v. Galloway, 976 F.2d 414, 436 (8th Cir.) (Bright, J. dissenting), *cert. denied*, 113 S. Ct. 1420 (1992). Commentators also have recognized that *Williams* and its progeny simply are inapposite in achieving the guidelines' objectives. Meeting these objectives "requires . . . a complete restructuring of the policies and practices of the federal sentencing system, since that system is and always has been predicated upon the concept of judicial discretion." Silets & Brenner, *supra* note 220, at 1079.

239 386 U.S. 605 (1967).

240 Galloway, 976 F.2d at 441 (Bright, J., dissenting).

241 McMillan v. Pennsylvania, 477 U.S. 79, 88-89 (1986).

242 United States v. Billingsley, 978 F.2d 861, 866 (5th Cir. 1992), *cert. denied*, 113 S. Ct. 1661 (1993); United States v. Galloway, 976 F.2d 414, 417 (8th Cir.), *cert. denied*, 113 S. Ct. 1420 (1992); United States v. Lam Kwong-Wah, 966 F.2d 682, 688 (D.C. Cir.), *cert. denied*, 113 S. Ct. 287 (1992); United States v. Restrepo, 946 F.2d 654, 659 (9th Cir. 1991) (en banc), *cert. denied*, 112 S. Ct. 1564 (1992); United States v. St. Julian, 922 F.2d 563, 569 n.1 (10th Cir. 1990), *cert. denied*, 113 S. Ct. 348 (1992).

The Seventh Circuit has sent contradictory messages regarding the proper burden of proof when fact-finding at sentencing greatly increases the length of the sentence. *Compare* United States v. Masters, 978 F.2d 281, 286-87 (7th Cir. 1992), *cert. denied*, 113 S. Ct. 2333 (1993) (Constitution does not require higher burden of proof) *with* United States v. Trujillo, 959 F.2d 1377, 1381-82 (7th Cir.), *cert. denied*, 113 S. Ct. 277 (1992) (agreeing with *Kikumura* holding that in some situations a higher burden of proof at sentencing is required) and United States v. Schuster, 948 F.2d 313, 315 (7th Cir. 1992) (same).

243 918 F.2d 1084 (3d Cir. 1990).

244 *Id.* at 1100-01 (citing McMillan v. Pennsylvania, 477 U.S. 79, 88 (1986)).

245 *Id.* at 1102-04.

246 929 F.2d 365 (8th Cir. 1991).

of proof, although the increase in *Townley* did not reach that point.[247] The "standard" with which the courts are left is that they should know that level of disparity when they see it.[248] This vague standard requires a two-level determination that is unnecessary and difficult. First, a court must identify whether the disparity is "a tail which wags the dog," that is, whether the additional penalty is so great as to raise due process concerns. Second, the court must impose the corresponding standard of proof.[249] Notably, *Kikumura* and related cases fail to identify a logical basis for creating a dual standard. Whether the defendant's sentence is increased by two months or twenty years, the defendant should have the same right to a valid decision based on reliable evidence.

This type of individual case analysis fails to recognize the importance of a systemwide change in the sentencing process. Under the guidelines, courts consider not just one factor, as in *McMillan*, but many factors. Some of these factors were traditionally considered at sentencing, but many could have been charged as separate crimes. At the same time the guidelines impose specific consequences for each of these factors. Consequently, the guidelines make it possible for the government to avoid the traditional, difficult choice of whether to charge an offense and attempt to prove it beyond a reasonable doubt or to forego seeking punishment because there is insufficient proof of

---

247 *Id.* at 370.

248 As in *Townley*, other courts confronted with increases in the length of a sentence have concluded without elaboration that the clear and convincing standard had not been triggered by the increase in defendant's sentence. *See* United States v. Galloway, 976 F.2d 414, 425-27 (8th Cir. 1992), *cert. denied*, 113 S. Ct. 1420 (1993) (three-fold increase in defendant's sentence did not violate defendant's due process rights); United States v. Lam Kwong-Wah, 966 F.2d 682, 688 (D.C. Cir.), *cert. denied*, 113 S. Ct. 287 (1992) (six level increase not significant enough to require clear and convincing standard); United States v. Trujillo, 959 F.2d 1377, 1382 (7th Cir.), *cert. denied*, 113 S. Ct. 277 (1992) (sentence increase of 4.5 years did not merit higher level of due process).

249 District courts anticipating the possibility of this two level standard may attempt to forestall the problem by acknowledging it. A number of appellate court decisions observe that district courts are specifying that their resolution of disputed sentencing facts satisfies both the preponderance of the evidence and the clear and convincing standards. *See, e.g.*, United States v. Mergerson, 995 F.2d 1285, 1291 (5th Cir. 1993); United States v. Corbin, 998 F.2d 1377, 1387-88 (7th Cir. 1993); United States v. Concepcion, 983 F.2d 369, 390 (2d Cir. 1992), *cert. denied*, 114 S. Ct. 163 (1993); United States v. Billingsley, 978 F.2d 861, 866 (5th Cir. 1992), *cert. denied*, 113 S. Ct. 1661 (1993). Use of both the preponderance and clear and convincing standards may indicate district courts' uncertainty and discomfort with the current vague standard.

Appellate courts routinely dismiss defendants' arguments that the beyond a reasonable doubt standard should be applied. *See, e.g.*, *Mergerson*, 995 F.2d at 1291; *Corbin*, 998 F.2d at 1388. At least one district court, however, has applied the reasonable doubt standard. *See* United States v. Trujillo, 959 F.2d 1377, 1382 (7th Cir.), *cert. denied*, 113 S. Ct. 277 (1992).

the conduct.[250] The judge has no basis under the guidelines for finding the low burden of proof was met but concluding that such a sentence would be excessive. The guidelines thus enable the government to obtain a much higher sentence for a much lower level of proof and expenditure of resources. Moreover, at sentencing a court may ignore a jury's verdict of not guilty on a particular count, even in a case of jury nullification.[251] The judge, if following current law, may not ameliorate the sentence. The traditional checks and balances of jury

---

250 An ongoing criticism of the guidelines has been that they transfer to the prosecution the discretion that historically was accorded to the judge. *See, e.g.*, United States v. Harrington, 947 F.2d 956, 963-70 (D.C. Cir. 1991) (Edwards, J., concurring); United States v. Stanley, 928 F.2d 575, 582-83 (2d Cir.), *cert. denied*, 112 S. Ct. 141 (1991); United States v. Boshell, 728 F. Supp. 632, 637-38 (E.D. Wash. 1990); Alschuler, *supra* note 16, at 926; Koh, *supra* note 16.

251 Eleven circuits have ruled that conduct underlying charges of which the defendant was acquitted may be considered at sentencing. *See* United States v. Paulino, 996 F.2d 1541, 1546-49 (3d Cir.), *cert. denied*, 114 S. Ct. 449 (1993) (while jury determined that approximately 390 grams of cocaine were involved in defendant's drug conspiracy, district court calculated defendant's sentence based on its finding that between 127 to 140 kilograms of cocaine were involved); United States v. Wright, 996 F.2d 312 (10th Cir. 1993) (sentencing court may sentence defendant for conspiracy although jury acquitted defendant of that charge), United States v. Lynch, 934 F.2d 1226, 1234-37 (11th Cir. 1991), *cert. denied*, 112 S. Ct. 885 (1992) (sentencing court took into account defendant's possession of a firearm although the jury had acquitted defendant of this possession); *see also* United States v. Boney, 977 F.2d 624, 635 (D.C. Cir. 1992); United States v. Galloway, 976 F. 2d 414, 422-25 (8th Cir. 1992), *cert. denied*, 113 S. Ct. 1420 (1992); United States v. Fonner, 920 F.2d 1330, 1332-33 (7th Cir. 1990); United States v. Duncan, 918 F.2d 647, 652 (6th Cir. 1990), *cert. denied*, 111 S. Ct. 2055 (1991); United States v. Rodriguez-Gonzalez, 899 F.2d 177, 180-81 (2d Cir.), *cert. denied*, 498 U.S. 844 (1990); United States v. Mocciola, 891 F.2d 13, 16-17 (1st Cir. 1989); United States v. Isom, 886 F.2d 736, 738-39 (4th Cir. 1989); United States v. Juarez-Ortega, 866 F.2d 747, 748-49 (5th Cir. 1989).

The Ninth Circuit is alone in concluding that a district court may not consider acquitted conduct at sentencing. United States v. Brady, 928 F.2d 844 (9th Cir. 1991). The *Brady* court reasoned that while a sentencing court may consider evidence of factors not part of the offense of conviction, "it does not follow that the Guidelines permit a court to reconsider facts during sentencing that have been rejected by a jury's not guilty verdict." *Id.* at 851.

Judge Newman of the Second Circuit has urged that the role acquitted conduct plays at sentencing "must be modified [because a] just system of criminal sentencing cannot fail to distinguish between an allegation of conduct resulting in a conviction and an allegation of conduct resulting in an acquittal." United States v. Concepcion, 983 F.2d 369, 396 (2d Cir. 1992), *cert. denied*, 114 S. Ct. 163 (Newman, J., dissenting).

An amendment proposed to the guidelines in 1993 by the Practitioners' Advisory Group would have precluded the sentencing court from considering conduct of which the jury had acquitted the defendant. Proposed Amendments to the Federal Sentencing Guidelines, 52 Crim. L. Rep. (BNA) 2194 (Feb. 3, 1993). An alternative proposal put forth by the same group would have required the prosecution to prove acquitted conduct by a clear and convincing standard. *Id.* While twenty-two proposals were accepted by the Commission for amendment, neither of these proposals were among those accepted. 58 Fed. Reg. 27,148, 27,148-60 (1993).

Additionally, a court may consider illegally seized evidence which was suppressed at trial. United States v. McCrory, 930 F.2d 63, 69 (D.C. Cir. 1991), *cert. denied*, 112 S. Ct. 885 (1992); United States v. Torres, 926 F.2d 321, 322-25 (3d Cir. 1991). A court may also consider evidence from the trial of co-defendants, so long as that evidence does not come

determination of the facts and judge determination of the sentence are eliminated.

Ironically, one court has stated that fairness to a defendant has substantially increased under the guidelines, even with the low standard of proof.[252] A comprehensive look at the procedural protections of the guidelines suggests otherwise. There is no requirement that the government present proof that would be admissible under the Federal Rules of Evidence. There is a presumption that the information in the presentence report is correct.[253] These procedural rules do not protect the defendant.[254]

---

as an unfair surprise to defendant. United States v. Morales, 994 F.2d 386, 389-90 (7th Cir. 1993).

252 United States v. Arrego-Linares, 879 F.2d 1234, 1238 (4th Cir.), *cert. denied*, 493 U.S. 943 (1989).

253 *See* United States v. Smiley, 997 F.2d 475, 483 (8th Cir. 1993) (Bright, J., dissenting) (noting that probation officer's sentencing recommendations in the presentence report are "often summarily approve[d]" by the court); United States v. Bartsh, 985 F.2d 930, 932 (8th Cir. 1993) (district court properly accepted presentence report's calculation of amount that defendant embezzled because defendant failed to object to this calculation); United States v. Harrington, 947 F.2d 956, 966 (D.C. Cir. 1991) (Edwards, J., concurring) (observing that "many trial judges appear to accept the Report as written"); United States v. Mir, 919 F.2d 940, 942-43 (5th Cir. 1990) (defendant's failure to present rebuttal evidence to presentence report's finding that he was a leader in a narcotics conspiracy and that he possessed a greater amount of drugs than he admitted to meant that district court could consider the report's findings when calculating defendant's sentence); *see also* FED. R. EVID. 1101(d)(3), Advisory Committee Notes (in sentencing, "great reliance is placed on the presentence investigation and report"); Heaney, *supra* note 16, at 169 n.22 and accompanying text.

Some appellate courts have reversed trial courts which relied on the presumption that the presentence report is correct without considering the quality of the underlying information. *See, e.g.*, United States v. Watkins, 994 F.2d 1192, 1195-96 (6th Cir. 1993) (in calculating the total amount of intended loss caused by defendant's check kiting scheme, sentencing court relied solely on the presentence report because the government did not present any evidence regarding this issue; reviewing court vacated the sentence and remanded for resentencing because the report was inadequate); United States v. Gilliam, 987 F.2d 1009, 1014 (4th Cir. 1993) (presentence report based quantity of drugs that defendant possessed on amount alleged in indictment for the entire conspiracy; appellate court's review of defendant's questioning of the probation officer led court to determine that the report lacked sufficient indicia of reliability and thus sentence was vacated and case was remanded for resentencing); United States v. Leichtnam, 948 F.2d 370, 381-82 (7th Cir. 1991) (sentence vacated and case remanded for resentencing by reviewing court which noted that information in the presentence report regarding drug quantity had been supplied by government attorney and was totally unsubstantiated).

254 *See* Silets & Brenner, *supra* note 220, at 1079. The preliminary draft of the guidelines established the burden of proof at sentencing as the preponderance of the evidence standard. *Id.* Although the Commission later decided to allow courts to determine the proper burden of proof, two critics of the preliminary draft recognized that the preponderance of the evidence standard, which is the de facto standard today, "puts the defendant in a perilous position." *Id.* at 1083.

B. The Use of Hearsay

Hearsay[255] evidence has raised the greatest concern with reliability of evidence at sentencing. At trial using hearsay may be prohibited by the Confrontation Clause or the Due Process Clause of the Constitution or by the Federal Rules of Evidence.[256] The exclusion of hearsay at trial, under a constitutional rationale, is not completely coextensive with the exclusions of the Federal Rules of Evidence, although both trace their origins to the concern in England with the unfairness of prosecution by affidavit.[257] Recent Confrontation Clause cases have permitted out-of-court statements that meet "firmly rooted exceptions" to the hearsay rule.[258] Thus, a right of confrontation at sentencing afforded either by the Constitution or by application of the rules of evidence would provide similar, although not identical, protection against unreliable hearsay.

The concern over hearsay stems from the widely accepted belief that cross-examination can reveal infirmities in testimony that arise from: (1) defects in perception, (2) defects in memory, (3) defects in sincerity or veracity, and (4) defects in narration, such as ambiguity.[259] Secondary reasons given for excluding hearsay are that the declarant is not under oath and the declarant's demeanor cannot be observed.[260] The Federal Rules of Evidence contain a definition of hearsay, a general ban on the use of hearsay, and twenty-nine exceptions to the exclusion, including "catch-all" exceptions.[261] The rules were designed to admit hearsay only when it arose in circumstances that support its reliability by identifiable guarantees of trustworthiness.[262] Consequently, as Judge Edward Becker and Professor Aviva Orenstein aptly noted, inadmissible, reliable hearsay is an "oxymoron."[263]

---

255 Hearsay is commonly defined as an out of court statement offered for the truth of the matter asserted. FED. R. EVID. 801(c).

256 FED. R. EVID. 801-05.

257 This history was recently recounted by Justice Thomas in Illinois v. White, 112 S. Ct. 736, 743-48 (1992) (Thomas, J., concurring in part and concurring in the decision).

258 *See, e.g.*, Bourjaily v. United States, 483 U.S. 171, 183 (1987) ("co-conspirator exception to the hearsay rule is firmly enough rooted in our jurisprudence that . . . a court need not independently inquire into the reliability of such statements").

259 LILLY, *supra* note 70, at 159.

260 *Id.* at 160.

261 FED. R. EVID. 801-04.

262 For example, statements for purposes of medical diagnosis or treatment are admitted under an exception to the hearsay rule. FED. R. EVID. 803(4). The premise is that an individual will truthfully state medical conditions in order to receive appropriate medical care.

263 Edward R. Becker & Aviva Orenstein, *The Federal Rules of Evidence After Sixteen Years—The Effect of "Plain Meaning" Jurisprudence, The Need for an Advisory Committee on the Rules of Evidence, and Suggestions for Selective Revision of the Rules*, 60 GEO. WASH. L. REV. 857, 889 (1992).

The Federal Rules of Evidence, other than the single rule governing privileges, explicitly do not apply to sentencing.[264] The Federal Sentencing Guidelines assume that hearsay will still be permitted, as it was under pre-guidelines discretionary sentencing.[265] Accordingly, courts anxious for improved reliability of evidence at sentencing have looked for a constitutional basis to exclude hearsay.

Courts assessing whether a right of confrontation exists at sentencing have looked to the Confrontation Clause of the Sixth Amendment and the Due Process Clause of the Fifth Amendment. Because the Supreme Court had concluded that sentencing based on hearsay did not violate the right to confrontation under pre-guidelines discretionary sentencing in *Williams v. New York*,[266] defendants or courts seeking a different result at guidelines sentencing had to emphasize its differences from discretionary sentencing. Making such a distinction did not appear to be an insurmountable hurdle, because the *Williams* Court's analysis was inextricably linked to the rehabilitative theory underlying discretionary sentencing. The *Williams* Court emphasized that sentencing courts needed full information about the defendant in order to meet the goal of rehabilitative punishment.[267] The Court also recognized that the benefits to the defendant under rehabilitative sentencing were significant, including more lenient penalties.[268] In *Williams*, the Court also emphasized that the defendant had not challenged the veracity of the hearsay information contained in the presentence report.[269]

Despite the significant changes in sentencing, most courts have held that guidelines sentencing is not so different from discretionary sentencing as to warrant a different analysis of the confrontation or due process right to preclude hearsay.[270] Judicial consideration of the issue, however, has revealed sharply divergent views. Two federal appellate court panels held that there was a right to confrontation at some sentencings.[271] En banc courts reversed both of these cases with strong dissents demonstrating the deep disagreement about the preclusion of hearsay.

---

264 FED. R. EVID. 1101(d) (3).

265 *See supra* note 193 and accompanying text.

266 337 U.S. 241 (1949).

267 *Id.* at 247.

268 *Id.*

269 *Id.* at 244.

270 United States v. Sciarrino, 884 F.2d 95, 96-97 (3d Cir. 1989), *cert. denied*, 493 U.S. 997 (1989).

271 United States v. Silverman, 945 F.2d 1337 (6th Cir. 1991), *vacated*, 976 F.2d 1502 (6th Cir. 1992) (en banc), *cert. denied*, 113 S. Ct. 1595 (1993); United States v. Wise, 923 F.2d 86 (8th Cir. 1991), *vacated*, 976 F.2d 393 (8th Cir. 1992) (en banc), *cert. denied*, 113 S. Ct. 1592 (1993).

In *United States v. Silverman*,[272] the Sixth Circuit, en banc, reviewed sentences that were founded on determinations of relevant conduct based on hearsay.[273] The majority upheld the sentences, concluding that the standards of *Williams* controlled, and that the use of hearsay did not violate the confrontation clause or the due process clause.[274] The court noted that other Sixth Amendment guarantees, such as the right to jury trial, are not available at sentencing.[275]

In a vigorous dissent, Chief Judge Merritt argued that *Williams* was inapplicable to the guidelines sentencing scheme:

> [T]he new system completely changes the discretionary, nonadversary, nonfactual nature of the sentencing process by introducing the adversary sentencing hearing, the need for precise and accurate findings of disputed facts about other criminal conduct and absolute rules to be applied without deviation requiring the district court to increase dramatically the sentence based on the unconvicted conduct.[276]

Merritt analogized guideline sentencing for relevant conduct to the enhanced sentencing system examined in *Specht v. Patterson*,[277] where the Supreme Court refused to extend the *Williams* rationale to a novel and substantively different sentencing system. Merritt argued that the *Specht* holding required application of the confrontation clause wherever that "[sentencing] scheme requires fact-finding in an adversary setting"[278] and "the sentence is based in part on multiple hearsay."[279]

In *United States v. Wise*,[280] the Eighth Circuit sitting en banc considered the procedural requirement at guidelines sentencing, again in the context of an increased sentence based on alleged relevant conduct.[281] The trial court had relied on hearsay evidence in finding that there was relevant conduct.[282] A panel of the Eighth Circuit reversed the trial court for failing to evaluate whether the reliance on hearsay violated the confrontation clause.[283] The en banc court reversed the

---

272 976 F.2d 1502 (6th Cir. 1992) (en banc), *cert. denied*, 113 S. Ct. 1595 (1993).

273 *Id.* at 1503.

274 *Id.* at 1508-11. Judge Nelson concurred in the judgment, but argued that hearsay should be admitted if it met the "probable accuracy" test mentioned in U.S.S.G., *supra* note 10, § 6A1.3(a). *Id.* at 1517 (Nelson, J., concurring).

275 *Id.* at 1511. For an argument that there should be a right to jury determination of facts that determine a defendant's sentence, see Colleen P. Murphy, *Integrating the Constitutional Authority of Civil and Criminal Juries*, 61 Geo. Wash. L. Rev. 723, 773-77 (1993).

276 *Silverman*, 976 F.2d at 1525 (Merritt, C.J., dissenting).

277 386 U.S. 605 (1967).

278 *Silverman*, 976 F.2d at 1526 (Merritt, C.J., dissenting).

279 *Id.*

280 976 F.2d 393 (8th Cir. 1992) (en banc), *cert. denied*, 113 S. Ct. 1592 (1993).

281 *Id.* at 396.

282 *Id.*

283 *Id.* at 395.

panel and affirmed the sentence.[284] Although the problem of hearsay was not critical to the court's decision, the opinion noted that neither a right to confrontation nor due process limited the trial court's consideration of evidence at sentencing.[285]

The importance of having testimony subject to cross-examination as the basis for sentencing is illustrated in *United States v. Simmons*,[286] a case in which a court had the opportunity to review the actual witness' testimony. In *Simmons*, the appellate court reviewed evidence relied upon by the trial court to determine the quantity of drugs distributed by Simmons' codefendant, Bowers.[287] The trial court relied in part on testimony from Pierce, a customer of Bowers. Pierce testified that she had bought between one tenth and one gram of cocaine base from Bowers on more than twenty occasions.[288]

During Pierce's cross-examination, however, the defense established that Pierce had committed perjury by testifying falsely about her own extensive use of crack.[289] Also, when repeatedly questioned about her drug dealings with the defendant, she answered inconsistently and imprecisely, admitting that the events "ran together."[290] The appellate court concluded that Pierce's testimony was not reliable and could not be a factor in determining the quantity of drugs distributed by Bowers.[291] Because the presentence report had relied on Pierce's statement, the appellate court vacated Bowers' sentence and remanded for a further factual hearing to determine the quantity of drugs distributed by Bowers.[292]

Simmons demonstrates the importance of firsthand testimony. Had Pierce not testified at trial, the prosecutor probably would have reported her information to the probation officer writing the presentence report. If the quantity had been challenged by the defendant, the government most likely would have asked an officer or agent who had interviewed Pierce to testify as to what she had said. The government would not have been obligated to put Pierce on the stand. There would have been no perjury. The officer undoubtedly would have been consistent and confident in answering questions. In assessing the credibility of witnesses for the prosecution and the defense, the court would have had a clean-cut government agent on one

---

284 *Id.* at 405.

285 *Id.* at 400-04.

286 964 F.2d 763 (8th Cir.), *cert. denied*, 113 S. Ct. 632 (1992).

287 *Id.* at 771.

288 *Id.*

289 *Id.* at 769.

290 *Id.* at 776.

291 *Id.*

292 *Id.*

side and a defendant convicted of distributing large quantities of narcotics on the other.

When hearsay is presented by an agent or in the presentence report, the court has no opportunity to assess demeanor, consistency of the informant's story, bias, or general credibility. Instead the court relinquishes to the government or the probation officer its opportunity to judge the credibility of the actual witness to the alleged criminal conduct. As a result, the witness is never questioned under oath or cross-examined by an adversary.[293]

Although hearsay was routinely relied on in pre-guidelines discretionary sentencing, judges had wide discretion to treat hearsay as they chose. As noted earlier, one judge has written that, under discretionary sentencing, judges usually omitted from consideration facts in the presentence report that the defendant denied, such as hearsay statements.[294] Clearly, however, neither statute nor case law *required* such omissions. At a minimum, under discretionary sentencing a judge could give evidence less weight if it seemed less reliable. The actual impact of hearsay at discretionary sentencing usually could not be determined because judges did not have to state the reasons for their sentences. Because hearsay was an acceptable basis for pre-guidelines discretionary sentencing, courts reluctant to permit it at guidelines sentencing must distinguish between the two sentencing schemes.

Despite the importance of firsthand testimony, as demonstrated in *Simmons*, and some persuasive dissents in circuit courts' en banc opinions, recent cases indicate that most federal courts are unlikely to preclude reliance on hearsay at most guidelines sentencings.[295] Accordingly, preventing consideration of unreliable hearsay must be achieved by other means.

C. Specialized Rules

Courts have varied dramatically in their determinations of evidentiary issues at sentencing. This variation is consistent with the practice under pre-guidelines discretionary sentencing, in which courts determined their own procedures for sentencing. Thus, for example, with no statutory or recognized constitutional rule against the use of hearsay at sentencing, most courts have accepted it and have required only some minimal indicia of reliability.[296] Similarly, most courts have con-

---

293 Reliance on hearsay by an agent is routine and much less troublesome at some points in criminal proceedings, such as a preliminary hearing, because the decision will be reevaluated by a grand jury and later by a judge or jury.

294 United States v. Clark, 792 F. Supp. 637, 649 (E.D. Ark. 1992).

295 *See* cases cited *supra* this section.

296 *See* United States v. Query, 928 F.2d 383, 384-85 (11th Cir. 1991) (hearsay evidence may be relied upon to establish quantity of drugs involved so long as defendant has the opportunity to rebut the evidence); United States v. Holmes, 961 F.2d 599, 603 (6th Cir.),

tinued to judge the evidence under a mere preponderance of the evidence standard.[297] However, some courts have developed, explicitly or implicitly, specialized evidentiary rules for sentencing. Scholars have also suggested specialized rules.

Many of the specialized rules developed through case law are designed to guide courts in deciding whether to rely on hearsay. For example, some courts have placed the burden on the defendant to show that the declarant lacked personal knowledge or had a reason to lie.[298] Other courts have placed a more general burden on defendants to rebut hearsay.[299] If the defendant fails to rebut the hearsay, the court accepts it as true.[300] This shifting of the burden, however, is contrary to the principle at trial that the government has the burden of proof on each element of the offense.[301] In the context of relevant conduct, the rule requires the defendant to prove the negative, that is, that the defendant did not engage in the alleged conduct.[302] Shifting the burden does not establish the reliability of the initial hearsay; instead, it permits the court to suggest that the defendant has control of whether or not the hearsay is credited. This illusion hides the underlying, critical need for reliable information in sentencing.

Although most courts have been reluctant to impose a higher burden of proof or to prohibit hearsay at sentencing, some courts have explicitly acknowledged their concerns with the potential unreliability of hearsay and have imposed rules regarding the adequacy of the hearsay evidence.[303] Some reviewing courts have required an ex-

cert. denied, 113 S. Ct. 232 (1992); United States v. Chavez, 947 F.2d 742, 746 (5th Cir. 1991); United States v. Griffin, 945 F.2d 378, 381-82 (11th Cir. 1991), *cert. denied*, 112 S. Ct. 1958 (1992); United States v. Shewmaker, 936 F.2d 1124, 1129 (10th Cir. 1991), *cert. denied*, 112 S. Ct. 884 (1992); United States v. Hubbard, 929 F.2d 307, 309-10 (7th Cir.), *cert. denied*, 112 S. Ct. 206 (1991); United States v. Sciarrino, 884 F.2d 95, 96-97 (3d Cir.), *cert. denied*, 493 U.S. 997 (1989).

297 *See supra* note 218 and accompanying text.

298 *See, e.g.*, United States v. Aymelek, 926 F.2d 64, 68 (1st Cir. 1991).

299 *See* United States v. Corbin, 998 F.2d 1377 (7th Cir. 1993); United States v. Addison, 1993 WL 318780 (6th Cir. 1993) (per curiam); United States v. Chavez, 947 F.2d 742, 746-47 (5th Cir. 1991); United States v. Griffin, 945 F.2d 378, 381-82 (11th Cir. 1991), *cert. denied*, 112 S. Ct. 1958 (1992); United States v. Hubbard, 929 F.2d 307, 309-10 (7th Cir.), *cert. denied*, 112 S. Ct. 206 (1991).

300 *See, e.g.*, United States v. Streich, 987 F.2d 104, 107 (2d Cir. 1993) (per curiam) (stating that the defendant's failure to contest a presentence report's hearsay allegations, which were based on interviews with informants, meant that sentencing court could accept the allegations as true).

301 *In re* Winship, 397 U.S. 358, 364 (1970).

302 *See infra* note 342 and accompanying text.

303 *See, e.g.*, United States v. Miele, 989 F.2d 659, 664 (3d Cir. 1993) (arguing that the sufficient indicia of reliability standard "should be applied rigorously").

planation of why hearsay is reliable.[304] In *United States v. Padilla*,[305] the Tenth Circuit required that the hearsay source be named.[306] Other courts have required corroboration of additional criminal conduct by other evidence.[307]

Each of these rules incrementally improves the factual basis for sentencing and reflects how people commonly deal with hearsay in nonlegal matters. Requesting an explanation for why hearsay is reliable essentially asks the proffering party, why do you believe this? Requiring that the ource be named may permit the defense to argue why that particular individual should not be believed. Requiring corroboration of hearsay enables the court to base its fact-finding in part on the other evidence.

Under the Federal Rules of Evidence, these incremental requirements would not suffice for admissibility. Hearsay that does not meet an exception may not be used for substantive evidence.[308] Bolstering hearsay with corroborating physical evidence or testimony does not make it admissible.[309]

The Federal Rules of Evidence treat the admissibility of evidence and the weight the fact-finder chooses to give that evidence as separate determinations. The rules concerning hearsay initially ensure that each piece of evidence admitted has sufficient reliability to be a factor in fact-finding.[310] At sentencing, however, decisions of admissibility and weight are essentially merged.

---

304 *See* United States v. Ortiz, 993 F.2d 204, 208 (10th Cir. 1993) (finding that the district court sentence was clearly erroneous for relying upon FBI agent's testimony which was based solely on the uncorroborated, out-of-court statement of a confidential informant).

305 947 F.2d 893 (10th Cir. 1991).

306 *Id.* at 895-96.

307 *See, e.g.*, United States v. Hubbard, 929 F.2d 307, 309-10 (7th Cir.) (finding that hearsay evidence of intent to cause bodily injury was corroborated by physical evidence), *cert. denied*, 112 S. Ct. 206 (1991); United States v. Zuleta-Alvarez, 922 F.2d 33, 36-37 (1st Cir. 1990) (stating that hearsay evidence of drug quantity was corroborated by other witness' teştimony at grand jury and trial), *cert. denied*, 111 S. Ct. 2039 (1991).

308 FED. R. EVID. 802.

309 The Federal Rules of Evidence provide that a hearsay statement which does not fall within a specified exception, but has "equivalent circumstantial guarantees of trustworthiness," may be admitted if the court determines that

> (A) the statement is offered as evidence of a material fact; (B) the statement is more probative on the point for which it is offered than any other evidence which the proponent can procure through reasonable efforts; and (C) the general purposes of these rules and the interests of justice will best be served by admission of the statement into evidence.

FED. R. EVID. 803(24); *see also* FED. R. EVID. 804(5) (same).

310 FED. R. EVID. 801-803. In addition to rules governing hearsay, other Federal Rules of Evidence impose standards of reliability. *See, e.g.*, FED. R. EVID. 602 (prohibiting testimony if witness lacks personal knowledge of the matter of the testimony); FED. R. EVID. 701 (limiting opinion testimony by lay witnesses); FED. R. EVID. 702 (allowing opinion testimony by expert witness only if that witness possesses knowledge, skill, experience, training,

Some courts have not explicitly acknowledged their concerns about reliability, but have demonstrated them by "discounting" the facts as established by hearsay evidence. Discounting occurs when a judge makes a finding that a specific amount of harm—such as a specific quantity of drug distribution—has been established by a preponderance of the evidence, but the judge nevertheless bases the sentence on a lesser amount. This implicit weighing of hearsay can occur when the testimony about the quantity of drugs is necessarily an estimate because the full quantity was not seized. A court may elect to err on the side of caution by taking the smallest amount stated and multiplying it by the number of transactions.[311]

Sometimes the discounting is more extreme. Substantial discounting may suggest that the court is not persuaded about the quantity, despite the evidence. For example, in *United States v. Epstein*,[312] a jury convicted Epstein of conspiring to possess with the intent to distribute cocaine.[313] He was acquitted of a charge of attempting to possess with the intent to distribute two kilograms of cocaine.[314] The government estimated that Epstein and his coconspirator distributed between fifteen and seventeen kilograms of cocaine.[315] At the sentencing, the court reached two critical factual conclusions. First, the court concluded that the coconspirator's "testimony was sufficiently credible to establish the amount of cocaine sold by the defendant."[316] Next, the court conceded that the coconspirator might have overestimated the quantity and noted that the coconspirator's testimony was not totally corroborated.[317] The court then discounted the quantity by fifty percent and held Epstein accountable for distributing between seven and a half and eight and a half kilograms of cocaine.[318]

Epstein suggests the discomfort some trial judges experience with low standards of reliability for evidence. One could argue that if the trial court was so uncomfortable it should have found that the evi-

or education regarding the subject about which the witness would testify); FED. R. EVID. 901 (providing for authentication or identification of evidence as a "condition precedent to admissibility"); FED. R. EVID. 1002 (generally requiring the original of a writing, recording, or photograph to prove the contents thereof).

311 *See, e.g.*, United States v. Montoya, 967 F.2d 1 (1st Cir.), *cert. denied*, 113 S. Ct. 507 (1992). A DEA agent testified at Montoya's sentencing that a government informant had reported purchasing two to five ounces of cocaine per week from Montoya for three months. The court sentenced Montoya for selling only two ounces of cocaine per week for the twelve week period. *Id.* at 4.

312 United States v. Epstein, No. 89-CR809-2, 1992 U.S. Dist. LEXIS 541 (N.D. Ill. Jan. 15, 1992).

313 *Id.* at *4.

314 *Id.*

315 *Id.*

316 *Id.* at *8.

317 *Id.* at *10.

318 *Id.* at *10-11.

dence lacked sufficient indicia of reliability. Instead, this court seems to have done what was possible before guidelines—weighted evidence without wholly accepting or rejecting what was proffered.[319]

The application of ad hoc rules by different judges in different cases raises the possibility of disparities that the guidelines were specifically intended to minimize.[320] When one judge discounts hearsay evidence about quantity by fifty percent and another does not, defendants may receive dramatically different sentences for similar crimes. While this compromise accounting may resolve the issue in an individual case, it works against the guidelines' goal of avoiding unwarranted or unnecessary disparity in sentencing.

Commentators have also advocated that specialized rules be applied to sentencing, both with respect to burdens of proof and to the admissibility of evidence.[321] Some have urged the adoption of a higher burden of proof at sentencing. Judy Clarke has argued, as did the dissenting judges in *United States v. Restrepo*,[322] that proof beyond a reasonable doubt should be required for criminal conduct that was not part of the offense of conviction.[323] She has also argued that the clear and convincing standard should apply to more traditional sentencing factors.[324]

Professor Margaret Berger has proposed three limitations on the use of hearsay at sentencing: first, prohibiting use of hearsay statements by cooperating individuals to prove relevant conduct; second, requiring corroboration for hearsay at sentencing; and third, limiting admissibility of multiple hearsay.[325] These proposed rules directly ad-

---

319 The *Epstein* decision highlights one benefit of the guidelines scheme. Because the guideline require courts to present their reasoning, the *Epstein* court was forced to reveal how it had weighted the evidence. As discussed in part I of this Article, the pre-guidelines sentencing system allowed judges to sentence without expressly stating what factors motivated the sentence. In contrast to the former system, the guidelines' mandatory disclosure of reasoning invites scrutiny and analysis, which facilitate improvements to the guidelines.

320 Congress specifically directed the Sentencing Commission to establish sentencing policies with the purpose of "avoiding unwarranted sentencing disparities among defendants with similar records who have been found guilty of similar criminal conduct." 28 U.S.C. § 991(b)(1)(B) (1988).

321 *See* Becker & Orenstein, *supra* note 263, at 890-91; Margaret A. Berger, *Rethinking the Applicability of Evidentiary Rules at Sentencing: Of Relevant Conduct and Hearsay and the Need for an Infield Fly Rule*, 5 Fed. Sentencing Rep. 96 (1992); Judy Clarke, *The Need for a Higher Burden of Proof for Fact Finding Under the Guidelines*, 4 Fed. Sentencing Rep. 300 (1992).

322 946 F.2d 654, 663 (9th Cir. 1991) (en banc) (Pregerson, J., dissenting), *cert. denied*, 112 S. Ct. 1564 (1992).

323 Clarke, *supra* note 321, at 302.

324 *Id.*

325 Berger, *supra* note 321, at 99. Berger also argues that the government should not be permitted to relitigate at sentencing a count on which a defendant was acquitted. This suggestion to prohibit evidence of acquitted counts is consistent with the Ninth Circuit's reasoning in United States v. Brady, 928 F.2d 844, 851-52 (9th Cir. 1991), that it is improper to penalize a defendant for conduct which was the basis for an acquittal. Along the same vein, Berger proposes an "infield fly rule" that would prohibit the government from

dress the reliability and accuracy of fact-finding by targeting some of the most common and troubling kinds of hearsay used at sentencing. Excluding hearsay by cooperating individuals would eliminate a common source of hearsay about the defendant's relevant conduct and role in the offense. Yet, this proposed rule does not address the very similar testimony by paid informants. Furthermore, as Berger points out, hearsay statements by cooperating individuals are often excluded under the Federal Rules of Evidence.[326]

Requiring corroboration of hearsay, consistent with some judicial rulings, raises the level of reliability, but does not address the underlying problem that occurs when part of the evidence is unreliable. Similarly, limiting multiple hearsay means that the testifying witness judges the credibility of the actual declarant, rather than another individual who reported to the in-court witness. This requirement still precludes the court from making its own assessment about the declarant's perception, narration, and sincerity.

Judge Edward Becker and Professor Aviva Orenstein have gone one step further, suggesting that the Supreme Court, acting through an Advisory Committee of the Rules of Evidence, amend the evidentiary rules to make selected rules applicable at sentencing.[327]

Each of these suggestions demonstrates the general concern with the inadequacy of existing procedural safeguards for guidelines sentencing. Each attempts to improve the accuracy of fact-finding in at least some cases or to shift the burden of proof so that an erroneous decision is less likely to harm a defendant. Adopting piece-meal rules, however, fails to recognize the fundamental concern that a defendant should be sentenced based on reliable evidence. Specialized rules achieve some desired results, such as limiting the sentencing increases for relevant conduct, but they fail to recognize that the substantive question of what constitutes relevant conduct and the evidentiary question of what is reliable evidence are best addressed separately. If there is a consensus that defendants should be sentenced on reliable evidence, then Congress and the federal judiciary should look for a comprehensive solution.

introducing evidence at sentencing of dropped or previously uncharged crimes. Berger, *supra* note 321, at 99. These suggestions may be viewed as substantive rules which address how relevant conduct should be defined, rather than how to accurately and reliably determine relevant conduct. They would greatly limit new evidence of relevant conduct at sentencing.

326 Berger, *supra* note 321, at 99.

327 Becker & Orenstein, *supra* note 263, at 909-14.

III
A NEW EXPLORATION OF FACT-FINDING AT SENTENCING

Despite the courts' substantial attention to guidelines fact-finding, the goal of increased reliability in fact-finding at sentencing has not been attained. A fundamental reason for this failure is the mistaken reliance on pre-guidelines cases to determine guideline procedures.[328] A different approach is necessary.

This section analyzes procedures for fact-finding at guidelines sentencing according to theories of evidence. The analysis evaluates two evidentiary protections with important differences: the impact of raising the burden of proof and the impact of requiring more reliable evidence at sentencing. The analysis then evaluates the extent to which these protections advance the sometimes inconsistent goals of achieving accuracy in fact-finding and not unfairly burdening defendants with errors. Factors affecting this evaluation include the likelihood that evidence offered at sentencing will be inculpatory and the probability that evidence will be false. The loss of discretion by judges in the sentencing process exacerbates the problem of unjust fact-finding because judges can no longer ameliorate the harsh effects of low standards of reliability and proof at sentencing. The section concludes by outlining appropriate procedures for reliable fact-finding at guidelines sentencing.

A. Raising the Burden of Proof

Raising the burden of proof is often considered as a way to improve the reliability of fact-finding at sentencing.[329] However, raising the burden of proof does not guarantee greater accuracy in sentencing determinations. Indeed, as illustrated below, raising the burden of proof may result in fewer accurate outcomes. The benefit to the defendant is that the government bears more of the errors in sentencing decisions if the government has a higher burden.

The impact of changing the burden of proof may be demonstrated by looking at the determination of guilt or innocence and evaluating how outcomes change if the burden of proof is lowered. Assume a null hypothesis that the defendant is guilty. For each defendant, one of two possibilities is correct: The defendant is guilty or the defendant is innocent. For each defendant, the jury will either acquit or convict. Assume the following results in 400 cases where the government's burden of proof is guilt beyond a reasonable doubt:

---

[328] *See* discussion *supra* Part II.

[329] *See, e.g.*, David N. Adair, Jr., *House Built on a Weak Foundation—Sentencing Guidelines and the Preponderance Standard of Proof*, 4 FED. SENTENCING REP. 292 (1992).

	Jury Convicts	Jury Acquits
DEFENDANT IS GUILTY (300 X)	220 (correct)	80 (Type I error)
DEFENDANT IS INNOCENT (100 X)	10 (Type II error)	90 (correct)

Under the assumptions used,[330] there are ninety errors. Only ten of these errors are instances in which the hypothesis is false, but accepted, referred to in statistics as a Type II error.[331] In this example, these ten Type II errors are instances of convicting the innocent. The other eighty errors are Type I errors, in which the hypothesis is true, but falsely rejected.[332] These eighty Type I errors represent guilty defendants who are acquitted.

Now, assume the burden of proof is lowered to a preponderance of the evidence, which results in an increase in convictions.

	Jury Convicts	Jury Acquits
DEFENDANT IS GUILTY (300 X)	256 (correct)	44 (Type I error)
DEFENDANT IS INNOCENT (100 X)	15 (Type II error)	85 (correct)

There are now fifty-nine errors, a reduction of thirty-one errors. However, fifteen of the errors are now Type II errors, representing innocent defendants who are convicted.

For determinations of guilt or innocence, a higher burden of proof means that the number of Type II errors decreases, despite the fact that the total number of errors increases. The principle used to justify the high burden is commonly cited as, "[i]t is far worse to convict an innocent man than to let a guilty man go free."[333]

---

330 These numbers are hypothetical. The numbers in this and in the next chart illustrate the principle that the number of convictions will increase as the burden of proof is lowered.

331 John Freund & Gary Simon, Modern Elementary Statistics 301 (1992).

332 *Id.*

333 Justice Harlan stated this principle in his concurring opinion in *In re* Winship, 397 U.S. 358, 372 (1970) (Harlan, J., concurring). He further noted that:

The questions of whether and how standards at sentencing should be raised can only be answered if one identifies what kind of error is most problematic. For example, the sentencing factor that has received the most attention with regard to the burden of proof is relevant conduct.[334] Many commentators have urged that the burden of proof should be at least clear and convincing for relevant conduct that will substantially affect a defendant's sentence.[335] Those who urge a higher burden of proof are actually lobbying for more total errors, but fewer Type II errors. Because the government has the burden of proof for relevant conduct, juries will find fewer defendants to have committed relevant conduct that they did not in fact commit, as is the case with the guilt determination at trial. However, more defendants who did commit relevant conduct will be found not to have done so, resulting in an increase in total errors.[336]

Historically, one reason given for the lack of procedural protections at sentencing was that, after conviction, the defendant should no longer be given the benefit of the doubt; the government and the defendant should equally bear the risk of inaccuracy at sentencing.[337] As long as the burden of proof is on one party, however, there will not be actual equality. That is, even with a preponderance of the evidence standard, if the evidence is fifty-fifty, the party with the burden of proof loses. Nevertheless, the preponderance of the evidence standard does present the most equal consequences possible. The question, then, is whether producing fewer total errors is preferable to more total errors with fewer borne by the defendant.

In each instance of shifting the burden there is a cost. When the guilty go free because of the beyond a reasonable doubt standard at trial, criminals who may victimize others are free to return to the community. The Constitution requires this cost, rather than convicting

---

> It is only because of the nearly complete and long-standing acceptance of the reasonable-doubt standard by the States in criminal trials that the Court has not before today had to hold explicitly that due process, as an expression of fundamental procedural fairness, requires a more stringent standard for criminal trials than for ordinary civil litigation.

Id.

334 *See supra* note 323. For a listing of several articles critical of the treatment of relevant conduct under the guidelines, see *supra* note 159.

335 Clarke, *supra* note 321, at 302; Husseini, *supra* note 16.

336 This analysis assumes that the same evidence will be presented under either burden of proof. This assumption, however, is likely to be inaccurate for sentencings. Because the burden on the government at sentencings now is so low, both as stated and as applied, the government has little incentive to present substantial evidence. If the burden of proof were raised for sentencings, an indirect result might be that the parties would present more and better evidence. This in turn could result in more accurate sentencing decisions.

337 Kadish, *supra* note 22, at 254-55.

more innocent defendants.[338] Adjusting the burden of proof for a sentencing factor also has costs. Raising the burden of proof for relevant evidence will result in more total errors, but fewer defendants who are innocent of the relevant conduct will be punished for it. The increase in total errors means that more defendants who have committed identical conduct will receive different sentences, contrary to the goal of reducing disparity, and that more defendants will not be punished for the full harm that they committed. Thus, the choice in burdens of proof is a choice between these costs.

Because sentencing for additional relevant conduct seems so similar to convicting for criminal conduct, one might conclude that the choice of which costs to bear should be the same. Yet, with other factors the goal may more clearly be one of accuracy, reflected by fewer total errors, rather than shifting more of the errors to one party. If so, then the lesser burden of preponderance of evidence is appropriate.

Even once the burden of proof is specified, such as by a preponderance of the evidence, courts may not actually apply the standard in the same way. There are two possible, but different, applications of the preponderance standard: either the evidence convinces the fact finder that the proposition is more likely than not, or the weight of the evidence, no matter how slight the total evidence, is in favor of the proponent.[339] The distinction between these applications is critical. The first application may impose a higher standard for the degree of certainty of the ultimate proposition. Under this application, even if the proponent presents substantially more evidence (qualitatively and quantitatively), the proponent will still lose if the fact-finder does not believe that the proponent has established that the proposition is

---

338 In explaining why the beyond a reasonable doubt standard is the correct one at criminal trials, the Court has stated that "the interests of the defendant are of such magnitude . . . they have been protected by standards of proof designed to exclude as nearly as possible the likelihood of an erroneous judgment. In the administration of criminal justice, our society imposes almost the entire risk upon itself." Addington v. Texas, 441 U.S. 418, 423-24 (1979).

339 V. C. Ball stated this difference as follows:

> In civil cases, putting aside certain special types, the finding must be based upon "a preponderance of the evidence." At this point the courts divide. One group treats this latter term as meaning any preponderance, while others require that the preponderance be a "fair" one, or that the jury "believe in the truth" of the fact, or be "satisfied" or "convinced."

V. C. Ball, *The Moment of Truth: Probability Theory and Standards of Proof*, 14 VAND. L. REV. 807, 808 (1961).

Justice Harlan also expressed concern about the two possible interpretations of the preponderance burden of proof: "The preponderance test has been criticized, justifiably in my view, when it is read as asking the trier of fact to weigh in some objective sense the quantity of evidence submitted by each side rather than asking him to decide what he believes most probably happened." In Re Winship, 397 U.S. 358, 371 n.3 (1970) (Harlan, J., concurring).

more likely than not.[340] Under the second application, the proponent would win.

Obviously differing applications of the same burden of proof may be a problem at the guilt phase as well as at sentencing. But there are several reasons why defining the burden of proof may pose a more significant problem with fact-finding at sentencing. First, courts are not accustomed to having to apply any burden of proof in sentencing decisions.[341] At discretionary sentencing, a sentence within the statutory range did not have to be premised on any particular evidence. A court could impose any sentence within the statutory range based on little or no evidence.

Second, courts do not routinely make ultimate fact determinations based on evidence that is inadmissible under the Federal Rules of Evidence. Courts generally apply the preponderance standard to evidence inadmissible under the Federal Rules of Evidence only when deciding preliminary matters such as a motion to suppress evidence. Although a decision regarding suppression is important, it is not final and can be reconsidered in the course of a trial. Using evidence of such low reliability in determining ultimate facts aggravates the confusion between the competing conceptions of the preponderance standard. If all of the evidence under evaluation meets standards of admissibility under the Federal Rules of Evidence, which ensure some reliability, then a finding of preponderance of the evidence is also more likely to be a finding of more likely than not. If, on the other hand, all of the evidence is hearsay deemed unreliable by the Federal Rules of Evidence, then a finding of preponderance of the evidence is less apt to rise to the level of more likely than not.

Third, the unique posture of the parties at sentencing compounds the problem of defining the burden of proof. Frequently, the government will propose an increased sentence because of specific behavior alleged to have been committed by the defendant. The only defense to the allegation may be to deny the occurrence of the event. Proving this negative is difficult.[342] Moreover, the government's evi-

---

340 Some have assumed that this application is undisputed:

> All would agree that what counts is the jury's belief in the existence (or nonexistence) of the disputed fact, and the extent to which the evidence actually produces that belief; surely we are not seeking the jury's estimate of the weight of evidence in the abstract, apart from its power actually to convince or persuade them.

Fleming James, Jr., *Burdens of Proof*, 47 VA. L. REV. 51, 53 (1961).

341 At pre-guidelines discretionary sentencing, no burden of proof was required because no specific factual determinations were required. *See supra* note 212 and accompanying text.

342 The problem of proving a negative proposition also arises in civil forfeiture proceedings aimed at illegal drug activity under 21 U.S.C. § 881. Under that statute, the government need only demonstrate probable cause to believe that the property facilitated

dence is often hearsay presented by a government agent, likely to be found credible by the court. As a convicted person, the denying defendant is much less likely to be found credible. If the government is required to have the informant testify in order to have the benefit of the informant's information, the court can at least judge the credibility of the informant, rather than relying on the agent's assessment. Absent such a requirement, courts frequently sentence after weighing a government agent's testimony of hearsay statements against a convicted defendant's denial.[343]

This situation of inequality between the opposing parties contrasts sharply with the common situation in which the burden of preponderance of the evidence is applied: a civil dispute in which the opposing parties approach the court as equals without prejudgment by the court of their likely credibilities. One reason the beyond a reasonable doubt standard is necessary at criminal trials is the imbalance in favor of the prosecution resulting from the greater credibility deemed to accompany government witnesses.[344] This imbalance in favor of the government may be an even more serious problem once the defendant has lost the cloak of the presumption of innocence, as is the case at sentencing.

The question presented in this context is: How can a trial court find such limited evidence, deemed unreliable by the Federal Rules of Evidence, to establish the relevant conduct as more likely than not? The outcome may depend on the reliance on a preponderance of the evidence standard that requires no minimum level of confidence in

---

illegal drug activity. The owner of the property then has the burden of demonstrating innocent ownership in order to retain the property. Marc B. Stahl, *Asset Forfeiture, Burdens of Proof and the War on Drugs*, 83 J. CRIM. L. & CRIMINOLOGY 274, 284 (1992). The claimant must prove a negative: the absence of knowledge of illegal activity. *Id.* at 288.

[343] *See, e.g.*, United States v. McFarland, 1993 WL 72429 (10th Cir. 1993) (government agent's hearsay testimony concerning amount of drugs credited over defendant's testimony; the reviewing court noted that the government could have called the informant who had supplied information to the agent, but that in accordance with U.S.S.G., *supra* note 10, § 6A1.3(a), government was not obligated to do so); United States v. Sherbak, 950 F.2d 1095, 1100-01 (5th Cir. 1992) (affirming the district court's decision to credit unsworn statement of Drug Enforcement Agency agent over the defendant's counter-assertions was upheld); United States v. Griffin, 945 F.2d 378, 381-82 (11th Cir. 1991), *cert. denied*, 112 S. Ct. 1958 (1992) (concluding that the state agent's testimony, based partly on a confidential informant's statement classifying drug possessed by defendant as crack cocaine rather than powder cocaine, was credible because defendant failed to rebut it).

[344] Another possible bias is an attempt by courts to please the more powerful of the represented interests. Richard Higgins & Paul Rubin, *Judicial Discretion*, 9 J. LEGAL STUD. 129, 130 (1980) (citing RICHARD A. POSNER, ECONOMIC ANALYSIS OF LAW 416 (2d ed. 1977)). At sentencings, there may be substantial support from victims or law enforcement personnel for a severe sentence, but there is rarely support for a lesser sentence except from the defendant's friends and family.

the decision.[345] Some courts have suggested that decisions based on weak evidence such as hearsay are acceptable if the defendant has the opportunity to rebut the testimony or call any witnesses he or she chooses.[346] This approach, however, transforms the government's burden of proof into the much lighter burden of production. Rather than having to convince the fact-finder, the government need only present some evidence with "sufficient indicia of reliability" for its proposition.[347] If the defendant fails to present any contradictory evidence, the court finds in favor of the government.[348] Sometimes this result occurs even when the defendant has denied the alleged facts.[349]

Applying a higher burden of proof at sentencing would avoid the problem of a court sentencing a defendant when the court does not have an abiding conviction of the factual basis for the sentence. The language "clear and convincing," although not assigned a mathematical probability, conveys the idea that the fact-finder must do more than simply weigh which side has the most evidence. However, if the goals are to minimize error and to ensure that a court bases its decision on evidence reliable enough to establish that the proposed fact is more likely than not, a higher burden is unnecessary and may add confusion while increasing total error.

The level of confidence in a decision is related to both the burden of proof and the reliability of the evidence considered. When the burden of proof is higher than the preponderance standard, either clear and convincing or beyond a reasonable doubt, the reliability of the evidence may not be an issue because the fact-finder's determination so clearly evinces an abiding belief in the evidence. However, when there is a possibility that the fact-finder may be evaluating the evidence on each side and deciding in favor of the party that has better evidence, the reliability of the underlying evidence becomes critical. Absent an adequate standard of reliability, the fact-finder's choice of which side has the better evidence may not instill confidence about

---

345 For a discussion on the significance of the burden of proof assigned, see *supra* part II.A.

346 *E.g.*, *Griffin*, 945 F.2d at 381-82; United States v. Hubbard, 929 F.2d 307, 309-10 (7th Cir.), *cert. denied*, 112 S. Ct. 206 (1991); United States v. Query, 928 F.2d 383, 384-85 (11th Cir. 1991); United States v. Mir, 919 F.2d 940, 943 (5th Cir. 1990).

347 U.S.S.G., *supra* note 10, § 6A1.3(a) (stating that a sentencing court "may consider relevant information without regard to its admissibility under the rules of evidence applicable at trial, provided that the information has sufficient indicia of reliability to support its probable accuracy").

348 *See, e.g.*, United States v. Mir, 919 F.2d at 943 (concluding that because defendant failed to offer evidence to rebut presentence report's calculation of the quantity of drugs and its finding that defendant was a leader in a narcotics conspiracy, district court could consider these factors into consideration at sentencing).

349 *See, e.g.*, United States v. Query, 928 F.2d 383, 384-85 (11th Cir. 1991) (finding that the sentencing court accepted hearsay statements although the defendant denied their accuracy).

the decision among the participants in or observers of the criminal justice system.

B. Requiring Reliable Evidence

The appropriateness of imposing limitations on the evidence a court will hear has long been a matter of debate. Some commentators contend that a judge, unlike a juror, is fully capable of giving even unreliable evidence the amount of credit it is due and no more.[350] This argument has been offered in support of the proposition that Federal Rules of Evidence should not apply or should be eased at bench trials.[351] The drafters of the Federal Rules of Evidence rejected this argument.[352]

The impact of considering evidence inadmissible under the Federal Rules of Evidence cannot be precisely modelled or quantified.[353] Even an imprecise model may be of assistance, however, in clarifying the significance of such evidence. Assume that the government is trying to persuade the sentencing court that a defendant sold an additional kilogram of cocaine and therefore should receive a longer sentence. Assume further that the government bears the burden of proving that fact by a preponderance of the evidence. For the purpose of this hypothetical example, assume that there are two categories of potential evidence: evidence admissible under the Federal Rules of Evidence governing reliability ("FRE admissible evidence") and evidence not admissible under the Federal Rules of Evidence governing reliability ("FRE inadmissible evidence"). An example of FRE admissible evidence is an eyewitness who says she saw the defendant with the drugs. An example of FRE inadmissible evidence is a witness who heard someone who claimed to be an eyewitness say that she saw

350 Dale A. Nance, *The Best Evidence Principle*, 73 Iowa L. Rev. 227, 229-30 (1988); Joseph F. Weiss, Jr., *Are Courts Obsolete?*, 67 Notre Dame L. Rev. 1385, 1391 (1992).

351 *See, e.g.*, Joseph F. Weis, Jr., *Are Courts Obsolete?*, 67 Notre Dame L. Rev. 1385, 1391 (1992).

352 Rule 1101(a) states that the rules apply to courts and magistrates and makes no exception for bench trials. Fed. R. Evid. 1101(a).

353 One recent research project attempted to measure how much jurors relied on hearsay. The study had jurors read different trial transcripts, some of which presented portions of the evidence via hearsay and some of which presented the evidence directly. The study concluded that there were no significant differences in the frequencies of verdicts among the jurors who read different transcripts. Richard Rakos & Stephen Landsman, *Researching the Hearsay Rule: Emerging Findings, General Issues, and Future Directions*, 76 Minn. L. Rev. 655, 661 (1992). Because a key criticism of hearsay testimony is that the factfinder has no opportunity to judge the demeanor of the declarant, studies based on transcripts are insufficient to assess the real concerns of hearsay.

the defendant with the drugs. Both items of evidence are clearly relevant.[354]

Consider what happens if the sentencing court only permits the FRE admissible evidence. Given the limitation, there may be many cases with little evidence and, because the government bears the burden of proof, there may be many cases where the court will *falsely* reject the hypothesis that the defendant sold the uncharged kilogram. This is acceptable because the purpose of the burden is to ensure there are more falsely rejected hypotheses, where a more culpable defendant receives a more lenient sentence, than falsely accepted hypotheses, where a defendant not culpable of distributing the additional kilogram receives a heavier sentence.

Now consider what happens if all relevant evidence, both FRE admissible and FRE inadmissible evidence is considered. There should be fewer errors if one assumes that all evidence is relevant and more likely to be true than false. But if we add one more assumption, that almost all evidence at sentencing is inculpatory, the result will be more *false acceptances* of the hypothesis that the defendant deserves a harsher sentence.

To see this more clearly, assume that all FRE inadmissible evidence is inculpatory. This evidence cannot reduce the number of false rejections, because at best, for the defendants, the evidence will be disbelieved, leaving the defendants where they started based on the FRE admissible evidence. Therefore, inculpatory FRE inadmissible evidence can only lead to increased sentences. More often than not—because the evidence has some expected net probative value—the result will be that defendants who would otherwise *falsely* get a lighter sentence will get the correct, heavier sentence. But on some number of occasions defendants who would correctly get the lighter sentence based only on FRE admissible evidence will falsely get a heavier sentence based on incorrect but admitted FRE inadmissible evidence.

As a consequence, admitting FRE inadmissible evidence at sentencing diminishes the significance of the government's burden by systematically making it easier for the prosecution to obtain a heavier sentence. If the additional evidence were equally divided between inculpatory and exculpatory evidence, admitting it might be justified because there would be fewer total errors. But, because the evidence is likely to be inculpatory, there may be fewer total errors only at the expense of more errors borne by the defendant.

The outcome is even more problematic if FRE inadmissible evidence is much more likely to be false than FRE admissible evidence.

354 Under the Federal Rules of Evidence, evidence is relevant if it has any tendency to make the existence of a consequential fact more probable or less probable. FED. R. EVID. 401 (1992).

This seems probable when one considers the nature of information provided by informants. Assume informant A tells a government agent that the defendant sold the additional kilogram of heroin. If the agent believes the information, the agent will tell the prosecutor.[355] This agent is the only one who had the opportunity to judge the credibility of the informant. The prosecutor may decide whether or not to rely on the agent's credibility, but neither the prosecutor nor the court has an opportunity to judge the informant's credibility. If the government were required to present FRE admissible evidence,[356] the agent, the prosecutor and the judge would be able to assess, first hand, the credibility of the informant. Three levels of scrutiny are much more likely to find a falsehood or discrepancy than one. According to the rationale of the rules of evidence, the informant is also somewhat more likely to tell the truth under oath, subject to perjury.[357]

If one accepts the probability that more FRE inadmissible evidence will be false or inaccurate, then a possible result is that there will be more errors in judging the additional alleged conduct and that more of these errors will be falsely accepted hypotheses where a nonculpable defendant receives a heavier sentence.

Such sentencing errors are particularly serious because there is little chance of correction on appeal.[358] When FRE inadmissible evidence is permitted, the appellate court will only be able to review the agent's testimony at the sentencing.[359] Essentially, this review is one of sufficiency: absent some glaring inconsistency in the testimony, an appellate court will not reject the trial court's assessment of credibility.[360]

This article posits that even with pre-guidelines sentencing, there should have been more stringent evidentiary standards at sentencing. To the extent that courts based their sentences in part on specific

---

355 This analysis assumes that the agents and prosecutors are acting honestly and ethically. A further problem is that the use of inadmissible evidence makes it more difficult to identify evidence that an agent or prosecutor has intentionally fabricated or exaggerated.

356 The Sentencing Guidelines now specify that the government need not call in the actual informant, but instead may simply call the agent who witnessed the informant's statement. *See* U.S.S.G., *supra* note 10, § 6A1.

357 Fed. R. Evid. Art. VIII (Advisory Committee's Introductory Note: The Hearsay Problem).

358 Appellate courts review fact-finding at sentencing under a "clearly erroneous" standard. 18 U.S.C. § 3742(d); *see also* Braxton v. United States, 111 S. Ct. 1854, 1858 (1991) (clearly erroneous is proper standard for reviewing district court's finding of fact).

359 For an example and full discussion of the importance of firsthand testimony for appellate review, see *supra* note 286 and accompanying text.

360 A district court's assessment of witness credibility will not be disturbed unless it is "clearly erroneous." 18 U.S.C. § 3742(d); *see also* United States v. Sarasti, 869 F.2d 805, 807 (5th Cir. 1989) ("[c]redibility determinations are peculiarly within the province of the trier-of-fact, and we will not disturb the sentencing judge's findings").

facts, the above analysis applies. There is, however, a potentially more severe impact from FRE inadmissible evidence at guidelines sentencing than there was at pre-guidelines sentencing. The sentencing guidelines do not permit sentencing along a broad spectrum to accommodate varying degrees of reliability of evidence. Once a factor relevant to the defendant's sentence is alleged by the government or the defense, the court must make a factual determination. Moreover, with guidelines sentencing each factual resolution directly affects the individual's sentence, increasing the importance of the reliability of the evidence.[361]

A secondary effect of heightened evidentiary requirements is that they encourage parties to seek and obtain more reliable evidence. For example, if hearsay inadmissible under the rules is not permitted at sentencing then the party proffering the evidence will try to present the declarant.[362] The court can then judge the credibility of the declarant and the opposing party can cross-examine the declarant. Absent some minimal requirement, there is little incentive for the parties to bring more reliable evidence to the court.

To avoid substantial errors and instill confidence in sentencing decisions, courts should rely on FRE admissible evidence and should insist that the evidence establishes that the fact alleged is more likely true than not.

IV
Applying Rules of Evidence at Sentencing

Applying the Federal Rules of Evidence governing reliability[363] at sentencing best achieves the goal of improving the reliability of fact-finding.[364] These rules provide consistent standards for the admissibility of evidence among courts and among defendants. Even if courts did develop their own heightened standards for consideration of evi-

361 As one commentator has noted, using the results of unreliable fact-finding "is like feeding bad data into a computer. The program may be flawless, and the execution of the program by the computer may be flawless, but the result will be wrong." Adair, *supra* note 329, at 294.

362 The commentary to U.S.S.G., *supra* note 10, § 6A1.3 now allows the government to present an agent as a witness giving testimony based on hearsay rather than requiring the government to produce the declarant. *See supra* note 175.

363 Many of the rules of evidence do not concern the reliability of evidence and would not be applicable at sentencing. For example, Rule 105 relates only to an instruction to a jury regarding limited admissibility. Fed. R. Evid. 105. Rules 301 and 302 regulate the use of presumptions only in civil cases. Fed. R. Evid. 301-02. Rule 407 concerns subsequent remedial measures, which are not a relevant issue at sentence. Fed. R. Evid. 401. Rule 408 relates to offers to compromise only in civil cases. Fed. R. Evid. 408.

364 The idea of applying rules of evidence at sentencings proceedings is neither new nor untested. Rules of evidence have been applied at sentencing hearings in the military, M. R. Evid. 1101(c), and in state proceedings. The experiences of courts in these venues demonstrate the feasibility of applying rules of evidence at sentencing.

dence at sentencing, disparity among courts could result, which, under the guidelines, translates into disparity in sentences for defendants.[365]

The Federal Rules of Evidence also offer the significant advantage of addressing the admissibility of a wide range of evidence. They were developed to reflect the long history of common law evidence. Now, after eighteen years of use, the Federal Rules have been applied to all kinds of evidence likely to be presented at sentencing. With the established body of law for interpreting the rules, parties can predict what evidence will meet the standards of admissibility.

Applying the same evidentiary standards at sentencing as at trial also would diminish the likelihood of defendants being charged with "base conduct" by prosecutors hoping to greatly increase the sentence by demonstrating relevant conduct at sentencing. With the hearsay rule applicable at sentencing, initially raising relevant conduct at sentencing would be less attractive. The government would still be able to present additional evidence of relevant conduct at sentencing, but the evidence would have to meet established admissibility standards. The government would have an easier burden than at a trial, because the standard of proof would be a preponderance of the evidence rather than beyond a reasonable doubt. But the government could not convict the defendant for "base conduct" and then increase the defendant's sentence with inadmissible hearsay evidence, even with corroboration.

While applying the Federal Rules of Evidence at sentencing would not prohibit evidence of uncharged conduct, it does highlight the distinction between standards of evidence and substantive determinations about relevant conduct. The Federal Rules of Evidence impose a reliability filter on the evidence that can be considered. The requirement of reliable evidence is distinct from the issue of whether courts ought to sentence defendants for significantly different criminal acts than were proved at trial.

Equally important, the Federal Rules of Evidence are largely neutral with respect to which party is offering the evidence.[366] The Federal Rules of Evidence governing reliability were developed after much discussion over what constitutes reliable evidence. Much of the

---

365 *See* discussion *supra* note 3.

366 Of the 63 Federal Rules of Evidence, three may be readily identified that contain special provisions for criminal cases depending on which party is using the evidence. Rule 404(b) permits evidence offered to prove a pertinent trait of character by an accused to prove action in conformity therewith, but limits the introduction of such evidence by the prosecution. FED. R. EVID. 404(b). The rape shield provision limits the admission of evidence of the victim's past sexual conduct. FED. R. EVID. 412. Finally, Rule 803(8) precludes the use of public reports setting forth matters observed by law enforcement personnel in criminal cases against defendants. FED. R. EVID. 803(8).

evidence currently offered at sentencing is presented by the government, particularly regarding relevant conduct and role in the offense. Personal history factors currently have little impact on a defendant's sentence. The guidelines are still developing, however, and commentators have urged greater consideration of personal factors.[367] Should the guidelines be so amended, the Federal Rules of Evidence would consistently apply to the newly relevant evidence.

Finally, the Federal Rules of Evidence are understood by the parties at sentencing. The rules would not bring in a new system that must be learned and interpreted. Reviewing the current sentencing procedures demonstrates how the rules would fit into the system. A look at the types of evidence commonly used at sentencing and an evaluation of those types of evidence under the rules of evidence reveal that the rules may be extended in full to the sentencing phase, with only minimal modifications.[368]

A. Compatibility with Existing Procedures

The sentencing proceeding is a forum easily adaptable to rules of evidence. The parties are each represented by legal counsel.[369] The court and counsel are familiar with the rules of evidence.[370] The issues to be determined are well defined by the guidelines.[371] The considerations about how to use the rules of evidence at sentencing involve trying to apply evidentiary rules to the existing sentencing procedure, without unnecessarily expanding the amount of time and resources needed for sentencing.

Two fundamental components of the current sentencing process are first, the court's acceptance of evidence from the trial or of the

---

367 Daniel J. Freed & Marc Miller, *Handcuffing the Sentencing Judge: Are Offender Characteristics Becoming Irrelevant? Are Congressionally Mandated Sentences Displacing Judicial Discretion?*, 2 FED. SENTENCING REP. 189 (Dec. 1989/Jan. 1990) (arguing that the guidelines have been read too narrowly, without regard for the enabling legislation which clearly contemplated continued consideration of personal characteristics). *See also* Koh, *supra* note 16, at 1127-28.

368 The applicability of rules of evidence to sentencing is further demonstrated by their use in military proceedings. In military proceedings the fact-finder also determines the sentence. The fact-finder may be a jury or a judge. In either case, the Military Rules of Evidence, which are almost identical to the Federal Rules of Evidence, are applied at the presentencing proceeding, albeit in a relaxed manner. M. R. EVID. 1101(c). The application of the rules of evidence at sentencing in the military is a result of the recognition that the presentence proceeding is still an adversarial one.

369 *Cf.* Michael H. Graham, *Application of the Rules of Evidence in Administrative Agency Formal Adversarial Adjudications: A New Approach*, 1991 U. ILL. L. REV. 353 (arguing that application of rules of evidence in administrative proceedings may be inappropriate because the parties are not represented by counsel).

370 *Cf.* Kenneth Culp Davis, *An Approach to Problems of Evidence in the Administrative Process*, 55 HARV. L. REV. 364, 396 (1942) (noting that parties in an administrative proceeding may not be familiar with the rules of evidence).

371 *See supra* notes 148-53 and accompanying text.

defendant's admission to the government's proffer at the guilty plea; and second, the use of the presentence report as a focal point for identifying disputed issues and providing notice prior to the sentencing hearing of any facts or conclusions in the presentence report that a party wishes to challenge.

1. *The Court's Acceptance of Trial or Plea Evidence*

For the approximately sixteen percent of federal criminal cases that proceed to trial,[372] most of the fact-finding necessary for sentencing will be based on evidence presented at the trial, which accordingly will have met the standards of the Federal Rules of Evidence.[373] The sentencing court is not bound by how the jurors viewed the evidence, as may be demonstrated by their verdict, but may reach its own conclusions about the credibility of witnesses or reliability of the evidence.[374] The evidence presented at trial will provide the core evidence for determining the level of the offense committed. Because the offense level is determined by all relevant conduct, the court may also consider evidence of criminal conduct beyond what was charged in the indictment[375] Such evidence frequently will have been the subject of testimony at trial as uncharged acts in a conspiracy or as other bad acts admissible to show motive or intent.[376] When there is relevant conduct that was not brought out at trial, the court may obtain additional information on that conduct.[377]

The remaining eighty-four percent of cases, which are resolved by guilty pleas, will obviously not have the trial record on which to rely. Nevertheless, the sentencing court does not start from zero. With a

---

372 In 1990, 40,452 of 46,725 federal criminal defendants pleaded guilty and the remaining 7,874 proceeded to trial. Bureau of Justice Statistics, U.S. Dep't of Justice, Sourcebook of Criminal Justice Statistics 528, tbl. 5.36 (1991).

373 A potential problem will occur when the trial judge is unavailable for sentencing, for example, if the trial judge is unavailable. In the vast majority of cases, however, the court which heard the trial will also sentence.

374 *See, e.g.*, United States v. Stanberry, 963 F.2d 1323 (10th Cir. 1992) (finding that a defendant convicted on drug-related charges was not entitled to a special jury determination of facts relevant only to sentencing). *See supra* note 251 (for additional cases in which the sentencing judge has disregarded the jury's view of the evidence).

375 U.S.S.G., *supra* note 10, § 1B1.3.

376 Rule 404(b) provides that if certain conditions are met, evidence of other crimes, wrongs, or acts is admissible at trial to prove "motive, opportunity, intent, preparation, plan, knowledge, identity, or absence of mistake or accident." Fed. R. Evid. 404(b). However, this evidence is not permitted if it is being used to prove "the character of a person in order to show action in conformity therewith." *Id.*

377 This discussion reflects the current guidelines rule requiring sentencing to be based on all relevant conduct. U.S.S.G., *supra* note 10, § 1B1.3. Many judges and scholars have expressed their dismay with this rule, particularly when combined with the low preponderance of the evidence standard. *See* discussion *supra* note 159. If the guidelines were amended to limit or exclude relevant conduct as a basis for sentencing, there would be a substantial decrease in the issues to be resolved at sentencing.

disposition by guilty plea, Federal Rule of Criminal Procedure 11 requires that the court establish that there is a factual basis for the plea.[378] This may begin with the court asking the defendant to describe the events of the offense that is the subject of the guilty plea. Or the court may initially ask the prosecutor to summarize the evidence that would be produced if the case were to go to trial or to state the relevant facts regarding the defendant's guilt. The prosecutor has great latitude in how detailed the factual proffer is. When a defendant is pleading guilty to an offense with a mandatory minimum sentence, however, the prosecutor must clearly state the factual basis for invoking the mandatory minimum. Often the proffer will be very specific, because this is the prosecutor's best opportunity to inform the judge of the facts of the case.

Pursuant to Rule 11, the court asks the defendant to confirm that the facts of the offense were stated correctly.[379] If the defendant confirms that the statement of facts was correct, that statement may be subsequently treated as fact in the sentencing process. If the defendant disagrees with a portion of the prosecutor's statements, the court should address the disputed facts. If the court believes that the disagreement is insignificant—such as regarding a specific time a crime occurred—then the court may find that the defendant agrees with the statement of facts in all material aspects.[380] Where there is disagreement as to a material element of the offense, the matter must be resolved before the plea of guilty may proceed. Consequently, at the time of sentencing, the only factual disputes that should arise as to the nature of the offense are ones arising from additional information obtained after the plea proceeding.[381]

In an effort to ensure that a plea "goes down," the court, the defense, or the prosecutor may try to avoid a full discussion of the facts at this stage. Prior to the guidelines, this avoidance posed few problems. If a defendant had admitted the elements of the crime, there was no need to discuss further details. When mandatory minimums were introduced, the only added fact to be established at the plea was the amount of the drugs or other element triggering the mandatory minimum. With the introduction of sentencing guidelines, the requirements for a guilty plea were not changed. Under

---

378 "The court should not enter a judgment upon such [a guilty] plea without making such inquiry as shall satisfy it that there is a factual basis for the plea." FED. R. CRIM. P. 11(f).

379 FED. R. CRIM. P. 11(f).

380 FED. R. CRIM. P. 11.

381 As noted in United States v. Peak, 992 F.2d 39 (4th Cir. 1993), courts routinely accept pleas before considering the presentence report. Because the presentence report often contains factual findings that the defendant will attempt to challenge, factual disputes after the plea proceeding are common. *Id.*

Federal Rule of Criminal Procedure 11, a court must determine that the defendant's plea is voluntary after ensuring that the defendant has been informed of the rights to trial and counsel and that the defendant understands the nature of the charge to which the plea is offered and any pertinent mandatory minimum or maximum sentence.[382]

Importantly, however, Rule 11 does not require that the defendant be informed of a preliminary assessment of the sentencing guidelines.[383] Most defendants are so informed by their counsel, and by the government if a plea agreement is involved.[384] But there is no requirement under either Rule 11 or under the sentencing guidelines that key sentencing issues be resolved at the plea stage.[385] For example, there is no requirement that the government inform the defendant of all the relevant conduct it intends to describe to the presentence report writer. Nor is the government required to inform the defendant if it intends to assert that the defendant was a supervisor or leader, such that the sentence could be raised under the guidelines.

At present, there is little incentive for the prosecutor to raise these issues at the plea[386] and in some cases the prosecutor will not yet have information about relevant conduct or the defendant's role in an offense. Even if the prosecutor does have the information, there is no requirement to have the defendant admit to such things as relevant conduct. Instead, the prosecutor may choose to present that informa-

---

382 FED. R. CRIM. P. 11(c).

383 United States v. Stephens, 906 F.2d 251, 253 (6th Cir. 1990) (finding that at the time defendant entered his plea, he "was adequately informed of the consequences of his plea, even if the specific Guideline range was not known by him"); United States v. Salva, 902 F.2d 483, 486-87 (7th Cir. 1990); United States v. Gomez-Cuevas, 917 F.2d 1521, 1526 (10th Cir. 1990); United States v. Rhodes, 913 F.2d 839, 843 (10th Cir. 1990), *cert. denied*, 498 U.S. 1122 (1991); United States v. Henry, 893 F.2d 46, 48 (3d Cir. 1990); United States v. Turner, 881 F.2d 684, 686 (9th Cir.), *cert. denied*, 493 U.S. 871 (1989); United States v. Fernandez, 877 F.2d 1138, 1143 (2d Cir. 1989).

384 *See, e.g.*, United States v. Craig, 985 F.2d 175, 179-80 (4th Cir. 1993) (erroneous estimate by defendant's counsel insufficient ground to allow defendant to withdraw plea).

385 The guidelines direct a district court to defer its decision to accept or reject a plea agreement until the court has considered the presentence report, unless the report is not required. U.S.S.G., *supra* note 10, § 6B1.1(c). This language indicates that the Commission wants the court to be aware of areas of disagreement before accepting a defendant's plea. However, courts routinely accept pleas before reviewing the presentence report. *See, e.g., Peak*, 992 F.2d at 40 (reviewing court noted that presentence investigations normally are not conducted until after the guilty plea is entered).

386 Effective November 1, 1993, the commentary to U.S.S.G. § 6B1.2 was amended to include a paragraph encouraging the prosecuting attorney to disclose to the defendant relevant facts and circumstances concerning the offense and offender characteristics before the defendant enters a plea of guilty or *nolo contendere*. U.S.S.G. § 6B1.2, *supra* note 10, at App. C, amend. 495. According to the Commission, the intent of the amendment was to promote "plea negotiations that realistically reflect probable outcomes." *Id.* The amendment specifies that it does not provide defendants with "any rights not otherwise recognized by law." *Id.*

tion in the course of the presentence investigation to the presentence writer.[387] Once such information is incorporated into the presentence report, most courts will accept it, noting that hearsay is admissible at sentencing, and will deny the defendant's challenge to the allegation of additional criminal conduct unless the defendant can present evidence to the contrary.[388] Thus, it becomes the defendant's burden to disprove alleged relevant conduct.

If the government were not permitted to rely on hearsay, particularly hearsay presented via the presentence report, the equation would change. If the government were required to establish facts by admissible evidence, even under the low standard of preponderance, the government would have a greater incentive to be candid with the defendant at the plea stage and to state the known facts reflecting relevant conduct, role in the offense, or other sentencing factors at the time of the plea.[389]

Presently judges decide individually whether to require that the defendant be under oath when concurring in the statement of facts that serves as the basis of the plea. Whether or not the defendant is under oath, any statement that the defendant agrees with the facts as presented by the prosecutor is an admission that would appropriately be admissible under the rules of evidence.[390] Thus, if the Federal Rules of Evidence are applied at sentencing, the prosecutor will have a substantial incentive to be candid with the defendant at the time of the plea. As a result, the sentencing process may be shorter than at present where lengthy disputes may occur regarding relevant conduct. The same incentives would exist for the prosecutor to candidly address other frequently disputed facts that affect the sentence imposed, such as whether the defendant supervised others in committing the criminal acts.

Thus, whether a defendant's conviction is by trial or plea, at the time of conviction there is a substantial factual basis for sentencing already established. With either a trial or plea, there may be additional evidence of relevant conduct that was not admissible at trial.

---

387 Noting that probation officers (who author the presentence reports) sometimes lack the resources to conduct independent investigations, Judge Heaney asserts that prosecutors often control the information contained in the presentence report. Gerald W. Heaney, *Revisiting Disparity: Debating Guidelines Sentencing*, 29 AM. CRIM. L. REV. 771, 777 (1992).

388 United States v. Montoya, 967 F.2d 1, 3 (1st Cir.), *cert. denied*, 113 S. Ct. 507 (1992). *But see* United States v. Leichtnam, 948 F.2d 370, 381-82 (7th Cir. 1991) (sentence vacated and case remanded for resentencing by reviewing court which noted that information in the presentence report was supplied by a government attorney and was totally unsubstantiated).

389 *See supra* note 386.

390 A statement offered against a party which is the party's own statement is deemed "not hearsay." FED. R. EVID. 801(d)(2)(A).

2. *The Use of the Presentence Report*

The presentence report provides the key factual summary for the sentencing process.[391] In preparing the report, the presentence writer may review court documents and interview government investigators, victims, employers and acquaintances of the defendant. The presentence writer will always attempt to interview the defendant and the prosecutor or the case agent.

The extent to which the factual basis established at a plea or trial is subsequently communicated to the presentence writer varies tremendously. The presentence writer will rarely have been present during the trial and thus the writer may obtain the first factual information about the offense from the prosecutor, defense counsel, or the defendant.[392] In the case of a plea, the presentence writer may have been in court during the plea proceeding and thus be familiar with the proffered statement of facts. Where this was not the case, the presentence writer again may have obtained the initial account of the facts from the prosecutor, the defense counsel, or the defendant. Otherwise, a transcript of the plea proceeding could be prepared and provided to the presentence writer so that all parties move forward to the sentencing phase with a common understanding of the facts.

Presentence reports now generally follow a standardized format designed around the sentencing guidelines.[393] The report may even include a work sheet showing how the presentence writer calculated the defendant's sentencing range according to the guidelines. Once the presentence report is completed, the presentence writer presents it to the court in private.[394] Prior to the scheduled date for sentencing, the report is provided to the defendant and the defendant's counsel and to the prosecutor.[395] At that time, each side reviews the report to assess whether there are any errors. A party who believes there is an error, in the stated facts or conclusions, notifies the court, probation office and opposing counsel. Because the presentence writer has consulted both sides prior to writing the report, there are often no disputes with the factual statements. More common are contentions that the facts have been misinterpreted. For example, the parties may disagree about whether the defendant's refusal to discuss

---

391 This report is mandatory "unless the court finds that there is information in the record sufficient to enable the meaningful exercise of sentencing authority . . . and the court explains this finding on the record." U.S.S.G., *supra* note 10, § 6A1.1.

392 *See supra* note 387 and accompanying text.

393 For an explanation of the contents of a presentence report, see *supra* note 202.

394 Fed. R. Crim. P. 32(c).

395 Fed. R. Crim. P. 32 (c)(3) requires that the report be provided "at a reasonable time" before sentencing. As long as that requirement is met, the guidelines allow courts to set their own procedures "to provide for the timely disclosure of the presentence report." U.S.S.G., *supra* note 10, § 6A1.2.

another's role in the offense indicates a lack of acceptance of responsibility.[396]

At the time of sentencing, the presentence report is accepted by the court as correct unless there are specified objections.[397] The court may decide what interpretation to give the facts or may hear argument from the parties and then resolve the issues. The court generally holds a hearing on disputed factual issues.[398] Because a party must notify the court and opposing party of any facts the party disputes, there is adequate notice for the parties to be prepared to present evidence and to respond to evidence. At this phase the Federal Rules of Evidence could easily be applied at hearings to resolve factual disputes. Currently, when the defendant disputes a fact contained in the presentence report, the defendant must present contrary evidence.[399] If the defendant fails to present such evidence, the court may accept the presentence report as accurate.[400] This unfairly shifts the burden to the defendant.

B. Key Evidence Under the Federal Rules

Much of the evidence currently considered at sentencing proceedings is already admissible under the Federal Rules of Evidence. Courts have acknowledged this in cases challenging the low standards of proof for evidence.

A key change would occur, however, in courts' reliance on hearsay at sentencing. Much of the hearsay presented to courts is in the presentence report. Consider how the rules would broadly address hearsay at sentencing. The definition of nonhearsay and the many exceptions to the hearsay prohibition still permit extensive hearsay, although the basic hearsay rule is stated in the language of a prohibition. Examples of hearsay commonly used at sentencing that would be admissible under the federal rules include statements by the defendant that are offered by the government, as admissions of a party opponent under rule 801(d)(2), and records of prior criminal conduct

396 *See, e.g.*, United States v. Sanchez, 984 F.2d 769, 774 (7th Cir. 1993) (defendant's request for reduction based on his acceptance of responsibility was properly denied because defendant failed to identify his drug supplier).

397 The presentence report need not be the only written material that the court reviews. The commentary specifies that in determining facts relevant to sentencing, the court may consider "any other relevant information" in addition to the presentence report. U.S.S.G., *supra* note 10, § 6B1.4, comment. For example, the parties may submit sentencing memoranda which are a mixture of facts and arguments. But the presentence report is usually the first sentencing document the court receives and comes with the imprimatur of impartiality and professional investigation by a probation officer.

398 *See supra* note 180 and accompanying text.

399 The court has discretion to allow the defendant to introduce evidence regarding alleged factual inaccuracies. FED. R. CRIM. P. 32(c)(3)(A).

400 *See, e.g.*, United States v. Rogers, 1 F.3d 341, 345 (5th Cir. 1993).

for which there was a conviction, admissible as judgments of previous convictions under rule 803(22).

Some appellate courts have already answered defendants' arguments that trial courts relied on hearsay at sentencing by pointing out that the hearsay was admissible under the Federal Rules. In *United States v. Johnson,*[401] the Tenth Circuit concluded that a letter written by the defendant and relied on at sentencing would not be hearsay because it was an admission under rule 801(d)(2). Under the same rule, the First Circuit, in *United States v. Wright,*[402] held that an admission by a defendant recounted to the court by a probation officer at sentencing was not hearsay.[403]

Examples of hearsay that would be excluded include an agent's testimony about an informant's estimate of the quantity of drugs a defendant distributed or about an informant's assertions of a defendant's ties to organized crime. Applying the hearsay rule to evidence such as the quantity of drugs distributed would greatly reduce the relevant conduct problems that have so troubled courts.[404]

C. Making the Rules Applicable to Sentencing

No statute requires rules of evidence to be applied at sentencing in federal courts.[405] The Federal Rules of Evidence, which were adopted in 1975, state that the rules, other than with respect to privileges, do not apply at sentencing.[406] Whether or not the Sentencing Commission has the authority to issue guidelines governing evidentiary standards at sentencing is a matter of some debate.[407] Clearly, however, the Federal Rules of Evidence could be amended to extend

---

401 971 F.2d 562 (10th Cir. 1992).

402 873 F.2d 437 (1st Cir. 1991).

403 *Id.* at 441.

404 *See supra* notes 159 and 272 and accompanying text.

405 The Military Rules of Evidence provides, however, that rules of evidence apply at the sentencing phase. M. R. Evid. 1101(c).

406 Federal Rule of Evidence 1101(d) states:

> (d) Rules inapplicable. The rules (other than with respect to privileges) do not apply in the following situations:
>
> (1) Preliminary questions of fact. The determination of questions of fact preliminary to admissibility of evidence when the issue is to be determined by the court under rule 104.
>
> (2) Grand jury. Proceedings before grand juries.
>
> (3) Miscellaneous proceedings. Proceedings for extradition or rendition; preliminary examinations in criminal cases; *sentencing*, or granting or revoking probation; issuance of warrants for arrest, criminal summonses, and search warrants; and proceedings with respect to release on bail or otherwise.

Fed. R. Evid. 1101(d) (emphasis added).

407 *See, e.g.*, Hutchison & Yellen, *supra* note 179, at 406 (observing that "[n]othing in 28 U.S.C. § 994 authorizes the Commission to prescribe evidentiary rules.").

application of the rules governing reliability to sentencing proceedings.

The Rules Enabling Act governs amendments to the Federal Rules of Evidence.[408] In accordance with this act, the Supreme Court can prescribe rules of evidence. The Standing Commission on Rules of Practice and Procedure of the Judicial Conference of the United States can make proposals to the Supreme Court to change such procedural rules.[409] When changes are prescribed by the Supreme Court, Congress has seven months to respond, amend the proposal, or delay the effective date of the amendment.[410] Inaction by Congress is taken as assent.[411] In the alternative, Congress may initiate changes to the Federal Rules of Evidence by legislation. Of the six substantive changes made to the Federal Rules of Evidence since 1975, Congress initiated three.[412]

A proposal to amend the Federal Rules of Evidence must specify which rules should govern sentencing.[413] Several of the rules would be inapplicable to the issue of reliability of evidence, including those that limit the introduction of evidence of a defendant's prior criminal conduct.[414] The rules applicable to sentencing should include those that impose reliability standards, such as the rules governing opinion and expert testimony,[415] hearsay,[416] authentication,[417] and contents of writings.[418] Application of these rules, which are neutral to the defendant and government, would fairly raise the reliability of evidence relied upon at sentencing.

---

408 28 U.S.C. §§ 2071-74 (1993).

409 28 U.S.C. § 2073 (1993). The Standing Committee consists of members of the bench and bar. *Id.* The Chief Justice appoints these members. Becker & Orenstein, *supra* note 263, at 860 n.6. The Supreme Court appoints separate Advisory Committees in the civil, criminal, appellate, and bankruptcy areas to propose rule changes. *Id.* at 860. However, no advisory committee has ever been established for evidence rules. The civil and criminal Advisory Committees currently are responsible for monitoring and proposing changes to the Federal Rules of Evidence. *Id.*

410 28 U.S.C. § 2074(a) (1993).

411 28 U.S.C. § 2074(a) (1993). A different procedure applies to changes affecting privilege rules; for those Congress *must* approve any changes. 28 U.S.C. § 2074(b) (1993).

412 Saltzburg & Redden, Federal Rules of Evidence Manual 774 (1990).

413 Fed. R. Evid. 1101(d)(3).

414 Under the current sentencing guidelines, such prior criminal conduct may be relevant, either as relevant conduct or as criminal history. U.S.S.G., *supra* note 10, §§ 1B1.3 and 4A1.1.

415 Fed. R. Evid. 701-06.

416 Fed. R. Evid. 801-06.

417 Fed. R. Evid. 901-03.

418 Fed. R. Evid. 1001-07.

Conclusion

Recent decisions have highlighted the concern about the reliability of fact-finding at guidelines sentencing. Some judges and scholars have urged that the Constitution requires more procedural protections at guidelines sentencing, but this argument has not prevailed. Others have urged adoption of specific rules for sentencing. Proposals have addressed the issues of kinds of evidence to be considered, burdens of proof and the quality of the evidence. Much confusion about these issues has arisen because of the lack of clarity about what errors are problematic and how burdens of proof and standards of reliability for evidence jointly affect the quantity and kind of errors.

This article has addressed this issue of error. For decisions where the least total error is desired, the preponderance of the evidence burden of proof is appropriate. But this burden should be applied to require that the fact-finder be persuaded that the alleged fact is more probable than not. For decisions similar to determining guilt, where the goal is to have fewer errors borne by defendants, imposing a burden of proof on the government of clear and convincing proof or proof beyond a reasonable doubt may be appropriate.

To achieve the level of confidence in the preponderance of the evidence standard for sentencing that now exists in civil cases, standards of reliability should be applied to the evidence presented at sentencing proceedings. This article suggests a simple solution: apply the existing Federal Rules of Evidence at sentencing. Fact determinations at sentencing now have a direct and identifiable impact on the penalty imposed. Accordingly, the reliability of fact determinations at sentencing is critical to achieving the goals of lessening disparity, sentencing fairly, and instilling confidence in sentencing decisions.

The fact determinations at guidelines sentencing are the type of specific judgments for which the Federal Rules of Evidence are designed. The rules provide a familiar guide to the admissibility of evidence. They consistently impose minimum standards of reliability, neutral to the government and defendant.

This proposal has another virtue. Judges, who understand the problems that have arisen from faulty fact-finding at sentencing, can use their authority under the Rules Enabling Act to adopt such rules. Or Congress may legislate the change. The Commission, even if it has the authority, has shown no inclination to exercise it. Courts have felt constrained by precedent in deciding individual cases, even though that precedent arose under a fundamentally different sentencing system. By amending the Federal Rules of Evidence to apply to sentencing, judges or Congress can affirmatively choose to have all sentences based on reliable evidence.

[16]

Sentences Without Conviction: From Status to Contract in Sentencing

by Richard Fox and Arie Freiberg*

Summary

The orthodox position that sentences are not to be imposed without a determination of guilt in the form of a conviction has been weakened. Modern statutory sanctions often provide that a conviction is merely optional. The formal diminution of an offender's legal status, which occurred in the act of conviction, added legitimacy to the later execution of coercive measures against that person. Nowadays, the legitimising function of conviction in sentencing is being replaced by that of consent. Yet the offender's consent to the "non-conviction sentence" may be less real than apparent. If the aim of such sentences is the reduction of unpredicted collateral legal disabilities and social stigma, it is not clear that this objective is being realised. Principles governing the exercise of judicial discretion whether or not to record a conviction prior to sentence are largely lacking, the concept of a "sentence" is itself being eroded, and the offender may be trading valuable appellate rights for vague benefits which might be better secured in other ways.

Introduction

The essence of punishment for moral delinquency lies in the criminal conviction itself. One may lose more money on the stock market than in a court room; a prisoner of war camp may well provide a harsher environment than a state prison; death on the field of battle has the same physical characteristics as death by sentence of law. It is the expression of the community's hatred, fear or contempt for the convict which alone characterizes physical hardship as punishment. (H. Hart, "The Aims of the Criminal Law", (1958) 23 *Law and Contemporary Problems* 401 at 404-405.)

---

*Readers in Law, Monash University.

This article is the text of a paper presented to the 5th Australian and New Zealand Society of Criminology Conference, Sydney, July 1989. The authors thank Dr Allan Borowski of Latrobe University for encouraging their discussion of some of the issues raised in this paper.

The end of an orthodox criminal trial, if successful from the prosecution's point of view, is marked by four features: first, an admission or jury finding of guilt; secondly, judicial acceptance of that finding of guilt by the recording of a conviction; thirdly, the announcement of the judgment, which is known as the sentence;[1] and finally, its execution.

It has long been thought fundamental to the protection of the rights of persons accused of crime that the sentencing powers of a court should not be exercised or executed without a prior formal judicial determination of guilt, usually manifested by conviction. However, in recent times, as statutory sentencing options have proliferated, there has been a tendency to weaken the orthodoxy of criminal justice that calls for conformity to the sequence: guilt, conviction, sentence and execution. In particular, the requirement of a conviction is becoming optional, or even being discarded. There has been a consequential debasement of the meaning of "sentence", and a slide into formal diversionary programmes. The latter rely on promises of non-conviction in order to induce suspects to consent to the implementation of powerful correctional measures without encumbering the prosecution with the need to prove its case, or burdening the court with an obligation to impose a sentence. This decline in convention is part of a general move to husband limited correctional resources and enhance dispositional flexibility in the interest of individualising sentences.

The "non-conviction sentence" made its initial appearance in the juvenile jurisdiction, but is now firmly entrenched in adult sentencing schemes. Such "sentences" come in various forms, but have common attributes. First, they are offered in the name of leniency, or in the hope of rehabilitation, even though they may be onerous in nature and lead to oppressive results on breach. Secondly, they purport to be contractual or consensual in character, even though the bargaining power of the parties is transparently uneven. Thirdly, while the accused trades away appeal and other legal rights to avoid formal conviction, the prosecution wins new appellate rights and the court continues to retain considerable dispositional power over the alleged offender. Fourthly, though purportedly seeking to minimise the discriminatory legal consequences of a conviction and its social stigma, the legislature is not willing wholly to expunge the criminal record.

There is no modern "non-conviction" sentence at common law. The closest to it, the so-called common law bond, depends upon the recording of a conviction. It allows persons convicted of indictable offences to be set at large on condition that they agree to appear for sentence if and when called upon and to be of good behaviour in the meantime. These undertakings are secured by a bond or recognisance requiring the payment of a sum of money to the Crown in the event of a breach. The procedure has its roots in a combination of the power of justices to bind persons

---

1 "The sentence passed by the court is the judgment of the court": Samsoondar Ramcharan [1973] A.C. 414, 426 (P.C.).

over to keep the peace[2] and the inherent jurisdiction of courts to defer imposing sentence on convicted persons.[3] The result is not a sentence, but its conditional deferral following conviction. As a consequence of its interim nature and of its consensual base, no appeal by the accused against the terms of the conditional release is allowed.[4] The prosecution, however, is usually permitted a statutory right of appeal against the leniency of such order. The consequences of failing to comply with the conditions of release on a common law bond are twofold. The amount of the bond or recognisance becomes immediately payable, and the convicted person is recalled to be sentenced for the original offence. If the conduct which constituted the breach is itself a crime, the offender will be subject to punishment for that as well, and thus open to a form of triple jeopardy.

The newest statutory criminal sanctions draw heavily upon this paradigm. However, they tend to do away with, or make optional, the formal conviction. This development has occurred in Australia without debate or analysis. As a result, where the new legislation allows a magistrate or judge the choice of whether or not to record a conviction prior to imposing a sanction, principles relevant to the exercise of that discretion are all but non-existent. Nor are the legal implications of non-conviction fully understood. Non-conviction measures may reduce stigma and irrelevant social and legal discrimination against those prosecuted for crime, but they have also created uncertainty regarding what counts as a prior conviction for other areas of importance. These include the plea of autrefois convict, legislative arrangements designed to simplify the proving of prior criminality, the application of higher penalty scales to second and subsequent offenders, the availability of fines in addition to or instead of other punishment,[5] and the availability of major ancillary sanctions such as orders for reparation or disqualification. Furthermore, the almost casual legislative relaxation of the requirement of a conviction might be seen to inadvertently weaken or remove an important legal and philosophical foundation for the state's significant intrusion into the life and property of a citizen through the sentencing process.

Conviction

There has long been uncertainty regarding what constitutes a conviction, and its precise jurisprudential nature. The word has been described as a "verbum aequivocum"[6] because it is used so inconsistently in case law

---

[2] P. Power, "'An Honour and Almost a Singular One': A Review of the Justices' Preventive Jurisdiction" (1981) 8 Mon. L.R. 69; *Penalties and Sentences Act* 1985 (Vic.), s. 80.

[3] R. G. Fox and A. Freiberg, *Sentencing: State and Federal Law in Victoria* (1985), 7.301.

[4] But an appeal against the substantive merits of the conviction may be pursued.

[5] *Penalties and Sentences Act* 1985 (Vic.), s. 6: "If a person is convicted of an offence, the court may . . . fine the offender in addition to or instead of any other punishment to which the offender may be liable."

[6] *Burgess v. Boetefeur* (1844) 7 Man. & G. 481 at 504.

and statute. Sometimes it is taken to mean the guilty verdict of the jury, at other times the sentence of the court (including orders of unconditional discharge or deferral of sentence); occasionally it is taken to mean both.[7]

Conviction is first and foremost a matter of status. It is a judicial act by which a person's legal condition is officially altered. The alteration effected by conviction is a diminution of rights and capacities. This follows automatically from the fact of conviction, and is not necessarily tied to the particular sanction which follows it.[8] In the earliest days, a person was said to be "convict" when a court, in a case of treason or felony, accepted a finding of guilt, but had not yet passed judgment.[9] The person thus came to be known as a convict, and his or her personal property was automatically forfeited to the sovereign. After judgment, which was then normally a sentence ordering the forfeiture of the person's life, that person was said to be "attaint". The latter meant that the person's real property was forfeited and his or her remaining civil rights and capacities were extinguished, so that he or she was considered "civiliter mortuus"—dead in law.[10] In the terms of Graveson's definition of status, that person's was "a special condition of a continuous and institutional nature, differing from the legal position of the normal person, which is conferred by law and not purely by the act of the parties".[11]

The most extreme features of forfeiture and attainder were formally abrogated in the United Kingdom by the *Forfeiture Act* 1870 (U.K.), and in this country[12] long after they had already become obsolete, and the term "convict" came to mean a person sentenced to death or penal servitude. Conviction for serious crime no longer meant the complete loss of legal personality. Though forfeiture and attainder had been abolished, some legal incapacities were retained as part of the statute law and still automatically followed the fact of conviction. They no longer flowed from ancient doctrines of forfeiture, escheat and corruption of blood, but

---

7 *S. (an infant) v. Manchester City Recorder* [1969] 3 All E.R. 1230 at 1246-1247 (H.L.), [1970] 2 W.L.R. 21 at 41; *Dixon v. McCarthy* [1975] 1 N.S.W.L.R. 614 at 617; *Hannan; Ex parte Abbott* (1986) 41 N.T.R. 37 at 39; *McNicholl v. Tothill* (1988) 47 S.A.S.R. 134 (S.A.S.C.).

8 *Sheridan* [1937] 1 K.B. 223 at 229; Blackstone, *Commentaries on the Laws of England* (1765), Vol. 4, p. 374.

9 Coke, *First Institute* (1628), p. 390b.

10 Blackstone, op. cit., pp. 373-382; *Dugan v. Mirror Newspapers Ltd* (1978) 142 C.L.R. 583 at 601-603. Ironically, this allowed the person to plead autrefois attaint as a bar to any subsequent indictment for treason or felony while the attainder was in force. The potential difficulties this created in the colony of New South Wales in relation to the exercise of civil rights by convicts whose sentence of death in England was commuted to transportation is noted by V. Windeyer, "A Birthright and Inheritance" (1961) 1 U.Tas.L.R. 635 at 662.

11 R. H. Graveson, *Status in the Common Law* (1953), p. 2.

12 For example, the *Forfeitures for Treason and Felony Act* 1878 (Vic.), now represented by the *Penalties and Sentences Act* 1985 (Vic.), s. 111. However, not all States completely abolished the common law forfeiture and attainder rules received in the Australian colonies as applicable English law; see, for example, *Dugan v. Mirror Newspapers Ltd* (1978) 142 C.L.R. 583.

were found in specific statutory provisions which singled out the fact of conviction, the class and category of offence, and the type and duration of sanction as the basis of some form of civil disqualification or adverse discrimination, including the special treatment of persons with prior convictions in the criminal law, or under the rules of evidence.

Common law generally regarded persons who had convictions as incompetent to act as witnesses, but this incapacity has been abolished by statute.[13] However, it is possible to raise and prove a person's previous convictions as the basis of discrediting him or her as a witness.[14] At common law it is now well understood that offenders are not to be punished again for their prior crimes,[15] but it is equally accepted that previous convictions are germane to establishing an offender's character and criminal propensity. The sentence of a person with prior convictions is not augmented because of his or her previous wrongdoing, but such person is disentitled to any mitigation on account of previous good conduct. This can be affected by statute. Many Acts specifically allow for escalated penalties for recidivists, but the trigger for that increase is inevitably the fact of a prior conviction rather than some other non-conviction measure.

The specific statutory provisions that single out the fact of a conviction as the basis of some form of divestment of office, licence or right are numerous, though not as global in their effect as were the common law doctrines of forfeiture and attainder. This means that though, in modern times, the legal consequences of acquiring the status of a convicted person are less comprehensive, they are also less well-known. Indeed, they have a variable, almost random quality. Because they depend upon the effect of a multiplicity of local State and federal laws, as well as those of overseas countries, their adverse consequences may appear in the most unexpected areas. The existence of a conviction[16] may be the legal reason for withholding occupational, employment and commercial rights or licences; electoral, political and civic rights; entitlements to migration or citizenship; the capacity to litigate, testify or act as a juror; or pension and inheritance rights.[17] Convictions may also affect rights or privileges outside the jurisdiction, such as the issue, by foreign countries, of entry visas. While these legal disabilities can be catalogued,[18] there is no system-

---

[13] *Evidence Act* 1958 (Vic.), s. 22.

[14] *Evidence Act* 1958 (Vic.), s. 33.

[15] *D.P.P. v. Ottewell* [1970] A.C. 642 at 650.

[16] Modern legislation sometimes distinguishes between older or more recent convictions, for example, *Penalties and Sentences Act* 1985 (Vic.), 104A: "A conviction for an offence against the *Shop Trading Act* 1987 or Part VI of the *Labour and Industry Act* 1958 is not to be taken to be a conviction for any purpose (including the purposes of any enactment imposing or authorising or requiring the imposition of any disqualification or disability on convicted persons) after the expiration of five years after the conviction was made."

[17] R. G. Fox and A. Freiberg, op. cit., ch. 6.

[18] See Australian Law Reform Commission, *Discussion Paper No. 25: Criminal Records*, A.L.R.C. (1985), Appendix C; Law Reform Commission of Western Australia, *Project No. 80: Report on the Problem of Old Convictions* (1986), Appendix IV.

atically collected Australian empirical data on how pervasive and disruptive are their actual effects, or how extensive is the social discrimination experienced by convicted persons. Employment disadvantages appear to predominate,[19] but this remains untramped ground for basic criminological research in this country.[20]

It was clear that a person's status in law not only immediately changed as the result of conviction, but could be further diminished as the result of the particular sentence awarded. The two components were divisible, and their effects need not be identical. To be convicted was, alone, enough to produce an alteration in status that carried legal disabilities. Whether a further loss of rights occurred depended on whether the sentence was one of imprisonment, a fine, or release on a recognisance to be of good behaviour.[21] This distinction is important because the disabilities which adhere to a particular sanction lapse at the expiration of the execution of that sanction[22] (except with the death penalty), but the status of being a convicted person is a permanent one, said to be allocated by the state for reasons of public security.[23] It continues indefinitely unless brought to an end by some further act of the state through the medium of a court competent to do so,[24] or by special legislation to expunge it.[25] Thus, even today, the result of a pardon by the executive arm of government is to relieve the offender of all penalties and forfeitures which attach to the offence pardoned, but not to reverse the conviction itself. The latter endures, and, under present law, may only be set aside by judicial order.[26]

The question of what amounts to the actual legal act of conviction is not without its obscurities. It is now accepted in this country that, at common law, the proffering of a guilty plea or the return by a jury of a verdict of guilty does not, of itself, constitute a conviction. That admission or finding must be expressly or implicitly accepted by the court.[27] A verdict is a decision not of the court, but of the jury.[28] To be invested with the status of a convicted person requires a judicial act. And it is this judicial act of conviction which justifies the next judicial step of sentence.

---

19 *Report on the Problem of Old Convictions*, op. cit., paras 3.28-3.33.

20 J. P. Martin and D. Webster, *The Social Consequences of Conviction* (1971).

21 *London County Quarter Sessions; Ex parte Metropolitan Police Commissioner* [1948] 1 K.B. 670 at 679-680.

22 *Penalties and Sentences Act* 1985 (Vic.), s. 104.

23 Graveson, op. cit., pp. 58 and 101.

24 For example, on appeal, or where, on a plea of guilty, the court accepts a later change of plea: *Phillips* [1967] Qd R. 237 at 288-289.

25 None of which exists in Australia. The spent convictions scheme under the *Criminal Law (Rehabilitation of Offenders) Act* 1986 (Qld) and the *Spent Convictions Act* 1988 (W.A.), as well as that proposed for national adoption in the Australian Law Reform Commission, *Report No. 37: Spent Convictions* (1987), are of the "statutory lie" type. The fact of conviction need not be disclosed after a certain period, but the conviction itself has not been expunged.

26 *Foster* [1984] 2 All E.R. 679; 3 W.L.R. 401.

27 *Tonks* [1963] V.R. 121 at 127-128; 335.

28 *Snow* (1915) 20 C.L.R. 315.

No court is obliged to accept a plea of guilty,[29] and a trial judge may refuse to act on a jury's verdict, at least on its first return, because of ambiguities or misunderstandings revealed in its terms.[30] But, conversely, when there is no admission or finding of guilt to accept, as where the only issue tried is that of unfitness to plead,[31] or in the case of the special verdict on a successful insanity defence,[32] there can be no conviction.

The acceptance of guilt necessary to found a conviction is usually implied in the act of passing sentence, or in the calling for reports preparatory to doing so. But it is not dependent on a sentence being handed down, and if the court defers sentencing the accused has nonetheless been convicted. Where the sanction to be imposed is one which, by statute, is not necessarily dependent on a conviction, the sentencer will create ambiguity, as occurred in New South Wales in *Griffiths'* case,[33] by failing to indicate, in some express fashion, whether guilt has been accepted as a conviction or not. Even when it has been so accepted, the sentencer is free to change his or her mind on hearing any subsequent sentencing plea in mitigation by the accused or counsel.[34]

When *Griffiths'* case reached the High Court, Jacobs J. discussed whether a conviction had to be "recorded" in some formal way before it would have legal effect. His Honour observed that the Return of Prisoners and the other modern paperwork that passed as the "record" of the court in criminal matters lacked the formality normally required to constitute an official court record. Nevertheless, this was not of great moment, because each judge of record was regarded as a living record of the court, and his or her act of judicial acceptance constituted a sufficient recording of a conviction for most purposes.[35] The understanding of what counts as a conviction may also be affected by statutory provisions, such as s. 376 of the *Crimes Act* 1958 (Vic.), which defines what is a previous conviction for the purposes of alleging priors in an indictment or presentment. The definition covers both convictions, properly so called, and other orders made as a consequence of a finding only of guilt.

A conviction is not merely a judicial alteration of legal status carrying with it collateral legal consequences such as civil disabilities, the risk of enhanced punishment for later crime, and the possible diminution of standing as a witness. It also represents an ethical statement or judgment of moral culpability which, in communal eyes, provides a declaration that the defendant is a person worthy of punishment, or in need of some other form of state intervention in the interests of suppressing crime.

---

29 *Tonks* [1963] V.R. 121.
30 *Griffiths* (1977) 137 C.L.R. 293 at 301-302, 313-317.
31 *Larkins* (1911) 105 L.T. 384 at 385.
32 *Felstead* [1914] A.C. 534; *Taylor* [1915] 2 K.B. 709 at 712.
33 *Griffiths* (1977) 137 C.L.R. 293.
34 *D.P.P. v. McCoid* [1988] V.R. 982.
35 *Griffiths* (1977) 137 C.L.R. 293 at 317-318.

For this reason, the very fact of conviction is properly regarded as a major act of condemnation and public stigmatisation,[36] and is, without more, treated as a significant sanction in its own right.

In a Canadian Law Reform Commission discussion paper on the moral foundations of sentencing, Weiler wrote:[37]

> "One of the most important sanctions available to the practice of punishment is *conviction* of the defendant—the public and authoritative certification of his guilt. We are operating here within the highly-charged atmosphere of an allegation of blameworthy conduct which has caused serious harm to an innocent victim. As a result, when we stigmatise a person as an offender, we inflict not only a damaging, but also one of the most enduring, sanctions which the state can mete out. . . . [B]ecause this practice both relies on and reinforces the deeply-felt moral standard of the community, the aura which is attached to its condemnation of the offender is a source both of its strength and dangers."

It is the danger of permanent stigmatisation by conviction that makes understandable the legal reforms which give sentencers the means of avoiding a formal conviction, yet the state's right to intervene and force an individual to bend to its will derives from the diminution of status effected by the conviction. It is the dual function of the conviction, as both a mark of condemnation (what has been called the "expressive" function of punishment[38]) and as a formal forfeiture of the individual's right to full autonomy and self-determination, that is the state's warrant for *imposition* of sentence. This legitimising function of the conviction was recognised by Vincent J. of the Supreme Court of Victoria when he wrote:[39]

> "There are serious questions to be considered in relation to the . . . increase in the options available to a sentencer which do not involve the recording of a conviction. I am not entirely convinced that this path should be followed too far as it has the potentiality of blurring the distinction between criminal law responses and those available under the civil law. In this context, for example, I believe that one of the unfortunate features of the debate which has occurred over recent times in relation to the position of victims has been that there has been a tendency to regard criminal behaviour as primarily the concern of the offender and the victim with the community agencies

---

36 "A conviction is a formal and solemn act marking the court's and society's disapproval of a defendant's wrongdoing," *McInerney* (1987) 29 A.Crim.R. 318 at 329; N. Walker, *Punishment, Danger and Stigma* (1980), p. 146.

37 P. C. Weiler, "The Reform of Punishment" in Canadian Law Reform Commission, *Studies on Sentencing* (1974), p. 107.

38 J. Feinberg, "The Expressive Function of Punishment" (1965) 49 *The Monist* 397.

39 Personal communication to the Attorney-General of Victoria in response to Report of the Victorian Sentencing Committee, 28 July 1988; extract reproduced with his Honour's permission (emphasis added).

simply adjusting the balance between them. *The significance of the recording of a conviction should not be underestimated as a statement of guilt and as providing the justification of the imposition of a penalty.*"

Sentence

The apparent erosion of the significance of the conviction in the interest of avoiding stigma runs parallel with a weakening of the concept of a sentence in the interests of individualising sanctions. If the criminal courts can make dispositive orders that are not sentences, perhaps it does not matter that they are not the result of a conviction. It is rare to find a general all-inclusive common law or statutory definition of what constitutes a sentence.[40] The legislative definitions that do exist are usually there to settle the meaning of the term for such purposes as disqualification, or the bestowal of rights of appeal. Any comprehensive definition of what is a sentence would have to acknowledge that, nowadays, the concept appears to catch measures imposed prior to the termination of the trial or hearing (for example, orders made on adjournment); that the sanction need not amount to a final disposal of the prosecution (for example, deferred or suspended sentences); that it is not essential that the order encompass some punitive purpose executed by criminal justice agencies (for example, hospital orders); and, possibly, that the sentence includes ancillary orders made concurrently by the sentencer, even though these are primarily designed to expedite processes of civil recovery (for example, orders for damages, restitution, or reparation).

The Canadian Sentencing Commission defined a sentence as "the judicial determination of a legal sanction to be imposed on a person found guilty of an offence".[41] This definition does not directly use conviction as the foundation of sentence, but builds on the notion of a finding of guilt. In *Griffiths*,[42] Barwick C.J. defined sentence as a "definitive decision by the judge on the punishment or absence of it which is to be the consequence of the conviction". Conviction was essential, but punitive consequences were not. Statutory definitions of sentence, dating from the introduction of the right of an accused to appeal against superior

---

[40] We offer: "any dispositive order of a criminal court consequent upon a finding of guilt, whether or not a formal conviction is recorded," R. G. Fox and A. Freiberg, op. cit., 1.101.

[41] Canadian Sentencing Commission, *Sentencing Reform: A Canadian Approach* (1987), p. 115. The Report stresses that it is a person upon whom a sentence is imposed (presumably a natural rather than legal person) and that the cause of his plight is the conviction for an offence, although this is not the wording of the definition.

[42] (1977) 137 C.L.R. 293 at 307.

court sentences in the early decades of this century, lent support to the Barwick view. They stated that a sentence included:[43]

> "Any order of the court or of the judge thereof made *on or in connexion with a conviction* with reference to the person convicted or any property or with reference to any moneys to be paid to him."

Though the definition was not exclusive of any meaning the term "sentence" had at common law, it was soon evident that orders not made on or in relation to a conviction were not appealable as sentences under this section.[44] This created problems when the introduction of Crown appeals against leniency in sentencing was under consideration. It was the allegedly inappropriate use of these non-conviction measures that the Crown wished to challenge in the public interest. As a consequence, the statutory definition of a sentence was extended to include orders which were not the result of a conviction, or were deemed not to be so.[45] However, that extension was only for the purpose of Crown appeals; the accused was still denied the right to appeal against being subject to a non-conviction sanction, or to challenge the onerousness of its terms. The reasoning behind this was that such measures "were introduced into the legislation as remedial provisions intended to be for the benefit of convicted persons".[46] There was also the additional bar that the offender had voluntarily agreed to accept and comply with the terms of the order. The latter argument was advanced notwithstanding the reality that, in most instances, a refusal to agree would have resulted in a custodial sentence.

This lack of symmetry in the respective positions of the Crown and the accused for the purpose of appealing against "non-conviction" sentences, and the suspect nature of the consent upon which the accused's deprivation of appeal rights is based, are instances of the problems which these forms of disposal of offenders have thrown up. That which follows is a closer look at some of the principal non-conviction or optional conviction measures. Victoria will be drawn upon for examples, but similar ones can be found in most Australian jurisdictions.

The Precursor—Probation

Probation was originally a form of common law bond with added elements of supervision.[47] As a statutory order, it had its Australian origins in the Children's Court, and migrated to the adult criminal justice

---

[43] For example, the *Crimes Act* 1958 (Vic.), s. 566, emphasis added. This definition is to be extended to cover specified non-conviction and other orders on the coming into force of the *Crimes Legislation (Miscellaneous Amendments) Act* 1989 (Vic.), s. 13.

[44] *Prior* [1966] V.R. 459; *Abedsamad* [1987] V.R. 881. Cf. *Magistrates' Court Act* 1971 (Vic.), s. 73: appeals to the County Court from the Magistrates' Court may relate to convictions *or orders*.

[45] For example, the *Crimes Act* 1958 (Vic.), s. 567(1A). See now changes effected by *Crimes Legislation (Miscellaneous Amendments) Act* 1989 (Vic.), s. 13.

[46] *Prior* [1966] V.R. 459 at 462.

[47] R. G. Fox and A. Freiberg, op. cit., 8.201-8.205.

system as a rehabilitative alternative to custodial sentences. Until its abolition in the adult jurisdiction in Victoria in 1986, probation was, in essence, the deferral of the imposition of a sentence for up to five years upon the defendant agreeing to accept the supervision and guidance of a person appointed by the court. Other conditions could be added. The supervision was normally provided by professional officers of a government-run probation service. Technically speaking, the accused had been convicted, but no sentence had been passed. However, it was thought that the rehabilitative objectives of the probation supervision would be compromised if those who agreed to its conditions were later stigmatised by a record of conviction.[48] The legislation therefore deemed the conviction not to have occurred. This fiction could not be sustained, and certain exceptions were immediately admitted.

This was necessary because, in dealing with recidivism, the courts wanted to be apprised of the person's previous "record". They feared that a repeater might continue to masquerade as a first offender. As a result, the legislation allowed for acknowledgment of the existence of the conviction in the proceedings themselves, or in action taken for any subsequent variation, discharge or breach of the probation order, or in any other proceedings initiated against the offender for a subsequent offence.[49] The last allowed the prosecution to refer to the offender's priors and the fact of release on probation. The fact that the order was deemed not to be the result of conviction also did not prevent the probationer from pleading autrefois convict in any subsequent prosecution for the same offence, nor did it prevent an appeal against the actual conviction, or certain consequential orders. Nonetheless, as the order was in the nature of a consensual deferral of sentence, there was no sentence, and no appeal by the offender against the probation order or any of its conditions could be entertained.[50] The only statutory right to appeal against such orders was that given to the prosecution.

Probation for adults has since been replaced in Victoria by the more compendious community-based order. Probation orders still exist in the Children's Courts in the State and they too are deemed not to be the product of a conviction.[51] The recently passed, but as yet unproclaimed, Victorian *Children and Young Persons Act* 1989 retains the probation order but now makes the recording of the conviction discretionary. This was never the case with adult probation. The new Act does not offer magistrates criteria that are specific to the decision whether or not to convict. Nonetheless, in its listing of matters to be taken into account in sentencing, the Act requires the court, as far as practicable, to have

---

[48] A. B. Teton, "Crime Without Conviction: Supervision Without Sentence" (1986) 19 John Marshall L.R. 547 at 548.

[49] See *Crimes Act* 1958 (Vic.), s. 520 (now repealed). The prosecution was given a statutory right of appeal.

[50] *Prior* [1966] V.R. 459.

[51] *Children's Court Act* 1973 (Vic.), s. 26(1)(c).

regard to "the need to minimise the stigma to the child resulting from a court determination".[52] Unlike the situation which previously applied to adults, a child can appeal against a probation order. It does not matter that the order may not be the product of a conviction, because appeals to the County Court are framed in terms of the right to appeal against "any sentencing order".[53] Notwithstanding that no conviction has been recorded, the new Act makes it clear that the court retains its authority to impose any order on the child for compensation, restitution, reparation, disqualification or other legal disability as if the defendant had been convicted.[54]

The Successor—Community-based Orders

The major non-custodial sanction in Victoria,[55] the community-based order, was introduced in 1986. It is deemed to be a non-conviction order, but the sentencer is now expressly empowered to order the contrary.[56] Here again, there is neither case law nor statutory guidance regarding what factors are relevant to that decision. The community-based order is an amalgamation of three previous measures, which it replaced in 1986: the probation order, which was a non-conviction order, and the attendance centre and the community service orders, both of which were the product of a conviction.

Like probation, the community-based order is a consensual one; but, unlike probation, not only must the offender agree to its terms, but the consent of the Office of Corrections must also be obtained, via a report from a community corrections officer that facilities are available for the implementation of the order and that the offender is suitable for such an order. Certain core conditions relating to reporting and good behaviour must be agreed to as being common to all orders, but the accused will be invited to accept one or more of eight programme conditions. The latter can have a significant impact of the offender's liberty. The restrictions may include the obligation, for up to a year, to undertake regular part-time attendance for educational and other activities at nominated centres or to perform unpaid part-time community work; being subject to supervision by a community corrections officer for up to two years; undergoing the assessment and treatment of drug, medical or psychological problems; submission to testing for alcohol or drug use; and compliance with such other conditions as the sentencer thinks necessary.[57] Normally the duration of a community-based order is not

---

[52] *Children and Young Persons Act* 1989 (Vic.), s. 139(1)(d).

[53] Ibid., s. 197. See also definition of "sentencing order" in s. 3.

[54] *Children and Young Persons Act* 1989 (Vic.), s. 137(3) and (4).

[55] Leaving aside the suspended sentence of imprisonment.

[56] *Penalties and Sentences Act* 1985 (Vic.), s. 39.

[57] Ibid., s. 29(2).

to exceed two years, but longer orders can and have been made.[58] Five years is not unknown.

If the statutory presumption that the order is a non-conviction one is overridden,[59] the sentencer is under no obligation to give reasons for doing so. But, as with probation, the protective cover against legal disability which comes with non-conviction is immediately partially withdrawn. The legislation declares that the community-based order is to be accepted as a conviction-based measure for the purpose of the making of the order itself (so as to allow for the plea of autrefois convict); for subsequent criminal proceedings; for the ordering of compensation for motor vehicle theft; and for the loss of motor vehicle licences.[60] It also makes clear that the sentencer has not lost the power to make additional orders against the accused for costs, damages, compensation, disqualification, suspension and the imposition of fines.[61] While the order is still counted as a conviction for the purpose of an appeal by the accused against being found guilty,[62] or an appeal against sentence by the prosecution,[63] it is denied the status of a conviction or a sentence for the purpose of any appeal by the offender against sentence. Furthermore, there is a threat of triple jeopardy in the event of a breach of the order. First, it is a finable offence to fail to comply with any conditions of the order. Secondly, the offender is liable to be re-sentenced for the offence for which the order was originally made.[64] Thirdly, the person is open to being punished separately for any offence that constituted the breach.

In the juvenile jurisdiction in Victoria, there is no direct equivalent of the community-based order. The closest in the *Children and Young Persons Act* 1989 (Vic.) is the "youth supervision order".[65] This is intended to be placed between probation and youth attendance orders in the order of seriousness of sanctions, and will have community service as one of its conditions. It, too, allows for a discretionary conviction.[66] It is subject to the same ancillary orders and rights of appeal as for youth probation.

---

58 Under s. 28(4)(b).

59 *Penalties and Sentences Act* 1985 (Vic.), s. 39(1) states: "Except where the court by which a community-based order is made otherwise directs, a conviction for an offence in respect of which a community-based order is made is not to be taken to be a conviction for any purpose (including the purposes of any enactment imposing or authorizing or requiring the imposition of any disqualification or disability on convicted persons . . .)"

60 *Penalties and Sentences Act* 1985 (Vic.), s. 39(1)-(4).

61 *Penalties and Sentences Act* 1985 (Vic.), s. 41.

62 Ibid., s. 39(4).

63 *Crimes Act* 1958 (Vic.), s. 567A(1A). There is a drafting anomaly in the latter section. Only one form of community-based order is open to appeal by the Crown, namely, one containing the supervision condition. The flaw arose when the word "probation" was being replaced in s. 567A(1A).

64 *Penalties and Sentences Act* 1985 (Vic.), s. 33.

65 *Children and Young Persons Act* 1989, (Vic.), ss 163-168.

66 *Children and Young Persons Act* 1989 (Vic.), s. 137(1)(g).

The Future—Monetary and Custodial Sanctions

The fine is the most common punitive sanction. Traditionally it has been a judicially-imposed, conviction-based measure. That situation is changing dramatically. Thus the *Magistrates (Summary Proceedings) Act* 1975 (Vic.)[67] provides an alternative procedure for the enforcement of infringement notices (more commonly known as on-the-spot fines) under various Acts. These are essentially non-curial, non-conviction exactions of financial penalties. A person expiating an infringement notice by the payment of the penalty is regarded as not having been convicted of the offence alleged. Use of this technique to extract non-conviction monetary penalties is increasing in popularity, and is moving from the field of traffic control to that of corporate regulation.[68] It generates admissions of liability by relying on the defendant's self-interest in avoiding both the inconvenience of a court appearance and the stigma of a conviction.

But even within the curial setting there is pressure to be able to impose fines without first convicting the offender. The Victorian Sentencing Committee, under the Chairmanship of retired Supreme Court judge Sir John Starke, reported:[69]

> "The Committee received submissions that in certain circumstances where there are relatively minor offences and in particular in relation to some traffic offences, the thought of conviction causes a great deal of distress to otherwise law-abiding citizens. It has been suggested therefore that in certain summary offences it should be open to a Magistrates Court to impose a fine but not count it as a conviction against the offender. The Committee believes that this would be an appropriate extension to the sanctions of a non-custodial nature now available to the courts."

The Committee's recommendation was translated into legislative form in two clauses in its Draft Penalties and Sentences Bill. By cl. 3, a fine would be defined as a "sum of money payable by an offender under an order of a court made on the offender being convicted or found guilty of an offence", and under cl. 47 it was intended that:[70]

> "If the Magistrates' Court convicts a person of a summary offence and imposes a fine on that person it may order that the conviction is not to be taken to be a conviction for any purpose whatsoever."

---

[67] Sections 89A-89R; *Magistrates' Courts (Penalty Enforcement by Registration of Infringement Notices) Rules* 1986.

[68] Similar procedures apply to the enforcement of *penalty notices* under the *Companies (Victoria) Code*, the *Futures Industry (Victoria) Code* and to the *Securities Industry (Victoria) Code*: *Magistrates (Summary Proceedings) Act* 1975 (Vic.), s. 89S-89ZE.

[69] Victorian Sentencing Committee, *Sentencing: Report of the Victorian Sentencing Committee* (1988), para 7.3.14 (Vol. 1).

[70] Ibid., Vol. 2.

The Committee did not discuss how this discretion was to be exercised, whether ancillary orders could be imposed at the same time, whether the conviction would count for the purposes of assessing recidivism, or whether a non-conviction fine was to be subject to appeal by either the defendant or the prosecution. To date, no action has been taken on this recommendation, but Victorian Children's Court legislation has, for some time, permitted magistrates a discretion whether or not to convict prior to imposing a fine.[71] This option is retained under the new Act.[72]

Immediate custodial detention, whether in a prison or in a youth training centre, is the ultimate sanction in the present sentencing hierarchy. So grave is the measure as a final form of disposition,[73] that both common law and statute requires conviction as a pre-condition.[74] The courts generally have the power to moderate a custodial sentence by suspending its immediate execution, but this still turns on a prior conviction. Hitherto they have had no means of trying to alleviate the disabilities that come with custody by manipulating the conviction itself. Cracks in the structure are beginning to appear. As usual, they are first visible on the juvenile front. Thus s. 53(1)(g) of the *Northern Territory Juvenile Justice Act* 1983 now allows a court to order detention or imprisonment on proof of a charge which does not necessarily count as a conviction. Inventive sentencers can find other ways in which custodial restraint can be achieved without altering the offender's status through conviction. Non-conviction orders, such as release on adjournment bond, are open to having special conditions attached which prescribe forms of "home detention". These involve an offender agreeing to remain within the confines of his or her home during curfew times (generally all non-working hours). The potential of these "consensual" orders has yet to be fully explored in this country.

Custody of the Mentally Disordered

The custodial detention of those caught up in the criminal justice system who are suffering from extreme mental disorder is bound up with the avoidance of a conviction. Custodial detention for punishment assumes that the person being punished is legally responsible for his or her act or omission, not only through his or her role in substantially causing the prohibited harm, but also by possession of the mental state which the law requires as providing the element of fault or blameworthiness. If the recording of a conviction marks the formal attribution of blame, a

---

[71] *Children's Court Act* 1973 (Vic.), s. 26(1)(d).

[72] *Children and Young Persons Act* 1989 (Vic.), s. 137(1)(e) and s. 150.

[73] As opposed to remand in custody.

[74] *Children's Court Act* 1973 (Vic.), s. 26(1)(f); *Children and Young Persons Act* 1989 (Vic.), s. 137(1)(i) and (j); *Penalties and Sentences Act* 1985 (Vic.), s. 5.

mentally disordered person who lacks the requisite culpability cannot be justly convicted or detained in custody for punishment. As Hart states:[75]

> "The . . . feature distinguishing punishment from treatment is that unlike a medical inspection followed by detention in hospital, conviction by a court followed by a sentence of imprisonment is a public act expressing the odium, if not the hostility, of society for those who break the law. As long as these features attach to conviction and a sentence of imprisonment, the moral objections to their use on those who could not have helped doing what they did remain."

Consistently with this principle, a successful insanity defence results in a verdict of acquittal. But the acquitted person is not discharged. The verdict is treated as a "special" one. The sanction it attracts in Victoria under s. 420(1) of the *Crimes Act* 1958 (Vic.) is indefinite detention in "strict custody" during the Governor's pleasure. In 1986, a second subsection was added to provide that, instead of making an order under subsection (1), the court could make one enabling the person to receive services under the *Mental Health Act* 1986 (Vic.), or the *Intellectually Disabled Persons Services Act* 1986 (Vic.). The aim was to facilitate treatment in a non-punitive setting. Similar indeterminate arrangements are in place under the *Crimes Act* 1958 (Vic.), s. 393(1) and (2), when persons are found unfit to stand trial. The latter group will not, of course, have had the benefit of a trial, nor the formality of a conviction.[76]

Yet, despite their non-conviction status, there is considerable doubt that, in Victoria, those subject to these special verdicts are treated any differently from, or any better than, those being punished on conviction for the substantive crime.[77] Persons ordered to be detained in "strict custody" will, more likely than not, be held in prison. Any ordered to "receive appropriate services" under the *Mental Health Act* 1986, or the *Intellectually Disabled Persons Services Act* 1986, will receive none, because the latter orders are ineffectual. This is due to the apparent failure, in those sponsoring the legislation, to keep in mind the procedural significance of the absence of a finding of guilt or a conviction. In setting out the powers of a court on a criminal trial, these two Acts allow for judges or magistrates to make hospital or like orders only in respect of persons who have been "found guilty"[78] or "convicted".[79] Ironically, this means that to be convicted, without raising mental disorder as a substantive defence, may provide better access to mental health or intellectual disability services through these two Acts than relying on such disorder or disability as a bar to conviction.

---

[75] H. L. A. Hart, *Punishment and Responsibility* (1968), p. 208.

[76] See A. Freiberg, "Out of Mind, Out of Sight: The Disposition of Mentally Disordered Persons Involved in Criminal Proceedings" (1976) 3 Mon. L.R. 134.

[77] Victorian Sentencing Committee, op. cit., p. 439.

[78] *Mental Health Act* 1986, s. 15(1)(a).

[79] *Intellectually Disabled Persons Services Act* 1986, s. 20(a).

The paradox of using the criminal justice system to continue to detain in custody persons whom the state has been unable to convict has been a source of continuing difficulty. The Victorian Sentencing Committee insisted on continuing to regard the acquittal of those found not guilty on the ground of insanity as a special class of acquittal which gave the court the power to detain instead of the duty to discharge. It wanted control to be retained under an enhanced range of possibilities. The options it recommended would include adjournments, diagnostic orders, discharge on condition of treatment and detention as a security patient for an indeterminate period. If it had its way, the Committee would require a person to be detained if he or she represented an "unacceptable risk to the safety or health of the public or of any member or members of the public or of the person".[80] The Law Reform Commission of Victoria, in its discussion paper on Mental Malfunction and Criminal Responsibility,[81] has adopted a similar stance.[82]

The opposing viewpoint is one which takes the fact of acquittal at face value and reinforces the moral significance of non-conviction by insisting that all questions of subsequent disposal of the person be left to civil procedures and tribunals, free of the punitive overtones of the criminal law. This was the preferred approach of the former Chief Justice of the High Court, Sir Owen Dixon. He described the continued detention of persons after their acquittal as "a confusion between the administration of criminal justice and the administration of the law relating to lunacy" and as a "discreditable chapter of the law".[83]

Ancillary Orders

Being a "non-convicted" person does not wholly avoid the status of being a convicted one. Parliament has made an effort to ensure that power to make important ancillary orders has not been lost. This is done either by framing the legislation governing the ancillary sanctions in such a way as to allow them to be imposed simply on the finding of guilt, irrespective of whether a conviction has been recorded, or by attaching to the non-conviction sanction an express power to make ancillary orders. The principal ancillary orders are those which direct that restitution be made, compensation be paid, licences be suspended or cancelled, goods, chattels or proceeds of crime be confiscated and/or forfeited, or that the offender suffer some form of disqualification or loss of office.

---

80 Victorian Sentencing Committee, op. cit., 10.9.53 and cl. 73 and 74 of its Draft Penalties and Sentences Bill.

81 V.L.R.C., Discussion Paper No. 14, August 1988.

82 Ibid., at pp. 33-34 and pp. 47-48.

83 O. Dixon, "A Legacy of Hadfield, M'Naghten and Maclean" (1957) 31 A.L.J. 255 at 261. The need for community protection is ample justification for other forms of civil intervention, including ones as protective of the security of the public as prison without its punitive overtones, D. Wood, "Dangerous Offenders, and the Morality of Protective Sentencing" [1988] Crim.L.R. 424.

In order to assist victims of crime to pursue civil remedies against the accused, most penal legislation bestows upon sentencers the power to make compensation or restitution orders. Though ordered in criminal proceedings, they must be enforced as a civil judgment. They are intended to be compensatory, not punitive. Typically, s. 92(1) of the *Penalties and Sentences Act* 1985 (Vic.) allows compensation to be ordered not only on conviction of an offender, but also when the offender is released under one of the non-conviction measures. Similar powers are given to the Children's Court "where a charge has been proven",[84] and to a court imposing sentences for offences against federal law, whether or not a conviction has been recorded.[85]

Divestment of licences or offices is more openly punitive and may occur as a consequence of different legal processes, not all of which turn on the exercise by a court of a sentencing discretion. Legislation may declare a specific incapacity to follow automatically either on commission of a certain type of crime (in which case the disqualification comes into effect notwithstanding that the alleged offender has not been convicted), or upon the recording of a conviction. There is a general provision in the *Road Traffic Act* 1986 (Vic.)[86] which gives a court the power to cancel, suspend or vary licences either on the court convicting the alleged offender or, without a formal conviction, being satisfied of his or her guilt. The most recent Victorian innovation in this field has been the power granted to the police to suspend the licence of an offender merely on a charge being laid. Neither a finding of guilt nor conviction is, at that stage, required. The suspension continues until the determination of that charge.[87]

Strictly speaking, the sanctions of forfeiture and disqualification fall within the field of sentencing only when the legislature directs or permits them to be included in the judgment by which a criminal court disposes of guilty persons.[88] In the majority of cases in which forfeiture is possible, it can only be ordered on conviction of a person charged with a specific offence, or on proof of guilt where no conviction has been recorded.[89] However, these two sanctions can also be found to take effect as an entirely automatic consequence of the commission of certain offences, particularly those against customs and revenue laws. In those contexts, the sanction operates irrespective of whether a charge has been laid, a finding of guilt has been made, or a conviction obtained.

---

84 *Children's Court Act* 1973 (Vic.), s. 26(3)(a) to be repealed and replaced by *Children and Young Persons Act* 1989 (Vic.), s. 137(3) and (4).

85 See *Crimes Act* 1914 (Cth), s. 21B, power not only on conviction, but on conditional discharge without conviction under s. 19B.

86 Section 28(1).

87 *Road Traffic Act* 1986 (Vic.), s. 51(1).

88 See Fox and Freiberg, op. cit., ch. 6.

89 For example, the *Drugs, Poisons and Controlled Substances Act* 1981 (Vic.), s. 85(2)(b).

The *Customs Act* 1901 (Cth) contains many provisions that declare that goods are forfeited to the Crown simply on the commission of an offence. Divestment of title does not depend on any person being charged or convicted, nor upon a judicial order being made. Conviction only has the effect of condemning the goods. Failure to obtain a conviction does not, however, establish that the goods are not condemned or create an estoppel, or otherwise determine the question of whether they were rightly seized. Section 229A of the *Customs Act* 1901 makes the proceeds of certain drug dealings liable to forfeiture. As with other non-judicial forms of forfeiture, the divestment of ownership does not turn on the conviction of any person.[90] Under s. 243A-243S of the *Customs Act* 1901, which provides for the imposition of pecuniary penalties, a judicial order is required, but the conviction of the alleged drug offender is not essential.

Recent Victorian and Commonwealth legislation dealing with confiscation of the profits of crime was the subject of considerable controversy over whether the power to confiscate should depend upon a prior conviction. Ultimately, in both jurisdictions, the view prevailed that before such a drastic measure could be invoked a conviction was necessary. This then led to the concept of conviction itself being manipulated. In the Victorian legislation, the term is given a statutory meaning wide enough to cover cases in which the person has been found guilty, but discharged without conviction, or in which the offence was taken into account in sentencing for other proceedings but no specific finding of guilt or conviction has been recorded in relation to it, or where the defendant has absconded and has thus never been found guilty or convicted of any relevant offence.[91]

The confiscation of profits of crime legislation is unusual in its scope and the way in which it deems persons to have been convicted. Nevertheless, there remain occasions when an offender can avoid a finding of guilt or a conviction as part of the trade-off for a willingness to accept a more expeditious imposition of a sanction. This occurs in arrangements for taking offences into account, or schemes for diverting offenders from the trial process altogether. In such cases, victims of crime may find themselves without access to the forms of reparation intended to be provided by general legislation creating these ancillary orders.

Offences Taken into Account

The general principle is that a person should only be sentenced for the offences of which he or she has been convicted,[92] but offences taken into consideration are an exception to the rule. It had been a convention in England, since at least the turn of the century, that, when fixing

---

[90] *Vickers v. Minister for Business and Consumer Affairs* (1982) 43 A.L.R. 389.
[91] *Crimes (Confiscation of Profits) Act* 1986 (Vic.), s. 3(2).
[92] *Wishart* (1979) 1 Cr.App.R. (S) 322.

sentence, the courts could take other admitted, but as yet unprosecuted, offences into consideration. This meant that, with the consent of the accused, and without recording additional convictions, or giving cumulative sentences, the court could impose a more severe sentence than would be possible if it were dealing with the defendant only for the offences then being proceeded against. Both sides benefited. The offender avoided being convicted in relation to the other offences and obtained a lesser sentence than would have been imposed if each impending charge were dealt with separately. The police improved their clear-up rate and the prosecuting authorities cleared their lists. The informal arrangement was placed on a statutory footing in Victoria in 1974[93] and by the Commonwealth in 1982.[94]

The defendant must be convicted of at least one offence (other than treason or murder) and must formally admit and request account to be taken of the other charged, but as yet unprosecuted, crimes. If the sentencer exercises the discretion in favour of the accused, he or she may increase the sentence on account of the other offences but not so as to exceed the maximum that might have been passed if no others had been taken into consideration. Theoretically, the offences taken into consideration can be subsequently prosecuted since the legislation expressly declares that offences taken into account in this way are not to be regarded as an offence of which the person has been convicted. Though this "non-conviction" disposal of the outstanding charges does not count as a conviction for the purpose of the plea of autrefois convict, the legislation[95] provides that thereafter no proceedings are to be taken or continued in respect of any of the offences taken into account unless the conviction in respect of which it was taken into account has been quashed or set aside. Because there is no conviction, the question whether a court is empowered to make any ancillary orders in respect of such offences arises. The Commonwealth has expressly made statutory allowance for such orders to be made in respect of offences taken into account,[96] but, under Victorian legislation, there is no such power.

Diversion Schemes

The international trend towards more informal systems of justice[97] is evident in Australian moves to deal with offenders by some form of pre-trial diversion from the criminal justice system. In essence, these schemes are an effort to achieve correction without conviction. Their introduction is stimulated by various factors. First, there is a desire to

---

[93] *Penalties and Sentences Act* 1985 (Vic.), s. 10.
[94] *Crimes Act* 1914 (Cth), s. 21AA.
[95] See s. 10(4) and also s. 21AA(8).
[96] Section 21AA(5). Appeal rights are given in respect of such orders under s. 21AA(6).
[97] See R. L. Abel, *The Politics of Informal Justice* (1982).

ease the pressure on the courts and on prison crowding. The schemes divert to community-based services which maintain offenders in the community and therefore with their families and in employment. Secondly, there exists a wish to reduce stigmatisation and avoid the reinforcement of further offending through conviction and criminal labelling. Thirdly, there is an attraction to the idea that consent is preferable to coercion. Finally, there is the ever-present promise of cost savings.

Pre-trial diversion programmes have long been used in the juvenile jurisdiction, with its premium on keeping youngsters out of the courts. They have also been utilised in various ways for adults in the United States, for example, in schemes of "deferred prosecution", "delayed prosecution", "pre-trial probation" and "adjournments in contemplation of dismissal". Diversion for adults involves, in essence, the suspension of formal criminal proceedings against an individual, on condition that the person do something in return, usually some form of participation in a rehabilitative programme.[98] For instance, there is in Massachusetts a pre-trial diversion programme for drink-drivers, under which the alleged offender may have the case adjourned subject to successfully completing an alcohol rehabilitation programme.[99] Likewise, Pennsylvania has a pre-indictment probation procedure known as the Accelerated Rehabilitative Disposition, in which, to avoid a conviction, the alleged offender must agree to in-patient treatment for drug dependency.[100]

In Australia, the most recent proposals for diversionary programmes are concerned with the treatment of sexual offenders. In New South Wales, the as yet unproclaimed *Pre-Trial Diversion of Offenders Act* 1985 (N.S.W.), which was a product of that State's Task Force Report on Child Sexual Assault, proposes that a person who is charged with, and pleads guilty to, a specified child sexual assault offence, can give an undertaking to a court to participate in a rehabilitation programme for a period of up to two years.[101] Once such an undertaking is given, the court is prevented from proceeding to convict or sentence the alleged offender. If the programme is successfully completed, no further pro-

---

[98] R. W. Balch, "Deferred Prosecution: The Juvenilization of the Criminal Justice System" (1974) 38 *Federal Probation* 46.

[99] K. L. Brekka, "Guilty Until Proven Innocent: Pretrial Diversion and Retroactive Criminal Status—The Constitutionality of the 1982 Massachusetts Drunk Driving Law" (1984) 19 *New England Law Review* 377.

[100] H. V. Ludwig, "Treatment and Sentencing: The Power of the Court, the Rights of the Defendant, and the Legal and Ethical Implications of Sentencing Alternatives" (1979) 8 *Contemporary Drug Problems* 381. For descriptions of other schemes, see J. M. Dean, "Deferred Prosecution and Due Process in the Southern District of New York" (1975) 39 (3) *Federal Probation* 23; J. Hudson, B. Galaway, J. L. Henschel, and J. Penton, "Diversion Programming in Criminal Justice: The Case of Minnesota" (1975) 39 (1) *Federal Probation* 11; A. L. Pirro, Jr., "Adjournment in Contemplation of Dismissal: Criminal Procedure Law Section 170.55" (1974) 38 *Albany Law Review* 223.

[101] Section 23.

ceedings may be pursued in respect of the offence.[102] If the undertaking is breached, the court may either extend the undertaking, or convict and sentence on the charge. The New South Wales Task Force felt that, while a pre-trial diversion programme might be criticised as insufficiently punitive and a "soft" option, it offered the greatest potential for protecting children and reducing the incidence of sexual abuse.

The Victorian Law Reform Commission, in its *Report on Sexual Offences Against Children*,[103] has raised the possibility of introducing a similar scheme in Victoria. It proposed arrangements containing the following elements:[104]

> "Under a *pre-trial diversion program*, a person charged with an offence who meets specified criteria is offered a program of treatment and counselling before the trial is held. To be accepted into the program, an accused person must formally admit guilt at a court hearing. . . . If the offender completed the program, the charge would be withdrawn. An offender could be expelled from the program for failure to comply with its conditions. In that event the prosecution would be reactivated, a conviction would be entered and the offender would be sentenced."

Pre-trial diversion programmes have been extensively criticised. Concern has been expressed about their potential for abuse. A common objection, namely, that no determination of guilt has been made by a court prior to the implementation of the sanction, is met, under the most recent Australian proposals, by the precondition that there be a formal admission of guilt by the accused in a court setting. This offer of guilt, which substitutes for the conviction, is thought to suffice because it and the later participation in the programme are considered to be voluntary.

Voluntariness of this sort is suspect. The inducements are extremely powerful. The promise of rehabilitation; the benefit of non-conviction; removal of the trauma, hardship and cost of a trial; the reduced chances of incarceration; and the avoidance of ancillary sanctions and publicity are an offer rarely to be refused.[105] Yet, once admitted to the programme, the alleged offender may find that the promises are unfulfilled, the conditions severe, and the threat of being prosecuted for failure to conform to the diversionary regime is as coercive as the sanction which was avoided. There is the further risk that prosecutors will use the diversionary

---

[102] However, for the purpose of making a compensation order under s. 437 of the *Crimes Act* 1900 (N.S.W.), the undertaking is deemed to have the same effect as a conviction. Under s. 31, the Commissioner of Police must maintain a record of all persons who have pleaded guilty under the Act and have given an undertaking.

[103] *Report No. 18*, November 1988, pp. 123-130.

[104] Ibid., pp. 123-124.

[105] See Balch, op. cit., 47. For an extensive discussion of the issues in pre-trial settlement, see Canada Law Reform Commission, *Working Paper No. 7: Diversion* (1975).

programme as a means of resolving a weak case which they doubt would survive a courtroom contest. Another worry is that a defendant might spend a substantial period of time in a pre-trial diversion programme, only to be told that, having failed rehabilitation, he or she must now return to court for prosecution and punishment. The recent Australian proposals do not place limits on how long a criminal prosecution might be suspended while an offender participates in the diversionary programme, nor what limits there are on the form, duration and invasiveness of the treatment to be offered.

The Victorian Law Reform Commission scheme has already come under attack. It has been assailed as creating a "trial-avoidance hearing", in which the accused is induced to plea-bargain by an offer of participation in a scheme whose treatment content is largely unknown and which leads to the automatic entry of a conviction on failure,[106] thus completely bypassing the long-established protections which the trial process offers accused persons.[107] It is interesting that, in her influential discussion paper on child sexual assault,[108] Hewitt expressed a strong preference for treatment programmes that were only offered by a sentencing court after conviction. In her view, once the offender had been formally convicted, the court was free to be more honestly and openly coercive in demanding that person's participation in a reclamation programme.

From Status to Contract

The above survey has revealed a steady, but unsystematic, growth of statutory non-conviction or optional-conviction orders. It seems that soon all sanctions open to use by sentencers, except possibly those involving detention in custody, will be freed of the need to impose a formal conviction. The change is motivated by a desire to avoid the civil consequences which continue as added punishment after the sentence itself has been executed. But the wish to promote civil rehabilitation clashes with the role of the conviction as a moral justification for the corrective action taken against the convicted person. Even in setting up the most modern of the non-conviction sanctions, the legislature is not fully prepared to expunge the offender's record of prior crime. One of the unintended consequences of moving unsystematically to non-conviction sanctions has been to restrict the ability of the courts to making ancillary orders which depend on the prior fact of conviction. This

---

[106] C. A. J. Coady, M. N. Coady and G. T. Pagone, "Child Abuse: Treatment, Punishment and Other Diversions" (1989) 63 *Law Institute Journal* 389.

[107] For a critical assessment of the merits of those protections, see D. J. McBarnet, *Conviction: Law, the State and the Construction of Justice* (1981), ch. 8.

[108] L. Hewitt, *Child Sexual Assault Discussion Paper*, Department of Community Services (1986).

problem has usually been resolved by some form of remedial legislation, though the coverage of such legislation is by no means complete, and can be improved.

Another major feature of the emergence of the non-conviction sentence has been the shift from conviction to consent as the moral justification for action against the accused. However, grave doubts have been expressed about the validity of that consent. Hitherto, conviction has been seen as central to sentencing, because of its impact on legal status. The devaluation of social status followed from the diminution of legal status. The confluence of the two raised the fact of conviction to a condemnatory sanction in its own right. Conviction-based sanctions continue to be ranked higher in gravity in the sanction hierarchy than non-conviction ones.[109] The degradation of conviction brings with it automatic and potentially permanent disabilities for the censured person. The latter accords with one of the core characteristics of status, namely, that it is a legally imposed condition which cannot be got rid of at the mere will of the parties without the interposition of some organ of the state.[110] Because, in modern times, the duration and extent of the disabilities which attach to convictions are less well-known and more unpredictable in their effect than they originally were, it is entirely understandable that law reform bodies and legislatures are attracted to schemes designed to allow the offenders to live down their past and to limit the use made of their criminal record. But, instead of passing legislation setting up machinery specifically to deal with spent convictions, or to repeal or reduce the scope of the disabling provisions, the moderation of the consequences of a sentence is being attempted through the abandonment of the concept of conviction.

Sir Henry Maine offered the famous generalisation that the movement of progressive societies up to his time was that from status to contract.[111] Graveson explained that the meaning of that statement was:[112]

> ". . . that the rights and duties, capacities and incapacities of the individual are no longer being fixed by law as a consequence of his membership of a class; but those former incidents of status are coming more and more to depend for their nature and existence upon the will of the parties affected by them . . ."

The new sentencing options seem to be demonstrating a similar shift from status to contract. On the one hand, the most severe sanction, detention in custody, still needs a formal alteration of the status of the offender through conviction as a justification for its unilateral imposition upon the person convicted. Neither the consent of the offender nor that of

---

109 For example, *Allison* (1987) 49 N.T.R. 38 (N.T.S.C.); *Children and Young Persons Act* 1989 (Vic.), ss 137 and 138.

110 Graveson, op. cit., p. 48.

111 H. Maine, *Ancient Law* (1860), p. 182.

112 Graveson, op. cit., p. 34.

the prison or prison authorities is required. On the other hand, the latest forms of non-custodial sanction are based solidly on consensual and contractual relationships. So marked is this shift from status to contract that, in Victoria, except for fines, every non-custodial sanction now requires the express agreement of the accused, and, more often than not, that of the receiving agency responsible for his or her supervision.[113] Justice by consent, rather than coercion, is becoming the norm.

Though the apparent heart of these negotiated sanctions is the principle that the sentencer is willing to respect the autonomy, self-interest and self-actuation of the offender as the basis of bringing that person in as an active participant in his or her own fate, the freedom of the accused person to enter such "contractual" relationships may be more apparent than real. The consent is being induced by the statutory promise of favours and the judicial threat of reversion to a conviction-based measure. The parties to the non-custodial, non-conviction sentencing contract are not equal. Maine's dictum was offered in the 19th century, when the aim of law was to secure individual rights and give freest expression of the will in contractual arrangements. The 20th century saw a move back to status, at least in areas in which inequality in bargaining power was apparent. Interestingly enough, there are signs that this is also manifesting itself in new sentencing provisions, particularly those at a federal level,[114] which emphasise the obligation of the court to ensure that the accused is fully informed and understands the nature of the undertakings and obligations which he or she is being invited to accept "voluntarily". What has not yet been addressed is whether there should be legislative limits on the open-ended nature of the conditions offered to the offender. As has been noted elsewhere,[115] some of the more "Orwellian" conditions to which offenders are invited to agree raise the question of whether, despite the intended beneficial effects of non-conviction, these sanctions have become, or are capable of becoming, so oppressive or onerous, that to be subject to a conviction-based sanction, such as custody with its known limits becomes attractive, and is not seen as a burden, but as a means of protection from abuse of power.

This issue is particularly acute in the proposed Australian sexual offender diversionary programmes, in which the accused is faced with a choice between trial and sentence, with all its attendant protections, or diversion, with an implied waiver of rights. Balch has argued[116] that, because diversionary programmes use the threat of the possibility of conviction to encourage an accused to do something, the element of

---

113 *Penalties and Sentences Act* 1985 (Vic.), ss 28(5), 48(1), 81(b) and 83(3). See also *Children and Young Persons Act* 1989 (Vic.), ss 137(5), 140, 142, 144(3), 163(2)(b) and 171(c).

114 *Crimes Act* 1914 (Cth), ss 19B(2), 20(2) and 20AB(2).

115 R. G. Fox, "Dr. Schwitzgebel's Machine Revisited: Electronic Monitoring of Offenders" (1987) 20 A.N.Z.J.Crim. 140.

116 Balch, op. cit., 47.

voluntariness is undercut. He particularly warns that, where a programme is regarded as "voluntary", humane and rehabilitative, due process rights are likely to be relegated to a secondary position, with the implication that dispositions have become "privileges", not burdens. As in juvenile justice, "the formal determination of guilt is seen as of small consequence",[117] with the end result being a relaxation of standards and a presumption of guilt.

Pressing offenders to enter into unequal bargains in order to avoid convicting them is designed to dodge the unexpected and unknown consequences of the alteration in status brought about by the conviction itself. It is submitted that this is an inefficient way of bringing the social and legal disabilities under control. Other techniques must be considered. There are a number of ways that relief can be granted from the consequences of conviction, other than by creating a discretion whether a conviction is to be recorded or not. They include the granting of pardons, the creation of expungement legislation,[118] or legislation "setting aside" convictions.[119]

It is not inappropriate to continue to rely upon the fact of conviction as an act of legal and social condemnation while, at the same time, trying to limit its random effects. But the uncertain ameliorating effects of giving sentencers a discretion whether or not to record a conviction is not the best way to go. What is needed is a more coherent and logical approach to the drafting of new sanctions. Three components must be addressed:

(1) *Definition of the offence and its attendant sanctions.* The sanctions should indicate whether they can be imposed with or without recording a conviction and, where a choice is allowed, an indication of the criteria relevant to the exercise of that discretion.

(2) *A separate set of provisions setting out the powers of the court and the rights of the accused in respect of non-conviction sentences.* This would include the power to make ancillary orders and the accused's rights of appeal. The unreal nature of the "consent" upon which the non-conviction disposition is based strongly suggests that the accused's rights in respect of non-conviction measures should be no less than those available upon a conviction. Likewise, in the public interest, the same parity between conviction and non-conviction measures should apply in respect of the making of ancillary orders.

(3) *The implementation of uniform national legislation dealing with the expungement of convictions.* This should contain a graduated

---

[117] Ibid., 50.

[118] See, for example, the *Rehabilitation of Offenders Act* 1974 (U.K.).

[119] See discussion in F. C. Zacharias, "The Uses and Abuses of Convictions Set Aside Under the Federal Youth Corrections Act" [1981] *Duke Law Journal* 477.

offence and time scale which limits the duration of the effect of each conviction, at least in this country. Consideration might also be given to obviating the need for non-conviction measures by creating the immediately expunged conviction. At the same time, there should be a review of all local legislation imposing disabilities and disqualifications on convicted persons, with a view to reassessing the desirability of their retention within the limits set by the spent convictions legislation.

So long as present legislation continues to invest sentencers with a discretion to convict or not, the judge or magistrate should observe the following protocol:

- first, select a sanction type and quantum that appears to be a sufficiently proportionate response to the offence committed;[120]
- secondly, given that a choice of convicting or not exists, consider whether the protection of the community will be adequately provided for by the conditions of the specific sanction in mind, or whether it requires the exercise of other special forfeiture or disqualification powers which may be invoked without recording a conviction;
- apply the principle of parsimony in appending no more than is needed of any such special ancillary orders. Since to record a conviction will produce further unpredictable consequences, no conviction should be entered;
- finally, if the sentencer believes that, within the proportionate limits of the sentence, community protection will be produced by the conviction effect, he or she should permit counsel for the accused to address the court on what, in reality, will be the impact on the offender's economic, social, political and occupational position if the court exercises its discretion to record a conviction.[121]

A better legislative structure and a willingness to define more clearly the purposes of the dispositional process, the sanction powers of the courts and the legal and moral foundations of those powers can only improve the present ad hoc system in which neither the legislature, nor the courts, appear to have the courage of their convictions.

---

[120] For example, *Graham v. Bartley* (1984) 57 A.L.R. 193 at 196, where it was held inexpedient to proceed without conviction under the *Crimes Act* 1914 (Cth), s. 19B, in relation to a "blatant fraud".

[121] For example, *Lanham v. Brake* (1983) 74 F.L.R. 284 at 293, where the factors of proportionality and possible professional disabilities were discussed; *Simmonds v. Hill* (1986) 38 N.T.R. 31, where no conviction was entered because of the possible effects of a conviction on a juvenile's proposed career.

Name Index

DISPOSED OF
BY LIBRARY
HOUSE OF LORDS